understanding GENESIS

How to Analyze, Interpret, and Defend Scripture

Dr. Jason Lisle

First printing: July 2015

Master Books®, P.O. Box 726, Green Forest, AR 72638

Master Books® is a division of the New Leaf Publishing Group, Inc.

ISBN: 978-0-89051-900-4

Library of Congress Number: 2015909401

Cover by Diana Bogardus

Unless otherwise noted, Scripture quotations are from the New American Standard Bible.

Please consider requesting that a copy of this volume be purchased by your local library system.

Printed in the United States of America

Please visit our website for other great titles:
www.masterbooks.com

For information regarding author interviews,
please contact the publicity department at (870) 438-5288.

Acknowledgments

I thank my friends and family for their support and encouragement as I wrote this book, and for helpful feedback. I especially want to thank Dr. Ken Gentry and Dr. Jim Johnson for reviewing various sections of this book and for providing helpful suggestions. Their expertise was essential in honing my arguments and in reducing mistakes. Any remaining errors are mine alone. I thank the Lord Jesus for His gracious salvation, His forgiveness of my sins, and for calling me to share and defend His Word.

Contents

Introduction

"That's *your* interpretation! The Bible doesn't really mean what you think it does." Such statements are common today when disputes arise over biblical issues. It's no longer enough to say, "Thus says the Lord," because people will respond, "But what does the Lord really *mean* by what He says? You are not interpreting the passage properly." Is the Bible really so hard to understand? People can only obey the Scriptures and respond to the gospel to the extent that they correctly *understand* the Scriptures. So, the correct interpretation of Scripture is not merely an academic issue. It is a matter of eternal life and death. In our age of rampant post-modernism, the faithful Christian must not only defend the inerrancy of the Bible, but must also defend its proper interpretation.

This is perhaps most obvious in modern interpretations of the first book of the Bible: Genesis. Does the Bible really teach that God created in six days, or were such "days" symbolic of long periods of time? Does Genesis really suggest that God separately and supernaturally created every kind of creature on earth, or is such language merely an allegory for God-guided evolution? Was Adam a real person, or simply a metaphor? Did physical death enter the world at the time of Adam's sin, or was this merely spiritual death? Was Noah's Flood really global in extent, or merely local? At no time in the history of the world have such questions been as relevant as they are today. Our need to be able to answer these questions — and logically defend our position — has never been greater.

But are such answers even possible? The post-modern mindset is deeply entrenched in our culture today, such that some people will treat the meaning of a biblical text as if it is *subjective* — relative to the person. Perhaps you have heard someone say, "That's not what the text means *to me*." Another person might say, "That's true for you perhaps, but not for me."

It's disheartening, but sometimes even Bible study leaders will ask, "What does this passage mean *to you*?" Can a Bible verse really mean different things to different people? Clearly, a biblical teaching might be *applied* differently to different situations. But can the *meaning* of a passage differ from person to person? On the other hand, if the text has one meaning, then why do people not always agree on what that meaning is? Why are there so many denominations of Christianity with such differing views on what the Bible actually means? Can we really know for certain what the author of Genesis intended? And if so, can we *defend* the proper interpretation of Genesis against those who have a compromised view?

Interpreting a Clear Text

It is my conviction that the Bible has one correct interpretation — the meaning intended by the author. And I submit that Almighty God knows how to communicate clearly with His creations, and that He has done so in the Bible. I will give reasons for this position later; for now, the skeptical reader may consider this claim as a hypothesis. If this view is indeed true, then the main portions of God's Word should not be hard to understand. Though there are some difficult passages that require careful study, I submit that the ordinary, literate person can read and grasp the main-and-plain basic doctrines of the Bible. And I intend to demonstrate this in the chapters that follow.

But I must first address a very common objection to this position: If the Bible is so clear, then why are there so many disagreements on what it means? We must admit that there are numerous denominations of Christianity with their various doctrinal positions. And there are countless cults that profess to believe the Bible while disagreeing on some very fundamental issues. Even within a conservative denomination there are often disputes over matters of theology: interpretations of the "end-times," applicability of Old Testament laws, the continuation or cessation of the prophetic gifts of the Spirit, the nature of election, mode of baptism, and so on.

Do such disputes prove that the text is unclear? Not necessarily. Interpretation of any document involves both the text and the reasoning of the reader. So when proper interpretation is not accomplished, logically this could be due to either a problem in the text *or* a problem with the reader. If the text of the Bible really is God-breathed as it claims to be (2 Timothy

3:16), then it cannot be in error. And so for all errors in interpretation the fault must lie with the reader. Human beings have any number of foibles that can prevent us from reasoning rightly from a text, even when the text is perfectly clear. Let's consider just two.

In some cases, sincere believers misunderstand the text because they are not reasoning properly. Conservative Christians with a sincere desire to understand the Bible nonetheless sometimes don't think clearly; they make mistakes in reasoning resulting in a faulty interpretation. The mistake is unintentional; but it is still a mistake. Optimistically, I submit that this problem accounts for many of the differences within biblically conservative denominations. The nice thing about these kinds of misinterpretations is that they can be resolved through education. A study of the principles of logic is immensely helpful in biblical interpretation. Christian denominations may be able to resolve many of their differences by learning to reason carefully from the text. My hope is that this book will be a starting point to that end.

Second, we must consider a more hideous cause of biblical misinterpretation, one that is far more difficult to alleviate: the sinful nature of mankind. In many cases, the text is very straightforward, but people do not want to accept the clear meaning of the text. Consequently, they are strongly motivated to interpret the text in an unnatural way, contrary to the intention of the author, so that they will not have to do or believe what the text actually indicates. In their minds, such persons are justified in saying that they believe the Bible, while simultaneously embracing unbiblical beliefs and perhaps even a sinful lifestyle. The heart of the problem is a problem of the heart, and cannot be remedied by mere education. It requires an act of repentance.

"But surely a Christian would not succumb to this type of temptation," some might say. But Christians are merely sinners that God saved by His grace and mercy. And that gift of salvation makes us righteous *in principle* before God, but we continue to struggle with sin until the Lord calls us home. Christians do sin sometimes in their interpretation of the Word, and our first inclination is to deceive ourselves about that very fact (1 John 1:8). Namely, people work very hard to convince themselves (and others) that they are not distorting God's Word to protect an unbiblical preconception, when in fact that is just what they are doing.

It's a strange thing to deceive oneself, and my purpose here is not to explore this perplexing aspect of human psychology.[1] Rather, I merely point out that self-deception is a very real phenomenon (James 1:22, 26; Galatians 6:3; 1 Corinthians 3:18), and Christians are not immune from this vice. Genuine Christians, saved by God's grace, can and do at times misunderstand God's Word because they are motivated to *not* believe what the text so clearly teaches. It's an easy trap that we must take great care to avoid.

The Book of Genesis is especially prone to this type of misunderstanding, precisely because it is so contrary to the popular beliefs of our pagan society. For example, the Bible teaches that God created in six days, implying an age of the universe of thousands of years. But some Christians will respond, "Sure, the text says six days. But what's a 'day'? Those were not literal, ordinary days, but vast ages — hundreds of millions of years each. The Bible is true, but your *interpretation* of what it means is simply wrong." Is such a response genuinely motivated by textual considerations, or is it driven by a preconceived opinion, perhaps being influenced by modern "scientific" opinion? And how are we to deal with such disputes?

Undoubtedly, few people would admit to intentionally misreading a text. Those who distort the teaching of Scripture are able to subconsciously convince themselves that they are reading the text properly — the aforementioned self-deception. They believe on some level that their interpretation is true.

The Stakes Are High

Misinterpretation of God's Word is always detrimental, but the consequences in some case are far more devastating than in others. Some misinterpretations result in eternal damnation — those that distort the essential message of the gospel. This is seen in countless cults that profess to be Christian, but deny any number of essential Christian doctrines: the Trinity, the deity of Christ, the virgin birth, the transcendence of God, the resurrection of the dead, eternal punishment for the wicked, and so on. Those who claim to be Christian but deny the essential gospel of Jesus will not enter His

1. To deceive oneself, one must do two things that are strangely inconsistent. First, he must believe a proposition (P) in order to do the deceiving. Second, he must be convinced that he does not believe that proposition (P) in order to be deceived. In categorical form we would say of this person that "S believes P," but also "S believes that S does not believe P." Self-deception is strange but true (James 1:22).

Kingdom (Matthew 7:21–23). Curiously, for the most part, these cultists are reading the same words of Scripture that the orthodox Christian is reading. They even quote the Scriptures to support their position! But they have failed to interpret the Bible correctly, to their own demise.

Eternity is at stake. Only the true gospel has the power to redeem sinners. Only the real Christ can save people from eternal destruction. Hence, if we truly love our neighbor, then we must be able to explain the proper interpretation of Scripture and defend that view against the heretics. This calls for us to study *hermeneutics.* **Hermeneutics** *is the study of the principles of the interpretation of a text.* If we are to obey Christ's instructions to make disciples of all nations (Matthew 28:19–20), then we must first have a correct hermeneutic so that we understand the Scriptures. And then we must be able to defend our hermeneutic against faulty views that distort God's Word.

The Literal View

It may come as a surprise to many that there should be any need to interpret the Bible at all. Some may ask, "Doesn't the Bible mean what it says? Isn't it pretty clear, and aren't we supposed to take the words as written?" Indeed, many Christians profess to interpret the Bible *literally* — in strict accordance with the primary meaning of the words. They might say that any alternative to literalism would not be faithful to the text. But this raises two concerns.

First, whatever view is the correct one, we must be able to *defend* that view against alternatives. Throughout history, not everyone has agreed that the Bible should be read literally. There are allegorical, mystical, pietistic, and accomodationist schools of interpretation, to name just a few. An allegorist might say, "Genesis is not to be taken as literal history. It's merely an allegory meant to convey the fact that God created. Jonah in the belly of the great fish, the parting of the Red Sea — these shouldn't be taken literally." Now I happen to think that such schools of interpretation are wrong — that they are not faithful to the intention of the author. But can I logically *demonstrate* this?

Second, while I am sympathetic to those who espouse to read the Bible literally, I must point out that even they do not take *everything* in Scripture in a strictly literal fashion. When God calls His people "stiff-necked" (e.g.,

Exodus 32:9, 33:3), do we believe that they *literally* had stiff necks? Most people, even if they claim to be literalists, understand this as a euphemism meaning "stubborn." That is a very natural reading of the passage, but it is *not strictly literal*, at least *not in English.*[2] Proverbs 25:15 teaches that "a soft tongue breaks the bone." It's not to be taken in a literal fashion. Do false prophets *literally* wear sheep's clothing, and are they *literally* wolves (Matthew 7:15)?

Consider the following verses: Daniel 2:35, Nahum 2:13, Revelation 13:1–2. Does anyone really believe that a mountain will grow to cover the earth, or that a sword will literally devour lions, or that God creates a seven-headed dragon with ten horns? There is no doubt that God has the power to do all these things, yet most people will insist that these are used as non-literal imagery. In some cases, the Bible explicitly tells us what the non-literal figures mean (e.g., Daniel 2:36–45; Revelation 17:7–18: Matthew 13:36–42). Clearly, a strictly literal interpretation of Scripture is too simplistic. Even if we grant that much of the Bible is to be taken literally, clearly, some of it is not.

Sometimes when people say that they read the Bible literally, they really mean "naturally" or *"literarily"* — reading the text in a mostly literal fashion, but allowing for figures of speech, and recognizing that some types of literature within Scripture require a non-literal reading (such as the Psalms). Now, I happen to think that a natural reading of Scripture is the right way to go. But this still leaves us with two issues that we must resolve. First, what does it mean to read the Bible naturally? That is, which sections should be taken literally, and how are we to interpret the non-literal sections? Second, can we prove that this is the right way to interpret Scripture? After all, it may personally benefit us to have a right view of hermeneutics, but this won't do others much good unless we can persuade them that this is indeed the right view.

Rightly Dividing the Word

The importance of correct hermeneutics cannot be overstated. Incorrect hermeneutics leads to bad theology. And bad theology destroys everything it touches. It has contributed to the downfall of individuals and entire cultures.

2. Some biblical phrases are literal in the original Hebrew, but have been translated somewhat figuratively in English.

Bad theology can destroy lives in this world and for all eternity. We can only live a life pleasing to God by faithful obedience to His Word. And this is only accomplished if we rightly understand His Word.

The goal of this book is two-fold. First, I intend to discover the principles of hermeneutics, the rules or principles by which we can correctly interpret God's Word, in order to arrive at the correct interpretation of Genesis and the other books of the Bible. Second, I aim to logically refute faulty interpretations of Genesis by showing how such views violate established hermeneutical principles. This book therefore is designed to serve as an apologetic resource to help Christians defend the Word against compromised positions, particularly when it comes to the foundational Book of Genesis.

Due to space constraints, I will not deal at length with the questions of biblical inerrancy. And I will only briefly touch on matters of transmission and translation. I start from the Christian position that the Bible is without error in its original autographs, and that it has been carefully transmitted and faithfully translated into modern English. Thus, I take as an axiom that the major modern conservative Bible translations are basically faithful to the original, and can rightly be called "the Word of God." For those who question biblical inerrancy or who have concerns about textual criticism, there are other fine works that discuss these issues. The subject of this book is the dispute that arises over methods of *interpretation*: disagreements about what the Bible means between two professing Christians who both affirm that the Bible is the inerrant Word of God.

It would be easy enough to list commonly accepted hermeneutical principles and show how certain individuals violate such principles, thereby ending up with atrocious misunderstandings of Scripture. But then critics might deny that the hermeneutical principles I have listed are the correct set of principles. After all, there is no reason to accept something as correct merely because it is commonly believed. So my goal in this book is to discover the *necessary* hermeneutical principles that lead to a correct interpretation of the text.

I will attempt to logically prove that each of the principles discussed in this book must be the correct principle. Often such proofs will be accomplished by showing how when a given hermeneutical principle is denied it leads to a contradiction or some other absurdity. I begin with questions about how to interpret a text in general, and then move on to ask how the Bible should be interpreted. After all, the Bible is not just any text. So should it be interpreted in the same way? I then explore the role of evidence external to the text. I will also consider how different types/styles/genres of literature should be treated. Then I will examine the role of logical reasoning in biblical interpretation, and how mistakes in reasoning can result in misunderstandings of the text.

Does the Bible itself give instructions or guidance on how to interpret it? That is a question I will address at length in chapter 9. Then I move on to application: examining specific doctrines commonly held by professing Christians to see if such views are consistent with hermeneutical principles. My primarily focus will be on the correct reading of Genesis, but I will also explore a few other important Christian doctrines. My goal is to expose faulty views of Scripture that stem from violations of hermeneutical principles.

At the end of each chapter, I have provided a summary and review of the basic principles covered in that chapter. This serves to reinforce the main points of the chapter while omitting the details. This book covers a lot of material, so summary reviews should be very helpful. After reading the book once, a student may want to reread the chapter reviews to help him or her remember the basic points without having to re-read the entire book.

The real fun begins in chapter 10, where I begin applying the now-established rules of hermeneutics to commonly held claims. In chapter 11 I investigate the claim of old-earth creation. In chapter 12, I explore the hermeneutic and motivation behind belief in deep-time (millions of years). Chapter 13 deals with theistic evolution, and chapter 14 examines the claim that the Genesis Flood was non-global. I have included two appendices. The first is an actual dialog I had with a young man who denied the deity of Christ. The second is a discussion of formal logical fallacies and the errors in biblical interpretation that stem from them.

Chapter 1

That's *Your* Interpretation!

The first thing we must establish and be able to defend is that there *exists* a correct interpretation of Scripture. That may seem silly or trivial, but in our post-modern culture some people claim that "truth is relative," and hence the notion that there is one correct interpretation of Scripture would be unnecessarily restrictive. Doesn't the Bible mean whatever you want it to mean? Isn't one person's interpretation of Scripture just as legitimate as the next? Isn't the important thing what it "means *to you*"?

In the post-modern view, there is no "correct" or "incorrect" interpretation of the Bible or any document since such a position presupposes that truth is objective and absolute. The absurdity of such a view is quickly revealed when we ask a post-modernist if it is a "correct" interpretation of *his statement* that there is no "correct" or "incorrect" interpretation of any statement. Moreover, principles of logical reasoning are predicated upon the objective and absolute nature of truth. Consider the definition of the word "proposition" as it is found in a textbook on logic. A proposition is a statement or claim that either affirms or denies something; "Grass is green" is a proposition. A given proposition is either true or false.

But some people today verbally deny that there is such a thing as objective truth. The position that truth is subjective (relative to the person) is called "relativism." A relativist might say that a particular claim is "true for you, but not for me." Is it possible for a claim to be true relative to one person, but false for another person?

A proposition like "My favorite color is blue" might seem like such an example. This proposition is "true for me" and for others who prefer blue. But it is false for everyone else, correct? Well, not really. A proposition is not merely a sentence, but the meaning behind that sentence — the claim that is being made. So when I say, "My favorite color is blue" this is a *different* proposition from when Mike says, "My favorite color is blue" even though the sentence is the same. The sentence I've uttered has the meaning "Dr. Lisle's favorite color is blue." Whereas Mike's sentence means "Mike's favorite color is blue." These are clearly two different propositions.

But can the same proposition be true for one person, and yet false for another person? The relativist says, "Yes. Truth is dependent upon the person. It is not absolute or objective." But in making such a claim, the relativist has uttered an *absolute statement*. He did not qualify his proposition by stating to which person or group of people it is true. Instead, he uttered it as if it were absolutely, objectively true, regardless of who makes the claim. Indeed, we may wish to ask the relativist, "Is your position (that truth is relative) absolutely true?" If he says, "no" then he has given up his position, since he has admitted that it is not necessarily true (for everyone). If on the other hand he says, "yes," then he has refuted himself, in stating that it is absolutely true that truth is not absolute. The relativist's self-contradictory position is reduced to absurdity.

For truth to be meaningful at all, it must be objective and absolute, because the alternative leads to nonsense. To say that something is "true for me, but not necessarily for others" is to reduce truth to something internal to the person, and not something meaningful about the external world. Essentially, the phrase "It's true for me" is synonymous with "I believe it." Certainly, different people can have different beliefs; beliefs are subjective. But the universe external to them is not affected by their beliefs.

Believing something doesn't make it so. And in his heart of hearts, every relativist knows this — and demonstrates that he knows it by his behavior. Even the most ardent relativist still looks both ways before he crosses the street. This is because he knows that the truth of getting hit by a car is objective and thus irrelevant to his personal beliefs or feelings on the matter. Relativism teaches that it is absolutely true that truth is not absolute — a contradiction. Relativism is internally inconsistent, and self-refuting. Thus, we must conclude that truth is objective and independent of the beliefs of a particular individual, since the alternative is self-refuting. We shall refer to the (absolute) view that truth is not absolute as the "relativist fallacy."

But just because there is an objective truth does not mean that it is discoverable, or that language necessarily conveys it. And so we must now ask the follow-up question: "Is language (either written or verbal) capable of conveying truth?" In other words, does language have *meaning*? If so, is the meaning objective, or is the meaning relative to the recipient? Other questions follow from this. Can a given proposition mean two different things to two different people? There is no doubt that people can (in some instances) read the same proposition, and come away with two different *beliefs* about what the proposition means. But is this because the proposition has more than one meaning? Does it have any meaning at all?

Do Words Have Meaning?

To say that a word (or combination of words) has "meaning" is to say that it represents a particular idea or limited range of ideas that the author/speaker is intending to convey to the reader/listener. When you read the word "lion" on a page, it likely conjures a particular thought in your mind. Although this thought may not be exactly identical to what another person thinks when reading the word (size, age, posture, mountain lion vs. African lion, etc.), it is very likely that the ideas will be very similar. It certainly won't conjure up the idea of a quasar, an apple, or waffles. The word has meaning since it represents an idea. And that meaning is objective since the word represents the same idea regardless of who reads it within the context of a given language.

The entire point of communication is to transfer an idea from one person to another person, often to induce a particular action in the recipient. Thus, genuine communication is only possible if words have objective meaning. Of course, it should be obvious from everyday observation that communication is possible. Ideas are indeed transferred from one person to another. Thus, it follows logically that words do have objective meaning.

But not everyone professes to agree with this reasoning. There are some people who would argue that words do not have any objective meaning. These "deconstructionists" would say that it is never possible to take away from a text the author's intended meaning. "Every reading is a misreading" is their creed. Deconstructionists have written some marvelous works espousing their point of view. They attempt to communicate their belief that words do not possess objective meaning, and thus that we can never get to the author's intent. But if that were true, then why did they bother writing such works? If words have no meaning, and cannot convey the author's intention, then why do deconstructionists attempt to use words to convey their intention to the reader? If genuine communication is impossible, then why do deconstructionists attempt to communicate this to their readers? Such inconsistency betrays the fact that even the most ardent deconstructionist really does believe in his heart of hearts that words do have meaning.

Words, within the context of a given language, do indeed have objective meaning. If they didn't, then writing and reading would be pointless. We could never learn anything from books or from teachers if words did not convey objective meaning. Yet, students do learn all sorts of information and skills from books and from their teachers. So, clearly, words do have meaning. The fact that even deconstructionists must use meaningful words to argue against the notion that words have meaning shows that words indeed have meaning. The alternative is self-refuting. The error of assuming that words do not have objective meaning we shall call the "deconstructionist fallacy."

How Many Meanings Does a Word or Statement Contain?

A given word can have more than one meaning. "Land" can be a noun, as in "I just bought some land." "Land" can also be a verb as in "Planes land on runways." Indeed, a typical dictionary will have over 20 different definitions (i.e., meanings) for the word "land." These are called *lexical* definitions — the definitions of a word that are found in a dictionary. However, when a given word is used in a particular context, only *one* of its lexical definitions will apply. Context, the surrounding words and sentences, indicates which one of the lexical definitions of a word is being used. In the above examples, there is no confusion as to what the word "land" means in each case. The context makes it clear. Any other definition would reduce the proposition to nonsense.

Generally, only one meaning of each word will allow a given sentence to make any sense. The word "plane" was used above and it also has multiple meanings. It can refer to an aircraft, or a two-dimensional geometric entity.

But this second meaning is disallowed in the particular context of the example above. It wouldn't make sense for a geometric plane to land on a runway. Both "land" and "plane" are clarified by their contextual relationship to each other. This is the *context principle*. And this particular sentence has only one meaning — a meaning that any English-speaking person would readily understand.

Of course, sometimes an author will inadvertently write an ambiguous sentence, in which the reader can't ascertain what the author intended to convey: "The school's music department is giving away free guitars on Saturday — no strings attached!" The last phrase is a bit perplexing because it isn't clear if the author means that the guitars literally do not have any strings on them, or whether the phrase is being used figuratively to mean that there is no "catch" or hidden fee. Either meaning fits the context, so the reader is left to wonder. This type of ambiguous grammatical construction is called an "amphiboly." The amphiboly is rightly considered to be a logical fallacy if it is used as part of a logical argument.

There are some situations where sentences are intentionally constructed to allow multiple meanings, but this is usually done in jest. Consider this old joke: "There are 10 kinds of people: those who understand binary, and those who don't." The joke makes use of an intentional ambiguity of the meaning of "10" — which we normally think of as "ten," but is also the number "two" in binary. The joke works by intentionally misleading the reader as to the meaning of "10," only to reveal an alternative meaning in the climax. The reader is supposed to take the meaning of "10" to be "ten" on the first pass, only to realize that it really must be "two" given the context. However, only one word in the sentence is ambiguous (initially) and only temporarily so. Thus, even in this case, the ambiguity is very, very limited. In most propositions, there is one meaning for each word, and one overall claim that is being made.

But there are exceptions. There may be certain situations in poetic literature where the words are left intentionally ambiguous so that the intent is to stir up thinking in the reader, rather than to convey a specific concept. But this type of usage is quite rare even in poetic literature. Generally, each statement is constructed to convey one specific idea to the reader. It is normally the case that an author has one meaning in mind when he or she constructs a particular proposition. It is this meaning that he or she hopes will be understood by the reader. Whether or not the reader actually understands this meaning is not yet our focus. The point here is that for the vast bulk of literature, there is one primary meaning for each stated proposition; this meaning is the idea that the author has intended to convey to the reader. But can we actually prove this assertion?

Consider the alternative. If a given proposition does not have one specific primary meaning that the author intends to convey to the reader, then logically, it must either have multiple primary meanings, or no meaning at all. In both cases, this leads to an absurd result. Let's consider these two possibilities in turn.

First, if a given proposition has multiple primary meanings, then how could they be faithfully communicated in a single statement? "Plane" has a number of meanings, and "land" has a number of meanings. But the sentence "The plane is ready to land" only makes sense when one of the lexical definitions is used for "plane" and likewise for "land." If the author intended to communicate two different things in a single proposition, how could he reasonably do so given the limited range of definitions of words? Indeed, it is hard to even construct a single simple proposition that could conceivably convey two equally primary points simultaneously.

If I want to convey the fact that (1) it is hot outside, and (2) dogs are mammals, I can't conceive of a way to do that in one simple proposition. Certainly, I could do it in one sentence by connecting the two points with "and" (e.g., "It is hot outside, and dogs are mammals"). But this compound proposition is still comprised of *two* simple propositions. Each of these simple propositions has only one meaning.

A single sentence can be used to convey different primary meanings by emphasizing different words: "We should not speak ILL of our friends" has a slightly different primary meaning from "We should not speak ill of our FRIENDS." The first suggests that we may speak of our friends so long as we do not say anything negative about them, whereas, the second suggests that we may speak ill of people so long as they are not our friends. The two meanings are similar, but not identical. Thus, these represent two different propositions. If we emphasized both words "ill" and "friends," would this convey two equally primary points? It is far more likely that the reader would be confused as to which point we are trying to make. *It is our natural expectation that a given proposition has only one primary meaning.*

To illustrate this last point, consider the aforementioned amphiboly: "The school's music department is giving away free guitars on Saturday — no strings attached!" As indicated earlier, the statement is confusing because we don't know whether the sentence means that the guitars don't have strings, or whether there is no hidden fee. But it doesn't even occur to most people that it might mean *both*. We can scarcely conceive of the notion that the author intended to convey both meanings simultaneously. The human mind naturally presupposes that only one meaning was intended, and that the author simply did not realize that his phrasing was ambiguous (unless it was done intentionally as a joke).

So clearly, a given proposition cannot have more than one primary meaning if it is intended to communicate, because any alternative leads to miscommunication. A proposition might accomplish its primary point by use of a secondary point or image. This is common in idioms. For example, "The early bird catches the worm" is not primarily teaching anything about birds or worms. Its primary meaning is that competitive opportunities favor those enthusiasts who arrive early. Rather than stating this directly, the idiom makes its primary point by the illustration of a specific example. But the sentence still has only one main meaning. This must be the case if it is to be understood. A given proposition, under ordinary circumstances, will have exactly one primary meaning, if it has any meaning at all.

Alternatively, we consider the possibility that a proposition has no meaning at all. If this is the case, then the reader cannot extract meaning from the passage because it is impossible to extract what isn't there. The reader might claim to find meaning. And he may genuinely think that he has discovered the meaning from the passage, but clearly this is impossible if there is no meaning in the passage. Anything that the reader takes away will be coming from his or her own mind, not the mind of the author. In that case, the author has not truly communicated, because none of his ideas were transmitted to the reader.

If propositions have no meaning, then reading is not an exercise in communication, but rather, an exercise in introspection. Like a Rorschach inkblot test, whatever a reader takes away from a passage would be a reflection of his or her own thoughts and feelings, and would have nothing to do with anything in the mind of the author. Again, we must conclude that communication — a genuine transfer of a thought or idea from one person to another — would not be possible if propositions don't have meaning. Therefore, the existence of successful communication is proof that propositions do have meaning. This isn't to say that a meaningless statement has never been uttered in the history of mankind. Rather, it simply means that a meaningless statement does not communicate anything. Given the success of human communication, we would therefore expect that such statements would be rare, and almost always unintentional.

There have been times when archeologists have uncovered a previously unknown written language. They can see that there are symbols used in a specific non-random, non-repeating sequence, but they do not know the meaning because they do not understand the language. Some scholars spend years attempting to decipher such ancient languages. Why? It is because they expect such sentences to contain meaning. It doesn't even occur to a scholar to suppose that the ancient symbols have absolutely no meaning at all. Obviously, someone wrote these symbols down because he or she was attempting to communicate — to convey an idea to a reader.

The notion that words do not have a primary meaning is a self-defeating position. No one can legitimately argue that "words have no meaning" because in stating that "words have no meaning" the person has assumed that they do! It must be the case that most propositions do have exactly one primary meaning if practical communication is possible.

And communication is indeed possible. Students are able to learn about mathematics, science, and the War of 1812 from their teachers and from textbooks. This would be utterly impossible if (A) words did not have meaning, or (B) if propositions generally had multiple meanings. Communication is not always successful of course. But the point here is that communication could *never* be successful if words did not have meaning. So the claim that propositions do not have one primary meaning is false, since it leads to the absurd conclusion that communication is impossible. We define the *one-meaning principle* as the fact that a given proposition generally has one primary meaning.

Can Human Beings Discover the Meaning of a Proposition?

Given that propositions generally do have one specific and primary meaning, it is natural to ask whether this meaning is able to be discovered by the reader. Communication is only achieved when the reader is indeed able to understand the meaning of a particular passage, and we have already seen that communication is possible and is happening all the time. Thus, it stands to reason that it is indeed often possible to discover the meaning of a proposition — but "often" is not the same as "always."

We also noted that communication is not always successful. People sometimes do not understand what a text means. Perhaps they do not know the language. Perhaps they do not understand the context. Perhaps the sentence is poorly constructed and ambiguous. Perhaps a person's own opinions and biases get in the way of proper understanding. For these and other reasons, a given proposition is not necessarily understandable to a given person.

So the answer to this question is more nuanced than the previous ones. Can human beings discover the meaning of a proposition? Often yes, but not always. And sometimes understanding can be achieved only with a great deal of effort. What then are the conditions under which a person can understand the meaning of a text?

Essential Requirements for Properly Understanding the Meaning of a Text

First, we note that an interpreter must have basic human perception and rationality. We can dismiss the silly examples of a person who is comatose, or one who is clinically insane. A person with an extreme mental or physical disability might not be able to read, least of all understand a text, nor can a newborn baby. Throughout the rest of this book we consider the average person to be of ordinary intelligence and having no severe mental or physical deficiencies that would inhibit thoughtful communication.

Second, it is clear that the reader must have sufficient knowledge of the language that he or she is reading. This includes basic knowledge of the rules of grammar, a sufficiently large vocabulary, and knowledge of common figures of speech. Knowledge of the topic under discussion is very helpful (though not always strictly necessary); a technical paper on the discovery of the Higgs boson might be very difficult for a non-physicist to understand, even if it is written in his native language. In a way, technical jargon can be thought of as its own language, or as an offshoot or dialect of the common language of the culture.

So, clearly, some level of proficiency in the language is necessary for understanding a given text. But this aptitude need not be a perfect knowledge of all aspects of the language. Who can honestly say that they know every English word? Yet such limitations do not stop people from reading books, and learning a great deal from such books. A reader with a very limited vocabulary can often understand words beyond her knowledge by their context. Even in cases where the context is not fully sufficient, partial understanding is often possible: "Karms are always red." Although you may not understand what a "karm" is (which of course you won't since I just made up the term), it is obvious from context that it is red in color, it is physical not conceptual (since concepts cannot have "color"), and that it is plural (not only from the "s" but also because of the verb "are") whose singular form is likely to be "karm." So language is surprisingly powerful in its ability to communicate ideas, even when the linguistic knowledge of the reader is quite limited.

Obviously, if a reader has no knowledge of a given language, he will be unable to understand text written in that language unless someone translates it for him or until he learns the language. There may be some languages that have been lost with time, such that no one alive today understands their vocabulary or grammar. Propositions written in an unknown tongue cannot be understood unless and until the language vocabulary and grammar are discovered. This was once the case with Egyptian hieroglyphics. No living human could understand them because the vocabulary and grammar had been lost. This was the case until the Rosetta Stone was uncovered at the turn of the 19th century. Since it had the same decree written in three languages, one of which is hieroglyphics, and another is (known) ancient Greek, the known language could be used to finally decipher the unknown language.

The reader only needs to know the language of a particular text as he or she reads it; this need not be the language in which the original author wrote the text. As long as the translator knows both languages sufficiently well, and presuming that he or she takes care to faithfully translate the original text into the new language, the meaning can be preserved. This isn't to say that this always happens — only that it's possible.

A lady once told me that because I have not read the Bible in its original languages (e.g., Hebrew, Aramaic, and Greek) that I hadn't really read it, and could therefore not understand it. But this view is easy to refute. Although ideas can be transmitted via language, they are not bound to a specific language. As one example, I learned the physics of relativity by reading a book on the topic that had been written by Albert Einstein. It is obvious that I understood the meaning of the book, because I now know relativity, as evidenced by the fact that I can correctly solve relativistic physics problems. Yet the book I read by Einstein was not originally written in English. What I had read was an English translation of his book, which was originally written in German. Yet I was able to learn relativity. It would be absurd to argue that I don't know relativity on the basis that I've never read about it in the original German.

Likewise, one need not know Hebrew and Greek to read and understand the basics of the Bible. Of course, knowledge of the original language can be very helpful in understanding nuances of specific passages. But as long as we are dealing with a faithful translation, the basic meaning of the original text will be preserved, and can (in principle) be understood by the reader even if he or she does not know Hebrew or Greek.

By analogy, a person can watch a VHS tape of a movie on an old "standard definition" television, or he can watch the same movie on Blu-Ray using a high-definition television.[1] Either way, the person should have no difficulty understanding the story. On the Blu-Ray he will experience a sharper picture, more vivid colors, and he might notice details that he missed on the VHS tape. But the basic plot of the movie is unchanged. So it is with reading the Bible in the original languages. You will get a sharper picture with more "color," and might notice some extra details. But the basic message is unchanged.

Another requirement for understanding is that the author of a given text must have been sufficiently clear in his writing. If the author were careless, he may have written an incomplete sentence, or failed to specify a referent that was clear in his mind but is not mentioned in the text. In this case, the defect is not in the reader, but in the text itself. Many texts have such errors.

But since our interest is primarily in understanding the meaning of the Bible, we must ask if such a defect is possible in Scripture. Clearly, the answer is no. Given our original premise, that the Bible is the inerrant Word of God, though written by men, it was guided infallibly by God. Its primary author is God, who makes no mistakes (linguistic or otherwise). When God communicates, He does so perfectly. If God leaves out a detail, this is by

---

1. http://www.icr.org/article/6918/.

design — not accident. We do leave open the possibility of rare transmission and translation errors by men; however, these are few and far between as even secular scholars will readily admit. Nonetheless, aside from these very rare cases, we must conclude that any error in understanding the Bible must be due to a fault of the reader, the copyist, or translator, but never a fault of the Author or the original text.

A certain degree of cultural awareness is necessary to understand certain references in literature. A reference to the victory of the Denver Broncos over the Cincinnati Bengals would be difficult for someone totally unfamiliar with American sports. Imagine someone interpreting such a statement as being about two groups of animals — literal Bengal tigers being attacked and defeated by literal broncos. Figures of speech are often cultural as in, "You are really in hot water now!" We know better than to take the expression literally because of our cultural understanding of this common expression. Not all propositions require such cultural awareness. But some do. And this is an issue that must be considered when we come to the topic of interpreting the Bible.

Some knowledge of laws of logic is necessary to understand a text. This doesn't mean that a course in logic is necessarily required (though it may be very helpful), but basic applications of the law of non-contradiction, the law of identity, *modus ponens*, and so on, will be necessary to properly interpret a text. This may seem too obvious to include in a list like this. But it turns out that many errors in biblical interpretation are due to basic errors in logic. We will address such issues in a later chapter.

We must also consider the problem of philosophical bias. Human beings are not emotionless automatons that objectively and neutrally process information to arrive at objectively inescapable conclusions. Rather, people have biases. They have beliefs and they have things that they strongly *want* to believe. Some people might believe that they are not subject to such a bias, that they would never believe in something simply because they wished it to be so. But this itself is a bias based on wishful thinking! An untruthful bias can cause a person to misunderstand a given text. Conversely, and perhaps surprisingly, a correct bias can actually help a person to understand a given text under certain circumstances. Let's consider some examples.

We start with an absurd case of someone who has the philosophy that "words are meaningless." Can that person ever properly understand a text?

Not if he genuinely believes that words are meaningless. He might be able to read a text, but he will interpret it as meaning nothing. He will get nothing out of it, and thus will never understand the author's intention. This is an extreme and unrealistic example of course. But it illustrates the point. A person who tenaciously and consistently held such a philosophy could never — even in principle — understand a text. Perhaps some people might think that they have a counterexample: someone who claims to have such a philosophy and yet does understand the meaning of a text. But such a person would merely be *professing* that "words are meaningless." If he genuinely believed that words had no meaning, then he wouldn't ever bother to say that words have no meaning, and he would never be able to understand any text.

Let's consider a more realistic scenario. One such bias that can affect our understanding of a written or verbal statement is when we overestimate the character of an individual. Steve says, "I didn't come into work because I was sick yesterday." But Brian saw Steve going for a bike ride last evening. Thinking the best of Steve, and believing him to be honest, Brian believes that what Steve actually meant was that he was sick for only the first part of the day, but then felt better by evening. His estimate of Steve's character motivates him to interpret Steve's claim in the best possible light. But in fact, Steve was simply lying. Steve intended to convey the (false) information that that he was sick all day in order to get out of work. Brian's bias caused him to misinterpret a statement that was really pretty clear.

I was recently conversing with a young man who denies the Trinity (see appendix A for the complete dialogue). I pointed out that John 1:1 teaches that the Word was with God and was God, and that John 1:14 explains that this Word is Jesus. But since the person was biased against this position, he did not want to interpret the "Word" to be a person, but rather an idea, or impersonal aspect of God that later was transformed into the person of Jesus.[2] But the text does not say that the Word was an *aspect* of God. Rather, it teaches that the Word *was God*. The text is very clear, but the young man could not correctly understand the passage because of his bias.

Let's consider a case where a bias can be helpful. Tom states, "Sarah just bought a new truck." But Josh knows that the truck Sarah just bought is a used vehicle, over ten years old. He also knows that Tom is an honest person,

2. We will see in a later chapter that this is an example of the superfluous distinction fallacy.

and would not normally lie. Josh therefore reasons that by "new truck," Tom probably meant to convey that the truck was "new" to Sarah, rather than "factory-new." This is a very reasonable interpretation of Tom's statement. Josh's accurate biases have provided additional information, which removed the ambiguity and helped him to correctly understand Tom's claim. Someone without such biases may have misunderstood — thinking that Tom was claiming that Sarah's truck is factory-new.

People can be very strongly motivated to interpret a text in light of what they *want* to be true. This turns out to be one of the most significant types of bias that results in major errors of biblical interpretation. Since many people rightly recognize the Bible as the Word of God, they know that it is authoritative; they understand that they are held accountable to what it teaches. But some of God's commands are not harmonious with the lifestyle that people wish to live. They are therefore strongly motivated to find a way to interpret the passage such that it allows them to live the way they *want* to live. This is a powerful vice and can ensnare even the most sincere believers.

Could it be that many of the disagreements over what the Bible means stem from the motivations of the reader? Is it possible that a misunderstanding of a text has nothing to do with any ambiguity in the text itself, but is due to the fact that the person does not want to accept what the text clearly teaches? We'll revisit this topic in greater detail later. The point here is that biases (rightly or wrongly) play a very strong role in how a person interprets a text. To interpret a text faithfully, we must be aware of our own biases, and be ready to correct them as necessary. The goal therefore is not to eliminate bias — this isn't possible. Rather, it is to understand how biases can affect our understanding of the text, for better or for worse, and be ready to give up a bias if and when it is shown to be wrong.

Do We Have the Freedom to Interpret a Text as We Wish?

We have seen above that texts do have meaning, and that it is often possible for us to understand that meaning. But how does this affect our *interpretation* of the text? The common sentiment "That's *your* interpretation" implies a critical but unproven assumption: that people have the right to interpret a given text as they wish. But is this assumption legitimate? Is it rational?

We can pose the question in two different ways. First, we might ask if we can interpret the text as we wish, in the sense of having the capacity or legal freedom to do so. The answer to this is rather obvious. People do have the *capacity* (for better or for worse) to interpret a text any way they wish, and many individuals exercise this freedom rather liberally. Hence, there are many different interpretations of Scripture (and other texts to a lesser extent) in use today. Many people want to interpret the Bible according to their own desires. Therefore, they will tend to choose this version of the question because it is obvious that we do have the capacity and legal freedom to interpret any text virtually any way that we wish.

But this is trivial. A more interesting and relevant question concerns whether it is *proper* to interpret a text as we wish. More specifically, does such an attitude allow us to consistently arrive at the *meaning* of a text? As we already established above, the meaning of a proposition is the idea that the author intends to communicate to the reader. And we saw that for a meaningful, well-constructed proposition, there is exactly one primary meaning. But since people have the capacity to interpret a text any way they wish, there are an unlimited number of interpretations of a text. But only *one* of those interpretations (at most) will correspond to the meaning of the passage since the passage has one meaning. This is a crucial point, which deserves some discussion.

A given text has an unlimited number of potential interpretations, but it has only *one meaning*. Thus, it is reasonable for us to define the term "correct interpretation" as *the interpretation that matches the meaning of a text* — the one that is faithful to the *author's intention*. All other interpretations will be "faulty" — that is, they are not true to what the passage means. Since communication involves the transmission of an idea, and since communication is only achieved when the recipient understands the meaning, it follows that only a correct interpretation of a text accomplishes genuine communication. Anything else is merely introspection.

Can we prove this point? Consider the alternative. Consider the man who says, "No, we are free to interpret statements as we see fit." I could respond, "Ah, then you agree with me that we are NOT free to interpret statements as we see fit." To this he would likely reply, "No, you misunderstood. I said that we *are* free to interpret statements as we see fit." I could then respond by saying, "I understood you perfectly. I interpreted your words according to my wishes. My desire is that you agree with me, so I interpreted your statement accordingly!"

When our hypothetical critic says, "No, you misunderstood," he is making the claim that proper communication was not accomplished, that I did not interpret his words *properly* (in accordance with his intention). But this contradicts his claim that any interpretation is acceptable. The very fact that people attempt to communicate shows that they do believe that communication is possible. And communication is only possible when the *interpretation matches the author's intention*. The claim that "multiple interpretations are acceptable" is self-refuting because it presupposes that the claim itself has only one correct interpretation. The multiple interpretations view is a form of the relativist fallacy.

"Sure, these principles make sense for any normal literature," says the critic. "But the Bible is not normal literature. It has special rules." How are we to deal with this claim?

Review

Can truth be relative to the individual? No, because the statement "truth is relative" is an absolute statement. If it's true, it's false. Therefore, it's false. To deny the absolute nature of truth is the *relativist fallacy*.

Do words have meaning? Yes. The statement "Words do not have meaning" is self-refuting because it presupposes that words do have meaning. If it is true, it's false. Therefore, it's false. To deny that words have meaning is the *deconstructionist fallacy*.

Does a proposition have meaning? Yes, generally, and only one meaning. If propositions did not generally have meaning, or if they had more than one meaning, then genuine communication could never occur. Thus, people could never learn anything from books or teachers. But communication is possible; people do learn from books and from teachers all the time. Therefore, the notion that propositions are generally meaningless (or have more than one meaning) is a self-refuting proposition. It's necessarily false.

Can human beings discover the meaning of a proposition? Yes — often. If it were never possible to discover the meaning of a proposition, then communication would be impossible. But we know that communication is possible. Concepts can be transferred by the use of language. Thus, it is indeed often possible to discover the meaning of a proposition — but not always.

Are there certain essential requirements necessary to understand a text? Yes, the reader of a text must understand the language of the text. This includes at least some of the vocabulary and the major rules of grammar. An understanding of the history and culture of the author may be necessary in some cases, but not in all cases. The reader must be able to reason logically, and have a philosophy that is compatible with proper interpretive methods, one that will not cause a misunderstanding of the passage. There may be others. But these provide a reasonable start.

Is it proper/appropriate to interpret according to our own wishes or standards? No, arbitrary interpretation does not generally extract the meaning of a passage. It merely reflects the reader's biases, not the author's intention. The notion that we are free to interpret a text by our arbitrary wishes is self-contradictory; anyone espousing such a view would have to assume that his statement would itself not be subject to arbitrary interpretation. The "correct interpretation" is defined to be the one that matches the meaning of a passage — the author's intention. The one-meaning principle is the fact that a given proposition generally has exactly one primary meaning, and thus exactly one correct interpretation.

Chapter 2

The Bible as a Work of Literature

For the most part, people can read a book and understand what the text means. There is no major dispute about what the author meant to convey in books like *the Hobbit*, a cookbook, or a textbook on American history. People are able to apply rules of textual interpretation with little effort and normally come to agreement on the main meaning of just about any book . . . except the Bible. Why is this?

For whatever reason, many people do not apply the same rules of hermeneutics to the Bible that they would to any other work of literature. Is that a reasonable thing to do? If so, what is the reason, and in what ways should biblical interpretation differ from that of any other text?

The Bible is much more than a work of literature. But it is *at least* a work of literature. Consequently, the rules of interpretation that we would apply to any other work of literature will generally apply to the Bible as well. In fact, it is a logical fallacy to exempt the Bible from the ordinary rules of interpretation unless there is a logically compelling reason why it should be exempt from a particular rule. This fallacy is called "special pleading," which is the fallacy of having a double standard.

It is fairly easy to demonstrate that interpreting a particular book by different standards (without a good reason) from other literature is fallacious. The person who argues otherwise would refute himself. Consider someone who states that the Bible is subject to different rules of interpretation than those used for other sources of information, yet he gives no particular reason. The fact that he expects us to understand his statement reveals that he has tacitly assumed that the rules of interpretation are *universal* — that they are not dependent on the source of information. Otherwise, we might interpret his words differently than someone else who says the same thing! If there were fundamentally different rules of interpretation for different sources, then language would not be objective and communication would be impossible. The meaning of a proposition does not depend on its origin. A given proposition in Scripture necessarily has the same basic meaning as the same proposition in another work of literature within the same context. So the same basic principles of interpretation that apply to literature will apply to Scripture.

Language necessarily has an objective quality to it; both the writer and the reader must agree on the rules of language if communication is to take place. To arbitrarily switch to a fundamentally different set of rules of interpretation for a different document is to commit the fallacy of special pleading, and will lead to an incorrect interpretation of the text. It is important to note the qualifiers "arbitrarily" and "fundamentally different." These are crucial because there are certainly some differences in rules of interpretation between different *styles* of literature. There are some differences in interpretive rules between poetic literature and historical narrative. But the primary rules are the same (e.g., context is important, linguistic relativism is fallacious in both poetic and historic literature, and so on). And for the differences, there is a good reason — it's not *arbitrary*. Yes, there is a reason to treat poetic literature somewhat differently from historical narrative since the two forms use a different style.

So there are two points to take away here. First, if we are to be logical and avoid the fallacy of special pleading, then we must interpret the Bible according to the same basic interpretive rules as other types of literature of the same style. That means we interpret the Bible's historical sections in the same manner as another history book, and its poetic sections as we would other poetic literature. The Bible is a work of literature and should be interpreted accordingly.

Second, any exceptions to this generalization must be logically warranted. Unlike any other work of literature, the Bible is the Word of God and is consequently inerrant. This does not make it cease to be a work of literature; and so hermeneutical rules still apply. But does the inerrant nature of God's Word warrant any distinctions in rules of hermeneutic from what would be used for errant literature?

The Bible as a History Book

The Bible is *basically* a history book. It records events that have happened in the past. The Bible does contain other types of literature as well. It contains poetic literature, such as the Psalms; prophetic literature, such as Revelation; and doctrinal teaching, such as the Book of Hebrews. But even the non-historic portions often contain a great deal of history, or elaborate on such history. The Book of Job, for example, which is considered part of the poetic "wisdom literature," is primarily historical in nature.[1] Even the way the Bible begins shows its historical nature: "In the beginning, God created the heavens and the earth." It is a simple statement of something that happened in the past — history.

Since the Bible is basically a history book, it follows from the above interpretive principles that it should be interpreted accordingly. This is the *genre principle*, and we will come back to it in greater detail in a later chapter. Those sections of Scripture that are historical in nature are to be read as a person would read a history book. How then do we read a history book? History books are read in a generally literal fashion. By "literal" we mean that the words are taken in their ordinary, primary, everyday sense. When a word has more than one meaning, we use context — the surrounding words — to determine which meaning fits.

Since the Bible is primarily historical literature, and since historical language is correctly interpreted in a generally literal fashion, we now have a very good starting point in biblical interpretation. We begin with the historical sections that are easy to interpret since they are primarily literal. Anyone can take the words at face value since this requires no special knowledge beyond being able to read. This will form a basic knowledge of what the Bible is teaching, and will aid us when we move on to the more difficult passages in other types of literature found in Scripture.

This also refutes a number of different positions on biblical interpretation. There are some people who claim that the Bible is to be taken in a metaphorical fashion. They see it as an artistic work, not to be taken literally. However, this view commits the fallacy of special pleading. These

1. Job is classified as poetic or wisdom literature because the speeches of Job and his friends employ a poetic style. However, these events happened historically.

same people take any other history book in a literal fashion; but they don't apply the same standard to Scripture. Moreover, they give no good objective reason as to why the Bible should be exempt from the ordinary rules of interpretation that would be applied to any other history book. Their approach is "reading into" the text, which is not true to the author's intention and is therefore, by definition, an incorrect interpretation. In the next chapter, we will explore some faulty views of hermeneutics, and see that they pay insufficient attention to the style of literature under investigation.

As with any other work of literature, we should be cognizant of the cultural and historical setting in which the text was written. This will help us understand any common figures of speech, or references to events or persons that are not explained in the text itself. But, since the historical sections of Scripture are largely literal, most of them can be understood without a lot of knowledge of the culture. Indeed, we can learn about the culture by reading the text with minimal interpretation. Many figures of speech can be decoded by their literary context. As our knowledge of the historical practices and idioms improves, we can apply this knowledge to the rest of Scriptures. The method of using the grammar of the text itself and knowledge of the historical setting to exegete a text is called the *grammatical-historical approach*. This approach is logically justified because it is designed to faithfully extract the author's intention, which is the goal of hermeneutics.

The Bible as the Word of God

The Bible is a work of literature, but it is different in some ways from all other works of literature. As such, we might expect that there may be a few rules of interpretation that are slightly different for Scripture than for other literature. This is logical if and only if there is a good reason for such a difference.

The key distinction between the Bible and other ancient books of history is the fact that the Bible is inspired by God. Virtually all other differences stem from this distinction. The Bible is "God-breathed." Therefore everything that the Bible affirms is what God affirms. This means that all its claims are true since God by His nature is truth (John 14:6). Scripture is inerrant text (entirely without error) in its original manuscripts. And this has implications for our interpretation of Scripture that would not necessarily apply to other literature.

The inerrant nature of Scripture does *not* mean that every sentence in the Bible is true, as a moment's reflection will make clear. The Bible truthfully records the false statements made by fallible people. For example, the Bible records the false statement, "There is no god." But it does not *affirm* that statement. In other words, the Bible is not claiming that there is no god. On the contrary, it explains that only a fool would believe something like that (Psalms 14:1). Likewise, when the Bible records in Genesis 18:15 that Sarah said, "I did not laugh," the Bible is not affirming Sarah's position but merely truthfully reporting her words (which were false). This is a crucial distinction. *What the Bible reports is not necessarily what the Bible endorses or affirms.* However, everything that the Bible affirms is true. And this distinguishes Scripture from other types of literature, which may be mistaken in what they affirm.

Since the Bible is inerrant in its affirmations, it will be tempting for us to interpret it in light of what we think we know. For example, "The Bible seems to be teaching X, but I know that the contrary claim Y is true, so the text must really mean Y since the Bible cannot be wrong." Such reasoning is very seductive and is probably responsible for a large number of faulty interpretations of the Bible. However, this approach is *not* exegesis and will not consistently arrive at the intention of the author because our beliefs about what is true have no bearing on the intention of the author. The approach of "reading into" the text based on our beliefs is called "eisegesis."

Eisegesis is fallacious because it presupposes that our fallible mind is superior to the clarity of the infallible Word of God. It is ridiculous to judge the inerrant by the standards of the errant. What we *think* we know is far less certain than what the Bible teaches, if indeed the Bible is the inerrant Word of God. Therefore, it is foolish to attempt to adjust what the Bible teaches to match with what we think we know. The logical approach is the reverse; we adjust our beliefs to match the teaching of Scripture. Eisegesis will not systematically lead to a correct interpretation of Scripture any more than it will for any other document. Like all other literature, the correct interpretation of Scripture must be *exegetical.*

Since it is inerrant, the Bible will not contradict itself. Again, this doesn't mean that it cannot record contradictions stated by people. But what the Bible affirms in one place will not contradict what it affirms in another place. This means that if two verses seem to be in contradiction, our interpretation of one or both of them is wrong. This would *not* necessarily be the case with any other work of literature. When we find an apparent contradiction in some other book, we might allow for the possibility that the contradiction is genuine; but this is not possible with Scripture due to its inerrancy. So this is a logically justified difference in interpretive method between the Bible and other literature.

Since the Bible cannot contradict itself, this leads to a hermeneutical rule: verses must be interpreted in such a way as to logically comport with each other. This is the *consistency principle*, or the *principle of non-contradiction*; a correct interpretation of the text of Scripture will never contradict a correct interpretation of another text of Scripture.

This rule is not terribly different from the corresponding rule that would apply to other documents. It is proper interpretation to give the benefit of the doubt to any literature that seems to make a statement that is factually wrong, or seems to contradict another statement in the same work. It is appropriate to presume that any perceived contradictions within a given text are resolvable unless and until it can be demonstrated that they are not. The reason for this is that people don't often consciously contradict themselves; thus, it is unlikely the author's intention is to both affirm and deny the same thing at the same time. And since the correct interpretation is the one that gets to the author's intention, it will usually be the case in most literature that apparent contradictions are only apparent.

Our everyday communication shows that we naturally abide by this principle. Suppose we asked someone, "Did you go to work yesterday?" And the person responds, "Well, yes and no." We would not normally accuse him of lying and contradicting himself. Rather, we would give him the benefit of the doubt and presume that he did go to work in one sense, and did not in another sense. There is no contradiction if the sense is different. We might ask the person for an explanation, but we would not jump to the conclusion that his statement is a contradiction until there is no doubt. He might clarify by saying, "Well, I did go to work in the sense that I went to the building. But the power was out due to a fallen power line, and they told us to go home. So I didn't actually go inside the building or do any work." Now his answer makes perfect sense, and there is no contradiction.

Only when all possible explanations have been eliminated should we conclude that a (non-scriptural) text contradicts itself. The generalization of giving the benefit of the doubt to a text applies to both biblical and non-biblical literature. But in the case of Scripture, the rule is absolute since Scripture *cannot* contradict itself; whereas for other literature, contradictions are merely improbable, but we do allow for the possibility since the authors are fallible. So the distinction is not as great as it might seem at first.

It is noteworthy that critics of the Bible often ignore this principle. Even if we grant for the sake of argument that the Bible could contain errors, it is still normal interpretive procedure to give any text the benefit of the doubt. To fail to follow this principle is fallacious for any text; it is an *appeal to ignorance* to assume without justification that a paradox is not resolvable. The critic who says, "These two verses seem to contradict; therefore the Bible is wrong" hasn't proved anything other than his own lack of scholarship. Only after showing that there is no possible way to reconcile two different claims within a text would it be rational to conclude that there is necessarily a genuine contradiction.

Divine Co-Authorship

The Bible claims to be the Word of God written by men (2 Timothy 3:16). Therefore, with the exception of a few chapters that were written by God without human involvement (Exodus 31:18), every section of Scripture has (at least) two authors — one human, and one divine. It is clear from the different styles of different books of the Bible that God did not override the thoughts and styles of the people He chose to write His Word. Rather, He used their different personalities and styles to write exactly what He wanted.

There is a great mystery here, because it is difficult for us to grasp how God could do this. How can God cause men to write His Words without overriding their personalities or styles, and yet every word of Scripture came out just as God wanted? We couldn't do this of course. But God is not bound by our limitations, and there is no logical contradiction in God creating men and inspiring them in such a way that what they write is exactly what God wanted. The sovereign King of kings is able to orchestrate human actions to accomplish His divine plan (Isaiah 46:10–11).

Hermeneutics is the attempt to understand the intention of the author. But the Scriptures have two authors — God and man. Is it possible that the two authors had a different primary intention in a given passage? The objective nature of language disallows such a possibility. Words mean the same thing to different people if communication is to take place. Therefore, what the human author of Scripture affirms is also what God affirms. Any alternative is contrary to the perspicuity of Scripture.

Nonetheless, God is omniscient, whereas human authors are not. It is therefore possible that God has in mind a specific meaning or application of a passage that goes beyond the knowledge of the human author. This second-level of meaning must be fully consistent with the intention of the human author (so as to be compatible with perspicuity), but will go beyond his understanding. The Bible contains many example of this. New Testament authors often quote Old Testament passages, but give a fuller explanation of them than would have been known by the Old Testament author. For example, in Psalm 22, David writes about the anguish of one who has trusted in the Lord and yet seems to be forsaken by Him (Psalm 22:1–3). This man trusted in God from his mother's womb (v. 10), yet is despised by the people (v. 6), mocked (v. 7), and pierced in the hands and feet (v. 16). His bones are out of joint (v. 14), and his garments are divided for those casting lots (v. 18). It is obvious from our New Testament perspective that this psalm refers to Christ (e.g., John 19:24). God clearly had the crucifixion of Christ in mind when He inspired David to write Psalm 22. But did David know that? It is certainly consistent with what he wrote, but due to New Testament revelation we have a fuller understanding of the passage than even David had.

The prophet Malachi wrote that God would send Elijah before the day of the Lord to restore the hearts of fathers to their children (Malachi 4:5–6). Not that Elijah himself would appear — but rather someone who would come in the spirit and power of Elijah. Did Micah know that this "Elijah" is John the Baptist? Probably not. But Jesus explains that this is indeed what was meant (Matthew 11:14, 17:10–13). That the Malachi passages refers specifically to John the Baptist was confirmed by Gabriel (Luke 1:11–20). Gabriel quoted Malachi 4:5–6 and applied this passage specifically to John the Baptist (Luke 1:17).

Was Gabriel misquoting Malachi? Of course not. The meaning of the Old Testament text did not change; Gabriel simply provided additional revelation from God that gave a fuller understanding of the passage in Micah. Likewise, the primary meaning of Psalm 22 can be understood on its own terms without New Testament enlightenment. David knew what he meant, and anyone reading the passage can understand it on its own terms. But the New Testament gives a more specific and rich understanding of the passage. It is perfectly appropriate to use later revelation from God to enrich our understanding of previous revelation.

A New Testament interpretation of an Old Testament passage will never contradict the primary meaning of the passage as it would have been understood by its human author. But New Testament interpretation may give additional insight that would have been unknown to the original audience. It is *not* the case, as some critics have alleged, that New Testament writers take Old Testament verses out of context and appropriate them for their own purpose. No. Any Old Testament author would endorse how the New Testament author interprets a verse, even though the New Testament interpretation gives a more complete picture than the Old Testament author possessed at the time. The redemptive-historical method of interpretation makes use of this fact to better understand Old Testament history in light of God's plan of salvation. Jesus Himself interpreted the Scriptures in such a way as He explained to His disciples how the Old Testament pointed to Himself (Luke 24:27, 44).

Note that the redemptive-historical method is not *contrary* to the grammatical-historical method, but is supplementary to it and relies upon it. The grammatical-historical method extracts the primary meaning of a passage as it would have been understood by its original audience, whereas the redemptive-historical method builds upon this and gleans additional insight from later biblical revelation to help Christians understand the Old Testament in a way that goes beyond what Old Testament believers would have understood at the time, while nonetheless being fully consistent with it.

Additional Distinctions in Biblical Interpretation

The divine nature of Scripture brings another distinction, related to the previous topic, concerning the way in which the different books of the Bible can be used to interpret each other. Since all Scripture is inspired by God and inerrant, it follows that any verse in Scripture that comments on another verse, does so with inerrancy. For example, in Hebrews 1:8, the author quotes Psalm 45:6 and ascribes the quote to God (the Father) as speaking to God the Son. Now if you read Psalm 45:6, it may not be obvious that this is God the Father speaking to God the Son. But in this instance, the Scripture provides its own interpretation, and that interpretation is inerrant. So there can be no doubt that Psalm 45:6 is speaking about God the Son, since the Bible elsewhere explicitly says so.

There is nothing unusual about using one portion of a text to help us interpret another portion of a text. This is perfectly appropriate for any work of literature. What is unusual about Scripture is the following: First, the words from one author in one book can be used to interpret the words of another author in another book. Second, such interpretations are inerrant. And third, interpretations are not limited to what a person would naturally be able to understand in his time and culture. Let's look at each of these separately.

If we want to learn what a particular author means by a particular statement, we would naturally look to other statements within that same work written by that same author to clarify. So naturally, when he himself tells us what he means, there can be no doubt, particularly when found within the same written text. An author's comments about his own writings are far more authoritative than anyone else's, because the author knows better than anyone what the text means; he wrote it!

Naturally, the best key to interpretation of a particular text (whether biblical or not) is what the author has said about the text within the text. The second best perhaps would be what the author says about the text in a later text. This is still very helpful because it is the same person. Yet it loses something because the person may have changed his mind on some issues, or may not remember his original intent.

Far less important is what a different person (a non-author) has to say about the text. Not that we should automatically dismiss his or her analysis, but we would expect the person to give a good argument for his or her position before we accept the position as the proper interpretation. A third party cannot read the author's mind, and so he or she must make an argument from the text — an argument that we should evaluate according to the principles of interpretation. But an author need not make such an argument; in the text itself he can simply say, "this is what I mean: ____." And that settles the matter.

But with Scripture, the rule *appears* to change slightly. An author from one book of the Bible is just as qualified to interpret the words of an author of another book as the author of that other book. For example, when the author of Hebrews explains the meaning of Psalm 2:7 in Hebrews 1:5, his interpretation is just as authoritative as if the Psalmist himself interpreted his own words. This is because in the ultimate sense, the author of Hebrews and the author of the Psalms are the same author: God.

So really, the rule hasn't changed. We simply need to keep in mind that the entire Bible has one ultimate Author who does not change His mind. God used human beings to write His Word; but He infallibly inspired them to do so such that what they wrote is exactly what God wanted them to write (2 Peter 1:21). He used their personalities and styles, but it is ultimately His Word. And so, Hebrews 1:5 is God explaining what He meant when He wrote Psalm 2:7. And no one is more qualified to interpret Scripture than God.

Add to this the fact that Scripture is inerrant, and we see that it is absolutely inescapable to conclude that whenever one portion of Scripture interprets another, it does so perfectly. That Scripture is the best guide to interpreting Scripture is often called "the analogy of Faith." To deny this principle is to deny inerrancy, and the inspiration of Scripture.

And we must remember that since the biblical authors were inspired by God, they had access to revelation far beyond what could be ascertained through normal sensory experience and human reasoning. For example, the author of Hebrews tells us what Abraham thought about the offering of Isaac as a sacrifice. Abraham trusted in God's promise to bring many descendants through Isaac, even if Isaac were sacrificed; Abraham believed that God could raise Isaac from the dead (Hebrews 11:17–19). The really interesting thing is that there is nothing in the Genesis 22 account about Abraham's thoughts on the resurrection. How could the author of Hebrews possibly know what Abraham *thought*? Unless Abraham had written down his thoughts in some other text that was still extant in the first century (though is now lost), the author of Hebrews could only have known this by divine inspiration. God knew what Abraham thought, and God revealed this to the author of Hebrews. Due to the principle of inerrancy, it must be the case that the Hebrews 11:17–19 analysis of Genesis 22 is exactly right.

Consider another example: Isaiah 7:14 prophesies that a virgin will conceive and bear a son. Critics have pointed out that the Hebrew word *almah*, translated as "virgin" need only refer to a "young woman," not necessarily a literal virgin. This is very unlikely in context, because there are no instances in Scripture where the word is clearly used of a young woman who is not a virgin. In any case, some of the more liberal translations (such as NRSV) do render that word as "young woman." Even if we allowed that as a possibility, when Matthew quotes this passage in the New Testament (Matthew 1:23) he uses the Greek word *parthenos* that can only mean a literal virgin. Matthew infallibly records that Isaiah did indeed mean to indicate a virgin — not just a "young woman." Since Matthew writes under divine inspiration, his interpretation of Isaiah 7:14 is absolutely authoritative.

This can be summed up in the following rule: the best guide to interpreting the text of Scripture is the text of Scripture — the "analogy of faith." When one section of the Bible interprets another section, it does so infallibly. There is absolutely no possibility for error. As a corollary to this rule, any interpretation of Scripture is in error if it is inconsistent with the Bible's interpretation of itself. Anyone wishing to deny this principle must deny the inerrancy of Scripture as well.

Conclusions

We must conclude that, in general, the Bible follows the same interpretive rules as other literature of the same style. The grammatical-historical hermeneutic recognizes this, and attempts to extract the intention of the author based on his words (grammar) in the historical setting in which he lived. We have seen that any alternative to the grammatical-historical approach is self-refuting. Yet, not all people agree. Why is this? What are some of the other methods that professing Christians use? And can we demonstrate that such methods are faulty?

Review

Do the rules of interpretation of literature apply to the Bible? Yes — and it's easy to prove with a simple syllogism: (1) rules of interpretation apply to works of literature, (2) the Bible is a work of literature, (3) therefore, rules of interpretation apply to the Bible. To exempt the Bible from the rules of interpretation that apply to all other literature without a good reason is to commit the fallacy of special pleading.

Are there any differences in rules of interpretation when applied specifically to the Bible? Yes, but only a very few, and they are only subtly different.

If a rule of interpretation is to be modified for Scripture, then there must be a compelling logical reason for the change. Since the Bible is the inerrant Word of God, the rules of interpretation that allow for errors in other documents must be adjusted for Scripture. This is not special pleading because we do have a good reason for the change: inerrancy and inspiration by God. Rules of interpretation that are unrelated to the divine aspect of Scripture will apply unchanged.

Is there a difference between the Bible and other texts in terms of how we deal with apparent contradictions? Yes — but it is a subtle one. Proper interpretation of any text always involves giving the text/author the benefit of the doubt in matters of fact or matters of apparent contradiction. People rarely self-consciously contradict themselves. Thus, contradictions are improbable in a given text by a given author. And for Scripture, contradictions are *impossible* due to its inerrant status as the Word of God. This is the *consistency principle*, or the principle of *non-contradiction*.

What type of literature is the Bible? It contains several types of literature, but the Bible is primarily a history book. As such, the rules of interpretation that are used for interpreting history books will apply to the main historical sections of the Bible. One such rule is that historical works are to be read in a natural fashion (i.e., literally, unless there are clear contextual clues suggesting otherwise). No one would take a book on American history as a metaphor for instructions on how to make waffles. Therefore, if we are to avoid the fallacy of special pleading, the Bible's historical accounts are to be interpreted as literal history. This is the *genre principle*, and will be addressed in greater detail in a later chapter.

What method is appropriate for interpreting Scripture? The grammatical-historical hermeneutic is appropriate by the impossibility of the contrary. Anyone wishing to argue against a grammatical historical approach would have to use a grammatical-historical approach to make his argument. That is, he expects us to take his words literally as constrained by the rules of grammar in our present historical context. The progressive nature of divine revelation allows us to glean additional insights into Old Testament passages by reading the New Testament. For example, a redemptive-historical approach examines Old Testament typology in light of New Testament revelation (e.g., Hebrews 8:1–5). This approach is not contrary to the grammatical-historical hermeneutic, but builds upon it.

What is the most authoritative interpretation of a given text? The author's own statements within a text about what he or she means in that text are absolutely authoritative. Correct interpretation is all about getting to the author's intentions, and no one understands the author's intentions better than the author. Comments by other people (non-authors) for a given text are not authoritative, but may be helpful if they make a good argument for their position. There is no reason to exempt the Bible from this rule. However, there is a subtle apparent change when it comes to Scripture: biblical authors *are* authoritative when commenting on other authors, because they write under divine inerrancy. This is not a genuine modification to the rule when we recognize that the entire Bible has one ultimate author: God. He interprets His own words better than anyone else.

What is the best interpreter of Scripture? Answer: Scripture. This follows from the previous rule. When one section of the Bible interprets another section, it does so infallibly. This is called the "analogy of faith." As a corollary to this rule, any interpretation of Scripture is wrong if it is inconsistent with the Bible's interpretation of itself. Anyone who denies that Scripture infallibly interprets Scripture must necessarily deny inerrancy.

Chapter 3

Exposing Faulty Methods of Hermeneutics

Given the definition of "correct interpretation" as that which matches the author's intention, and knowing that the Bible is not exempt from the rules of interpretation that apply to other literature, we are now in a position to expose the errors in faulty methods of hermeneutics. Namely, a hermeneutical method is faulty if it leads to incorrect interpretations — those that do not match the author's intention. But how are we to know the author's intention?

Some critics claim that it is never possible to understand the author's intention, and thus all hermeneutical methods are pointless. "After all," they say, "you would have to be able to read the mind of the author in order to know what he or she intends." This is a form of the deconstructionist fallacy. And we have already seen that this is a self-refuting position since this critic expects us to understand his intention. An easy response is, "I don't have to read a person's mind to know what he's thinking if the person *tells* me what he's thinking! That's the point of language." The critic who argues for deconstructionism has attempted to use words to convey his thought that words cannot convey thoughts — a self-defeating argument.

The purpose of words is to reveal the thoughts and intentions of the speaker/author. That is the entire point of communication — to transfer a thought from one person's mind to another. Therefore, if we are to understand an author's intention, which is the goal of hermeneutics, *we must take his own words as the primary means of revealing his intention.* A correct hermeneutic must be based principally on what the author himself has written. This may seem trivial, yet many hermeneutical methods do not take the author's words as their primary focus. As a result, such methods do not consistently arrive at the author's intention; in other words, they result in an incorrect interpretation of the text.

We will cover the details of analyzing the author's words to better understand his intention in later chapters. But we don't have to know these details to see that many modern hermeneutical methods are faulty. All we have to do is show that they are not primarily motivated at understanding the author's intention through an analysis of his words. Namely, any hermeneutic that takes some other standard as its primary criterion, rather than the author's words, is faulty and unreliable. Such methods will not consistently arrive at the meaning of the text because that really isn't their goal. A faulty hermeneutic might, by sheer accident, occasionally happen upon the right answer. But since its goal is wrong, such accidents will be uncommon. Let's examine the goal and method of some common views of hermeneutics.

The Allegorical Method

Consider first the *allegorical* method of interpretation. This system takes elements of the narrative portions of Scripture as symbolic only, but not necessarily as literal history. Of course, the Bible does use non-literal language on occasion and the grammatical-historical approach recognizes this. However, proper interpretation demands that the author's own words should be the primary way to distinguish the literal sections from the figurative. And this is where the allegorical method falls short.

Genesis is usually the first casualty of this hermeneutic. In many cases, the allegoristic interpreter takes Adam and Eve as metaphors conveying spiritual truth, but not as literal people who actually lived. Historically, this hermeneutic was employed by such men as Philo of Alexandria (1st century) and Augustine of Hippo (4th century). The allegorical method has seen some resurgence in our modern culture, perhaps due to the desire to reconcile Darwinian evolution with Genesis. Jewish scholar Dr. Jeffrey

Tigay defends this hermeneutic as applied to Genesis in his article "Genesis as Allegory."[1] His article begins:

> In showing that the Universe had a beginning, science has come closer to the teachings of the Bible than ever before. Nevertheless, there is still a considerable distance between current scientific thought and the details of the biblical account of creation. According to the latter, the physical world and the many species of living things were created essentially as we know them less than six thousand years ago over a period of seven days. Astronomy, geology, biology, and related sciences indicate that the process was a gradual one that took billions of years. Earlier geological strata of the earth's surface show the different stages through which the earth passed and approximately how long they lasted, while fossils and remains of extinct species such as dinosaurs show that the different species of living creatures evolved slowly from a common ancestor.

Already we see some fallacious reasoning. Tigay has committed the fallacy of reification (see chapter 8) in personifying "science" as if a method could have a belief about such things as evolution or the age of the earth. But more importantly, this introduction reveals something about Tigay's motive for using the allegorical approach. By relegating Genesis to a fictional, non-literal story, Tigay is able to reconcile in his mind the words of Genesis with what he believes to be the true history of the universe, namely evolution and vast ages. He goes on to say this:

> In the Middle Ages, Saadia Gaon argued that a biblical passage should not be interpreted literally if that made a passage mean something contrary to the senses or reason (or, as we would say, science . . .). Maimonides applied this principle to theories about creation. He held that if the eternity of the universe . . . could be proven by logic (science) then the biblical passages speaking about creation at a point in time could and should be interpreted figuratively in a way that is compatible with the eternity of the universe.

---

1. http://www.myjewishlearning.com/article/genesis-as-allegory/.

Tigay defends Saadia Gaon's approach: that when "science" conflicts with a narrative of Scripture, it is supposedly appropriate to take the words of Scripture as figurative, regardless of the grammar, style, or context of the passage.[2] Tigay's comment reflects a misunderstanding of the scientific method — science was never designed to study supernatural or historical events, such as creation. Of course, scientific evidence in the present can have a confirmatory though non-decisive implication for various views of history. But Tigay seems to have uncritically accepted what the majority of secular scientists (currently) believe about origins as an unquestionable fact, to which the Bible must submit. But let's put all these errors aside since our focus is on his hermeneutic. Notice the one thing that Tigay does not even begin to consider in any of his argumentation. That's right: he doesn't even touch on the *intention of the author*.

As we are not mind-readers, we can only ascertain an author's intention by considering his words. And this is precisely what Tigay fails to do at any point in his essay. He never even considers what the author of Genesis had to write about the purpose of Genesis. And he openly admits that his motivation for an allegorical interpretation is to make Genesis line up with the "senses, reason, and science," by which he apparently means current secular views of origins. Tigay is not alone; other advocates of the allegorical method do likewise. That's the point of allegorical interpretation. The method imposes a figurative interpretation on various texts of the Bible without any consideration as to what the texts themselves say about their own style or purpose.

No doubt, some portions of Scripture are non-literal; we saw this in the previous chapters. But we must use the author's words to discern between the literal and non-literal if we are to arrive at the meaning, rather than imposing a system contrary to the author's intended meaning. Since the intention of the author is, by definition, the goal of correct interpretation, and since this is not the goal of the allegorical method, we can conclude that the allegorical method is a fundamentally incorrect method

2. There is a difference between reason and science, though Tigay equates the two. Science is a procedure for observationally testing certain kinds of truth claims, and is sometimes used to mean the body of knowledge or beliefs attained by such procedures. "Reason" has multiple definitions. It can refer to what seems sensible ("reasonable"), which is very subjective. It can refer to proper reasoning — which is objective. The Bible everywhere presupposes the correct use of reasoning, but it does not assume modern "scientific" opinion.

of hermeneutics. It does not get to the meaning — the author's intention — of a text. It was never designed to do so.

Pietistic Interpretation

Another hermeneutic that has seen recent resurgence in some denominations is the pietistic approach. In this method, the reader's interpretation of the biblical text is guided and controlled by the "inward light" — the non-audible leading of the Holy Spirit. When considering what a biblical passage means, the pietistic interpreter prays and waits upon the Holy Spirit to "whisper in his ear" the correct answer. This may sound very biblical on the surface. We know that the Holy Spirit does indeed enlighten our mind to understand the Word (1 Corinthians 2:12–14). However, the pietistic interpreter goes beyond this, and takes his internal feelings about the leading of the Holy Spirit to be the *ultimate standard* for biblical interpretation, at the expense of the grammar and context of the written text.

The problems with this approach are numerous. First, we readily observe that various pietistic interpreters frequently come to very different and contradictory interpretations of a given text. But how could this be if the Holy Spirit told each of them what the passage means? Would the Holy Spirit tell Jim that the text means one thing, and then tell Jenny the opposite? If so, then He has lied to at least one of them. That would make no sense. And how would a third party decide which person was truly hearing from God? Subjective feelings about the leading of the Holy Spirit are not something that other people can verify. When two pietistic interpreters disagree on what the Spirit said to them, we must conclude either (1) they have misunderstood what the Holy Spirit "whispered in their ear," or (2) it wasn't the Holy Spirit at all who was speaking to them.

This raises an important issue: how does the pietistic interpreter know that this "inner light" is really the leading of the Holy Spirit, as opposed to his own inner voice, or Satan for that matter? Whenever anyone claims to hear a private word from the Lord (e.g., "God told me to sell my house and move to Africa") we must ask, "Was this impression a message from God leading you, or was it a message from Satan tempting you? And how do you know?"

God certainly can speak to people, but Satan can as well (Matthew 4:1–3). And people can say things inwardly to themselves (e.g., Psalm 10:6,

11). How are we to discern the difference? The grammatical-historical hermeneutic provides us with an answer — we compare any supposed new revelation from God with what God has already revealed in His Word. Since God does not deny Himself, new revelation that is genuinely from God will always be consistent with previous revelation. But the pietistic interpreter has no good answer to the question. Since his "inner voice" is the standard by which he interprets the written text, he cannot then use the written text to evaluate the validity of his inner voice. He may strongly feel that his feelings are from God, but how does he really *know*? Feelings are not proof.

Subjective feelings are notoriously unreliable. Yet the pietistic hermeneutic relies on subjective feelings as the ultimate standard of interpretation. He has assumed that such feelings were initiated by the Holy Spirit, but it is just as possible that they were not. It's hardly surprising that this approach leads to wildly different opinions on what the Scriptures mean. The interpreter is left to believe whatever fanciful view his own imagination can concoct, untethered by the constraints of reason or textual analysis. Any conclusion is more likely to be a result of the interpreter's indigestion than anything relevant to the author's intention.

Yes, we should listen to what the Holy Spirit says. But inward feelings are not necessarily from the Holy Spirit. *The Bible* on the other hand is (2 Peter 1:21). The written Word is the primary way that the Holy Spirit speaks to people. The Holy Spirit will not contradict in private what He has written openly (2 Timothy 2:13). The Bible is objective (open to inspection by all) and has already established itself to be God's Word.[3] Reason compels us to test alleged new subjective revelations against the established and objective revelation of the Bible — and the Bible itself teaches this as well (Deuteronomy 13:1–5; Acts 17:11; 1 John 1:4). The pietistic approach does precisely the reverse, and is thus contrary to Scripture and sound reason.

It is also worth noting that the pietistic approach has a fatal internal flaw — one that actually compounds the perceived problem rather than alleviating it. The problem of how to interpret the biblical text is said to be resolved by a private message from God. Even if we grant, for the sake of argument,

3. See Jason Lisle, *The Ultimate Proof of Creation: Resolving the Origins Debate* (Green Forest, AR: Master Books, 2011), for a proof demonstrating that the biblical worldview is true, and is given by God.

the dubious assumption that the private message really is from God, we are compelled to ask, "How do you know you have *correctly interpreted the alleged private message from God*?" With the text of Scripture, we can ask others to look at the text and analyze our reasoning. The Bible itself extols the wisdom of consulting others to verify a matter (e.g., Proverbs 15:22, 20:18, 11:14; Deuteronomy 19:15). But a private message from God is not open to the investigation of others. There is no objective method by which we can evaluate the content of the message, let alone its interpretation.

If clear, objective text is sometimes subject to misunderstanding, how much more so a subjective feeling that was allegedly initiated by the Spirit? Perhaps the pietistic interpreter will then claim that he received a second message from God confirming that the first message was properly interpreted. But then we must ask how he knows he correctly understood this second message, and so on, leading to an infinite regress that establishes nothing. At some point a message must be interpreted by its own content. Why not do this with the objective original text, instead of unnecessarily compounding the problem?

God does not contradict Himself (2 Timothy 2:13). Therefore, subjective feelings attributed (rightly or wrongly) to the Holy Spirit may not override the objective words of the Holy Spirit recorded in the text of Scripture. The pietistic approach violates this principle. Once again, this hermeneutic does not accept the words of the author as the primary key to interpretation. Thus, the pietistic method is faulty and will not reliably arrive at the correct interpretation of the text.

The Accommodation Method

Accommodation is the act of simplifying a complex principle for the purpose of explaining that principle to someone else. Since God is infinite and cannot be fully comprehended by finite man, He explains some things in a simplified way so that we can understand the basic concept without necessarily knowing all the nuances. This is a biblical principle.

The *accommodation hermeneutic*, however, is something quite different. The accommodationist interpreter assumes that anything in Scripture that is contrary to modern secular opinions is merely an accommodation to the understanding of the time. Advocates of this position assert that God used the accepted (though false) views of the day, especially the ancient near-east cosmology, to teach true spiritual principles such as monotheism. The view was proposed by 18th-century rationalist Johann Semler.

The accommodationist hermeneutic is attractive to some because it allows professing Christians to justify beliefs that appear contrary to the biblical text. As one example, Jesus affirmed that Moses authored the Pentateuch — the first five books of the Bible, often simply referred to as "the law" (Luke 24:44; John 5:46–47, 7:19). But some liberal scholars reject Mosaic authorship, and yet profess to be Christians. Dr. Peter Enns is one example. He uses the accommodationist hermeneutic to get around Christ's statement. Enns writes, "But more important, I do not think that Jesus's status as the incarnate Son of God requires that statements such as John 5:46–47 be understood as binding, historical judgments of authorship. Rather, Jesus here reflects the tradition that he himself inherited as a first-century Jew and that his hearers assumed to be the case."[4] In other words, Enns thinks that Jesus merely repeated a false view in order to teach a greater truth.

When it comes to Genesis, an accommodation interpreter would say that the author is not affirming any of the details of creation as literally or historically true. Rather, Genesis is simply accommodating the original readership, namely the ancient Hebrews, who believed that the world had been created in the recent past, with all the various organisms according to their kinds. Rather than correcting these false (according to accommodation advocates) views, God simply uses them to communicate the more important fact that He is the Creator.

It seems to me that the accommodation hermeneutic can be summarized as "God uses lies to teach truth." Advocates of that method might dislike my characterization, but how could they argue against this assessment? This "accommodation" is different from genuine, biblical accommodation that uses simplifications of truth to teach truth. The notion that God would use a lie to teach the truth is contrary to His nature as God (Titus 1:2; John 14:6; see also Matthew 12:25). And it leads to an insurmountable problem. If God is willing to lie in His Word, then how could we ever know which parts are true?

Moreover, the accommodation method smacks of chronological snobbery. It implies that the ancient Hebrews were too stupid to understand

4. Peter Enns, *The Evolution of Adam: What the Bible Does and Doesn't Say about Human Origins* (Grand Rapids, MI: Brazos Press, 2012), p. 153.

what we now know about the cosmos; thus, God had to use a false and simplistic view of cosmology to teach them the truth that God created. But there is no logical reason to suppose that ancient man was less intelligent than modern man. Such a mindset stems from evolutionary bias, not evidence. Moreover, if all God wanted to teach was that He is Creator, then only the first verse of Genesis 1 would be necessary. Why take the rest of the chapter to lie about the details?

But again, these considerations are secondary to our central question: does this method take the text as the primary means by which to understand the intention of the author? Clearly it does not. Peter Enns states, "The Old Testament is not a treatise on Israel's history for the sake of history, and certainly not a book of scientific interest, but a document of self-definition and persuasion: 'Do not forget where we've been. Do not forget who we are — the people of God.' "[5] But where does Enns get this idea? It's certainly not from the *text*. The text of Scripture indicates that it is indeed a treatise on history; Genesis 2:4a states, "This is the *account* of the heavens and the earth when they were created." And Genesis 5:1a states, "This is the book of the generations of Adam" (ESV). The text indicates that these portions are historical in nature.

The accommodation method does not take the text itself as the primary means by which to understand the meaning of the passage. Rather, it is driven by external, modern opinions of history and science. It is therefore not a reliable means of extracting the meaning of a passage.

The Mythical Theory

The *mythical hermeneutic* presupposes that biblical narratives of the Old Testament are mostly non-historical myths. The New Testament stories are supposedly largely based on these myths. Advocates of this method, such as David Friedrich Strauss, came up with a list of rules to distinguish the portions of Scripture that really happened from those portions that are mythical. One such rule is that a narrative should not be considered historical if it violates laws of nature. Hence, most miracles are regarded as fiction.[6]

5. http://biologos.org/uploads/resources/enns_scholarly_essay3.pdf p. 10, accessed 6/24/2014.
6. I am considering for the sake of argument only those miracles that violate laws of nature. Not all miracles need do so. God can do an extraordinary action (a miracle) without violating laws of nature if He so pleases. Alternatively, God can suspend laws of nature if He so chooses. It may not be possible to know which type of miracle God does in a given instance, for the simple reason that we don't know what all the laws of nature are.

The method reduces creation to mere myth, as well as the Resurrection of Christ.

The "Jesus Seminar" movement of the mid 1980s embraced this type of hermeneutic, accepting or rejecting Scripture based on a preconceived list of criteria. The narratives in which Jesus does a miracle were rejected as non-historical, since miracles violate natural law. Texts in which Jesus predicted the future are similarly rejected since no one can predict the future (according to advocates of the position). Of course, we must ask how the Jesus Seminar advocates could possibly *know* that miracles are impossible, or that no one can predict the future. These are preconceived opinions, and not something that we could conclude from reading the Bible. These preconceptions merely beg the question.

The Jesus Seminar focused primarily on the Gospels, and its founding members voted on the probability that any given claim was actually true, based on their preconceived opinions of what is possible. They decided that less than 20 percent of the words of Jesus recorded in the Gospels actually were spoken by Him. The rest are alleged to be myth, having been constructed long after the earthly ministry of Christ.

It's hard to take this view seriously because it is completely arbitrary and lacks any rational justification. The Jesus Seminar uses the personal opinions and philosophies of its members to construct a list of rules by which the Scriptures are judged to be true or untrue. Putting the arrogance of this method aside, we note that modern opinions and philosophies have absolutely nothing to do with the intention of the author. The mythical theory makes no attempt whatsoever to extract the meaning of a passage. Rather, it summarily rejects or accepts certain passages based on preconceived (and unbiblical) opinions of what is or is not possible. It is a hermeneutic in name only, and will not faithfully interpret the meaning of the Bible.

Naturalistic Methods

Several interpretive schools of thought, including the mythical view and some versions of the accommodation view, can be classified as "naturalistic." Such methods reject all supernatural agency as either non-literal or false. Any perceived miracles are merely phenomenological, or literary exaggeration. For example, Jesus walking on water (Matthew 14:25–27) was really

Him walking along the shore, not on the sea.[7] And Jesus feeding the five thousand (John 6:10–14) is explained as follows: the generosity of the boy who gave his fish and bread to feed others (John 6:9), inspired others to give what little they had, which inspired others, and so on, until everyone had been fed.

We need not give a point-by-point refutation of such methods to see that they are inherently faulty. They take a preconceived philosophy — in this case naturalism — as the standard by which the text of Scripture is interpreted. But nowhere does the text of Scripture itself even hint that this is what the *authors intended*. Naturalistic methods may appease the whimsical bias of the reader, but they are logically irrelevant to the meaning of the text. They do not even consider the intention of the author according to his own words, and are therefore faulty.

The Common Thread

One reason many of the above faulty views of hermeneutics are not more readily recognized as faulty, is because they have an element of biblical truth, though taken to an unbiblical extreme. The allegorical method may not seem so offensive at first because there are indeed some areas of the Scriptures that are figurative. The flaw in allegorical interpretation is in failing to allow the text itself to determine which portions are figurative. Likewise, the pietistic approach may seem good at first blush because the Holy Spirit indeed illumines our reasoning from the Scriptures. But the approach allows subjective feelings attributed to the Holy Spirit to override what the Holy Spirit objectively wrote. The accommodation method might seem plausible because the Bible does use accommodation. But biblical accommodation is quite different from the accommodation hermeneutic. In the former, God uses simplified true principles to teach truth. In the latter, God allegedly uses false information to teach truth.

Another reason that faulty views of hermeneutics persist is because of the popularity of evolution and "deep time" (vast ages). Our society is highly motivated to not believe in the biblical account of creation. And the above methods allow the reader to take Genesis contrary to the intentions of the author, so that it may be reconciled with modern secular views of

7. This view would make Peter's sinking (on solid land) all the more miraculous! (Matthew 14:29–30).

origins. This might be emotionally satisfying to the reader, but such procedures will not consistently arrive at the meaning of the text because they do not evaluate the author's intention by his written words.

The Grammatical-Historical Method

In order to arrive at the meaning of the text, we need to have the right goal and the right method. First, our goal must be to understand the intention of the author. That is because this is the definition of the correct interpretation — the meaning of the passage. Second, we must take the words of the author as the primary method by which we come to understand his intention. This is because we are not mind-readers, and can only know a person's thoughts if that person reveals them by his or her words. All of the methods listed above fail at least one, if not both, of these two requirements.

This brings us to the grammatical-historical method of interpretation. Unlike all the previous methods, this hermeneutic is motivated by the primary goal of understanding the author's intention by the method of considering his own words. This is the only possible hermeneutic that can yield the correct interpretation, because it is the only one that has the right goal and the right method.[8] The grammatical-historical approach takes the author's own words as the "Supreme Court" by which to judge what the author means.

Granted, people can be committed to the right hermeneutic and still make mistakes in reasoning. So adherence to the grammatical-historical approach does not guarantee that its advocates will always draw the right conclusion. Rather, it is the only method that makes it *possible* for readers to consistently derive correct interpretations. The remaining chapters of this book will serve to flesh out the details of the method, and help readers to avoid mistakes in reasoning.

The grammatical-historical approach is exactly the hermeneutic that is applied to all other literature, and the one that people use in their everyday communication. To exempt the Bible from the method of interpretation used in all other literature is the logical fallacy known as "special pleading." Recall, those who argue against the grammatical-historical method must

8. The redemptive-historical hermeneutic might seem to be "another" correct method, but it is more of an extension, or logical continuation, of the grammatical-historical hermeneutic rather than a separate method entirely. The former rests atop the latter, and could not exist independently of it.

inherently assume the grammatical-historical method if they expect their words to be interpreted properly by their audience.

"Grammatical" is in reference to the fact that the author's words are paramount. But what about "historical"? Grammar is historical in nature. That is, rules of grammar are (somewhat) a matter of convention — they are something that all people of a given language must agree to if communication is to be achieved. But cultures change with time. And therefore languages change with time. The meaning of words can drift slightly over the centuries. Grammatical constructions can change too. And thus, we must know something about the history and the culture of the writer if we are to fully understand his grammar, by which we understand his intention.

In many cases, we can learn this history by what the author himself says in the document.[9] But is it ever necessary to know history that is not contained in a document in order to understand the meaning of the document? If so, is the Scripture such a document? If knowledge of history is helpful in biblical interpretation, is there other knowledge outside of Scripture that would be helpful or perhaps necessary for proper understanding? What might that be?

Review

The goal of hermeneutics is to arrive at the meaning of the text — the intention of the author. Since we lack the ability to read minds, we can only know an author's thoughts by his words. Therefore, a correct method of hermeneutics must focus on the author's words as the final standard of interpretation. Hermeneutical views that do not treat the text as the primary standard of interpretation, or are not motivated by the goal of understanding the author's intention, are faulty — they will not faithfully or consistently extract the meaning of the text.

The allegorical method treats some historical narrative passages in Scripture as figurative, despite grammatical and contextual evidence to the contrary. The pietistic method is based on the subjective feelings of the reader, on the assumption that such feelings are from God. But such a view makes it impossible to know if such feelings really are from God, or if

9. Knowledge of history may not be necessary to get the gist of many biblical narratives. By reading such narratives, we begin to learn something about the history of Israel and its culture. This helps us to understand these narratives even better on the second pass. This hermeneutical circle will be discussed in detail in chapter 9.

they have been interpreted properly. The accommodation method (which should not be confused with legitimate biblical accommodation) assumes that God uses the common views of the original audience to teach biblical principles, even if those views are false. The mythical hermeneutic treats most historical narratives in Scripture as fictional myths, made up by people who came much later in history. Naturalistic hermeneutics (of which the mythical view is one type) treat all supernatural elements in Scripture as non-literal or untrue. The common thread in all these methods is that they do not treat the text itself as the primary source of information about the author's intention. Most of these are not motivated by the goal of getting to the author's intention, so none of them will consistently extract the correct meaning of the text.

The grammatical-historical method uses the author's written words as the primary source of information by which to understand the author's intention. This hermeneutic alone has the right method and goal to extract the primary meaning of the words of Scripture. The grammatical-historical hermeneutic is proved by the impossibility of the contrary: anyone arguing against this hermeneutic must use this hermeneutic in order to communicate his point.

Chapter 4

Me, My Bible, and the Holy Spirit

Many years ago, I recall asking one person what resources he used to help him in Bible study. He responded with a polite but firm, "It's just me, my Bible, and the Holy Spirit." It sounds very pious. But is it biblical? Should we use resources beyond the Bible, such as commentaries, to help us understand it? Or do such resources only detract from a proper understanding of Scripture?

The sad reality is that there are many bad commentaries in existence. Such guides mislead people, hindering their understanding of the Bible through fallacies, inaccuracies, and unbiblical philosophical baggage. So I have some sympathy for those who want to reject commentaries altogether. Indeed, it would be better to use no commentaries at all and just read the Bible carefully without outside help, than to use a misleading commentary.

But we are not limited to only those two choices. Good commentaries do exist — those that can shed light on difficult passages. There are study guides that give historical background in certain biblical topics, which can greatly illuminate our understanding of a particular passage. Some commentaries give helpful information on the original language, which can be very useful in understanding the nuances of a particular verse. But how are we to know which commentaries are good?

The good commentaries and study guides are those that faithfully expound upon the meaning of the Scriptures. But in order to evaluate if the guide is faithful to the text, it might seem that we would have to already know the meaning of the text. But the meaning of the text is the very thing we are consulting the study guide to find! It would seem that we are stuck in a "catch-22." How can we escape this vicious circle?

To what extent should we use outside help, such as commentaries, to aid our interpretation of Scripture? And how do we distinguish good commentaries from bad ones? Should we use knowledge of history to guide our interpretation? What about the role of science in hermeneutics? Should the writings of the church fathers be a factor? What about the internal leading of the Holy Spirit?

The Use of External Evidence in Biblical Interpretation

Can external evidence be used to help us understand a portion of Scripture? In a way, we've already answered this. Rules of grammar and vocabulary must already be known (at least partially) in order to understand a given text. These rules of grammar are seldom explicitly stated within the text, and only a fraction of the words in a text are defined within the text itself — unless you happen to be reading a dictionary. Language is something that must be learned *outside* the text, before the text can be properly interpreted. So a given text does require some outside knowledge of language at the very least in order to be understood.

This fact might bother some very sincere Christians who rightly have a very high view of the Bible. If the Bible is indeed the inerrant Word of God, then it should be our ultimate standard — the lens through which all evidence is to be interpreted and by which all other claims are judged. But how can it be the ultimate standard if external knowledge is necessary in order for us to understand what the Bible means? If external knowledge is the Supreme Court that interprets the Bible, then how can we escape the conclusion that this external knowledge — and not the Bible — is the true ultimate standard? What if the external knowledge we use to understand the Bible turns out to be wrong? Then how can we possibly end up with a correct interpretation of Scripture?

We will begin to address these issues here, and explore them more fully in a later chapter. For now, we note that a person must have some basic understanding of language in order for him or her to understand anything in the Bible. And this understanding of language is not something that can be gleaned from the Bible alone. Thus, some external knowledge is actually required in order to understand the Bible. People learn language from their parents and teachers, and it is this knowledge of language that allows them to read and interpret the Bible. This refutes the "me, my Bible, and the Holy Spirit" view, as well-intentioned as it may be. The notion that we don't need anything but the Holy Spirit to interpret Scripture is sometimes called the "maverick fallacy."

Consider the hypothetical case of a child who was raised by wolves, and knows nothing of human language or communication. If this person comes across a Bible (or any other text) will he ever be able to understand it merely by carefully scrutinizing it? It doesn't seem plausible. Another person who already knows a human language must teach the child language in order for him to ever be able to understand any written text. External knowledge of language is a prerequisite for understanding the Bible. But this prompts us to ask, "Is any *other* external knowledge required? And if so, what?"

Does Science Play a Role?

It is common for many Christians to be guided in their interpretation of Scripture by modern scientific knowledge. Is this a good interpretive principle? There is no doubt that many people have embraced what they consider to be a scientific fact which later turns out to be false, and have wrongly interpreted the Scriptures according to that false claim. It will be a great temptation to interpret the Bible in light of what we think we know. However, this can lead to drastic errors.

There are ancient Greek texts that teach that the earth is a flat disk that floats on water. It would be totally inappropriate to interpret such texts in light of modern science as follows, "They must have meant that in a symbolic sense, because we all know the earth is round. They probably meant that only the continents were 'relatively' flat, and that they merely 'appear' to float, but that the world is truly round." Such an interpretation is not true to the intention of the author, and is therefore wrong by definition. The text is perfectly clear. The author meant to convey his (incorrect) belief that the world is flat. The proper interpretation is to admit that the author clearly taught a flat earth, and that he was wrong about that claim. It is not appropriate to use modern science to interpret an ancient text.

The person who says, "The Bible teaches X, and means X, but it is wrong — I believe Y" is a better interpreter than the person who says, "The

Bible teaches X, but actually means Y — and I believe Y." Neither person has been faithful to God, but the first one was at least doing proper exegesis. The meaning of a text is not determined by the wishes of the reader or by modern claims. Therefore, it is inappropriate to "read into" the text ideas that would have been foreign to the author or the original audience. Reading "into" the text what the author has not intended is called "eisegesis" and will not consistently yield a correct interpretation.

This leads naturally to the following hermeneutical principle: external evidence is helpful when it accurately helps us get at the *author's intention*, and is irrelevant or misleading otherwise. This follows logically from our definition of the "correct interpretation." External evidence of the use of language, historical evidence pertaining to the time the text was written, and knowledge of ancient customs/language/figures of speech can all be helpful in understanding the author's intention. These are things that would have been known to him. This is part of the grammatical-historical hermeneutic. However, modern scientific insights, contemporary philosophy, personal preferences, and current political opinions cannot logically be used to arrive at the meaning of an ancient text since these things would have been completely foreign to the author. This seems apparent, and most people follow this principle when it comes to any ancient document *other than Scripture.* Why do people want to exempt the Bible from this obvious rule of interpretation?

There are two reasons why people often fail to follow this critical principle when it comes to interpreting the Bible. First, unlike any other book, the Bible is the authoritative Word of God. As such, it has total jurisdiction over every aspect of our lives. We are obligated to do what it says ought to be done. But people don't always want to do what the Bible commands. People are therefore strongly motivated to bend the Scriptures to their desires, rather than the reverse. Such self-deception rarely happens in a fully self-conscious way — but it does happen. Human beings are masters of self-deception (James 1:22). For any other text, people are generally content to interpret it properly and simply disagree if they don't like what it teaches.

Second, since the Bible is written by a perfect God, it must be totally inerrant in all aspects. This includes areas where the Bible seems to be wrong, at least according to modern scientific consensus. Knowing that the Bible cannot truly be wrong, many Christians are therefore inclined to read it in light of what they "know" to be true. Of course, one fatal problem with this is that what we think we know can turn out to be wrong.

An additional problem with interpreting the Bible in light of modern science is that this denies the *principle of perspicuity*. The perspicuity of Scripture is the concept that the Bible is "clear" in its main teachings, and that the Bible was written to be understood by the people living at the time it was written and anyone willing to study it. In other words, the Bible does not require any advanced specialized knowledge in order to be understood. Contrast this with a graduate level textbook on nuclear physics, which by design requires a strong background in the topic in order to be comprehensible. We presume that God did not write the Bible to be understood only by a small percentage of elite experts, and that the Bible therefore does not require advanced scientific insight in order to be understood. But can we *prove* this supposition?

Consider the alternative. If the Bible does require advanced knowledge of modern science in order to be understood, then it follows that the Bible was not properly understood for the millennia preceding such modern scientific insight. But then we must ask, "How do we know that we *currently* have sufficient scientific knowledge to understand the Bible?" The present is just another point in time. Five hundred years from now, the science of today will seem as antiquated and primitive as the scientific knowledge of five hundred years ago. So why would we arbitrarily assume that the start of the 21st century is the moment in time when we finally acquired sufficient knowledge of science to understand the Bible? We could equally well suppose that humanity will not reach a sufficient level of knowledge until A.D. 3000. So, the problem with assuming that advanced scientific knowledge is necessary to understand Scripture is that we could never know if we had reached that level, and thus we could never have any confidence that we understand the Bible at all. And if we can't have any confidence that we can understand the Bible, then there is very little point in bothering to read it.

Modern scientific insight cannot be used to govern the meaning of an ancient text. The Bible is not exempt from this rule. Though people are motivated to interpret the Bible according to their preferences (or their opinions of what is scientific fact), such preferences have no bearing on the author's intention, and thus will not lead to a correct interpretation. The view that modern scientific insight should be used to interpret the Bible magisterially is refuted because it leads to the absurd conclusion that we could never really know that we understand the Bible at all. Science may be used in a ministerial role, to make educated (though not inerrant) guesses on matters where the Bible is silent. But eisegesis is not a reliable or logically sound way to arrive at the meaning of a text.

Any reasoning of the following form is an example of this: "The Bible states 'X.' But it obviously cannot mean X because science has shown that Y is true instead. So when the text states, 'X,' it really means 'Y.' " This type of reasoning stems from a low view of Scripture, and a high view of man's intellect. It's a low view of Scripture because it supposes that God is not able to communicate clearly: that when the Bible clearly states "X," it might mean something totally different. If God is not able to communicate clearly, then this challenges His omnipotence. He's not really God if He can't even write a good book. This view gives far too much respect to man's intellect in supposing that man cannot possibly be wrong about matters of modern science. Such a view is absurd in light of the history of science; many mainstream scientific positions of the past are now defunct.

The Two-Books Fallacy

The science-above-Scripture view is irrational because it effectively ascribes far more ability to finite man than to the infinite God — a logical impossibility. Few people who hold to the science-above-Scripture view will explicitly acknowledge that this is what they are doing. They would rather think of science and Scripture as two different but equal revelations from God. They would say, "Any apparent conflict is due to either a misinterpretation of nature, or a misinterpretation of Scripture." This makes it sound like science and Scripture are on equal footing, since either is subject to human error when it comes to interpretation.

But such a claim commits the equivocation fallacy on the word "interpretation." The word is used in two different senses to make two things seem equal, when in reality they are not. To "interpret" Scripture means to understand the meaning of the propositions. But is this what we mean when we speak of "interpreting" nature? No. Nature is not comprised of propositions. When scientists "interpret" nature, they are *creating* (not interpreting) propositional statements that they believe to be true. For example,

"This rock has a high concentration of iron; it is probably a meteorite." These propositions must then be interpreted (in the linguistic sense) by the reader/listener in order to understand the meaning.

So, to understand the claims of a scientist involves *two* levels of interpretation: we must interpret his claim (linguistically), which is itself an interpretation (a propositional hypothesis) of nature. But to understand the propositions of Scripture involves only one interpretation (linguistic) of *inerrant* propositions. Of the two different senses of "interpretation," which is the most error-prone? We must admit that the hypothesis-creating "interpretation" of nature is highly error prone. Many hypotheses have come and gone. But interpreting language is far easier. People do occasionally misunderstand the meaning of a sentence — but it is pretty rare!

Understanding the meaning of a text is a far easier task than creating correct hypotheses about the universe. The science-above-Scripture advocate hopes to conceal this fact by rolling the two meanings of "interpretation" into one, and making it sound like "interpreting" nature is on the same level as interpreting Scripture. But they really aren't.

When we interpret the Bible we are (fallibly) attempting to understand the meaning of an inerrant text. There is only one step, and thus only one possibility for error. But when scientists "interpret" nature, they create a fallible hypothesis about the world. Their hypothesis is based on their understanding of the universe (which is extremely limited when we consider how big the universe is), and is therefore highly subject to error. Moreover, the world is cursed and full of sin; it can be misleading to even the most knowledgeable individuals. Additionally, we must then linguistically interpret the meaning of what the scientists say. This is also subject to error in the same way that our understanding of the biblical text may be subject to error; except in the case of science, the text is not at all inerrant.

Sometimes this hermeneutical fallacy is disguised by the claim that "God has written two books: the Scriptures, and the book of nature." The intention is to elevate the claims made by scientists to the level of Scripture so that those claims may be used to interpret Scripture. The obvious problem with this view is that nature is not a book. It is not comprised of propositional statements that can be evaluated as "true" or "false." People can create statements about nature. But those statements will not be inerrant, and therefore are not on the same level as Scripture.

Since we have shown that such a view is fallacious, we shall refer to the concept of interpreting the Bible in light of the "book" of nature as the "two books fallacy." It is noteworthy that a distinguishing feature of many cults is that they consider some other book besides the Bible to also be inerrant. Canonization of "nature" or "science" is a very serious theological and hermeneutical error.

We can summarize all of the above with this rule of hermeneutics: external claims from science may not be used to interpret a text in a way contrary to its meaning as determined from grammar and context. No matter how tempting it may be, if the grammar and context of a verse indicate that it means "X," then we must interpret it as teaching "X" even if most scientists teach "not-X." This is the principle of *sola scriptura* or "Scripture alone." *Sola Scriptura* does not deny the use of external evidence, even scientific evidence, in biblical interpretation. Rather, it merely denies that such evidence has equal or greater authority than the Scriptures themselves. Science may not be legitimately used to override the clear meaning of the text.

Some people are inclined to limit *sola scriptura* to matters of salvation and holiness. But this is the fallacy of special pleading, since there is no rational warrant to separate these issues from other topics on which the Bible touches. If the Bible is truly the inerrant Word of God as it claims to be, then it will be the final authority on all matters.

Science can be used in a faithful, ministerial sense — as a servant to Scripture. On matters where the Bible is genuinely silent, we may use our knowledge of science to construct reasonable hypotheses. These will be fallible of course. Also, science may give us greater insight into a passage, so long as it does not alter the meaning of a passage. For example, the Bible uses the "stars of heaven" as a metaphor for a humanly uncountable number (Genesis 22:17; Jeremiah 33:22). Modern astronomy has revealed that our galaxy has over 100 billion stars, and there are at least as many galaxies as stars in our own. What a wonderful confirmation of Scripture! This gives us greater appreciation for passages like Genesis 22:17 and Jeremiah 33:22, but it does not alter their meaning.

The Role of Commentaries

Although the best interpreter of Scripture is Scripture, this does not mean that external sources cannot be helpful as well. It simply means that they are not infallible, and must be used with discernment. They may not be used to override the clear teaching of Scripture in violation of *sola scriptura*. How can we separate the good ones from the bad, unless we already know the meaning of the text? There are two ways.

First, we now have some rules of hermeneutics that must not be violated if we are to arrive at the correct interpretation of a passage. If a commentary violates these rules, then it is not a good commentary. We don't need to know the meaning of a text of Scripture to see that a commentary is violating proper hermeneutical procedure. Those commentaries that interpret Scripture in light of modern opinions about science, those that commit the two-books fallacy, or those that fail to interpret historical passages in a primarily literal fashion are not good commentaries because they are not faithful to the author's intention. Such resources are eisegetical rather than exegetical, and will not consistently arrive at the actual meaning of the text.

When reading a commentary, carefully examine the *reasoning* of the author. Does he give a reason for his view? If not, then we can dismiss it.[1] Is his reasoning cogent? Is it self-consistent and also consistent with the rest of the Bible? A good commentary will give compelling reasons for why a text should be understood in a particular way, and will also show how alternatives fail. Although we may not initially understand a particular text, we can always examine the reasoning of the commentator to see if it stands up to scrutiny.

Second, although we may not understand the meaning of every verse in Scripture, we have shown above that the historical sections of the Bible are to be interpreted in a primarily literal fashion. And that means that we can indeed know the meaning of many texts of Scripture with very little difficulty. When the Bible states that the Israelites wandered in the wilderness for 40 years (e.g., Numbers 32:13), this means that they wandered in the wilderness for 40 years. Historical sections are easy to understand. If a commentary doesn't get these easy sections right, it is reasonable to presume it won't consistently get the more difficult passages right either. On the other hand, if a commentary does faithfully treat biblical history as literal events, then it deserves to be considered on other more difficult issues.

We would do well to remember that commentaries are written by fallible people. The authors have biases and opinions that may not be correct. And these will influence the way they treat the Bible. Therefore, we should

1. See chapter 6.

remember: (1) Commentaries on the Bible are inferior to the Bible because they are not inerrant, whereas the Bible is inerrant. (2) If a commentary author has an incorrect bias on a given issue, this will adversely affect his or her interpretation of biblical passages dealing with this issue. (3) Commentary authors may have incorrect biases on some issues, and correct biases on other issues; therefore, it is possible for them to give good interpretations on some matters, and poor interpretations on other matters. These are important considerations to keep in mind even after we have evaluated a commentary to be basically good. There are other things to consider as well, which we will address later.

In general, I have found that older commentaries tend to be more accurate and helpful than modern ones. Specifically, I mean commentaries that were written before Darwin. Many (though not all) modern commentaries have been influenced by evolutionary thinking. And this does nothing but detract from proper interpretation.

Note that all of the above considerations also apply to the church fathers. As fallible people, they do not have the authority to tell us that we must interpret the Bible according to their opinions. We should examine their reasoning just as we would any other commentary. If they abide by proper hermeneutical principles, and treat biblical history as literal, then we should strongly consider their analysis and conclusions. Otherwise, we reject their opinions as we would any other bad commentary. The only substantial difference between the early church fathers and modern commentaries is that the church fathers were closer to the time that the New Testament was written, and therefore may have additional insight into cultural customs and common figures of speech in use at the time, as well as access to historical documents that are no longer extant. The same can be said of early non-Christian historians such as Josephus.

When it comes to any source of information external to the Bible, it is appropriate to evaluate the reasoning based on its internal merit, not the person giving the interpretation. To reject or accept an interpretation merely because a particular (fallible) person has made it is called the *genetic fallacy*. If a highly intelligent person gives a bad interpretation of a text, it's still a bad interpretation. The person has nothing to do with it. Only if the original author himself gives the interpretation of which he has written, or if God does so, should we accept it without additional reasons. Yes, the human author and God know exactly what the passage means; all others must give good reasons using proper hermeneutics if we are to accept their interpretation as correct.

The Role of the Church

The local church body can be very helpful when it comes to understanding the Scriptures. The Church is not an invention of fallible humans, it was founded by Christ and belongs to Him (Matthew 16:18). The Church was created to guard Christian doctrine, to preserve the integrity of the Word of God, and to teach others to rightly interpret and apply it (Ephesians 4:11–13). Therefore, all Christians should be part of a local church body and voluntarily submit themselves to the authority of their biblical pastors. To fail to do this is sin (Hebrews 10:25). The Church is designed to help guide Christians to rightly interpret the Bible.

However, we must also keep in mind that a church is a collection of fallible people, and is itself fallible. Pastors and other church teachers do err from time to time. We are not to consider their words to be on the same level as Scripture. Scripture is given by inspiration from God, and is without error (2 Timothy 3:16; Psalm 119:160). Though God used fallible men to write His Word, He infallibly guided them so that what they wrote is absolutely inerrant (2 Peter 1:21). But *nowhere* does the Bible teach that the Christian church is infallibly directed by God. On the contrary, the Bible gives examples of how various churches had departed from the truth (e.g., Galatians 3:1–3, 4:10–11; 1 Corinthians 5:1–2, 6:5–8, 11:18).

Given that the Bible is infallible and that pastors are fallible, it follows that we should test everything the pastor teaches with what the Bible teaches (1 Thessalonians 5:21). Scripture alone is our ultimate authority. Pastors and other teachers are important and are appointed by God (1 Corinthians 12:28). But their teachings are to be tested by the written Word (Galatians 1:8-9; Matthew 4:4). Therefore, we are to take Sunday morning sermons much as we would take a commentary. They can be very helpful, but we need to be discerning and test what was spoken to see if it aligns with Scripture (Acts 17:11).

Helpful External Guides

There are several external sources of information that can help us understand the author's intention. Historical works written around the same time as the Bible can shed light on customs, language, grammar, and figures of speech in use at the time. Modern resources that translate and consolidate such ancient writings can be very helpful insofar as they are accurate. Their accuracy can be estimated by comparing them with other such works, by their internal consistency, and by their ability to shed light on the Bible in a way that comports with how the Bible interprets itself.

Lexicons are books containing lists of words used in the Bible along with their definitions. The words are usually given as the original Hebrew or Greek word, along with the most commonly used English equivalent. The first verse of the Bible ends in the word "earth," which in Hebrew is *'erets*. A Hebrew lexicon shows that this word has a range of meanings depending on context; it can mean the entire earth, a particular region, land in general, soil, the inhabitants of a land, etc. A lexicon that I frequently use also shows how often the word is translated in a particular way in the King James translation of the Bible. For example, *'erets* is translated as "land" 1,543 times, as "earth" 712 times, as "country" 140 times, and so on. These translations show that the Hebrew word (in this case) is very similar to our English word "earth," which has roughly the same range of meanings. Lexicons are not infallible of course, and therefore must be used with discernment. But often a lexicon will give specific verses where the word is used as translated, giving us the opportunity to see that the suggested translation is indeed accurate.

Concordances give verses in which a given word occurs in a particular English translation of the Bible. This can be very helpful when studying a specific concept in Scripture, because we can see all the other places where the same word is used. Caution is warranted though, because sometimes the various occurrences of a particular English word may come from several different Hebrew or Greek words with perhaps different meanings. But they are very helpful when a person has forgotten where a verse is found. Topical concordances and cross-references are helpful in locating verses that have a similar theme.

Maps can be very helpful in understanding certain situations in Scripture. How far is Jerusalem from Bethlehem? A map makes this very clear. Why did Jesus have to pass through Samaria in going from Judea to Galilee (John 4:3–4)? A map of the area at the time makes it obvious. It's not that the passages are incomprehensible without a map; but since the original author would have been familiar with the country (and we often are not) it is very helpful to have a map of the ancient world to give greater clarity. Most Bibles include at least some maps for this very reason.

Alternate translations of Scripture can also be useful in overcoming the language barrier. I often read several different English translations of a particular text so that I better understand the nuances. This sharply reduces any possible bias that may have been introduced inadvertently by the translators in any one version. It also helps us to better understand how a particular word is used in context. For example, in 1 Peter 3:15 we are told to be ready to give an answer, and to do so with "fear" (in the King James Version). What kind of "fear" is indicated — fear in the sense of being afraid, or fear in the sense of respect? The same word is translated in the New International Version as "respect" and in the New American Standard Version as "reverence." Consulting multiple versions clears up the ambiguity. At the very least, it indicates what the translators believe it means.

Here is the point: All these sources are helpful in interpretation because they give information that is *relevant to the author's intentions.* The author knew about his own culture, his own language, the common figures of speech, and the topography of the area. So these are relevant for us to know as well, so that we can better understand his writing. Lexicons and alternate translations are useful in overcoming the fact that the author wrote in a different language than most of us can read. Used with discernment, these can shed great light on the meaning of the text.

The Role of the Holy Spirit

The regeneration and internal leading of the Holy Spirit are crucial to properly understand the Scriptures. This bothers some people — particularly non-Christians. They would like to believe that their own mind is sufficient to understand a given text. After all, they don't have a problem understanding other books. So why should the Bible be different?

But the Bible is not just any book. It is the Word of God. And it presents an uncomfortable truth — that all human beings fall utterly short of God's glory and deserve His wrath (Romans 3:23, 6:23). In our sin nature, we willfully rebel against this truth and cannot accept it without God's help. First Corinthians 2:14 states, "But a natural man does not accept the things of the Spirit of God, for they are foolishness to him; and he cannot understand them, because they are spiritually appraised." The "natural man" in this passage refers to someone who has not received Christ as Savior and Lord. The Bible teaches that such a person "cannot understand" the spiritual things of God. The unbeliever may have an intellectual grasp of the basic meaning of the words, but he cannot truly know or accept them and they indeed seem foolish to him. Why?

Let me give the wrong answer before I give the right one. The wrong answer is that the Bible requires some sort of mystical experience, or thinking that is beyond logic in order to understand it. This is the gnostic view. Unbelievers may think that they are perfectly rational, and that Christians want them to have some sort of mystical enlightenment in order to understand the supra-logical truths of Scripture. They see biblical truths like a Zen koan; something that only makes sense if you abandon normal logic. But this is not what the Bible teaches.

Now the right answer: the Bible is perfectly logical. It is the unbeliever who isn't (2 Corinthians 4:4; Ephesians 4:17–18). The Bible describes unbelievers as being spiritually dead (Ephesians 2:1; Colossians 2:13; 1 John 3:14). They cannot understand the things of God, because they cannot think fully rationally when it comes to spiritual issues (1 Corinthians 2:14). Now this does not mean that they cannot be rational about other things. God has given everyone a certain degree of grace, and that includes the ability to reason and acquire knowledge. And so unbelievers can build rockets, and program computers, and solve math equations. But when it comes to spiritual issues, they fail to reason in a fully logical way. The Holy Spirit is not an emotional experience, nor is He contrary to logic. The Holy Spirit is God, and as such He is perfectly logical. To be logical is to reason correctly, and God always reasons correctly. The Holy Spirit helps our fallen fallible mind to reason properly.

It is the same reason that if I handed a book to Albert Einstein, he would not be able to read or understand it. It's not because he's stupid; it's because he's dead. Likewise, unbelievers are not stupid; they are spiritually dead and must be resurrected in order to understand the spiritual things of the Bible. They may understand *some* biblical issues by God's grace. But unbelievers will not consistently correctly interpret Scripture because they are not capable of consistently reasoning logically about spiritual issues. Nor do they want to. The Bible teaches that it is the hardness of their hearts, their stubborn rejection of the biblical God, that leads to the ignorance within them (Ephesians 4:17–18). However, God does give some enlightenment even to unbelievers (Romans 1:19), and so their ignorance is not total, nor is it excusable (Romans 1:20).

What then are the implications of the fact that the Holy Spirit must enable us to understand His Word? First let us consider the implications in our personal Bible study. If we are to consistently and correctly understand God's Word, we must be saved; we must have received Christ as Lord and Savior and have experienced the resurrection of our "dead" spirit (Ephesians 2:1–6). Second, we must have an attitude of humility, always ready to give up our prideful opinions and be corrected by God as needed (James 4:6).

We must listen to God, and obey Him always. Some people think this means listening for a mystical voice to "whisper in our ear" what we should do. People are far too quick to attribute their own subjective feelings to the prompting of the Holy Spirit. But the Bible is the primary way that the Spirit speaks to us (2 Peter 1:21; Hebrews 3:7, 10:15–16; Acts 1:16, 28:25; Ephesians 6:17). He regenerates our mind so that we can understand what He says in His Word (Romans 12:2; Titus 3:5).

In reasoning with an unbeliever, we must remember the role of the Holy Spirit. Without the Spirit, the unbeliever will not fully understand many aspects of Scripture. Indeed, apart from the work of the Holy Spirit, the unbeliever *cannot* come to understand that Jesus is Lord (1 Corinthians 12:3). Again, this is not because the unbeliever needs to make some sort of non-logical "leap of faith" in order to understand. Rather, it is because his mind is spiritually dead, and cannot reason properly apart from the Holy Spirit. I have had a number of conversations with unbelievers in which they simply cannot think about a particular issue in a logical and consistent way. Yet a Christian child can understand the argument. It is amazing to see this principle in action. Experience confirms the scriptural principle that unbelievers cannot reason properly about spiritual matters.

This principle turns out to be far less significant in debates between two Christians. When two believers have a disagreement about the proper interpretation of a verse, it is inappropriate to use the internal leading of the Holy Spirit as a debate point. In other words, it would be unfitting to say, "The Holy Spirit is saying to me that your interpretation is wrong." This is not effective for three reasons.

First, the internal leading of the Spirit is not objective; it is not open to the investigation of others, and as such is not useful in a debate. How can the other person in the debate really know if the Spirit is speaking to his friend? For that matter, how can the person making the claim know that it is truly the Holy Spirit, and not simply his own feelings? He would have to check what he thinks the Spirit says against the Scriptures, which we know are what the Spirit says. But why not just go to the Scriptures directly then?

Second, the Holy Spirit is God and therefore does not contradict Himself (2 Timothy 2:13). So whatever the Holy Spirit tells person A, it must match what He tells person B. Any dispute over the meaning of the Scriptures cannot be the result of the Holy Spirit saying different things to different people. Moreover, wherever the Holy Spirit leads someone, it will necessarily be consistent with what is recorded in the objective Scriptures. So again, why not just go to the Scriptures? The Scriptures are the objective words of the Holy Spirit, available for inspection by anyone. Thus, the Bible is the final arbitrator of the interpretation of the Bible.

Third, as a matter of debate strategy, if anyone says, "The Holy Spirit told me X," I could equally well say (not that I would necessarily), "Well, that's odd, because He told me the exact opposite!" We need to be very careful about claiming that God has said something if that something is not in the Bible. To claim to speak for God something that is not truly from God is blasphemy — a particularly detestable sin (Deuteronomy 18:20). Even if the person softens the statement, "*I believe* the Spirit is indicating that this interpretation is correct," his opponent could always respond by saying, "I believe the Spirit is telling me the opposite." Clearly one of them is wrong, since God does not contradict Himself. And such subjective statements are not useful in terms of a debate. It is far more reasonable to adhere to the Words of the Holy Spirit as recorded objectively in the Bible. So once again, we see that the best interpreter of Scripture is Scripture.

A particularly vile misuse of the "leading of the Spirit" is when a person claims that God told him or her to do something that is contrary to the Scriptures. The Bible, for example, teaches that believers should not marry unbelievers (2 Corinthians 6:14). Imagine a woman saying, "Well, I prayed about this. And I believe that God told me it's okay to marry this guy — even though he is not a believer." Wrong! It was the Holy Spirit that inspired 2 Corinthians 6:14; it is the Holy Spirit that tells Christians not to marry non-Christians. And God does not contradict Himself. Thus, we can rest assured that the woman in this example was not listening to the Holy Spirit at all.

I wish that the above example were hypothetical. But this is a common mistake among Christians. Remember, the *Bible* is the primary way and the objectively authoritative way that the Holy Spirit speaks to us. It is true that the Holy Spirit must enable us to understand the Scriptures. But He will never do this in a way that is contrary to the Scriptures. Therefore, the final guide to interpreting the Scriptures will always be the Scriptures.

Review

Is external knowledge necessary to understand Scripture? Yes, the use of external knowledge to aid in scriptural interpretation is unavoidable, but must be used with discernment if we are to arrive at a correct interpretation. Clearly, we must have some knowledge of language and grammar in order to read and understand the Bible. This refutes the maverick fallacy. External knowledge leads to correct interpretation when it helps us understand the author's intention (by definition).

Is external knowledge always helpful in interpreting Scripture? No, external knowledge that is foreign to the original audience or author of an ancient text will not systematically lead to a correct interpretation. Using information that was not known to the author (such as modern philosophy, scientific insights, personal opinions, etc.) is reading into the text, and is the fallacy of "eisegesis." It cannot be a correct interpretation because by definition such things are irrelevant to the author's intention.

Can knowledge of science govern our interpretation of the Bible? No. Science cannot be used in a magisterial role to judge the meaning of a biblical text for three reasons. First, there would be no reason to assume that we currently have a sufficient level of scientific knowledge, and consequently we could never have any confidence in our understanding of Scripture. Second, it denies the principle of perspicuity — that the Bible is meant to be understood by different cultures at different times; it is not just for experts or modern readers. Third, scientific "knowledge" is rarely certain, and often changes with new discoveries; it is therefore logically fallacious to judge the certain by the standards of the uncertain. Science does not have magisterial authority over the Bible. This is one form of the fallacy of eisegesis.

Are nature and the Bible on the same level of divine revelation? No. The Bible is comprised of clear statements. Nature is not. The Bible is inerrant. Nature is not. The Bible is perfect, but nature is cursed. To say that "both nature and the Bible are inerrant, but our *interpretation* of each is fallible" is to commit the fallacy of equivocation, since the word "interpretation" is used in two different senses that are made to sound equivalent. But the "interpretation" of nature is not linguistic. Rather, it involves the creation of fallible propositions (a highly error-prone process), which must then be linguistically interpreted. On the other hand, biblical interpretation is linguistic interpretation of infallible propositions.

Is the "record of nature" on the same level as Scripture? No. Nature is not perspicuous; it is not propositional truth. It cannot legitimately be called a "book" or a "record." Therefore, it is fallacious (and heretical) to treat nature (or "science") as a 67th book of the Bible. The view that nature and Scripture are two equally authoritative revelations by God is the two-books fallacy. The "Bible plus some other book" view is a distinguishing characteristic of cults.

Are commentaries helpful in biblical interpretation? Yes, if and only if they help us arrive at the author's intention. Helpful commentaries obey the rules of hermeneutics. A commentary that violates such rules cannot be considered reliable in its conclusions. Such rules include: interpreting Scripture consistently with Scripture, not reading into the text based on information that would be foreign to the author and culture, taking historical narrative in a generally literal fashion, and so forth. Likewise, the church fathers must also follow hermeneutical principles if their interpretations are to be considered reliable. All comments about Scripture that are found outside of Scripture must be consistent with how the Bible interprets itself if such external comments are to be considered reliable. Only the interpretations by the writers of Scripture can be considered inerrant, since they were infallibly guided by the mind of God. The most authoritative interpreter of Scripture is Scripture — this principle is called the "analogy of faith."

What other external sources can be legitimately used to aid in biblical interpretation? Lexicons, concordances, alternative translations, historical works written at the time of the Bible, and maps can all be helpful in understanding the text. These either give us information that would have been known to the author and the original audience (and are thus relevant in understanding his intention), or help us deal with the language barrier. However, they are not inerrant.

Does the Holy Spirit have a role in biblical interpretation? Yes — an essential one. Only those people who are saved — whose minds have been regenerated by the Holy Spirit — can consistently understand and accept the things of God. Unbelievers may intellectually apprehend portions of the Scriptures by God's grace.

Can we appeal to the internal leading of the Holy Spirit in our defense of a particular interpretation? No. The regenerating power of the Spirit is certainly needed in order for us to understand spiritual things. But this isn't useful in a debate between two Christians because the Holy Spirit will tell them both exactly the same thing since He does not deny Himself. And it will not be useful in a debate between a believer and unbeliever because the unbeliever resists the Holy Spirit. However, it is important to remember that unbelievers will not be able to reason properly about certain spiritual issues, since their spirit has not been regenerated by God.

Can the Holy Spirit speak something contrary to the Scriptures? No. God does not contradict or deny Himself (2 Timothy 2:13). It is fallacious to use a supposed leading of the Holy Spirit to override the clear teaching the Bible. The Scriptures *are* the words of the Holy Spirit (2 Peter 1:21).

Chapter 5

Types of Literature in the Bible

In one sense, the Bible is one book with one author: God. In another sense it is many books with many different authors — the human authors who physically inscribed the words. Some of the books of the Bible are written in different styles than other books are. As we saw previously, we must consider the type of literature if we are to correctly extract the meaning of a passage. It would be fallacious to read poetry as history or history as poetry. So what are the different types of literature in the Bible? And how should we interpret each style?

Commonly, the books of the Bible are listed in six categories: Law, History, Wisdom, Prophecy, Gospels, and Letters. The prophetic portions are often further divided into the Major Prophets, the Minor Prophets, and Revelation. The epistles are often further divided into the Pauline epistles, and the general epistles. These categories are not defined in the Bible itself, and so there is no reason to take such classification as inerrant. But this is a useful starting point. Using this system, the books of the Bible are placed into these categories as follows.

Genesis, Exodus, Leviticus, Numbers, and Deuteronomy are the books of the Law. These were all written primarily by Moses (Deuteronomy 31:24). The books of History in the Old Testament are Joshua, Judges, Ruth, 1 and 2 Samuel, 1 and 2 Kings, 1 and 2 Chronicles, Ezra, Nehemiah, and Esther. The only New Testament book classified as "history" is Acts.

There are five books of Wisdom/poetry: Job, Psalms, Proverbs, Ecclesiastes, and Song of Solomon.

There are 5 Major Prophets in the Old Testament: Isaiah, Jeremiah, Lamentations, Ezekiel, and Daniel. There are 12 Minor Prophets: Hosea, Joel, Amos, Obadiah, Jonah, Micah, Nahum, Habakkuk, Zephaniah, Haggai, Zechariah, and Malachi. The "Major" versus "Minor" concerns only the length of the book — not the estimated importance of the topic or author. Lamentations is the exception to the rule, being a small book but included in the Major Prophets due to its author, Jeremiah. Revelation is the only New Testament book classified as prophecy. Technically, Revelation is also an epistle, since it is a letter written by the Apostle John. But it is almost always listed separately from the other epistles due to its unique heavy emphasis on prophecy.

The Gospels are Matthew, Mark, Luke, and John. The epistles written by Paul are Romans, 1 and 2 Corinthians, Galatians, Ephesians, Philippians, Colossians, 1 and 2 Thessalonians, 1 and 2 Timothy, Titus, and Philemon. (Some scholars believe that Paul also wrote, or was a co-author of, the Book of Hebrews; but many do not.) The general epistles are Hebrews, James, 1 and 2 Peter, 1, 2, and 3 John, and Jude.

Historical Literature

Although there are six major divisions by this system, several of these fall under the same basic literary type. For example, the Gospels are historical reports of the life and major teachings of Jesus. They are books of history, even though they are not usually included in the same category as the other books of history. The Gospels are singled out due to their special importance in God's history of redemption, and there is nothing wrong with doing that. But from a literary standpoint, they are the same genre as Acts. Likewise, the books of the Law (also called the Pentateuch or the Torah) are primarily historical in nature. Even knowledgeable critics of the Bible must concede that Abraham was a real person who lived in history, just as the Bible records in Genesis. Many of the events recorded in the Pentateuch have been confirmed through archaeology.

As we saw previously, works of history must be interpreted in a primarily literal fashion if we are to correctly understand their meaning. It would be absurd to read a history book metaphorically, as poetic, as a self-help book, or as a recipe for making brownies. History books report historical events in a straightforward way. To exempt biblical historical books from this principle without cause is the fallacy of special pleading. So, the Books of History, the Gospels, and the Pentateuch are to be read in a primarily literal fashion. The words basically mean what they say, with allowances for occasional figures of speech that are obvious from context.

Critics may deny that the events recorded in these biblical books actually happened.[1] But this is utterly irrelevant to the matter of *interpretation*. Interpretation of a text is about understanding the author's intention. And there can be no doubt that the authors of the historical books of the Bible were intending to convey matters of historical fact. Below we will deal with the indicators found within these books that mark them as historical.

Letters

The term "epistle" is from the Greek and means "letter." In modern usage, an epistle is a letter written by or endorsed by an Apostle — one of the followers of Jesus who witnessed Him in His earthly ministry. Most of the epistles in the Bible were written by Paul (13 of 21). The remaining 8 letters were written by James, Peter, John, Jude, and one person whose name is not recorded: the author of Hebrews.[2] There can be no doubt that these are letters due to the way they are written: they usually include a "from" and a "to" somewhere in their introduction. How shall we then interpret these letters?

A letter is just that: it's a message from one or more persons to one or more persons, written to convey information. Such information might express the feelings of the author such as gratitude (Romans 1:8) or concern (Galatians 4:11; 1 Corinthians 11:18). The information may contain instructions from the author to the recipient (1 Corinthians 11:1–17). It may contain important teaching (Ephesians 2:8–9). An epistle may contain historical information (Galatians 1:17–19). It may provide interpretations of Old Testament passages (Hebrews 8:7–8, 11:17–19). And what do all these types of messages have in common? They all use language in the ordinary way. Letters are primarily literal, as everyday experience confirms.

1. Archeology continues to be a source of embarrassment for critics of Scripture. Many of the claims of Scripture that were once denied by critics have now been verified by archeologists.
2. Revelation chapters 2 and 3 also contain seven very short epistles addressed to the seven historic churches that then existed in Asia Minor. These letters were dictated from the Lord Jesus Christ Himself.

When we receive a letter from a friend, we do not assume that it was written in a cryptic or metaphorical way. We take the text as written unless there is a contextual reason to take it another way.

Therefore, when interpreting an epistle it is appropriate to approach the text in a literal fashion. We do make allowances for figures of speech. But non-literal usage of text within an epistle must be justified by the context. As with the historical sections of the Bible, epistles use language in a primarily literal, straightforward way. This makes them rather easy to interpret.

The alternative to this view is self-refuting. Those who deny that letters are to be taken literally often write articles explaining their position. But an article of that sort is basically a letter to be read by many, and to convince them. And naturally, the author expects readers to take his letter literally, in order to argue that we should not take letters literally — a contradiction. It is apparent from our everyday experience that letters from one person to another or to a group of people are primarily literal in nature.

A *Mostly* Literal Approach

It is sometimes said when it comes to interpreting the Scriptures, "If a literal sense makes sense, seek no other sense, or you'll end up with nonsense." Although this little saying may not be appropriate for the poetic sections of the Bible, it is a pretty good hermeneutical principle for the historical sections and the epistles. Just as with modern history books or modern letters, people tend to use language in the ordinary way when communicating in these styles. This is good news for those who wish to understand the Bible correctly without having to read through volumes of commentaries, or getting a doctorate in Hebrew. The vast bulk of the Bible falls under the literary categories of either history or letters, and both genres employ a primarily literal use of language, which is the easiest to interpret. So, of the 66 books of the Bible, 43 are properly interpreted simply by taking the text at face value — something any literate child can do.

In the New Testament, it's even easier; 26 of the 27 books are either historical or letters and are therefore primarily literal! Only the Book of Revelation falls under a different literary style. It's not surprising that many people find the New Testament easier to understand than the Old Testament. The primarily literal style is easy to comprehend even with very little background information. So our preliminary assessment suggests that roughly two-thirds of the books of the Bible should be taken essentially at face value, and therefore should be very easy to correctly interpret.

How shall we approach the remaining 23 books of the Bible? Consider that although these are not classified as history or letters, some of them contain substantial historical sections. Therefore, these portions will be primarily literal as well. For example, the Book of Job — though classified as part of the wisdom literature — is primarily historical in nature. It records some of the events of Job's life, and it does so literally. Why then is it classified as a book of Wisdom/Poetry? The book reports the speeches of Job and his friends, and these speeches are poetic in nature. But when the book is reporting historical events, it does so in the normal, literal style. Another example is the Book of Daniel. It is classified as prophetic literature — and much of it is. But parts are historical narrative (e.g., Daniel 1, 6) and are written in a historical, literal way.

Conversely, there will be occasional sections of poetry in the historical books, and they are clearly identified. For example, Exodus 15:1–21 records the song of Moses, which makes use of some poetic language. This is in the context of literal history; the Israelites literally sang this song as a matter of historical fact (Exodus 15:1). But the contents of the song are poetic. So it would be inappropriate to take the text in verse 15 to mean that the inhabitants of Canaan literally melted. Rather the text indicates that this is literally what the Israelites sang. Some sections of the Gospels contain non-literal usage, such as when Jesus tells a parable. But even here, we are to understand that Jesus literally told the parable just as the text reports.

There are some cultural differences in the use of language between the ancient Israelites and our modern society. We are a low-context culture, meaning that we use relatively few word-pictures. However, the ancient Hebrews were a high-context culture, and the Hebrew language makes a very rich use of verbal imagery. They were far more inclined to use word-pictures and other idioms, even in otherwise literal, historical literature. If these types of phrases were translated word-for-word into English, they would sound very non-literal. Yet they would have been easily understood by the original readership.

As one example of non-literal language, *hyperbole* is very common in the Bible. Hyperbole is the exaggeration of something for the purpose of emphasis. Critics might claim that exaggeration is dishonest. But that would only be so in cases where the person *intends* to be taken literally, and exaggerates only slightly so that his claim is believable literally. For example, someone who catches a fish and exaggerates slightly about its size hoping to impress others as they take his claim literally, is being deceptive. But suppose he exaggerates in a way that is obvious for emphasis, for example, "That fish was huge. It was a million feet long!" There is nothing wrong with hyperbole in the appropriate context. No one would accuse a person of being deceptive for using hyperbole as in "If I've told you once, I've told you a thousand times!" The number is exaggerated for emphasis, not for deception.

In the Hebrew culture, hyperbole was quite common; it was offered non-literally, and taken non-literally, and no deception was intended. Jesus often used hyperbole as His normal teaching style. Consider Luke 14:26. Here Christ says, "If anyone comes to Me, and does not hate his own father and mother and wife and children and brothers and sisters, yes, and even his own life, he cannot be My disciple." We know that Jesus doesn't intend this literally, because He commands us elsewhere to love our neighbor and to honor father and mother (Matthew 19:19). Rather, Jesus uses hyperbole to stress that we ought to love Him so much more than our earthly family that the latter is essentially "hate" by comparison. The difference between the two degrees of love has been exaggerated for dramatic effect.

But such non-literal exceptions are generally obvious from context. Historical literature is largely literal by its very nature. And thus, a correct interpretation of historical sections of Scripture will be to take the words at face value, except where context suggests that an idiom is in use.

Poetic Literature

The first thing to note is that biblical poetic literature is very, very different from poetry in English. When we think of a poem, we often think of words that have a certain rhyme and meter. However, the ancient Hebrews did not think or write this way. Instead, Hebrew poetry focused entirely on one essential feature: parallelism.

Consider Psalm 145 to see examples of parallelism. Verse 2 states, "Every day I will bless You, and I will praise Your name forever and ever." The verse contains two phrases that go together in parallel. "I will bless You" is very similar to "I will praise Your name." Furthermore, "every day" means something that is continual or ongoing, just like the phrase "forever and ever." The two parts of the verse are connected; they mean basically the same thing but use different words to say it. This is parallelism — the distinguishing and essential feature of Hebrew poetry. Hebrew poetry is *always* characterized by copious use of parallelism. And Hebrew poetry is only properly interpreted by considering how the two (or more) parallels go together. We'll come back to the issue of interpretation later in the chapter. For now, let's focus on *identifying* poetic literature in the text, and examine the characteristics of this type of literature.

The Book of Psalms is perhaps the supreme example of poetic literature in the Bible. The book is a collection of various songs, praises, and prayers to God. It would be hard to argue otherwise; many of the Psalms are even labeled as such (e.g., Psalm 3, 4, 5, 6, 7, 8, 9, etc.). As far as I know, no one claims otherwise. So it makes sense to use the Psalms as a starting point for identifying and interpreting biblical poetic literature.

Unlike the historical books, the Psalms are not primarily concerned with recording events that have transpired in the past, nor are they primarily concerned with giving specific instructions to a particular person or persons as with the epistles. They may touch on these things, of course, but the Psalms are primarily given as examples of prayers and praises to God, given by a human author (usually David) under the inspiration of the Holy Spirit. In general, poetic literature is not as literal as historical narrative. But there are some caveats to consider.

The distinction between literal and non-literal is perhaps not as sharp as we might first assume, particularly when dealing with the Hebrew language. "Literal" refers to the ordinary, common meaning of a word or phrase, as opposed to a figure of speech. But what happens when a figure of speech is used very commonly? It *becomes* the ordinary, common meaning. Hebrew word pictures were so common that, in a sense, they can be said to be literal with respect to the original readership. But when translated word-for-word into English, we would see them as non-literal, since we don't use the same figures of speech.

Also, there are some cases where the original language is literal, but the translators chose to use an English idiom to best express the meaning. The reverse is also possible. So when we come across a figure of speech in an English Bible, we cannot automatically assume that it was non-literal in the original language, though it *may* be. Nonetheless, we should take it as the figure of speech that the translators intended if we are to correctly understand the original intention of the author. Most people reading this book read the Bible in English. So for the rest of this chapter, I will consider the literal/non-literal nature of a passage *as it is expressed in English translations.* With this caveat in mind, let us examine some biblical examples of poetic literature.

Consider the eighth chapter of Psalms. It begins (as many of the Psalms do) with an introduction: "For the choir director; on the Gittith. A Psalm of David." This introduction indicates that this Psalm, like so many others, is the lyric to a song and it was written by David. The melody has been lost to time, but its message is preserved forever in Scripture. We note that the introduction is itself literal. There is no symbolism, only matters of fact: the author, the intended recipient, and the nature of the writing. Then the actual Psalm of praise begins: "O LORD, our Lord, How majestic is Your name in all the earth, who have displayed Your splendor above the heavens!"

We immediately see that this style is very different from the matter-of-fact recording of events that we find in the historical narratives. It is an expression of praise to God.

Verses 3-4: "When I consider Your heavens, the work of Your fingers, the moon and the stars, which You have ordained; What is man that You take thought of him, and the son of man that You care for him?"

The parallelism is almost palpable. "The heavens" go together with "the moon and stars," just as "the work of Your fingers" goes along with "which you have ordained." "Man" goes along with "the son of man," just as "take thought of him" goes along with "care for him." There can be absolutely no doubt that this is Hebrew poetry because the parallelism is so clear. Given that this is poetic, we should not expect a physical or rigidly literal interpretation — that wouldn't be true to the author's intention.

In these verses, David ponders the majesty of the universe, and wonders why God would care for something as small and seemingly insignificant as humanity. The meaning is clear, but the passage is not primarily literal. When the text states, "the work of Your fingers" we should not conclude that God literally has fingers. The clear teaching from the literal/historical sections of the Bible is that God is a spirit (John 4:24), which is a non-material being without flesh and bone (Luke 24:39). Granted, God the Son took on human nature at the incarnation; but the Psalms are written in the Old Testament when none of the persons of the Trinity had a human nature. God's "fingers" are not literal. Rather, the Psalms are using an anthropomorphism to express the actions of God in creating the universe. An anthropomorphism is the poetic device of attributing human qualities to something that is not human. Any Scriptures that treat God the Father or the Spirit as a physical being with a face, or hands and the like, are using anthropomorphic language, since we know from the literal portions of Scripture that a spirit is non-physical.

The parallelism in this verse is one of agreement rather than one of contrast. Notice that the phrase "What is man that You take thought of him" is very similar in meaning to the phrase that follows it: "And the son of man that you care for him?" Both phrases are essentially asking, "Why would the God who made something as spectacular as the universe care or even think about something as seemingly insignificant as human beings?" But they pose the question using slightly different words. The first phrase uses the term "man" while the second uses the phrase "son of man." But obviously, every son of man is also a man. So the terms are really equivalent. Moreover, "take thought of him" has basically the same meaning in this context as "care for him." The two phrases are synonyms. Hence, this type of poetic literature is referred to as *synonymous* parallelism.

Take a look at the copious use of synonymous parallelism found in Psalm 19. The first part of the Psalm in verse 1 reads, "The heavens are telling of the glory of God" while the second part reads, "And their expanse is declaring the work of His hands." The two phrases have basically the same meaning: that the universe reveals the majesty of God through what He has made. The "heavens" from the first phrase is basically the "expanse" from the second phrase. The phrase "are telling" from the first part is basically the same as "is declaring" from the second part. And the "glory of God" matches nicely with "the work of His hands," though the two are not exactly the same.

Verse 2 exhibits the same pattern: "Day to day pours forth speech, and night to night reveals knowledge." "Day to day" and "night to night" are both basically ways of saying "continually." That is, the heavens reveal God's glory all the time — day and night. The phrase "pours forth speech" is not exactly the same as "reveals knowledge," but they nonetheless go well together. Speech is the way that knowledge is revealed, or "poured forth." Of course, the universe does not literally speak; but since this section is poetic, it is not intended to be taken in a literal fashion.

Synonymous parallelism usually comes in two parts, but sometimes it has three or more parts. Consider Psalm 1:1: "How blessed is the man who does not walk in the counsel of the wicked, nor stand in the path of sinners, nor sit in the seat of scoffers!" This passage has a threefold parallel structure. "Walk," "stand," and "sit" are three different physical images that represent being in cooperation ("council," "path," or "seat") with another person. And "the wicked," "sinners," and "scoffers" are all synonyms for an unrighteous person. The imagery is beautiful, but not strictly literal. The meaning of the passage is nonetheless clear: we are blessed if we do not align ourselves with wicked people.

The other basic type of parallelism found in Scripture is called "antithetical parallelism." In this case, rather than the two parts of the poem saying the same thing, the second part gives the flip side (the "antithesis") of the first part. Psalm 1:6 is an example of this: "For the Lord knows the way of the righteous, but the way of the wicked will perish." The two parts of this go together like the two opposite sides of a coin. On the one hand, if we are righteous before God, then He knows us and directs our path; but, on the other hand, if we are not righteous before God then our path is a dead end and we will perish. The first part of the verse deals with the godly path, and the second part with the path of the ungodly.

Why parallelism? We often think of and recognize poetry by rhyme and meter. Modern English poetry often has a certain rhythm, and the words at certain parts of the pattern tend to rhyme. But the culture of the ancient Hebrews was different. To them, a good poem was one that exhibited good parallelism. And we should be grateful for this. If biblical poetry were concerned primarily with rhyme and meter, then its beauty would be lost as it is translated from the original language into English. Isn't it wonderful that God chose to use the Hebrew culture with its emphasis on parallelism in poetry to record His Word! The beauty of poetic parallelism transcends the specific language and is evident even in our modern English translations.

The fact that poetic sections of the Bible abound in parallelism will be very useful when it comes to interpreting those sections. The meaning of the passage is revealed in what the first part of the parallel has in common (or contrasts) with the second part of the parallel. We can use this fact to interpret these passages, as we do later in this chapter. For now, we simply note that it is extremely helpful in *identifying* which sections of the Bible are poetic (and by contrast, which sections are not)!

For example, there can be no doubt that the Proverbs are rightly classified as poetic literature since they contain abundant parallelism. Proverbs 1:8 shows synonymous parallelism: "Hear, my son, your father's instruction and do not forsake your mother's teaching." Proverbs 10:17 shows antithetical parallelism: "He is on the path of life who heeds instruction, but he who ignores reproof goes astray." In English translations of Proverbs, the parts of synonymous parallelism are usually connected by the word "and," whereas the two parts of antithetical parallelism are almost always connected by the word "but."

The Proverbs are usually stated as generalizations — things that are generally true most of the time. Critics sometimes attempt to discredit the Proverbs by pointing out that some of its generalizations have exceptions. Well yes, most generalizations do. But that doesn't in any way disprove the generalization itself. The Proverbs were never intended to be taken as exception-less. So when Proverbs 22:6 tells us that we are to train up a child in the way he should go and when he is old he will not depart from it, this is a generalization. The text does *not* say, "In all cases, *every* child that is trained up will never, under any circumstances, depart from that path for his entire life." We should not assume that there has never been an instance of a child with good biblical training who nonetheless ended up rebelling against God. Rather, the Proverb indicates what occurs *most of the time.*

We can see why Job, Ecclesiastes, and Song of Solomon are classified as wisdom/poetic literature due to their abundant use of parallelism. Consider Job 3:3, Ecclesiastes 3:1, and Song of Solomon 2:1 as three examples of obvious poetic parallelism, among many that can be found in these books. But there are also sections in other books that contain poetry, and are therefore non-literal. Exodus 15:1–19 records the song that the Israelites sang about their escape from Egypt. The song exhibits parallelism and is not meant to be taken as a literal account. Consider Exodus 15:6 as an example: "Your right hand, O Lord, is majestic in power, Your right hand, O Lord, shatters the enemy." As we saw previously, God is a spirit, and therefore does not have literal hands. But the "right hand" is imagery of God's power —

and it was that power that "shatters the enemy." Of course, the enemy was not literally "shattered," but rather drowned (Exodus 14:27–28). But the poetic imagery of the word "shatters" makes a powerful point.

Additional Literary Indicators of Poetry

Parallelism is the key identifier of biblical poetry. But there are additional literary devices that are employed frequently in poetic sections of the Bible. Although these additional figures of speech are not exclusive to poetic passages, they are far more frequent there than in the narrative or didactic sections. Repeated use of these devices is therefore a clear indication of poetic literature.

Synecdoche is the substitution of a part for the whole, or the whole for a part. "Jim could really use a raise for the sake of his family; he has seven mouths to feed!" In this example, "mouths" really means "people" and indicates that Jim is providing for seven family members. The entire person needs to eat. The mouth is simply the part of the person most associated with eating, which is why it is poetically substituted.

Proverbs 6:16–19 gives some fantastic examples of synecdoche. It lists things that the Lord hates beginning with "Haughty eyes, a lying tongue, and hands that shed innocent blood." But it is not literally the eyes, the tongue, or the hands that are displeasing to God. It is the entire *person* who sins. The eyes, the tongue and the hands are merely the parts of the person that are associated with the particular sins. The part has been substituted for the whole. Verse 18 continues with "A heart that devises wicked plans, feet that run rapidly to evil." Are we to believe that God is really displeased with the literal heart or the physical feet of the sinner? It is the entire person who has offended God.

Note the unusual phrasing of verse 16; "There are six things which the Lord hates, yes, seven which are an abomination to Him." This is clearly synonymous parallelism, but the number (six) increases by one in the second part of the phrase. It reads strangely in English. We are tempted to ask, "Which is it: six or seven?" Of course there is no contradiction here because seven includes six. That is, if you have seven things, you necessarily have six things (and one more). But this X, X+1 parallel is very common in Hebrew, and is a clear marker of poetic language. It is called "graded numerical parallelism." For other examples, see Job 5:19, Proverbs 30:15, 18, 21,

29; Amos 1:3, 6, 9, 11, 13, 2:1, 4, 6; Micah 5:5; Ecclesiastes 4:6, 12, 11:2; Jeremiah 3:14; Isaiah 17:6; and Hosea 6:2. Note that these are all poetic or prophetic books and *none* are historical narrative.

Reification is another figure of speech commonly found in poetic literature. Reification is the act of attributing a concrete or personal characteristic to an abstraction. My favorite example of this in the Scriptures is Proverbs 8. This chapter reifies wisdom as if it were a woman. Wisdom is described as crying out with a voice (verse 1), as having a mouth (verses 7-8), as loving people (verse 17), as giving commands (verses 32–33), as having the power to give people wealth (verse 21), as witnessing creation (verses 22–30), and as rejoicing (verses 30–31). Wisdom is even quoted as if speaking in the first person beginning in verse 4.

But wisdom is a concept, and cannot literally do any of these things. This chapter is painting a word-picture. It describes a powerful scene in which we see the benefits of seeking after wisdom. We get the point, and the emotional impact is far greater than if this Proverb had been written in a literal way. Reification is always non-literal. Sometimes people today use reification incorrectly, in a quasi-literal way to get around a problem, as in "Evolution guided the development of life on earth." But this is fallacious because evolution is a concept and cannot literally guide or do anything. Reification is therefore considered a fallacy when used literally as in a scientific argument. But it is perfectly acceptable, and quite beautiful when used in poetry.

Prophetic Literature

Isaiah is a book abounding in prophetic imagery. One of the characteristics of prophecy in Old Testament literature is that it is often written in a *poetic* form. This is apparent from their copious use of parallelism. Consider Isaiah 49:1, "Listen to Me, O islands, and pay attention, you peoples from afar. The LORD called Me from the womb; from the body of My mother He named Me." Or Jeremiah 1:5, "Before I formed you in the womb I knew you, and before you were born I consecrated you; I have appointed you a prophet to the nations." The synonymous parallelism in these verses is very obvious. *Prophetic passages often use the same types of poetic imagery found in the wisdom literature.* This is a clear indicator that the authors intended that such passages should not be taken in a strictly literal sense. Again, we should remember the caveat that a given passage may have been more literal in the original Hebrew language than it appears in English translations.

It is relatively easy to show that prophetic literature wasn't intended to be taken in a fully literal way. Consider Isaiah 19:1: "The oracle concerning Egypt. Behold, the LORD is riding on a swift cloud and is about to come to Egypt; the idols of Egypt will tremble at His presence, and the heart of the Egyptians will melt within them." The notion of an omnipresent God literally riding on a cloud or literally coming to Egypt is contradictory. When God judged Egypt, its idols didn't literally tremble, nor did the hearts of the Egyptians literally melt. But we get the idea. The imagery conveys impending, devastating, divine judgment.

In some cases, the Scriptures themselves explicitly and literally state the meaning of the poetic/symbolic images used in a particular prophecy. In Daniel 2:31–35, God gave a prophecy to King Nebuchadnezzar through a dream. The dream contained many symbols and visual imagery — a statue made of different types of material, and a stone that destroyed the statue and grew into a mountain that grew until it filled the entire earth. It is doubtful that anyone would take this prophecy as meaning that a literal statue would be literally constructed out of different materials, and then literally destroyed by a literal stone that grew to encompass the earth. And it wasn't meant to be taken that way. Even Nebuchadnezzar knew better than to take it literally; he expected an interpretation of the non-literal symbols. Daniel, under the inspiration of the Holy Spirit, gave the interpretation of the prophecy in verses 36–45. There can be no doubt that this interpretation is correct, because it is given by direct inspiration of God Himself! The point is that the original prophecy was non-literal in nature, and contained dramatic imagery with symbolic meanings.

As far as I know, there is no Bible scholar who seriously believes that the beast with seven heads and ten horns that comes out of the sea in Revelation 13:1 is a literal creature. Does God have the power to make such a creature? Of course. But Revelation is a book of prophecy, and it uses the same kinds of non-literal imagery as the prophetic books of the Old Testament. So we don't expect the beast to be literal. Some might be wondering, "If it is non-literal, what then does it mean? How are we to interpret the sections of the Bible that use non-literal language?" We do so by context and by considering what the parallel parts have in common. We will look at some examples later. For now, it is sufficient to recognize that biblical prophecy contains abundant elements of Hebrew poetic literature, and therefore is not to be taken in a strictly literal sense.

Parables

There are no books of the Bible that are classified in the category of "parable." All the Scriptures fall primarily into one of the six categories that were listed at the start of this chapter. But we have already seen that books of one primary literary style may contain sections of another style. And such is the case with parables. The Gospels, which are primarily historical narrative, contain parables that are not.

As with Exodus 15, we have an example of one type of literature found within another type. We are to understand that Jesus literally and historically spoke the parables as recorded in the Gospels, but the parables themselves are not necessarily meant to be understood as historical events.

A parable is a short story that teaches a spiritual principle. A parable is written in a literal, non-poetic way about familiar things, and uses these to teach a principle that goes beyond the mere events of the story. Most parables communicate by analogy. An analogy is where one thing is used to represent another, due to some important similarity between the two. This is a very effective way of teaching. Modern astronomers and physicists will often use analogies to teach the basics of very complicated mathematical truths to non-experts.

Are parables literal? The stories are told in a literal way, but they illustrate a truth that goes beyond the literal words of the story. The elements of the story symbolize something else. Consider the parable of the wheat and the tares in Matthew 13:24–30. How are we to properly interpret this parable? What does it mean? This one is easy because Jesus tells us exactly what it means. He interprets His own parable in Matthew 13:36–43. He explains what the wheat symbolizes, what the tares symbolize, what the field symbolizes and so on. There can be no doubt that parables are meant to be symbolic expressions of spiritual truths because that is how Jesus — God incarnate — interprets them. We recognize this truth only because we take the Gospels as literal history, and therefore Jesus really did teach and interpret the parable as the Gospels record. Parables are unique in that they are not literal or historical records, but are also non-poetic. They are found primarily in the Gospels, and were one of the main methods that Christ used in His teaching ministry.[3]

Recognizing Types of Literature

We can think of the Bible as containing two basic types of literature: literal, and not-so-literal. There are then sub-categories of each of these two main divisions. The not-so-literal portions of the Bible are mainly the wisdom literature and prophecy. These sections are written in a poetic way. Even poetry uses many literal words and phrases, of course; hence, "not-so-literal" may be a better description of these sections than "non-literal." But poems make generous use of metaphors, and verbal imagery. Therefore, we should not press the details beyond the verbal imagery that the author intended to convey.

The poetic/not-so-literal sections are characterized in the following ways. (1) Parallelism; either synonymous or antithetical parallelism. This is an *essential* distinctive of Hebrew poetry. If you don't have parallelism, you don't have poetry. (2) Verbal imagery — metaphors, similes, symbols, and other figures of speech. (3) The introduction or title of the book; namely, poetic sections are found primarily (but not exclusively) in the wisdom literature (Job–Song of Solomon), and prophetic literature (Isaiah–Malachi, and Revelation). (4) The lack of markers of history or epistles as shown below.

Conversely, the literal sections of the Bible will generally lack the above characteristics. The books of the Bible that are written in historical narrative do not use parallelism, unless they are literally reporting a song or poem performed by someone in history (e.g., Exodus 15:1–21). There is some use of figures of speech, but it is not as common as in the poetic sections. The introduction of the books of history (including the Gospels and the Law) often makes clear that the type of literature is primarily literal. The same is true of the epistles.

Historical narrative is further characterized by what some people might consider "boring" details. Names of specific people or places, dates of events, lists of genealogies, the number of years a person lives, and so on, are all characteristics of historical narrative. Genesis chapter 5 is a wonderful example of such historical details and contains a long list of genealogies. It cannot be classified as poetry; Genesis 5 would make a terrible poem! The

3. The Old Testament contains a few parables as well. See Ezekiel 17:1–24, 24:1–14.

attention to detail is characteristic of literal historical narrative, and is a sure indication that we are to take the text as written.

As with poetic literature, the title and introduction of the book can reveal the type of literature. The epistles are usually addressed as letters from the author to a person or group of people, so it is clear that such writings are to be treated as literal letters. Likewise, the historical literature is often introduced as such. Consider the first verse of the Book of Deuteronomy: "These are the words which Moses spoke to all Israel across the Jordan in the wilderness. . . ." Can there be any doubt that the author is attempting to convey what historically happened?

Historical narrative in the Old Testament is easy to recognize, and there are additional linguistic indicators in the original language that are not as apparent in English translations. For example, Old Testament narrative makes frequent use of a Hebrew construction called a "waw-consecutive." This is where a sentence starts with "And" followed by a verb. The verb follows "And" in the original Hebrew word order, which is not necessarily the English word order. For example, Genesis 5:3 states, "And Adam lived an hundred and thirty years . . ." (KJV). In Hebrew, the order is "And lived Adam . . ." so it is a waw-consecutive. So are verses 6, 7, and so on. All of those verses that start, "And ____ lived . . ." are waw-consecutive. In general, anywhere in the Old Testament where the KJV translation renders a long list of events with each one starting with "And" or sometimes "Then" (from the same Hebrew word) it is waw-consecutive. Though an individual waw-consecutive may occasionally be found in poetic sections of the Bible, long lists of waw-consecutive occur *only* in historical narrative, never in poetic literature. Therefore, a long list of "and this happened, and that happened, etc." is a sure sign of historical narrative. Please note that some English translations do not always include the "and" because the translators felt that the passage would read more naturally in English without it.[4]

In summary, historical narrative is characterized by the following. (1) It lacks the parallelism of poetry. (2) It uses fewer similes, metaphors, and figures of speech than the poetic or prophetic literature. (3) It makes frequent mention of specific details, some of which are not directly relevant to the

4. The New American Standard (NASB) translation is one that has changed on this issue. The 1977 version of the NASB included the "And" in verses such as Genesis 5:9. However, in the 1995 version, most of these were removed.

topic — specific names, places, dates, ages. (4) It is often indicated by the title or introduction to the book. (5) It makes frequent use of the Hebrew waw-consecutive (Old Testament only).

Basic Literary Rules of Interpretation of Various Genres

The historical sections of the Bible and the letters are primarily literal. We've seen that the alternative is self-refuting. This makes sense because modern history books are always primarily literal, and so are letters. Such literature is roughly two-thirds of the books of the Bible. For these sections, the key to proper interpretation is therefore to read the words according to their ordinary, literal meaning, using context and the standard rules of grammar, as well as all the other rules we have previously discussed. For the most part, interpretation of these sections is very easy. The words mean just what they say.

Interpreting the not-so-literal sections of the Bible will not be quite as straightforward because the words will not necessarily mean what they most commonly mean in ordinary speech. Since the literal sections of Scripture are easier and more straightforward to interpret than the poetic/prophetic sections, this leads very naturally to a rule of hermeneutics. *The clearer sections of Scripture must be used to help interpret the less clear passages. As a corollary to this, the historical sections of the Bible and the epistles should be used to interpret the poetic and prophetic passages — not the reverse.* A poetic passage may shed additional light on an historical passage. But it should not be used to override the clear meaning of an historical text. The historical texts should constrain our interpretation of the poetic and prophetic texts. It makes sense, yet not all interpreters follow this rule. Nonetheless, we can prove that this rule is true by showing that the alternative leads to absurdity.

Proving the Principle of "the Narrative Constrains the Poetic"

Suppose, for argument's sake, that we ignore the principle of interpreting the poetic/prophetic sections in light of the literal sections, and instead choose to do the opposite. If we were to ignore the poetic markers found in Old Testament prophecy and read such sections in a fully literal way according to our English translation, we would have to conclude that Jesus is *not* the Messiah! Consider the following texts.

Isaiah 8:14–15 indicates that the Messiah will become "a stone to strike and a rock to stumble over, and a snare and a trap for the inhabitants of Jerusalem." But Jesus did not literally become a stone, a snare, or a trap for the inhabitants of Jerusalem. Therefore, He cannot be the Messiah if the Isaiah passage is fully literal. Jeremiah 30:9 teaches that the Messiah would be the resurrected King David, but Jesus is not literally King David. Ezekiel 34:23 states of the Messiah, "Then I will set over them one shepherd, My servant David, and he will feed them; he will feed them himself and be their shepherd." Not only is Jesus not literally David, but He is not literally a shepherd; He was a carpenter by trade (Matthew 13:55; Mark 6:3).

According to Isaiah 7:14, the mother of the Messiah "will call His name Immanuel." But Mary named her son "Jesus" (Luke 1:30–31). Conversely, Zechariah 6:12 states that the Messiah's name will be "Branch." Now if either Isaiah or Zechariah is to be taken literally, then Jesus is not the Messiah. Furthermore, Zechariah 6:12 states that this Branch "will build the temple of the LORD." But Jesus didn't build a literal/physical temple; the temple had been built long before the birth of Jesus. And so He cannot be the Messiah if Zechariah is to be taken literally.

Isaiah 11:4 says of the Messiah that "He will strike the earth with the rod of His mouth, and with the breath of His lips He will slay the wicked." But Jesus did not literally do these things. Malachi 4:5 teaches that Elijah the prophet would be sent before the Messiah to prepare the way. But John the Baptist was literally the one who preceded Jesus. And John the Baptist is not literally Elijah. Many other examples could be given.

If Jesus is the Messiah (and indeed He is) then these prophetic passages cannot be strictly literal. They are all true, but are only rightly interpreted according to the author's intention in the context of the style of literature in which they are found. Jesus isn't literally a rock, but He is figuratively (1 Peter 2:8). John the Baptist isn't literally Elijah (John 1:21), but he represents Elijah (Luke 1:17, Matthew 11:14, 17:12–13). Jesus didn't build a physical temple, but He built the spiritual temple of God — the church (1 Corinthians 3:16–17). Jesus is, genealogically, the "branch" of David (Jeremiah 33:15). And Immanuel ("God with us") is one of His many names (Matthew 1:23). Jesus is, spiritually, a shepherd — not of literal sheep but of people (John 10:11). The Old Testament authors used verbal imagery and common idioms to communicate truth in the prophetic sections of the Old Testament; that was their cultural norm. Why do so many people today ignore this?

In our modern-day arrogance, too many people assume that the Bible was written primarily for 21st-century Americans. Consequently, they think it should be read according to our modern customs and styles, which are fairly low-context (using fewer idioms and verbal imagery than high-context cultures like ancient Israel). But the Bible was written almost entirely by Jews, and primarily *for* Jews. Those of us who are Gentile believers have been grafted in to the family of God (Romans 11:17). And we ought to have the humility to learn to read the Bible the way its authors intended — according to *their* styles and customs. Anything less is not exegesis, but eisegesis.

Our tendency to hyper-literalize poetic literature may partly stem from an overreaction to liberal interpretations of the historical-literal sections of Scripture. It is morally wrong and unscholarly to interpret the historical sections of Scripture as poetic or non-literal because this is contrary to the intention of the authors. However, it is equally morally wrong and unscholarly to interpret poetic or prophetic sections in a hyper-literal way, for exactly the same reason — it is contrary to the intention of the authors. Either mistake violates the *genre principle* and can lead to serious heresy. We've already seen that we would have to conclude that Christ is not the Messiah. But consider how our view of the nature of God becomes incredibly distorted when we hyper-literalize prophetic and wisdom literature.

Orthodox Christianity has always taught that God is an immaterial (non-physical) spirit, not a man; God is omnipresent and invisible. This position is well-justified scripturally (John 4:24; 1 Samuel 15:29; 1 Kings 8:27; 1 Timothy 1:17). But if the poetic and prophetic passages are taken literally, we could conclude the opposite of each one of these! We would conclude that God has a physical body with hands and a face (Job 1:11; Psalm 10:12, 63:8, 13:1, 27:8), who sits on a chair like a man (Daniel 7:9). God cannot be an omnipresent spirit if He is a physical being literally located on a throne in a literal temple (Revelation 4:2; Isaiah 6:1). And what does this God literally look like? He's not invisible if he can be seen and looks like a man (Ezekiel 1:26), with white hair (Daniel 7:9), but whose body is like precious stones (Revelation 4:3), is bright as the sun

(Revelation 21:23), has wings (Psalm 17:8) with feathers (Psalm 91:4), and whose loins are on fire (Ezekiel 1:27)! But to take such passages as a literal description of a physical being violates the genre principle and the principle of accommodation (discussed in chapter 6). Such hermeneutical errors led to the fourth century heresy called "audianism" — the notion that God has a physical form.

To be clear, I am not for a moment suggesting that it is wrong to use poetic passages to draw theological conclusions. On the contrary, we can learn a great deal about the nature of God from the Psalms and other poetic literature. The problem is when people take more from such passages than is really there, particularly when such an interpretation contradicts the historical narrative passages. The more straightforward nature of the historical passages rightly constrains the poetic literature.

We know that Christ applied this principle in His earthly ministry. When Jesus was fasting in the wilderness, Satan tempted Him by quoting and misapplying a poetic section of Scripture (Psalm 91:11–12 quoted in Matthew 4:6). Jesus responded by quoting from the historical narrative (Deuteronomy 6:16 quoted in Matthew 4:7). Christ's response is cogent *only if the narrative constrains the poetic.*

Consider another example. Exodus 14 records the history of the escape of the Israelites from Egypt, and the crossing of the Red Sea. It is written in the normal historical narrative style. Exodus 15:1–18 records a song that the Israelites sang about this event; it contains all the expected markers of Hebrew poetic literature. The appropriate way to interpret Exodus 15:1–18 is in light of the literal history of Exodus 14. If we reverse this principle, then we end up with nonsense. If we take Exodus 15:1–18 literally, then God's literal right hand (verse 12) was stretched out, and shattered the enemy rather than drowning them (verse 6). God blew air out of His literal nose to move the waters (verse 8), and His anger literally burned the enemy to death (verse 7). The inhabitants of Canaan turned into liquid — they literally melted (verse 15), but not before they were frozen solid so that they could not move (verse 16).

Now wouldn't it be ridiculous to take chapter 15 literally, and then interpret chapter 14 symbolically to match? As far as I know, no one does this with these two chapters. Why then do some Christians violate this principle in other portions of Scripture? One such error concerns the interpretation of the first chapters of Genesis. There are some individuals today who claim that the early chapters of Genesis can only be properly understood in light of the poetic books of the Bible. They use Job, Proverbs, and Psalms specifically. But this is an obvious violation of the literary rules of hermeneutics. With such an error, we can equally well "prove" that Jesus is not the Messiah.

Biblical texts must be interpreted according to the type of literature in which they are found if we are to arrive at the meaning of the passage. We will call this the *genre principle*. The genre principle indicates that historical sections of the Bible and the epistles should be interpreted in a primarily literal fashion. The genre principle indicates that poetic sections, prophetic sections, and parables should be interpreted in a not-so-literal way. Since literal sections are easy to interpret, it is only reasonable to interpret poetic sections in light of the literal sections. This is one of the most important hermeneutical principles pertaining to the different types of literature found within Scripture. When this principle is violated it leads to ridiculous and often heretical results.

Application — Historical Passages

Let us take the first chapter of Genesis as an example of how to properly apply the genre principle. First, we need to answer the question: "What type of literature is Genesis?" The first verse states, "In the beginning God created the heavens and the earth." This is a simple statement recording a past action. This type of introduction is very typical of historical literature (e.g., Leviticus 1:1; Numbers 1:1; Deuteronomy 1:1; Joshua 1:1).

We notice that there are virtually no indications of poetic literature in Genesis 1:1. There is no obvious use of similes, metaphors, reification, synecdoche, or graded numerical parallelism ("X, X+1" patterns). There is no synonymous or antithetical parallelism. Some people have tried to argue that the repetition of the phrase "and there was evening and there was morning" (verses 5, 8, 13, 19, 23, 31) is synonymous parallelism. But it cannot be such because no *synonyms* are used. With synonymous parallelism, the same idea is conveyed two or more times using *different words* with similar meanings. The repetition of a single phrase verbatim is not parallelism.

Some Psalms do repeat a phrase verbatim several verses later (Psalm 46:7, 11; 57:5, 11; 67:3, 5; 80:3, 7, 19). The Psalms were sung originally, and repeated phrases are the refrain. Some people have argued that the "evening and morning" in Genesis are such a refrain. But this is false because the day changes — a second day, a third day, and so on. Such would not be the case in a refrain. The "evening and morning" are repeated to emphasize that each day consisted of one evening and one morning, thereby disallowing any long-age interpretation. Genesis 1 is certainly not a song or poem.

Genesis 1 also gives details that would not be included typically in poetic literature — such as the order of events. The text indicates that the stars were created on the fourth day. But when poetic literature describes the creation of the stars, such details are omitted (e.g., Psalm 8:3, 33:6, 136:7–9). Notice also how many sentences in Genesis 1 begin with the word "And" in the King James Version. This is no error; these are instances of the Hebrew waw-consecutive. Indeed, every verse in Genesis 1 after verse 2 uses the waw-consecutive. Such repeated usage never occurs in poetic literature. Genesis 1 fits all the qualifiers of literal historical narrative, and none of the qualifiers of poetry.

How then shall we interpret Genesis 1? Literally. When Genesis 1:5 indicates that the first day was composed of one evening and one morning, the correct interpretation is that the first day was composed of one evening and one morning. It is really not confusing or difficult at all. When Genesis teaches that God created the luminaries on the fourth day (Genesis 1:14–19), the correct interpretation is that God created the luminaries on the fourth day.

Now, people may not want to accept this as true. They may wonder how God could do such in six days, or how the earth could have day and night before the sun.[5] But if people can't understand how God did something, then that's *their* problem — not God's. People may choose to incorrectly interpret Genesis to match their preconceived ideas about creation. But from the rules of hermeneutics, there is absolutely no doubt that the *meaning* of Genesis 1 is that God created in six days, in the precise order and exact way that the text states.

---

5. Only a light source and a rotating planet are necessary for day and night. The sun isn't required. Of course, the Bible indicates that there was a temporary light source for the first three days (Genesis 1:3). And the planet was rotating because there was evening and morning (Genesis 1:5).

Application — Poetic Passages

As an example of applying hermeneutical principles to poetic literature, consider the 19th Psalm. The introduction states, "For the choir director. A Psalm of David." The introduction leaves no doubt that this is poetic literature, a song of praise. We have already seen above how the first two verses exhibit synonymous parallelism — an obvious indicator of poetic literature. But what do the passages mean?

Remember that in synonymous parallelism the two parts mean basically the same thing. The key therefore is to consider *what the two parts of the parallel have in common — their essential core.* "The heavens are telling of the glory of God" and "their expanse is declaring the work of His hands" (verse 1) are each a word picture of the universe speaking about God's glory. The genre principle indicates that we should not take this to mean that the universe literally or audibly speaks. Nonetheless, we can learn something about the glory of God by understanding the universe, *as if* it were speaking to us.

Verse 2 states, "Day to day pours forth speech, and night to night reveals knowledge." The parallelism is obvious, but what does it mean? "Day to day" and "night to night" are both synonyms for something that happens on an ongoing basis. We are to understand that the non-literal message of the universe is *continual.* And "speech" is the way that knowledge is revealed. The verse indicates that the sky continually reveals God's glory. Verse 3 has some translational issues, so we will return to the question of its interpretation in the next chapter.

Verse 4 states, "Their line has gone out through all the earth, and their utterances to the end of the world." The commonality in the two phrases is the universal nature of general revelation. Not everyone has read the Bible, but everyone has experienced the glory of God as revealed in the created world. This theme is emphasized in the next verses. The sun is personified as a groom coming out of his chamber and a strong man rejoicing as he runs his course. Verse six describes the rising of the sun and its circuit through the heavens. This indicates the apparent path of the sun in the sky and the fact that it can be seen by all people. This is clear from the context of the previous verses that describe the universality of general revelation. The last phrase in verse 6 further confirms that this is the meaning: "And there is nothing hidden from its heat." Hence, no one can escape God's general revelation.

Some people have tried to read into verse 6 that it is endorsing a geocentric solar system. Others have suggested that this is divine insight into the orbit of the sun around our galaxy. But both of these interpretations violate the contextual principle. The text is not addressing models of the solar system or galaxy. Rather, the Psalmist is describing God's general revelation to man; hence, he uses observational language to illustrate the fact that all people have experienced God's revelation. The earth rotates in such a way that nothing on its surface is hidden from the heat of the sun, which is part of God's general revelation. The passage indicates the universality of general revelation using the sun as an example — nothing more, nothing less.

In verses 7–14, the topic switches from God's general revelation to God's special revelation — the text of Scripture. Note that verses 7–9 poetically describe various aspects of the Word of God — the law, the testimony, the precepts, the commandment, the fear, and the judgments of the Lord. Each of these aspects is praised in some way as "perfect, restoring the soul" or as "sure, making wise the simple." This seems to be an example of synecdoche — all these aspects of God's Word represent the whole of Scripture. That is, the entire Bible is perfect, sure, right, pure, clear, and true.

Verse 10 must be very difficult for those who want to put general revelation on the same level as Scripture, for this verse takes the things that men most desire in the natural world, and indicates that Scripture is *better*! Those aspects of Scripture mentioned in the previous verses are to be desired more than gold, and are sweeter than the drippings of the honeycomb. God's Word is better than the best parts of God's world. The world is cursed after all. Scripture is not.

Verse 11 indicates that the Scriptures warn God's servant of the hazards of sin — a great reward indeed for keeping God's commandments. In verses 12–14, we learn that the Scriptures can discern even the hidden sins of a person, and can lead him away from sin's power. They can lead him to repentance and forgiveness so that the man of God may be acceptable in God's sight.

Overall, Psalm 19 presents us with a wonderful comparison of God's general and special revelations. Each has its place. General revelation's main advantage is that it is absolutely universal and inescapable. Special revelation is not. But on all other fronts, special revelation is superior. It alone has the ability to bring salvation and sanctification to man, and is therefore to be desired more than anything in the world.

Review

There are six major categories of books in Scripture: Law, History, Wisdom, Prophecy, Gospels, and Epistles. Of these, the books of the Law, the books of History, and the Gospels are written in historical narrative style. These historical books and the Epistles are written using ordinary language, with only occasional figures of speech. This is just like letters and historical works that are written today. The Wisdom literature and biblical prophecy have the characteristics of Hebrew poetic writings. Just as with poetry today, there is abundant non-literal usage of words — metaphors, similes, and various figures of speech. The author's intention therefore, is that the poetic/prophetic sections are not to be taken in a wooden literal sense. Hence, if we are going to interpret the Bible correctly, we must take the historical sections and epistles in a primarily literal fashion (with allowances for occasional figures of speech), and we must *not* take the poetic and prophetic sections in a strictly literal fashion. We note that works of literature of one type may contain within them literature of another type (historical books may contain songs or parables that were historically verbalized).

Poetic sections of Scripture are characterized by the following: (1) Parallelism (either synonymous or antithetical). Parallelism is *the key distinctive* of biblical poetry. (2) Increased usage of similes, metaphors, symbolism, verbal imagery, and other non-literal figures of speech such as reification and synecdoche. (3) The introduction of the book. (4) A lack of indications of characteristics of historic narrative, such as detailed genealogies. These criteria are characteristic of the Psalms, which both Christians and critics agree is poetic, non-literal literature. Such characteristics are also found in the other books classified as Wisdom literature, and also in the books of Prophecy.

Historical sections in Scripture are characterized by (1) a lack of parallelism, (2) fewer figures of speech (similes, metaphors, symbolic imagery) than the poetic literature, (3) attention to details — including specific names of individuals or places, genealogies, dates, ages, (4) the introduction of the book, (5) frequent use of the waw-consecutive (in the Old Testament) which in English versions often shows up as a string of sentences that all begin with "And" or "Then." The books of the Law, the books of History, the Gospels, and the Epistles have these characteristics.

Since the literal sections of Scripture are clearer and more straightforward to read (by definition) than the less-literal sections, it is a natural principle of interpretation that the less-literal should be interpreted in light of the literal. As a corollary, the Poetic/prophetic sections of Scripture must be interpreted in light of the literal historical or doctrinal sections. If this principle is reversed, we could "prove" that Jesus is not the Messiah, or any number of other anti-biblical heresies. Without this literary principle, biblical interpretation is reduced to nonsense.

In poetic sections that use synonymous parallelism, the meaning of the two (or more) parts of the verse must go together. This constrains their meaning. In antithetical parallelism, the two parts of the verse must contrast. This constrains their meaning as well.

Chapter 6

Common Hermeneutical Principles and Fallacies

It can be very helpful to have a name for each of the rules or principles of biblical interpretation. This allows us to succinctly justify our interpretation of a given text. Rather than repeat an argument for a given hermeneutical procedure it is more efficient to say, "The text must mean this because it follows from the principle of ______." For each principle of hermeneutics there is a corresponding fallacy — a mistake in reasoning — when that principle is violated. Hermeneutical fallacies occur when the reader fails to correctly apply a principle of hermeneutics. In this chapter, we demonstrate and examine some additional principles of hermeneutics. These will be summarized at the end of the chapter. For completeness, we also summarize hermeneutical principles covered in previous chapters.

The Contextual Principle

When we look up a given word in a dictionary, more often than not, it will have several different definitions. Each definition is called a "lexical definition." However, within a given proposition, a given word will have only one meaning. It will generally be one of the lexical definitions. Which definition applies is always determined by context — the surrounding words. This is the contextual principle.

One form of context is the immediate context — the words in very close proximity to the word in question. Suppose we wanted to know the meaning of the word "land" in the sentence, "The plane is about to land." The immediate context of the words "about to" instantly informs us that "land" is being used as a verb in this context, in the infinitive form. Therefore, we can immediately eliminate all of the definitions of "land" in which the word is used as a noun. Those would be out of context. The term "plane" further constrains the meaning of land down to one of its lexical definitions: "to bring or set on the ground."

The way in which words are used grammatically will often instantly reduce the range of possible meanings in a given context. For example, if a sentence begins with the two words, "The land," we instantly know that "land" is not a verb because it wouldn't make sense grammatically. Grammatical rules are an important contextual constraint.

The context can also be the broader framework, such as the sentences or paragraphs surrounding the word in question. It might even be the context of the entire book. The sentence "The Bengals were a big hit this year" means one thing if it occurs in a book on NFL sports, and means something entirely different if it occurs in a book on zoo-keeping. The broader context might also include what we've already defined as the genre principle. The type of literature in question will certainly be relevant to the meaning of the text. Context is absolutely essential for proper biblical interpretation.

In situations where the broader context might imply one meaning, but the immediate context implies something else, the immediate context is paramount. For example, suppose we read a book about a person named "April." The book is biographical, telling about many of the events of April's life. The broader context would suggest that apart from any evidence to the contrary, a reference to "April" in the book would be a reference to this main character. But we then come to a passage that describes what happened "on the day of Sunday, April 17." Clearly, the immediate context implies that the word "April" here refers to the month, not the main character, despite the broader context.

As a biblical example, some critics have said that Jesus was mistaken in referring to the mustard seed as the smallest of all seeds (Matthew 13:31–32). Orchid seeds are known to be smaller. Was Jesus mistaken? Context, however, shows that Jesus was considering *garden plants* (verse 32), that is, kosher plants that Jews planted for food. He was not making a claim about all plants in the universe, but only illustrating the growth of the kingdom by using a Jewish garden. And of those plants used in such gardens that could grow into a tree, the smallest seeds were indeed mustard seeds.

The contextual principle is proved by noting that communication would be impossible if this principle were ignored. A typical word might have 20 different lexical definitions. So a sentence with only five words would have up to 3.2 million different meanings if the meaning of each word were not constrained by context! We couldn't have any confidence in communication if there were only a 1 in 3.2 million chance of picking the right meaning of all five words simultaneously. Clearly, the context of the surrounding words allows us to instantly reduce the possibilities to a few, and in most cases, down to one.

When the contextual principle is violated, we say that the interpreter has "taken the text out of context." When text is taken out of context, the interpretation will not, in general, be correct. Just because a word means a particular thing in one verse does not necessarily mean that the word has the same meaning in another verse. Only if the context is sufficiently similar is it right to argue that the words must mean the same thing. Context always determines the meaning.

There are two specific forms of this fallacy that often occur in matters of biblical interpretation. One involves ignoring the contextual constraints of a particular word in a given text, and insisting on a lexical definition that does not fit the context. This fallacy is called "the unwarranted expansion of an expanded semantic field." A very common example of this fallacy can be found in some texts of old-earth creationists and theistic evolutionists who argue that the days of creation were actually vast ages.

The argument goes something like this: "The Hebrew word translated as 'day' in Genesis chapter 1 is *yom*. This word has a number of meanings, one of which is a long, but finite, indefinite period of time. Therefore, the days of creation might not be ordinary days; they could have been vast ages, perhaps hundreds of millions of years each." This argument ignores the contextual principle by failing to note the context in which *yom* is used in Genesis 1. Although an "indefinite period of time" is one of the lexical definitions of *yom*, it is not the most common meaning. *Yom* normally means an ordinary day, and is almost always translated that way. In Genesis

1, the word *yom* occurs in the context of "morning" and "evening," which would only make sense if *yom* is referring to an ordinary day. The old-earth creationist has committed the fallacy of the unwarranted expansion of the expanded semantic field, by selecting a definition of *yom* that is beyond the range allowed by the immediate context.

A similar fallacy is called the "unwarranted *restriction* of an expanded semantic field." Sometimes, a word in a given context is used in a broad or non-specific way. When this occurs, it would be fallacious to force a specific sub-meaning on the word when this is not supported by context. For example, some people have argued that the Bible teaches a geocentric solar system because the text states that the world shall not be moved (Psalm 93:1). They take "moved" to mean "motion relative to a Newtonian inertial reference frame." Although Newtonian motion may well be a subset of the meanings of the Hebrew word for "moved" (*mot*), there is nothing in the context to warrant restricting the meaning to that specific sub-meaning. The word *mot* can also mean "to fall, to be overthrown, to slip, to dislodge" — none of which are references to Newtonian physics.

The "Explicit Constrains the Implicit" Principle

Closely related to the contextual principle is the principle that the explicit constrains the implicit. An explicit teaching is something that is stated directly like, "For in six days the LORD made the heavens and the earth, the sea and all that is in them" (Exodus 20:11). An implicit teaching is something that is implied, but not directly stated in the Scriptures. "There was no death of the living animals before Adam sinned" is not directly stated in the Bible, but it can be cogently argued from the Scriptures such as Genesis 1:28–31, 3:14; Proverbs 12:10; Romans 8:20–22; 1 Corinthians 15:26.

It is always far easier to defend an explicit teaching of Scripture than an implicit teaching, because we can simply point to the verse that states it directly. Since explicit teachings are clearer and more direct than implicit teachings, it makes good sense to use the former to guide our understanding of the latter. Just as we use literal passages to help us understand the poetic passages, it is always the case that the clear teachings of Scripture must be used to guide our interpretation of the more difficult passages.

A fallacy is committed when this principle is ignored. For example, some people have argued that the "young-earth" position is wrong, because the Bible teaches that the mountains are ancient (Deuteronomy 33:15), and the "heavens were of old" (2 Peter 3:5). They take this to mean billions of years old, and then interpret the days of Genesis as long ages to match. But this is using the implicit to override the explicit. The mountains and the heavens are indeed old — thousands of years old! "Old" is an implicit, non-specific term. It is the Genesis account and other explicit teachings in Scripture that tell us *how* old.

The Substitution Principle

The substitution principle of mathematics states, "if A=B, then A may be substituted for B." This principle works just as well in biblical interpretation. If X means Y, then X may be substituted for Y without altering the meaning of the passage. In this case, X is what the Bible explicitly states, and Y is what it means (the correct interpretation). If the interpretation is correct, then we can substitute the interpretation for the text (we can paraphrase) without altering the meaning. The substitution principle is axiomatically true, and we can prove it easily. We simply point out that if substituting Y (the interpretation) for X (the text) alters the meaning, then Y is necessarily not the correct interpretation of X, since the correct interpretation by definition is the one that captures the meaning.

As an example of this principle, in the second part of John 3:16, "eternal life," doesn't just mean everlasting existence (both believers and unbelievers experience that). Rather, we know from the rest of the Scriptures that it means "living forever enjoying God's gracious presence." Furthermore, the phrase "believes in Him" doesn't just mean believing that God exists (the demons do that and it doesn't save them), rather it refers to a saving faith: trusting in Christ for forgiveness of sins and affirming Him as Lord. Therefore, by the substitution principle, John 3:16(b) is teaching that if we trust in Christ for forgiveness of sins and affirm Him as Lord, then we will live forever enjoying God's gracious presence. This paraphrase seems to me to be capturing the essence of the verse. If it doesn't, then that means that my interpretation of "eternal life" or "believes in Him" (or both) is wrong.

This principle is very helpful in refuting false interpretations of Scripture. For example, in Mark 10:6 Jesus states, "But from the beginning of creation, God MADE THEM MALE AND FEMALE." Jesus is responding to the Pharisees' question about divorce by explaining that God intended marriage to be one man and one woman united by God for life, and was that way from the beginning of creation. This passage bothers many old-earth creationists because they do not believe that human beings were around at the "beginning of creation." Indeed, of the 13.8 billion years that old-earth creationists and evolutionists believe in, they say that human beings have only been around in the *last* 0.001 percent of history. Whereas the Bible teaches that Adam and Eve were made on the sixth day — they were there at the first week of creation, which certainly counts as the beginning.

To get around this problem, some old-earth supporters have claimed that Jesus' statement in Mark 10:6 is not referring to the beginning of creation, but rather the beginning of marriage. We can show that this is nonsense by the substitution principle. If "beginning of Creation" really meant the beginning of marriage, and we understand that "God made them male and female" is the institution of marriage, then we can substitute this and we find the paraphrased text says, "But from the beginning of marriage, God instituted marriage." But such a statement is trivial and worthless. Everything exists from its own institution. If Jesus meant to say that marriage existed from the institution of marriage, then His statement has no power and is a useless tautology. The actual meaning is that God instituted marriage from the beginning of *creation* — it was part of His original plan and existed from the first week of time itself.

The Fact-Value Principle

The Bible does not affirm as right everything that it records as true. There is a difference between what *is* and what *should be*. And that difference will persist until this world passes away. This principle must be considered when we examine the actions or words of biblical persons. As an argument against Scripture, critics will sometimes complain that various biblical persons did this or that wicked thing. But this is irrelevant to the *truth* of the biblical record. Yes, people do wicked things sometimes. That's why we need a Savior.

One of the unique things about the Bible in contrast to other ancient literature is that it records the weaknesses of its heroes of the faith. King David had Uriah killed in order to take his wife. The Bible records this wicked act (2 Samuel 11:2–27), but it certainly does not endorse it as right. On the contrary, the Bible explicitly states that David's actions in this matter were "evil in the sight of the LORD" (2 Samuel 11:27). It is not proper biblical interpretation to assume that the Bible necessarily endorses the actions of an individual, unless there is a textual reason to conclude this.

This principle includes words that are spoken by individuals. For example, the Bible correctly records the lie spoken by the old prophet in 1 Kings 13:18, but it certainly does not endorse the old prophet's statement. What about the words spoken by believers — those who trust in the Lord and strive to obey Him? Great caution should be observed here. Often, the statements of godly individuals are exactly right, and should be heeded. But even very godly people sometimes sin, both in actions and in words. Sarah was a godly woman (Hebrews 11:11; 1 Peter 3:6), and yet her statement denying that she laughed was false (Genesis 18:12–15), and is not endorsed by God as true. So we need to examine these on a case-by-case basis, and compare the statements made by people with the authoritative affirmations of Scripture.

Peter, a godly man and indeed an Apostle of Jesus, made an incorrect statement when he denied that Jesus would be crucified. He states, "God forbid it, Lord! This shall never happen to You" (Matthew 16:22). The Bible does not endorse Peter's statement. It merely infallibly reports it. Peter was factually wrong and morally wrong to contradict His Lord. The same Apostle lied about knowing Jesus three times (Matthew 26:69–75). Scripture is not teaching that Peter's statements were true, or that it was morally right for him to deny Christ. Quite the opposite. The Scriptures accurately report Peter's sinful statements.

Yet, we do take the words in the books of 1 and 2 Peter as authoritative and inerrant. These were written by the same Apostle. So it may seem perplexing at first that we should take Peter's words as wrong in some instances and as absolutely inerrant in another. The key to this difference is found in 2 Timothy 3:16. When Peter penned the two epistles that now bear his name, he was writing under the inspiration of God, and therefore could not be mistaken in what he wrote. Second Timothy 3:16 is clear that this is the case with all Scripture. When Peter lied about the crucifixion of Jesus, and when he denied Jesus three times, he was acting out of his own sin nature. So the words spoken by Peter in the Gospels are not necessarily endorsed by God as true; but the words of Peter that he penned in his epistles were directed and inspired by God, and are therefore authoritative.

The Bible does not endorse as true all the words spoken by people; it merely accurately reports them. What the Bible does endorse or affirm as right are its direct teachings, and any words spoken by God Himself. God, by His nature, is truth (John 14:6). Therefore everything God says is true, and everything that is affirmed in God's Word is true.

The Incidental Fallacy

One way in which the fact-value principle is violated is the incidental fallacy. This occurs when a reader takes an historical text as prescriptive rather than descriptive. We've already seen one example of this; the fact that David committed adultery with Bathsheba does not mean that we should do likewise. Furthermore, even when God does approve of something for one person in history, this doesn't necessarily imply that the same action would be right for all people in history. Some of God's commands are general and for everyone; but others are for a specific individual at a specific time. Context distinguishes the two.

It would be fallacious to conclude that we should all offer our child as a burnt offering on the basis that God commanded Abraham to do such. That command was given to Abraham and was for him alone. How many sermons have I heard that God has "plans for our welfare to give us a future and hope" on the basis of Jeremiah 29:11? But this promise was given specifically to the Jewish exiles in Babylon (Jeremiah 29:1) and concerns God's plans for *them*. To apply this to all people at all times is to commit the incidental fallacy. After all, God sometimes plans for His people to suffer and even to be martyred (John 13:36).

The Red Letter Principle

In general, we cannot assume that the words spoken by a human being in Scripture are necessarily affirmed as true or right by God in Scripture. The reason is simple: humans are not God; we make mistakes. But there is one human who is God and therefore never makes mistakes. Therefore, we can conclude that all statements made by Jesus are true, right, and endorsed by God. The red letter principle is not an exception to the fact-value principle, but rather a corollary of it. The fact-value principle acknowledges that everything God says is true and everything He does is morally commendable. The red letter principle simply acknowledges that Jesus is God. Therefore, what Jesus says is always true, and what He does is always right.

The Accommodation Principle

In Isaiah 55:8–9, God states, " 'For My thoughts are not your thoughts, nor are your ways My ways,' declares the LORD. 'For as the heavens are higher than the earth, so are My ways higher than your ways and My thoughts than your thoughts.' " God's knowledge, His way of thinking, is so far beyond us that it is like comparing the size of the universe to the earth. For this reason, the extent to which we can understand God will always be only partial. We can never "come up" to God's level to understand His ways. Therefore, when God wishes to communicate to us, He must "come down" to our level. He uses analogy and metaphor to give us a basic, simplified understanding of a complex truth. This is the accommodation principle.

Human beings also use the accommodation principle, particularly when teaching young children. We use analogy and metaphor when a literal and precise explanation would be beyond the child's understanding. These literary devices give the child an approximation of reality in cases where the child cannot comprehend the full reality. "Electricity in a wire is like water flowing through a hose. A resistor is like a narrow spot in the hose that slows the water." From this analogy, a child could correctly conclude that resistors reduce the flow of electricity in a wire. It's a good analogy — but it's not the full reality. It would be wrong to conclude that breaking an electric wire will make you wet, since breaking a water hose will make you wet. The analogy has limits.

God uses accommodation in a number of ways — and none of these should be pressed beyond the limit of the analogy. For example, God often uses anthropomorphic language to describe Himself or His actions. An anthropomorphism is when a human trait is figuratively attributed to something that is not human. God is a spirit (John 4:24). As such, He does not have a physical body (though of course, Jesus, the second member of the Trinity, now has a body since He has added a human nature to His divine nature). So when the Bible speaks of God having fingers (Psalm 8:3), hands (Exodus 7:4), arms (Exodus 6:6, 15:16), feet, or a face (Exodus 33:20), these are anthropomorphic examples of accommodation. They are not meant to be understood as literal/physical, but rather are the best analogy that we can comprehend.

What then do such figures of speech actually mean? To extract the meaning of the passage, we look at the essential aspect of the analogy or metaphor. As one example, our hands are perhaps the most fundamental body part that we use in terms of physical labor. Our hands are how we accomplish our work — especially our dominant hand which is the right hand for most people. So by analogy, it makes sense that God's "hand" represents His ability, His power to accomplish His will. This is indeed how the term is used in the Scriptures (Exodus 7:5, 9:3, 13:16, 15:6, 32:11; 1 Chronicles 29:12; Psalm 17:7, 18:35, 44:3, 60:5, 77:10, 98:1). Notice that many of these refer to the "right hand" specifically. These passages are not intended to teach that God has literal, physical hands; that would violate the explicit teaching in John 4:24 that God is a spirit.

Likewise, the "face" often symbolizes the *full presence* of a person. When two people have a conversation, they talk face to face, not to their feet or their left hip or their right elbow. Why is that? The face is where we express emotion, where we take in most of our sensory experiences, where we communicate with others. The face is the essence of our personhood. Even today, we often use the expression "face to face" to indicate a conversation in which both people are present, as opposed to a phone conversation. Likewise, the face of God is used in the Scriptures to indicate the fullness of His presence (Deuteronomy 31:17–18; 1 Chronicles 16:11; 2 Chronicles 7:14; Psalm 11:7, 27:8, 30:7, 31:16, 80:19; Jeremiah 18:17). In fact, in the Hebrew language, "face" and "presence" are the same word: "panim." To seek God's face is therefore to seek the fullness of His presence, and when God "hides His face" it means that He withholds some of His gracious fellowship from people. These verses should *not* be taken to mean that God is a physical man with a literal face, since that would contradict the literal portions of Scripture (e.g., John 4:24; 1 Kings 8:27).

Sometimes God's emotions are anthropomorphized. In Genesis 6, we read that the wickedness of mankind was very great. In verse 6, the text states, "The LORD was sorry that He had made man on the earth, and He was grieved in His heart." The term "sorry" has a number of meanings. We often think of it as regretting something in the sense that we now consider what we did to have been a mistake. Alternatively, it can simply mean to feel "bad" about an unfortunate circumstance. Does Genesis 6:6 teach that God regretted His earlier actions in creating man? Did God change His mind about making people? No. God makes no mistakes and never changes (Malachi 3:6). He does not repent in the sense of regretting an earlier decision and reversing it (Numbers 23:19). Therefore, we are to understand that this text is an accommodation to human understanding. The sadness that God felt over the wickedness of mankind is being described in the best terms that we finite humans can understand.

The Bible speaks of God forgiving our sins in such a way that He no longer even remembers them (Jeremiah 31:34; Hebrews 10:17). Does He *literally* forget them? We can certainly remember many of our own sins. Does this mean we know some things that God doesn't know? Clearly not. God knows all things (Colossians 2:3; Psalm 147:5; Proverbs 15:3). So when the Bible says that God does not remember our sins, this is an accommodation to human understanding. It is the closest analogy that we can understand to the level of forgiveness extended by our Creator. God has forgiven our sins to such an extent, that it is *as if* He can't even remember that they happened. He will treat us *as if* we had never sinned. But God remains omniscient.

Another example is found in Genesis 22. Here, God commands Abraham to offer his beloved son Isaac as a burnt offering. Abraham obeyed, and was about to slay his son when the Angel of the Lord stopped Him. The Angel of the Lord in this instance is Christ since He refers to Himself as the Lord (verses 12, 15–16). In verse 12 the Lord says, "Now I know that you fear God, since you have not withheld your son, your only son, from Me." The phrase "Now I know" would be bothersome apart from the principle of accommodation. Didn't God know beforehand what Abraham would do? Of course He did; God knows everything. Though God knew from all eternity that Abraham would pass the test, He uses accommodationist language to express His pleasure since Abraham's faith had now been expressed in a way that could be observed by other people.

In addition to anthropomorphism, there are other analogies that God uses to help us understand at least partially His nature, or the nature of spiritual things. Eternity in the Lake of Fire for those who reject God's gracious offer of salvation is referred to in Scripture as "the second death" (Revelation 22:14). We are not to think that this death is literal or physical in the sense of an organism ceasing to function. Rather, death is the closest analogy that we can understand to what the Lake of Fire is like. Death, the ultimate tragedy, the finality of it, the thing that people fear above anything else, the regrets, the pain and humiliation, the knowledge that everything you've worked for in life will no longer matter to you, the total lack of hope — all of these things, but forever! That is what the Lake of Fire is like. Physical death is a mere shadow of the bitter, eternal reality that awaits those who have continually rejected God. The analogy of "death" to the eternal existence of unbelievers is certainly fitting.

Parables are a form of accommodation. We may not fully understand the kingdom of heaven; so Jesus relates it to things that we do understand. It is like a merchant seeking fine pearls (Matthew 13:45), like a dragnet cast into the sea (Matthew 13:47), like a king with servants (Matthew 18:23), like a landowner who hires laborers (Matthew 20:1), like a king who gives a wedding feast for his son (Matthew 22:2). None of these analogies is exactly the same as the kingdom of heaven of course, and we shouldn't take them that way. But each of these analogies captures certain aspects of the kingdom of heaven that we can at least partially understand.

The accommodation principle is not contrary to the literal principle, but the two balance each other. The literal principle reminds us that the doctrinal and narrative parts of God's Word are to be taken in a plain, straightforward way unless there is contextual reason to suggest otherwise. The accommodation principle reminds us that when it comes to God's nature, we are not to press analogies beyond what is indicated by the text.

The Progressive Revelation Principle

God has revealed Himself to all people (Romans 1:19). He has "hardwired" human beings in such a way that we know God. When we look at what God has made, we instantly know in our heart of hearts that God exists and we have some understanding of His attributes (Romans 1:18–20). This is often called "general revelation" because it is available to all people at all times. From Adam to today, people have always had some knowledge of the Living God.

The Scriptures are called "special revelation" because this specific revelation is only available to those who read the Scriptures. The Gospel message is one such example because it is found only in Scripture, not in nature (Romans 10:17). God, in His wisdom, has chosen to reveal His plan of salvation progressively — in stages. The Bible was written over a timespan that likely exceeds 2,000 years. Adam had some knowledge of God and of salvation, and we can read about this in Genesis. The Israelites of the Old

Testament had more revelation. We who live in the era of the New Testament have more revelation from God than those who lived in the era of the Old Testament because we have the complete Bible (1 Peter 1:10–12).

What are the implications of progressive revelation on biblical interpretation? Progressive revelation implies that the New Testament authors understood more of the specific details of the Gospel than the writers of the Old Testament. Therefore, we expect that the New Testament will fill in many of the details of salvation, the nature of God, and other spiritual issues that were dealt with in less detail in the Old Testament. The New Testament gives us a fuller explanation of many of the teachings in the Old Testament, such as salvation. The Old Testament does teach about salvation in Christ, but it does so primarily using symbols — analogical foreshadows (Hebrews 9:8–9, 10:1; Galatians 3:24).

Progressive revelation implies that later books of the Bible will tend to be more explicit in their details than earlier books of the Bible. Following the "explicit constrains the implicit" principle, we will therefore expect that later revelation should be used to interpret earlier revelation. As a corollary to this, the New Testament should be used to interpret the Old Testament. This is not to say that the Old Testament could not be properly understood until the New Testament was written. It certainly could. Nor is it to say that the New Testament is any more inspired than the Old Testament. Both are inerrant revelations from God. Rather, the New Testament gives us greater detail and clarity when it touches upon the truths that were first revealed in the Old Testament.

For example, Deuteronomy 25:4 states "You shall not muzzle the ox while he is threshing." This Old Testament command is clear enough on its own. Oxen were used to tread grain, and they liked to eat some of it as they wer[illegible]. The Old Testament tells us that it would be wrong to muzzle the ox [illegible]e he is threshing, so that he cannot eat some of the grain. But the New [illegible]tament gives greater illumination on this passage. The New Testament explains that this passage was not primarily written for the benefit of the ox (1 Corinthians 9:9–10). Rather it was teaching a general principle, of which the ox is merely one example. Namely, God's creatures should be free to enjoy the fruit of their labor. It is therefore wrong to withhold payment from those who have worked for it. See also 1 Timothy 5:18. The New Testament explains in greater detail the Old Testament passage.

Progressive revelation does *not* mean that later passages will change the meaning of earlier passages. They merely provide a more explicit understanding of earlier concepts. Since the meaning of a passage is the author's intention when he wrote the passage, the meaning cannot change with time. Old Testament passages still mean in the New Testament what they have always meant. The Old Testament ceremonial laws could certainly be understood on their own. But we now have a much better understanding of the Messiah to which those Old Testament symbols pointed (Galatians 3:24–25). The Old Testament prophets who wrote about the coming Messiah did not have the details of Christ's earthly ministry that we can now read in the Gospels (1 Peter 1:10–12). However, nothing in the Gospels is contrary to the writings or intention of the Old Testament prophets.

The progressive nature of special revelation also implies the crucial necessity of reading and understanding the Old Testament. Though the New Testament explains in greater detail the doctrines found in the Old Testament, these doctrines cannot be fully appreciated apart from the elucidation provided in the Old Testament. In other words, if you don't read the Old Testament, you will not fully understand the New Testament. And if you don't read the New Testament, then your understanding of the Old Testament will not be as rich or detailed.

As an example of this, consider the "proto-Gospel" found in Genesis 3:14–15. In this passage, God responds to the sin of Adam and Eve. He promises that the "seed," a descendant of Eve, would crush the head of the serpent (and by implication, the power behind the serpent — Satan). Moreover, the serpent would bruise the heel of the woman's descendant. The implication is clear enough on its own. God is promising to deal with the problem of sin. A descendant of Eve would be "bruised" by the serpent, indicating a damaging attack, but not enough to stop the descendent. This "seed" would then crush the head of the serpent, destroying his power once and for all. Adam and Eve were not given any other details, at least none that are recorded. It was enough for them to know at that time that one of Eve's descendants would destroy the power of the serpent, allowing people to be redeemed from the power of sin.

At a later time, God revealed more information about this promised Messiah. He would be a descendant of David (Jeremiah 23:5), despised by men (Isaiah 53:3), righteous (Isaiah 53:11), would be pierced for our sins (Isaiah 53:5), would justify many (Isaiah 53:11), that he would die among sinners (Isaiah 53:12), that He would be God Himself (Psalm 45:7; Zechariah 12:10; Isaiah 45:21–22). And then in the New Testament, God reveals all sorts of additional information about this Messiah. All of this later revelation is perfectly consistent with previous revelation, but is much more detailed than the basic proto-Gospel given to Adam and Eve. The New Testament sheds greater light on all the Old Testament verses that refer to the Messiah.

But — and this point is crucial — the New Testament information about Christ is rooted in previous revelation, going back to Genesis. The later revelation would not make sense apart from previous revelation. Why did Jesus come to earth? Why did He have to die to pay for sins? What is sin, anyway? The Old Testament answers these questions and sets the stage for the more detailed illumination provided in the New Testament.

The Text Principle

It's so obvious, and yet it is one of the most violated principles of hermeneutics. The text principle is simply this: the Scriptures should be interpreted based on what they actually state. It's pretty evident, or so we would think. But it never ceases to amaze me how many ridiculous interpretations of Scripture stem from a sloppy, careless reading of the text. People often go on to do "biblical interpretation" on a statement that does not exist anywhere in Scripture.

People may criticize the Bible for teaching that animals do not change and then they observe that animals do adapt within a certain range to their environment. But the Bible doesn't anywhere teach that animals do not change — only that there are basic "kinds." Critics may argue that the Bible is wrong to teach that two of every species of animal on earth could fit on the ark. But where does the Bible ever say anything about "species"?

A person recently e-mailed me to criticize my understanding of the Genesis account of creation. He explained that I was ignoring the fact that the Bible teaches that the "birds and the stars" were "created in the same place." But where does the Bible state this? Certainly stars were put in the sky, and birds fly across the face of the sky, but that need not mean the same part of the sky, or the exact same location. The Hebrew word for "sky" or "heavens" is *shamayim,* and includes both the atmosphere and the farther celestial realm. The word is in a dual form that indicates two-ness, and may suggest that the sky is two-chambered — perhaps a reference to the atmospheric portion and then the celestial portion. Nowhere do the Scriptures teach that birds and stars were created in the same location or "chamber" of the sky. This person simply had not read the text carefully.

Some misreadings of the Bible get repeated often and circulate within the Christian church. Perhaps you have heard that there were three wise men who rode on donkeys and that they visited Christ at the manger. We've all heard how the angels sang at the birth of Christ, and that Adam ate an apple. Surely the phrase "spare the rod and spoil the child" is in Scripture, right? Doesn't Revelation teach that the "Antichrist" will come and rule the world? What about the "curse of Ham?" You can search all you like, but these claims are not found anywhere in the Bible.

Critics of creation frequently make the mistake of reading the text in a careless fashion (or not reading it at all), and then argue against their made-up misrepresentation of the Bible. This is called a "straw man fallacy." Here are some I found on some atheist websites, with my comments following. (I'm not making this up!)

"The Bible says that God took an entire day to create something called a firmament." (Does the Bible say that God "took an entire day" to create it, or does it just say He created it, and that happened on the first day?)

"God was so tired from creating things over six days that he needed a full day for rest and recuperation." (What verse says that God was "tired" from creating, or that He "needed" a day of rest?)

"In Genesis, God says that all of creation is 'very good,' including parasites, predators and predation, natural disasters, and all the nasty things that cause death and suffering." (The "very good" part is scriptural, but where does the Bible teach that the original world included any of these "nasty things"?)

"According to Genesis, the first book of the Bible, Adam was lonely — apparently God didn't foresee that problem. As absurd as that is, though, God adopts the even more absurd solution of creating all the animals just to find a 'help meet' for the lone human." (Where does the text state that Adam was lonely? Where does the Bible say that God made the animals to find a help meet for Adam?)

"Genesis has contradictory accounts of when and how Eve, the first woman, was created. The Bible's first creation story says that Eve was created at the same time as Adam." (It does? What verse says they were made "at the same time"?)

The Silence Principle

The flip side of the text principle is that we should not draw hard conclusions based on what the Bible does *not* say. The Bible does not mention Noah having any daughters. But we cannot conclude from this that Noah had no daughters. It could simply be that they are not mentioned. The silence principle is proved by virtue of the fact that the Bible is not exhaustive truth; it does not record everything that has ever happened or everything that is true and therefore we cannot use the absence of something in Scripture as evidence of non-existence. To reason based on what the text does not say is called "an argument from silence."

An argument from silence is not always fallacious, but it is never conclusive. There are places in Scripture where there is a *conspicuous* absence — where we have good reason to believe that something would have been reported if it had happened. Consider the Gospel according to Matthew. Matthew frequently called attention to the fulfillment of prophecy (Matthew 1:22, 2:15, 2:17, 2:23, 4:14, 8:17, 12:17, 13:14, 13:35, 21:4, 26:56, 27:9, 27:35). Matthew also records Christ's prophecy that the Jewish temple would be destroyed (Matthew 23:38, 24:1–2). But Matthew does not record anywhere the fulfillment of this prophecy — an event that took place in A.D. 70. It is reasonable to infer that Matthew wrote his Gospel before this event happened, since it would be out of character for him to fail to report such a spectacular fulfillment of prophecy, particularly since he did record the prophecy itself.

This seems a reasonably cogent argument, though it is an argument from silence. It is likely, but not conclusive, since Matthew could have had some unknown reason to leave out this particular event. However, if an absence is not conspicuous or unusual, then appealing to what is *not* found in a text is considered fallacious. It is a version of the fallacy of *denying the antecedent*, which is covered in Appendix B. In summary, an argument from silence is fallacious unless the absence of an expected report is highly unusual or conspicuous.

The Superfluous Distinction Fallacy

Certain words have distinctions — slightly different meanings in different contexts. As one example, what does the "law" mean when used in the Bible? It is used in multiple ways and may refer to the Pentateuch (John 1:45), the Mosaic administration (Luke 2:22), God's moral commandments (Romans 2:26), the Old Testament ceremonial commandments (Hebrews 10:1; Galatians 3:24–25), all of God's commandments (Joshua 22:5), the written text of God's commandments (John 1:17), the unwritten internal knowledge of morality (Romans 2:15), and so on. We are supposed to distinguish between these various uses by looking at the local context.

When the local context does not warrant a distinction, it is fallacious to assume a distinction unless the larger context of Scripture requires such a distinction in order to remain logically coherent. This is justified since God does not contradict Himself. In other words, all distinctions must be justified from the text either explicitly or implicitly from the need for textual coherence. For example, in Matthew 5:18, Christ indicates that the law is more permanent than the universe. Yet, in Hebrews 7:12, 18–19, we read that the law was changed with Christ. Since God does not contradict Himself, we are rationally justified in concluding that these two passages are addressing *two different aspects of the law*. Christ speaks of the abiding validity of God's law in general, with emphasis on the unchanging moral standards of God, whereas Hebrews addresses the Old Testament ceremonial law (e.g., animal sacrifices, circumcision, etc.) that foreshadowed Christ and was set aside in the New Testament.

The *superfluous distinction fallacy* is the failure to follow this principle. It occurs when a person draws a distinction that is *not* rationally warranted by the Scriptures. This unsupported distinction is usually made in an attempt to defend a preconceived idea. For example, a heretic might say, "God the Father and God the Son are not omnipresent. In their essential nature, they have a form that resembles that of a man. Only the Holy Spirit is omnipresent." A Christian might point the heretic to Jeremiah 23:24 where the Lord Himself indicates that He fills the heavens and the earth — God is omnipresent. And since the Father and Son are God, it follows that they are omnipresent. Suppose the heretic responds, "Ah, but Jeremiah 23:24 is only referring to the Holy Spirit — not the Father or Son." This would be a superfluous distinction fallacy because there is nothing in Jeremiah 23:24 that suggests that only one person of the Trinity is involved, and there is no need for such a distinction in order to bring the rest of the Scriptures into logical coherence.

The superfluous distinction fallacy is absolutely insidious. It is one of the most dangerous and deceptive fallacies for two reasons. First, it is subtle; most people are unaware of this fallacy, and therefore cannot spot it in a conversation. Second, it can lead to any number of heresies. Quite literally *any* unbiblical claim at all can be defended if we allow for arbitrary distinctions to be drawn. Consider the heretic who claims that Jesus is the Son of God, but not God. Yet in Hebrews 1:8, God the Father speaks to God the Son and refers to Him as "God." The heretic might respond, "Ah, but that title is merely an *honorary* one, since the Son is acting under God's authority." But there is absolutely no textual indication of this, and it is not necessary to bring about biblical coherence. The superfluous distinction fallacy is a form of arbitrariness. And we will see in the next chapter that arbitrariness in interpretation is illogical and leads to absurdity.

The Reliability of Ignorance Fallacy

It stands to reason that people who study a particular topic, such as mathematics or geology, should have a great deal of understanding when it comes to those specific topics. A young child with little training in math might be able to read a textbook on calculus, but it is unlikely that his understanding of the topic will come close to that of a mathematics professor. For whatever reason, some people reverse this principle with Scripture. They claim that to correctly understand the meaning of a passage, we ought to read it like a child would, with no theological preconceptions and taking all the words at face value. Essentially, this position claims that the more ignorant the person, the more reliable his or her interpretation of Scripture will be.

It doesn't take a lot of reflection to realize the absurdity of this notion. A child might think that Revelation 17:3 means that there will be a literal beast with seven heads and ten horns. That's what the text states, right? A child might read John 5:29 and think that good works are what cause people to go to heaven, and bad works send people to hell. A child might think that God in the essence of His divinity is a physical being with white hair, a body like ours, with glowing eyes, and a literal sword coming out of His mouth (Revelation 1:13–16). And in all instances, the child would be wrong.

I suspect that the *reliability of ignorance fallacy* stems from a reaction to the prejudicial, unbiblical interpretations of some scholars. Yes, there are some highly educated people who have been taught improperly. They have a faulty philosophy, causing them to distort God's Word and they teach others to do the same. Because of their theological pre-understanding, they do not read the Bible rightly. And so some people suggest that the solution to such biases is to let the uneducated be the main interpreters of Scripture, especially children who have not yet been tainted by the biases of the education system.

The problem with this reasoning is that children are not exempt from biases. They have a sin-nature and also a theological pre-understanding, though they probably have not consciously reflected on it to the same extent as the scholar. Their unspoken, subconscious biases influence their interpretation of the text just as those of the most educated scholar. Bias is inevitable. Lack of education does not alleviate the problem.

So it is not ignorance that leads to a reliable understanding of the text, but diligent study of the text with an attitude of humility and the illumination of the Holy Spirit. Those people with the best understanding of the text will therefore be those people who have studied the text for a very long time, have reasoned rightly from what they have read, and have had the humility to be corrected when necessary.

There is a reason why we don't ask children with no training in math to teach classes on math. And for exactly the same reason, new converts to Christianity are not the best interpreters of Scripture. Yes, the Bible is sufficiently clear that even new converts will be able to understand much of it on the first pass — particularly those passages that are literal historical narrative. But they will not understand the more difficult sections.

The Bible indicates that it contains both "milk" (passages that are easy to understand right away) and "meat" (passages that are difficult to understand at first). Furthermore, the Scriptures describe new believers as being like newborn babies that can only digest the "milk" of the Word at first — not the "meat" (Hebrews 5:13–14; 1 Corinthians 3:1–2). The Bible specifically singles out the "unlearned" (the uneducated) as those who are very prone to distort the more difficult passages in Scripture (2 Peter 3:16).

All Christians begin their new life in Christ as "spiritual babes" that cannot handle the "meat" of the Word. But we are not supposed to remain in that condition. The Bible instructs us not to be like children in our thinking, but to be mature (1 Corinthians 4:20). We are supposed to study the Word (2 Timothy 2:15) and reason from it, thereby exercising our ability to discern (Hebrews 5:14). Furthermore, the Bible commends the Bereans who studied God's Word carefully (Acts 17:11). These passages should dispel the notion that ignorance is helpful in biblical interpretation.

"The Point Is" Fallacy

There is a tendency for those who profess Christianity to overlook details in Scripture that are contrary to intuition or common opinion, even when these details occur in the historical/literal sections. This is especially evident in Genesis, where the details of God's creation do not align with the majority secular view. There exists a strong temptation to dismiss biblical inconveniences with the sweeping claim: "Those details aren't the point. The *important* thing is _____." In this view, the reader is allowed to consider biblical affirmations as false as long as such affirmations are not the primary point of the passage.

This view has serious problems. First, it denies inerrancy and makes God a liar. We would certainly grant that a particular text has a main point; but it is not rational to assume that the details surrounding that point are false or non-literal when those details are recorded in the historical narrative or didactic texts. In many cases, the main point is *established* by the supporting details. So if the details were not true, then there would be no reason to assume that the main point of the passage is true.

For example, suppose I claimed that Eric is a really lousy driver. "He has received three speeding tickets in the last month. He has been in four automobile accidents in the last three years. He never signals when changing lanes, and often runs red lights. I'm afraid to ride with Eric." Clearly, the point of this story is that Eric is terrible driver. Can we therefore dismiss the supporting details as false? Would it be rational to respond as follows? "It doesn't really matter whether those details are true. I don't think Eric really received any speeding tickets or ran any red lights, or that he has been in any traffic accidents at all. The point is: he's a bad driver." But without the details, there is no rational justification for accepting the main point of the story.

A common example of this fallacy when applied to Scripture is in Genesis. The critic says, "The creation story in Genesis 1 wasn't intended to give any literal or scientific details of how God created. So we need not accept the order of events, or the notion that it was only six days. The *important thing* to take away is that God created." Perhaps the main point of Genesis 1 is indeed that God created. But does this mean that we are free to ignore the secondary points — the details God provided that describe the way in which He created? If God didn't think the order of events of creation or timescale of creation were important, then why did He write anything beyond the first verse of Genesis? Is the rest of Genesis just filler so that God could get the word count up? Would God lie about details in order to establish a main point?

"The point is" fallacy denies biblical inerrancy, in deeming sections of the Bible to be untrue — those sections that are auxiliary to the central teaching. Is the main point of the Pentateuch that Moses's mother is named "Jochebed"? Of course not. Is knowledge of Jochebed's name a requirement for salvation? Clearly not. But the Pentateuch does state that this was her name (Exodus 6:20; Numbers 26:59). And so if the Bible is truly inerrant then we must accept that it is correct about this detail — even though its doctrinal significance may be low.

Jesus said that we are to live by every Word that proceeds from the mouth of God (Matthew 4:4) — not just those words that we deem to be the main point of a passage. Second Timothy 3:16 indicates that *all* Scripture is given by inspiration of God and useful for teaching — not just what we consider to be the main point.

The Root Fallacy

Sometimes people will try to glean the nuanced meaning of a word by studying its etymology — the origin of the word. For example, the Hebrew word for man is *adam* and is very similar to the Hebrew word for land/soil/ground *adamah*. This makes sense, because the first man was created from the dust of the ground. That may indeed be why the words are so similar. There is nothing wrong with attempting to study the historical development of words. But there are two potential problems with applying the etymology of a word to the exegesis of a passage.

First, in many cases we don't really know the etymology of a word. Two words that have similar spellings may indeed have a historical connection. Then again, they may not. It's not a crime to speculate on how one word may have been historically derived from another. But in most cases such conjectures will remain conjectures. There is no way to prove them, and hence any conclusions drawn from them should be considered uncertain at best.

Second, the goal of hermeneutics is to discover the author's intention: what he means at the time he writes, and *not* what the words once meant in the distant past. For example, suppose I said, "I'm working on some math problems and I need a new calculator." You probably pictured a small electronic device with buttons and a digital display that performs basic arithmetic. That is indeed what I meant, but it is not what the word "calculator" used to mean. Before the mid-20th century, a "calculator" was a person — someone that you could hire to perform tedious computations. That job was made obsolete by the invention and affordability of the electronic calculator. Eventually, since there was no competition, the "electronic" adjective was dropped, and today it wouldn't occur to anyone to think of a calculator as a person. To understand what I mean by "calculator," we only need to know how the term is used today; information on what the term used to mean is utterly irrelevant.

But sometimes a word in an ancient text is so obscure that we have not much to go on except how it might be etymologically related to a similar ancient word. If a conjecture is the best we can do, so be it. But it must remain a conjecture, and must not contradict the immediate or larger context of a passage. The root fallacy is committed when people give too much weight to the alleged origin of a word, at the expense of context. The root fallacy is somewhat subjective, because it is a judgment call as to what constitutes "too much weight." Suffice it to say that context must always trump etymology.

The Semantic Anachronism Fallacy

The meaning of a word is determined by the way it is used in a given society. After many generations, the meaning of a word can shift as people gradually start using it in a different way. We must keep this in mind when we read an ancient text. We must always interpret a given word as the author understood it if we are to arrive at the correct interpretation. To force a modern meaning on an ancient word would not be true to the author's intention. This error is called the semantic anachronism fallacy.

A common example stems from the King James translation of Genesis 1:28 where God instructed Adam and Eve to "replenish the earth" (KJV). People sometimes assume that "replenish" here means to "refill," and hence implies that the earth was once full but became empty through some sort of catastrophe. But in reality, the Hebrew word translated "replenish" is *male* (maw-lay') and simply means "to fill." This is not an error in the King James Version, because when it was translated in the early 1600s, "replenish" simply meant to fill completely. That meaning has shifted slightly, and today "replenish" means to "fill again." Since the author of Genesis had in mind the meaning of the word at the time it was written (and not a modern meaning) it is incumbent upon us to interpret it as he intended. The principle is proved by noting that the meaning of a passage is what the author intended; and the author could not intend a meaning that didn't exist at the time.

Very young students sometimes commit this fallacy when reading Genesis 1:29–30 in the King James Version. These verses teach that human beings and all animals were originally vegetarian. But children sometimes think the opposite, since these passages mention "meat." Of course, in old English, "meat" simply means "food" in a general sense. Context makes clear that all food was originally plant material; only after the Flood were humans permitted to eat animal flesh (Genesis 9:3).

The Translation Principle and Bible Translations

Most of us cannot read the Bible in the original languages in which it was written. When we read an English Bible, we should be conscious of the fact that we are reading a translation of the inspired text, not the original inspired text. If you read a good modern translation such as the King James Version, the New King James Version, the American Standard Version, or the New American Standard Bible, then what you are reading is about as close as linguistically possible to the original language without actually having to learn Hebrew and Greek. And 99 percent of the time, you will understand the meaning of the text just as the author intended, with very little difficulty.

But there are some cases in which the words and phrases or the grammar of the original language make an exact translation into English impossible. This could be because a Hebrew or Greek word does not have an exact synonym in English. Or it could be that the tense or grammar of the original cannot be fully captured in English. In some cases, the translators will drop or add a word so that the sentence will make sense to modern readers.

As one example, in the Hebrew language there is a word *et* that connects a verb to its object. There is no equivalent in English, and so this word is simply dropped. Genesis 1:1 contains this word twice in the original Hebrew: "In the beginning God created [*et*] the heavens and [*et*] the earth." The Hebrew word shows that the heavens and the earth are the objects of God's creating.

Likewise, sometimes words are added in the English version for readability — words that are not necessary in the Hebrew grammar. Many Bible translations (such as ASV, KJV, NKJV, and NASB) put these words in italics to indicate that they are not in the original. Genesis 1:11 in many English Bibles has an "and" preceding "the fruit tree" or "fruit trees." This word is not in the original text. It has been added because in English grammar we always put an "and" before the final item in a list, as in "Jim, Joe, Pat, and Sally."

But some Hebrew phrases have no direct parallel in English. In such cases, the translators have a difficult choice to make. They can choose to render the individual words as close to the original as possible, even though it may sound awkward in English. Alternatively, they may choose to use a different English word or phrase that better captures the idea, even though the words do not exactly match the original language.

Consider the first phrase of Romans 6:2, which in Greek is *mē genoito*. The first word is an emphatic denial and the second word has the meaning of "come to pass" or "happen." So, it could be literally rendered as "Not come to pass!" But that doesn't read well in English. The NASB translates it as "May it never be!" which is reasonably close to the original, but it makes sense in English too. The KJV translates this phrase as "God forbid," whereas the NKJV renders it as "Certainly not!" The NIV (New International Version) translates the phrase as "By no means!" And the NLT (New Living Translation) renders it as "Of course not!"

Notice that all these translations capture the basic meaning: Paul is answering his previous rhetorical question with an emphatic "NO!" In this instance, the NLT wording is probably the most natural expression that we would use in modern English to emphatically answer in the negative a rhetorical question. Yet it is perhaps the least similar to the original inspired Greek text. The NASB is closer to a word-for-word translation in this instance, but is perhaps the least natural in terms of how we would say things in English. These are the issues that translators must face when translating from Hebrew and Greek into English. There is not always one perfect solution. Rather, there is always a balance between clarity in English and fidelity to the original language.

With this in mind, there are two different approaches in which a translator may attempt to render a biblical text into English. These are called "formal equivalence" and "dynamic equivalence." Using the formal equivalence method, a translator attempts to render the text word-for-word as much as possible, with only minor deviations to make allowances for readability and grammatical structure in English. The individual words are considered to be the basic unit of translation. The KJV, NKJV, NASB, and ASV are all formal equivalence. Formal translations can be difficult to read in places where the grammar or phrasing of the original language makes the English word-for-word translation sound unnatural or awkward.

On the other hand, using dynamic equivalence, a translator attempts to render verses in a thought-for-thought fashion. Phrases, rather than individual words, are considered to be the basic unit of translation. So rather than being concerned with a word-for-word match between the original language and its English counterpart, the translator attempts to use whatever English words or phrases he or she can use to best convey the meaning of the original phrase. The NIV and NLT are both dynamic equivalence translations. Such translations can be easier to understand than their formal equivalence counterparts because the translators have emphasized readability.

Sometimes people have the impression that dynamic equivalence is somehow less "true" to the original than formal equivalence. It is important to recognize that both methods attempt to faithfully convey to the reader the meaning of the original text. Whether this is best accomplished by a word-for-word equivalence or a thought-for-thought equivalence depends very much on the reader's comprehension of the culture and language of the writers.

Consider the first phrase of Proverbs 11:25, which the KJV renders as "The liberal soul shall be made fat." This is an accurate word-for-word translation, but its meaning may be lost on some readers. The word "liberal" has a certain connotation in our politically charged climate. Does this Proverb mean that those who vote for Democrats will gain weight? The ambiguity disappears in the 1984 NIV, which renders the passage as "A generous man will prosper." Although this is not a word-for-word translation, the meaning is much clearer. To be "liberal" in the biblical sense of the word is to be generous. "Soul" means an individual person or "man" in this context. And in the ancient world where most people made their living by physical labor, only a wealthy person could be "fat." So "fat" was used as a synonym for "wealthy" or "prosperous" in many instances in the Bible (Jeremiah 5:27–28; Deuteronomy 31:20; 1 Samuel 2:29; Nehemiah 9:25; Psalm 92:14; Proverbs 13:4, 15:30, 28:25; Isaiah 30:23, 58:11; Ezekiel 34:16).

A reader unfamiliar with the above facts might not understand the KJV word-for-word translation of Proverbs 11:25. But the same reader could easily understand the NIV thought-for-thought translation of this same passage. Therefore, dynamic translations are excellent for new Christians, who do not yet know a lot of the background details of Old Testament life, culture, and language.

However, there are disadvantages to a thought-for-thought translation. Dynamic equivalence assumes that the translators correctly understand what the passage means. In most cases, they do; these are superb Bible scholars. And new Christians should have some degree of confidence in the ability of the translators to correctly understand a passage and render its equivalent in English on the major Christian doctrines. However, translators are not free of bias (no one is). And so when it comes to the nuanced interpretation of certain difficult passages, we should remember that a dynamic equivalence is more susceptible to the biases of the translators than a formal equivalence. Also, there are some cases in which the specific words in the original language have significance that may be lost in a thought-for-thought translation.

On the other hand, formal translation is more susceptible to incorrect understanding by the reader. The differences in grammar between English, Hebrew, and Greek can make certain word-for-word translations difficult to understand in English. Therefore, I usually recommend a dynamic translation for new Christians. For what it's worth, I believe the 1984 edition of the NIV to be the best dynamic translation; it is both readable and accurate.[1] For those who have been Christians for many years, a formal translation is better in terms of getting at the specific nuances of those verses that require us to know the actual words used. Detailed study and memorization of the Scriptures are best with formal equivalence since there is less possibility of translator bias. There are several good formal translations. KJV is very good, but can be difficult for some readers to understand due to the old English. NKJV, ASV, and NASB are all excellent translations. By contrast, RSV and NRSV are *not* good because their translators were not committed to biblical inerrancy, and therefore apply an incorrect hermeneutic in places.

There are also "paraphrased" Bibles. These works attempt to make the text even easier to read than a dynamic translation by using language in a very casual and modern way. I do not consider paraphrased "Bibles" to be authoritative because they are not a translation of God's Word, but rather someone's opinion of what God's Word means. Of course, there is nothing wrong with reading someone's opinion of what God's Word means, as long as this is not confused with the actual text of Scripture. This follows from the text principle. In general, I don't recommend paraphrases. They often look physically like Bibles, and I am concerned that people will be inclined to think that they are reading Scripture, rather than someone's opinion of Scripture. It's better to get a dynamic translation like 1984 NIV if you want a very readable Bible. But again, it's not a sin to read a paraphrase as long as it is understood as such.

The matter of formal versus dynamic translation is not an all-or-nothing issue. Even dynamic translations will render a text word-for-word if it makes good sense in English. And formal translations will deviate from an exact word-for-word parallel if the English translation would not be understood. So there is a range. The NASB is one of the most formal translations, followed respectively by the ASV, the KJV, and the NKJV. The 1984 NIV

1. The 2011 edition of the NIV attempts to reduce gender bias by replacing many masculine pronouns (he, him) with non-gender-specific plural pronouns (they, them). In my opinion this is not as faithful to the original text as the 1984 edition of the NIV. It is best to translate the pronouns as they are in the original language, and then use footnotes, when necessary, to explain that many of these principles apply to women as well, in light of Scriptures such as Galatians 3:28.

is dynamic, but is probably the closest to word-for-word of all the dynamic translations.[2] The NLT is further up on the dynamic scale. The Living Bible and the Message are paraphrases.

The translation principle reminds us that we are reading a translation of God's Word, and therefore we must consider that the English word or phrase may not exactly capture the meaning of the original Hebrew or Greek. As one example, critics sometimes mock the Bible for teaching that rabbits chew the cud (Leviticus 11:6). But this ignores the translation principle because the Hebrew words translated as "chew the cud" have a somewhat broader meaning than what "chew the cud" means in English.

In English, to "chew the cud" refers to ruminants. These animals (such as cows) have four stomach compartments. They will partially digest food in one chamber, then regurgitate and chew on it, and then swallow into another chamber. The Hebrew expression certainly would include ruminants, but it also allows for other animals including rabbits as demonstrated in the following.

The Hebrew words translated as "chew the cud" are *gerah* and *alah*. *Gerah* refers to partially digested food that was previously swallowed, and *alah* has the basic meaning of "to take up again." So in the original language, the text teaches that rabbits take up again partially digested food that was previously swallowed. Although rabbits are not ruminants, they do "take up again food that was previously swallowed." Rabbits produce two types of feces: a hard kind, and a softer pellet called a "cecotrope." Cecotropes are only partially digested, and so rabbits will ingest them again to complete the digestion. (This may sound disgusting to us, but apparently the rabbits don't mind.) So rabbits do "take up again food that was previously swallowed" — just as the original text of Scripture teaches.

The best way to deal with the translation principle is to read the text in the original language, or at least look up the words in a Hebrew/Greek lexicon and see how they are defined, and how they are used elsewhere in Scripture. We can then have confidence in how a word is being used in the context of a particular verse. This gives us insight into the nuances of

2. As indicated in a previous endnote, the 2011 update to the NIV seems to have taken a step backward. The translators have rendered many masculine terms in a gender-neutral way. Although many masculine terms (such as the "brethren") may be legitimately applied to both men and women, it may have been better to leave the terms as they are in the original language, and then explain such in a footnote.

the word as it was originally used. And there are various Bible computer programs available that make study of the original language relatively easy. I use Larry Pierce's "Online Bible," which is very powerful and ridiculously inexpensive (the basic starter pack is free).[3]

The second best way to deal with the translation principle (and this can be used in concert with going back to the original language) is to compare several different English translations. This drastically reduces the chances of translator bias since different translators with different biases are responsible for the different English versions. In the overwhelming majority of cases, there is no fundamental difference in how a verse is translated in any of the major versions. This gives us confidence that the main English translations are very faithful to the original text, and accurately convey the intention of the author. But on the rare occasions in which two different translations conflict, we must do further study to see which (if either) is faithful to the original text.

Consider Psalm 19:3, which is part of a passage that poetically describes the heavens declaring God's glory. The 1984 NIV renders this as "There is no speech or language where their voice is not heard." This wording implies that the "voice" of the heavens is *always* heard. But when we compare with another translation we see an inconsistency. The NLT renders Psalm 19:3 as "They speak without a sound or word; their voice is never heard." So which is it? Is the "voice" of the heavens always heard as the NIV suggests, or never heard as the NLT suggests? They cannot both be true. This is one of those very few places in Scripture where one of the translations is simply wrong.

The KJV and NKJV translate Psalm 19:3 as "*There is* no speech nor language *where* their voice is not heard." This seems to confirm the NIV translation of the passage: that the voice of the heavens is always heard. Notice that the word "where" is in italics, meaning that it is not in the original Hebrew text but was added for clarity. But the addition of this word changes the apparent meaning. Reading it again without that word we find, "*There is* no speech nor language; their voice is not heard." This confirms the NLT translation of the passage. The NASB also confirms this: "There is no speech, nor are there words; their voice is not heard."

3. Despite the name, the Online Bible is primarily used offline. However, new modules are often posted online and available for download: http://onlinebible.net/.

Psalm 19:3 indeed teaches that the message of the heavens is a silent message. It is never heard. We can look up the verse in the original text and confirm that the word "where" is not present in the Hebrew text. Once that word is dropped, the synonymous parallelism in the passage becomes clear: no speech, no words, not heard. The message of the heavens is not an audible message. It does not use words or human speech, and for that reason the "voice" of the heavens cannot be heard. We can understand the true meaning of the passage even before going to a Hebrew lexicon just by comparing several translations, and recognizing that words in italics have been added.

Review of Hermeneutical Principles and Fallacies

The contextual principle is the recognition that a given word has a range of possible meanings, only one of which is appropriate in the given context. The correct interpretation of a word in context is that which fits with the surrounding words, causing the sentence to make sense, and which fits the broader context of the paragraph, chapter, book, or the entire Bible. Without the contextual principle, communication would be impossible, since we could never determine which meaning of a particular word is in use.

The "explicit constrains the implicit" principle acknowledges that detailed descriptions should be used to interpret inferences, not the reverse. The clear interprets the less-clear. The reason for this is fairly obvious; it is far easier to correctly interpret a clear, explicit statement than it is an implicit teaching.

The substitution principle states that if Y is a correct interpretation of X, then Y may be paraphrased as X without altering the meaning. The substitution principle is true by construction, and can be used to expose faulty interpretations of Scripture.

The fact-value principle acknowledges that the Bible records statements and actions that it does not necessarily endorse. For example, the Bible truthfully records statements made by people, even when their statements are false. Therefore, we cannot assume that the words spoken by an individual and recorded in Scripture are necessarily true, unless the Bible endorses them as factual. This applies even to believers in the Bible since they too are sinners, albeit forgiven sinners. On the other hand, the words written by the biblical authors in the Bible are authoritative and inerrant since they are written under the divine guidance and control of the Holy Spirit.

The incidental fallacy occurs when a reader takes an historical text as prescriptive rather than descriptive. This includes the error of taking commands that God gives to a specific individual that were intended only for that individual, and applying them to others.

The red-letter principle is a corollary of the fact-value principle. It explains that since Jesus is God, everything that Jesus said is true, and everything that Jesus did is morally commendable.

The accommodation principle is the recognition that limitations of human understanding and human language make it impossible for us to communicate with God on His level. Therefore, God comes down to our level when He communicates with us, explaining things using analogies and word pictures that we can understand. Such figures of speech are not intended to be fully literal, but are designed to give us an approximation of reality at a level that we can understand.

The progressive revelation principle is the biblical doctrine that God has increased His special revelation to mankind over time. We have more knowledge of God today recorded in the Scriptures than the Jews of the Old Testament; and they had more revelation than the early patriarchs. Later revelation is always consistent with previous revelation (this follows from the consistency principle), and helps us interpret it by expanding upon and clarifying previous revelation. Since later revelation builds upon previous revelation, the New Testament will not be fully understood apart from the Old Testament.

The text principle is the obvious truth that biblical interpretation must be applied to the actual text of Scripture — not what someone falsely claims that the text states. Some of the most ludicrous interpretations of the Bible are due to a sloppy reading of the text, and are easily refuted simply by reading what the text actually states.

The silence principle is the fact that when we don't find something in a text, this doesn't necessarily disprove the existence of that thing. An *argument from silence* is generally considered fallacious or very weak. The only exceptions would be if there is a compelling reason why we would expect something to be mentioned if it were true.

Distinctions in the meaning of a word or phrase must be justified from context or from the need for logical coherency in the Bible. The superfluous distinction fallacy is the violation of this principle — when people draw a distinction to protect their pre-understanding of the text when such a distinction is not warranted by the text itself.

The reliability of ignorance fallacy is the claim that people with less knowledge of the Bible tend to have more reliable interpretations of the text than people with more knowledge of the Bible. Scripture teaches the opposite: that unlearned individuals tend to distort the more difficult sections of God's Word (2 Peter 3:16), that new Christians can initially handle only the milk of the Word, not the more difficult "meat" portions (1 Corinthians 3:1–2; Hebrews 5:13–14). The Apostle Paul instructs us not to remain like children in our thinking (1 Corinthians 14:20).

"The point is" fallacy claims that sections of the Bible may be untrue, as long as they are not the main point of the passage. This is fallacious, because the author certainly intended for us to understand that the details are true, otherwise he would not have included them. The fallacy denies biblical inerrancy by allowing God to be mistaken or deliberately lying about auxiliary details.

The translation principle acknowledges that English Bibles are not the original inerrant text, but rather translations thereof. Although the major Bible translations are very faithful to the original text, there is no logical or scriptural reason to suppose that any particular translation is as inerrant as the original. We must look to the original text if we are to be certain of the meaning of a passage.

Formal equivalence is the method of translation that treats the word as the basic unit of translation, and attempts to translate word-for-word whenever possible. Dynamic equivalence is the method of translation that treats phrases as the basic unit of translation, and attempts to translate thought-for-thought. Dynamic equivalence is often easier to read, but is more subject to translator bias than the alternative. Formal equivalence is closer to the original language word structure, but can be hard to read for precisely that reason. The KJV, NKJV, ASV, and NASB are good formal translations, whereas the 1984 NIV and NLT are good dynamic translations.

Review of Hermeneutical Principles from Previous Chapters

The one-meaning principle is the fact that propositions generally have exactly one primary meaning. Those who argue that a particular text means several different things are violating this principle. A given text has one primary meaning. It is usually possible to get at that meaning by studying the context. We might consider several possible interpretations in an attempt to get at the one meaning. In some cases, due to human fallibility, we may not be able to decide which interpretation is the correct one. But even in these cases we can often narrow the options to only a few.

The genre principle is the recognition that the Bible contains several different types of literature, each with its own principles of interpretation. It is inappropriate to interpret poetry as if it were history, just as it is inappropriate to interpret history as if it were poetry. There are six main categories of Bible books, but some are basically the same style. Books of one primary style may contain sections of another style. Broadly speaking, the historical narrative sections of the Bible, including the Gospels, the books of history, and the Pentateuch, along with the didactic sections (the epistles) are properly interpreted in a primarily literal way. The books of wisdom and the prophetic works are often highly poetic in nature, and should not be interpreted in a strictly literal fashion, though they do have some literal content. The genre principle, along with the "explicit constrains the implicit" principle, indicates that poetic and prophetic passages should be interpreted in light of the literal-historical or didactic passages.

The two-books fallacy is the error of treating nature as if it were a book that contained propositional statements that have equal authority to Scripture. The problem of course is that nature is not composed of propositional statements. People can make statements about nature, but these statements are subject to error, and are thus not infallible. In practice, the two-books fallacy is committed when people adjust their interpretation of the infallible text of Scripture to match the fallible statements of men.

The literal principle acknowledges that non-poetic literature in the Bible should be interpreted literally, unless there is a clear contextual reason to take it another way. The literal principle does allow for figures of speech even in otherwise literal sections of the Bible. But these must be justified from the culture, grammar, and context — not arbitrarily assumed.

The consistency principle alludes to the internal cohesiveness of Scripture. God does not deny Himself; therefore a correct interpretation of one passage in Scripture cannot contradict a correct interpretation of another passage in Scripture. The consistency principle is one way in which the Bible is "self-interpreting."

The inerrancy principle acknowledges that the Bible is without any mistakes in its original autographs. This principle must not be used as an excuse to interpret the Bible to match what are assumed to be "facts," since our beliefs are subject to error. But it does provide illumination when considering several possible interpretations of a passage; the correct interpretation will not contradict any of the facts reported elsewhere in Scripture. A correct interpretation may indeed contradict what fallible people consider to be a "fact."

The analogy of faith principle recognizes that the best interpreter of Scripture is Scripture. When one Scripture comments on another Scripture, it does so without error. This follows logically from inerrancy.

The principle of perspicuity is the doctrine that the Bible is written with clarity. It was designed to be understood by its readers at the time it was written and also afterward. Perspicuity denies that the Bible is written in a cryptic way that could only be understood by someone with modern scientific knowledge or gnostic insight. When people claim to have discovered some "new truth" in Scripture that was never seen before, we can rest assured that their interpretation is false.

Chapter 7

The Role of Logic in Biblical Interpretation

Logic is the study of the principles of "correct reasoning." If people do not reason logically (correctly) then there really isn't any reason to trust their conclusions. Why would scriptural interpretation be an exception to this?

People use laws of logic (the rules of correct reasoning) every day. This occurs mainly on the sub-conscious level, but it happens constantly. You couldn't get up in the morning without using laws of logic. You know that if you get out of bed, you will no longer be in bed. Imagine your surprise if you got out of bed and found yourself still in bed! That outcome doesn't even occur to us because we know that such a thing would be contradictory. To be in bed and not in bed at the same time in the same way violates logic.

What does it mean to be logical? If logic indeed means "correct reasoning," then who gets to decide if a given line of reasoning is correct? Since God is the truth, it is His reasoning that is ultimately the standard for correct reasoning. Hence, to be logical is to think in a way that is consistent with the character of God as revealed in the Bible.[1]

To what extent should we apply logic to Scripture? Using the substitution principle and the definition of logic, the question becomes: To what

1. This presupposes that we have a correct understanding of God and of Scripture, which requires proper hermeneutics. Fortunately, the Lord knew that we would need to use logic before ever reading in the Bible about the God who is the foundation for it. So He "hard-wired" us to be able to think rationally, at least in a limited capacity. Of necessity, we begin to use our ability to be logical before we come to understand that the biblical God is the rational foundation of logical principles. This hermeneutical spiral is discussed in chapter 9.

extend should we apply correct reasoning to Scripture? And of course the answer is: to the fullest extent! We should *always* be logical in our approach to Scripture. To do less is dishonoring to our Lord. The Bible throughout presupposes that we are to reason from what it explicitly sets forth.

Again, many people are inclined to exempt the Bible from the ordinary rules of logic that apply everywhere else. One reason they might give is that "God is supernatural!" Yes, He is. But *supernatural* does not mean *illogical.* God can do things that go beyond laws of nature. But God is always logical because, as God, He always thinks correctly.

Another reason people might offer is that "the Bible gives principles that are not logical, like the Trinity or 'love your enemy.' " But these principles are *not* illogical. Rationality should not be confused with intuition — our natural expectation or feeling of what seems right. It may feel uncomfortable to love your enemy, but it violates no laws of logic. Some biblical principles may go beyond our ability to fully comprehend, but that does not make them *illogical.* They are merely counter-intuitive in some cases.

"Doesn't the Trinity violate the law of non-contradiction? How can God be one and also three?" The law of non-contradiction states that **A** and **not-A** cannot both be true at the same time *and in the same sense*. The last part of this definition is important, because God is one in one sense and three in a *different* sense. Namely, God is one in nature or essence, but three in persons. If God were only one in essence and also three in the same essence, then we would have a contradiction — but that's not the Trinity. The Trinity may be hard to understand, but it does not violate any laws of logic.

"Isn't the fact that Jesus is both God and man a contradiction?" No. A contradiction would be to say that Jesus is God and *not God* at the same time and in the same sense. But to say, "Christ is God and man" violates no rules of logic. A person can be both a brother and a friend — there is no contradiction, because there is nothing in the definition of "brother" that excludes an essential aspect of "friend." Likewise, there is nothing in the essential nature of God that precludes Him from taking on the essentials of human nature as well. So the Bible may be counter-intuitive at times, but it is never irrational.

God cannot be illogical, because He cannot make a mistake in reasoning. Therefore, the Bible should not be exempt from laws of logic. The Bible is inerrant; but if we fail to reason correctly, our interpretations of Scripture will be unreliable.

God expects us to use logic and draw proper conclusions from the text of Scripture. In fact, you cannot know that you are saved without using logic. Here's why. The Bible nowhere states, "Dr. Lisle is saved." Instead it states, "If you confess with your mouth Jesus as Lord, and believe in your heart that God raised Him from the dead, you will be saved" (Romans 10:9). Furthermore, I know that I have confessed with my mouth that Jesus is Lord, and I have believed in my heart that God raised Him from the dead. I conclude logically that I am saved.

To draw this conclusion, I have used a law of logic called *modus ponens* (see appendix B). All sane people know how to use this law of logic, even if they don't know the name of it. The Bible says that we can know that we are saved (1 John 5:13). But as we have seen, the Bible does not explicitly name the people who are saved today. It is only possible to know that you are saved if you trust the Bible *and* use logic. Therefore, the Bible presupposes and endorses the proper use of logic by its readers. But what are the marks of proper logical reasoning?

We will address some specific principles of correct reasoning (and by contrast, the fallacies that occur when they are violated) in the next chapter. In this chapter we discuss the most foundational principles of logic. There are two main characteristics that distinguish correct reasoning from poor reasoning: (1) a good thinker has an objective reason or reasons for his or her position, and (2) these reasons are self-consistent, obeying laws of logic. Sometimes it is easiest to prove these principles by contrasting them with their opposites: arbitrariness and inconsistency.

Arbitrariness

To be arbitrary means "to not have an objective reason." When you decide to wear a red shirt rather than a blue one, and you really don't have a reason that someone else could check, such a decision is arbitrary. Or when you decide to drink grape juice instead of orange juice, if you have no specific reason in mind, then your choice is arbitrary. We make countless arbitrary and often unconscious choices every day. Did you start walking with your left foot or your right? You probably don't know, and it really doesn't matter too much one way or the other.

There is nothing wrong with such a whimsical attitude when it comes to unimportant items or subjective preferences. However, when consequences matter, we had better have a good reason for our choice. The decision of whether or not to wear a parachute when jumping from a plane will have a profound effect on the outcome. And so this is not a decision that we would want to leave to the flip of a coin.

Likewise, when it comes to interpreting the text of Scripture (or any matter of fact), we are not supposed to be arbitrary, because the consequences of our approach matter. Namely, if we don't have good objective reasons for our interpretation, then it will very likely be wrong. Picking an interpretation on a whim could lead to an essentially infinite number of possibilities. But since there is only one correct interpretation (only one that corresponds to the author's intention), the probability of an arbitrary approach leading to the correct interpretation is nearly zero.

A logical person has a reason or reasons for his or her interpretation of a text. This is the whole point of rational debate. The goal is to show that we have a good *reason* or several good reasons for our position (that it is not arbitrary), and therefore other people should believe it too. In a debate, to be arbitrary is to concede defeat. It is to say, "I don't really have a good reason for my position."

Whenever a person says something like this, "I believe X and you should too," there will be a natural question on the part of the hearer: "Why? Why do you believe X and consequently why should I?" If the person is not able to give an objective reason for his belief in X, then there is no reason why the hearer shouldn't believe the exact opposite.

So, if you want your beliefs to correspond to reality, then you should always have a good reason for them. If you don't, then the belief is just as likely to be wrong. The more important the belief, the more crucial it is to have a good reason, because the consequences are more devastating if you are wrong. As a corollary to this, if your interpretation of Scripture is to correspond to its meaning, then you should have a good reason for your interpretation. I will grant that an arbitrary belief might occasionally turn out to be true by accident. But since there are far more wrong interpretations than the (one) correct interpretation, this will be highly unlikely. *Arbitrary beliefs are unreliable.*

Little children don't often recognize this. They tend to be very arbitrary. They firmly believe there is a monster in the closet, and they act on their belief by pulling the bed sheets over their head. Do they have a good reason for their belief? Of course not. Children are irrational, and we expect this from them. As people grow up, we are supposed to become rational. We are supposed to learn to have good reasons for our beliefs. And we are supposed to discard beliefs that don't have good reasons. This is the mark of rationality.

You may think that this is all perfectly obvious. And most of the time, it is. But in debates on scriptural interpretation, you will find that people are often very arbitrary. They want to exempt the Bible/theology/religion from the standards of reasoning that apply to everything else. And you will actually have to explain to them that this is not rational. People are supposed to give a good reason for their beliefs, and not just state them and then get upset when others don't agree. The whole point of a debate is to see which side has the best reason for his or her respective position.

If you do not have a reason for your interpretation of a passage of Scripture, then there is no reason (literally) why we shouldn't believe the exact opposite. There is no reason to expect that your interpretation is correct. There may be rare occasions when someone does not have a good reason, but ends up with the right interpretation by accident. Yes, even a blind squirrel gets an acorn every once in a while. But we would not expect people to consistently arrive at the correct interpretation of the text when they do not have good reasons for their position. Arbitrary thinking is unreliable. And so this leads to what is perhaps the most important rule of hermeneutics: *for an interpretation of Scripture to be considered reliable, you must have an objective reason for it. It cannot be arbitrary.*

Inconsistency

The other mark of rationality is consistency. Truth is always self-consistent. This stems from the nature of God. God does not deny Himself (2 Timothy 2:13). The Lord has "hardwired" us to know that truth is self-consistent. Therefore, if a person makes two claims that are inconsistent with each other, we can be certain that at least one of them is false. This applies to the text of Scripture as well. If a person holds two contrary interpretations of a passage, or an interpretation of one passage that contradicts his interpretation of another passage, then we can be certain that at least one of his interpretations is wrong. Recall from a previous chapter that it would be irrational to allow for genuine contradictions in an inerrant text.

The most obvious types of inconsistency are those that are outright contradictions. Clearly, if a person says, "Aliens exist and it is not the case that aliens exist," then he is in error. His thinking is inconsistent and thus irrational. Of course, not all apparent contradictions are actually contradictions. The hypothetical individual above might clarify that he is using the term "alien" in two different senses. Perhaps he believes that extra-terrestrial aliens do not exist, but illegal aliens do. There would be no inconsistency there. A contradiction is "A" and "not-A" *at the same time and in the same sense.*

Outright contradictions are rarely stated as explicitly as above, nor are they often stated back-to-back as above. If they were, then they would be immediately obvious and the debate would be over. Instead, contradictions tend to be separated by time or obscured in terminology. This can make them difficult to spot.

Another form of inconsistency is the behavioral inconsistency. This occurs when a person's actions do not match his or her words. I've dialogued with Christians who claim that *all* the Old Testament ceremonial laws are still binding on Christians today. But then those same people will drive a car on Saturday, which violates the Old Testament Sabbath day laws since engines involve kindling a flame (Exodus 35:3).

Unfortunately, Christians are often very inconsistent. If asked how they know that Christ was raised from the dead when it is not known scientifically how that could be possible, many Christians would rightly respond, "God can do as He wishes. He is not bound by laws of nature. And we know Christ was raised from the dead because it is recorded in the pages of Scripture. The text is clear." But then again, when asked about the age of the earth, many of those same Christians would respond, "Well, the scientists say it's billions of years old. So, maybe the days in Genesis weren't really 'days.' " This is very inconsistent reasoning.

Logical fallacies are marks of inconsistency. Fallacies are arguments that may sound logical on the surface, but violate a law of logic. Fallacies tend to be persuasive. That is why they are so common. We have already seen that the claim that "our interpretation of nature is on the same level as our interpretation of Scripture" is a fallacy of equivocation. In the next chapter, we will look at specific logical fallacies that commonly occur in matters of biblical interpretation.

Review

Proper reasoning cannot be arbitrary. This is easy to prove. Anyone who states that "arbitrariness is perfectly acceptable — you don't need reasons to believe things" can be refuted with this simple retort: "Oh yeah? Prove it." If the person says nothing, then his claim is dismissed. If he says anything, his claim is refuted because he is attempting to give reasons for why he does not need to give reasons. If reasons are not needed to back up a claim, then we can simply state that "reasons *are* needed to back up a claim" and the person must accept it without any reason, otherwise he denies his own position!

Proper reasoning must be self-consistent. A correct interpretation of Scripture cannot contradict itself since truth is always self-consistent. Laws of logic cannot be violated in any way if we are to end up with a reliable interpretation. It is easy to prove this. The critic who claims that it is acceptable to violate laws of logic in some cases can be refuted with this statement: "Then it is *not* acceptable to violate laws of logic at any time." How can the critic respond? If he says, "No, that's not true because it contradicts what I just said" then he has assumed the law of non-contradiction — this shows that he really does believe that laws of logic do apply at all times. But any other response will not answer the objection. The claim that laws of logic need not apply at all times is a self-refuting proposition.

The most important rule of hermeneutics is that you should have an objective reason for your interpretation. The second most important rule is that the reason must be good (self-consistent, not violating rules of logic, etc.). All the other rules simply flesh out these two.

Chapter 8

Logical Fallacies in Biblical Interpretation

I have previously written about logical fallacies, but never from a hermeneutical perspective.[1] So there will be new examples in this chapter, and I will only cover the most common logical fallacies involved in biblical interpretation. For readers interested in a more complete list of informal fallacies, specializing in examples that occur in debates over origins, have a look at my previous book *Discerning Truth: Exposing Errors in Evolutionary Arguments*.[2]

"Logic" is the study of the principles of correct reasoning. A "logical fallacy" is a common mistake in reasoning. Often these can be found in a person's interpretation of Scripture. Even if people follow all the principles of hermeneutics listed at the end of chapter 6, they can still end up with a faulty interpretation of Scripture if they don't reason properly. Putting it another way, even if people correctly understand the meaning of individual verses, they can fail to reason properly from these truths — resulting in a faulty theology. In this chapter, we explore the correct use of logic in reasoning from the Scriptures by contrasting it with fallacious reasoning from the Scriptures.

1. I have written previously on logical fallacies that are common in arguments put forward in defense of particles-to-people evolution in the book *Discerning Truth: Exposing Errors in Evolutionary Arguments* (Green Forest, AR: Master Books, 2010), and more briefly in *The Ultimate Proof of Creation* (Green Forest, AR: Master Books, 2011).
2. Lisle, *Discerning Truth: Exposing Errors in Evolutionary Arguments*.

Informal Fallacies

Informal fallacies, also called "ordinary language fallacies" are the common mistakes in reasoning that happen in ordinary everyday language. These stand in contrast to *formal* fallacies: mistakes in reasoning that are due to the "form" or structure of the argument. Formal fallacies are covered in appendix B. There are three categories of ordinary language fallacies. The first category encompasses fallacies of ambiguity, in which the argument is unclear in some way. The second involves fallacies of presumption, in which the argument assumes something that is dubious. Sometimes fallacies of presumption can be ameliorated by supplying evidence for the questionable assumption, but when such evidence is not supplied, the fallacy remains. The third category covers fallacies of relevance, in which the argument's premises are not strongly relevant to the conclusion.

Fallacies of Ambiguity

Equivocation is the fallacy of switching the meaning of a term within an argument. Since context constrains the meaning, equivocation is a violation of the contextual principle. The word "creation" can refer to the act of creating (as in "the creation of the universe"), or the thing that was created (as in "look at my latest creation"). The term is used both ways in English translations of the Bible. Romans 1:20 refers to the act of creation. "For since the creation of the world. . . ." On the other hand, Romans 8:22 refers to what God created (the universe). "For we know that the whole creation groans. . . ." The same word is used in the Greek in each case.

Psalm 104 is often called a psalm of creation. There is a popular speaker who commits the fallacy of equivocation when he claims that Psalm 104 is describing events during the creation week since it is a psalm of "creation." But is the term "creation" in this context referring to the *act* of creation, or the *object* of creation (the present universe)? Verse 16 speaks of the cedars of Lebanon, and verse 26 mentions ships in the sea. But Lebanon and ships did not exist during the act of creation. Verse 21 speaks of lions roaring after their prey; but Genesis tells us that all animals were vegetarian when the world was first created (Genesis 1:29–30). The death of creatures is mentioned in verse 29 — but death is an enemy (1 Corinthians 15:26) and would not have been present before Adam sinned (1 Corinthians 15:21; Genesis 1:31; 3:21).

So it should be obvious that Psalm 104 is speaking about the present world, the object of creation, not the creation week. The chapter does allude to the act of creation in spots. It mentions in verse 19 the fact that God created the moon. But this is a past action, not a present account. There are also references to the global Flood (verses 6–9). The Flood didn't happen during the creation week. Clearly, Psalm 104 is teaching about God's providence throughout history and in the present world.

A heretic might argue this way: (1) God cannot be tempted (James 1:13), (2) Jesus was tempted in all points (Hebrews 4:15), and (3), therefore, Jesus cannot be God. This is the fallacy of equivocation because the word "tempted" is being used in two different ways. It can mean to be "tested." Jesus was tempted in the sense of being tested in all ways, and did not fail any test (He did not sin) as Hebrews 4:15 explains. God the Father was also tempted in this way by the Israelites (Exodus 17:7; Deuteronomy 6:16; Psalm 78:13, 95:9). But "tempted" can also mean "enticed" in the sense of being drawn away by lust. This is the sense in which the term is used in James 1:13, because the next verse plainly states this. God is never enticed. Jesus, being God, was never enticed by any type of lust in His earthly ministry, nor will He ever be.

Another common example of the equivocation fallacy is when someone argues that our interpretation of Scripture is just as prone to error as our interpretation of nature. The word "interpretation" is used for both in order to make scientific claims sound as credible as scriptural claims. But the word is used in two different senses that are *not* equally authoritative. To interpret Scripture means to understand the meaning of the propositional claims of Scripture. But to "interpret" nature means to *create* propositional claims about the world. The latter is surely a more difficult and error-prone task than reading a book. Hence, the *two-books fallacy* is an example of equivocation.

Was Abraham justified by works or justified by faith? Romans 4:2–3 teaches that Abraham was justified by faith — not by works. But critics will point out that James 2:21–24 teaches that Abraham was justified by works too. Is this a contradiction? No, it's an equivocation fallacy on the word "justify." To justify can mean (1) to be in the right, or (2) to demonstrate before others that you are in the right. The former type of justification is by faith in God and not works. But the latter type can only be by both faith and works, since mortal people cannot see faith except as it is manifested by works (James 2:18). The context of Romans and James respectively makes clear which type of justification is being addressed.

Amphiboly is the fallacy of shifting the meaning of a phrase. It is very similar to equivocation — the only difference is equivocation involves a single word. The amphiboly fallacy is committed when someone takes a phrase in an incorrect way, or in a *potentially* incorrect way. Revelation 13:8b (KJV) reads all "whose names are not written in the book of life of the Lamb slain from the foundation of the world." What is the referent of the phrase "from the foundation of the world?" Does it refer to the Lamb, or to the names written in the book of life? Was the Lamb slain from the foundation of the world, or were the names written in the book of life from the foundation of the world?

The wording in Greek leaves the referent ambiguous. The KJV rendering implies that the referent is the Lamb. But the NASB wording suggests it is the names written in the book of life: "everyone whose name has not been written from the foundation of the world in the book of life of the Lamb who has been slain." To argue for one rendering from this verse alone is to commit the fallacy of amphiboly, since the Greek wording allows both possibilities.

In some other cases, any perceived ambiguity can be eliminated by careful analysis of the verse. Jesus promised that the repentant thief on the cross next to Him would be with Him in paradise that very day. In Luke 23:43, Jesus says, "Truly I say to you, today you shall be with Me in Paradise." Not everyone likes that view however. Certain Christian cults teach "soul sleep" — that those who die do not experience any conscious existence until the resurrection. They usually try to get around Luke 23:43 by arguing that the comma has been misplaced. (The Greek did not use a comma anyway). They suggest that the phrase should be read, "Truly I say to you today, you shall be with Me in Paradise." Phrased this way, it sounds like Jesus is merely assuring the thief that he would someday in the future be with Him in paradise, and the "today" refers to when Christ makes the statement.

This is an amphiboly fallacy because this second interpretation does not stand up to scrutiny. It would reduce the word "today" to a triviality. When else would Jesus say it? Everything anyone says, he says on the day he says it. The Lord does not waste words. He clearly meant to convey to the thief that they would both be in paradise on that day.

A Unitarian once told me that 1 Corinthians 8:6 proves that Jesus is not God. The passage reads, "But to us there is but one God, the Father, of whom are all things, and we in him; and one Lord Jesus Christ, by whom are all things, and we by him" (KJV). He said that this passage shows that there is one God, the Father, and separately, there is one Lord: Jesus Christ. He assumed that this passage was addressing two different beings merely because two different titles were used. This is an amphiboly fallacy, because the passage clearly is referring to one being as *both* God and Lord, just as Thomas referred to Jesus as "my Lord and my God" (John 20:28). Thomas wasn't referring to two different people! The Son is both Lord and God, and the Father is both Lord and God (Matthew 11:25; Luke 10:21).

The fallacy of accent is the alteration of the meaning of a phrase by emphasizing the wrong word. "We should not speak *ill* of our friends" has a slightly different meaning from "We should not speak ill of our *friends*." The first constrains the *type of things* we might say about our friends, and the second constrains the *people* of whom we might speak ill.

Exodus 20:3 states, "You shall have no other gods before Me." Sometimes people misinterpret this verse by placing unwarranted emphases on the last two words "*before Me*." They suggest that we can indeed have other "gods" or "idols" so long as we put the Living God first. This is the fallacy of accent. The Hebrew words translated "before Me" really have the meaning of "in My presence." And from other Scriptures we learn that God's presence is everywhere (Psalm 139:7–10; Jeremiah 23:24). Therefore, Exodus 20:3 means that we are not to have any other gods — period. The "before Me" or "in My presence" clause is for emphasis; it reminds us that God's presence is everywhere and is not to suggest that we can have other gods as long as we put them after God.

Reification is the poetic device of attributing concrete or personal characteristics to an abstraction. It is perfectly acceptable in poetic literature. However, it should be avoided in logical arguments because it can obscure the relevant facts. In such cases, reification is a fallacy.

One of the most common examples can be found when people argue for their position because it is what "science says." Science, being a concept, does not "say" anything. Scientists do say things, since they are people and can express their opinions on a matter. But science — as a concept — cannot say anything at all. Why do people not then just argue, "Scientists say, ____"? One reason is that it would be immediately obvious that not *all* scientists say _____. There are those who disagree. And that makes the case much weaker. Moreover, scientists are people, with biases, opinions, and other philosophical baggage that makes their conclusions less than objective and ultimately fallible. The phrase "science says" sounds so objective and monolithic. This reification fallacy attempts to obscure the fact that scientists are fallible people who often disagree with each other.

What about "the Bible says ___" or "this book claims ___"? These are not so much reification, but metonymy. Metonymy is a figure of speech in which a person is represented by a related concept, such as the book he or she wrote. We are all familiar with phrases such as "the White House issued a press release today. . . ." In this example, the White House actually represents the person or persons who issued the release. And we all understand this. Since there is no misdirection here, metonymy is not generally considered a fallacy. "This book claims" is simply a shorter way of saying, "The author of this book claims." Metonymy would only be a fallacy if it were used in an overly literal way to obscure a difficulty.

Fallacies of Presumption

The sweeping generalization is taking a principle that is true most of the time and applying it as if it had no exceptions or qualifications. There are many rules that have one or more caveats. To ignore the exceptions is fallacious. The Book of Proverbs contains many wonderful examples of generalizations: things that are true most of the time. Bible critics sometimes mischaracterize these Proverbs as if they were exception-less rules.

Proverbs 15:1 states, "A gentle answer turns away wrath, but a harsh word stirs up anger." The critic might say, "Tim answered Kevin very gently. But Kevin got angry anyway. So the Bible is clearly wrong about that." No, *generally* a gentle answer does indeed turn away wrath. The Proverbs do not say that this happens *in every instance*.

Proverbs 22:6: "Train up a child in the way he should go, even when he is old he will not depart from it." Suppose a married couple has a wayward son or daughter. Can we conclude that they did not train up their child in the right way? No. It's a possibility, but it's not necessarily the case. Proverbs indicates that most of the time when children are reared biblically, they will become biblical adults — but not always.

The critic may argue against Scripture in the following way. "The Bible says 'You shall not murder' in Exodus 20:20. But then God says that certain crimes should be punished by death — Exodus 21:16. So the Bible is contradictory." This is a sweeping generalization fallacy because a "murder" is the "unlawful killing of a person" and God has specified certain situations where it is lawful to kill a person. As one example, God has authorized the government to execute criminals who have been found guilty of crimes that God has deemed capital offenses (Romans 13:1–7). So whereas it is generally unlawful to take a human life, God has defined several appropriate exceptions.

A hasty generalization is the fallacy of drawing a generalization from too few specific instances. "Psalm 18:6–8 is not literal. Proverbs 8:1–6 is not literal. Revelation 17:3–6 is non-literal. Therefore, the Bible is not meant to be taken literally." Though parts of the Bible are non-literal, it is fallacious to conclude that the Bible — in general — is non-literal.

The false-cause fallacy is committed when people assume a cause-and-effect relationship that is not warranted by the evidence. Two things are "correlated" if they go together or are linked in some way. But knowing that A and B go together does not necessarily imply that A is the cause of B. It could be that B is the cause of A. Or, perhaps both A and B are caused by C. Example: "People with wrinkled skin have a much higher death rate than those with smooth skin. Thus, wrinkles must cause death." While there is a correlation between wrinkles and death rate, one is not the cause of the other.

Certain cults teach a works-salvation. They think we can earn our way to heaven by doing good deeds. There are many biblical verses they use to prove their point. One such passage is John 5:28–29. This passage refers to the resurrection of the dead and the judgment that follows. ". . . all that are in the graves shall hear his voice, and shall come forth; they that have done good, unto the resurrection of life; and they that have done evil, unto the resurrection of damnation" (KJV). Does this verse teach a works-salvation?

The cultist has done one thing right. She has recognized in this verse that there is a correlation between doing good and salvation, and doing evil and damnation. Then she fallaciously concludes that good works are the *cause* of salvation. But the Bible nowhere teaches this. On the contrary, it expressly teaches that this is not the case. Christians are saved by God's grace received through faith in Christ — not by works (Ephesians 2:8–9). Why is there a correlation between salvation and good works? Genuine salvation will *result* in the person wanting to obey God and doing good works (1 John 2:3–6, 3:7–9). So there is a correlation, but salvation is not the result of good works, rather, it is the *cause*. The Bible teaches good works are the result and evidence of salvation (1 John 5:2–4; James 2:14–18).

The bifurcation fallacy is committed when two options are presented as the only possibilities when in fact there is a third option. "Either the traffic light is red or it is green" is a bifurcation fallacy because the light could be yellow. In some claims, there really are only two options: either you are pregnant, or not pregnant. There is no fallacy here. But when a third option exists, the claim of "either A or B" is a bifurcation fallacy.

Christ's disciples committed the bifurcation fallacy in John 9:2. Having passed by a man who was blind from birth, the disciples asked, "Rabbi, who sinned, this man or his parents, that he would be born blind?" They had assumed that there were only two possible reasons for the man's blindness — either (1) his own sin or (2) the sin of his parents. Christ rejected both of those options and gave the third, correct answer. In John 9:3, Jesus answers, "It was neither that this man sinned, nor his parents; but it was so that the works of God might be displayed in him."

The critic asks, "Who raised Jesus from the dead? First Peter 3:18 indicates it was the Holy Spirit, but John 2:19–21 and John 10:17–18 indicate that it was Jesus Himself. And Acts 2:24, 32 indicates that God did it. Which is right?" The answer: they all are. All three persons of the Trinity were involved in the Resurrection of Christ. There is no contradiction here. In suggesting that only one of the verses can be true, the critic has committed the bifurcation fallacy.

As an example of an alleged contradiction in Scripture, one critic asks, "Did God write the Ten Commandments with His own finger as indicated in Exodus 34:1, or did Moses write them as indicated in Exodus 34:27?" This bifurcation fallacy is easily answered: both! God wrote the Ten Commandments on the tablets of stone (Exodus 34:1), and commanded Moses to write them (again) which is why they are also part of the Book of Exodus (e.g., Exodus 20). If Moses had not written them after God did, then we would have no record of the Ten Commandments in Scripture; they would have been written only on the stone tablets in the ark of the covenant.

"Does God sovereignly control every aspect of the universe, or do human beings have the freedom to make genuine choices?" Both are scriptural (Isaiah 46:10–11; Deuteronomy 30:19). God is able to use human choices to accomplish His will. This may seem counter-intuitive to us, perhaps because such calculations are far beyond our intellectual capacity. But there is no contradiction nor is there any violation of logic in recognizing that God sovereignly uses human choices.

The critic asks, "Was there one demon-possessed man by the tombs as recorded in Mark 5:2–13 and Luke 8:27 or were there two men as recorded in Matthew 8:28–32?" This is a bifurcation fallacy because both claims are true. The number one is a subset of two. If there are two people then there is necessarily one (and one other). Why didn't Mark and Luke mention the other one? The Bible does not say. Perhaps the one was more violent or had far more demons than the other. Christ and the disciples apparently only followed up with one of these two people later on (Mark 5:15–20). In any case, the account of Matthew is fully consistent with the accounts of Mark and Luke.

Begging the question is when the argument tacitly assumes its own conclusion as a premise. "The opening chapters of Genesis are clearly poetic. Therefore, they should not be taken in a literal fashion." The conclusion is merely assumed by the premise, and is unproved.

The **complex question** is the interrogative form of begging the question. "If Genesis were meant to be taken literally, then why is it written in such a poetic style?" Of course, Genesis isn't written in a poetic style; there is no parallelism. The question tacitly assumes the point in question, rather than making a case for it.

The **question-begging epithet** occurs when people use loaded language in place of logic to persuade. "It's so obvious that the days of creation were long periods of time that no further argument needs to be given. Any intelligent person can see this." Such a sentence is nothing but a rhetorical attempt to intimidate the reader — to persuade by appealing to the person's desire to appear intelligent — instead of using logic. There is a place for emotional language. But it is fallacious to substitute such language *in place of* a logical argument.

Fallacies of Relevance

The naturalistic fallacy is the assumption that something is morally right simply by virtue of the fact that it exists or happens. It is of the form, "____ happens, therefore _____ is right." For example, "Lying can't be all that wrong; after all, everybody does it." These arguments are fallacious because what people in fact do is not necessarily what they *should* do. There is a distinction between what *is* and what *should be*. The naturalistic fallacy violates the fact-value distinction by falsely assuming that a behavior is morally right simply because it occurs. We noted previously that the Bible does not endorse or affirm as morally right all of the events that it records as true.

Critics will sometimes suggest that the Bible endorses polygamy since some of the patriarchs had multiple wives and there was no civil penalty for it. This claim commits the naturalistic fallacy because the Bible is not endorsing polygamy when it merely records that some people engaged in this unethical behavior. Furthermore, not all morally despicable behavior has a civil penalty attached to it (e.g., Exodus 20:17). The only type of marriage that the Bible endorses as morally right is that of one man united by God to one woman for life (Genesis 3:17; Matthew 19:4–9; Leviticus 18:18).

The moralistic fallacy is the assumption that because something *should be* a certain way, that in fact it is that way. The assumption is fallacious because in an imperfect world, things are not always as they should be. Like the naturalistic fallacy, the moralistic fallacy violates the fact-value distinction; however, it does so in the opposite direction. The naturalistic fallacy starts with the way the world is, and then draws a moral conclusion. The moralistic fallacy starts with what is morally right, and then illicitly draws a conclusion about the way the world is.

Common examples of the moralistic fallacy are when people argue that God wouldn't allow something to happen because it would be morally detestable. For example, "I don't think human cloning is possible because that would violate God's design of the family." Such arguments are fallacious because God does allow morally detestable things to occur, and the Bible is full of examples (e.g., Judges 2:11, 3:12, 4:1, 10:6; 1 Kings 15:26, 16:25). Horrendous theologies can stem from the moralistic fallacy, "It is terrible that people should reject God and spend an eternity in hell. Therefore, I think that God forgives everyone. Hell doesn't really exist." But such an argument is fallacious and heretical. Although it is tragic that many people reject God and end up in hell, this is the reality that the Bible describes. Until the eternal state, there will continue to be a distinction between what is and what should be.

The genetic fallacy is the mistake of assuming that something must be false due to its source. Hermeneutically, this occurs when a critic dismisses a biblical claim solely on the basis that the claim is biblical. "You don't really believe that Jonah was in the belly of a great fish do you? The Bible is an old collection of stories written by sheepherders." The problem with such reasoning is that the antiquity of the Bible and the vocation of its authors have absolutely no bearing on the correctness of its claim. Rationally, an argument should be evaluated on its merit, not its *source*.

The appeal to force or fear is also called the *ad baculum* fallacy. This mistake in reasoning is committed when people try to persuade by instilling fear, rather than by making a logical argument. "Believe _____ or else there will be negative consequences!" Sometimes people will appeal to fear in an attempt to persuade someone to accept their interpretation of Scripture. "If you don't believe that the days of creation were millions of years each, then you'll look silly, and educated people will laugh at you." But the consequences of believing a claim are irrelevant to the truth value of the claim. Some first-century Jews used the *ad baculum* fallacy to discourage people from following Jesus (John 9:22).

The faulty appeal to authority is claiming that something must be true simply because a fallible expert believes it. This fallacy is tricky, because there is nothing wrong with citing an expert to support a particular claim. The argument becomes a fallacy when any of the following occur: (1) the expert is not an expert in the area in which he or she has made the claim, (2) the expert's claim is itself shown to be fallacious or contrary to evidence, (3) other experts in the same field take the opposite position, or (4) a fallible expert is treated as infallible.

For example, "Dr. Collins is an expert on genetics, and he believes that Genesis chapters 1 and 2 are poetic. So they definitely are." This is a faulty appeal by any of the above standards: (1) being an expert in genetics does not imply expertise in biblical interpretation, (2) the claim is shown to be false by examination of the text itself, (3) experts in biblical Hebrew make the opposite claim, (4) Dr. Collins is not infallible, and thus his claims cannot be considered infallible, even in his own field of study.

The appeal to ignorance is the fallacy of assuming that something is true on the basis that it has not been demonstrated to be false. "We will have wings and be able to fly in heaven. After all, the Bible doesn't say that we won't." But just because something has not been disproved does not automatically mean that it must be true. Appeals to ignorance are always reversible. We could equally well say, "We will not have wings nor be able to fly in heaven. After all, the Bible doesn't say otherwise."

This is only a sample of the most common informal fallacies. For a discussion on formal logic and formal fallacies, see appendix B.

Review

Equivocation is the fallacy of switching the meaning of a term within an argument.

Amphiboly is the fallacy of shifting the meaning of a phrase.

The fallacy of accent is the alteration of the meaning of a phrase by emphasizing the wrong word.

Reification is the poetic device of attributing concrete or personal characteristics to an abstraction.

The sweeping generalization is taking a principle that is true most of the time and applying it as if it had no exceptions or qualifications.

A hasty generalization is the fallacy of drawing a generalization from too few specific instances.

The false-cause fallacy is committed when people assume a cause-and-effect relationship that is not warranted by the evidence.

The bifurcation fallacy is committed when two options are presented as the only possibilities, when in fact there is a third option.

Begging the question is when the argument tacitly assumes its own conclusion as a premise.

The complex question is the interrogative form of begging the question.

The question-begging epithet occurs when people use loaded language in place of logic to persuade.

The naturalistic fallacy is the assumption that something is morally right simply by virtue of the fact that it exists or happens.

The moralistic fallacy is the assumption that because something *should be* a certain way, that in fact it is that way.

The genetic fallacy is the mistake of assuming that something must be false due to its source.

The appeal to force or fear (also called the *ad baculum* fallacy) is the mistake committed when people try to persuade by instilling fear, rather than by making a logical argument.

The faulty appeal to authority is claiming that something must be true simply because a fallible expert believes it.

The appeal to ignorance is the fallacy of assuming that something is true on the basis that it has not been demonstrated to be false.

Chapter 9

The Bible's Instructions on Interpretation

Does the Bible have anything to say about how we should interpret it? If it does, how could we possibly understand such instructions unless we already knew how to interpret it?

Years ago, when VCRs were relatively new, someone told me about a particular brand with an interesting issue.[1] Rather than including an owner's manual with written directions on how to connect the VCR to the television and other equipment and how to operate the device, the manufacturer decided it would be far more helpful to visually *show* people how to do this. So they recorded a short video showing someone making all the correct connections from the VCR to the television and then loading and playing a tape. They included this presentation on a video cassette tape with the VCR at the time of purchase. Of course, in order to view the tape, the customer would need to have the VCR already properly connected. And if it's already connected, then there is no need to view the instructions on how to connect it.

Likewise, the Bible does give some instructions on hermeneutical principles. But in order for us to properly interpret the Bible's instructions on hermeneutics, wouldn't we already have to know hermeneutical principles? It seems that we are in a logical dilemma: how can we understand the Bible's instructions on how it should be interpreted unless we already know how

1. I don't know if the story is historical or fiction. But it is true that someone shared this with me.

the Bible should be interpreted, thereby abrogating the need for any such instructions?

Some Christians have suggested that the way to resolve this dilemma is to get our principles of hermeneutics from outside the Bible. But this alleviates one dilemma by creating another one that is actually worse. First, how do we know we are correctly interpreting this other standard? By what hermeneutical principles do we read this other standard in order to understand it correctly, so that it can then tell us how to read the Bible? This new standard would face the same challenge in principle that people have with Scripture.

Second, if some non-biblical standard were the "Supreme Court" that judges what the Bible means, then this non-biblical standard would be *more authoritative* than Scripture. If the Bible states, "Do not murder," but then suppose the standard by which we interpret the Bible declares: "by 'murder' the text really means 'chew gum.' So this prohibition means we shouldn't chew gum." If we avoided chewing gum because of what this other standard claims the Bible says, then which standard are we *really* following?

But doesn't Jesus say that *His Word* is to be the foundation for all our thinking (Matthew 7:24–27)? Are we not to "take captive" to obedience of Christ *all* our thoughts (2 Corinthians 10:5)? If the Bible is the ultimate standard for all truth claims, then it cannot be subject to some external, allegedly superior standard. The Bible is that ultimate standard for all knowledge — the standard by which all other standards are judged.

When I state that the Bible is the ultimate standard for all knowledge, I do not mean that all knowledge is found directly in Scripture. As far as I know, the physics formula $E=mc^2$ is not in Scripture, and yet it is true. Rather, Scripture provides the *foundational worldview* in which science, logic, and math are possible. All things that are true are compatible with Scripture, and could not be known if the universe were not precisely the way the Bible says it is. Ultimately, it is only by God's revelation that we can know anything. So, the laws of physics could never be justified apart from the worldview established in the Bible.[2]

2. One reason for this is that the discovery of any law of nature is predicated on the principle of induction, whereby we infer a general principle from specific instances. Induction presupposes an underlying orderliness in nature that can be discovered by observing various specific instances. Induction is rationally justified in the Christian worldview since God upholds the universe in a consistent way for our benefit (Colossians 1:17; Hebrews 1:3). Apart from the Christian worldview, no one has been able to discover a rational basis for the principle of induction.

If the Bible really is the ultimate standard for knowledge, the rock on which we must build all our thinking (Matthew 7:24–27), then everything we think and do should be based on the biblical worldview. And hermeneutics is something that we think and do. Therefore, hermeneutical principles should be based on the biblical worldview. We dare not appeal to some allegedly greater standard to get our hermeneutical principles. And so the dilemma remains: hermeneutical principles should be based on what the Bible teaches, but how can we correctly interpret what the Bible teaches without correct hermeneutical principles?

The Understandability of the Bible

The resolution to the paradox is found in the marvelous way that God has designed the human mind, and the way He has revealed Himself in Scripture. The Lord has created the mind with a built-in ability to use logic and induction to learn to communicate through language.

Consider how quickly little children can learn to communicate. It's quite astonishing. Even before they take a single class in logic or grammar, they quickly learn to understand much of what their parents say. Certainly, children will make mistakes. But the human mind has an amazing capacity to understand language without any explicit training in logic, grammar, or hermeneutics. Clearly, children must have some innate knowledge of hermeneutics because they are able to correctly interpret (most of the time) human language.

This makes sense in the Christian worldview. The Lord is a linguistic being. He speaks and the universe responds: "For He spoke, and it was done; He commanded, and it stood fast" (Psalm 33:9; see Genesis 1:3, 6, 9, 14, 20, etc.). And God has created people in His image (Genesis 1:26–27) with linguistic ability — the ability to learn and use language (Exodus 4:11). God is able to communicate with His people using language. From the very beginning, God communicated and reasoned with Adam (Genesis 3:9–12) and engaged his capacity to rational speech (Genesis 2:19–20).

God's rational communication to us is accomplished primarily through His written Word, although God has also spoken audibly with certain individuals in the past (Genesis 3:9–12, 8:15; Numbers 12:7–8). God knows how to communicate. Clearly an omnipotent God has the ability to write a book that His rational creatures will be able to understand.

Hence, His challenge to Israel: "Come now, and let us reason together" (Isaiah 1:18).

Apparently, God has created the human mind in such a way that even children instinctively know some principles of logic and hermeneutics long before they read the Bible. They evidence this by their ability to use logic and to correctly understand language. The fact that children also make mistakes in reasoning and in linguistic interpretation shows that their innate understanding of logic and hermeneutics is incomplete and imperfect. As Paul says, "When I was a child, I used to speak like a child, think like a child, reason like a child" (1 Corinthians 13:11). Nonetheless, children have *some* ability to understand and use words.

Though our initial hermeneutic is incomplete and fallible, it is sufficient to correctly understand much of what the Bible states. Putting it another way, the Bible is clear enough in its main teachings, that the average literate person will be able to understand them, despite his or her incomplete and faulty hermeneutic. Theologians call this understanding the "perspicuity of Scripture." This is not to say that every passage in the Bible is equally clear, or that all Scripture will be properly understood when people use a faulty hermeneutic. The Bible itself claims that parts of it are hard to understand (2 Peter 3:16). But its most basic teachings cannot be missed.

And what of the more difficult portions? The Bible teaches that it must be studied carefully if we are to rightly understand it (Acts 17:11; 2 Timothy 2:15). In Proverbs 2:1–2 we read the call of wisdom (which ultimately is found in God's Word, Psalm 19:7): "My son, if you will receive my words and treasure my commandments within you, make your ear attentive to wisdom, Incline your heart to understanding." It continues by urging us to "cry for discernment," and directing us to "seek" and "search" for it (Proverbs 2:3–4).

Later, God rebukes Israel for not understanding, and then calls them to maturely study His truth more carefully: "To whom would He teach knowledge, and to whom would He interpret the message? Those just weaned from milk? Those just taken from the breast? For He says, 'Order on order, order on order, line on line, line on line, a little here, a little there.'" (Isaiah 28:9–10).

The Bible also warns that unlearned persons will inevitably distort the more difficult sections (2 Peter 3:16). Notice in this passage that

Peter specifically identifies a lack of education ("unlearned") as one of the primary reasons people misunderstand the more difficult sections of Scripture. This observation should be sufficient to refute arguments based on the "reliability of ignorance fallacy." Nonetheless, the clarity with which God has written Scripture is sufficient for its main sections to be understood by anyone willing to accept them. And Christians can come to understand even the more difficult passages in time, through careful study and reflection of the Word.

Jesus rebukes the Pharisees as the teachers of Israel for not carefully listening to the Scripture's message: "You search the Scriptures because you think that in them you have eternal life; it is these that testify about Me" (John 5:39). In Hebrews 5:12–14 we find a powerful rebuke to those who have not studied the Word and grown in their understanding of it: "For though by this time you ought to be teachers, you have need again for someone to teach you the elementary principles of the oracles of God, and you have come to need milk and not solid food. For everyone who partakes only of milk is not accustomed to the word of righteousness, for he is an infant. But solid food is for the mature, who because of practice have their senses trained to discern good and evil." In Jeremiah, God warns: "The wise men are put to shame, they are dismayed and caught; behold, they have rejected the word of the LORD, And what kind of wisdom do they have?" (Jeremiah 8:9).

A child can usually understand the literal teachings of his parents. And as he grows, he learns to understand the non-literal usage of language — the common figures of speech of his culture. Likewise, the average person can understand most of the literal portions of the Bible without advanced knowledge of hermeneutics. And he can come to understand the non-literal portions by proper study.

Consider that the Lord has written the Bible in such a way that most of it is quite literal. We have seen that 43 of the 66 books are either historical narrative or letters. The nice thing about these literal portions is that they do not require a sophisticated and well-developed philosophy of hermeneutics and logic — only a very basic knowledge of language is required to understand them. Consider John 11:35 which states, "Jesus wept." It's hard to imagine that anyone could fail to grasp the meaning, regardless of his or her knowledge of hermeneutics.

The Foundational Nature of God's Word

The Bible is foundational to all human knowledge, because it is the revealed Word of God who is the source of all knowledge (Proverbs 1:7; Colossians 2:3). This doesn't mean that all truth is found in Scripture. But it does mean that all Scripture is true (John 17:17; 2 Timothy 3:16–17). And the truth of Scripture frames the basic worldview that is necessary in order for us to discover the truth of anything else.

Logic, as one example, is rooted in the nature of God. God is fundamentally logical and is the source of all truth (John 14:6; Romans 3:4). Therefore, truth will never violate laws of logic. The law of non-contradiction (that two contradictory propositions cannot both be true at the same time in the same way) stems from the nature of God. It is because God, who is the source of all truth, does not deny Himself (2 Timothy 2:13; Hebrews 6:18); that truth will never contradict itself. Hermeneutical principles, laws of logic, orderliness in nature, standards of morality, and all other aspects of knowledge have their foundation in the truth of Scripture.

Critics generally make two objections to this position. First, the critic will complain that the Bible cannot be the source of logic, hermeneutics, morality, etc., because all people know these things to some extent, regardless of whether or not they believe the Bible. In other words, even an atheist is able to use laws of logic to reason properly about some things. That's certainly true. But it does not refute the position. The claim is not that people must profess to believe in the Bible in order to use logic, hermeneutics, morality, and so forth. Rather, the argument is that the Bible must be *true* in order for such things to be meaningful. What the person professes is utterly irrelevant to what is true.

By way of analogy, a fish might not profess to believe in water. Perhaps the fish lacks the intellectual capacity to understand what water is. But the fish's beliefs (or lack thereof) about water do not change that fact that the fish relies upon water as essential for its survival. Likewise, a critic may doubt that the biblical worldview is necessary for logic, hermeneutics, and morality to be meaningful, but this has no bearing on the reality of the situation. After all, the Bible warns that the unbeliever is actively suppressing the truth in unrighteousness so that he will not (so he believes) have to give an account before God (Romans 1:18, 2:1).

Second, a critic might deny that the Bible is foundational for things like logic and hermeneutics because these intellectual tools are necessary to understand the Bible. If we must know these things first, then how can the Bible be their source? To be sure, we must already have some knowledge of logic and basic hermeneutic principles in order to understand the Bible. Does this mean that the Bible is not their foundation, since our understanding of Scripture comes *after* our initial knowledge of logic and hermeneutics?

We must recognize an important distinction between the logical primacy in reasoning and the chronological order of discovery. By way of analogy, consider Linda who is quietly reading a book when a baseball smashes through her front window. Startled, she runs to the front window and looks outside to see a group of boys playing a game of baseball. One of the boys is holding a bat, and is staring fearfully at Linda. Linda figures he was the one responsible for breaking the window. He is the cause; the ball smashing through the window is the effect.

The young batter is "foundational" to the broken window in the sense he is responsible. Without him (or some other batter) the window would not have been broken. But Linda is first made aware of the broken window, and only later discovers its cause. She has knowledge of the broken window *before* she discovers the reason for it! Likewise, people have been given a basic knowledge of logic, hermeneutics, and morality before they discover the reason for these things — the all-ordering God of Scripture.

God knew that we would need some principles of logic and some understanding of language in order to read His Word. When we read the Bible, we come to understand that it provides the logical foundation for such principles. So the Lord gave us an innate rudimentary ability to reason and to learn language. And He has written the Bible such that our incomplete hermeneutic cannot miss the main truths presented in the literal sections. But are we to remain like children with a primitive hermeneutic, and understanding only the main teachings of Scripture? No. We are supposed to grow in our understanding of the Word (1 Corinthians 14:20; Hebrews 5:14, 6:1,). The Bible teaches that although we initially understand only the "milk" of the Word, we are morally obligated to study the Bible to eventually understand the "meat" of the Word (Hebrews 5:12–14; 1 Corinthians 3:2).

No one mocks a child for believing in the Easter Bunny. But if an adult believed in the Easter Bunny, that would suggest a mental disorder of some sort. Likewise, grace is available when new converts to Christianity misunderstand some of the harder doctrines. That's hardly surprising. But Christians should not remain in such a state (1 Corinthians 14:20; Hebrews 5:12–14; 1 Corinthians 13:11). How then do we improve our hermeneutic so that we can understand the more difficult sections of Scripture? This comes from accepting and thinking about the parts of the Bible that we do understand. Scripture will systematically correct the hermeneutics of those who want to be corrected.

The sections of the Bible that we can understand in our first reading will provide insight into how the remaining sections should be interpreted. That is, even a partial understanding of Scripture will lead to an improved understanding of hermeneutical principles. With an improved hermeneutic, we can understand the Bible even better on the second pass, which will further improve our developing hermeneutic and so on. Of course, this presupposes that we have the humility to allow the Holy Spirit to correct our thinking — something that unbelievers will resist.

The Hermeneutical Circle

So how then are we able to understand the Bible since it is the foundation for hermeneutical principles? The dilemma is resolved by recognizing that our understanding of Scripture improves progressively as the Scriptures correct our understanding of hermeneutics. This "hermeneutical circle" is bothersome to some people. It may go against our intuition and our preferences. We would like to have some system of interpretation that allows us to understand the Bible perfectly on the first pass. But if we accept that the Bible is the ultimate standard for everything we think and do, then the hermeneutical circle is logically inescapable. Obviously, the only "Supreme Court" that can authoritatively tell us what the Bible means is the Bible! Appealing to any other standard would make the Bible less than ultimate (consider the implications of Hebrews 6:13; Job 40:1–5).

Note that the hermeneutical circle is not "circular reasoning" in the sense of two claims where the conclusion of each is the premise of the other. Rather, the hermeneutical circle is an application of the analogy of faith — that the best interpreter of Scripture is Scripture. Therefore, any interpretation of Scripture is wrong if it goes against how the Scriptures interpret the Scriptures. This allows us to systematically reject unbiblical approaches to hermeneutics, and become increasingly more accurate in our understanding of the Bible. For this reason, the approach is sometimes called the "hermeneutical spiral" because it progresses outward, enlarging and correcting our understanding of Scripture on each pass.

Why are people sometimes reluctant to accept, in principle, the spiral nature of hermeneutics? It may be that this is different from the linear approach that we use for many other truth claims. However, there is nothing irrational about the hermeneutical spiral. The fact is that some truths are discovered in a spiral, rather than linear progression. Let's consider some examples.

The Logical Necessity of Knowledge Spirals

How do people learn language? How do they learn what words mean, what the rules of grammar are, how to conjugate verbs, and so forth? Most students learn about such things from a teacher. And what does the teacher use to teach students language? He or she uses *language* — words, grammar, verbs, and so on. Clearly, students must already have some knowledge of language in order to understand the teacher. But if they already know language, then what is the purpose of them taking a class on language?

The obvious answer is that students can improve their knowledge of language by taking a class on language. A student needs only a rudimentary knowledge of language in order to benefit from the words of his or her teacher. There is nothing fallacious or unreasonable about a teacher using language to teach students to have a better understanding of language. If that's perfectly reasonable, then why can't the Bible teach us to have a better understanding of the Bible?

Consider the laws of logic by which we reason. How would we demonstrate to ourselves or to our students that laws of logic are correct or reasonable? We could certainly construct a valid, sound argument showing the necessity of various laws of logic. But in that argument, we would have to use laws of logic in order to draw any valid conclusions whatsoever. Should we then abandon logic since some principles of logic must be known in advance of their own demonstration? Of course not. By using principles of logic, we can investigate these principles and improve our understanding of logic. There is nothing fallacious about that. If we can use logic to examine and improve our understanding of logic, why can't we use Scripture to examine and improve our understanding of Scripture?

Even in the realm of science, some types of knowledge are acquired in a spiral, non-linear fashion. A student might be asked to measure the mass of some object using a balance scale. The object of unknown mass is placed on one side of the balance, causing that side to tip down. Then the student puts some combination of known masses on the other side of the scale until the two plates are level. The sum of the known masses reveals the mass of the object.

But this is not a one-step process. The student does not *initially* know what combination of known masses will cause the scale to balance. He must make an initial guess based on how heavy the unknown mass feels in his hand as compared with the known masses. It is exceedingly unlikely that his initial guess will be exactly right. But it will probably be relatively close. The direction in which the scales tip after this guess informs the student whether he should add or subtract known masses. And the speed at which the scales adjust tells him how close he is to the right answer. As long as the student is willing to adjust the known masses according to the readings on the balance, it will not be long until he has the precise answer. Likewise, precise interpretations of Scripture sometimes require multiple steps and considerable study.

Because of our sin nature, we prefer quick, one-step solutions. But some things just aren't that way. And the Scriptures indicate this. As one example, the Bible teaches that sanctification is *progressive*; it is not instantaneous, but is something we should pursue daily (2 Peter 3:18; Hebrews 12:14). Sanctification is the process of becoming set apart as holy to God. Although we are saved by God's grace, we don't immediately become perfectly righteous in practice (Romans 7:19). It is a lengthy process (Romans 5:3–4; James 1:3–4) — one that ultimately does not reach perfection until we enter heaven. The Bible uses the analogy of silver and gold being purified by fire (Zechariah 13:9; Psalm 66:10; Job 23:10; Proverbs 17:3; Malachi 3:3; 1 Peter 1:6–7). When gold is heated to a liquid state and stirred, impurities float to the top and may be skimmed off. But not all the impurities are removed in one pass. The process must be repeated until the gold is pure.

We might prefer to be instantly perfect at the moment Christ saves us. But regardless of our wishes, the Bible teaches that sanctification is progressive, not instantaneous. What about hermeneutics? The same principle must apply because correct hermeneutics is an aspect of sanctification! Reading the Bible correctly is a *moral obligation* and therefore something that should improve as people grow in the Lord (2 Timothy 2:15). We are sanctified by progressively understanding and living God's Word (John 17:17).

The principles of the hermeneutical circle can be summarized as follows:

1. People are born with a pre-packaged hermeneutic: basic rules of linguistic inference.

2. Our pre-packaged hermeneutic is incomplete and is corrupted due to our sin nature.

3. Nonetheless, our initial hermeneutic, along with the language we learn from our family, is sufficient to understand the most basic biblical doctrines. This is especially true in the literal portions of Scripture, as long as we approach such doctrines in a spirit of humility and repentance.

4. The Bible's basic doctrines have the ability to systematically correct our understanding of hermeneutics.

5. When we re-read the Bible with our improved hermeneutic, we will understand the Bible even better than we did on the previous pass.

6. Our improved understanding of the Bible leads to an even more improved hermeneutic.

7. Go to step 5.

Steps 5 and 6 are repeated indefinitely and can lead to proper understanding of even the difficult portions of the Bible. We have seen from previous chapters that external documents may be helpful in understanding the biblical text if, and only if, those documents shed light on the intentions of the author. Even in those cases, external guides should always be considered secondary; the biblical text is primary. This follows from the analogy of faith.

If indeed the Bible is the foundation for all knowledge — even knowledge of hermeneutical principles — then the principles of hermeneutics we have discovered in the previous chapters should be grounded in the Bible. Any such principle may be either an explicit teaching, logically deducible from biblical principles, or it may be implicit by example. If we understand the hermeneutical spiral, then there is no logical reason why we cannot get our hermeneutical principles from Scripture itself. In fact, we *must* do this if the Bible really is the ultimate standard.

If we understand and accept the hermeneutical circle, we should have no objection to getting our hermeneutical principles from the Bible itself. In fact, we have been using this principle all along. In chapters 1–8, the truth of the Bible was implicitly assumed throughout. In fact, in a number of places the Scriptures were explicitly cited in order to prove a hermeneutical point. If readers did not accept the hermeneutical circle, then they should have objected to this early on: "Wait just a minute, Dr. Lisle! You cannot use Scripture to make your point until *after* you have established all the rules of hermeneutics! After all, we cannot understand the text until we have a complete and well-established hermeneutic."

But this objection probably did not occur to most readers precisely because *we all inherently accept the hermeneutical circle.* We know what the main-and-plain literal sections of Scripture mean, even without having a perfect hermeneutic. And we can build on these basic truths to improve our understanding of the more difficult truths. No one objects that it is impossible to learn language from a teacher who teaches while using language. By the same reasoning, no one *should* object that it is impossible to learn biblical principles of hermeneutics from the Bible while using it.

God's Word is the ultimate standard for knowledge. It follows then that all the principles of hermeneutics that we have discovered in fact have their logical foundation in Scripture. That foundation may be very obvious in some cases, and more indirect in others. Some hermeneutical principles will be directly stated in the Bible, others are logically deduced from what is directly stated. Still others are implied or given by scriptural example. Although previous chapters did give some scriptural support for the principles we discovered, it seemed inappropriate to give the full argument from Scripture until after some discussion of the hermeneutical circle. But now that we know that getting our principles of interpretation from the Bible itself is proper, biblical, and logically inescapable, let's revisit this issue in greater detail.[3]

Let's explore some of the specific hermeneutical principles we discovered in previous chapters and see if they really are taught in Scripture. We won't hit all of these for the sake of space and because some are very obvious. Let's begin with two most important rules of hermeneutics:

1. You must have a reason for your interpretation.
2. Your reasoning must be self-consistent.

We will then move on to the other hermeneutical principles we have discovered, to confirm that these indeed have a scriptural foundation.

The Biblical Necessity of Self-Consistent Reasons

In chapter 6, we saw (1) the importance of having a reason for our beliefs and (2) the importance of consistency in our thinking. Not surprisingly, these principles are scriptural. That we should have a reason for our beliefs is implicitly required in 1 Peter 3:15. This passage indicates that we must be able to give a defense (a rational argument) to anyone who asks for a *reason* of the hope that is within us. We could give no defense if we did not have a reason. Our thinking should not be baseless, being blown about like an untethered balloon in the wind (Ephesians 4:14) or shifting like a house built on sand (Matthew 7:26–27). We are supposed to reason (Isaiah 1:18, 41:1, 21). The Apostle Paul, by example, reasoned with people (Acts 17:2, 18:4). Our thinking should be anchored in reasons ultimately stemming from the Word of God (Matthew 7:24–25).

And our thinking must be self-consistent because God is. He does not deny Himself (2 Timothy 2:13), and we are supposed to emulate His character (Ephesians 5:1) since we are not only originally created in His image (Genesis 1:26–27) but also since as Christians we are re-created in His image (2 Corinthians 3:18; Ephesians 4:24; Colossians 3:10). Since all truth is in Christ (John 14:6), truth will never contradict itself (John 10:35). The law of non-contradiction has its rational foundation in the

3. This method is itself somewhat of a hermeneutical circle. Namely, we began to systematically discover hermeneutical principles before we discussed the fact that such principles are rooted in Scripture. Scripture is logically primary to hermeneutical principles even if the principles are discovered chronologically first. Even the laws of logic by which we reason are themselves grounded in the nature of God as revealed in His Word. See Lisle, *The Ultimate Proof of Creation: Resolving the Origins Debate.*

Christian worldview. Because God is faithful, our words should not be "yes and no" (2 Corinthians 1:18). That is, we should not contradict ourselves. This also confirms that the Bible has one primary meaning for each of its propositions — not "yes and no." So the two most important principles of hermeneutics are indeed scriptural principles.

The Bible on the Interpretation of Historical and Doctrinal Texts

Let's now explore the *literal,* the *genre,* and the *"explicit constrains the implicit"* principles. Together these principles indicate that:

1. The historical narrative and doctrinal sections of Scripture are to be interpreted in a mostly literal fashion.
2. The poetic and prophetic sections are not as literal.
3. The literal sections constrain the meaning of the less-than-literal sections.

We have already seen that most of the Bible is historical narrative or direct doctrinal teaching (the epistles), both of which are to be understood in a primarily literal way. Does the Bible itself interpret these texts literally? Jesus did. For example, in Matthew 19:3–8, Jesus quotes verses from Genesis 1 and 2 as the literal historical basis for marriage. He acknowledged that Moses was a real person, not a symbol or poetic metaphor (John 5:46–47; Mark 12:26; Luke 20:37). Jesus believed in the creation of Adam in the beginning of creation (Matthew 19:4), the literal historical reality of Abel (Matthew 23:35), Noah (Matthew 24:37–38), Abraham (John 8:37, 58), Isaac and Jacob (Luke 13:28; Matthew 22:31–32), David (Matthew 12:3–4), and Solomon (Matthew 6:29; Luke 11:31). Christ interpreted biblical history literally.

So did the Apostles. Paul affirmed the historical reality of Adam (Romans 5:14; 1 Corinthians 15:22, 45; 1 Timothy 2:13–14), Eve (2 Corinthians 11:3; 1 Timothy 2:13), Abraham (Romans 4:1–3, 9:7, 11:1; 2 Corinthians 11:22; Galatians 3:6–9), Isaac and Rebekah (Roman 9:10), Jacob and Esau (Romans 9:13), and David (Acts 13:36; Romans 1:3; 2 Timothy 2:8). Peter affirmed the historical truth of Noah and the Flood (1 Peter 3:20; 2 Peter 2:5), and Abraham and Sarah (1 Peter 3:6). James confirmed the historicity of Abraham and Isaac (James 2:21). Jude confirmed the historical existence of Adam and Enoch (Jude 14). The author of Hebrews affirmed the historical nature of just about every major person in the Old Testament (Hebrews 11:1–40). Many others could be listed, and we can find no counterexamples where the Bible takes history as non-literal. There can be no room for doubt that the New Testament interprets Old Testament history as speaking of literal persons and events. Therefore, so should we.

The epistles are also interpreted literally by their own authors. All the apostles expected that their instructions to the church should be literally followed (e.g., Philemon 2:12; 2 Thessalonians 3:14, 3:6; 2 Corinthians 2:9). John criticizes an individual who refused to do so (3 John 9). Paul explained that his instructions are the Lord's (literal) commandment (1 Corinthians 14:37). Jude quotes 2 Peter 3:3 as literal doctrine (Jude 17–18). Therefore, we must conclude that the Bible endorses the literal interpretation of doctrinal and historical passages.

The Bible on the Interpretation of Poetic and Prophetic Passages

We naturally expect poetic literature to express truth using non-literal figures of speech — that's a common characteristic of poetry, even of Hebrew poetry. So it is not surprising that this is exactly how the Bible interprets its own poetic passages. In Romans 3:13, the Apostle Paul quotes Psalm 5:9 and Psalm 140:3. He speaks of people whose "throat is an open grave" and that the "poison of asps is under their lips." Paul applies these metaphors to the deception of sinners. He certainly is not arguing that sinners literally have the poison of asps under their lips, or that their throats are literally open graves. But the word pictures of poison and death are very striking.

Second Peter 2:21–22 deals with the topic of those who were once enslaved to sin, were then exposed to the gospel, and enjoyed the blessings of Christian community, but who then return to a sinful lifestyle. The Apostle explains that this disgusting pattern is described in Proverbs 26:11 as "like a dog that returns to its vomit." Peter understood this as an analogy for such foolish behavior — a very fitting one.

A particularly interesting example of proper and non-literal interpretation of a poetic passage is found in Hebrews 10:5, which quotes Psalm 40:6. At first glance, it seems like a misquotation because the Hebrews passage has Christ saying, "a body You have prepared for me," whereas the Psalm passage states, "My ears You have opened." The discrepancy is because the author of Hebrews is quoting from the Septuagint — the Greek translation of the

Old Testament. Was this an error on his part? Clearly not — the author writes under divine inspiration. Which word captures the right meaning of Psalm 40:6 — ear or body? The author of Hebrews recognized (along with the translators of the Septuagint) the poetic device of *synecdoche* — the substitution of the whole for the part, or the part for the whole. The ear is part of the body and is used to represent the entire body in Psalm 40:6. Only by recognizing the non-literal poetic usage of "ear" do we end up with the correct interpretation of Psalm 40:6 — the interpretation given by the author of Hebrews.

Likewise, the Bible interprets its own prophetic passages in a less-than-literal way. This isn't surprising considering that such passages usually have ubiquitous indicators of poetic literature. Consider Malachi 4:5–6 that states, "Behold, I am going to send you Elijah the prophet before the coming of the great and terrible day of the LORD. He will restore the hearts of the fathers to their children. . . ." Does this literally refer to Elijah? The New Testament interprets "Elijah" non-literally to mean "in the spirit and power of Elijah" and that this figure actually refers to John the Baptist (Luke 1:17). Jesus confirms that the Old Testament prophecy of the coming of Elijah is referring to John (Matthew 11:13, 17:12). John the Baptist is not literally Elijah (John 1:21), rather the prophet Malachi used Elijah metaphorically to represent John.

A great example of prophetic symbolism is found in Isaiah 28:16 where God says, "Behold, I am laying in Zion a stone, a tested stone, a costly cornerstone for the foundation, firmly placed. He who believes in it will not be disturbed." Is this a literal stone, literally placed in Zion? Not according to Scripture. The Apostle Peter quotes this passage and explicitly applies it to Christ (1 Peter 2:5–6). Jesus is not literally a stone of any sort. But He is metaphorically the cornerstone of the Church.

In some cases, the Bible explicitly interprets its own prophetic imagery. Revelation 17:3–6 describes a woman sitting on a scarlet beast. The beast had seven heads and ten horns. We are not supposed to take this as a literal animal that God physically created. In Revelation 17:7–18, the angel explains to John what the beast and woman *symbolize*.

In some prophecies, the symbolism is so obvious that no interpretation is needed and none is given. Consider the prophecy revealed to Joseph in his dreams in Genesis 37:6–10. Joseph's family did not need an interpretation of what the sheaves or the celestial luminaries symbolized. They immediately understood what the dreams meant — that Joseph would one day rule over them, and that they would bow down in respect to him (Genesis 37:8, 10). The prophetic vision came to pass (Genesis 42:6, 44:14) and had nothing to do with literal stars or literal sheaves.

The Scriptures also affirm that their literal sections must constrain the meaning of their poetic sections. As we saw earlier, Jesus in Matthew 4:7 used the literal historical passage of Deuteronomy 6:16 to correct Satan's misinterpretation of Psalm 91:11–12. The author of Hebrews also affirms this principle in verse 29 of chapter 11, which refers to the Israelites crossing the Red Sea. There he refers to the literal/historical fact that the Egyptians drowned. This confirms that the historical account of Exodus 14:27–28 constrains the poetic retelling of the story in Exodus 15:1–18. The poetic song uses non-literal imagery in which the Egyptians were burned to death (Exodus 15:7), shattered to pieces (Exodus 15:6), and swallowed by the earth (Exodus 15:12).

Although the poetic and prophetic sections are less literal than the historical sections, they are often easy to understand. In some cases, no explicit interpretation is needed because the symbolism is so obvious. In other cases, the Bible explicitly gives the interpretation. And in all cases, the larger historical and doctrinal passages can be used to constrain the meaning of the less literal. Even the poetic and prophetic portions of the Bible were written to be understood.

Other Principles of Hermeneutics in Scripture

We have seen that the most foundational principles of hermeneutics *are themselves found in Scripture* either explicitly by direct teaching, or implicitly by example or necessary inference. This is also true of the other principles of hermeneutics. It is instructive to look at the hermeneutical principles listed in chapter 6, excluding those that we have already demonstrated, to see their biblical basis. This will confirm that indeed the Bible is the ultimate standard for how it should be interpreted. These principles will be covered briefly before giving a more expanded investigation of the Bible's teaching on the perspicuity of Scripture.

The "contextual principle" — that the meaning of a given word is determined by its grammatical-historical context — is taught implicitly throughout the Scriptures. As one example, Jesus indicated that He would be killed and then rise again after three days (Mark 8:31). Although the Greek word for "day" (*hēmera*) can in some contexts simply mean "time" in a general sense (e.g., John 8:56, 16:23; Hebrews 3:8), the context of Christ's statement indicates that these are earth-rotation days because it occurs in the historical narrative section and there is a number associated with them — "*three* days." That these are literal days is confirmed by the fact that Christ indeed rose on the third day (Matthew 28:1–6; Acts 10:40).

The account of the Resurrection also confirms the grammatical-historical hermeneutic — that the words are to be understood according to the grammar and the historical setting of the original readers. In this case, first-century Jews considered the beginning of the new day to start at sunset — not sunrise or midnight as we might think today. They also considered part of a day to count as an entire day (the use of synecdoche). So if you work for only one hour on Monday, it is fair to say you worked on Monday. There are many other scriptural examples of part of the day counting as a day, such as 1 Kings 20:29. Here the Israelites camped for "seven days," yet the seventh day was only partial because the text says that they joined the battle *on the seventh day*. Similarly, Genesis 42:17–18 and 1 Samuel 20:12–13 also demonstrate this principle.

The Resurrection confirms that the Gospel writers used the terms in just this way. Namely, Christ died on Friday before sunset (Luke 23:53–54; John 19:31; Mark 15:42) and was buried. In Hebrew thinking, that fraction of a day counts as a day. Christ was in the tomb from Friday sunset to Saturday sunset — a second day. Then He rose on Sunday before sunrise (Matthew 28:1; Luke 24:1), and by Jewish reckoning, Sunday began at sunset at the end of Saturday evening. This counts as the third day (Luke 24:7).

The "substitution principle" is implicitly used throughout the Bible. This principle states that if Y is a correct interpretation of X, then Y may be paraphrased as X without altering the meaning. We saw earlier that the meaning of "ear" in Psalm 40:6 is really "body," where the Psalmist has used synecdoche — the part to represent the whole. The author of Hebrews makes use of the fact that "ear" means "body" in this instance and substitutes it in Hebrews 10:5 without altering the meaning of the passage.

The "fact/value principle" acknowledges that the Bible records statements and actions that it does not necessarily endorse. For example, the

Bible affirms that murder and adultery are wrong (Exodus 20:13–14), and yet it records the fact that David committed adultery with Bathsheba and murdered her husband Uriah (1 Samuel 11:3–5, 15). The Bible explains that David's actions were evil (2 Samuel 11:27), and thus not endorsed by God.

The "incidental fallacy" is the violation of the fact/value principle. It happens when someone takes an historical text as prescriptive rather than descriptive. Just because the Bible records something that happened doesn't mean that we should do that thing today. The Bible teaches this principle in Deuteronomy 6:16. In this passage God (through Moses) commands Israel that they are not to put the Lord to the test as they had done previously at Massah. So the Bible records their past (sinful) action, and yet specifically instructs them *not* to do this in the future.

The "red-letter principle" — that all Christ's affirmations are true and that all His deeds are morally commendable is confirmed in 1 Peter 2:22, which teaches that Christ "committed no sin, nor was any deceit found in His mouth." Hence, everything Christ affirms is true and everything He does is good. At Christ's baptism and again at the transfiguration, God the Father affirms His full confidence in what Jesus does and says (Matthew 3:17, 17:5).

"Accommodation" is the principle that since we cannot think on God's level, God communicates on our level, sometimes using figures of speech that help us to understand the main idea without necessarily understanding the nuances. That God's thinking is infinitely above ours is revealed in texts such as Isaiah 55:8–9, " 'For My thoughts are not your thoughts, nor are your ways My ways,' declares the Lord. 'For as the heavens are higher than the earth, so are My ways higher than your ways and My thoughts than your thoughts.' " That God is willing to condescend to our level is demonstrated most conclusively by the incarnation (Philippians 2:6–8). Many examples of accommodation are found in the Old Testament: references to God's hand (Exodus 13:9, 14, 16, 15:6) or God's arm (Exodus 15:16; Deuteronomy 5:15) are used as metaphors for His power, since we know that God in the essence of His divinity does not literally have a body (John 4:24; Luke 24:39). Jesus often used analogies and figures of speech to explain kingdom principles (e.g., Matthew 13:31, 33, 44, 45, 47) — these are all forms of accommodation.

The "progressive revelation principle," that God has revealed Himself increasingly with time, is taught explicitly in passages such as Hebrews 1:1–2 and 1 Peter 1:10–12. The first of these passages states, "God, after He spoke long ago to the fathers in the prophets in many portions and in many ways, in these last days has spoken to us in His Son, whom He appointed heir of all things, through whom also He made the world." Thanks to New Testament revelation, we now know the details of the incarnation of Christ, of His atoning death, and of His Resurrection — things that Old Testament believers could only anticipate (Matthew 13:17; 1 Peter 1:10–12).

The Bible repudiates relativism — the notion that a proposition can be true for some people and false for others. Jesus affirms the objective nature of truth when He says, "I am the way, and the truth, and the life" (John 14:6). The absolute nature of truth is rooted in the eternal God. And such truth is objectively revealed in God's Word. Christ says, "Sanctify them in the truth; Your word is truth" (John 17:17). The Apostle Paul denounces relativism in 2 Corinthians 1:18, "But as God is faithful, our word to you is not yes and no."

The "text principle" states that biblical interpretation must be applied to the actual text of Scripture — not what someone falsely claims that the text states. Jesus illustrated this principle masterfully when He refuted the Sadducees in Matthew 22:23–33. The Sadducees were attempting to refute the Resurrection by showing that earthly marriages could not possible persist in heaven. Of course, the text of Scripture *does not anywhere* teach that earthly marriages continue in heaven. The Sadducees had not read the text carefully, and Jesus knew it. "Jesus answered and said to them, 'You are mistaken, not knowing the Scriptures nor the power of God. For in the resurrection they neither marry nor are given in marriage, but are like angels of God in heaven' " (Matthew 22:29–30; NKJV).

Another example is found in John 21:22–23. Here, the disciples had not listened carefully to Christ's actual words, and began claiming that John would not die until Jesus returned. But that wasn't actually what Jesus had said. Rather, He said, "*If* I want him to remain until I come, what is that to you?" (emphasis added). The statement was a (conditional) hypothetical proposition, not a categorical one. Jesus was not asserting that John will not die; He was merely pointing out that *if that were the case* it wouldn't be anyone else's concern.

The "argument from silence" is fallaciously concluding that something doesn't exist or didn't happen, simply on the basis that it is not mentioned. But the Bible affirms that many things are true that have not been recorded in Scripture (John 20:30, 21:25; Revelation 10:4).

The "superfluous distinction fallacy" is when a non-textual distinction is arbitrarily imposed to protect a preconceived thesis. However, legitimate distinctions must be justified by the text itself or by the need for logical consistency within the text. For example, the Bible teaches that God is all powerful (Jeremiah 32:17, 27), and that there is nothing He cannot do (Job 42:2; Luke 1:37; Matthew 19:26). Yet, the Bible also teaches that God cannot lie or deny Himself (Titus 1:2; 2 Timothy 2:13). So we are to understand that God's omnipotence means that He can do anything *that is consistent with His nature.* This distinction is warranted because the Bible does not contradict itself — a principle that itself stems from the fact that God cannot lie or deny Himself.

The principle is illustrated in the Apostle Paul's reasoning in 1 Corinthians 15:27. Here Paul explains a warranted distinction in Psalm 8:6 which teaches that God the Father has put all things in subjection under Christ's feet. Paul explains that "all" is qualified; it refers to everything *except* God Himself. This distinction isn't because the psalm mentions that God is an exception; rather, it is required for logical consistency, since God is sovereign and therefore cannot be involuntarily subject to anyone (Deuteronomy 32:39; 2 Chronicles 20:6; Hebrews 6:13).

The Pharisees and scribes had introduced all sorts of superfluous distinctions into the commandments of God. As one example, the fifth commandment "Honor your father and your mother" implies providing financially for elderly parents. But the Pharisees and scribes claimed an unbiblical exception to this rule; they held that elderly parents need not be honored financially if the money is instead given to the temple of God. But the Bible nowhere justifies such an exception, nor is it necessary to preserve logical consistency. It was wrong, and Jesus sharply rebuked them for this in Matthew 15:3–9.

"The point is" fallacy is readily refuted by 2 Timothy 3:16. The fallacy is invoked when people dismiss details of a biblical passage that are not central to (what they deem to be) the main point of the passage. But 2 Timothy 3:16 teaches that *all* Scripture is "God-breathed" and profitable for teaching — not just the portions that some people consider to be the important points.

The "translation principle," that the Bible is inerrant in its original autographs and language but not necessarily in copies or translations, is implied in a number of ways throughout Scripture. Jesus indicates that not one "jot" or "tittle" from the Scriptures will pass away until heaven and earth do (Matthew 5:18). A "jot" is the smallest letter of the Hebrew alphabet, and a "tittle" is a very small extension of a line — again in the Hebrew language. This indicates that God's law, *as it was originally written in its original language*, is what Christ endorses as inerrant and unalterable. Moreover, the fact that the Bible warns us not to add or subtract from God's Word (e.g., Deuteronomy 4:2; Proverbs 30:6) implies that it is possible (though morally wrong) to do so. This can happen by being careless in either transmission (copying) or translation.

The Bible refutes deconstructionism and implicitly endorses the one-meaning principle in the 14th chapter of 1 Corinthians. In verse 10, Paul states, "There are, perhaps, a great many kinds of languages in the world, and no kind is without meaning." The Bible uses language, and indicates that language always has meaning. Thus, the Bible has meaning. Furthermore, each of its affirmations has one primary meaning, because each is from God who denounces double-mindedness as sinful (Psalm 119:113; James 1:8, 4:8).

The fact that people can (often) understand the meaning of a proposition is confirmed in texts such as Ephesians 3:4, which states, "By referring to this, when you read you can understand my insight into the mystery of Christ." This demonstrates that, at least in some cases, reading the text results in understanding.

That knowledge of language is necessary for understanding a particular proposition is demonstrated in 1 Corinthians 14:11. Here, Paul says, "If then I do not know the meaning of the language, I will be to the one who speaks a barbarian, and the one who speaks will be a barbarian to me." Paul explains that those who speak in an unknown language will not benefit those who don't know the language: "For no one understands, but in his spirit he speaks mysteries" (1 Corinthians 14:2). "So also you, unless you utter by the tongue speech that is clear, how will it be known what is spoken? For you will be speaking into the air" (1 Corinthians 14:9).

The notion that we may interpret Scripture according to our wishes is sharply refuted by Christ. One example of this is Matthew 15:6 where Jesus indicts the Pharisees and scribes for invalidating the word of God for the sake of their tradition. In Galatians 1:7–9, the Apostle Paul condemns those who "want to distort the gospel of Christ." The Apostle Peter also speaks negatively of those who distort the Scriptures (2 Peter 3:16). In 2 Timothy 2:15, Paul encourages believers to accurately handle the word of truth. This implies that there is a right way and a wrong way to interpret Scripture. Therefore, the word of God is certainly not something that we are permitted to distort or interpret according to our own desires.

The "inerrancy principle" is confirmed throughout the Scriptures. Jesus said, "Sanctify them in the truth; Your word is truth" (John 17:17). Psalm 119:160 (NKJV) states, "The entirety of Your word is truth, and every one of Your righteous judgments endures forever." Second Timothy 3:16 states, "All Scripture is inspired by God and profitable for teaching, for reproof, for correction, for training in righteousness." Even the smallest "jot" and "tittle" of God's Word will not fail (Matthew 5:18).

The Bible on the Perspicuity of the Bible

Finally, the "perspicuity of Scripture" is itself a biblical principle. This issue deserves special attention because it is very important and is sometimes misused. Most of the Bible is written in a literal style. It doesn't take any advanced hermeneutical skill to read a text literally. The perspicuity of Scripture is therefore confirmed by the literary style of the majority of the text of Scripture — historical narrative and doctrinal teaching. This is not to say that even these sections are strictly literal. There are occasional figures of speech in otherwise literal literature as well as cultural references that might be difficult for us to understand without further study. But God has made the primary doctrines so clear that anyone who genuinely seeks the truth will come to understand. The Bible itself teaches this in many ways.

First, there are verses that directly indicate the perspicuity of Scripture. Paul explains that His writings are not convoluted or deceptive but straightforward and plain: "Rather, we have renounced secret and shameful ways; we do not use deception, nor do we distort the word of God. On the contrary, by setting forth the truth plainly we commend ourselves to every man's conscience in the sight of God" (2 Corinthians 4:2; NIV84).

To have a basic understanding of the primary doctrines of God's Word, believers need only read the Word. Ephesians 3:4 states, "By referring to this, *when you read you can understand* my insight into the mystery of Christ" (emphasis added). Paul thereby indicates that reading the text results in understanding — the very essence of perspicuity. In Psalm 119:104, David writes, "From Your precepts I get understanding." And Psalm 119:130 states this even more directly, "The unfolding of Your words gives light; it gives understanding to the simple." Proverbs 2:6 states, "For the Lord gives wisdom; from His mouth come knowledge and understanding." All these passages reveal that simply reading God's Word results in understanding.

God Himself tells us that His Word is not difficult. In Deuteronomy 30:11–14 the Lord states, "For this commandment which I command you today is not too difficult for you, nor is it out of reach. It is not in heaven, that you should say, 'Who will go up to heaven for us to get it for us and make us hear it, that we may observe it?' Nor is it beyond the sea, that you should say, 'Who will cross the sea for us to get it for us and make us hear it, that we may observe it?' But the word is very near you, in your mouth and in your heart, that you may observe it." Although this text refers specifically to the ease of obeying God's commandments, such obedience would be impossible if such commandments could not be understood.

Second, the Bible implicitly teaches that it can be understood; there are certain verses that only make sense if the primary doctrines of Scripture are able to be understood by the average person. Romans 10:17 teaches, "So faith comes from hearing, and hearing by the word of Christ." In order for hearing God's Word to produce faith in a person, it must be *understood* by that person. An incomprehensible message would not result in faith. Psalm 119:105 states that God's Word is "a lamp to my feet and a light to my path." But God's Word can only serve as a guide if it is understood (1 Corinthians 14:9). Second Timothy 3:16 teaches that all Scripture is profitable for teaching, for reproof, for correction, and for training in righteousness. But it wouldn't be profitable for any of those things if its meaning could not be understood.

In the context of discussing the gifts of tongues and prophecy, the Apostle Paul explains that words only benefit people if those words are clear and understandable (1 Corinthians 14:1–6). He states, "For if the trumpet makes an uncertain sound, who will prepare for battle? So likewise you, unless you utter by the tongue words *easy to understand*, how will it be known what is spoken? For you will be speaking into the air" (1 Corinthians 14:8-9; NKJV, emphasis added). And the Bible teaches that it does benefit people (e.g., Psalm 19:7–11, 119:9, 11; Matthew 7:24–27). Therefore, the Bible must be clear and understandable.

Third, the nature of God is such that His Word is necessarily clear, not vague, ambiguous, or confusing. God is not the author of confusion (1 Corinthians 14:33). He gives understanding to people (Proverbs 2:6; 1 John 5:20; 2 Timothy 2:7; Daniel 2:21). It is God's pleasure to give wisdom and understanding to anyone who asks (James 1:5; Proverbs 2:3–6). God is a linguistic being. He spoke the universe into existence (Genesis 1:3, 6, 9; Psalm 33:9). He is able to communicate with His creations (John 10:27). So the Bible itself endorses the perspicuity of Scripture.

It really shouldn't surprise us that an omnipotent, omniscient God is able to write clearly. God created language; Adam was able to speak the very day he was created. And God gave clear linguistic information to Adam and Eve. Such revelation from God was eventually written down, and has been passed on to us. The clear literal teaching of the majority of passages in Scripture therefore serves as a basis for interpreting the more difficult passages.

Misunderstanding the Basics

Given that the primary doctrines in Scripture are so very clear, we must ask, "Why do so many people miss these basic truths?" Many people profess to be Christian but then deny obvious truths of Scripture: the Trinity, creation, the deity of Christ, the Second Coming of Christ, eternal punishment for unbelievers, and so on. A group of people that professes to be Christian but rejects one or more of these essential Christian doctrines is often deemed a "cult." Since cults are so common these days, it may cause us to ask, "Is the Bible really as clear as it seems?"

Scripture teaches that God grants understanding to anyone who sincerely asks for it (Proverbs 2:6; James 1:5). Therefore, those who do not understand the Bible are those who *have not genuinely asked* — those who are not truly seeking understanding. Sometimes cultists will claim that they have tried very hard to understand the Bible. But after much study and prayer, they just don't see the Scriptures as a Christian does. They claim they honestly cannot find any evidence of the deity of Christ, or eternal punishment, or other such fundamentals of the faith, despite reading the Bible with humility and an "open mind." But such a position is disallowed by the Bible. Scripture is clear on this: *Those who do not understand the basics of God's Word are those who do not want to understand* (John 8:43; 2 Corinthians 4:3; Matthew 22:29).

In Ephesians 4:17–18, Paul explains the reason why the unbelieving Gentiles lacked understanding. It was because of the "ignorance that is in them, because of the hardness of their heart." The phrase "hardness of their heart" indicates a stubborn rebellion against God. People who have read the Bible but do not come to understand it are those who do not *want* to believe what it teaches. They would prefer to serve a god of their own imagination, a god that is pleasing to their desires, rather than submit to the living God. They prefer to live in self-deluded ignorance (James 1:22), and God honors their wish (Psalm 81:11–12; 2 Thessalonians 2:10–12).

Quoting the prophet Isaiah regarding those who do not know Christ as Lord, Jesus says in Matthew 13:14, "You will keep on hearing, but will not understand; you will keep on seeing, but will not perceive." In the next verse, the Lord explains the cause of their lack of understanding, "For the heart of this people has become dull" (Matthew 13:15). In John 8:43, Jesus states of the unbelieving Jews, "Why do you not understand what I am saying? It is because you cannot hear My word." The unbelieving Jews could not accept ("hear") Christ's word because they didn't want the truth (John 8:45). Jesus affirms this pattern in Mark 8:17, "Do you not yet see or understand? Do you have a hardened heart?" Lack of understanding the Scriptures is never God's fault. It is always the result of man's hardened heart — man's stubborn refusal to accept the truth.

Recall the aforementioned analogy of the balance scale. The science student can discover the unknown mass *only* if he allows the balance scale to correct his initial inaccurate estimate of the mass. He must have the humility to recognize that the balance scale is superior to his intuition about mass. Indeed, he must submit to the scale as the true standard by which masses are measured. He is required to adjust his beliefs about the unknown mass to the readings of the scale. Likewise, we must submit to the Word of God as the ultimate standard by which it is interpreted if we are to have correct understanding.

Suppose the science student refused to submit to the readings of the balance scale. He says, "My intuition about mass is so good that I can't possibly be wrong in my initial estimate. I know the scale indicates that I have overestimated the mass. But I just can't be wrong, so clearly the scale needs to be adjusted since it has underestimated the mass." The student then proceeds to gently push on the beam and level the balance — adjusting it to his preconceptions. Would this allow the student to obtain the right answer? Of course not. Likewise, if a person refuses to allow Scripture to correct his thinking, is there any realistic chance that he will end up with good theology?

Since the Bible itself indicates that its teachings are perspicuous, any misunderstanding of Scripture is *always* the fault of the reader — never the fault of the text. But such failings are not limited to cultists. Christians, those who have a genuine saving faith in Christ, sometimes misinterpret the non-essential doctrines as well. But how can this be? Christians don't have the hardened heart of an unbeliever, do they? There are a number of ways in which a sincere Christian might misunderstand a biblical text.

First, we note that the redeemed are saved by grace, not merit (Ephesians 2:8–9), and yet they continue to have a sin-nature that wars against God (Galatians 5:16–17). As such, and to our shame, we sometimes resist biblical teaching just as unbelievers do. Salvation initiates the process of sanctification in the believer, but that process isn't complete until we pass into eternity. We sometimes succumb to the temptation to resist God's Word in areas of our life that are not completely yielded to God. We may not be consciously aware of an area of hard-hearted pride in our lives, but such areas exist nonetheless.

Second, a Christian might misunderstand a text simply because he or she hasn't studied it sufficiently. The person may sincerely want to understand the text, but hasn't taken the time to read the Bible as thoroughly and frequently as is appropriate. As we saw previously, some sections are harder than others and require substantial consideration. The fault is still on us — not God. Failing to study God's Word is a sin of omission.

Of course, scribal errors and translator errors can result in a text that is not completely true to the original, and a sincere Christian might misunderstand a doctrine from reading a distorted copy of the text. But the fault still lies with human fallibility, partly on the scribe/translator, but also partly with the reader. After all, it is incumbent upon the reader to *study* the text, not just read it. This involves some degree of textual analysis, checking to make sure that his or her copy of the text is a faithful translation of the original.

Third, a Christian might understand the individual words or phrases of the biblical text, but then fail to reason properly from that information, resulting in faulty theology. I suggest that this is one of the main reasons why there are so many different denominations of Christianity in the world today. Again, the fault lies in us, not in God's Word. If we don't reason correctly from the text, it would be absurd to blame the text.

The solution to these latter two errors is education. This could include formal education, but it wouldn't have to. Taking a college class on logic could be very helpful. Alternatively, a less expensive option could be to purchase a textbook on logic, and go through it by oneself or as part of a small group. To know the Bible better, one must spend time reading it. Reading multiple translations can alleviate many misunderstandings. Hebrew and Greek concordances are indispensable for understanding the nuances of biblical words. Computer Bible software has taken biblical analysis to a new level of ease. Cross-references, concordance look-up, and word searches are practically instantaneous. The fellowship of sincere believers can prod us to study further, and can help us reason through difficult issues.

Errors involving prideful resistance to God's Word are more difficult to correct. The solution in these instances is the progressive sanctification that follows from salvation. Christians *should* have an attitude of humility that seeks to be corrected from unbiblical theology and behavior. Indeed, it is impossible to be saved without repenting, confessing Christ, and submitting to Him as Lord (Luke 13:3; Romans 10:9; 1 Corinthians 12:3). These things cannot be done in pride (James 4:6). Therefore, true Christians will exhibit humility and will grow in their understanding of the text as part of their ongoing sanctification. But what about non-Christians?

The Ignorance of the Dead

Unbelievers do not understand God's Word because they don't want to — because of the hardness of their heart (Ephesians 4:17–18). But the problem is even worse than this. Not only are unbelievers unwilling to correctly understand basic Christian truths, but they are *unable* to fully understand such truths (Romans 8:5–9; 1 Corinthians 2:14). The spiritual truths of God seem foolish to the unbeliever.

The Bible speaks of unbelievers as being "dead" in their sins (Ephesians 2:1; Colossians 2:13). It is clear from the context that this is not a reference to physical death. We know that unbelievers have physical life and breath (Acts 17:25). But spiritually, they are dead. What does it mean to be "spiritually dead"? One aspect of our being — our spirit — is able to commune with God. This spirit is in all people. But in those who have not received Christ as Lord, their spirit is "dead." This does not mean that their spirit ceases to exist. Rather, their spirit is not able to function as originally designed. By analogy, a dead animal does not cease to exist, but it does cease to function.

The unbeliever is spiritually dead in the sense that his spirit is disabled so that he cannot understand spiritual truths in an affirming way. This does not mean in any way that unbelievers are unintelligent or stupid. But it does mean that there will be limitations on what unbelievers can understand about Scripture. Of course, not everything in Scripture is strictly "spiritual." The Bible deals with very practical matters — matters of history, for example. The unbeliever should have no difficulty understanding that Genesis 21:27 teaches that Abraham gave sheep and oxen to Abimelech. But when it comes to basic doctrines like the hypostatic union (that Jesus is both God and man), unbelievers cannot grasp what is right before their eyes. They cannot think rationally about spiritual matters without spiritual renewal from God, in the same way a dead man can't understand anything at all unless God resurrects him.

Even worse, unbelievers often misunderstand their own misunderstanding. They will read a passage like 1 Corinthians 2:14 (that the natural man cannot understand the things of God) and think that the Bible is teaching a form of gnosticism. This is the idea that some "secret knowledge" above and beyond ordinary logic is necessary to understand certain truths. But that's not what the Bible teaches. The unbeliever does not need God's help to think in a way that is beyond logic, but rather to think *logically*. By God's grace, the unbeliever is able to understand some things. But there are other things that he cannot accept due to his faulty worldview, resulting from a stubborn rebellion against God — a "hardened heart."

The supreme example of this is the understanding that Jesus is God incarnate. It is a basic truth that all true Christians know. The Apostle John declares that Jesus was the Word and the Word was God (John 1:1); Christ claims equality with the Father God who fully approves of Him (John 5:18; Matthew 3:17); Thomas calls him "My Lord and my God" (John 20:28); and so forth. Is any truth more obvious than that Jesus is God in the flesh? Yet unbelievers cannot receive this truth. They may intellectually understand the meaning of the claim "Jesus is Lord." But they cannot accept the claim itself because their spirit is dead.

This might cause some people to ask, "How then can anyone be saved? Understanding and professing that 'Jesus is Lord' is a requirement for salvation (Romans 10:9–10). Yet, the understanding of such spiritual matters is only possible for believers — those who are already saved. How then can any unbeliever become a believer?" The answer, of course, is that salvation is a miraculous work of God (Ephesians 2:8). The disciples asked the same question in a somewhat different context, "Then who can be saved?" (Matthew 19:25). Christ's response answers our question as well as theirs, "With people this is impossible, but with God all things are possible" (Matthew 19:26).

Some may think that a temporal paradox arises since belief in Christ as Lord is both a requirement for salvation and only possible for the saved. Does faith in Christ come first, and then salvation follows? But that would be contrary to 1 Corinthians 2:14, since a natural man (an unbeliever) cannot accept the things of the Spirit of God. Or does salvation come first, and then faith in Christ follows? But that would contradict Romans 10:9–10 which indicates that faith in Christ is necessary for salvation. It seems to me that the paradox is easily resolved if we understand that faith in Christ and salvation are simultaneous. When God saves someone, He enables them to understand that Christ is Lord (1 Corinthians 12:3) at the same time that He resurrects their dead spirit (Ephesians 2:1–5). This may seem counter-intuitive, but it does not violate any laws of logic and is consistent with the Scriptures.

It is very uncomfortable to many people that we cannot choose to love and serve God without His help. We'd like to believe that in our own natural wisdom, we saw the need for a Savior and chose to follow Christ. But our emotional preference is irrelevant to the truth of the matter. Truth is determined by God's Word. So what does the Bible say about the cause of our coming to Christ?

God is the one that gives us the faith by which we receive His grace (Ephesians 2:8–9). Without the help of the Holy Spirit, we would be unable to affirm that Christ is Lord (1 Corinthians 12:3). In our sin nature, we like to think that we have mustered up the faith to believe God by our own initiative. But Jesus is the author of our faith — not us (Hebrews 12:2). Even our ability to repent from sin is something that God gives (Acts 5:31; 2 Timothy 2:25). Jesus Christ is both the author and perfecter of our faith (Hebrews 12:2).

This fact is why it is impossible to "reason someone into heaven." Yet, paradoxically, God calls us to reason with unbelievers, to give a rational defense of our faith (1 Peter 3:15). What then is the benefit of such reasoning? Why defend the faith to someone whose dead spirit cannot understand the faith?

First, God commands us to. That is sufficient for a Christian. Second, we need to remember that God ordains not only the end, but the means as well. God often uses human activity to accomplish His will (Isaiah 46:11). "Why should we give a defense of the Christian worldview to someone who cannot (without God's help) understand it?" Answer: because God may very well help that person to understand. The Lord in His sovereignty may choose to use human conversations as part of the means by which He draws people to Himself. "Why does God use fallible man to defend His Word and proclaim His Gospel and draw others to Himself?" I don't know for sure, but it is a great honor that God has chosen to use us in this way.

The take-away of this section is that the Bible is perspicuous. It is understandable, and the Bible itself indicates this in a number of ways. The fact that many people reject the Bible and misinterpret it is not due to any problem in the text. The problem is *always* with people. Even Christians continue to have a sin nature, and hence a tendency to distort God's Word. This may be on the sub-conscious level. But we must strive to have our thinking conformed to Christ, asking God to continually give us the rational mind to understand the clear teaching of His Word, and the humility to accept it (Romans 12:2). This is a prayer that God loves to answer; He freely gives wisdom to those who ask (James 1:5; Proverbs 2:6).

Review

What is the ultimate standard in which hermeneutical principles are grounded? Answer: The Bible. This follows logically; if the Bible is the ultimate standard on all matters, then it must be the ultimate standard for its own interpretation. Some will ask, "But if the principles of correct interpretation are grounded in the Bible, then how could we understand the Bible when we first read it?" Answer: God has created us to know *some* biblical principles even before we read of them in Scripture. There is a distinction between logical primacy, and chronological discovery. We are already aware of some hermeneutical principles even before we read the Bible and discover their justification.

"If the Bible is the ultimate standard for its own interpretation, how could we ever come to understand it? Wouldn't we already need a correct hermeneutic to understand the Bible? And if we have a correct hermeneutic already, then why attempt to discover hermeneutical principles in the Bible?" The answer to all the questions is found in the "hermeneutical circle" or "hermeneutical spiral." Namely, we are born with an imperfect hermeneutic that is sufficient to understand some of the Bible on the first pass. If we allow the Bible to systematically correct our hermeneutic, we will understand it even better on the second pass, and so on. Our understanding of hermeneutical principles grows with our knowledge and understanding of the biblical text.

Although some people are bothered by the hermeneutical circle, many things in life are discovered in such a way. Students in school can learn the principles of language from a teacher, who uses language to convey those very principles. Students need only a basic knowledge of language in order to use language to improve their knowledge of language. No one complains that this is fallacious. So why not let the Bible correct and improve our knowledge of biblical interpretation? If our hermeneutical principles are rooted in something other than the Bible, then they are fallible. Moreover, it would mean that the Bible is not our ultimate standard for all things.

The principles of hermeneutics that we explored in previous chapters are all grounded in Scripture. In some cases, the principle is stated very directly. For example, that our reasoning should be self-consistent and non-contradictory is taught in verses such as 2 Corinthians 1:18 and James 4:8. In other cases, the principle is implied or illustrated by example. Jesus used the literal historical texts of Scripture to constrain the meaning of the poetic sections (Matthew 4:5–7). The Bible interprets its own history literally. It interprets its poetic and prophetic portions in a not-so-literal way.

The hermeneutical spiral is itself taught in Scripture. The Bible indicates that some portions are "milk of the Word" that new believers can easily understand; other portions are "meat of the Word" that require some maturity in biblical interpretation (1 Corinthians 3:1–2; Hebrews 5:12–13). The Scriptures teach that we are supposed to become mature in our thinking, and not remain like infants who are only able to understand the milk of the Word (1 Corinthians 14:20, 3:1–2). The Bible itself is what gives us the wisdom to become mature in our thinking (Proverbs 2:6). God's Word is to be the foundation for all thinking if that thinking is to stand up to scrutiny (Matthew 7:24–27, 4:4). This necessarily includes knowledge of hermeneutical principles, since all knowledge is in Christ (Colossians 2:3).

The Scriptures are fundamentally clear. This is the doctrine of the perspicuity of Scripture. The principle is itself taught in Scripture explicitly (Deuteronomy 30:11; Ephesians 3:4; Psalm 119:104, 130) and implicitly (Romans 10:17; 1 Corinthians 14:9). Not all Scriptures are equally clear, however. Some are difficult; this is the "meat of the Word" that requires some hermeneutical skill to understand.

There are a number of reasons why people sometimes misinterpret the fundamentally clear text of Scripture. Unbelievers are spiritually "dead," and therefore cannot understand and accept the spiritual things of God (Ephesians 2:1, 5; 1 Corinthians 2:14). The hard-hearted sinful rebellion of man resists understanding the Bible (Ephesians 4:17–18; Romans 1:21–22). God grants repentance to some, and resurrects their dead spirit to live in Christ (2 Timothy 2:25; Acts 5:31; Ephesians 2:5–9). However, Christians do not cease to struggle with sin while they remain in this world; they sometimes have an attitude of pride that inhibits proper biblical interpretation.

Lack of sufficient study or improper reasoning can also lead to incorrect interpretations. The Apostle Peter explains that lack of education in biblical matters is one reason that some people distort the more difficult doctrines (2 Peter 3:16). In all cases of misinterpretation, the fault lies with the reader, not with the biblical text. God has given us other believers — the church — to help us to rightly discern His Word. We are here to help each other, challenging our brothers and sisters in Christ to rightly interpret God's Word as they challenge us to do the same (Proverbs 27:17).

Chapter 10

Application – Common Hermeneutical Errors

Mistakes in biblical interpretation abound. Some are just annoying. Others are heretical. But all bad theology has one thing in common: a violation of one or more principles of hermeneutics. There are many books written by people who constantly violate hermeneutical principles. It can be depressing. But there is a positive aspect: bad theology is a great way to practice spotting hermeneutical fallacies. Seeing many examples of fallacious interpretation can actually help us learn to interpret the Bible properly — by avoiding the fallacious with which we have become familiar.

Geocentrism

Before Copernicus, most scientists believed in a geocentric solar system in which the planets and the sun orbit the earth. The earth was thought to be the motionless nonrotating center of the universe. Modern astronomers embrace heliocentrism — the view that the planets (including earth) orbit the sun. There are today some very well-meaning Christians who reject heliocentrism and embrace a form of geocentrism because they think the Bible teaches the latter. While this is not a heretical view by any means, it is unscriptural and is rather embarrassing to other Christians who understand that such a view is (1) not anywhere taught in Scripture, and (2) easily refuted by logic and empirical science. Geocentrists sometimes attempt to bolster their claim by misapplying certain principles of science. But here we are only interested in their interpretation of Scripture, and their reasoning from it.

We need to understand precisely what the modern geocentrists are claiming before we can compare such claims against the teaching of Scripture. First, the modern form of geocentrism really should be labeled "geostationarity," because the belief is not primarily about the position of the earth, but its alleged lack of motion. Modern geocentrists believe that the earth does not rotate and that it does not revolve around the sun; they teach that earth is absolutely stationary. If this were the only claim, we might not have a genuine disagreement with the geocentrists, since the earth is stationary from our perspective as inhabitants on its surface. The earth is a perfectly legitimate frame of reference, and does not move relative to itself. Of course, *the same is true for any other object.*

But many geocentrists go further and claim that heliocentrism is wrong. Specifically, they would say that it is not true that the earth orbits the sun. They would say that the earth alone is stationary, and that it would be wrong to say that any other planet is stationary since they are all in motion relative to earth. Moreover, they claim that the Bible does not allow for a moving earth. To test this claim, we will need to define some terms and think through their implications. We must first ask, "What is meant by the term *motion*?"

According to the dictionary, motion is "a change of position in space." If a person is in the back seat of a car, and then at a later time is in the front seat, motion has occurred. He or she has *moved.* So for motion to be meaningful, we must be able to define and measure *positions* at various times. The position of an object or person is only meaningful when given in reference to another object or person. In the example above, the position of the person is given in relation to the interior of a car. We could have picked another object though. Perhaps a person is 37 miles north of Denver, and then moves to a different position 21 miles south of Denver. That's perfectly meaningful.

Without a point of reference, position is meaningless. Suppose I phone a friend and ask, "Where are you?" She responds, "I'm 42 miles." The answer is worthless and gives me no information on my friend's position because she did not give a point of reference: 42 miles *relative to what*? She might clarify, "42 miles away from my destination" or "42 miles away from my starting point" or "42 miles north of Dallas." Those all make sense because we have a reference point.

Since position is only meaningful when given relative to an object, and since motion is defined in terms of a change in position, it follows logically that motion is only meaningful when given relative to an object of reference. For example, suppose that there was only one thing in the universe. Is that thing in motion? The question makes no sense because there is nothing *else* by which we can measure the object's position to see if it has changed with time.

Therefore, all motion is inherently relative. Motion is meaningful only when given in terms of a known frame of reference. That reference frame can be anything at all. It could be a person: "I'm moving closer to James"; an airplane: "I'm getting moved up to first class"; a building: "I'm moving from the second floor to the fourth floor"; or a city: "I'm moving from the south side of Dallas up to Farmers Branch." So whenever anyone asks, "Is this object in motion or is it stationary," we must ask, "relative to what?"

So our first question to the geocentrists who say that the earth is stationary is, "Stationary relative to what?" If they respond, "It's just absolutely stationary — there is no reference frame," then we can dismiss their claim as meaningless. They are not using the terminology correctly. Absolute motion is an oxymoron — it's right up there with the "sound of one hand clapping."

They might respond, "The earth is stationary relative to itself." This is a good answer, and it is true. But it doesn't support their position. Remember, they are not only arguing that geocentrism is true, but also that heliocentrism is false. But *everything* is stationary relative to itself. Relative to the sun, the sun is stationary and the earth revolves around it. Relative to Mars, Mars is stationary, and both the sun and the earth revolve around it. Yet, the geocentrist rejects these latter two views. But he cannot do it with his current answer and be consistent. He singles out the earth for no given reason — the fallacy of special pleading.

The geocentrist might respond that the earth is stationary relative to an invisible, undetectable "ether." There was a time when scientists thought that this might genuinely be the case. But despite many experiments, no such ether has ever been discovered. And there is no reference to it in the Scriptures. So this answer amounts to an appeal to ignorance. I could equally well say, "No, the earth is moving relative to the ether, but Mars is stationary relative to it," and there would be no observational evidence to favor the geocentrist's claim over mine. They are equally arbitrary. The geocentrist cannot therefore logically argue that heliocentrism is wrong on the basis of an undetectable ether.

As a last resort, the geocentrist might claim that the earth is stationary relative to the spiritual realm — the third heaven. This is a form of the reification fallacy. The third heaven (2 Corinthians 12:2) is the spiritual realm, in contrast to the two physical heavens (the atmospheric region and outer space, e.g., Genesis 1:14, 20). It is not a physical location within space, but a reference to the presence of God. This is what we mean when we say that believers "go to heaven" when they die. We mean that their spirit is in the presence of God (2 Corinthians 5:8; Philippians 1:22–23).

God is not a material being with a physical location (John 4:24; 1 Kings 8:27). So naturally, the third heaven is not something that has a location within space. To describe the position or motion of something relative to the third heaven is therefore meaningless. Recall that the definition of motion is defined as a "change of position in space," and that it is only meaningful when specified relative to another object within space. It is meaningless to say that an object is moving relative to something that has no physical location. It would be like saying, "I'm moving at 32 miles per hour relative to *justice*." Justice is an immaterial concept, and has no physical location in space. It cannot be used as a frame of reference for motion.

So geocentrism (or "geostationarity") is that claim that the earth is stationary, and no other celestial objects can truthfully be called stationary. However, the geocentrist's claim is meaningless unless he specifies a reference frame. But he cannot specify any detectable, meaningful reference frame other than the earth itself. And all things are stationary relative to themselves. So the geocentrist cannot cogently argue that other reference frames are wrong. With this in mind, let's look at how the geocentrist attempts to gain support from the Scriptures.

Psalm 93:1 states, "The Lord reigns, He is clothed with majesty; the Lord has clothed and girded Himself with strength; indeed, the world is firmly established, it will not be moved." Geocentrist Gerardus Bouw, in his book *A Geocentricity Primer*,[1] claims that this verse supports geostationarity. Already we see indications of a violation of the genre principle. Psalm 93 is poetic literature as indicated by the nature of the book itself and the obvious

1. Gerardus D. Bouw, *A Geocentricity Primer* (Cleveland, OH: The Biblical Astronomer, 2004).

synonymous parallelism in this verse. To literalize such a passage in defense of a particular model of science is suspect at best.

What does the passage really mean when it indicates that the world "cannot be moved"? Since the passage (like all of the psalms) is poetic, the two parallel phrases *must* be interpreted as a unit. Any alternative will not arrive at the meaning of the passage — the author's intention. Thus, the phrase "established" must be directly comparable to "cannot be moved." The Hebrew word translated as "established" is *kûn* (appearing as a passive participle), and indicates the ongoing and passive result of God's action of establishing the world. In other words, because of God's sovereign sustenance of the world, as its controller, the world has an ongoing stability that He continues to provide. The action verb here has the idea of becoming or being stable — to be firm, fixed, stable, secure, or established. Notice that this stabilizing action does not require an object to be *stationary*. Rather, the basic action signified by the Hebrew verb *kûn* is stabilizing, not causing something to be stationary.

This security or stability must then be directly comparable in meaning with "cannot be moved." The Hebrew word translated "moved" is *mot*. Using a concordance, we can see how the Bible uses the Hebrew verb *mot* — it basically means to move, to move from, to remove, to fall from, to tear or slip away from, to be loosed from, etc.[2] Then, we can notice that *mot* action is negated in Psalm 93:1. The negative of such action has the idea of losing one's set or proper place, which could refer to being loosed from a fixed location or it could mean being removed from a fixed relationship to something that is itself in motion.

For example, the verb appears in Psalm 17:5, 38:16, and 94:18, all three of which verses refer to someone's foot slipping. No one expects a foot to be attached to a motionless body, so a non-slipping foot is not an example of a motionless object! Rather, the idea in those verses is that a human foot can and should move (in relation to the human body it is attached to) in directional synchronization with where the brain and the rest of the body are aimed. It is not movement *per se* that constitutes a foot that "slips"; rather, it is an errant foot's misstep that qualifies the foot's action as "slipping." Likewise, David uses the same Hebrew word when He writes, "I shall not be moved" (Psalm 16:8, 62:6; KJV). Does he mean that he intends to

2. See *Young's Analytical Concordance to the Bible.*

remain physically stationary for the rest of his life? Clearly he means that he is established in God — he will not deviate from the path that God has set before him.

Since the first part of the phrase in Psalm 93:1 indicates stability, the second part must parallel this when it indicates that the world cannot be "moved." Interpreting Scripture with Scripture, the verse must mean that the earth cannot be overthrown, slip, or fall. It will not deviate from the path that God has created for it, just as David says he will not deviate from his spiritual path. The Psalmist is not talking about motion, but rather about stability. The verse therefore does not suggest that the earth is motionless in some absolute or Newtonian sense.

The next verse states, "Your throne is established from of old; You are from everlasting." But God's throne is not a physical object within space. The "established" throne of God refers to its permanence, not its lack of motion through space. This reinforces the point that the Psalmist is writing about stability, and not about motion in the sense of modern physics.

Another passage concerns the sign that was given to Hezekiah. God gave a miraculous sign to Hezekiah — making the sun go backward ten degrees in its diurnal path as measured by a sundial. One reference is found in Isaiah 38:8 which states, "Behold, I will bring again the shadow of the degrees, which is gone down in the sun dial of Ahaz, ten degrees backward. So the sun returned ten degrees, by which degrees it was gone down" (KJV). Bouw claims that this "indicates that the sun did the moving, not the earth."[3] Bouw does not state a reference frame however. So we must ask, "The sun did the moving *relative to what*?" Without a reference frame, motion is meaningless.

When a reference frame is not explicitly stated, it is very natural and appropriate to take the earth as the frame of reference. Yes, the sun rises and sets relative to the earth. But how does this exclude the notion that the earth moves relative to the sun? Remember, Bouw's position is that heliocentrism is false. But merely showing that things are in motion relative to the earth does not accomplish this. Modern astronomers also refer to sunrise and sunset and the diurnal path of the sun in the sky. But they don't deny heliocentrism. Why does Bouw think that similar language in Scripture somehow supports his position?

3. Bouw, *A Geocentricity Primer*, p. 23.

In this case, Bouw's error is indefensible because the Bible explicitly gives the frame of reference: the sundial. The sun is said to return ten degrees as measured by the shadow on the sundial. The sundial is on earth of course. So there can be no doubt that the Scriptures are using earth as the reference frame in this instance. Nowhere does the Bible suggest that earth is the *only* legitimate frame of reference. But without that premise, Bouw has no argument.

Bouw also attempts to use the account of Joshua's long day as an evidence for his version of geocentrism. The relevant passage is Joshua 10:12–14. Verse 13 states, "So the sun stood still, and the moon stopped, until the nation avenged themselves of their enemies. Is it not written in the book of Jashar? And the sun stopped in the middle of the sky and did not hasten to go down for about a whole day." Bouw states, "The geocentric implication of this passage is obvious. Instead of the sun's motion through the sky being due to the rotation of the earth, here it states that the sun and moon daily move around the earth. The sun is commanded not to move or rise; it is not the earth which receives the commandment to stop turning."[4]

Again, the Scriptures use the earth as a convenient reference frame. Notice that the Bible gives the reference frame explicitly when it states that the sun stopped in the *middle of the sky*. The sky is the visible arc of heaven as seen from the surface of earth. The sun and moon were said to stop their daily motion in earth's sky. But how does this remotely support Bouw's claim that the earth is not rotating? He thinks it is significant that the command was given to the sun and moon, not to the earth to stop turning. But the sun and moon are not sentient beings that literally understand a command and then respond by stopping. The language is observational; it appears from the surface of earth as if the sun and moon were consciously responding to orders.

Since all motion is relative to a specified reference frame, Joshua's command makes perfect sense in light of his position on the surface of earth. Again, modern astronomers do this all the time. We say things like, "What time does Saturn rise tonight?" or "The sun sets early this time of year." In no way are we suggesting that the earth does not rotate relative to the rest of the universe. Neither does Scripture.

In describing the sun, Psalm 19:6 states, "Its rising is from one end of the heavens, and its circuit to the other end of them; and there is nothing

---

4. Ibid., p. 34.

hidden from its heat." Bouw claims, "The geocentric import of Psalm 19:6 lies in the fact that the sun, not the earth, is described as moving."[5] Since the sun does move relative to earth's reference frame just as the earth moves relative to the sun, we must ask why Bouw thinks that this passage even remotely supports his position. Psalm 19:6 refers to the circuit of the sun in the heavens (earth's sky) and nothing on earth's surface is hidden from the sun's heat. There can be no doubt that the Bible is using the earth as a convenient and appropriate reference frame. But the Bible does not even hint anywhere that other reference frames are wrong, as Bouw seems to think.

Claims that the Bible supports geocentrism are based on a sloppy reading of the text and fallacious reasoning.

Annihilationism

Annihilationism is the view that the soul of unbelievers eventually ceases to exist rather than spending an eternity in the Lake of Fire. Some annihilationists believe that the soul of an unbeliever ceases to exist when the person dies. Others believe that the soul of an unbeliever does spend a finite amount of time in the Lake of Fire, and then ceases to exist. Either way, they deny eternal punishment. We can certainly understand the psychological motivation to believe in annihilationism. An eternity in the Lake of Fire is too horrible to contemplate. In our flesh, we certainly don't want it to be true.

But wishing for something doesn't make it so. The Word of God clearly teaches that those who continue to reject God's offers of mercy will indeed experience eternal punishment. In Matthew 25:46, Jesus says about unbelievers, "These will go away into eternal punishment, but the righteous into eternal life." Other Scriptural support is found in passages such as Mark 3:29, 2 Thessalonians 1:9, Hebrews 6:2, and Daniel 12:2.

A person recently wrote me a letter in which he rebuked me for teaching eternal punishment for unbelievers. This person (whom I'll refer to as "Tim") is obviously an annihilationist. Here are the relevant portions of his letter, along with my comments:

> *Tim: [Your book] is beautifully designed and well written. Regretfully, I will not be able to share it with anyone because at the end you demonstrate that you hold to the pagan presuppositions of the immortality of the soul and hell.*

---

5. Ibid., p. 71.

Here, Tim commits the fallacy of the question-begging epithet. He uses loaded language rather than logic in an attempt to persuade when he refers to the "pagan presupposition" of the immortality of the soul and hell. What evidence does he have that these are pagan concepts? He presents none. In fact, the Bible teaches that hell is indeed eternal (Matthew 18:8, 25:41; Jude 1:7; Revelation 20:10), and that punishment of unbelieving souls is indeed eternal (Matthew 25:46; Mark 3:29; 2 Thessalonians 1:9; Hebrews 6:2; and Daniel 12:2.) These are biblical concepts, not pagan ones.

> *Tim: The Scriptures clearly state that only the Almighty has immortality (1 Timothy 6:16).*

Tim here ignores the contextual principle, and the consistency principle. First Timothy 6:16 states that God "alone *possesses* immortality" (emphasis added). Does this mean that only God is immortal? No. Angels are immortal (Luke 20:36). Believers live forever with God — they too are immortal (John 5:24; 1 Corinthians 15:52; John 3:16). So, clearly, the passage cannot mean what Tim wants it to mean — that only God lives forever. That interpretation contradicts other Scriptures and is therefore wrong. In context (1 Timothy 6:13), the passage indicates that God alone is the source of eternal life; it is His alone to give to others (John 5:21, 26, 6:33, 63; Romans 4:17; 2 Corinthians 3:6).

> *Tim: . . . and the soul that sins will die (Ezekiel 18:4, 20)*

That's right. But where does the text say that the soul that sins will "cease to exist"? The Biblical words "die" and "death" do not equate to popping out of existence, or being blotted out of existence. Not only has Tim failed to do a proper word study on the Hebrew word for "die," Tim again ignores the contextual principle. What does "the soul" refer to in this instance? The Hebrew word *nephesh* has a number of meanings: soul, life, person, mind, heart, creature, and so on. Which one fits the context?

Is this saying that a human's "soul" will be permanently annihilated for sinning? Not at all. Does this mean that those sinners are punitively popped out of existence forever? Of course not. In Scripture, as a systematic study of the topic will confirm, human death and dying always refer to the complete breakdown (i.e., division) of the body-and-soul unity (such as when Christ "died" yet later "rose again" — when Christ "died" He did not cease to exist!). When Christ argued against the Sadducees, He refuted their denial of physical resurrection, showing that death is not the permanent end of the person. When I die, my body decays but my soul is immediately present with the Lord (2 Corinthians 5:8). It does not cease to exist.

In Ezekiel 18, the "soul" refers to the person, in reference to his punishment. The passage discusses the complaint of the Hebrews in captivity that they were being unfairly treated by God on account of the sins of their fathers (Ezekiel 18:1–3). God rebukes them. In verse 4 and verse 20, God explains that He holds people accountable for their own sins — not that of their fathers. "The soul (person) who sins shall die" in context means that a person will be held accountable for his own sins, not that of his parents. This is particularly obvious in verse 20. Tim pulled only the first part of the verse out of context to support his point. But the entire verse reads as follows, "The soul who sins shall die. The son shall not bear the guilt of the father, nor the father bear the guilt of the son. The righteousness of the righteous shall be upon himself, and the wickedness of the wicked shall be upon himself" (NKJV).

> *Tim: Also, how could eternal life be a gift (Romans 6:23) if a person already has it?*

Eternal life is not the same as eternal existence. The Bible is clear that all people will exist forever. But only those who have received God's gracious salvation will enjoy eternal life. Tim has set up a straw-man argument. He argues that Christians teach that unbelievers have eternal life, when really the Christian position is that unbelievers have eternal conscious existence apart from the gracious presence of God. They do not have "life" in the sense of enjoying God's presence. Tim also seems to equivocate on the meaning of the word "life." The Bible uses the term in more than one way, with context determining the meaning. More on this below.

> *Tim: It seems that almost all mankind from the beginning of time including most "Christians" believe the first part of the devil's lie that they would not die (Genesis 3:4).*

I'm not aware of any Christians who argue that people, in general, will not die (physically). So this is another straw-man fallacy. The Bible uses the term *life* in at least two ways. "Life" can refer to our physical body's ability to move and breathe — physical life. In this sense, all people are alive if they have a pulse. Alternatively, "life" can refer to our spirit being made right in the eyes of God and enjoying His indwelling presence — spiritual life. Only believers experience this life.

Likewise, the Bible speaks of two "deaths" — one physical, one spiritual (Revelation 20:14). Everyone experiences physical death. But only unbelievers will experience spiritual death in the Lake of Fire. Jesus affirms the two deaths in John 11:25–26. Believers will die (physically), but will live again (physically) — John 11:25. And believers will never die (spiritually) — John 11:26. The two verses would contradict if we did not understand that Jesus is referring to two different types of death. Yet Tim does not seem to be aware of this distinction, and blurs the meaning of "life" in his letter.

> *Tim: Apart from this lie there isn't one test in all the Scriptures that even intimates that the soul is immortal.*

That just isn't true. Matthew 25:46, Mark 3:29, 2 Corinthians 4:18, Galatians 6:8, 2 Thessalonians 1:9, Hebrews 6:2, Jude 1:7, all indicate the eternal existence of human beings either in the presence of God or apart from Him.

> *Tim: As a result "Christianity" developed the most horrible doctrine of eternal torment.*

The doctrine is rightly called Christian, since Christ taught it (Matthew 25:46).

> *Tim: When I have asked pastors if they believe in eternal torment some of them have answered affirmatively with glee in their voices and as I tried to convince them otherwise they have gotten angry.*

I find it hard to believe that men of God would have "glee in their voices" when speaking of eternal torment. I suspect this is an incorrect inference on Tim's part due to his bias. But even if they did, pointing it out is merely an *ad hominem* fallacy. The Bible teaches the doctrine of eternal punishment, even if professing Christians do not have the right attitude in discussing the issue. In any case, they were right to affirm what Jesus taught (Matthew

25:46). By the way, anger is not always wrong (e.g., Matthew 21:12–13). If Tim continued to deny the biblical teaching of eternal torment after these pastors showed him the verses that teach it, then they were right to become angry (and yet they still should not sin) (Ephesians 4:26).

> *Tim: This is almost incomprehensible to me when the Almighty Himself says that He has no pleasure in the death of the wicked (Ezekiel 33:11).*

I'm presuming that this is in reference to what Tim believes to be the inappropriate attitude of pastors talking about eternal punishment. But this is irrelevant to the issue of whether or not the Bible teaches the doctrine of eternal punishment versus annihilationism. To distract from the topic is called a red-herring fallacy. The reason that God has no pleasure in the death of the wicked is because He knows that an eternity in the Lake of Fire awaits them. God would rather the wicked turn from their sin and live — that is what the rest of Ezekiel 33:11 states. Tim referred to only the first part (out of context).

> *Tim: How can anyone believe that Yahweh is love (1 John 4:7–16) and at the same time believe that hideous doctrine?*

Just because God is love doesn't mean that He must always do what Tim thinks He should do. We need to remember that God is also just. It would be completely unjust for God to cause unbelievers to cease to exist, rather than to allow them to pay the penalty for their sin in the Lake of Fire. An honest judge does not let a criminal go free without full punishment. Tim is ignoring a crucial aspect of God (justice) in order to emphasize another aspect of God (love).

Because God is love, He doesn't force people into His presence against their will. He allows them to reap the consequences of their choices. He graciously sustains their existence apart from His loving presence, just as they have asked Him to do their entire lives.

> *Tim: In fact it would not even be* just *if Yahweh made someone suffer for eternity for a few years of sinning.*

Scriptural support? Tim has it backwards; he is trying to tell God what is right, rather than allowing the Scriptures to inform him of what is right.

Since God is an infinite Being, a sin against Him is infinitely immoral and deserves an infinite penalty. As one example of this, Jesus refers to blasphemy against the Holy Spirit as an "eternal sin" (Mark 3:29). Sin against an infinite God requires an infinite penalty. To think that we could pay for our high treason against God by spending a finite amount of time in hell is to reduce God to a finite being — which is heretical.

> *Tim: The false concept of hell is not supported by the Scriptures.*

Jesus affirmed the existence of hell, and had quite a lot to say about it (Matthew 5:22, 29–30, 10:28, 18:9, 23:15, 33; Mark 9:43–47; Luke 12:5).

> *Tim: When you see the word hell expecially [sic] in older versions of the Scriptures it is translated from the Hebrew word* sheol *which simply means the grave or from the Greek word* hades *which also means the grave or from the Greek word* gehenna *which was a place for burning garbage outside of Jerusalem.*

Tim's descriptions of *sheol* and *hades* here are not bad. However, "death" has two chambers — one for believers who are comforted with God, and one for unbelievers who are in agony (Luke 16:25). It is not possible to pass between these two chambers (Luke 16:26). *Hades* normally refers to the chamber that holds the unbelievers (Luke 16:23). The word that Jesus used to describe the eternal destination of unbelievers was *Gehenna,* which alludes to the place outside Jerusalem where garbage and dead animals were burned. It is obvious from context that when Jesus used the word *Gehenna,* He was referring to the eternal hell, because the place outside Jerusalem is not eternal — but Christ's descriptions of hell are eternal. In any case, none of this supports Tim's claim, and so he commits the fallacy of irrelevant thesis.

> *Tim: The* parable *of the rich man and Lazarus (Luke 16:19–31) was not a discussion of the after-life.*

Actually, that's exactly what it is — just read it. By the way, does the Bible say that this is a *parable*?

> *Tim: The Saviour was using the common false presupposition of hell to get across the point. . . .*

So Tim is claiming that Jesus was using a lie to teach people about the truth? (Matthew 12:25–26). This is inconsistent with the nature of God (Titus 1:2). Tim has ignored the consistency principle; he is not interpreting Scripture with Scripture.

> *Tim: . . . that if people didn't listen to Moses and the prophets they wouldn't be persuaded even if a person rose from the dead to tell them.*

That's certainly one of the points that Jesus makes. Why has Tim assumed that Jesus is not also teaching other principles? One of the main points of Genesis 1 is that God is the Creator. Does this mean we are free to ignore the other details? Stories can illustrate more than one truth. Tim has committed "the point is" fallacy.

Many Jews at the time of Christ had the faulty view that wealthy people must have been pleasing in God's eyes since God had blessed them with good finances, and that those who were poor probably deserved it. In the story of Lazarus and the rich man, Jesus refutes this notion. He reminds us that in this present world sometimes the wicked prosper and the righteous suffer — but not in the eternal state.

> *Tim: To believe that this parable was an actual description of the after-life would be ludicrous — as if there could be communication between people in "hell" and heaven.*

If Jesus tells us that this is what the afterlife is like, who is Tim to argue? Even if we were to grant that Jesus took some license in this story, it would not help Tim's point. If the rich man ceases to exist, then he cannot be suffering, nor would he be worried about his living relatives.

> *Tim: There are a few misunderstood texts that are used to support the false presupposition of hell and eternal torment. Matthew 3:12 mentions unquenchable fire. All that means is that it can't be put out until whatever is burning is burned up.*

This is the fallacy of the superfluous distinction. Tim hasn't given any reason for his view of what he thinks "unquenchable" means. His statement is arbitrary, and therefore can be readily dismissed. There is no logical reason to think that unquenchable means anything other than unquenchable. Moreover, Tim has ignored the consistency principle — he's not interpreting Scripture with Scripture. Other passages in Scripture describe the punishment of the wicked as an *eternal fire* (Matthew 18:8, 25:41; Jude 1:21; Revelation 20:10). Tim's view must be rejected because it contradicts these other passages in Scripture.

Further scriptural evidence against Tim's view is found in Mark 9:44, 46, 48 which quotes Isaiah 66:24. These passages speak of those who have transgressed against God and state that "their worm will not die, and their fire will not be quenched." The Isaiah passage is using synonymous parallelism, so clearly the first part must have a similar meaning to the second. Since the first part indicates that the worm does not die, the second part must indicate that the fire is *never* quenched. Tim's interpretation is inconsistent with the parallelism.

> *Tim: Hebrews 12:29 states that "our Elohim is a consuming fire" which means to burn up completely; to annihilate. Sinners are annihilated by Elohim's presence.*

In a violation of the "explicit constrains the implicit" principle, Tim assumes that the metaphor of God as a consuming fire means that He consumes the souls of unbelievers such that they cease to exist. He then uses this idea to reinterpret the clear texts that indicate that unbelievers experience eternal punishment (Matthew 25:46; Jude 7). The statement, "For our God is a consuming fire" is a metaphor. We should not think that the Bible is teaching that God is a physical flame with literal heat that can be put out by water.

Even in the analogy, Tim's argument fails. When logs are "consumed" by a fire, they don't cease to exist. They are merely transformed. Fire changes the properties of what it touches, but it doesn't annihilate anything; the number of atoms remains unchanged. Tim wants to believe that sinners are annihilated by God, but the Scriptures do not teach this. They do teach that unbelievers (and believers) will exist eternally.

Tim seems to have some translational problems as well. *Elohim* is the Old Testament Hebrew word for God. Hebrews 12:29 is written in Greek and uses the term *Theos* — not *Elohim*.

> *Tim: Jude 7 says that Sodom and Gomorrah suffered the punishment of eternal fire. Are they still burning? Of course not.*

Again, Tim exhibits a sloppy reading of the text. Jude 7 does not say that Sodom and Gomorrah "suffered" (past tense). Rather it says that they "are exhibited" [present tense] "as an example in undergoing the punishment of eternal fire." The people of those cities are still today suffering punishment of eternal fire, and since it is eternal, they always will. This passage actually disproves Tim's theology.

Tim seems to have missed the metonymy in this passage. He argues that the cities of Sodom and Gomorrah are not burning, so the fire must not really be eternal. But the names "Sodom and Gomorrah" are used as a figure of speech to refer to their inhabitants. It's just like a newspaper article that says, "According to NASA. . . ." Jude 7 is obviously using metonymy because it says of Sodom and Gomorrah that they "indulged in gross immorality and went after strange flesh." This is not something that a city (in the sense of its location or its buildings) can literally do. It is something that the *people* of those cities did. Jude 7 teaches that the people of Sodom and Gomorrah are now and forever suffering punishment of eternal fire. They did not cease to exist as Tim would like to believe.

> *Tim: Revelation 20:10 says that the devil will be cast into the lake of fire and be tormented day and night. . . . Verse 15 says that [the unrighteous are] thrown into the lake of fire. It doesn't say they will be tormented day and night.*

Revelation 14:10–11 does. Verse 11 states, "And the smoke of their torment goes up forever and ever; they have no rest day and night, those who worship the beast and his image, and whoever receives the mark of his name." So it is not just the devil that is tormented eternally, but all those who have rebelled against our infinite Creator.

> *Tim: The following is a partial list of texts that oppose the doctrines of eternal torment and the immortality of the soul: Psalm 5:6; 6:5; 9:5, 6; 21:9–10; 37:10, 20, 38; 68:2; 73:27;* ***92:7****; 94:23; 97:3 145:20; Proverbs 12:7; 19:9; 21:28; Ecclesiastes 9:10; Isaiah 1:28, 13:9, 26:11, 14, 33:12, 14–16,* ***41:11–12****, 47:14, 60:12; Ezekiel* ***18:4, 20****, 33:11; Malachi* ***4:1, 3****; Matthew* ***10:28****; John 3:15–16; Romans 2:12, 6:23; 2 Thessalonians 1:9; Hebrews 10:27, 12:29; 2 Peter 3:9; 1 John 3:15. (The texts in bold are especially significant).*

None of these passages state that the soul of an unbeliever ceases to exist at some point in time as Tim wants us to believe. And Tim gives no argument as to why he thinks these verses prove his point. Notice that of the 45 verses listed, only 9 are from portions of Scripture that are literal history or epistles. The other 36 are poetic/prophetic passages using not-so-literal language. Although there is nothing wrong with using poetic passages, these must be interpreted in light of the literal passages, not the reverse, as Tim has done. The clear doctrinal teaching is that punishment for unbelievers is eternal (e.g., Matthew 25:46)

The only one of these references that even hints at a person "ceasing to exist" as opposed to perishing or dying, is Isaiah 41:11–12. This passage states, "Behold, all those who are angered at you will be shamed and dishonored; those who contend with you will be as nothing and will perish. You will seek those who quarrel with you, but will not find them, those who war with you will be as nothing and non-existent." Do these verses really teach that the soul ceases to exist?

The synonymous parallelism in the passage is striking, and reminds us that the passage should not be over-literalized. Notice that the passage does not say that unbelievers will "become nothing and non-existent." Rather it says that they will be "*as* nothing and non-existent." That little word makes a big difference. It shows that the author is using a simile — a comparison of two different things using "like" or "as." The passage teaches that unbelievers will be removed from the sight of the righteous in this world to the extent that it is *as if* they did not even exist. But the passage does *not* suggest that their souls are annihilated.

Most of the other passages refer to the death, the perishing, or the destruction of the wicked *in this world*, but not an alleged annihilation in the afterlife. When the body dies, it does not cease to exist. Likewise, the Hebrew word often translated as "perish" or "destroy" is *abad*. It does not indicate lack of existence. In Exodus 10:7, Pharaoh's servants were complaining that Egypt had been "destroyed" (*abad*) by the plagues. But Egypt did not cease to exist. Tim's entire argument seems to be based on an equivocation fallacy; he is equating death with non-existence. Many of the above passages clearly do not support Tim's claim when they are read carefully. Isaiah 13:9 states that the wicked will be exterminated *from the land* — not from existence.

Tim singles out Psalm 92:7, which states, "That when the wicked sprouted up like grass and all who did iniquity flourished, it was only that they might be destroyed forevermore." However, two verses later we read that the wicked will perish and be scattered. People cannot be scattered if they do not exist. Clearly, destruction in this sense is referring to their downfall, the eternal humiliation and punishment brought on by their disobedience to God.

Second Thessalonians 1:9 is also on Tim's list, but a moment's thought shows that the verse actually *refutes* his position. The text states, "These will pay the penalty of eternal destruction, away from the presence of the Lord and from the glory of His power." If "destruction" in this context meant that they would at some point "cease to exist" as Tim believes, then the adverb "eternally" would make no sense. How can a one-time action be happening *eternally*? Obviously, the destruction of unbelievers is a continual separation from the glory of the Lord and lasts forever. That such a separation is eternal is clear in this passage, and utterly refutes Tim's position.

> *Tim: Many preachers especially Jonathan Edwards used and some preachers today are still using the doctrine of eternal torment to scare people into accepting the Saviour.*

Jesus warned people in exactly this way. (Matthew 5:29–30, 10:28, 18:8–9, 25:41, 46; Mark 9:43–48). Pay particular attention to Mark 9:48 because this is where Jesus is warning them that their discomfort in hell will never end: "their worm does not die, and the fire is not quenched."

> *Tim: As a result a great number of people claim to be a follower of the Saviour because they don't want to burn forever in "hell." . . .*

That seems like a pretty good reason to me. Jesus apparently thought so too (Mark 9:43–48; Luke 12:5; Matthew 10:28). Jesus warned people of negative consequences to induce repentance and righteous living (e.g., John 5:14). Tim seems to think that Jesus was wrong to argue that way.

> *Tim: When the true motive a person becomes a follower of the Saviour should be that they have seen a revelation of Yahweh's love. Yahweh does not want people to fellowship with those who are scared of Him. That is a form of force and true love cannot be forced.*

Scriptural support? This is a bifurcation fallacy: "Either we serve God out of love, or out of fear." *Both* are biblical reasons to serve God. We should have a healthy, respectful fear of God (Proverbs 1:7) — particularly when we are in rebellion against Him. Jesus affirmed that we should fear God: "But I will warn you whom to fear: fear the One who, after He has killed, has authority to cast into hell; yes, I tell you, fear Him!" (Luke 12:5).

> *Tim: Because of the doctrine of eternal torment Satan has been very successful in instilling in people a negative concept of the Heavenly Father.*

The reverse is true. Annihilationism is the unbiblical view. And it gives people a negative concept of the Heavenly Father — that He is unjust in allowing unrepentant people to escape their rightful punishment.

> *Tim: I will now quote from your book (page 112) "Since our shortcomings offend His infinite holiness, the punishment must also be infinite. Either we must suffer such a punishment, or else a substitute must endure it in our place." Where is that found in the Bible?*

Romans 3:23, Ecclesiastes 7:20, Isaiah 64:6, 1 John 1:8, 10 (our shortcomings offend).

Revelation 4:8, 1 Isaiah 6:3, Psalm 71:19, 1 Samuel 2:2, Leviticus 11:44, Isaiah 55:9, Hebrews 4:15, Deuteronomy 32:4 (His infinite holiness).

Matthew 25:46, 25:41, Jude 7, Daniel 12:2, Mark 9:43–48, 2 Thessalonians 1:9, Revelation 14:10–11, 20:10, 15, Leviticus 24:19–20, Exodus 21:22–25 (the punishment must also be infinite).

Revelation 20:12,15, Mark 16:16, Hebrews 10:29, Ezekiel 14:10, Hebrews 2:2-3 (either we must suffer such a punishment).

Isaiah 53:6, 1 Peter 3:18, 2 Corinthians 5:12, Leviticus 1:2–3, 1 John 2:2, 4:10 (or else a substitute must endure it in our place).

> *Tim: Going by your rules of logic, if the Saviour suffered eternal torment in our place then He should still be on the cross or burning in "hell."*

Actually, they are God's rules of logic. And Tim isn't using them correctly. An infinite penalty must be paid, since our crime is against the infinitely holy God. We as beings of finite value would take an eternity to pay an infinite penalty. But Jesus is God. His life is of infinite value. Therefore, He was able to pay an infinite penalty by dying once for all (Romans 6:10; Hebrews 7:27, 9:12; 1 Peter 3:18).

> *Tim: When the Saviour cried "My El, My El, why have you forsaken me," He was showing that He was in the same state of mind as everyone who is about to suffer the second death: without any hope of an after-life, which is annihilation.*

This is an arbitrary speculation on Tim's part, and easy to refute from the Scriptures. Jesus was certainly *not* "without any hope of an afterlife." He knew that He had the power to lay down His life and take it up again (John 10:18). He knew that He would be resurrected (Matthew 12:40) and He rebuked the disciples for their lack of faith in His Resurrection (Luke 24:25). What about "My God, my God, why have you forsaken me?" Jesus was quoting Psalm 22.

In summary, we see that Tim's position stems from a very sloppy reading of the Scriptures, hermeneutical fallacies, and errors in reasoning.

Chapter 11

The Age of the Earth

Applying proper principles of hermeneutics, we must conclude that the earth is "young" — approximately 6,000 years old. This number is arrived at by the following reasoning. God created the universe in six days (Genesis 1–2:4; Exodus 20:11). Human beings were made on the sixth day (Genesis 1:26–31). The Bible gives the age when certain patriarchs had children, and does the same for their children (e.g., Genesis 5:3–32). This gives us the span of time between the generations.[1] These all occur in historic narrative sections of Scripture, and therefore require a literal interpretation. Also, timespans between certain other events are provided (e.g., Daniel 9:25). These timespans can be added to give the total timespan between Adam and Christ at roughly 4,000 years.

From other historic records we know that Christ's earthly ministry took place around 2,000 years ago. Only the last step in this calculation depends on any extra-biblical information. And it is undisputed — even critics acknowledge that the earthly ministry of Jesus occurred around 2,000 years ago. Therefore, the total age of the earth is around 6,000 years.

1. Could the children listed in Genesis really be grandchildren or great-grandchildren? In other words, could there be gaps in the genealogies? For the purpose of computing the age of the earth it makes no difference whatsoever because the age of person A is given at the time of the birth of person B regardless of whether any people came in between these two. The possibility of gaps in the genealogies of the Old Testament therefore does not allow for an old-earth; http://www.icr.org/article/4124/.

The scriptural age of the universe is not a popular position today, particularly in academic circles. Most scholars have embraced secular philosophies such as uniformitarianism or naturalism. Such worldviews are not compatible with recent creation. They require billions of years to (allegedly) account for the universe we see today. Christians who have become enamored with secular academia are therefore strongly motivated to read the Bible in such a way as to allow for billions of years. All such attempts violate hermeneutical principles. Let's examine some of the common arguments that people use to claim that Scripture teaches or at least allows for billions of years.

In particular we are going to examine the arguments put forward by Dr. Hugh Ross.[2] He is an astronomer who believes in the big bang, an "old earth" (4.5 billion years old) and an even older universe (13.8 billion years old). He also professes Christianity and argues that the Bible is perfectly compatible with a big bang and an "old earth." My critique of Ross's arguments should not be construed as a personal attack. I've met Dr. Ross in person, and he is quite likeable. The Bible tells us, however, that we are to test doctrine by the standards of Scripture (1 Thessalonians 5:21; Acts 17:11), and we are to cast down arguments that are raised up against the knowledge of God (2 Corinthians 10:5).

I have selected Dr. Ross because he is well known, has written extensively on this topic, and is one of very few old-earth creationists who have even attempted to argue for their position *from Scripture*. Though I don't agree with his reasoning, I commend Ross for at least attempting to deal with the biblical claims instead of simply dismissing them. Most other old-earth creationists admit that the Bible seems to teach a young earth, but they feel compelled to believe otherwise due to scientific considerations. But Ross has argued that the correct interpretation of *Scripture* will lead to a billions-of-years-old earth. This is a hermeneutical claim, and is therefore a great place to apply the biblical principles of interpretation that we have discovered. In that spirit, let us see if Dr. Ross's claims are hermeneutically sound.

Are the Days of Creation Really Days?

In chapter five of his book *Creation and Time*,[3] Dr. Hugh Ross lists nine reasons why he believes that the Scriptures teach that the days of Genesis were not ordinary days, but long periods of time. Let us examine each of these.

2. Dr. Ross's statements are inset in italics throughout this chapter.
3. Hugh Ross, *Creation and Time* (Colorado Springs, CO: NavPress, c1994).

> *The meaning of the word day, of course, is the focal point of the creation time-scale controversy. Does it, or does it not, represent a contradiction between Scripture and science? The answer to that question depends on whether the time period indicated must be a twenty-four-hour day or whether it can refer to something like millions of years.*

Already we can see some problems. The phrase "a contradiction between Scripture and science" is not meaningful because science is a conceptual tool, not a proposition. Scripture is propositional of course. But science is a procedure that people use to construct propositional statements about nature. His choice of words suggests that Ross has committed the reification fallacy in thinking that "science" (a concept) has an opinion on the age of the earth — something that only a person can have.

It would have been clearer for Dr. Ross to ask whether there is a conflict between Scripture and *what most scientists believe*. Then we would be correctly comparing propositions with propositions. But that would expose Ross's ultimate standard (the opinions of the majority of scientists) for the fallible standard that it is. It would become obvious that he is comparing an inerrant text with the mere opinions of men — a fact that Ross apparently wants to conceal.

Giving Dr. Ross the benefit of the doubt, perhaps he refers to science as the body of knowledge obtained by the scientific process, rather than the process itself. Essentially, the question becomes, "Is what we know from science compatible with what the Bible teaches?" But this merely replaces one fallacy with another. It begs the question. What we "know" about the universe depends greatly on our understanding of history. And for Christians, our view of history should be largely informed by what the Bible teaches. Only by rejecting the plain teaching of Genesis can Ross claim that the secular scientists have rightly interpreted the evidence by which they conclude billions of years. He cannot then use such opinions as a basis for rejecting the plain teaching of Genesis without reasoning in a circle.

1. A day — like a thousand years?

> *The length of God's days. The same author of Genesis (Moses) wrote Psalm 90:4, "For a thousand years in your sight are like a day that has just gone by, or like a watch (four hours) in the night." Moses*

> *seems to state that just as God's ways are not our ways (Isaiah 55:9), God's days are not our days.*

Several fallacies occur here. First, Dr. Ross has completely disregarded the contextual principle. Is Psalm 90:4 commenting on creation, Genesis, or the days of creation? Not at all. The first several verses of this chapter contrast the eternality of God with the short lifespan of man. To apply the verse as if it were addressing the days of creation is a terrible distortion.

Second, Ross has ignored the genre principle and the "explicit constrains the implicit principle." Psalm 90 is poetic literature. It is not historical narrative, and cannot be used to alter the meaning of the literal/historical passages in Genesis. On the contrary, the literal historical passages teach us how to understand the poetry. The explicit and clear teaching of Genesis 1 guides our interpretation of the Psalms — not the reverse. Genesis is foundational to other books of the Bible because it records the earliest history and introduces the words and phrases used in later books. It is similar to the way a legal contract defines its terms at the start — like "Richard Smith, hereinafter called 'Employee.' " Later uses of the term must agree with previous usage.

Third, Ross engages in linguistic relativism, which is self-refuting. Namely, he has suggested that words have different meanings when spoken by God than when used by human beings — "God's days are not our days" he said. But communication would be impossible if words meant different things to different people. If words have different meanings to God, then when He says, "you shall not steal" (Exodus 20:15), it might really mean, "Eat more pancakes!"[4]

Interpreting the verse properly in its poetic context, we find that the passage means that God does not experience time as we do. This is because He is beyond time — He is eternal. Therefore, when God does use time words, it is always for our benefit and to be understood in the normal way. Anything else would lead to nonsense.

2. The Hebrew word — **yom**

> *The Hebrew word yom, translated day, may be used (and is) in biblical Hebrew, as it is in modern English, to indicate any of three time periods: (a) sunrise to sunset, (b) sunset to sunset, (c) a segment*

4. See *Creation Basics and Beyond* (Dallas, TX: Institute for Creation Research, 2013), p. 33.

of time without any reference to solar days (anywhere from weeks to a year to several years to an age or epoch).

Dr. Ross does not state his conclusion. But the implication is that he thinks that this implies (or at least allows for) the days *of creation* to be long periods of time. (If this were not his conclusion, then his statements are logically irrelevant.) But in leaping to this conclusion Ross has violated several principles of hermeneutics and logic.

For one, he has committed the fallacy of the unwarranted expansion of an expanded semantic field. This happens when people ignore the contextual principle and instead select a meaning of a word that does not fit the immediate context. The question Ross is supposed to be addressing is, "What are the days of creation?" not "What is the total range of meanings of 'day' in various contexts?" That the word *yom* might mean a period of time longer than 24 hours in some contexts does not remotely establish that it can mean such in Genesis 1 unless the context is considered. So we must ask, "Can the Hebrew word for 'day' (*yom*) mean a long period of time *in the context of Genesis 1*?" The answer is clearly "no" for the following reasons.

First, each of the days of Genesis 1 is bounded by (and even defined as) one evening and one morning (e.g., Genesis 1:5, 8, 13). A long period of time would not be. Second, God defines "day" as the light portion of the cycle in Genesis 1:5. This is clearly "day" in the sense of "daytime" and could not possibly be an epoch of time. Third, day is contrasted with night in Genesis 1:5. While we might use an English idiom such as "back in my father's day," we would not say, "back in my father's night."[5] Fourth, each of the days of creation is used with a number — "a second day," "a third day," and so on. Such sequential enumeration is always indicative of ordinary days in all biblical historical narrative, and is always translated as such.

Fifth, we note the *lack* of indicators in Genesis of the metaphorical use of *yom* as a long period of time. Just as evening, morning, night, and numbers in context with *yom* imply ordinary days, so prepositional phrases like "the day of the Lord" (e.g., Zephaniah 2:3) may indicate a longer period of time usage. And yet, we find no such phrase in Genesis 1. Moreover,

5. The English idiom "back in my father's day" is not used in Hebrew. Scripture only refers to the days (plural) of Noah, Lot, etc. This is literal usage because it really does refer to the days (albeit many of them) in which those people lived.

non-literal usage of *yom* occurs primarily in poetic literature — it would be unusual to find it in historical narrative.

Sixth, we note the that the plural form of the word *yamim* — translated as *days* — is never used to denote "long periods of time." Rather, it always refers to ordinary days in historical literature. Yet this is precisely the word used in Exodus 20:11 — "For in six *days* the LORD made the heavens and the earth, the sea and all that is in them, and rested on the seventh day. . . ." *Yamim* does not allow for a day-age interpretation.

Additionally, Dr. Ross has committed the logical fallacy of the undistributed middle (see appendix B). This is clear when we restate his argument as a standard syllogism:

> 1. Some instances of *yom* are long periods of time. (Some Y are P.)
> 2. The days of Genesis 1 are instances of *yom*. (All D are Y.)
> 3. Therefore, the days of Genesis 1 are long periods of time. (All/some D are P.)

The argument is fallacious because the middle term (instances of *yom*) is not distributed in either premise — it does not refer to all its members. Therefore, there is no necessary link between the major and minor term (the days of Genesis 1, and long periods of time).

3. Testable chronology

> *A study of other chronologies in the Bible reveals a common characteristic: They record sequences that are both significant and discernible to the reader. The timing and order are important because they show the careful unfolding of God's plans and affirm His control. The discernibility provides a tool for validating the message of God's spokesman.*

Ross's argument here is vague. But it seems that he is suggesting that all temporal sequences given in the Bible can be used to test or validate the accuracy of God's Word. According to Ross, God lists specific timing of events so that we can later verify their accuracy, confirming that the message indeed comes from God.

> *Examples from my own theological perspective include: Jeremiah 31:38–40 (a prediction, now fulfilled, of the location and construc-*

> *tion sequence of Jerusalem's nine suburbs during the second rebirth of Israel as a nation); Daniel 9:24–27 (a timetable for the rebuilding of Jerusalem, the Messiah's coming and death, the destruction of Jerusalem, years of desolation, and final restoration); and Daniel 11:2–35 (a prediction, since fulfilled, of the chronology of victories, defeats, and intrigues of various kings and kingdoms of the Greek and Roman eras). The supernatural accuracy of such chronologies not only proves their inspiration but also gives assurance for today and hope for tomorrow.*

Regardless of the fidelity of Dr. Ross's interpretation of these prophecies, we would not dispute that fulfilled prophecy is a powerful confirmation of the authority and divine nature of the Bible. But the days of creation are not prophecy. They are recorded history. Ross violates the genre principle, treating the historic narrative in Genesis as if it were prophetic. Historic narrative was not given to show future events whose fulfillment could be observed. Rather, historical narrative was given to show past events which cannot be observed in the present.

> *For the creation days, long time periods during which increasingly complex life-forms were created, indeed, are verifiable and essential to validate the supernatural accuracy of the writer's statements. But if all creation were completed in six twenty-four-hour days, the most sophisticated measuring techniques available, or even foreseeably available, would be totally incapable of discerning the sequence of events. Thus a major use of the chronology would be thwarted.*

Dr. Ross commits several fallacies here. First, he commits the hasty generalization fallacy. Ross explains that some sequences of events recorded in prophetic literature can later be observationally verified as they occur. But then, in a remarkable leap in logic, Ross concludes that this must be true of *all* sequences of events in Scripture, and hence must apply to Genesis 1 as well. Such a generalization is completely unwarranted. We can easily find many sequences in Scripture that have never been verified by any modern "measuring techniques." Consider the genealogies and ages listed in Genesis 5. Have any of these ages been verified by modern scientific methods? Is there any way such ages could be measured in the foreseeable future? In fact, none of the chronologies in the historical narrative passages in Scripture can be observed today.

Ross treats age like a substance that can be measured by scientific means. But age is a *concept* of history, not a physical object that can be measured empirically. Dr. Ross has committed the fallacy of reification. Moreover, he has conflated empirical/observational science with forensic/origins science. Furthermore, Ross simply gets his facts wrong when he states "long time periods during which increasingly complex life-forms were created, indeed, are verifiable. . . ." How exactly were long time periods verified? What experiment allows us to observe these alleged long time periods, or perform tests on them? Such ages are *assumed* — not observed. Science — empirical science that enables us to create computers and put men on the moon — necessarily involves observation and repeated experimentation. Speculating on what happened in the past does not fall under this category.

Ross violates the inerrancy principle in stating that verifiable long time periods are "essential to validate the supernatural accuracy of the writer's statements." Essential? Is Ross saying that we cannot know that the Bible really is the Word of God unless its claims are verified by the methods of observational science? Many of the Bible's claims cannot be verified by observational science. Repeated observations and experiments in the present cannot confirm the virgin birth, the Resurrection of Christ, any of Christ's miracles, or even mundane things like the ages of the patriarchs. Is Ross really suggesting that we cannot know for sure that these sections are supernaturally inspired since they cannot be validated by science?

Dr. Ross violates the text principle as well. The Bible nowhere teaches that God created increasingly complex organisms as the creation week unfolded. On the contrary, fruit trees are highly complex but were made on day 3. If Ross wants to use the secular timescale as validation of the biblical order of events, then he's got a problem because they do not match. The secular timescale puts fish before fruit trees, reptiles before birds, and stars before the earth. Genesis 1 is contrary to all of these.

There is no suggestion anywhere in Scripture that God listed any historical chronology for the purpose of being verified later by any sort of scientific method. None.

4. Unusual syntax

> *Looking at the word-for-word translation of the Hebrew text, one finds this phraseology: "and was evening and was morning day X." . . .*

> *If "day X" were intended as the noun complement for the one evening and morning together, the linking verb should appear just once, in plural form (as the King James Version renders it): "And the evening and the morning were the Xth day." . . . This syntactic ambiguity does not constitute proof. However, it does suggest that "day" here is to be taken in some unusual manner.*

This is the fallacy of appeal to ignorance. Essentially Ross asks, "What is the reason for the particular syntax in Genesis 1?" He doesn't know. So he concludes that it "suggests that 'day' here is to be taken in some unusual manner." But that doesn't follow logically. And Ross presents no evidence to support it. Why would we automatically assume a non-standard meaning for *yom* on the basis of "unusual syntax"?

The fact that Dr. Ross doesn't know why the text is worded as it is does not give him the logical warrant to make up a reason. God had a very specific reason for wording the text as He did. The meaning would be subtly altered if it were reworded as Ross suggests. "The evening and the morning were the second day" does indicate ordinary days, but that's all. The biblical phrase "and there was evening and there was morning, a second day" (Genesis 1:8; NASB) indicates not only that the evening and morning constitute that second day, but also that they happened. There *was* evening. There *was* morning. These occurred. This is more powerful than Ross's suggested alternative.

There is not the slightest hint that these are to be anything but ordinary days. In fact, the association of evening and morning with the days of creation is one of the contextual reasons we know that these days are genuine days.

5. The uniqueness of the seventh day

> *Of the first six creation days Moses wrote: "There was evening, and there was morning — the Xth day." This wording indicates that each of the first six creation days had a beginning and an ending.*

Actually, the wording indicates that each of the days had a *morning* and an *evening,* not merely a beginning and an ending. Dr. Ross can't accept that the days are marked by one literal morning and one literal evening because that would only be possible with ordinary days. Therefore, he takes evening and morning in a metaphorical sense to mean ending and beginning. However, the Hebrew words for morning and evening are never used that way in any biblical historic narrative. Ross has subtly substituted his alternatives for evening and morning without making any argument for it. Very slippery, Dr. Ross!

> *However, no such wording is attached to the seventh creation day, neither in Genesis 1–2 nor anywhere else in the Bible. Given the parallel structure marking the creation days, this distinct change in form for the seventh day strongly suggests that this day has (or had) not yet ended.*

Dr. Ross's argument in standard form is:

1. If the seventh day had a recorded evening and morning, then it has ended.
2. The seventh day does not have a recorded evening and morning.
3. Therefore, it has not ended.

The argument is the fallacy of denying the antecedent (see appendix B). Just because the evening and morning are not mentioned on the seventh day does not mean that it didn't have one. From a hermeneutics perspective, Ross's fallacy is the "argument from silence." Just because something isn't mentioned in the Scriptures doesn't mean it doesn't exist or didn't happen. The third Wednesday after creation is not mentioned in Scripture, but we should not conclude that there was no such day.

Moreover, the fallacious argument proves too much. For argument's sake, let's accept Dr. Ross's interpretation of evening and morning to be an ending and beginning. Ross argues that the seventh day is still continuing because no evening (ending) is mentioned. But also, no morning (beginning) is mentioned. Therefore, by Ross's reasoning, the seventh day has not yet begun. But this refutes his belief that we are currently living in the seventh day.

Is the seventh day different? Yes — qualitatively, but not quantitatively. For one, it's not a "creation day" as Ross falsely labels it. Rather, it is a day of rest (Genesis 2:2–3). It was the first day of rest, and a day that God blessed and set apart from all other days (Exodus 20:11).

> *Further information about the seventh day is given in Psalm 95 and Hebrews 4. In these passages we learn that God's day of rest continues.*

Ross asserts that Psalm 95 and Hebrews 4 teach that "God's day of rest continues." But neither text states this. Hebrews 4:4 quotes Genesis 2:2, which mentions God resting on the seventh day, but it does not even hint that the day continues until now. Rather, both Psalm 95 and Hebrews 4 affirm that there remains a "rest" that God's people may enter into — not a "day of rest." Note that only the people of God may enter God's rest according to Hebrews 4:2–3, 9. But if the "rest" were a long age corresponding to the present time, then everyone would be a part of it. Obviously, Hebrews 4 refers to a spiritual rest that is analogous in some ways to God's resting on the seventh day.

> *According to this passage, the seventh day of the creation week carries on through the centuries, from Adam and Eve, through Israel's development as a nation, through the time of Christ's earthly ministry, through the early days of the church, and on into future years. King David in Psalm 95:7–11 also refers to God's seventh day of rest as ongoing.*

In a blatant violation of the text principle, Ross asserts that Psalm 95 teaches that God's seventh day of rest is ongoing. In fact, Psalm 95 does not so much as mention the seventh day, or a "day of rest." Ross just doesn't seem to be reading the biblical text carefully at all. He seems to assume that since God's rest continues, so the day of rest continues. This is the fallacy of affirming the consequent: 1. If the day continued, then the rest would continue. 2. The rest continues. 3. Therefore the day continues.

The silliness of Ross's blunder can be exposed by analogy. Suppose I said, "Thursday, I did laundry and worked on the car. Friday, I worked on my taxes all day. Saturday I rested. And today, I'm still resting." Would that imply that today is still Saturday?

> *From these passages we gather that the seventh day of Genesis 1 and 2 represents a minimum of several thousand years and a maximum that is open ended (but finite). It seems reasonable to conclude then, given the parallelism of the Genesis creation account, that the first six days may also have been long time periods.*

This struck me as remarkably inconsistent. Dr. Ross has just made the case that the seventh day is long because it is referenced so *differently* from the other days. Now he argues that the other days are probably long periods too, given their *similarity* to the seventh day.

> *Supporting evidence for the seventh day as an ongoing period of rest from creating comes from John 5:16–18. Here, Jesus defended His healing on the Sabbath by saying that God, His Father, "is always at his work to this very day, and I too am working."*

It is unclear why Dr. Ross thinks that this verse supports his view. God is always working. But His work of the creation of the physical universe ended by the seventh day. He continues to rest from His work of creation, but this doesn't remotely suggest that every day is the seventh day. If it did, then we shouldn't work ever, since work is forbidden on the Sabbath Day (Exodus 20:8–11).

> *The fossil record provides further confirmation of an ongoing seventh day. . . .*

Here we have a great example of the two-book fallacy.[6] Ross attempts to interpret the inerrant text of Scripture according to sinful man's fallible understanding of a cursed world.

6. The events of the sixth day

Dr. Ross argues that too many events happened on the sixth day for it to be an ordinary day. This is a violation of the "explicit constrains the implicit" principle. The length of each of the specific events on day 6 is not recorded. But the text does give the length of the sixth day — it was a day, as bounded by evening and morning (Genesis 1:31). The explicit information — that this occurred on the sixth day — should be used to constrain the implicit time of the events (their sum was no more than 24 hours).

> *[On the sixth day] First, God planted a garden in Eden, making "all kinds of trees to grow out of the ground."*

Yes. And there is no reason to think that this supernatural creation by God took any "normal" length of time. God can do things quickly that would take time or never happen in nature. Jesus turned water into wine essentially instantaneously. Likewise, the planting of the Garden may have taken

6. http://www.icr.org/article/two-book-fallacy/.

no time at all. To assume that all processes must happen through slow-and-gradual naturalistic rates is the fallacious assumption of uniformitarianism.[7]

> *Then Adam, after receiving instructions, worked and cared for the Garden of Eden.*

Where does the biblical text say that "Adam worked and cared for the Garden of Eden"? The text only says that God placed Adam in the Garden to [for the purpose of] cultivate and keep it. The Bible does not say that Adam began working immediately. Even if he did, the Bible does not say for how long. So there is no reason to think that any time elapsed here. So far (including the planting of the Garden) we are up to a total minimum time of zero (or negligible).

And what about the instructions Adam received from God? Only one is recorded. "From any tree of the garden you may eat freely; but from the tree of the knowledge of good and evil you shall not eat, for in the day that you eat from it you will surely die" (Genesis 2:16–17). How long did it take God to give this instruction? It takes only about ten seconds to read these words out loud at a relaxed pace. This brings our minimum time required for the events of the sixth day up to a total of ten seconds. Perhaps God gave Adam other instructions on cultivating the garden — though the text does not say this. This might add a few minutes. But there is no evidence of any lengthy conversations in Genesis 2.

> *After that, he carried out his assignment from God to name all the animals (the nephesh creatures — i.e., all the birds and mammals).*

Actually, Adam only had to name the birds, the cattle, and the "beasts of the field," which is a small subset of the *nephesh* (living) creatures. Nonetheless, this is the one event on the sixth day that probably did take actual time. But would it take more than a day? First, the biblical answer. According to the "explicit constrains the implicit principle," we know that it took less than a day for Adam to name all the animals. It is a hermeneutical fallacy to argue that the biblical timescale must be adjusted simply because we don't think all that could be done in one day. It's no different from arguing that Jesus really took a long time to turn water into wine, since we all know that wine takes time to ferment.

7. http://www.icr.org/article/8165/.

So even if we didn't have the details, we know from Scripture that Adam took less than a day to name the animals. But we do have some details. Adam didn't have to name fish or any insects since these are not classified as "beasts of the field." Nor are amphibians, and so these would not have been counted either. This leaves around 11,000 known species. But not all of these are "beasts of the field." We don't know the exact number, but it would be less.

Moreover, the Bible nowhere says that Adam had to name each species. The Bible doesn't even use the word "species." It does use "kind" on many occasions. "Kind" seems to represent the reproductive limit on an organism — different kinds are biologically unrelated (e.g., Genesis 6:19–20). Breeding experiments have shown that "kind" often matches up closely with the genus or family levels of our modern taxonomic system. If Adam named each kind, then this lowers the number to around 2,000 to 3,000. This is a fairly generous upper limit, because Adam may have named only groups of kinds rather than individual kinds — for example: large birds, small birds, large mammals, small mammals. That's probably an unrealistic lower limit. The point is that the true number is likely much less than 2,000.

So how long would it take? The process was efficient since Adam didn't have to find or gather the animals; Genesis 2:19 states that God brought the animals to Adam. And Adam in his unfallen state would have been able to focus on his task most effectively. Even given the upper limit of 3,000 animals, and if Adam named an animal every five seconds or so, this would take just over four hours to name them all — perhaps five if he took breaks. This again would be an upper limit. The point is that this can easily be done within a single day, just as the Bible teaches.

> *In the process Adam discovered that none of these creatures was a suitable helper and companion for him. Apparently Adam had sufficient interaction with the plants and animals of the garden to realize that something was missing from his life.*

Does the text say that Adam discovered that none of the animals "was a suitable helper and companion for him?" No. It merely states that they were not suitable. Whether or not Adam realized this, the text does not say. Again, Dr. Ross has pulled more from the Bible than what it really teaches. Even if Adam did realize that none of the animals were suitable for him, there is no reason to think that such a realization took a long time. Perhaps the animals came to Adam in male-female pairs. If so, it would quickly become obvious to Adam that he did not have such a companion.

> *Next, God put Adam into a deep sleep, performed an operation and, after Adam awoke, introduced him to the newly created Eve.*

And how long did this take? The text doesn't say, other than we know it happened all on the sixth day, which from context was an ordinary day. It doesn't take long to fall asleep, and only seconds to wake up. To introduce a person takes only seconds. So there is no problem with those all happening within a few minutes. How long does it take to turn a rib into a woman? We have no basis for comparison. It's something only God can do, and He only did it once. But God made Adam from the dust apparently rapidly. So there is no reason to believe that the creation of Eve took significant time.

> *Adam's exclamation on seeing Eve is recorded in Genesis 2:23 as happa'am [sic]. This expression is usually translated as "now at length" (see also Genesis 29:34–35, 30:20, 46:30; Judges 15:3), roughly equivalent to our English expression "at last."*

Does Adam's response suggest that the events took longer than a day? Dr. Ross thinks so. But even if we accepted his dubious translation of *ha pa'am* as "at last" or "now at length," does this imply longer than a day? When I've had a hard day at work, and it is finally time to go home, I might say to myself, "At last!" But that doesn't mean I've been continuously working for more than a day. Again, Ross violates the "explicit constrains the implicit" principle in using the unclear amount of time for the creation of Eve to modify the clear amount of time given in Genesis 1. It's hermeneutically backwards.

Moreover, *ha pa'am* is never translated "at last" or "now at length" anywhere in the KJV, NASB, NKJV, or ASV. It is the same Hebrew phrase used in Genesis 18:32 when Abraham asks God "yet but this once" to withhold judgment on Sodom for the sake of ten righteous people. Did Abraham's request come after a long period of time in excess of a day? No, it happened in a single afternoon (Genesis 18:1). So the same phrase in the similar context of Genesis 2:23 certainly does not imply long ages. It seems that the KJV, NASB, ASV, and NKJV rightly translate the phrase "This *is now* bone of my bones. . . ." (In fact, the literal meaning of *pa'am* has the idea of an event occurring at a "point in time," such as "now" or "at that instant in time" — see Genesis 33:3, 43:10, 46:30; Exodus 10:17, 23:17; Leviticus 4:6; Deuteronomy 16:16; Judges 6:39; 1st Samuel 18:11; etc.)

> *Still later on the sixth day Adam and Eve received instructions from God concerning their responsibilities in managing the plants, animals, and resources of the earth, a lengthy communication, one can imagine. Altogether, many weeks', months', or even years' worth of activities took place in this latter portion of the sixth day.*

Where does the biblical text say that God had a "lengthy communication" with Adam and Eve on the sixth day? There is no such text. Ross suggests that "one can imagine" a lengthy communication — but imagination that deviates from the text's plain meaning is no substitute for proper exegesis. All the Bible states regarding God's instructions after the creation of Eve on the sixth day are recorded in Genesis 1:28–30. God told them "Be fruitful and multiply, and fill the earth, and subdue it; and rule over the fish of the sea and over the birds of the sky and over every living thing that moves on the earth. Behold, I have given you every plant yielding seed that is on the surface of all the earth, and every tree which has fruit yielding seed; it shall be food for you; and to every beast of the earth and to every bird of the sky and to every thing that moves on the earth which has life, I have given every green plant for food."

How long did it take for God to say all that to Adam and Eve? It takes me about 30 seconds to say aloud those verses at a casual pace. Where on earth does Ross get the idea that "lengthy communication" taking many weeks, months, or even years(!) took place? Not from Scripture. Ross invents an imaginary conversation between Adam, Eve, and God that lasts for months but is not found in the Bible, so that he can then say that day 6 was not an ordinary day. This isn't exegesis at all. It's distorting the Scriptures — plain and simple.

7. The day in Genesis 2:4

> *This verse [Genesis 2:4], a summary statement for the creation account, in the literal Hebrew reads, "These are the generations of the heavens and the earth when they were created in the day of their*

> *making." Here the word* day *refers to all six creation days (and the creation of the universe that took place prior to the first creative day). Obviously, then, this is a period longer than twenty-four hours.*

The conclusion of Dr. Ross's enthymeme is that the days of Genesis are therefore longer than 24-hour days. But this does not follow logically. Once again, Dr. Ross has ignored the contextual principle, resulting in the fallacy of the unwarranted expansion of the expanded semantic field. That *yom* can mean a period of time longer than a day in some contexts (Ross argues this is the case for Genesis 2:4) does not imply that it can mean that in other contexts.

From a logical perspective, Ross has (again) committed the fallacy of the undistributed middle.

> (1) Some instances of *yom* are long periods of time, e.g., Genesis 2:4.
>
> (2) The days of creation in Genesis 1 are instances of *yom*.
>
> (3) Therefore, the days of creation in Genesis 1 are long periods of time.

The argument is still logically invalid as it was in Dr. Ross's point number 2.

In addition, there is no obvious reason to suppose that even Genesis 2:4 is not an ordinary day — the first day when God created the heavens and the earth. It's not necessary to assume that Genesis 2:4 must refer to the entire creation week. But even if it did, this cannot be used as rational justification for taking the days in Genesis 1 to be long periods of time, since their context excludes such an interpretation.

> *Hebrew lexicons verify that the word for generations (*toledah*) refers to the time between a person's birth and parenthood or to an arbitrarily longer time span. In Genesis 2:4 the plural form, generations, is used, indicating the multiple generations have passed.*

Ultimately, lexicons are not the final authority on what a Bible word means — rather, its usage in the context of Scripture, by God Himself, is what is ultimately authoritative.[8] But Ross does no careful word study on the noun "generations" (*toledoth*), so his conclusions are arbitrary and capricious. The Hebrew word *toledoth* has a number of meanings, but its most basic and

8. www.icr.org/article/5684.

literal meaning is identified by how it is used in Scripture, including how its root verb is used in Scripture. The root verb of *toledoth* is the Hebrew verb *yalad*, which means to bear or deliver in the sense of childbirth, i.e., to generate, to produce, to give issuance to.

But as usual, Ross picks a definition that is incompatible with the context of the passage.[9] This again is the fallacy of the unwarranted expansion of an expanded semantic field. *Toledoth* can refer to (human) "generations," but it can also mean "account," "birth," "descent," "history," or "proceedings." Of all those possible meanings, the only one that definitely cannot apply to Genesis 2:4 is "human generations" because there were no humans when the universe was first created. Yet this is the very definition that Ross arbitrarily picks. Genesis 2:4 tells us that the preceding verses are the "account" or "history" of the heavens and earth, the "proceedings" of their "birth." Ross here has also violated the translation principle in falsely assuming that *toledoth* implies that multiple generations have come and gone.

8. Biblical references to the antiquity of the earth

> *In describing the eternity of God's existence, several Bible writers often compare it to the longevity of the mountains or the "foundations of the earth." The figures of speech used in Psalm 90:2–6, Proverbs 8:22–31, Ecclesiastes 1:3–11, and Micah 6:2 all depict the immeasurable antiquity of God's presence and plans.*

In a clear violation of the "explicit constrains the implicit," Ross attempts to use poetic passages to modify the meaning of the clear historical narrative. All the passages he lists are from poetic or prophetic-poetic literature. They invoke non-literal figures of speech. The faithful reader is supposed to interpret these passages in light of the clear historic narrative, not the reverse.

Moreover, none of these passages even hint that the creation days were longer than 24 hours each, or that the world is billions of years old. All these references are perfectly compatible with an earth that is a few thousand years old. We need to remember that although a 6,000-year-old earth is often called a "young earth" position today, 6,000 years is really very old. It is only in contrast to the secular view of billions of years that thousands of

9. God's command in 2 Timothy 2:15 indicates that we must study how God uses a given word in its biblical context to properly understand its meaning.

years could be considered "young." The earth is old — thousands of years old! And these Scriptures confirm it.

> *The brief span of 3000-year terrestrial history (in the context of the wisdom literature) seems an inadequate metaphor for God's eternality.*

The metaphor "seems inadequate" *to whom*? Only secular thinking would consider 3,000 years a "brief span" of terrestrial history. Just think of how this United States has changed in the last 100 years. Ross asserts that 3,000 years just isn't a good metaphor for the eternality of God. But he thinks the concept of billions of years is. Why? Neither thousands nor billions of years is even one percent of eternity. Nor are trillions, or quadrillions of years, or even a googolplex of years. Dr. Ross's assumption that billions of years are sufficient, but not thousands, is totally arbitrary. Really, any timescale that significantly exceeds a typical human lifespan can seem like eternity from our perspective.

> *The fact that the Bible does consider the antiquity of the founding of the earth a suitable metaphor for God's eternality suggests the biblical view of a very ancient earth.*

The earth is very ancient. It is the historical narrative passages that tell us how ancient — thousands of years. Ross uses the implicit to re-interpret the explicit — a hermeneutical fallacy. From a logical perspective, Ross's argument is completely arbitrary. He has assumed that billions of years count as ancient, but that thousands of years do not. But he gives no biblical or logical support for this.

9. More biblical references to the antiquity of the earth

> *Habakkuk 3:6 directly declares that the mountains are "ancient" and the hills are "age-old." In 2 Peter 3:5, the heavens (the stars and the universe) are said to have existed "long ago."*

We are tempted to ask, "So? How does this in any way support the notion of *billions* of years?" The hills *are* ancient — thousands of years old. The heavens and earth have existed from long ago — they are far older than any human being. These verses do not even hint at the billions of years that Ross needs to support his position. Ross again has used the implicit to interpret the explicit — a severe violation of hermeneutical principles.

Dr. Ross continues in his next chapter to argue for long creation "days." His first three reasons in that chapter are really an attempt to justify eisegesis — interpreting the text in light of modern opinions of science. We will deal with those claims in the next chapter, because it is somewhat off-topic here.

10. The vastness of the universe

Dr. Ross lists several verses (Genesis 22:17; Jeremiah 33:22; and Hebrews 11:12) that describe the humanly uncountable number of stars, and then argues that the universe must be very vast. Although I agree with his conclusion, his argument doesn't actually support it. A large number of stars doesn't automatically imply a *vast* universe because the Bible does not tell us how big stars are or how much space is in between them. For example, the number of atoms in a cup of water is also humanly uncountable; but does this mean that the cup of water is "vast"? Nonetheless, I do think there is scriptural support for a vast universe (e.g., Isaiah 55:8–9; Job 22:12; Psalm 36:5, 103:11), but Ross did not list these verses. In any case, we all agree that the universe is vast. But that doesn't make it "old."

Dr. Ross concludes that the universe is larger than 56,000 light years. I won't list his argument since I agree with the result. He then makes the leap to arguing that the universe must therefore be old:

> *Since no material in our universe moves more rapidly than the velocity of light, and since the velocity of light must remain constant for life to exist (see pages 97–99), we can conclude that the biblically stated* minimum *age for the universe is 56,000 years.*

First, Dr. Ross again violates the "explicit constrains the implicit" principle. The Bible explicitly teaches that God created the universe in six days — Exodus 20:11. It implicitly teaches that the universe is big, but it doesn't say how big (e.g., Isaiah 55:8–9). The text of Scripture certainly doesn't teach anything about 56,000 light-years. But even if it did, this is a size — not an age. In a leap of logic, Dr. Ross decides that the universe must also be 56,000 years old. But this just doesn't follow.

Presumably, Ross is referring to the "distant starlight problem," though he doesn't provide enough details for us to know for certain. The idea is that since light takes a time of one year to travel a distance of one light year, and since we see stars that are more than 56,000 light-years away (implying that the light has traveled from there to here), the universe must be older than 56,000 years. Aside from the arbitrary assumptions of naturalism and uniformitarianism involved in such an argument, there are a number of scientific problems with it as well. Not the least of these is that it assumes that the one-way speed of light is defined to be isotropic (the same in all directions). I have dealt with the distant starlight issue in other literature.[10] The point here is that the argument is scientific in nature — not biblical!

Dr. Ross's argument is no different from an argument against the Resurrection of Jesus on the basis that modern operational science has never documented resurrection from the dead.[11] From all we understand about observational science today, it is not possible for a person to walk on water, or to turn water instantly into wine. Should we then interpret the historical narrative portions of Scripture that teach such things as mere allegory? Ross's argument here is pure eisegesis — not exegesis. It's not surprising that this argument follows after his extended attempt to rationalize eisegetical readings of Scripture (which we will address in the next chapter).

Some might retort, "But the Resurrection of Jesus was supernatural, as were his miracles of turning water into wine, and walking on water." But can't (indeed, must not) the same be said of the creation of the universe from nothing? It is absurd to interpret the supernatural in light of what is possible in the natural. Dr. Ross seems to anticipate this point when he states the following:

> *Note: God certainly has the power to construct the universe at a more rapid rate than the velocity of light, but the physical evidence indicates that He did not do so (astronomer's observations of the past, see pages 97–100).*

It's an amusing argument: apparently we *know* that God didn't do a miraculous work here because of physical evidence. But how can we use physical evidence to discount the possibility of a miracle? A supernatural action by God is — by definition — something that would not happen by the ordinary principles of nature. So how can the ordinary principles of nature

10. https://answersingenesis.org/astronomy/starlight/anisotropic-synchrony-convention-distant-starlight-problem/. See also *Creation Basics and Beyond*, chapter 47.
11. Cases of momentary "clinical death" aside, we have not shown a scientific way to reanimate a person who has been dead for days.

exclude the possibility of something beyond them? It's a bit like arguing that all the evidence inside a house proves that there is nothing outside the house. Ross lists what he believes to be evidence that God did not use supernatural means to get light from galaxies to earth in pages 97–100. But these all boil down to circular reasoning and are summed up in his conclusion on page 100:

> *Because of the time it takes for light to travel from the stars, galaxies, and other sources to the astronomers' telescopes, their telescopes operate like time machines into the past. Astronomers can literally measure the heavens to see what God did in the past.*

So how does Ross know that God used natural means to get the light from there to here? He says this is because he can see what God did in the past, since light takes a long time to get from distant stars to the telescope. But how do we know that light takes a long time to get to the telescope? Because God used natural means to get the light here. Ross is reasoning in a circle. His argument is nothing but a question-begging fallacy.

> *Let me repeat an earlier point: A consistent pattern in God's revelations is that when He does perform miracles, He does not purposefully remove or intentionally hide the evidence of those miracles from us.*

Apparently, Dr. Ross is trying to persuade us that God's actions during the creation week — at least as they pertain to light-travel in the early universe – were not miraculous. He argues that this must be the case because there is no evidence of such, and God doesn't hide evidence of the miraculous. But what is the physical evidence today that Jesus once turned water into wine, or walked on water, or calmed the storm? There is no physical evidence of these things in the present – we know of them only from the pages of Scripture. Is this because God "hid" the evidence of these things? Of course not. Yet, by Ross's logic we should reject such miracles since there is no evidence of them today outside the Bible.

This sort of argument — the idea that it would be deceptive of God to create in six days because the universe "looks" older — is really another example of the "two-books fallacy." The universe doesn't literally say anything about its own age: it's not propositional truth. The Bible is. The ironic thing about this argument is that its opposite is true. Namely, it would necessarily be deceptive for God to *not* create in six days and then write in His Word that He *did* create in six days! What could be more deceptive than a deliberate lie?

11. Sabbath days and Sabbath years

> *The Sabbath day for man and the Sabbath year for the land are analogous to God's work week. God's fourth commandment says that the seventh day of each week is to be honored as holy, "For in six days the Lord made the heavens and the earth... but he rested on the seventh day" (Exodus 20:10-11) [sic].*

It's a pity that Dr. Ross quotes only a portion of the text, because the relevant passage actually begins in verse 8. Exodus 20:8–10 explain that we are to remember the Sabbath day, to keep it holy; we are to work six days, but we are *not* to work on the seventh day, or our family, or hired help, or guests, or cattle. Verse 11 is the *explanation* for why. It explains that we are to work six days and rest one day because God worked six days and rested one day when he made the universe. This context is very important, as we will see shortly. Note also that this passage says nothing about Sabbath *years*.

> *This passage is often cited as proof positive for the twenty-four-hour-day interpretation. Evangelical Hebrew scholar Gleason Archer disagrees: "By no means does this demonstrate that 24-hour intervals were involved in the first six 'days,' any more than the eight-day celebration of the Feast of Tabernacles proves that the wilderness wanderings under Moses occupied only eight days."*

Here Archer has recklessly committed the fallacy of the false analogy. He argues that the timescale of creation cannot be linked to our workweek because the timescale of the Feast of Tabernacles is not linked to the timescale of the wilderness wanderings. The problem is that the Bible directly teaches that the timescale of the workweek *is* connected to the timescale of creation — Exodus 20:8–11. But the Bible does *not* link the timescale of the Feast of Tabernacles to the 40 years of wandering. In other words, the Bible does not say, "You shall observe the Feast of Tabernacles for seven days, because you wandered in the wilderness for seven days." But it does teach that we are to work six days and rest one because [for] "in six days the Lord made the heavens and the earth. . . ." Archer has ignored the context principle, and has simply not read the text carefully.

> *Sometimes the Sabbath is a full year (cf. Leviticus 25:4).*

The Sabbath *day* is always a day. Dr. Ross apparently doesn't realize that the word "Sabbath" simply means "to rest." The day of rest is a Sabbath day, and a year of rest is a Sabbath year. Ross has committed the fallacy of equivocation on the word Sabbath, in confusing Sabbath years (which are longer than a day) with Sabbath days (which are not). Sabbath years in Scripture are never linked directly back to creation — only Sabbath days.

> *Clearly, the emphasis in Exodus 20 is on the pattern of one out of seven, not the literal duration of the days of creation.*

If that were true, then we would expect other patterns of seven in Scripture to reference back to the creation days. But we never do. Dr. Ross's claim here is untenable. He's basically indicating, "That aspect of the text [duration] is not important. Pay no attention to that detail. What is important is. . . ." He's ignoring the inspiration and inerrancy principles. *All* the details of Scripture are important and inerrant (2 Timothy 3:16). This necessarily includes the duration of the creation week being the same as our seven-day week (Exodus 20:8–11).

> *Just as the high priests of Israel served "at a sanctuary that is a copy and shadow of what is in heaven" (Hebrews 8:5), the days demarked by the rotation of the earth are copies and shadows of the days distinguished by God in the Genesis creation record.*

Scriptural support? Dr. Ross doesn't provide any. So his claim is nothing but a false analogy fallacy. The Bible nowhere suggests that the days of our week are shadows of what is in heaven. The days of creation are specifically indicated to be earth-rotation days, because each one is comprised of exactly one evening and one morning (e.g., Genesis 1:5, 8, 13). Exodus 20:8–11 does not teach that we are to work in day "shadows" because God worked in "heavenly" days (whatever those might be). Rather it teaches that we are to work for six days and rest for one because that's what God did — using the same word for "days" in the same context.

Ross also seems to be unaware that Exodus 20:11 uses the plural word for "days" which is *yamim. Yamim* is *never* used to mean a long period of time, but always refers to ordinary days in all historical narrative in Scripture.

> *The human and the temporal always are copies and shadows of the divine and the eternal, not vice versa. The seven days of our calendar week simply follow the pattern established by God.*

Ross's first claim is the hasty generalization fallacy. There *are* some human, temporal activities that are designed to be copies or "shadows" of the divine reality — such as the Temple and sacrificial system used in the Old Testament. The Bible teaches that. But it does not follow logically that *all* human and temporal activities are symbolic shadows of the heavenly realm. There is no logical reason to make that leap, and there is no scriptural support for such a generalization.

Dr. Ross's second claim is true, but it refutes his main point rather than supporting it. The pattern established by God during the creation week was that God worked in six days — each comprised of one evening and one morning — and then rested one day. We are supposed to follow this pattern, which is why we have a seven-day week. If God had really created over long ages, and then rested for a long age, then we are not truly following His pattern by having a literal week.

> *God's "work week" gives us a human-like picture we can grasp.*

Notice that Ross puts "work week" in quotes indicating metaphorical usages. But the Bible doesn't treat it this way. The Bible teaches that God really did create in six days and then rested one day as a pattern for us.

> *Scripture frequently speaks of God's hand, His eyes, His arm, even His wings. The context of each of these passages makes it obvious that none of these descriptions is meant to be taken concretely. Rather, each word presents a picture to help us understand spiritual reality about God and His relationship to us.*

This is correct. But it doesn't help Dr. Ross's case. References to God's eyes, arms, wings, and so on, occur primarily in the poetic literature, where we expect such non-literal figures of speech. But Genesis is historical narrative. Yes, God accommodates human understanding by giving us anthropomorphisms. But are the days of creation anthropomorphic? Not at all. Ross says that word pictures in Scripture help us understand spiritual reality. I agree. But billions of years is not a "spiritual reality." So it would not make sense to take the days of creation as representing some kind of spiritual truth. That is not consistent with the historical narrative genre of the passage. Is Genesis teaching us about the nature of God through metaphors and word pictures? No. It is teaching us about literal history.

> *The difference is not literal versus figurative.*

Actually, it is. God's hands, eyes, and wings are not literal; they are figurative. If Ross wants us to take the days of creation in the same way, he really should admit that this is figurative.

> *The difference is between an interpretive method that does not recognize context (including the immediate textual context, the literary genre of the passage, and the broader theological context) and one that does.*

The ironic thing is that Dr. Ross's approach to Scripture does not recognize such things. Ross treats poetic passages as if they were accounts of creation, and he treats the account of creation as if it were poetic. He does not recognize the context of Genesis (history), and instead treats it as if it were an anthropomorphic reference to God, like Psalm 23.

> *What I am suggesting here is not a gratuitously figurative or symbolic interpretation of God's creative week, but rather a recognition of anthropomorphic usage that is clearly commonly used elsewhere in Scripture to describe God and His relationship to His creation and His creatures.*

What is Dr. Ross's evidence for taking Genesis as anthropomorphic? I suspect Ross really means "symbolic" or "non-literal" because "anthropomorphism" is giving human attributes to something that is not human (in this case God). References to God's arms, wings, eyes, hands, and so on are all anthropomorphisms. But we don't see that in Genesis 1. The only thing I can find in Genesis 1 that might count as anthropomorphic language is God "speaking" — especially in verse 26. This may not be speaking exactly as we do it (creating sound waves in air), but is as accurate a description as our finite minds will allow. Genesis 1 is not primarily teaching about the nature of God, but rather about what God did in history. So, from context, we would not expect a lot of anthropomorphic language. Ross has violated the genre and contextual principles.

Most significantly, taking "days" to mean "vast ages" is *not* anthropomorphic. It's non-literal, but it is not attributing a human attribute to a non-human. Nor has Ross provided any textual evidence whatsoever that the days are symbolic rather than literal. He has merely stated it, and shown other Scriptures that use language in a non-literal way. But no one denies figurative language in some sections of Scripture. The question is: What is the evidence of such figurative language *in Genesis*? Dr. Ross hasn't provided any. Given the historical narrative genre of the book, we wouldn't expect a lot of figurative language anyway.

One other very interesting thing to note is that Dr. Ross has contradicted himself. He has provided two *mutually exclusive* arguments for his day-age interpretation. In other words, if one of these arguments is correct, then the other one can't be correct. Let me explain. Here, Dr. Ross is arguing that the days of creation are to be taken figuratively — as anthropomorphic language. But he has previously argued that one of the *literal* definitions of *yom* (day) is "a segment of time without any reference to solar days (anywhere from weeks to a year to several years to an age or epoch)." If that's a literal definition of the word *yom*, then it is *not* figurative to take it as a long period of time. Dr. Ross has argued both that the days of creation are literal and that they are non-literal. At least one of those arguments is necessarily wrong.

> *We need to recognize that the analog of our Sabbath to God's Sabbath does not demand seven twenty-four hour days. Age-long creation days fits the analogy just as well, if not better.*

Here, Dr. Ross commits the linguistic relativism fallacy in claiming that "Sabbath" means something different to God than it does to us. If words really meant different things to God than to us, then reading the Bible would be pointless, because we could never know what God actually intended. Imagine a murderer attempting to justify his actions biblically by claiming, "The command to not murder is from God's perspective, not ours. God's definition of 'murder' is just an *analogy* for our 'murder.' We must recognize that this analogy does not demand that we take the command literally."

12. Death through sin

> *"Death through sin" is not equivalent to physical death. Romans 5:12 says, "Sin entered the world through one man, and death through sin, and in this way death came to all men, because all sinned."*

Here, Dr. Ross switches to a defensive posture and begins a hermeneutical argument that sin brought into the world only spiritual death, not physical death. His motivation for this argument stems from his acceptance of the secular timescale. Secular scientists believe that living creatures have been living and dying on earth for billions of years. This is long before human beings existed, by either secular or biblical thinking. Therefore, Ross accepts that physical death of animals was in the world long *before* Adam sinned. Consequently, he must explain the many passages in Scripture that teach that death is a *result* of Adam's sin. Ross's solution is to claim that all such references are referring to spiritual death. He quotes Romans 5:12 to support this. But it is not at all obvious that this passage is referring to spiritual death.

> *Some have interpreted this verse as implying no death of any kind for any creature existed before Adam's sin and, therefore, only a brief time could have transpired between the creation of the first life-forms and Adam's sin.*

Dr. Ross commits *two* straw-man fallacies in this single sentence. First, I've not heard anyone claim that the lack of death before Adam's sin implies "only a brief time could have transpired between" creation and Adam's sin. Biblical creationists teach that the world was perfect before Adam sinned, without death and suffering of the living creatures, and that it would have remained that way forever if human beings had not sinned. The timespan between creation and Adam's sin may indeed have been brief, but no one could reasonably infer that from the lack of death before sin.

Second, and more importantly, Ross has stated that some (creationists) believe that "no death of *any kind*" existed before Adam's sin. But I'm not aware of anyone who holds such a position, and it is certainly not the position held by mainstream biblical creationists. Rather, we would say that the Bible teaches no death of any *living creature* before Adam sinned. There are things that are not "alive" in a biblical sense that could have "died" even before sin, such as plants or microorganisms.

The Bible uses a particular Hebrew phrase to refer to *living* creatures: *nephesh chai*. This phrase is used of human beings (Genesis 2:7), and also of animals (Genesis 1:24). But it is never used of plants. Many of us learned in school that plants or individual cells are classified as "alive" — but this is a different classification system than the Bible uses. Biblically, plants are not alive; they are food for living creatures. The biblical use of physical life and physical death can only literally refer to human beings or animals. Ross confuses the modern taxonomic system with the biblical one.

> *The proponents of such a view fail to realize that the absence of physical death would pose just as great a problem for three twenty-four-hour days as it would for three billion years. Many species of life cannot survive for even three hours without food, and the mere ingestion of food by animals requires death of at least plants or plant parts.*

First, this is obvious eisegesis. Dr. Ross is not reasoning from the text, he is reasoning from his understanding of principles of nature, and then concluding that the text cannot mean what it really says. Essentially, Ross is claiming that God could not have sustained a universe with living creatures without any death. If that is so, then we have no hope that heaven will be any different. Moreover, God would not really be omnipotent.

Second, Dr. Ross conflates the biblical definitions of life and death with the modern technical/biological ones. No, plants are not alive by the Bible's definition (*nephesh chai*). Hence, their consumption by an animal does not constitute death by the Bible's definition. Plants are not volitional creatures that can feel pain or suffer loss. They are food to be eaten. In the paradise of God we will eat plants (Revelation 2:7), yet there will be no death in the eternal state (1 Corinthians 15:26).

> *A rebuttal to this problem suggests that the verse is referring to "soulish" rather than physical death.*

This is also a straw-man argument, though I suspect it is unintentional. Dr. Ross has not understood what creationists have taught about sin and death, and has attempted to refute a position that no one holds. Biblical creationists teach that physical death (not "soulish" death) of living creatures entered the world when Adam sinned. The Hebrew word *nephesh* is sometimes translated as "soul," and so those creatures that are *nephesh chai* are sometimes called "soulish creatures" in contrast to plants or microbes.

> *The difficulty with this adjusted interpretation remains: are birds and mammals condemned to "death through sin"?*

The biblical answer is "yes." The Bible teaches in Romans 8:19–22 that all creation groans under a bondage of corruption. Verse 20 makes clear that the creation was subjected to such futility unwillingly. God cursed the entire creation because of Adam's sin. Animals are condemned to death — not by their own sin, but because of Adam's. Why Ross thinks that this is a "difficulty" is unclear. When a leader makes a bad decision, all those under his authority suffer as a result.

> *Of all life on earth, only humans have earned the title "sinner." Only humans can experience "death through sin."*

This faulty reasoning is exposed with a simple analogy. "Only the leaders of our government can make and enforce laws. Therefore, only they can suffer the effects of bad laws." If that's a silly argument, then it is also absurd to think that animals cannot suffer the effects of human sin. Animals die, not because they have rebelled against God, but because we have. And we were put in charge of the animals (Genesis 1:26, 28). They feel the effects of our poor leadership decisions, just as we feel the effects of the poor decisions of our leaders.

> *Note that the death Adam experienced is carefully qualified in the text as being visited on "all men" — not on plants and animals, just on human beings (Romans 5:12, 18–19).*

This is the fallacy of the argument from silence. Ross assumes that since animals are not specifically mentioned, they must be excluded. But the cited text does not say one way or the other. The Bible is written for people. So its primary doctrines concern the relationships between God and man. We wouldn't expect an extended discussion in Scripture on animals and their interaction with God because this doesn't concern us. Romans 5 doesn't specifically address the death of animals because that's not the topic of discussion. By itself, Romans 5 neither affirms nor denies that animal death was introduced at the Fall. But other Scriptures do, as we will explore shortly.

> *Romans 5:12 addresses neither physical nor soulish death. It addresses spiritual death. When Adam sinned, he instantly "died," just as God said he would ("In the day that you eat of it, you shall surely die" — Genesis 2:17 NKJV). Yet, he remained alive physically and soulishly (i.e., mentally, volitionally, and emotionally). He died spiritually. He broke his harmonious fellowship with God and introduced the inclination to place one's own way above God's.*

The argument Ross has made is basically this: (1) God promised that Adam would surely die in the day he ate of the forbidden fruit. (2) Adam did not die *physically* in the day he ate of the forbidden fruit. (3) Therefore, God must have meant that Adam would die spiritually, not physically. (4) Romans 5:12 is a reference back to this event in Genesis. (5) Therefore, Romans 5:12 is also speaking of spiritual death.

Premise 4 is correct, and so is premise 2. But notice something very peculiar about this argument: it contradicts Dr. Ross's previous arguments! His argument here hinges on the fact that Adam did not physically die *in the day* that he ate the fruit. But Ross has previously argued that "days" in Genesis are long periods of time — many millions of years each. If that is true, then Adam did indeed die physically on the same "day" that he ate the fruit. So if Ross's earlier arguments about days are correct then premise 2 of his current argument is false, and the argument fails. On the other hand, if premise 2 is established, then the days of Genesis are ordinary days, and all of Ross's previous arguments for long days are faulty!

The correct interpretation of Genesis and also of Romans 5:12 requires that we pay careful attention to the text and the context. Let's start with Genesis 2:17. The last part of this verse is often rendered something like "for in the day that you eat from it you shall surely die" in most English translations. The last part "you shall surely die" makes sense in English. But the Hebrew wording would be more literally translated "dying you shall die." The double use of death indicates the *certainty* of it.

In Hebrew, the phrase uses a double verb — it combines an infinitive absolute verb with an imperfect second person singular verb, both of which are simple active verbs. In English translations, the tense indicates a future fulfillment of the death, "dying you *shall* die" — that is, in the future. And so it is not *instant* death that God promises will happen on the day that Adam eats of the forbidden fruit, but the *certainty* of death. We might paraphrase this by saying, "On the day you eat of it your dying process-that-leads-to-death begins," "on the day you eat of it, you will become mortal," or "on the day you eat of it, your (future) death will be certain." On the very day that Adam ate of the forbidden fruit, his death went from a hypothetical possibility to an unstoppable experience of slow disintegrating, leading to an unavoidable destiny. The process of death began instantly. And though that dying process took hundreds of years to culminate, the outcome was certain on the (literal) day that Adam sinned.

Of course, I have no doubt that Adam's sin also incurred spiritual death — a "separation" from a perfect communion with God (Isaiah 59:2). But from context, we know that the penalty for sin is (at least) physical death. This is confirmed in Genesis 3:19 as God explains the consequences of Adam's sin: ". . . till you return to the ground, because from it you were taken; for you are dust, and to dust you shall return." Can there be any doubt that Genesis 3:19 refers to physical death? If the penalty for sin is merely spiritual death, then why did Jesus die *physically* (not spiritually) on the Cross? The Bible makes clear that we are saved by Christ's shed blood (Ephesians 1:7; Romans 5:9; Revelation 1:5) — His physical death. So there can be no doubt that Genesis, and therefore Romans 5 as well, is referring (at least) to physical death that fell upon man as a result of sin.

> *In the same manner, it has been established that 1 Corinthians 15:21 ("since death came through a man") also must refer to spiritual death rather than to physical death. As the following two verses in 1 Corinthians explain, "For as in Adam all die, so in Christ all will be made alive. But each in his own turn: Christ, the firstfruits; then, when he comes, those who belong to him" (verses 22–23).*

A moment's thought reveals the impossibility of Ross's interpretation of 1 Corinthians 15:21. Verse 22 compares the death brought into the world by Adam's sin with the Resurrection that Christ brings — "For as in Adam all die, so also in Christ all will be made alive." But if the death in this passage is only spiritual, then the resurrection must be spiritual as well — the salvation that Christ imparts to believers (Ephesians 2:5). But does a spiritual resurrection fit the context? No, for two reasons.

First of all, 1 Corinthians 15:22 states that in Christ *all* will be made alive. But not all people experience spiritual resurrection (salvation) — only believers (John 5:25). The only resurrection that all people experience is the *physical* resurrection (John 5:28–29). Even if we take 1 Corinthians 15:22 as hyperbole, suggesting that at some point almost everyone will be saved, the "spiritual death and spiritual resurrection view" is very difficult to reconcile with the next verse: "But each in his own order: Christ the first fruits, after that those who are Christ's at His coming" (verse 23). This verse indicates that the resurrection under discussion here takes place at the Second Coming. This is the physical resurrection (John 5:28–29), not the spiritual resurrection which happens all the time, whenever someone receives Christ as Lord (John 5:25; Ephesians 2:1, 5). The verse also teaches that Jesus is the "first fruits" — the first to be resurrected this way. Jesus never needed to be resurrected spiritually because He is perfect. His Resurrection was physical. Therefore, the type of death under discussion in 1 Corinthians 15:21–23 is unquestionably physical death.

> *Christ grants eternal life through His crucifixion and resurrection, and will give believers indestructible bodies at His return. Christ's crucifixion and resurrection conquered sin and removed the barrier Adam erected between humanity and God. Any person choosing spiritual life in Christ will receive it. Eventually, at Christ's second coming, the eternal spiritual life that the believer in Christ already possesses results in eternal physical life.*

This is essentially correct, but it refutes Ross's claim that 1 Corinthians 21 merely refers to spiritual death. Here, Dr. Ross admits that *physical* resurrection and *physical* eternal life are granted to believers at the Second Coming of Christ. This is what 1 Corinthians 15:22–23 teaches. Therefore, the death mentioned in verse 21 must also be physical, otherwise the passage would be "comparing apples and oranges."

> *My point is that only human beings, spiritual beings, are "made alive in Christ." First Corinthians 15 refers only to those creatures who experience sin and desire to be delivered from sin. This excludes*

> *all species of life on the earth except humans. Therefore, just as in Romans 5, no reason is found to deny physical death for nonhuman life previous to Adam's sin.*

Again, Dr. Ross's reasoning just doesn't make sense. The fact that Christ will resurrect all people does not prove that animals don't experience death as a result of Adam's sin. Besides, God promises to make *all* things new — not just people (Revelation 21:5; 2 Corinthians 5:17; Galatians 6:15). All creation will be redeemed (Romans 8:21; Acts 3:21) as a result of Christ's obedience on the Cross. This doesn't necessarily imply a one-to-one resurrection of each individual *nephesh*-bearing animal that has ever died (although that is not textually ruled out). But it does clearly indicate that all creation is currently suffering from the Curse, and will be delivered from it in the eternal state.

Note too that Dr. Ross hasn't dealt with the Scriptures that biblical creationists would actually use to show that there was no death of living creatures before sin. Romans 5 and 1 Corinthians 15 deal primarily with human life and death, so it would be inappropriate to use these texts in isolation to argue either for or against animal death. Where are animals mentioned in such passages? Rather, we use such verses in context with others, such as Romans 8. Romans 8:18–23 clearly teaches that the Curse due to Adam's sin has touched all of creation. This necessarily includes animals, since they are part of creation.

Dr. Ross ignores Genesis 1:31, which teaches that "God saw everything that He had made, and behold, it was very good." Note that everything God made was very good — not just people. Yet, in Ross's view, the world was already full of death and suffering, disease and bloodshed when God finished creation. Are we to believe that such things are "very good"? The Bible teaches that God cares about animals too (Luke 12:6; Exodus 34:26; Deuteronomy 25:4, 22:6). Indeed, the Bible says that a "righteous man has regard for the life of his animal" (Proverbs 12:10). God is not so cruel as to create a world in which animals suffer and die and call it "very good." The original world was perfect because all of God's works are perfect (Deuteronomy 32:4). But since God put Adam in charge of the world, the entire world suffered the effects of Adam's treason against God.

And what did God do to cover the shame of Adam and Eve? He sacrificed an animal, or animals, to provide skins of clothing (Genesis 3:21).

Yes, the Lord instituted animal death at the time of Adam's sin. The Lord commanded animal sacrifice in the Old Testament as a continual reminder of the effects of sin (e.g., Exodus 29:18, 42; Leviticus 1:17, 4:29), until the Savior would come to pay the penalty for such sin once and for all. So there really cannot be any doubt from the Scriptures that sin brought physical death to all living creatures. Dr. Ross has ignored all these Scriptures, and focused on refuting a straw-man argument from Scriptures that don't address animals at all.

> *Genesis 3 records that after Adam and Eve died (spiritually) through sin, God sent an angel to block their access to the tree of life. Apparently Adam and Eve had the potential for eternal physical life before and after sinning against God. Knowing that eternal physical life in their newly acquired sinful condition ultimately would be disastrous for them and their descendants, God barred their access to it. God would not allow His plan to be thwarted.*

Dr. Ross does not give an argument for his interpretation; he simply states it. When we interpret Scripture with Scripture, we can see that his interpretation is false. Did Adam and Eve have "the potential for eternal physical life" even *after* sinning against God? No. God said that when they ate from the tree they would surely die, "dying you shall die" (Genesis 2:17), indicating the certainty of their mortality. God did *not* say, "dying you shall die, unless you quickly get to the tree of life and eat its fruit." That this is physical death is confirmed in Genesis 3:19 — man returning to dust is physical death, not spiritual.

The angel blocked Adam and Eve's access to the tree of life as an outward manifestation of the spiritual reality that Adam and Eve no longer enjoyed immortality and direct face-to-face access to God. That is the effect of sin. The tree of life was a literal tree that represented the direct access to God that people once had. The redeemed will again have such direct access in the eternal state (Revelation 2:7), but that is because of what Christ did 4,000 years later on another "tree" — the Cross.

> *Physical death for humans became a blessing designed to restrain the spread of evil and make way for the redemption of willing men and women.*

It's hard to believe that Dr. Ross would claim that physical death for humans is a blessing. This view just cannot be reconciled with Scripture. Death was the *punishment* for Adam and Eve's sin (Genesis 3:19). If death were a blessing, then God punished them by giving them something *good*. The Bible describes death as an enemy that will be abolished — not a blessing (1 Corinthians 15:26). The blessing of God, His gift to us, is not death. Rather it is the opposite of death — eternal life (Romans 6:23).

> *One point of concern remains. Some people think that the death of [living animals] before Adam's sin ascribes evil to the Creator. I have met men and women who deny that a God of love could be responsible for carnivorous behavior. They believe that carnivorous activity must be the result of sin and not of God's design.*

One of the characteristics that the Bible associates with evil men is that they shed innocent blood without cause (Proverbs 1:10–11; Psalm 94:22). So if God has been slaughtering animals by the millions for millions of years for no particular reason other than to watch them suffer, then it would be hard to think of that as anything but evil. Animals do suffer, but as a result of *our* sin. It's our fault — not God's. The Bible says that a good man regards the life of his animal (Proverbs 12:10). Would God hold people to a higher standard than His own?

Blaming God for animal death and suffering is particularly insulting to Him considering that animal death and suffering are due to our sin. When we attribute to God a failing in ourselves, it is reminiscent of Adam's response to God. Adam didn't take responsibility for his crime; instead he tried to cast blame on both Eve and God. In Genesis 3:12, Adam says, "'The woman whom You gave to be with me, she gave me from the tree, and I ate." Notice the qualifier that Adam uses: "whom You gave to be with me." Did Adam add this qualifier to distinguish Eve from all the other women? Clearly not. It seems that Adam was reminding God that Eve had been given by God, subtly suggesting that none of this would have happened if God hadn't made that dreadful mistake.

And what about the reference to carnivorous activity? The Bible is extremely clear that all living creatures were originally vegetarian, as were Adam and Eve (Genesis 1:29–30). Verse 30 states that plants were to be food for *everything that moves on the earth* which has life (*nephesh*). It wasn't until after the Flood that humans were given permission to eat meat (Genesis 9:3). The Bible doesn't say when animals began to eat meat. But it would have been after sin, since carnivorous activity involves the death of a living creature. Genesis is explicit that all living animals were originally created as plant eaters. Why does Dr. Ross argue for the carnivorous behavior before the Fall of man?

The answer, again, lies in the opinions of secularists. The secular timescale has carnivorous activity existing millions of years ago. And since Ross accepts this timescale, he is forced to interpret Genesis 1:30 in an unnatural and non-exegetic fashion to match. Perhaps he thinks it simply means that all animals eat things that are *derived* from plants; the carnivores eat the herbivores which eat plants. Aside from the fact that there is no suggestion of this meaning in Genesis 1:30, we note that this idea leads to absurdity.

Remember that Adam and Eve were given the same command as the animals in Genesis 1:29. So if this meant that they were to eat anything *derived* from plants — including other animals, then God's instructions to Noah in Genesis 9:3 would make no sense. This is where God says, "Every moving thing that is alive shall be food for you; I give all to you as I gave the green plant." But if they were already eating meat, then Noah could have said, "Excuse me, Lord, but apparently you forgot that we've already been doing that with your blessing for over a thousand years." That would be nonsense of course.

Recent Publications

Creation and Time is one of Dr. Ross's earlier publications. Some readers might be wondering if he continues to use these kinds of arguments. After all, I have debated Dr. Ross on several occasions and pointed out the fallacious nature of his claims. We might be inclined to think that he would accept constructive criticism from a brother in Christ and concede that some of these arguments are not sound. To the best of my knowledge, Ross has not retracted these claims, but he has started emphasizing different issues in some of his more recent works. Let's examine his more recent book, *Navigating Genesis* (published 2014),[12] to see if Ross's hermeneutical

12. Hugh Ross, *Navigating Genesis: A Scientist's Journey through Genesis 1–11* (Covina, CA: RTB Press, 2014).

skills have improved. A point-by-point analysis of the book would be time consuming, so here we shall only focus on those issues pertaining to hermeneutical approach and the age of the earth.

A Personal Journey

Navigating Genesis begins with a brief autobiographical sketch. Some writers use this to establish a deeper connection with the reader, and there is nothing inherently wrong with that. Nor should we argue from Ross's circumstances that any given argument he makes is necessarily wrong — that would be a circumstantial *ad hominem* fallacy. However, it is appropriate to take an author's own statements about his approach to hermeneutics as a basis for judging his approach to hermeneutics.

Dr. Ross begins with some good things to say about Scripture: that it claims to be divinely inspired and that people have rejected that claim for no good reason. Quite right. He correctly notes that the first chapters of Genesis are some of the most attacked portions of Scripture (although he does not admit that he himself *effectively rejects* those chapters). Of these he states,

> *The language of these chapters is remarkably clear and specific. The words repeatedly associate spiritual events with physical events, and physical events are, in a word, testable. As a scientist I would say these events beg to be tested.*

The first sentence here is true, but struck me as strangely contrary to Dr. Ross's approach to Genesis. After all, he believes that "days" don't really mean "days" that when God "made" the stars, He didn't really make them then but that they merely "appeared," that dinosaurs were made before birds, while the biblical text says that flying creatures are made on day 5 and land animals on day 6, and so on.[13] In other words, in Ross's view, the text doesn't mean what it says at all. How could that be "remarkably clear and specific"?

And what are we to make of the notion that the "physical events" of the creation week are "testable"? How? We certainly cannot do this by scientific observation. What experiment can we do in the present to prove that God created plants on the third day? There are scientific principles that confirm

13. Note that the Hebrew language uses a different word for "make" than it does for "appear." So it is exegetically wrong to take God's description of making the stars as simply a statement that the stars merely *appeared* on the fourth day.

biblical creation. But how can science, a procedure that requires observation and experimentation in the present, ever truly *test* a past event?

Perhaps Ross thinks that the order in which fossils are found can be used to scientifically test the order of events in Genesis. If so, then there would be two problems with such an approach. First, there is no logical reason to assume that the vertical order in which organisms are found in strata directly links to the chronological order in which God created them. Ross may think that such layers are deposited over millions of years as God progressively created, and thus that there is some correlation. But that would beg the question.

Second, the order does *not* match. That is, if we assumed that the vertical order of fossils represents their chronological order of creation, then the Bible would be wrong. Fish are found in lower strata than fruit trees, but Genesis puts the creation of fruit trees two days before fish. Land creatures are found in lower layers than birds, yet Genesis places the creation of birds first.

Most disturbing is Dr. Ross's statement that "these events beg to be tested." This is reification, of course. Events cannot beg or desire anything. So who is really doing the begging? Is Ross suggesting that God is inviting us to test Scripture by the standard of science? Wouldn't that make science more authoritative than Scripture? What did Jesus say about putting God to the test (Matthew 4:7)? Some might ask, "But how can we trust God without putting Him to the test?" The answer is that God has laid down the criteria by which all things are to be judged — and that standard is recorded in His Word. This includes the standard by which it is to be tested, as shown in chapter 9. It's not the events of the Bible that are to be tested by secular standards; rather, secular opinions are to be tested by the standard of the Bible.

Dr. Ross continues:

> *However, as if the implied invitation here in Genesis to test were not enough, the apostle Paul exhorted his readers to "test everything" to see what holds water and what does not, and to keep only what does. For Genesis 1–11, the content is largely natural history. So many of the appropriate tests will come from relevant disciplines of science.*[14]

14. Ross, *Navigating Genesis*, p. 9.

Is this reasonable? Paul does tell us to "test all things" in 1 Thessalonians 5:21. Does this support Ross's claim? Two questions need to be asked. (1) What is to be tested? (2) What is the standard by which it should be tested? From his previous paragraph, we know that Ross is attempting to persuade us that we should test the events recorded in Genesis — that we should test God's Word. But that is not what Paul is referring to in 1 Thessalonians 5:21. Paul is instructing the church in Thessalonica to test prophecies/doctrine (verse 20) *by* God's Word.

For Paul, the standard by which all doctrine should be judged is *Scripture* (2 Timothy 3:16; Acts 17:11)! Paul is not suggesting that we should test God's Word by some other standard, as Ross implies. Ross has taken the text out of context. Dr. Ross explicitly states his standard by which Genesis 1–11 is to be judged: "many of the appropriate tests will come from the relevant disciplines of science." This should make abundantly obvious to any reader that Ross's ultimate standard is not the Bible, but science. It is also an obvious example of the "two-books fallacy."[15]

While observational science is a good secondary standard for testing certain types of truths claims (those that are observable/testable in the present), it is not infallible and is not well-suited to evaluating past events. On the other hand, the Bible is the infallible Word of God and is thus right on everything it touches — whether these are spiritual matters or issues of science and history. Why does Ross judge the infallible by the standard of the fallible? And when the practical application comes, it is clear that it isn't real-world science at all that Ross uses to test the Bible. Rather, it is the consensus opinion of secular scientists that is held to be the standard against which all Scripture is to be judged. This isn't exegesis at all.

This approach is confirmed in the paragraph that follows:

> *With the help of many remarkable advances in astronomy, physics, geophysics, chemistry, paleontology, biochemistry, and anthropology, the words of the first eleven chapters can be subjected point by point to rigorous investigation. They can be verified or refuted with greater precision and to a greater depth than previous generations might have imagined possible.*[16]

15. http://www.icr.org/article/two-book-fallacy/.
16. Ross, *Navigating Genesis*, p. 9.

As a Christian, I find it deeply offensive that Ross thinks he is in a position to judge God's Word, particularly by his fallible and limited understanding of the natural sciences. More importantly, God is offended when His Word — including the books of Moses, such as Genesis (see John 5:45–47) — is dishonored by those who fail to recognize its authority and verity. On the final day, it will not be man that judges God's Word, but God's Word that judges man (Romans 2:12; Revelation 20:12–13; James 2:10; Deuteronomy 27:26; Matthew 4:4).

I understand that Ross may be addressing unbelievers and that he thinks that God's Word will pass the tests. But the attitude of saying that God's Word "can be verified *or refuted*" by some man-made test is extremely conceited.[17] Heaven and earth will pass away, but God's Word will not (Matthew 24:35). It is God's Word that will judge the mind of man, not the reverse (Revelation 20:12). In any case, Ross's ultimate standard has been revealed, and it certainly isn't the Bible.

Ironically, a few paragraphs later, Dr. Ross states, "The desire for autonomy of thought and freedom from God's authority combined with peer pressure from the surrounding culture typically results in people's testing by *their* standards and according to *their* notions rather than God's"[18] (emphasis in the original). I agree. But isn't Ross doing exactly that when he proposes to test Genesis by "the relevant disciplines of science"?

Dr. Ross then begins his personal testimony:

> *Until I was in my late teens, my singular passion was science, astronomy in particular. My life's purpose was to learn more and more about the universe. By the time I turned sixteen, I had studied enough cosmology to become convinced that of all the origins models ever proposed, the big bang model best fit the observational data.*[19]

Apparently, Hugh Ross did not have the benefit of a Christian upbringing. Instead, he had been thoroughly indoctrinated with secular views on the

17. It is also logically impossible. The standards of science and logic are epistemologically grounded in Scripture. That is, apart from the biblical worldview, there would be no reason to trust in the methods of science or laws of logic as reliable means of evaluating truth claims. Hypothetically, if the Bible were to be refuted by the methods of science or logic, then we would lose any rational foundation for these methods, thereby invalidating their supposed refutation.
18. Ross, *Navigating Genesis*, p. 10.
19. Ibid., p. 11.

origin and evolution of the universe, for example, the big bang. The reason I mention this is because it comes to bear on Ross's approach to biblical interpretation. He did not have the guidance of godly parents or a Bible-following church to teach him how to rightly understand God's Word. The Bible itself teaches that people will tend to have difficulty understanding its message until a believer comes alongside to help (see Acts 8:30–37). Indeed, Ross claims not to have known anyone who had read the Bible at the time he first read it. Consequently, much of his interpretation suffers from the maverick fallacy.

I appreciate Ross's passion for science — I share it. However, the Bible tells us that we are to test external claims (such as the big bang) against the standard of Scripture, to build our thinking on the rock of God's Word and to cast down any argument that is contrary (Matthew 4:4, 7:24–27; Acts 17:11; 2 Corinthians 10:5). Dr. Ross's approach is the opposite. Namely, he tests the Bible by the "established scientific record" (by which he means those popular claims of scientists that he happens to accept). Ross states that at the age of 16, he read the opening chapters of Genesis and found that "the four initial conditions and the sequence of major creation events — not just one or two, but nearly a dozen — all matched the established scientific record."[20] We've already seen that the sequence of events in Genesis does not match the order proposed by the secularists. So either Ross's theology or his understanding of secular origins claims (or both) are severely distorted.

After 18 months of reading through the Bible, Ross claims to have found not one provable error. And having concluded that this was extremely improbable by chance, he decided it must be of divine origin. He writes, "With some delays and more than a little wrestling with personal pride, I did make a transfer of trust, inviting God, the Creator of the vast cosmos, to be my God, the Master of my destiny, through Jesus Christ His Son."[21] I pray that is so. However, there is no evidence in any of Hugh Ross's writings that he has transferred his trust from secular opinions about *origins* to the Bible (with the sole exception of biological evolution between kinds). Indeed, it seems that he continues to judge God's Word by secular standards.

20. Ibid., p. 12.
21. Ibid.

> *How could the two "books" of revelation from the same Source — that is, the book of nature and the Bible — tell anything other than the same message? They will always match up when we come to understand them more fully and interpret them responsibly.*[22]

Here we have a spectacular example of the two-book fallacy.[23] How is it that the "book of nature" might not "tell anything other than the same message [as the Bible]"? Answer: because nature is not a book and doesn't tell any message at all. Ross has committed an atrocious reification fallacy in thinking that nature has a literal message. He also commits the fallacy of equivocation on the word "interpret." He applies this word to both nature and Scripture in the same phrase, thereby concealing the fact that it has a very different meaning in the two instances. It's disappointing that Ross continues to commit these fallacies when I have corrected him in person on these issues multiple times.

Creation of the Cosmos

In addressing Genesis chapter 1, Dr. Ross states,

> *Something happens between verses 1 and 2 that powerfully impacts the reader's comprehension of the story to follow. Here, the frame of reference for the creation account shifts from the entire cosmos (the heavenly objects that make up the universe) explicitly to the surface of earth. Perhaps because it comes so abruptly, this transition is easily missed, even by distinguished Bible scholars. I am persuaded that my immersion in science prepared me to see it.*[24]

Actually, Hebrew grammar disallows the possibility that "something happens between verses 1 and 2." Namely, verse 2 begins with "And the earth" — a Hebrew grammatical construction called a "waw-disjunctive." The construction occurs when a sentence starts with "and" followed by a non-verb, such as a noun. The waw-disjunctive indicates a break or interruption in the narrative. This is often for the purpose of providing additional information about what was previously stated. When used this way, it functions much the way we would use parenthesis in English — it shows

22. Ibid., p. 13.
23. http://www.icr.org/article/two-book-fallacy/.
24. Ross, *Navigating Genesis,* p. 28.

that verse two is a comment on verse one. Verse two does not necessarily follow in time, but is a parenthetical description of the conditions of the earth that was mentioned in the previous verse. Thus, it is impossible for something to happen between verses one and two because there is literally no time between the two. I realize, of course, that Ross is not a Hebrew scholar and probably didn't know that. But if he is going to write on these issues, then he has a moral obligation to research these issues or at least check with someone who is knowledgeable in Hebrew. Ross has violated the translation principle.

The text principle has also been violated. Where does the text mention or imply a "shift" in the "frame of reference"? Dr. Ross mentions a shift from the heavenly objects that make up the universe to earth. But if he had read Genesis with any degree of care, he would know that the heavenly objects were not made until day 4 (Genesis 1:14–19). It seems that the best explanation as to why "distinguished Bible scholars" missed this "transition" is because it isn't there. It has been imposed *on* the text, not exegeted *from* the text. The real motivation for inventing such a transition is found in Ross's comments that follow:

> *The observer's vantage point is clearly identified as "the surface of the deep . . . over the waters." Yet the vast majority of Genesis commentaries mistakenly proceed as if it were still high in the heavens, somewhere in the starry realm above earth. This one oversight seems to account for more misunderstanding, more attacks on the credibility of Genesis, than all other interpretive errors combined. The problem glares from the page at anyone slightly aware of how nature works. If the storyteller's viewpoint lies in the heavens above, the unfolding sequence of creative events contradicts scientific record. It violates much of well-established earth (and life) history. For example, it would place the production of plants before the formation of the Sun, Moon, and stars.*[25]

Ross mentions "the observer's vantage point," to which I must ask: "What observer?" Only God was present during the creation week, and He is omnipresent and thus has no unique "vantage point." That an alleged problem is seen by "anyone slightly aware of how nature works" is a question-begging epithet, not a rational argument. It's also a form of the "no true Scotsman

25. Ibid., p. 31.

fallacy." The goal here is to intimidate the reader — essentially, "if you don't agree with me, then you are pretty dim and don't really have even the slightest understanding of how nature works." That type of semantic game may persuade some people by emotion, but it has no rational force.

Likewise, the "well-established" history of "earth (and life)" is a question-begging epithet. That the earth is billions of years old is the very claim in dispute, yet Ross has already dismissed any alternative with one sweeping rhetorical claim. We could equally well respond, "Hugh Ross is wrong because he denies the obvious fact that the earth is around 6,000 years old." Would he accept that claim in place of rational argument? If not, then neither can we accept his epithets.

I would argue that the well-established history of earth and life *is the Bible*. When secular scientists speculate about what allegedly happened millions of years ago, that isn't history because it is not a record. On the other hand, the Bible *is* a written record of past events — it is recorded history. Most scientists therefore refer to their ideas of what happened millions of years ago as "prehistoric" — that is, before people began keeping written records.

But the most obvious problem with Dr. Ross's comments above is found in his last sentence. Without a shift in reference frame, he acknowledges that the Bible must be teaching that plants were made before the sun, moon, and stars. Of course, that is exactly what the Bible does teach. Plants are made on day 3 and the celestial luminaries are made on day 4 (Genesis 1:11–19). But that would go against Ross's pre-commitment to the secular (evolution-based) timescale. The "shift in reference frame" is not motivated by any textual considerations whatsoever. It was invented to protect a preconceived thesis. It is an example of the superfluous distinction fallacy. Ross's approach makes no attempt to understand the author's intention by an analysis of the author's words. It is a quasi-naturalistic hermeneutic (as refuted in chapter 3), and does not follow the grammatical-historical approach.

> *A look ahead to the third creation day reveals that water initially covered earth's entire surface (Psalm 104:6) "You [God] covered it [the earth] with the deep as with a garment; the waters stood above the mountains."*[26]

26. Ibid.

The conclusion is more or less correct; the initial earth was covered with water (and apparently was water) until God brought forth land on day 3 (Genesis 1:2, 9–10). But Ross's reasoning is abysmal. To prove the point, he cites Psalm 104:6. But is Psalm 104:6 referring to the first three days of creation? It mentions waters standing above the mountains — what does this reference? The same expression is used in Genesis 7:19–20 referring to Noah's Flood. But it is not used during the creation week; there were no mountains as yet because the earth was water (2 Peter 3:5). It was during the global *Flood* that God covered the world with the ocean and the waters stood above the mountains, as explicitly taught in Genesis. Ross has taken the text out of context, and has also violated the genre principle in failing to use the historical narrative of Genesis to discern the meaning of Psalm 104:6. Dr. Ross continues:

> *The book of Job makes reference to both the darkness and the water. Job 38:9 says that the earth's surface was dark because of opaque enshrouding clouds. God says in reference to "the sea" that covered earth's surface, "I made the clouds its garment and wrapped it in thick darkness."*[27]

Job 38 is a wonderful example of Hebrew poetic literature; the synonymous parallelism is quite striking. So again we must ask, why is Dr. Ross looking to the poetic literature to interpret Genesis, rather than the reverse? He's not following the genre principle.

And what does Job 38:9 really teach? Does it really say that "the earth's surface was dark because of opaque enshrouding clouds"? Not at all. Ross has committed the false cause fallacy — falsely assuming a cause-and-effect relationship between clouds and darkness, when the two are merely *correlated* (because they both happened during the creation week). Using the genre principle, we turn to the historical narrative of Genesis to find the reason for the darkness; it was because God created the earth before He created light (Genesis 1:1–3). Once God created light, the day side of the earth was illuminated, regardless of whether the sky had clouds at that point. I think it is more likely that the clouds were made on day 2 when God separated waters above from waters below (clouds are liquid water droplets in suspension). And thus, Job 38:9 likely includes aspects of day 1 and day 2, which is perfectly acceptable in poetic literature.

27. Ibid.

> *In analyzing the structure and grammar of Genesis 1:1 and 1:2 Hebrew linguists have determined that those texts proclaim that the creation of the universe and the formation of earth must predate the events described in the six creation days by an unspecified but finite duration of time.*[28]

In other words, Dr. Ross is suggesting that the creation of the heavens and the earth happened sometime *before* the six days of creation, presumably millions or billions of years earlier. He suggests that Hebrew linguists have determined this (and not merely that this *might* be so, but that it "*must*" be so). In fact, Biblical Hebrew philologists who respect the perspicuity of the Genesis text have concluded *just the opposite* of what Ross posits.[29]

Of course, Ross fails to document why this must be true in this case, even if we allow that it is grammatically possible in other contexts — a hasty generalization fallacy. But more importantly, he has failed the Berean test (Acts 17:11); he has not searched the Scriptures to see if this is claim is true. If he had, he would have found that Exodus 20:11 disallows such a notion.

Exodus 20:11 states, "For in six days the Lord made the heavens and the earth, the sea and all that is in them, and rested on the seventh day; therefore the Lord blessed the Sabbath day and made it holy." The phrase "in six days" indicates that these events happened within that time span, and therefore not before it. The heavens (the universe), the earth, the oceans, and everything within them — everything in the earth and the rest of the universe — these were made within the span of six days. This disallows the notion that the earth and universe were created before the creation week. Ross has violated the analogy of faith in failing to interpret Scripture consistently with Scripture.

> *Consequently, whichever one of the four usages... one might choose for the Hebrew noun* yôm *(translated "day") to delineate the duration of the six creation days, Genesis 1 allows for both the universe and earth to be as old as astronomers' and physicists' measurements have determined.*[30]

---

28. Ibid, p. 32.
29. http://www.icr.org/article/gap-theory-trojan-horse-tragedy/; Johnson, James J. S., "Does Bereshith Mean 'in a Beginning'?" *Creation Matters*, 18(3):6-7 (May-June 2013).
30. Ross, *Navigating Genesis*, p. 32.

We again see that the motivation for interpreting the text this way has nothing to do with the author's intention, but is designed to allow "for both the universe and Earth to be as old as astronomers' and physicists' measurements have determined." Again, Hugh Ross's ultimate authority has been revealed. It's the secular scientists that have "determined" the age of the universe — not God. And they have done this allegedly by "measurements," not *estimations*. But age is not a substance that can be measured by the tools of empirical science.[31] Ross has committed another reification fallacy. I am tempted to call attention to the word "choose" in reference to discovering what *yôm* means, as if we were free to choose rather than the meaning being determined by context. But that would be nit-picking.

In a section entitled, "How long are the creation days?" Dr. Ross states,

> *. . . most nouns in biblical Hebrew possess multiple "literal definitions" or common usages. The Hebrew noun,* yôm, *translated "day" in Genesis 1 is no exception. It has four distinct literal definitions:*
>
> 1. *part of the daylight hours; for example, from noon to 3 PM*
> 2. *all of the daylight hours*
> 3. *a 24-hour period*
> 4. *a long but finite time period*[32]

Actually, in any language, most words have multiple meanings. And we have seen in earlier chapters that context determines which meaning is appropriate for a given sentence. But what about Ross's claim that *yôm* has four *literal* definitions? Dictionary.com lists the meaning of "literal" as: "in accordance with, involving, or being the primary or strict meaning of the word or words; not figurative or metaphorical." A word is used in its literal sense if it is used in primary sense, as opposed to a rare or figurative sense. The Hebrew word *yôm* normally means "day." This corresponds well to the first three definitions that Dr. Ross lists.

In fact, these first three definitions are merely shades of the same basic meaning — a solar day. Definition #1 isn't that different from definition #2 when we understand that the Hebrew style is to count a fraction of something as the whole. If I worked for half a day on Monday, it is fair to say that I worked on Monday. And definition #3 isn't so different from definition

31. http://www.icr.org/article/genesis-critics-flunk-forensic-science/.
32. Ross, *Navigating Genesis,* p. 35.

#2 when we consider that the beginning of one period of daylight is separated from the next by 24 hours. In other words, if I say that something will happen in three days, it matters not whether I am thinking of 24-hour days, or merely 12 hour periods of daylight separated by 12 hours of night. Either way, we end up with the same answer. This is the literal definition of *yôm* — a day. It is literal because this is how the word is used in well over 95 percent of biblical instances.

Can *yôm* ever refer to a period of time longer than 24 hours? Perhaps, but if so it is very rare. There are approximately 2,000 instances of the word *yôm* in the Old Testament, including the plural form *yamim*. But only a handful of them could possibly be interpreted as something other than a literal day. And even these exceptions are found primarily in the poetic literature, where non-literal usage is to be expected. And in such instances, the word is part of a prepositional phrase, such as "the day of the Lord."[33] So is the "long period of time" definition of *yôm* a literal usage? No — by definition. *Literal* refers to the ordinary, common usage of a word. And since the "long period of time" usage is not remotely the common usage, it is not proper to refer to it as literal. Ross is demonstrably wrong on this issue.[34]

It would be more proper for Ross to say, "The Hebrew word for 'day' may be used in some contexts in a figurative sense to indicate a long, but finite period of time." That is (potentially) accurate. He could then say, "And I believe that is the way it is used in Genesis," and then we could debate the issue. Why does he insist that the figurative usage should be called "literal"? How does Ross treat Christ's figurative usage of the noun "door" when referring to Himself, in John 10:9? Does Ross call that a "literal" usage of the noun "door"? Or what about when John the Baptist, in John 1:29, called the Lord Jesus "the Lamb of God" — would Ross say that Jesus was then a "literal" lamb? Sometimes when people cannot defend their position on logical grounds, they resort to rhetorical twisting. Could that be what is happening here?

Ross continues, "While modern-day Hebrew has two words for an extended, finite-duration time period, in biblical Hebrew no other word besides *yôm* possesses the meaning of a long but finite period of time."[35]

---

33. Even the "day of the Lord" can refer to a 24-hour day in which the Lord does something truly unprecedented and spectacular.
34. www.icr.org/article/4537.
35. Ross, *Navigating Genesis,* p. 35.

Really? What about *olam*? This biblical Hebrew word is used to indicate a long but finite period of time, and does so throughout the Scriptures. In Genesis 6:4, this word is used of the men "of old." In fact, (unlike *yôm*) the primary, literal meaning of *olam* is a long duration that is beyond ordinary perception. Clearly the word was in use in biblical Hebrew, because the Bible uses that word in passages like Genesis 6:4, or to describe the ancient Hills in Genesis 49:26. It would have been a great choice for Genesis 1 if God had really intended to convey the notion that he created over six long ages of time.

Or what of the Hebrew word *qedem* which can mean "old" or "ancient" as in the "ancient mountains" in Deuteronomy 33:15. This word is used to indicate "ancient times" in 2 Kings 19:25, Nehemiah 12:46, Isaiah 37:26, 45:21, and elsewhere. That certainly seems to indicate "a long but finite period of time." Again, there is no doubt that the word is used in biblical Hebrew because it occurs throughout the Old Testament. Wouldn't that be a better word to use than "day" if God wanted to communicate that creation took vast ages?

Still other Hebrew words were available to indicate vast ages that would be far more appropriate than "day." The Hebrew word *dôr,* which denotes a "generation," can refer, in a secondary sense, to time in general and is translated as such in passages like Genesis 6:9 (NASB, NKJV). For that matter, the Hebrew word *tamîd* is used for something that is continual (as in Exodus 25:30, 27:20, 28:29–30, 38), but not necessarily forever (Number 9:16, 28:3, 6). Clearly, Hugh Ross is badly mistaken in thinking no biblical Hebrew words besides *yôm* can denote a long finite period of time.

He continues, "Therefore, if Moses wanted to communicate a creation history consisting of six eons, he would have no other option but to use the word *yôm* to describe those eras."[36]

This is a (rather obvious) bifurcation fallacy. And, as a matter of Biblical Hebrew philology, this is outrageously, irresponsibly, flat-out false. Putting aside for the moment that there are many Hebrew words that are far more appropriate than *yôm* to indicate a long period of time, if these words were not available would Moses use the word that normally means "day" to mean "time" without any qualifiers indicating non-literal usage? Wouldn't that be highly misleading? Has Ross overlooked some other options?

---

36. Ibid.

In English, if we had no words to indicate any time longer than a day, would it be impossible for us to express longer times? Hardly. Could we indicate a "year" without using the word "year"? Certainly. We could speak of 365 days. If we wanted to indicate a long, finite period of time, we could say "thousands upon thousands of days." If we wanted to indicate billions of years, we could say, "the days are uncountable, like the number of sand grains on the beach." If we finite humans can easily think of such solutions, how much more can God communicate His intention with clarity? God knows how to use similes and other figures of speech to convey large numbers (Genesis 22:17, 32:12, 41:49). We've seen previously that the context of Genesis demands the ordinary, literal usage of *yôm* as an ordinary solar day. The bottom line is that Hugh Ross's transmogrifications of the Genesis text are a denial of the perspicuity of God's Word.

Message of Day Seven

In chapter 9 of *Navigating Genesis*, Dr. Ross makes some additional arguments for an old earth. Most of these stem from his understanding of the seventh day — the day God rested from His work of creation. Let's examine some of the relevant claims. Regarding the mention of the seventh day in Genesis 2:2–3, Ross states the following:

> *Now the writer seizes the moment to drive home a lesson: Remember that God is the one who established, by example, the pattern of one work-free day (of 24 hours) in seven for humans and a work free "day" (of one year) in seven for tilled land.*[37]

But does Genesis 2:2–3 really teach these things? It does state that God rested on the seventh day, and sanctified it. But does it tell us that people are to have one work-free day in seven? I can't find that in the text of Genesis 2. Of course, Exodus 20:8–11 tells us quite explicitly that we are to have one day of rest in seven on the basis that God created in six days and rested one. And the Bible teaches that the land is to experience a Sabbath year, one year of rest in seven in which crops are not to be planted (Exodus 23:10–11; Leviticus 25:2–4).

But does the Bible anywhere teach that the basis for a Sabbath *year* is the creation week? No. And why not? It is because God didn't create in six

37. Ibid., p. 85.

years, and rest one *year*; rather He created in six days and rested one day. So the creation week cannot be the basis for Sabbath years. The Bible teaches that our *work week* is based on the creation week — but, contrary to Hugh Ross's claim, it never teaches that Sabbath *years* are a result of the creation week. Ross has committed the text fallacy — not reading the text carefully, and basing a conclusion on what the Bible does *not* say.

It seems that Ross has implicitly committed "the point is" fallacy. Namely, he seems to be arguing that the *important thing* that Genesis conveys is a pattern of 6 and 1, and that other details may be disregarded. He suggests that the units of time are not important. But this won't do, because the text *does* specify the amount of time — six *days*. If God wanted to specify six units of time of unspecified length, there are a number of ways to do that in Hebrew. The principle of inerrancy demands that we take the specified time units as true — days, not long ages.

There is also something very revealing in Dr. Ross's claim. He says, that "God is the one who established, by example, the pattern of one work-free day (of 24 hours) in seven for humans. . . ." But where does he get the "of 24 hours" part? The Bible nowhere says that our workweek is made of days that are explicitly said to be 24 hours long. The text simply says "days" (Exodus 20:8–10). Dr. Ross has (correctly) reasoned that these must be literal, 24-hour days, from context. But how did he come to that conclusion?

Obviously, Dr. Ross knows on some level that the numerical prefix "six" indicates that the Hebrew word for day(s) is being used in its ordinary, literal sense. But this same prefix is used for the days of creation referred to in Exodus 20:11. God has linked our workweek to the creation week using precisely the same words and phrasing. So if the days of creation were really "long but finite periods of time" then so would be the days of our week — in which case Ross would lose all rational basis for saying that our work week is made up of days "of 24 hours."

Then we come to what appears to be a central argument in Dr. Ross's claim that the days of creation are not truly "days," but vast ages — the alleged continuation of the seventh day. He states:

> *In Genesis 1, each of the six creation days (except the seventh) is marked off with the same refrain "There was evening, and there was morning." . . . Until day seven, that progression continues. We see God's work of transforming the world from darkness, as a symbol of*

> *chaos, toward light, as a symbol of order until that day. But, by the seventh day the transformation God intended is complete, and that day remains open-ended.*[38]

In other words, since the phrase "there was evening, and there was morning" is not mentioned for the seventh day, Ross concludes that the seventh day has continued even until now. How does he reach this conclusion? It is based on a number of logical and hermeneutical fallacies. First, it seems that Ross does not take morning and evening literally, otherwise he would have to take the days literally. After all, a day is composed of one evening and one morning. A long period of time would be composed of many evenings and many mornings. In failing to take evening and morning literally in this historical narrative portion of Scripture, Ross has violated the genre principle.

Perhaps Dr. Ross thinks that evening and morning are used merely to indicate the beginning and ending of each age of creation. If that is so, then he has committed "the point is" fallacy. It is as if to say, "the actual literalness of evening and morning doesn't matter; the point is that each 'day' had a beginning and an ending." But the Hebrew words for "evening" and "morning" are never used to indicate any sort of generic beginning or ending in any historical narrative text of Scripture. They always mean "evening" and "morning."

Even if we ignored these errors, Dr. Ross's reasoning is still fallacious. Essentially, he has argued that since the ending of the seventh day is not mentioned in Scripture, it has not happened. We immediately recognize this as the fallacious "argument from silence." Just because something isn't mentioned doesn't mean that it didn't happen. And, as mentioned earlier from his other book, this argument proves too much. If evening and morning represent the beginning and ending of the seventh day, and if not mentioning the end of the seventh day means it hasn't happened yet, then we would also have to conclude that it has not yet begun! After all, neither *evening nor morning* is mentioned.

> *This picture of an ongoing seventh day receives mention in other portions of Scripture. Psalm 95:7–11, John 5:16, and Hebrews 4:1–11 (each by a different writer) indicate that the seventh day began, from an earthly perspective, after the creation of Adam and Eve and extends*

38. Ibid., p. 88.

> *through the present year to a future time. Revelation 21 tells us that the seventh day will eventually end for us, when God's purposes for this cosmos have been fulfilled and God unveils an entirely new heaven and earth for us, a new creation with new physical laws, appropriate, as always, to the fulfillment of His divine purposes and plans for life beyond cosmic time.*[39]

Do any of these Scriptures indicate that the seventh day is ongoing? Not at all. Psalm 95:7–11 and Revelation 21 don't even mention the Sabbath day at all. Ross has violated the text principle. John 5:16 refers to Christ's healing on the Sabbath day; but that doesn't refer to the *first* Sabbath day — the day after God ended His work of creation. The Sabbath day is *recurring* (Exodus 20:8–11), and it's hard to believe that Ross doesn't understand that. Hebrews 4:4 does mention the Sabbath day, but does it say that this day continues until now? Clearly not. Rather, it indicates that God's *rest* continues until now.

There is a difference between what a person does on a particular day, and the day itself. If I played ping-pong on Wednesday, and continued to play ping-pong until Sunday, could we conclude that Wednesday lasted until Sunday? Likewise, God rested from His work of creation on the seventh day, and God's rest continues today since His work of creation is complete. But this in no way suggests that today is part of the seventh day.

Ross later repeats one of his errors in translation: "In biblical Hebrew, as opposed to modern Hebrew, no other word besides *yôm* carries the meaning of a long but finite time period."[40] And we have seen that at least four biblical Hebrew words carry just such a meaning: *olam, qedem, dôr,* and *tamîd.* And these *literally* indicate a long period of time, which would make them far more suitable than the rare and figurative use of *yôm* if God had intended to communicate that He created over long periods of time.

> *Because the Bible contains dozens of lengthy texts on various themes relevant to creation (see table 9, "Relevant Biblical Creation Texts"), it provides a means for testing and amplifying interpretations of the Genesis 1 account. An integrative analysis of all these passages leads to the conclusion that* yôm *refers to a long, but finite, time period.*

39. Ibid.
40. Ibid., p. 89.

> *This understanding of "day" yields a consistent reading of all the Bible's creation texts. It eliminates any internal contradictions. To interpret the Bible literally is not enough; one must also interpret it with internal (as well as external) consistency.*[41]

Much of that sounds pretty good. It appears on the surface that Dr. Ross is attempting to interpret Scripture with Scripture, honoring the principle of consistency and the analogy of faith. After all, it is quite true that a correct interpretation of one Scripture will not contradict a correct interpretation of another. And Ross provides a table (listed below) of pertinent texts that he believes can only be read consistently if the creation days were actually vast ages.

So what's the problem? Well, Dr. Ross provides absolutely no evidence at all that any of the verses he lists require the creation days to be vast ages. No argument is made and no examples are given. He's made an unsupported claim. It is hopelessly arbitrary and this violates the most important principle in hermeneutics — you must have a cogent reason for your interpretation. Ross provides none. And having looked at every text he provided, I can't find a single example that requires or even suggests that creation was anything other than six literal days. And strangely absent from Ross's list are the many verses that would *not* make sense if creation had taken billions of years. Such verses include Exodus 20:8–11, which teaches that our workweek is based on the creation week, or Mark 10:6, where Jesus states that the first humans were made "from the beginning of creation" and not billions of years later.

Note also that Dr. Ross's hermeneutic attempts to achieve internal "as well as external" consistency. By external consistency, he apparently means that his interpretation of Scripture will be consistent with secular models of earth history. But this violates proper interpretation, because it is irrelevant to the author's intention and is not based on the author's words. Ross's approach is a soft form of the naturalistic method of interpretation, which was refuted in chapter 3.

Here are the verses that Dr. Ross provides in his Table 9 as "Relevant Biblical Creation Texts": Genesis 1, 2, 3–5, 6-9, 10–11; Job 9, 34–38, 39–42; Psalm 8, 19, 33, 65, 104, 139, 147–148; Proverbs 8; Ecclesiastes 1–3, 8–12; Isaiah 40–51; Romans 1–8; 1 Corinthians 15; 2 Corinthians 4;

41. Ibid.

Hebrews 1, 4; 2 Peter 3; Revelation 20–22.[42] He provides a brief summary of what he believes to be the "creation theme" in each of these passages. Note that over half of these are from poetic/prophetic literature, where some degree of non-literal/non-narrative usage would be expected.[43] Yet Ross uses these poetic passages to override the clear teaching in the historical narrative of Genesis 1 — a clear violation of the genre principle.

We also see an egregious equivocation fallacy on the word "creation." This word can refer to the act of God creating, as in the "creation of the universe described in Genesis 1." Or it can refer to that which God created, as in "this world is God's creation." This latter usage of creation is basically synonymous with "the world" or "the universe" and is spoken of throughout the Scriptures. The former usage, the act of God creating, is most clearly described in the historical narrative of Genesis 1 and 2, though some other passages refer back to it. These two meanings are very different and should not be confused.

Of these two meanings of "creation," which is relevant to the days of the creation week? Clearly only the former meaning, *the act of God creating*, is pertinent. The latter meaning, "the universe," tells us nothing about how or when the universe came in to existence — only that it was created. Yet Ross conflates these two meanings. His list includes many verses that have absolutely nothing to do with the creation week; rather they refer to the world as it now is — the created order. Consider Psalm 19. This psalm tells us of God's revelation in the world. But there is absolutely nothing in this chapter that references the *act* of creation. Psalm 19 does not even mention the creation week, and doesn't so much as hint that the days of creation were anything but ordinary days.

We saw in a previous chapter that Psalm 104 uses creation primarily in the latter sense. It describes God's present provision in the created order. It's certainly *not* a retelling of the act of creation in Genesis, though it does allude back to the creation week in spots. But it is obvious that this Psalm refers to the present time in which the author wrote it, because it refers to

42. Ibid., p. 90.

43. As we saw in chapter 5, the Books of Job, Psalms, Proverbs, and Ecclesiastes are part of the poetic wisdom literature. They make extensive use of synonymous and antithetical parallelism, confirming their not-so-literal poetic style. Likewise, Isaiah is a prophetic book that makes heavy use of poetic figures of speech, and so does Revelation. Yet Ross refers to all these as "biblical creation texts" as if they were historical narrative. They are not.

the city of Lebanon and ships in the ocean (Psalm 104:16, 26). These did not exist during the creation week. Moreover, the passage refers to carnivorous activity (verse 21), but Genesis teaches that animals were originally created vegetarian (Genesis 1:29–30).

Do we have an exception in 2 Peter 3? Doesn't verse 5 teach that the heavens are old? Yes, it does, because the universe *is* old — very old — *thousands* of years old! Second Peter 3 doesn't tell us how old the universe is though, only that it's old. Applying the "explicit constrains the implicit" principle, we use the specific details of Scripture to learn precisely how old the universe is, and it is these details that provide an estimate of around 6,000 years.

Doesn't 2 Peter 3:8 teach that a day is like a thousand years? And if so, does this mean that the days of creation could be thousands of years each? Second Peter 3:8 is not referencing the days of creation at all, and so it would be out of context to take it as such. In context with verses 9 and 10, we can see that the Apostle Peter is explaining God's patience by reminding his readers that God is beyond time. From God's perspective, it is no harder to wait a day than a thousand years — those two very different units of time are similar in the sense that God is beyond them both. The verse does not say that a day *is* a thousand years. Rather, it means that it is *like* that to God, and a thousand years as a day.

Some might say, "So when God speaks about time, it could mean anything." Not so. God is beyond time, but He can enter time and He certainly knows how to tell time. Since God is beyond time, when He communicates units of time it is always for our understanding and therefore to be understood on human terms. It's absurd to think that because God is beyond time He cannot communicate time events in ordinary language. God is beyond space as well. So can we conclude that when God speaks of locations in Scripture, we need not take these locations literally? Context does not support such interpretations.

It seems that this list of "biblical creation texts" is nothing more than the fallacy of elephant hurling — listing many items that are said to support an argument without giving a single example or explanation of how. Perhaps Dr. Ross thinks that no one will bother to actually look up these passages. But when we do, we see that none of them require creation to be anything other than ordinary days. Don't just take my word for it; read them yourself.

> *The idea that the beginning of the universe, earth, and life on earth dates back only a few thousand years dismisses — at best — all the sciences and infuriates scientists. Some, who might be open to considering the good news of redemption in Christ, never give the biblical message a chance because of its seeming nonsense about creation.*[44]

It is hard to avoid the conclusion that Dr. Ross's approach to hermeneutics is not remotely motivated by a desire to understand the author's intention, but rather to accommodate modern secular opinions about the age of the earth and of the universe. Namely, many people have been persuaded that science proves a multi-billion-year-old cosmos, and then have trouble accepting the Bible because of "its seeming nonsense about creation."

But the problem is not with the text of Scripture. God doesn't need Hugh Ross to correct the Scriptures to make them line up with secular opinion. Rather, people with unbiblical opinions on the age of the earth are badly mistaken, and need to be politely but firmly challenged. No, science does not establish an ancient world. But more importantly, modern "scientific" opinions about age have no bearing on the *meaning* of the Scriptures. Rather than attempting to accommodate the ignorance of secularists about origins, it is far better to educate them on the truth about origins. After all, the "good news of redemption in Christ" makes no sense apart from the literal history of Genesis. If death is a normal part of the world, having preceded mankind for billions of years, how can it be the result of Adam's sin? And if death is not the penalty for sin, then why did Jesus die on the Cross?

Dr. Ross then appeals to church history:

> *Ante-Nicene scholars (those prior to* A.D. *325) devoted some two thousand pages of commentary to the "hexameron," the portion of Genesis 1 describing the six creation days. No other section of Scripture received more of their attention. Yet in all their pages of commentary, only about two address the meaning of "day" or the time frame for creation. Their comments on the subject remained tentative, with some favoring the day-age (typically a thousand-year period) interpretation — and their studies preceded the influence of science. Not one explicitly endorsed the 24-hour-day interpretation. But all believed*

44. Ross, *Navigating Genesis*, p. 89.

> *that God was intimately involved in the creative process, and that this creation doctrine — the who and the how of creation but not the when — makes a difference in how we respond to God and His Word.*[45]

Many errors have been packed into this single paragraph. Let's take them one at a time. First, the "hexameron" refers either to Genesis 1 or the early theological commentaries on Genesis 1. The name itself is from the Greek, *hexa,* meaning "six," and *hemer,* meaning day.[46] So even the name that was applied to this type of literature shows that early scholars did believe that Genesis meant to convey six days — not vast ages.

Second, the *earliest* extant hexameron is attributed to Basil, and dates to around A.D. 370 — *after* the council of Nicaea. Third, when we consult this earliest hexameron, we find that it explicitly confirms creation in six 24-hour days. Basil wrote,

> Since the birth of the sun, the light that it diffuses in the air, when shining on our hemisphere, is day; and the shadow produced by its disappearance is night. . . . Evening is then the boundary common to day and night; and in the same way morning constitutes the approach of night to day. . . . If it therefore says "one day," it is from a wish to determine the measure of day and night, and to combine the time that they contain. Now twenty-four hours fill up the space of one day — we mean of a day and of a night; and if, at the time of the solstices, they have not both an equal length, the time marked by Scripture does not the less circumscribe their duration. It is as though it said: twenty-four hours measure the space of a day, or that, in reality a day is the time that the heavens starting from one point take to return there. Thus, every time that, in the revolution of the sun, evening and morning occupy the world, their periodical succession never exceeds the space of one day.[47]

And what of Dr. Ross's claim that "Not one [ante nicene scholar] explicitly endorsed the 24-hour-day interpretation"? Ross gives no support for this,

---

45. Ibid., p. 91.
46. *Hemera* is the Greek word normally used for a literal day. It is the same word used for Resurrection of Christ on the third *day* in Matthew 16:21, 17:23; Mark 9:31, 10:34; Luke 9:22, 18:33, 24:7, 24:46; 1 Corinthians 15:4.
47. Basil, *Homily II on the Hexaemeron.*

but the claim is demonstrably false. Justin Martyr (A.D. ~100–165) believed in literal creation days. In his first defense he writes, "But Sunday is the day on which we all hold our common assembly, because it is the *first day on which God,* having wrought a change in the darkness and matter, *made the world*; and Jesus Christ our Saviour on the same day rose from the dead."[48] Irenaeus (A.D. ~130–202) also explicitly stated his belief in a six-literal-day creation, as we show below. Theophilus of Antioch (2nd century A.D.) affirmed a six day creation.[49] So did many others.

Some of these, such as Irenaeus, believed that the literal days of creation *also* suggested and symbolized future human history, with each day foreshadowing a future thousand-year period. But they didn't deny that the creation days themselves were ordinary 24-hour days. Irenaeus says, "For in as many days as this world was made, in so many thousand years shall it be concluded. . . . and in six days created things were completed: it is evident, therefore, that they will come to an end at the sixth thousand year."[50] I don't find hermeneutical support for such prophetic dualism. But clearly Irenaeus believed in a six-day-creation. Thus, Ross's claim is solidly refuted.

Fourth, Dr. Ross's point about there being little early discussion of the timespan of creation doesn't automatically imply his conclusion: that this is because the issue was unimportant. Rather, it could equally well mean that there was little debate on the matter, and thus it was unnecessary to defend the obvious. There isn't a lot of early literature defending the fact that the Israelites wandered in the wilderness for 40 years as opposed to 40 *billion* years. Why? It is because the text is clear.

Fifth, what of Ross's claim that the early non-literal-day supporters "preceded the influence of science"? This again is false. The science of that time period was based largely on Greek thinking. And the Greeks believed in a very ancient universe. That did influence early Christian thinking, and not for the better. It is therefore not surprising that some early Christians rejected the six-day timescale in order to accommodate Greek "science." The ideas of evolution and deep time are not new; they have merely taken a new form with the advent of Darwinian evolution and the big bang.

Sixth, Ross's final sentence is an example of "the point is" fallacy. Namely, he suggests that the "*Who* and *how* of creation" in contrast to the

48. Justyn Martyr, *The First Apology*, chapter 67.
49. Theophilus of Antioch, Book II, chapter 12.
50. Ireneaus, *Against Heresies* (Book V, chapter 28, section 3).

"*when*" is what "makes a difference in how we respond to God and His Word." In contrast, the Apostle Paul states that "*All* scripture is given by inspiration of God, and is profitable for doctrine" (2 Timothy 3:16; KJV), not just the "Who and how." If Scripture specifies the timescale of creation, which it does, then this timescale is correct. God makes no mistakes. If we accept some parts of Scripture, but then dismiss the parts we don't like, such as the timescale of creation, then this will indeed "make a difference in how we respond to God and His Word."

Seventh, a crucial principle of hermeneutics is that any information gleaned from early Church leaders must be considered secondary and supplementary to the text of Scripture itself. And we have already seen that the Scriptures do teach a six-day creation. If some early Christian writers failed to properly interpret the text, this has no effect on the meaning of the text itself, and should not dissuade us from applying proper hermeneutical principles. Ross argues as if he were a Roman Catholic, as if he believed that the opinions of the early Church fathers were somehow authoritative. Even a casual study of early Church history reveals that the "early Church fathers" committed all sorts of theological blunders. A review of how the Church systematically corrected the mistakes of its early fathers would be of some value. But the only authoritative interpreter of God's Word is God's Word.

> *The inclusion of day seven in the creation story, with its clue to the meaning of "day" as an extended time period, has become a treasured gift from the One who inspired the Word — if we recognize and accept its implications. However, the pressure to resist what it tells us about long days springs from a powerful source, a highly emotional reaction to the idea that death of any kind must have been part of a "very good" creation prior to humanity's act of rebellion against God.*[51]

We have already seen that proper interpretation of the seventh day does not have the implications that Hugh Ross desires. Namely, it does not allow for vast ages. In fact, the numerical prefix "the seventh" constrains the seventh day to be ordinary, along with the other six. Unable to deal with the logical arguments that have destroyed his position, Ross rhetorically suggests that his opponents are merely reacting emotionally in assuming that death could

51. Ross, *Navigating Genesis*, p. 91.

not be in the world before Adam's sin. This is a question-begging epithet fallacy. Actually, we have seen that the six days of creation can be defended purely on the textual grounds of the creation account in Genesis 1 — apart from any reference to death. Rather, the entrance of death into the world as the result of Adam's sin is a scriptural teaching that serves to confirm the already-established biblical timescale.

First, we note Ross's equivocation and straw man fallacies involving the word "death." The word has more than one meaning in Scripture, and even more meanings in modern English. We can speak of a "dead" battery, or say that the phone line is "dead." We can speak of a dead plant or a dead animal. The surface of human skin is composed of "dead" cells. These are all different types of death, and not all of them fit the biblical definition of death. Biblical creationists recognize this. It is only the biblical definition of death that is excluded — on biblical grounds — before the Fall. Ross has equivocated on this term. So Ross's claim that his opponents reject "death *of any kind*" prior to sin is a straw-man argument. I don't know of any biblical creationist that believes that "death" of plants or skin cells or bacteria is disallowed before the Fall.

The Hebrew term for "life" is *nephesh*, often used in sequence with the Hebrew word *chai* or *chaiyah* which can also mean "living" or "alive." When God created the land animals on day 6, He made "living life" (*nephesh chai*) often translated as "living creatures" (Genesis 1:24). The term is also applied to birds and water creatures (Genesis 1:20) and to human beings (Genesis 2:7). It does not apply to soul-less organisms such as bacteria and (most likely) insects. Only soul-possessing animals and humans are *alive* in the biblical sense of the word.

However, plants are never referred to in Scripture as *nephesh chai*. They are not alive in the biblical sense of the word. Can plants die? If they are not alive in the biblical sense, then it is absurd to think that they can die in the biblical sense of the term. The same principle applies to bacteria; they have no *nephesh* life and so there is no "death" in the biblical sense if one is eliminated. So when the Bible speaks about death entering the world as a result of Adam's sin (e.g., 1 Corinthians 15:21–22; Romans 5:12), it is not a reference to plant "death" or skin-cell "death," but rather true death of things that are truly alive. This would refer to animals and human beings. Ross has violated the translation principle, and the context principle.

> *The statement "it was good" appears six times in Genesis 1. In the concluding remarks in verse 31, God evaluates the sum of all His creation work as "very good." Many Christian leaders, including a number of prominent creationists, interpret all these declarations of the goodness of God's creation as proof that no disease, parasites, or carnivores could have existed before Adam and Eve's sin against God in the Garden of Eden. They go so far as to conclude that no death or suffering of any kind occurred previous to that rebellious act.*[52]

What other conclusion could we rationally infer? Would God create a world full of pain, suffering, disease, bloodshed, animals ripping out the innards of other animals, and then look at it all and pronounce it "very good"?[53] What kind of person does Ross think God is? More importantly, what kind of person does *the Bible* say that God is? Is God a cruel being who enjoys watching His creatures as they suffer and die? If not, then Ross has no hermeneutical grounds for his belief in a "very good" world that is full of death and suffering.

If we entertain the hypothesis that God's definition of "very good" is that His creations are to suffer disease and ultimately death, then rationality demands that we must be consistent with that principle. Don't bother to pray for people who are sick, since it's "very good" and approved by God that they are sick. Don't mourn the death of a friend — because death is "very good." Feel free to mistreat your pets, because their suffering and death are "very good" things. If these conclusions are to be rejected, then to be rationally consistent, we must also reject the premise that "very good" includes death, disease, and suffering.

Perhaps Ross will argue that only human death is bad, and thus only human death entered the world at the time of the Fall. But this cannot be defended biblically. God cares about animals too (Luke 12:6), though not to the same extent as humankind, of course (Luke 12:7). The Lord states that a righteous man values the life of his animals, and thus unnecessary cruelty to animals is wicked (Proverbs 12:10). The character of God as revealed in the text of Scripture shows that it would be contrary to His nature to create animals and make them suffer and call it "very good." Instead, God gave Adam dominion over a very good world; and it was Adam's sin that caused all under his dominion to suffer.

52. Ibid.
53. See *Creation Basics and Beyond*, chapters 1 and 7, available at www.icr.org.

Moreover, when Adam sinned, was only human death instituted at that moment? No, God instituted animal death at the time of the Curse. God sacrificed an animal or animals to provide skins of clothing for Adam and Eve, a bloody but effective illustration of the devastating consequences of sin (Genesis 3:21).

And what of carnivorous activity? Hugh Ross requires carnivores before the Fall of man because he accepts the secular timeline. But the Bible teaches that all animals were originally vegetarian before sin. This would have to be the case because there was not yet death (of any living creatures). But it is also explicitly mentioned in Genesis 1:29–30: "Then God said, 'Behold, I have given you every plant yielding seed that is on the surface of all the earth, and every tree which has fruit yielding seed; it shall be food for you; and to every beast of the earth and to every bird of the sky and to every thing that moves on the earth which has life, I have given every green plant for food'; and it was so."

> *These leaders overlook three critical points. First, Adam was not the first fallen created being. That distinction belongs to Satan. The Bible is silent on how long before Adam's rebellion Satan's mutiny occurred.*[54]

Presumably, Dr. Ross means to blame Satan for animal suffering. Why? The secular timeline, which Ross accepts, has animals living, suffering, and dying for hundreds of millions of years before humans arrive on the scene. So obviously, animal suffering cannot be blamed on Adam if it was occurring billions of years before Adam existed. But Satan was apparently created earlier — so Ross implies that perhaps Satan's sin resulted in a cursed world. But there are three problems here.

First, Satan was never given dominion over the earth, so it would be unjust for creatures that are not under Satan's dominion to suffer for his sin. Second, the Bible explicitly blames Adam for the sin that entered the world (Romans 5:12, 8:20–22). Yes, Satan sinned before Adam did. But the earth remained a paradise because Satan was not its steward. The Bible teaches that God gave man dominion over the earth (Genesis 1:26–28).

Psalm 8:4–8 states, "What is man that You take thought of him, and the son of man that You care for him? Yet You have made him a little lower

54. Ross, *Navigating Genesis*, p. 91.

than God, and You crown him with glory and majesty! You make him to rule over the works of Your hands; You have put all things under his feet, all sheep and oxen, and also the beasts of the field, the birds of the heavens and the fish of the sea, whatever passes through the paths of the seas." It was the sin of Adam, the one that God had placed in charge of His creation, that resulted in the Curse on the ground (Genesis 3:17).

Third, on the sixth day — after God had made Adam and Eve — God saw everything He had made and it was *very good* (Genesis 1:31). "Everything" must include Satan, since Satan was created by God. Thus, Satan had not yet sinned at the time of the creation of Adam and Eve. And therefore, the sin of Satan cannot account for any alleged millions of years of death and suffering before Adam and Eve.

> *Second, God possesses total foreknowledge. Before He created the universe He knew when, where, and how Adam's rebellion would occur. Consequently, He possesses the capacity to design the universe, earth, and earth's life ideally in advance of the future advent of human sin.*[55]

Dr. Ross's unstated conclusion seems to be that God may have cursed the earth due to Adam's sin even before Adam sinned, since God knew it was coming. But this is unjust. It is fundamentally unethical to force punishment on people for a crime that they have not yet committed.[56] Furthermore, this explanation doesn't make sense of God's statement that everything was "very good" on the sixth day. That simply doesn't mesh with a world full of death and suffering, regardless of the cause of that death and suffering.

> *Third, while the present creation is "good" and "very good," it will some day be replaced by a far superior creation — the new creation described in Revelation 21-22.*[57]

Where does the Bible say that the *present* creation is "very good?" It doesn't. Dr. Ross has again violated the text principle. The Bible instead teaches that the present creation is under a bondage of corruption (Romans 8:21) and groans and suffers pain (Romans 8:22). There are certainly aspects of

55. Ibid.
56. See *Creation Basics and Beyond*, chapter 7, esp. pages 61–64, available at www.icr.org.
57. Ross, *Navigating Genesis*, p. 91.

the world that are still good, because God is still working in this world (Romans 8:28). But there is evil and tribulation in the world due to sin (John 16:33).

> *In the new creation there will be no death, decay, suffering, grief, evil, sin, disabilities, disease, or restrained free wills.*[58]

Aside from "decay," I largely agree with this because it follows from the nature of God (the nature of "decay" will be covered below). Because the Bible teaches that God is good, I am confident that he would not make a new creation full of death, suffering, disease, and so on. And for exactly this reason we can conclude that God did not make the first earth with these things. But Ross rejects this reasoning. He does not find it inconsistent with the nature of God for God to create a world full of death, disease, and suffering. So on what basis does he conclude that the new earth will not have these evils?

It won't do for Dr. Ross to say that the text teaches that there will be no death, pain, or curse (Revelation 21:4, 22:3), because the text also teaches that of the *original* earth (Romans 8:20–22; Genesis 3:17–19, 1:31; Isaiah 24:5–6) — a doctrine that Ross rejects. Indeed, the Bible teaches that the consummated new earth will be a *restoration* of the original (Acts 3:21). So it makes no sense to think that the future eternal state will be a paradise if the world was not a paradise originally. Dr. Ross is again dreadfully inconsistent.

> *The present creation is very good in that it is the best possible creation for God to redeem those humans who so desire freedom from their slavery to sin. To put it another way, it is the perfect creation for God to eradicate evil and suffering and enhance the free will capacity of redeemed humans to experience and express love.*[59]

Here we have a particularly heinous example of the superfluous distinction fallacy. To protect his preconceived thesis, Dr. Ross suggests that the world was *not* "very good" at its beginning, but was merely very good *for the purpose of redeeming people from sin.* But is there any textual basis for adding this clause? Is this qualification needed to produce internal consistency? Not

58. Ibid.
59. Ibid., p. 91–92.

at all. The text of Scripture simply teaches that the world was initially "very good." Period. The text does not add or imply any qualifiers, and therefore neither should we.

To be consistent, Dr. Ross really should add similar qualifications for the new heavens and new earth. Imagine if he claimed, "There will be no death, suffering, evil, sin, disabilities, nor disease — *for angels*. But of course people will continue to suffer these things. The eternal state will be perfect, in the sense that it will be perfect for angels, but not for people." That little two-word qualifier "for angels" drastically changes the meaning. And of course, Ross doesn't claim that. But if it would be inappropriate for him to add the qualifier "for angels" to the new heaven and new earth, then why does he think it is acceptable to add "for God to eradicate evil and suffering" to the "very good" of the original world? The Lord makes no such qualification, and therefore neither should we.

Unequal or Overlapping Days?

Dr. Ross goes on to argue that the days of creation are not necessarily of equal length, but are not overlapping. The first issue is moot, since we have already seen that textual exegesis indicates that these are ordinary days — the same as our work week. The days are non-overlapping because that wouldn't make any sense with a numbered list. Obviously, the fourth day cannot overlap the fifth, or they wouldn't be the *fourth* and *fifth* days respectively.

Fortunately, Dr. Ross accepts that the days of creation are not overlapping, but this puts him in a logical bind. Even if we grant for the sake of argument his view that these were actually six long ages, the order of creation acts does not match the secular timeline. Fruit trees are made on day 3, and fish on day 5 — the opposite of the secular order. Birds are made on day 5, and land animals on day 6 — the opposite of the secular order. So, How does Ross attempt to deal with these incongruities, if indeed the days don't overlap? He writes:

> *On each creation day God initiates a specific transformative event. On that basis, Genesis 1 indicates no sea mammals or birds were created until day five. However, God's* initial *creation of bird and sea mammal species on day five would not mean He created no more of these creatures on day six.*[60]

60. Ibid., p. 92.

So Dr. Ross's solution is to claim that each day marks only the beginning of the things God creates on that day — and that God may have created more at a later time. But is this hermeneutically defensible? It seems like another superfluous distinction fallacy, where "and God made ____" really allegedly means "and God *began to make* _____." But there is no hint of this in the text. On the contrary, the text indicates that God made all of the kinds of organisms on the day when He says He made them. Consider Genesis 1:20—23:

> Then God said, "Let the waters teem with swarms of living creatures, and let birds fly above the earth in the open expanse of the heavens." God created the great sea monsters, and every living creature that moves, with which the waters swarmed after their kind, and every winged bird after its kind; and God saw that it was good. God blessed them, saying, "Be fruitful and multiply, and fill the waters in the seas, and let birds multiply on the earth." There was evening and there was morning, a fifth day.

The text does *not* say "God *began* to create ____." Rather, it says, "God *created* ____." But has it been translated properly? The Hebrew construction is a waw-consecutive; this occurs when "and" (*waw* in Hebrew) is followed by a verb in the original Hebrew word order. The verb for "create" (*bara*) is in the qal imperfect, which when prefixed with *waw* has the translation value of a perfect verb — that is, the action verb is narratively reporting activity that is completed action, *not* activity that is just beginning to occur. Such a construction generally denotes past action, and is typically the way a sequence of past events would be recorded in Hebrew. In other words, it means "God created" (e.g., at that time) — not "God started to create" (and continued for some time thereafter).

The same waw-consecutive construction is used in Genesis 1:4 and 1:5 "God saw. . . . God called. . . ." Did God merely *begin* to see the light, and *begin* to call it "day" on that first day? Likewise, many of the verbs in Genesis 1:6–11 use exactly the same construction. Clearly, these all involve past action which was completed on the day mentioned. It's not surprising that every major English translation renders these verses (and Genesis 1:20–23) in past tense, denoting completed action, and not as Ross has mistakenly proposed.

However, even if Ross were not mistaken about the verb tense, his rendering of Genesis 1:20–23 would not solve the problem. Even if God had merely *started* creating birds and swimming mammals on day 5, this is still before the first land creatures were made on day 6. Yet advocates of the secular timescale imagine the first birds and whales (swimming mammals) coming hundreds of millions of years after land animals. So even if the text allowed for the continued creation of birds and swimming creatures after day 5 (which it doesn't), it would not help Ross at all. The order is still wrong.

Notice also that Ross mentions only sea *mammals* and birds; but the Bible teaches that "every living creature" that was to fill the waters was made on day 5. This would naturally include fish. All swimming life and flying life was made on the fifth day. Why does Dr. Ross mention only swimming mammals? The secular timescale has fish evolving long before mammals and birds. And so Ross reads the text in such a way as to accommodate this. But this isn't exegesis at all. The text tells us that fruit trees were made on day 3 (Genesis 1:11–13), two days before the swimming creatures. Yet the secular timeline has this reversed. Even if we assumed that only the first fruit trees were made on day 3, and only the first fish on day 5, the order is still opposite of the secular timeline. Why not just take God at His Word?

> *Romans 8:18–23 declares that the law of decay (a.k.a. the second law of thermodynamics, law of entropy, or Murphy's law) that permeates the entire universe must remain in effect until the fullness of the number of human beings who are destined to receive God's redemptive gift and the eternal salvation that accompanies it has been attained.*[61]

In the above paragraph, we have an example of an equivocation fallacy. Dr. Ross equates the "decay" mentioned in Romans 8:21 with the second law of thermodynamics. But is this legitimate? Is the Bible speaking of thermal energy transfer in Romans 8, or some *other* type of decay?

The second law of thermodynamics describes the universal tendency of thermal energy to go from a useful state (in which it can perform work such as powering a machine) to a useless state. In particular, the net flow of thermal energy (heat) will spontaneously move from a hot object to a cold object and not the reverse. For example, if an ice cube is placed in hot coffee the thermal energy will flow from the coffee into the ice cube. Since the coffee is losing thermal energy, it cools off. And since the ice cube gains

61. Ibid.

energy, it heats up. Theoretically, you could use this flow of energy to power a machine of some sort — to cause motion or electricity. But eventually, the ice cube melts and comes to the same temperature as the surrounding coffee, resulting in lukewarm, diluted coffee. At that point, the energy is useless and can no longer be used to power any machine.

The second law of thermodynamics involves a type of "decay"; thermal energy goes from a useful state to a useless state. But it seems *extremely* unlikely that this is what the Apostle Paul had in mind in Romans 8. Ross's claim smacks of the semantic anachronism fallacy. After all, *in context* the passage is not dealing with heat, temperature, or thermal energy. Rather, it is dealing with the effects of sin. The Greek word that is translated "decay" in many English translations of Romans 8:21 is *phthora*. It denotes moral or physical decay and is usually translated "corruption." Indeed, most of the major Bible translations translate the word as "corruption" in Romans 8:21 (ASV, KJV, Darby, Douay, ERV, Geneva, NASB, NKJV, Rev Webster, Webster, YLT). But I cannot find any instance where the Greek word is used to indicate "decay" *in a strictly thermodynamic sense*. The word *might* include that sense, but it certainly is not limited to it. Likewise in English, when we speak of a "corrupt" politician, we don't mean that he has reached thermodynamic equilibrium with his surroundings!

In fairness to Dr. Ross, some "young-earth" creationists that I highly respect have made a similar error, in thinking that the second law of thermodynamics was a result of the Curse and in using Romans 8 to justify this. After all, Romans 8 does speak of decay. And a person might speculate that such decay includes the decay of thermal energy (going from useful to a useless state). But such a speculation goes beyond the text, and does not stand up to careful reasoning. After all, Romans 8 does not teach that *all* forms of decay are a deleterious result of the Curse.[62] On the contrary, some types of decay are "good," even essential for life, and are therefore not associated with the Curse. The decay of animal waste as it is recycled back into the environment is a process for which we should all be immensely grateful.

62. If it did, then we could conclude that the second law did indeed begin at the Fall, using a categorical syllogism as follows: (1) All types of decay began at the Fall. (2) Thermodynamic decay is a type of decay. (3) Therefore, thermodynamic decay began at the Fall. The argument is valid but unsound because the first premise is false. Correcting that premise, the argument becomes: (1) Some types of decay began at the Fall. (2) Thermodynamic decay is a type of decay. (3) Therefore, thermodynamic decay began at the Fall. This new argument is invalid (and thus unsound); it is the fallacy of the undistributed middle (see appendix B).

Thermodynamic decay is also in this category — it is "good," is essential for life, and therefore existed before the Curse. How do I know this? Consider the following.

The second law describes the tendency of energy to flow from a hotter object to a cooler one. And we know this took place during the creation week because the Bible describes light flowing from the sun to the earth (Genesis 1:17). So, obviously, the second law was already in effect from the beginning. The chemistry in our bodies is designed to use the second law, and would not function apart from it. We require the second law to digest food, and the Scriptures teach that Adam and Eve were given food to eat before the Curse. Even our ability to walk requires friction, which is a consequence of the second law of thermodynamics. So this is a good law, essential for human life, and is not associated with sin or the Curse described in Romans 8.[63]

Additionally, Dr. Ross equates the second law of thermodynamics with "Murphy's law." But the latter is not a real law at all, merely the pessimistic adage that "anything that can go wrong, will go wrong." Murphy's law is not true, nor is it biblical.[64] Yet Ross has falsely equated it with the second law of thermodynamics, which he has falsely equated with the moral and physical decay that resulted from sin.

Moral decay is evil, and the Bible condemns it (Isaiah 5:20). And moral decay (sin) entered the world through Adam, because Adam was given dominion over creation. Certain types of physical decay, such as physical death, resulted from the Curse. But the good and necessary types of decay did not.

> *In another book I explain how the physics of decay operates as a tool in God's hand to restrain the expression of evil. Because the law of decay plays a role in constraining evil, one can conclude that decay is the result of the fall.*[65]

This continues Ross's equivocation fallacy. *Moral* decay was indeed a result of the Fall, and so were certain types of physical decay — such as disease and suffering. But thermodynamic mixing was not; we know from Scripture

63. Jason Lisle, "The Search for a Cursed Cosmos," *Answers Magazine*, July 2009.
64. Contrast "Murphy's law" with what the Bible states in Romans 8:28.
65. Ross, *Navigating Genesis*, p. 93.

that such mixing occurred before the Curse. Since Ross conflates these two very different types of "decay," he is forced into a logical dilemma. Dr. Ross knows that the second law is necessary for the chemistry of our bodies, such as the digestion of food. But he also knows that (moral) decay is the result of sin. And conflating these two, Dr. Ross is led to believe that the second law of thermodynamics is the result of sin. But we have already seen that the second law was in effect from the beginning. Adam could not have survived without it. So what is Ross's solution?

> *God (in His foreknowledge) knew that the fall of Satan and later that of Adam would occur. In advance of those events He would have designed the universe with the best possible physics to restrain the evil resulting from those falls.*[66]

After having just stated that decay is a result of the Fall, Ross then claims that it *preceded* the Fall. This violates causality. The effect of something cannot happen before its cause. Although God is beyond time and knows the future, He is righteous, and therefore does not force punishment on people in *advance* of their crimes.[67] The Curse upon the ground followed *after* Adam's sin, not before (Genesis 3:17). Again, Ross mentions Satan's fall. But Adam was God's steward on earth, not Satan (Genesis 1:26). And thus Satan's sin did not bring sin or death *upon the world* — Adam's sin did (Romans 5:12).

> *(The Bible is silent on the timing of Satan's fall. His rebellion may have occurred before the cosmic creation events.)*[68]

Several problems are evident in Dr. Ross's parenthetical comment. First, we've already seen that the Bible is not entirely silent on the timing of Satan's fall. Satan's sin must have happened after day 6, because on the sixth day "God saw everything that he had made, and, behold, it was very good" (Genesis 1:31; ASV). Since Satan is part of the "everything" that God had made, it stands to reason that Satan also was very good at that time. Satan's fall must have happened sometime after the sixth day and before the sin of Eve (since Satan lied to and tempted Eve).

---

66. Ibid.
67. See *Creation Basics and Beyond*, chapter 7.
68. Ross, *Navigating Genesis*, p. 93.

There is also a severe logical problem with Satan's rebellion allegedly occurring "before the cosmic creation events." Time begins with the creation of the universe: "In the beginning God created the heavens and the earth." Satan is a created being. Thus, he was created during the creation week, because the Bible states that everything was made within that span (Exodus 20:11). So how could Satan rebel before his own creation, indeed before the beginning of time? Ross's suggestion sounds like he thinks Satan is beyond time and had existence before the creation of the universe. But God alone is beyond time (Revelation 1:8; Micah 5:2). Everything else is God's creation and cannot exist before the beginning (John 1:3).

> *Those who believe animal death prior to Adam's sin implies a cruel God need to consider again what God was willing to suffer for our sake. Nothing was more costly and painful for Him than allowing His Son to die for all our sins. Jesus' death was the ultimate expression of God's love.*[69]

Does this argument make any sense? No one is suggesting that killing is always an act of cruelty if it is done for morally commendable reasons. Did God have a good reason for allowing Jesus to suffer and die? Yes — it atoned for our wickedness. It was the right punishment for sin — our sin. It accomplished justice while allowing God's people to be redeemed. Moreover, Jesus volunteered. God the Father did not ask His Son to do anything that the Son was unwilling to do, and so there was nothing morally unjust about it in the ultimate sense. But did the creation volunteer to be subject to death and suffering? No — the Bible says it was *not* willing (Romans 8:20).

Thus, God's action in striking the earth with death and suffering of animal life is needlessly cruel and unjust *unless* it was the right punishment for sin. Adam, as the representative head of creation, rebelled against God, and thus it was right for God to punish Adam and corporately everything under Adam's charge. But any alleged animal death and suffering before Adam cannot be the result of sin, because the Bible is explicit that sin entered the world due to Adam's sin. Thus, animal death and suffering before Adam would be needlessly cruel, not morally commendable. A good

69. Ibid.

person does not needlessly harm an animal (Proverbs 12:10). How much more offensive it is to think that the perfectly Holy Creator would needlessly harm His creations!

> *These same individuals also need to ponder anew the pervasive New Testament message that the only way to truly live is to die (Philippians 1:21).*[70]

The unstated conclusion of Ross's enthymeme appears to be, "Since the Bible commends death, death is good and therefore could have preceded Adam's sin." But is physical death and suffering the kind of death that the New Testament commends? Clearly not. Ross has violated the context principle. The New Testament commends "dying to sin" — a metaphorical crucifixion of our wicked sin nature so that we might live more fully to God (Galatians 2:20, 5:24; Matthew 16:24). But literal death is not good, and is in fact an *enemy* that Christ will one day abolish (1 Corinthians 15:26).

Moreover, note that Philippians 1:21 is not addressing "the pervasive New Testament message that the only way to truly live is to die." Rather it expresses Paul's dilemma. On the one hand, he wants to be in the full presence of His Lord, which can only happen when he dies. On the other hand, Paul knows that he can only help others in this world if he continues to live in this world and suffer its afflictions. The context (Philippians 1:22–26) makes this very clear, and Ross has apparently not read the passage very carefully. This violates the text principle.

> *They also need to consider that Romans 5:12 declares that "sin entered the world through one man, and death through sin, and in this way death came to all people." By saying "all people" rather than "all life" and by specifying "death through sin" Paul here clarifies that Adam's fall did* not *inaugurate animal death.*[71]

The fallacy here is an argument from silence. Animal death as a result of Adam's sin is not specifically mentioned in Romans 5:12, therefore, Ross concludes, animal death was not the result of Adam's sin. But just because something isn't mentioned doesn't mean it didn't happen — particularly when other passages do implicitly teach that animal death came as a result

70. Ibid.
71. Ibid.

of the Fall. Romans 5:12 also does not state that Adam ever "went to the bathroom." Can we conclude therefore that he never did?

We know from other Scriptures that death (in the biblical sense of the word) is an enemy and thus would not have been part of God's original "very good" creation (1 Corinthians 15:26; Genesis 1:31). The effect of Adam's sin was not limited to human beings, but extended to all creation since Adam was given dominion over creation (Romans 8:18–23; Genesis 1:26). In fact, the Bible teaches implicitly that the Lord killed an animal as a result of Adam's sin to provide skins of clothing (Genesis 3:21). Perhaps this was a picture of salvation to come. In any case, when we let Scripture interpret Scripture, we can come to no other conclusion than that death of living creatures is the result of Adam's sin.

In the final paragraph of this chapter, Ross rhetorically asks, "How can physical death be entirely bad when it is the only means by which we can gain true life?"[72] He has confused the penalty with the payment of that penalty. The penalty of a crime must be something very unpleasant, otherwise it is not a fitting penalty. Death is a fitting penalty for our rebellion against God who is life. It is an enemy of God, and one that He will abolish at the resurrection (1 Corinthians 15:25–26).

Imagine being a billion dollars in debt. What would that be like? You would owe so much, that you couldn't possibly ever pay it back in ten lifetimes. All of your possessions have been taken and applied toward your debt, but this hasn't made so much as a dent. Then imagine that someone comes along and pays your debt for you, and restores all your possessions. This is much like the gospel, except our debt is much greater. Dr. Ross's statement is a bit like asking, "How can being a billion dollars in debt be entirely bad, when it is the only means by which we can be made debt-free?" It's not the debt that makes us free, but that someone else paid it. Likewise, it is not death (the penalty for sin) that gives us life, but rather that Someone else paid that debt.

It turns out then that none of Dr. Ross's arguments from Scripture are hermeneutically sound. Each of his arguments commits at least one, and often more than one, substantial hermeneutical or logical fallacy.

---

72. Ibid.

Chapter 12

A Case for Eisegesis?

It's doubtful that anyone could seriously argue that the Bible itself teaches a billions-of-years-old earth. There just isn't any hint of deep time in the Scriptures. And we have seen that old-earth arguments that use Scripture are always fallacious — committing logical or hermeneutical fallacies. Therefore, most old-earth Christians must appeal to evidence external to the Scriptures to make their case. Their interpretation of Scripture is then adjusted to match. This is eisegesis — reading into a text based on external opinions foreign to the original audience. Many old-earth advocates are even honest about this eisegetical approach, and see no problem with it.

We've already seen that such an approach is fallacious. Eisegesis is not faithful to the intentions of the author, and therefore will not consistently arrive at the correct interpretation. But since secular interpretations of scientific evidence are the only evidence available for the old-earther, Christians who hold such a position must find a way to rationalize eisegesis — although they probably would not admit that this is what they are doing. Do such arguments stand up to scrutiny? Let's consider some arguments from chapter 6 of Dr. Hugh Ross's book, *Creation and Time.*

By way of introduction, it seems that Ross's argument for his approach to Scripture is based on two errors: (1) implicitly assuming that general revelation is propositional (made up of true sentences) and that its message is as clear, truthful, specific, and easy to interpret as the words of Scripture, and (2) that what scientists believe about the universe is the same thing as general revelation.

Both of these are errors. First, general revelation is that which God has made evident to us through what has been created — not through words (Romans 1:19–20; Psalm 19:3, NASB). Since it is not composed of words, it doesn't make sense to talk of it as being true, at least in a literal sense. A rock is not "true" or "false," it simply *is*. God's general revelation is not a literal message, but the innate knowledge we have of Him that we immediately recognize when we look at what God has made. Since it is not a literal message, it makes no sense to think of general revelation as having the propositional truth or linguistic clarity that the Bible has.

Second, the opinions of (primarily secular) scientists are not general revelation. On the contrary, most secular scientists flatly deny their knowledge of God, suppressing the truth in unrighteousness as Romans 1:18 teaches. Evolution and billions of years are hardly God's message; rather, they are a secular alternative to creation made up by people who are in rebellion against God. Let's look at the details of the Dr. Ross's argument.[1]

1. God does not deceive

> *God is truthful and desires to reveal truth, both in creation and in the written Word. He does not trick or deceive. . . . Many familiar Bible verses explicitly declare that God is truthful and that He does not lie, either in word or in deed.*

Well said. The strange thing about this claim is that it hurts Dr. Ross's case. If God does not lie, then when He says He made everything in six days (Exodus 20:11), we can trust that He really did. If God does not trick or deceive, then we can trust that He would not use language in a misleading way — saying "days" when He really meant "long ages" for example. It is because God does not lie or deceive that we can trust that the biblical age of about 6,000 years is the true age of the universe.

> *Whatever objects of His [God's] creation we subject to scientific analysis will reveal their true age . . .*

Scriptural support? The Bible nowhere claims that scientific analysis of something will reveal its age. The methods of science are well-suited to

1. Dr. Ross's statements are inset in italics throughout this chapter.

discovering facts about the present world. But age is a concept of history, and is not a substance that can be measured by scientific analysis (observation and experimentation). There is nothing wrong with using methods of science to measure present rates and processes and then make an educated guess about an object's age. But that guess will be influenced by the person's view of history, and will only be as good as the assumptions that went into it. Moreover, there isn't the slightest hint in Scripture that such guesses will be invariably accurate as Ross implies. As one example, we know that radiometric dating is generally unreliable because it gives wrong answers when tested on rocks of known historical age.

> *. . . provided the analysis is theoretically valid, correctly applied, and accurately interpreted.*

Even if all these conditions are met, there is no guarantee that the resulting educated guess about age will be accurate. But these conditions are not always met. Only if people embrace biblical history will they have a tendency to correctly interpret the evidence with regard to historical events.

> *For created things to show a deceptive appearance of age would seem a direct violation of God's own stated character and purpose.*

Here, Dr. Ross has committed the fallacy of reification. He has attributed "appearance" to "age." (He's arguing that the appearance of age is real, not "deceptive.") But since age is a concept of history, it cannot have an "appearance." To be fair, some biblical (i.e., "young-earth") creationists have also made this mistake. Regardless, age is not a substance that can be seen. Ross's fallacy here is very crafty because we do often talk of things or people "looking old" or "looking young." Is this fallacious?

What do we really mean when we say that a person "looks old"? It's not as though people come with their age stamped on their forehead so that we could tell by simply looking. But there are certain characteristics that we often associate with the aging process. Wrinkles, spots on the skin, grey hair, thinning hair, no hair: these things tend to increase as we age. People who have a combination of these traits in abundance we tend to say "look old." But we are not being literal; we cannot see age. What we really mean is that such people have *observable physical characteristics that are typical of the elderly but rare among youth.*

But how do we know that such characteristics are associated with the elderly? The only way we could learn this on our own is to observe many people whose age is known (because they've told us, or we observed their birth) and note that certain characteristics are typical in certain age ranges. We can figuratively say that a person "looks about 40 years old" because we know many people who are about that age and have similar characteristics. Even this is very inexact, because people don't age exactly the same.

But would it make sense to apply this to the earth? Can we say the earth "looks" billions of years old because we've seen many other planets of various ages (each of the planets told us how old it was), and the earth has characteristics similar to other planets that are around 4.5 billion years old? Clearly not. Aside from the Bible, we do not have any historic information on the age of any planet, and so there is no way to distinguish the appearance of "old" planets from "young" ones. According to the Scriptures, the celestial objects were made on the fourth day of creation — this would include the planets. So biblically, all the planets are the same age (except for earth which is just three days older than the other planets) — about 6,000 years. It appears that this present earth is exactly what a 6,000-year-old earth looks like.

Second, it is particularly fallacious to apply "appearance of age" to something that is supernaturally created. Many good Christians have stated that when Adam was first created he probably looked about 30 years old. But if we could somehow travel back to the day after Adam was made and ask him how old he thinks he looks, I find it hard to believe that he would say, "About 30." Having no basis for comparison, and knowing that he had just been created, it seems far more likely that he would say, "Apparently, this is what a one-day-old person looks like." Eve's appearance certainly would not have challenged his hypothesis.

We would probably consider the reification to be non-fallacious when someone says a *person* looks "old" since (1) we have a large sample of people whose ages are known historically with common age groups having certain observable characteristics in common, and (2) these people were born in the natural way — they were not created *ex nihilo*. But for the earth, there is no sample of planets of multiple ages for which to make the comparison, and earth was created *ex nihilo*. It is therefore an egregious fallacy of reification to argue that the earth must be old since it "looks old," because, frankly, it just doesn't. If people think the earth "looks old," this is due to unbiblical thinking on their part, not any deception on God's part.

Dr. Ross goes on to explain that, yes, Adam and Eve did not have to grow to adulthood. But he then reasons:

> *Reliable age indicators for human beings do exist, however. Liver spots on the skin, scar tissue, muscle and skin tone, visual acuity, blood and bone chemistry, and memories of past events provide fairly accurate measurements of human age. I'm willing to speculate that tests of these age indicators in Adam and Eve would have revealed their true age.*

Many of these effects (scar tissue, liver spots) would not have existed before sin entered the world. As to the others, what makes Ross think that tests on Adam and Eve would reveal their true age? What kinds of test does he propose? New human beings today take considerable time to develop bone, muscle, and skin. If we could go back and test Adam and Eve's bones, muscles, and blood, and then computed their age assuming that they developed at today's rates, our estimate would be off by a factor of perhaps 10,000 or more. Dr. Ross can speculate all he wants, but this isn't correct hermeneutics.

> *Another biblical example sometimes quoted as evidence for appearance of age is Jesus' first public miracle: turning water into wine. The text (John 2:7–10) states, however, that the wine Jesus miraculously made had superb flavor, flavor which in this case did not necessarily come from an acceleration of the aging process. Modern methods exist for measuring the true age of a wine, but taste is not one of them.*

Ross has completely missed a crucial point. By turning water into wine, Jesus showed that He (as God) can do instantaneously what would take a long time in nature. So when Ross argues that it must have taken God billions of years to form the universe and the earth, he is forgetting this very text. God doesn't require any time to do anything.

People at the wedding in Cana may have assumed that the wine came about in the ordinary way, and probably believed that the wine was well-aged due to its taste. But Jesus did not create the wine with appearance of age. Rather, He made it good. Likewise, God did not create the earth with appearance of age. He made it to work. If people apply unbiblical, naturalistic assumptions to how the earth formed, and then come away thinking it "looks" billions of years old, well, it's not God's fault.

Again, Ross commits the fallacy of reification in saying, "modern methods exist for measuring the true age of a wine." Age is not a substance and cannot be measured.

> *Neither Adam and Eve nor the water Jesus turned into wine are available for accurate age testing. . . . Therefore, neither should be brought forward as evidence supporting appearance of age.*

I actually agree with Dr. Ross's concluding sentence, but not for the reasons he puts forward. These lines of evidence do not support "appearance of age" because age cannot literally have appearance. The creation of Adam and Eve shows that God can do instantaneously (or nearly so) something that today takes a long time by natural processes. When Jesus turned water into wine, it showed the same thing. If people were to assume that Adam, or Eve, or the wine, came about by natural processes, their age estimate would be grossly inflated. Likewise, the universe was supernaturally created. If people were to assume that the universe came about by natural processes, their age estimate for the universe would be grossly inflated. Ross seems oblivious to this simple fact.

> *But the universe and the earth are available. The abundant and consistent evidence from astronomy, physics, geology, and paleontology must be taken seriously.*

Here Dr. Ross reveals his eisegetical approach to Scripture. Sometimes old-earth supporters will attempt to hide the fact that their interpretation of the Bible is subject to the secular scientists' opinions of earth's history. Not here. Ross takes the secular interpretations of scientific evidence and uses these to guide his understanding of the Bible. It is undoubtedly the "secular interpretations of the scientific evidence," not scientific evidence itself, that drives Ross's view. Scientific evidence (data) always requires interpretation in order to generate the propositional claims that Ross uses to guide his hermeneutic. I actually appreciate the fact that Ross is honest about his procedure. This is bad hermeneutics of course. But at least he admits it.

Modern scientific claims must not be used to interpret biblical claims. We saw the reasons for this in chapter 4.

2. Creation reveals God

> *The Bible affirms that the creation reveals God's existence, His handiwork, His power, and His divine nature.*

Creation does reveal God and His divine attributes, but not age.

> *It seems reasonable to conclude, then, that honest investigation of nature leads to discovery of truths, including truths about God and about His otherwise invisible qualities.*

Okay — but does it do so *infallibly*? There is no doubt that we can often learn truths through the systematic investigation of nature. But are we always led to the right conclusion if our investigation is "honest"? If Ross answers "yes," then he doesn't know anything about the history of science. Honest scientists draw incorrect conclusions all the time. We never have all the evidence, so we do our best to interpret the evidence we do have correctly. But often new evidence is discovered that overturns previous theories. If Ross answers "no," then why would he use fallible information to interpret the infallible Word of God?

> *We are "without excuse" because the physical universe speaks truly.*

The fallacy of reification is quite obvious here. The universe doesn't speak at all, let alone speak "truly." Ross has also violated the text principle. The Bible does not teach that men are without excuse "because the physical universe speaks truly," or because they have infallibly understood the evidence by their own scientific reasoning. Not at all. Romans 1:18–20 teaches that God has revealed Himself to men. People know about God's nature because He has "made it evident to them" (verse 19). This comes not from science, nor from a talking universe, but directly from God.[2]

Notice that Romans 1:18–20 does *not* say that people can learn from nature how old the universe is. That is not something that God has revealed in nature — only in His Word. In fact, Romans 1:20 confirms the biblical timescale of thousands — not billions — of years. Here is why. In the

---

2. See chapter 4, section on "the two books fallacy."

secular view, human beings have "only" been around for less than a million years in a universe that is 13.7 billion years old. So humans occupy only the *last* 0.007 percent of earth's history. Conversely, if we take Genesis as literal history, then human beings were made on the first week — they were right there during the creation of the world. Notice that Romans 1:20 tells us that people have been able to know about God's nature "since the creation of the world." Now how could that be if people weren't around until the last 0.007 percent of the history of the universe?

> *How could we be held accountable by God for our response to a distorted message?*

Several problems with this claim stand out. First, to what *message* does Ross refer? A message always involves language. It contains encoded information. But nature does not. This seems to be a continuation of the fallacy of reification — the idea that nature "speaks."

Yes, we can learn from nature, but it is not a *message*. Nature is not a distorted message, nor a true message because it is not a message at all. The only message God has given us is His Word — the Bible. Of course, if the Bible doesn't really mean what it says in Genesis, then its message is distorted. So Dr. Ross's question backfires on him. We are supposed to believe God's Word, but how can God hold us accountable to a distorted message?

> *. . . God certainly had the power to alter the laws of physics at the instant that Adam sinned against God. But we can be confident that He did not since the astronomical record shows no evidence of such an alteration.*

I won't address Ross's scientific blunders here. This chapter is about his biblical interpretation and reasoning. Dr. Ross is reasoning in a fallacious circle. He argues that astronomy shows that the laws of nature have always been constant. But astronomy is predicated on the assumption that laws of nature are constant. We could not predict the future positions of planets if the laws of nature change in the future. So in assuming that the methods of astronomy are reliable, Ross has already presupposed that the laws of nature have always been constant. He then concludes that they have always been constant. He has begged the question.

It should be very obvious that Dr. Ross is using secular science to constrain his understanding of Scripture, a clear violation of the principles of hermeneutics. It turns out that his arguments here are not so much an argument for eisegesis, but merely a manifestation of it.

3. Is nature also God's Word?

> *The Bible affirms that the Word of God includes not only the words of the Bible but also His words written on the heavens and the earth.*

What words has God "written on the heavens and the earth?" And where exactly does the Bible claim that the "Word of God" includes God's "words written on the heavens and the earth?" Ross violates the text principle, because there simply is no such teaching in all Scripture. The "Word of God" in Scripture always refers to the words that God Himself has spoken — the Scriptures (e.g., Acts 13:44, 46), or to Jesus Christ (e.g., Revelation 19:13). The Bible does teach that God reveals Himself in nature; but natural revelation is never referred to as the "Word of God." Ross's claim here is unscriptural and untrue.

> *Many young-universe creationists limit the Word of God to the words of the Bible.*

That's because the Bible is the one and only written Word of God. One of the distinguishing features of cults is that they almost always have some other book besides the Bible that they also take to be the Word of God. The position that "the Bible plus this other book are both inspired by God" is generally and rightly considered heretical.

> *Since the Bible declares that only God and His Word are truth, these creationists consider information from any source outside the Bible as inferior and suspect.*

Does Dr. Ross really believe that the fallible information outside the Bible is on equal footing with the infallible information within the Bible? No one doubts that there is information to be found outside the Bible. But the faithful Christian should not put such information on the same level as the inerrant information in the Bible.

> *To them, extrabiblical data holds little value for clarifying what the Bible teaches on any issue or for prompting correction of faulty interpretation.*

This is a straw-man fallacy for three reasons. First, biblical creationists do value extra-biblical information "for *prompting* correction of a faulty interpretation." In other words, external information may give us the motivation to go back to the Bible to make sure that our interpretation was truly driven by the text. The discovery that the planets orbit the sun prompted some Christians to check whether their interpretation of the Scriptures that allegedly supports geocentrism was sound. Of course, it wasn't. There is no verse in Scripture that teaches geocentrism, and Christians should never have thought so in the first place. It was a scientific discovery that provoked them to double check the Scriptures. But the external evidence from science should not influence the interpretation itself. It merely prods us to double check.

Second, we do believe that external evidence (historical, linguistic) can and should be used to help us understand the Bible. But external evidence is not infallible, and therefore should not be used in a magisterial way to override what the Bible clearly teaches. External historical documents can be helpful in understanding biblical events. But if an ostensibly historical document contradicts the history in Scripture, we should reject the external document outright, and should not attempt to alter the clear teaching of Scripture.

Third, although some external evidence can be helpful in getting at the meaning of the text, by definition this is only if it helps us understand the author's intention. This would be limited to translational issues, so that we may better understand the author's original language, or historical information that *would have been known to the author* and the readers of the time. Modern scientific ideas, opinions, or traditions would not have been known to the ancient world, and therefore cannot be used to better understand the author's intention.

> *Yet the Bible more than once says that God speaks through the creation.*

This is a bait-and-switch fallacy. Ross is trying to prove that (1) the Word of God is more than just the Bible, but also includes God's "words written on the heavens and the earth" and (2) that extra-biblical information is not inferior to biblical information and may therefore be used to clarify biblical information. Now he shifts to argue that God has given general revelation — which is a different point.

The Bible never calls general revelation the "Word of God," nor does it ever put general revelation on the same level as Scripture. On the contrary, the Bible teaches that it is superior in propositional specificity to general revelation, as we will see shortly. Moreover, general revelation is not the same as the statements and opinions of scientists, which is what Ross really wants to use to interpret the Bible. Yes, God has indeed revealed Himself through nature. No, this cannot be considered the "Word of God," nor is it on the same level as Scripture, nor can it be legitimately used to constrain our understanding of the Scriptures.

To support his claim that God speaks through creation, Dr. Ross next quotes Psalm 19:1–4. He quotes from the NIV, which incorrectly renders verse 3 (see chapter 6). It's a pity Ross didn't check a few other translations, or check the Hebrew, because he would have seen that Psalm 19:3 actually *refutes* the point he's trying to make. Namely, the Hebrew wording of verse 3 indicates that the "speech" of creation is not a literal message with language or words, and it cannot be literally heard. It's also a pity Ross didn't continue reading the chapter, because Psalm 19 clearly indicates the superiority of God's Word over general revelation — the opposite of Ross's position. In verse 10, the Psalmist contrasts the Word of God with creation, and indicates that God's Word is *better* than the most desirable aspects of creation (gold and honey are used as examples).

> *Psalm 85:11 reads, "Truth springs from the earth; and righteousness looks down from heaven" (NASB). The Hebrew word for truth, emet, basically means "certainty and dependability."*

Notice that Dr. Ross is trying to build up a theology primarily from the poetic literature, and then using this to modify the meaning of the historic passages, like Genesis. This of course violates the genre principle and the "explicit constrains the implicit" principle. The clear literal teaching of Scripture is that its words are infallible, and superior to anything in creation (2 Timothy 3:16). Jesus contrasted nature with His Word in Matthew 24:35, "Heaven and earth will pass away, but My words will not pass away."

It would be a gross violation of the genre principle to take Psalm 85:11 as teaching that the earth literally speaks truthful statements. Rather, the text gives us a poetic word picture — truth abounding among men as if it had sprouted out of the earth, just as righteousness "looks down" from heaven. Here, righteousness is personified to complete the parallelism; righteousness and truth go together just as heaven and earth go together. The passage does not even hint that men can extract an infallible message from creation, as Ross seems to suggest.

> *Addressing his three friends, Job challenges them: "Ask the animals, and they will teach you, or the birds of the air, and they will tell you; or speak to the earth, and it will teach you, or let the fish of the sea inform you." (Job 12:7–8). It would follow from these and other verses that, in addition to the words of the Bible being "God-breathed, . . . useful for teaching, rebuking, correcting, and training in righteousness" (2 Timothy 3:16), so also are the words of God spoken through the work of His hands.*

The problem with Ross's claim is obvious: there are no *literal* "words of God spoken through the work of His hands." The Bible *nowhere* teaches that there are literal words to be found in nature. Ross has committed the two-books fallacy.

He has also violated the genre principle. Job is part of the wisdom literature, and makes heavy use of poetry. The parallelism in this passage is clear: ask animals — speak to the earth, they will teach you — [they] will inform you. It is obviously non-literal; we shouldn't think that Job is literally suggesting that his friends should ask animals, birds, the earth, or fish a question, and expect a literal (linguistic) response. The passage says nothing about an infallible message from nature that could be used to interpret Scripture. But that's what Ross is suggesting.

Dr. Ross has also violated the contextual principle. In context, Job is explaining to his three friends that he is well aware that the Almighty has brought this calamity upon him (Job 12:3). Job uses hyperbole to make his point; Job is essentially saying, "It's so obvious that even animals could tell you that" (Job 12:7–9). The power of the statement lies in the fact that nature *cannot* literally speak. Job is saying that what his friends have told him is so obvious that even things that cannot speak could tell them that. The power of the hyperbole would be lost if nature really did have a literal message in words.

> *In other words, the Bible teaches a dual, reliably consistent revelation. God has revealed Himself through the words of the Bible and the facts of nature.*

This is the two-books fallacy. The Bible does not teach that God's revelation in nature is on the same level as His revelation through Scripture. In fact, it clearly teaches in many ways the superiority of God's Word over any other standard (2 Timothy 3:16; Matthew 24:35; Matthew 7:24–27; Psalm 119:72, 103, 127; Job 23:12). God's revelation in nature is not propositional, whereas God's special revelation is.

Jesus consistently used the Scriptures alone as His ultimate standard, saying "It is written" and "Have you not read?" (Matthew 4:4, 7, 10, 12:3, 5, 19:4, 22:31; Mark 7:6, 12:26, 14:21, 27; Luke 19:46, 24:46; John 6:45). On the other hand, Jesus never appealed to nature as His ultimate standard, nor did he ever use "the facts of nature" to adjust or constrain His interpretation of Scripture. Indeed, Jesus explained that the Word of God ("Moses and the prophets") is superior to the most spectacular evidence we could find in nature (Luke 16:24–31).

What are the "facts of nature"? Ross doesn't say. And yet this is crucial to his argument. If he means facts in a literal sense — something that is true — then his statement isn't wrong but doesn't help his case. The universe is not truly 13.8 billion years — this is *not* a fact. Dr. Ross may claim that it is, but this begs the question. He's supposed to be proving this claim, not arbitrarily assuming it. If on the other hand he takes "facts of nature" figuratively to mean "what people generally think to be true — what we *take* to be fact" then his statement is false. People do take things to be fact that are contrary to Scripture — like the "fact" that people cannot walk on water, or the "fact" that the dead cannot come back to life.

Since nature is not propositional truth, any facts about nature must either be stated in Scripture or discovered by human beings. There can be no disparity between the facts about nature revealed in Scripture and the words of Scripture, because the former is a subset of the latter. Yes, the Bible agrees with what it says about nature. That's tautologically true. But what about the facts of nature discovered by people? The problem with facts discovered by people is that it is hard to know for certain that they are truly facts, rather than merely beliefs. Things that people assume to be facts are sometimes later disproved.

According to Psalm 19:1–4, the "words" of God proclaimed through the stars and galaxies are constantly being read by all peoples unto the ends of the earth.

Dr. Ross rightly put "words" in quotes indicating non-literal usage. This shows that even Ross knows that nature does not have a literal message comprised of literal words. God's general revelation is available to all people — true enough. But that revelation is not comprised of words or written in a language. It is therefore not of the same clarity as Scripture, and not something that can be used to interpret Scripture because general revelation is not propositional.

Colossians 1:23 states that salvation "has been proclaimed to every creature under heaven."

When this verse is read in context, it does not support Ross's argument. Colossians 1:23 states, "if indeed you continue in the faith firmly established and steadfast, and not moved away from the hope of the gospel that you have heard, which was proclaimed in all creation under heaven, and of which I, Paul, was made a minister." Paul is writing about the gospel message when he says, "you have heard, which was proclaimed in all creation under heaven." Is Paul referring to general revelation? No. He is referring to special revelation because only this can be *heard*. The gospel is found only in Scripture, not in nature. Apparently, by the time Paul wrote Colossians, the gospel message had spread to the point where it could be called universal. Paul may be using some hyperbole here; the point is that he is addressing the gospel — God's Word, not general revelation.

So God's revelation is not limited exclusively to the Bible's words.

No one is suggesting otherwise. We all believe in general revelation. But Ross is making two errors: he conflates general revelation with scientific consensus, and he treats general revelation as if it were comprised of propositional statements.

The facts of nature may be likened to a sixty-seventh book of the Bible.

This is the two-books fallacy. Dr. Ross's statement here is disturbingly close to heresy. Adding anything to Scripture is forbidden by God Himself (e.g.,

Deuteronomy 4:2). The "facts of nature" — whether genuine facts or things merely believed to be factual — are not like another book of the Bible. And keep in mind what Ross is considering to be the "facts of nature" are really just the opinions of secular scientists. We dare not elevate such statements to the level of Scripture.

> *Just as we rightfully expect interpretations of Isaiah to be consistent with those of Mark, so too we can expect interpretations of the facts of nature to be consistent with the message of Genesis and the rest of the canon.*

Dr. Ross's argument here fails in several ways. First, it is *not* the case that interpretations of Isaiah are always consistent with those of Mark. Bible critics often misinterpret both, and then argue that the Bible is contradictory. Perhaps what Dr. Ross meant was that *correct* interpretations of Isaiah will be consistent with *correct* interpretations of Mark. That's certainly true. But then to complete the analogy he would have to say that only *correct* interpretations of the facts of nature will be consistent with Scripture. But then the conclusion does not support his philosophy; Ross wants to take the consensus opinions of secular scientists, which are often *incorrect* interpretations of nature, and use them to interpret the Bible. But there is no reason to suspect that incorrect interpretations of nature will match the Scriptures.

Second, Dr. Ross commits the equivocation fallacy on the word "interpretation." When applied to a book of the Bible, "interpret" means "to provide the meaning of the words." But to interpret nature means "to explain" in the sense of constructing a sentence with meaningful information. The former linguistic type of interpretation involves understanding the meaning of words that already exist. The latter involves the creation of sentences that didn't previously exist, which must then be linguistically interpreted in order to be understood. There is no reason to mechanically assume that sentences created by human beings are necessarily true. But all sentences affirmed by God are true. Coming up with a correct scientific model is a far more difficult task than simply understanding God's Words which are guaranteed to be true and understandable (2 Corinthians 1:13).

> *Many Bible passages state that God reveals Himself faithfully through the "voice" of nature as well as through the inspired words of Scripture. Here is a partial list of such verses: Job 10:8–14, Job*

> *12:7, Job 34:14–15, Job 35:10–12, Job 37:5–6, Job 38–41, Psalm 8, Psalm 19:1–6, Psalm 50:6, Psalm 85:11, Psalm 97:6, Psalm 98:2–3, Psalm 104, Psalm 139, Proverbs 8:22–31, Ecclesiastes 3:11, Habakkuk 3:3, Acts 14:17, Romans 1:18–25, Romans 2:14–15, Romans 10:16–18, Colossians 1:23.*

We immediately recognize the fallacy of irrelevant thesis. No one denies that God has revealed Himself through nature. But Ross wants to argue (1) that general revelation guides our understanding of special revelation, and (2) that general revelation is the same as modern views of science. But none of these verses (or any text in Scripture) proves either of these points. The Bible never even hints that God's revelation in nature is as clear as His revelation in Scripture, such that the former should be used to understand the latter. Nor does the Bible ever equate the beliefs of people about nature with general revelation. *Man's understanding of nature is not the same as God's revelation through nature.*

It is worth repeating that last sentence because it highlights one of the main "bait-and-switch" fallacies that Hugh Ross repeatedly employs as he conflates God's revelation with mankind's claims. Man's understanding of nature is not the same as God's revelation through nature.

This second truth is very important. Just because some people believe that life evolved from a common ancestor does not mean that this is God's revelation. Just because some people believe in a big bang and billions of years, it does not suggest that this is God's "voice" in nature. None of the verses that Ross lists remotely hint at such a thing. On the contrary, the biblical pattern is that the Scriptures should be used to correct man's beliefs about the world (e.g., Acts 17:11, 18:28; Isaiah 8:20, 34:16; John 5:39; 2 Timothy 3:16).

Again we see that Dr. Ross appeals primarily to the poetic sections of the Bible, with very few references to the epistles. In any case, these verses only indicate that general revelation exists, not that it is on the same level or has the same clarity as God's special revelation. And most of them really are not addressing general revelation at all (e.g., all the Job passages; Psalm 8, 98:2–3, 104, 139; Proverbs 8:22–31; Habakkuk 3:3).

> *Some readers might fear I am implying that God's revelation through nature is somehow on an equal footing with His revelation through the words of the Bible.*

Yes, that is certainly the impression I get, particularly when Ross states that "The facts of nature may be likened to a sixty-seventh book of the Bible." In his next two sentences, Dr. Ross does not deny this impression; instead, he defends it:

> *Let me simply state that truth, by definition, is information that is perfectly free of contradiction and error. Just as it is absurd to speak of some entity as more perfect than another, so also one revelation of God's truth cannot be held as inferior or superior to another.*

Here Ross commits the fallacy of irrelevant thesis. The issue at hand is not the "superiority" of special revelation, but rather the nature and propositional *clarity* of Scripture. Special revelation is comprised of truthful propositions. General revelation is not comprised of propositions at all. General revelation is not "truth" as Ross defines it (information that is perfectly free of contradiction and error), because general revelation is not *information* at all. Information always involves language — words — either written or spoken. Nature has no words. Special revelation may not be superior to general revelation, but it is definitely linguistically *clearer* and more specific.

Truth never contradicts itself. The problem is that we don't always know what is true when it comes to nature. It is fallacious to assume that human opinions about the universe are as consistently true as the words of Scripture.

> *It could be different, just like the content of Ezra is distinct from that of Romans, but it cannot be better or worse.*

First, no one is suggesting that special revelation renders general revelation unimportant; rather, biblical revelation is superior in its power to teach truth because it is (1) unfallen and (2) linguistically clearer and more specific. The Apostle Peter considered Scripture to be "more sure" than his own first-hand observations of Christ's Resurrection (2 Peter 1:16–21).[3] Therefore, the

3. Students of presuppositional apologetics will appreciate why this must be the case. Sensory observation is generally reliable, and is rightly considered good evidence for a particular claim. But the Bible is even "more sure." Logically, this must be the case because the basic reliability of senses is contingent upon the Bible. That is, we can trust that our senses are basically reliable because they are not products of accidental chance, but rather God has created them as recorded in Scripture (Proverbs 20:12). But if the Scriptures were not true, then we would have no rational basis for trusting our sensory observations at all. Since the Scriptures are foundational to the reliability of sensory observation, it is impossible for sensory observation to be more epistemologically certain than the thing upon which it is based — Scripture.

former (special revelation from Scripture) must guide our understanding of the latter (general revelation from the physical creation), not the reverse. Both revelations have their place. Ross wants to treat them as the same type of revelation. To prove this, he likens the situation to two different books of the Bible. This is the false analogy fallacy. Ezra and Romans are both propositional truth; they both have linguistic clarity. But general revelation does not.

> *Thus when science appears to conflict with theology, we have no reason to reject either the facts of nature or the Bible's words.*

Notice the bait and switch fallacy. Suddenly Ross has switched from discussing "general revelation" to "science" as if these were the same. And the "Word of God" is now replaced with "theology" — as if these were the same. The term "science" can mean a number of things. But primarily it means either (1) the systematic study of nature by observation and experimentation, or (2) the body of knowledge accumulated by such a procedure. The problem is this: neither of these is general revelation.

The first definition doesn't comport with Dr. Ross's statement at all, because a procedure cannot appear to conflict with theology since a procedure is not propositional. So we give Ross the benefit of the doubt and presume that he means science in the sense of the body of knowledge accumulated by the scientific process. This would include things like the mass of a proton, the formula for gravity, the composition of a star, the rotation rate of Mars, and so on. These are facts that we have learned from observation and experimentation.

But the "facts" of science are not always truly facts. Sometimes we learn that what was previously taken to be fact is wrong. Science textbooks are updated from time to time as new research overturns previous research. *Science is fallible.* Scripture is not. Dr. Ross is mistaken to put them on the same level.

When scientific propositions conflict with the propositions affirmed in God's Word, the scientific propositions are simply wrong. This is what the Bible affirms (Romans 3:4; Titus 1:2; Hebrews 6:18). It is fine to have some respect for traditional scientific wisdom. However, such traditions are ultimately fallible, and must not be used to override Scripture. Notice what Jesus said to those who interpreted Scripture in light of the traditions of their time:

> And He answered and said to them, "Why do you yourselves transgress the commandment of God for the sake of your tradition? For God said. . . . But you say. . . . You hypocrites, rightly did Isaiah prophesy of you: 'This people honors Me with their lips, but their heart is far away from Me. But in vain do they worship Me, teaching as doctrines the precepts of men' " (Matthew 15:3–9).

When Ross puts the opinions of scientists on the same level with Scripture, is this not "teaching as doctrines the precepts of men"?

> *Rather, we have reason to reexamine our interpretations of those facts and words because sound science and sound biblical exegesis will always be in harmony.*

What reason does Dr. Ross provide for his claim that "sound science and sound biblical exegesis will always be in harmony"? He doesn't list any, and the claim is not intuitive. After all, science is a fallible process, and therefore any knowledge resulting from the scientific method will always be subject to error and revision. Not so with Scripture. The Bible is inerrant, and it teaches that it is understandable. Sound biblical exegesis will never need revision. But science — even when done perfectly — is by nature not certain and is always subject to error.

> *From both the Bible and the record of nature we can establish that God is totally responsible for the existence of the universe.*

What is the "record of nature" of which Dr. Ross writes? He's been discussing his view that general revelation is on the same level as Scripture. Then he substituted "science" for "general revelation." And now he seems to be substituting the "record of nature" for "science." But is "science" a record of nature? Is general revelation?

A record is "an account in writing or the like preserving the memory or knowledge of facts or events." General revelation is certainly not a record because it's not in writing. Nature is not composed of propositional statements, and therefore cannot be a record. Could the "record of nature" be a reference to science? Although scientific theories may be written down, they do not generally preserve the memory of events that have transpired in nature. History books do this. History books record past events in writing.

What then would be the history book that records the details of nature — how the world was made, and how it came to be the way it is today? The "record of nature" is the Bible!

Not only that, the Bible is the *only* literal "record of nature." It is the only account in writing that records the details of how nature was created and the timeline of the major natural events (e.g., the Curse, and the Flood). Scientists may speculate about how the world began, but this is not a *record.* Dr. Ross's statement is very crafty because it makes it sound like science is a "record of nature" just like the Bible, and that both are on equal footing. In reality, there is only one record of nature — the Bible. Ross has committed the two-book fallacy.

The Alternative View: A Case for Exegesis and *Sola Scriptura*

Sola Scriptura is the biblical principle, retrieved and revived by the Protestant Reformation, that Scripture alone must be our ultimate standard. It does not deny the existence of lesser standards, but these must always be evaluated in light of Scripture. This stands in contrast with the view of Roman Catholicism that tradition, as defined by the Catholic Church, is equally authoritative with the Scriptures. The Roman Catholics teach that the Church alone may infallibly interpret the Scriptures — effectively making their church leaders the ultimate standard by which all truth claims are judged, including the claims of Scripture.[4]

Protestants rightly reject the Roman Catholic view, and yet many Christians (some genuine but erring, others "Christian" in name only) have embraced their own version of the pope. There are those who tell us that we must interpret the Scriptures in such a convoluted way as to agree with the opinions of the majority of secular scientists — including the big bang, deep time, and evolution. This makes man the judge of God's Word. Such a view is unscriptural. We do not need a Protestant pope to understand God's Word. We affirm genuine *sola scriptura.*

The Bible teaches that it alone is the ultimate standard by which all other truth claims are to be judged. It teaches this in a number of ways. Second Timothy 3:16 states, "All Scripture is inspired by God and profitable for teaching, for reproof, for correction, for training in righteousness."

4. Effectively, Hugh Ross treats secular claims about science as a substitute Vatican, in a system of thought that deviates from the sola Scriptura epistemology of the Protestant Reformation.

The text does not say, "Scripture *and nature* are profitable for teaching. . . ." Scripture alone, and all of it, is what we are to use as our standard.

The Apostle Paul continues, "Preach the word; be ready in season and out of season; reprove, rebuke, exhort, with great patience and instruction" (2 Timothy 4:2). It is the Word that is to be preached, not the Word *and some other message*. Paul continues as if he were speaking directly to our situation today, "For the time will come when they will not endure sound doctrine; but wanting to have their ears tickled, they will accumulate for themselves teachers in accordance to their own desires, and will turn away their ears from the truth and will turn aside to myths" (2 Timothy 4:3–4). With the myths of the big bang, deep time, and evolution so prevalent in our culture today, it is difficult to avoid the impression that we are living in the time that Paul was discussing (see 1 Timothy 6:20).

Does the Bible allow for another ultimate standard in addition to itself? Consider what Christ has to say about attempting to serve two masters: "No one can serve two masters; for either he will hate the one and love the other, or he will be devoted to one and despise the other. You cannot serve God and wealth" (Matthew 6:24).

It is logically impossible to have *two* ultimate standards. There would necessarily be some difference between the two standards. (If two standards are exactly the same, then we really have one standard.) How would we decide which is correct in areas where the two standards disagree? Obviously, we would need a third standard to judge which of the two is correct. But since the third standard is judging the other two, it is necessarily more ultimate than they are. This third standard is exposed as the one true ultimate standard held by the person.

Applying this principle to those who believe that Scripture and science are equally authoritative, what happens when the majority of scientists disagree with what the Bible teaches on a particular issue? Most scientists believe in deep time (billions of years), whereas the Bible teaches creation in six days. Many professing Christians expose their confidence in men and lack of faith in God's Word by attempting to reinterpret the Bible to match with deep time. But then again, the majority of scientists would say that turning water into wine is not possible, nor is resurrection from the dead. Perhaps this time, the Christian sides with Scripture. He judges that the Scriptures are right in this instance, even though they are wrong about the timescale of creation in his view. But in both cases the Christian has revealed that his ultimate standard is not God's Word; it is his own mind. *He* decides which Scriptures to accept and which to reject (or "re-interpret").

This problem is not new. It is common to all of us, going back to Adam and Eve. Eve sinned when she ate of the forbidden fruit, but she failed the test before this outcome. Her arc of sin began when she decided that her mind and her senses were sufficient to judge God's Word. God had said that Adam and Eve were not to eat of the tree, and that if they did they would surely die. Satan challenged this claim, and Eve decided that she would judge for herself. God's Word was obviously not her ultimate standard. Eve believed her mind was the ultimate standard to judge God's claims, and Adam followed suit. It is our fallen human nature to want to be our own ultimate standard, to judge by our own mind (Deuteronomy 12:8; Proverbs 12:15, 16:25, 21:2; Judges 17:6, 21:25; Numbers 15:39).

Anyone who puts anything else on the level of Scripture, be it scientific consensus, the "facts of nature," or the teachings of the Roman Catholic church, has not been faithful to God's Word. Such a person has decided that he will be his own ultimate standard. He arrogantly assumes that his mind is sufficient to judge God's Word. Perhaps God's Word will pass the test. But the person has already failed. He has not realized that God's Word is not the thing on trial. It is God's Word that will judge his mind — not the reverse.

Chapter 13

Theistic Evolution

How did God create life on earth? Did He supernaturally create various kinds of organisms at the beginning, to have them reproduce with large-but-limited variation? Did God progressively create new organisms by modifying organisms that He had made previously? Did God set up the laws of nature so that they would slowly build and modify organisms over millions of years, without any supernatural intervention? What does the Bible say?

We have seen in previous chapters that (1) Genesis is written in historical narrative, and (2) that historical narrative is properly interpreted in a primarily literal fashion. Therefore, we conclude that Genesis is properly interpreted in a primarily literal fashion. The words mean what they state. So what do they state?

Although a number of Christians hold to theistic (God-guided) evolution, I am convinced that the Bible disallows any form of particles-to-people evolution. The biblical constraints on the age of the earth that we discussed in previous chapters disallow any slow-and-gradual evolution. Clearly, evolution cannot happen over millions of years if millions of years are not available. But even if we set aside the age of the earth, I am convinced that the Bible disallows Darwinian evolution. Organisms show a great degree of variation and adaptability, but they remain the same basic kind of organism as their supernaturally created ancestors. Consider the following.

Genesis 1:21 teaches that God created the creatures of the sea and flying creatures on the fifth day of the creation week. Note that God didn't modify previous creations to merely shape or form new animals; rather He *created* them. The implication is that God by His will alone called into existence something qualitatively new — from nothing — that had no previous existence.

The Hebrew word translated "created" is *bara*, and indicates creation from nothing. God spoke into existence that which had no previous existence. *Bara* is the same word used in Genesis 1:1 when God *created* the heavens and the earth. He created the universe from nothing, because there wasn't anything before the beginning (otherwise it wouldn't be the beginning). Appropriately, the word *bara* is only ever used literally with God as the subject.[1] This makes sense. Human beings can form, or make, or shape, but only God can create something from nothing. Since the swimming and flying creatures were created, they did not come about by an evolutionary process.

Furthermore, God created these animals "after their kind," and instructed them to go and multiply. This suggests that all swimming and flying animals come in discrete "kinds" grouped according to certain essential common features that define a given kind. The instruction to go and multiply seems to at least suggest that animals will reproduce according to their kind. This is illustrated more persuasively in Genesis 6:20. Here, God explains that two of every kind of land creature, including birds, would come to Noah and board the ark to preserve their lives. Hence, a "kind" appears to be the reproductive limit of an organism. There may be great variation within a kind, but organisms do not cross kinds; otherwise it would not have been necessary to bring two of each kind aboard the ark to preserve life.

What of the land animals? Genesis 1:25 states that God made them as well; He made everything that creeps along the ground. Here the Hebrew word for "made" is *'asah* and means "to do, fashion, accomplish, make." *'Asah* doesn't necessarily specify that God made these animals from nothing, though it does not preclude that option either. So, could these animals have been made from previous animals?

Context disallows such a notion because again God made each of these animals "after its kind." If they had been made from a previous kind of animal, then God would have made them "after a *different* kind." Again, the Flood account shows that two of each *kind* of land animal boarded the ark in order to preserve that *kind*. This only makes sense if animals reproduce according to their kind. We might expect great variation within a kind. But

1. The Hebrew word *bara* is used sarcastically with people as the subject in Joshua 17:15. Here Joshua suggests that the people should create land for themselves, obviously something that they cannot literally do.

such variation will have limitations. Note also that of the specific kinds that are mentioned as token examples of God's creation on days 5 and 6, they are the same kinds of animals that we have on earth today: fish, birds, cattle. Animals have remained the same basic kind since creation.

And what of plants? Genesis 1 doesn't directly say that God "made" or "created" plants; instead God commanded the earth to sprout vegetation, and the earth did so (Genesis 1:11). Does this allow for an evolutionary origin from a common ancestor? No, the text states that all the plants sprouted "after their kind" — not "from a common, previous kind." The text specifically mentions grass (or vegetation), plants yielding seed, and fruit trees as token kinds. Note that the fruit trees then sprouted with fruit already on them (Genesis 1:12) — a unique aspect of the creation week that is not open to a naturalistic interpretation.

Genesis categorically disallows any evolutionary origin for human beings. The creation of our first parents is described in greater detail than that of the animals. God formed Adam from the dust of the ground and breathed life into him, at which point Adam become alive. Adam did not come from an ape, nor do apes and man share a common ancestor. Rather, Adam was made from dirt (Genesis 2:7).

Could this "dirt" be a metaphor for an ape? The genre of Genesis excludes such an interpretation. The historical nature of Genesis requires a literal reading with allowances for the occasional idiom. But there is no hint that the "dust" of the ground is a figure of speech. A metaphor must have an essential feature in common with what it represents; but we can hardly think of anything so different from an ape as dirt.[2]

Furthermore, consider the Curse of Genesis 3:19. Here God promises that Adam would one day return to the dust of the ground. If dust of the ground were symbolic for an ape, then God is promising that Adam would one day again become an ape! Clearly, we cannot interpret the creation of man in an evolutionary way without doing violence to the Scriptures.

The Theological Importance of a Literal Creation

The timescale of creation itself disallows any possibility of particles-to-people evolution. Evolution is supposed to work over hundreds of millions of years

2. If God had wanted Moses to use the word "ape" in Genesis 2:7, He could have done so, but He didn't. The word "ape" [*qôph*] fits the facts of 1 Kings 10:22 and 2 Chronicles 9:21, so it is used there, but the word "ape" does not fit the history reported in Genesis 2:7.

as tiny changes accumulate, gradually changing one kind of organism into another. But we saw in chapter 11 that the text of Scripture is not compatible with millions of years of alleged prehistory. According to the Bible, the universe is several thousand years old; and everyone agrees that evolution cannot possibly happen in such a period of time. But there are other biblical reasons to reject evolution.

In modern taxonomy, human beings are classified as part of the animal kingdom. But in Scripture, humans are distinct from animals from the beginning of creation. God made mankind in His own image and gave them dominion over all the animals (Genesis 1:26–28). This shows that there has always been a distinction between human and animal, and that humans are superior to animals in terms of authority and intrinsic value (e.g., Matthew 10:31). It is perfectly biblical therefore for a man to kill and consume an animal (Genesis 9:3). But to murder a person is forbidden because people, and not animals, are made in God's image (Genesis 9:5–6). If evolution were true, then this important Christian principle would have no rational foundation.

The gospel message itself would be without a rational foundation if evolution were true. The gospel is predicated on the fact that (1) death resulted from and is the penalty for man's sin, (2) all people are descended from Adam and are therefore sinful from conception, and (3) Jesus is a descendent of Adam, yet is also God and without sin, and is therefore qualified to represent us and pay our penalty on the Cross. But if evolution were true, then none of these things could be defended. (1) Death cannot be the result of sin or penalty for sin if millions of years of death occurred *before* Adam existed or sinned. (2) In the standard evolutionary view, there is no Adam — people today are allegedly descended from a group of individuals that branched off from the apes. (3) Apart from a literal Genesis, there is no guarantee that Jesus is descended from Adam and thus eligible to pay our debt.

In Acts 17:26, Paul explains that God made all people from "one blood," a reference to the bloodline of Adam. Since Christ is also in this bloodline, He is our relative and His death on the Cross can redeem us from sin. The Bible explains that the blood of bulls and goats cannot take away sin (Hebrews 10:4). This is because we are not of the same bloodline — we are not biologically related to bulls and goats. This doctrine would be lost if evolution were true, because we would indeed be related to bulls and goats.

Every major Christian doctrine has its rational foundation in the literal history of Genesis, and could not be defended apart from that history. Why are we morally obligated to obey God's law? Answer: Because God is our Creator and holds us accountable for our actions (Genesis 1:27, 2:16–17). Why are people morally obligated to wear clothing — in contrast to *all* animals? Answer: Because of original sin, clothing was introduced as a temporary covering for the shame of sin (Genesis 2:25, 3:7, 21).

What about the doctrine of marriage? Christians teach that marriage is the God-ordained union of one man and one woman for life. The logical foundation for this doctrine is Genesis 1–2. Eve was made from Adam's side to be of him and to help him. Scripture directly states that it is "*for this reason*" that a man marries a woman (Genesis 2:24). Jesus recognized this truth. When defending biblical marriage to the Pharisees, Jesus quoted from Genesis 1 and 2, thereby affirming the historical basis for marriage (Matthew 19:4–6). Thus, if God did not actually create Eve from Adam's side, then marriage would have no reason — no logical foundation. As our culture increasingly rejects Genesis, is it surprising that the institution of marriage is also under attack? Apart from the history of Genesis, why can't people redefine marriage to be anything they want?

Why have laws in evolutionary universe? Laws are designed to protect the weak from the strong. But evolution is based on the strong dominating the weak. Laws are anti-evolutionary by their very nature, because they inhibit the strong from abusing the weak. According to evolution, a species is only able to advance as its weaker members are eliminated. How contrary to the entire earthly ministry of Christ! Jesus healed the sick, and had compassion on the poor and weak.

The Evolution Bias of the Culture

Evolution is undoubtedly one of the most popular origins myths of our time. Students in most government-funded schools are taught from a very young age that life on earth began when chemicals — by chance — formed the first self-replicating cell. Through mutations and natural selection, this cell multiplied and diversified over billions of years, giving rise to all variety of life. Every person, every animal, every plant, every fungus, and every bacterium on earth are said to be biologically descended from a single, common ancestor. Evolution is not simply "change" in a generic sense, but a story to explain how all life came about without any need for God. This story comforts the atheist and gives him hope that he will not have to answer to God for his misdeeds.

Strangely, this story is often found in science textbooks, particularly those dealing with biology. Furthermore, the story is often required learning in *biology* classes. This is peculiar because science deals with how the universe operates today. It uses testable, observable, and repeatable experiments and observations. Evolution is none of these things. Why would a myth about the past be found in a science textbook?

This would seem to be a propaganda tactic enforced by evolution's followers. We rightly have confidence in the methods of science, and the body of knowledge acquired by scientific reasoning. We have all benefitted from the technological and medical advances made possible by scientific discoveries. Perhaps if an origins myth like evolution were linked to science, people would start believing the myth due to their confidence in science. If evolutionists can convince people that evolution is science, then they don't need to provide any evidence for evolution; people will be persuaded merely by association.

This method seems to have enjoyed some success. World culture has become increasingly comfortable with evolution, and as people increasingly reject the history of the Bible, the more they will feel free to follow their own desires, unconstrained by the tether of God's law. There can be no doubt that this happens. It happened in England. And it is now happening in the United States.

It may seem surprising at first that Christians have begun embracing evolution, or at least a God-guided version of it. Have these Christians considered the inconsistency? What could be more contrary to the nature of God than evolution? God is compassionate, merciful, fair, righteous, and good. Evolution is the most horrific version of origins that one can imagine. It allegedly proceeds by the ruthless conquest of the strong destroying the weak. It is a gruesome tale of death, suffering, disease, and bloodshed, in which the victors are the most efficient at killing any competition.

Theistic evolution is about the worst option we can logically consider. Even the name is paradoxical. Evolution by its very nature is supposed to be based on random mutations, guided not by God but by *natural* selection. Evolution was invoked to explain the origin of life without appealing to God. Why then would a professing Christian be inclined to think that God created this way?

We can speculate, but ultimately we know what is *not* the reason: careful hermeneutics. No one can rightly claim that he or she believes in theistic evolution because it is what the Bible teaches. We've seen above that the foundation of Christian doctrines always links back to the literal history of Genesis. We have seen that Genesis is historical narrative, which requires a literal interpretation. And Genesis literally teaches that God created in six days. The universe and life on earth are not the result of a slow natural process, but were spoken into existence by the power of God's Word (John 1:1–3; Psalm 33:6–9).

Nonetheless, it is very tempting to compromise God's Word with what we think we know about the world. Therefore, there will always be some Christians who read their Bible in a non-hermeneutical way in order to accommodate the latest secular notions. In the remaining sections, let's consider just a few of the arguments that professing Christians have put forth in favor of theistic evolution.

The Language of God — by Francis Collins

If anyone could make a good case for theistic evolution, it should be Dr. Francis Collins. He headed up the Human Genome Project, and now serves as the director of the National Institutes of Health. Dr. Collins earned a PhD in physical chemistry from Yale, and he professes to be a Christian. He holds to theistic evolution, and wrote a book on the topic called *The Language of God: A Scientist Presents Evidence for Belief.*

Clearly, if a professing Christian is to believe in evolution, he must somehow come to terms with the creation account recorded in Genesis and affirmed throughout the Bible. How does a theistic evolutionist deal with death before sin? Unfortunately, Collins does not even touch on this crucial issue anywhere in his book. How does Collins reconcile the different order of events between Genesis and the secular timeline that he embraces? Again, it isn't addressed. What hermeneutical argument does Collins make that the author of Genesis meant to convey the idea that God created over millions of years of evolution? You can search all you like, but no argument *from the text of Scripture* is made. Nonetheless, Dr. Collins does make some biblical claims, and these need to be analyzed to see if they are hermeneutically sound.[3] He states the following:

3. Dr. Collins' statements are inset in italics throughout this chapter.

> *A few months later I spoke to a national gathering of Christian physicians, explaining how I had found great joy in being both a scientist studying the genome and a follower of Christ. Warm smiles abounded; there was even an occasional "Amen." But then I mentioned how overwhelming the scientific evidence for evolution is, and suggested that in my view evolution might have been God's elegant plan for creating humankind. The warmth left the room. So did some of the attendees, literally walking out, shaking their heads in dismay. What's going on here? From a biologist's perspective, the evidence in favor of evolution is utterly compelling. Darwin's theory of natural selection provides a fundamental framework for understanding the relationships of all living things. The predictions of evolution have been borne out in more ways than Darwin could have possibly imagined when he proposed his theory 150 years ago, especially in the field of genomics.*[4]

We get a glimpse into Collins's mindset. In his view, evolution is a well-established fact. And hence, if the Bible is true, it must be read in such a way as to accommodate evolution. This violates one of the most basic principles of hermeneutics. The correct interpretation of a text must be based *on the author's words*, not on modern opinions of science or origins, regardless of the validity of those opinions. Dr. Collins isn't doing exegesis at all. He accepts evolution as the unquestionable reality, and then reads Scripture in such a way as to match, regardless of the context or genre of the text.

I could stop here. In order to demonstrate that an interpretation is unreliable, all I have to do is show that it is not motivated by the primary goal of understanding the author's intention by analyzing the author's words. And clearly, Dr. Collins is not motivated by that goal; rather, his goal is to accommodate evolution. His interpretation of Genesis is thereby refuted. But we will continue to see additional examples of this faulty hermeneutic.

Additionally, I'm curious as to what "predictions of evolution" Dr. Collins believes have been verified. He doesn't back up this statement with any examples, so we are left to wonder. I challenge his statement, and ask him to provide documented examples of predictions made according to the evolution model that were not also predicted by creation and were later discovered.

---

4. Francis S. Collins, *The Language of God: A Scientist Presents Evidence for Belief* (New York: Free Press, 2006), p. 146.

> *If evolution is so overwhelmingly supported by scientific evidence, then what are we to make of the lack of public support for its conclusions?*[5]

Could it be that evolution is *not* overwhelmingly supported by scientific evidence? That could certainly explain the lack of public support. Yet Collins doesn't give even a moment's consideration to that option. A good scientist ought to be willing to consider alternatives, if only to find good reasons why they are not possible. An inability or unwillingness to consider alternatives tends to result in beliefs that are ultimately arbitrary, and indefensible.

> *The problem for many believers, of course, is that the conclusions of evolution appear to contradict certain sacred texts that describe God's role in the creation of the universe, the earth, all living things, and ourselves. In Islam, for instance, the Qur'an describes life developing in stages, but sees humans as a special act of creation "from sounding clay, from mud molded into shape" (15: 26). In Judaism and Christianity, the great creation story of Genesis 1 and 2 is a solid bedrock for many believers.*[6]

First, we note that Dr. Collins is aware that the "conclusions of evolution appear to contradict" the Bible. And since he professes to believe the Bible, Collins has a rational obligation to either (1) defend a hermeneutically sound interpretation of Genesis that accommodates evolution or (2) relinquish either the Bible or evolution. Nonetheless, Dr. Collins makes no *hermeneutical* argument for evolution in his book.

It is strange that Dr. Collins lumps the Koran in with the Bible and even quotes from the Koran. The Bible is the only inspired Word of God, while the Koran is not. And as someone who professes to be a Christian, Collins ought to know that. Perhaps by linking the silliness of rejecting a scientific claim on the basis of the Koran, Collins hopes to persuade that it is equally silly for Christians to reject a claim on the basis of Scripture. But this is surely a false analogy. If the Bible really is the inerrant Word of God, then we should indeed reject any claim contrary to its proper hermeneutically derived teachings.

I also note that Collins refers to Genesis 1 and 2 as a "story." While this isn't necessarily wrong, Genesis really is a historical record. That's how it

5. Ibid.
6. Ibid., p. 149.

refers to itself (e.g., Genesis 5:1), and thus proper hermeneutics demands that we think of it that way as well. Collins states that this creation "story" is "a solid bedrock for many believers." But shouldn't it be? In His earthly ministry, Jesus often appealed to the history of Genesis to explain Christian doctrine (e.g., Matthew 19:3–9, 11:23–24, 24:37–39; Luke 17:29; John 8:56–58). Shouldn't a Christian — a Christ follower — do the same?

> *If you have not recently read this Biblical account, find a Bible right now and read Genesis 1:1 through Genesis 2:7. There is no substitute for looking at the actual text if one is trying to understand its meaning. And if you are concerned that the words in this text have been seriously compromised by centuries of copying and recopying, do not worry very much about this — the evidence in favor of the authenticity of the Hebrew is in fact quite strong.*
>
> *There is no question that this is a powerful and poetic narrative recounting the story of God's creative actions. "In the beginning God created the heavens and the earth" implies that God always existed. This description is certainly compatible with scientific knowledge of the Big Bang. The remainder of Genesis 1 describes a series of creative acts, from "Let there be light" on day one, to the waters and the sky on day two, to the appearance of land and vegetation on day three, the sun, moon, and stars on day four, fish and birds on day five, and finally on a very busy sixth day, the appearance of land animals and male and female humans.*[7]

The first paragraph is fine; I included it for context. But then we jump to this bold claim, "There is no question that this is a powerful and *poetic* narrative. . . ." No evidence for this claim is given, at least not here. It is merely asserted that chapters 1 and 2 of Genesis are poetic. What evidence *from the text* do we have that might suggest a poetic genre? Recall the list of indicators from chapter 5. Do we have copious use of synonymous or antithetical parallelism? No — Genesis 1 and 2 contain nothing of the kind. And this is *the key*, distinctive feature of Hebrew poetry. Since there is no parallelism, we can say definitively that Genesis 1–2 is *not* poetry.

But just to drill it home, there are additional indicators that Genesis is *not* poetic. The introduction to the book, the lack of verbal imagery, the

7. Ibid., p. 150.

frequent use of the waw-consecutive, the detailed names, locations, and genealogies all indicate that Genesis is historical narrative. There is not so much as a hint of poetic form in Genesis 1–2.

And what of Dr. Collins's claim that "This description is certainly compatible with scientific knowledge of the Big Bang?" First, the big bang is neither knowledge nor scientific. It cannot be confirmed or repeated in a laboratory or observed today. People may observe stars or microwave radiation and *interpret* such as the result of a big bang — but interpretation is not evidence.

Second, is Genesis 1:1 really compatible with the big bang? No. Genesis 1:1 teaches that both the heaven (the universe, apparently the very fabric of space-time) was created at the beginning *along with the earth*. But big-bang supporters teach that the universe came into existence *9.3 billion years before earth*. Also, we note that chapter 1 of Genesis doesn't end at verse 1. It continues to describe the creation of the universe in a way that is very different from the big bang. As one obvious example, the big bang has stars coming into existence billions of years before earth; but Genesis 1 teaches that the stars were created on the fourth day — *after* earth.

Third, Collins correctly summarizes what happens on each day of creation, but he seems oblivious to the fact that this contradicts the secular timeline that embraces. Namely, Genesis 1 teaches that fruit trees came before fish, birds came before land animals, and water came before land. The secular timeline reverses all of these.

> *Genesis 2 then begins with a description of God resting on the seventh day. After this appears a second description of the creation of humans, this time explicitly referring to Adam. The second creation description is not entirely compatible with the first; in Genesis 1 vegetation appears three days before humans are created, whereas in Genesis 2 it seems that God creates Adam from the dust of the earth before any shrub or plant had yet appeared. In Genesis 2:7, it is interesting to note, the Hebrew phrase that we translate "living being" is applied to Adam in exactly the same way it was previously applied to fish, birds, and land animals in Genesis 1:20 and 1:24.*[8]

8. Ibid., p. 151.

Is it true that "The second creation description is not entirely compatible with the first"? That violates the consistency principle. The inerrancy of God's Word guarantees that no part of what it affirms in one place will contradict what it affirms in another. Collins has violated one of the most basic principles of biblical interpretation. When a person thinks that one part of God's Word is incompatible with another, this proves positively that the person's interpretation of one or both of those parts is wrong.

Moreover, the example he provides does not prove his point. He says, "in Genesis 1 vegetation appears three days before humans are created, whereas in Genesis 2 it seems that God creates Adam from the dust of the earth before any shrub or plant had yet appeared." Dr. Collins seems to have in mind Genesis 2:5–7. Verse 5 states, "Now no shrub of the field was yet in the earth, and no plant of the field had yet sprouted, for the LORD God had not sent rain upon the earth, and there was no man to cultivate the ground." Then the description of the creation of man is recorded in verse 7. Does this contradict Genesis 1, which teaches that plants were created before man?

Apparently, Dr. Collins didn't read the text very carefully. Genesis 2 does not teach that no plants had yet been created at the time of Adam's creation. Rather it states that no plants *of the field* had yet *sprouted*. The phrase "of the field" is from the Hebrew word *sadeh* which refers to *cultivated plants*. That is, there were not yet any plants that had sprouted as a result of human agriculture. Genesis 2:5 also explains *why* there were not yet any cultivated plants: "there was no man to cultivate the ground."

Dr. Collins points out that the Hebrew phrase "living being" is applied to Adam "in exactly the same way it was applied to fish, birds, and land animals." Yes it is. What is his point? Adam, fish, birds, and land animals are all alive, so it's not surprising that the Hebrew phrase for a living being is applied to all of them. But the text also says that God created/made each of these animals *after their kind* — not from a common ancestor. And Adam was made from the *dust of the ground* — not an ape or any previous animal. Collins seems to ignore any texts that contradict his preconceived belief in evolution.

> *What are we to make of these descriptions? Did the writer intend for this to be a literal depiction of precise chronological steps, including days of twenty-four-hour duration (though the sun was not created until day three, leaving open the question of how long a day would have been before that)? If a literal description was intended,*

> *why then are there two stories that do not entirely mesh with each other? Is this a poetic and even allegorical description, or a literal history?*[9]

Here, Dr. Collins has asked a very appropriate question — what did the writer *intend*? The hermeneutically appropriate way to answer this question is to consider the writer's words. How does the writer interpret himself? The analogy of faith — that God's Word is the ultimate interpreter of God's Word — is the right answer. The writer of Genesis indicated that it is a book of history (e.g., Genesis 5:1). Unfortunately, this is not the answer that Collins selects.

Dr. Collins seems to think that if he can show a contradiction between Genesis 1 and Genesis 2, that this will give him license to disregard the details of these chapters under the pretense that they are merely "poetic." But in fact, an apparent contradiction is an indication that a person has not studied the text sufficiently. Even poetic sections of the Bible will not contradict other poetic sections when each has been properly interpreted. Poetry is not exempt from the law of non-contradiction.

Also, we see the oft-repeated claim that the days of the creation week might not have been 24 hours long because the sun didn't exist for the first three days. But the sun has little to do with the length of a day — it merely provides light from a fixed reference. The rotation rate of the earth is primarily responsible for the length of a day. Genesis teaches that God provided a temporary light source for the first three days (Genesis 1:3–5), and the earth was already rotating because it experienced evenings and mornings (Genesis 1:5).

By careful study of the text itself, we can ascertain the author's intention and easily answer all of Dr. Collins's questions. "Did the writer intend for this to be a literal depiction of precise chronological steps?" Yes, that's why the author specifies what happens on each, and notes that each day consists of one evening and one morning. "Why are there two stories that do not entirely mesh with each other?" This is the fallacy of the complex question. Genesis 2 is a more detailed account of the events of day 6. If it doesn't seem to "mesh" with chapter 1, then you are reading it wrong; go back and study the text carefully. "Is this a poetic and even allegorical description, or

9. Ibid., p. 151.

a literal history?" It is literal history; the author says so: Genesis 2:4, "This is the *account* of the heavens and the earth. . . ." Genesis 5:1, "This is the book of the generations of Adam. . . ." Genesis 6:9, "These are the *records* of the generations of Noah. . . ." Genesis 10:1, "Now these are the *records* of the generations of Shem, Ham, and Japheth. . . ." And so on. How many times does God have to say this before people will accept it? There is no parallelism, and thus no poetry.

> *These questions have been debated for centuries. Nonliteral interpretations since Darwin are somewhat suspect in some circles, since they could be accused of "caving in" to evolutionary theory, and perhaps thereby compromising the truth of the sacred text. So it is useful to discover how learned theologians interpreted Genesis 1 and 2 long before Darwin appeared on the scene, or even before geologic evidence of the extreme age of the earth began to accumulate.*[10]

Nonliteral interpretations of Genesis existed before Darwin, but how is this relevant to the *correct* interpretation of Genesis? There were some early interpretations of the gospels that denied the deity of Christ, or denied the Trinity. Does that mean these interpretations are correct? Of course not. There is some value in looking at the early writings of the Church, but these may not override the clear teaching of the *Scriptures*. In any case, the orthodox position of the Church in history has always been that of creation, not naturalistic evolution.

Dr. Collins seems to recognize here that people today are motivated to interpret Genesis in a non-literal fashion due to the influence of Darwin. So he sets out to explore some non-literal interpretations of Genesis that preceded Darwin. But does Collins think that evolutionary thinking and long ages began with Darwin? The ancient Greeks had ideas comparable to evolution and deep time. Their philosophies have had a large impact on the world. Romans 1:20–25 shows the influence of evolutionary thinking in the first century. Darwin merely popularized a more modern version of a very old idea — an idea that was already prevalent by Christ's incarnation. It's not surprising that a handful of scholars in the early Church latched on to the secular ideas of their time and attempted to interpret the Scriptures accordingly. This is exactly what Collins and many others do today. He says,

10. Ibid.

> *The Hebrew word used in Genesis 1 for day (*yôm*) can be used both to describe a twenty-four-hour day and to describe a more symbolic representation. There are multiple places in the Bible where* yôm *is utilized in a nonliteral context, such as "the day of the Lord" — just as we might say "in my grandfather's day" without implying that Grandpa had lived only twenty-four hours.*[11]

We have already seen the many problems with this view in previous chapters, so I will just briefly point out that context is what determines the meaning of a word. And context is exactly what Collins has ignored. Yes, "day" may indeed be used in a non-literal way when used in non-literal sections of the Bible — but context always makes this clear. And the context of Genesis requires the days to be literal, as they are composed of one evening and one morning, with many other indicators as well. One thing that Dr. Collins got right that Dr. Hugh Ross often gets wrong is that when "day" is used to mean a "long period of time," this is a *non-literal* usage. The word is, perhaps, occasionally used that way in the poetic and prophetic sections of Scripture. Collins goes on to say,

> *Ultimately, Augustine writes: "What kind of days these were, it is extremely difficult, or perhaps impossible for us to conceive." He admits there are probably many valid interpretations of the book of Genesis:*[12]

Of course, Augustine's views on Genesis or any other issue are not relevant to the truth of those issues. Augustine was frequently wrong in his theology — sometimes he added to Scripture, and sometimes he subtracted from Scripture. Whatever Augustine did or did not believe may be important to a Roman Catholic, who trusts church "tradition." But Augustine's opinions are not at all authoritative, and a Bible-believing Christian should recognize this. Proper hermeneutics involves studying the *text* to ascertain the author's intention, not simply a fallacious appeal to authority. And what of this idea that "there are probably many valid interpretations of the book of Genesis?" This violates the one-meaning principle — a foundational principle of hermeneutics upon which all legitimate interpretations must be based. No more than one interpretation of Genesis can be correct, because there

11. Ibid, p. 152.
12. Ibid.

is only one that corresponds to the author's intention. All the others will be wrong.

> *Diverse interpretations continue to be promoted about the meaning of Genesis 1 and 2. Some, particularly from the evangelical Christian church, insist upon a completely literal interpretation, including twenty-four-hour days. Coupled with subsequent genealogical information in the Old Testament, this leads to Bishop Ussher's famous conclusion that God created heaven and earth in 4004 b.c. Other equally sincere believers do not accept the requirement that the days of creation need be twenty-four hours in length, though they otherwise accept the narrative as a literal and sequential depiction of God's creative acts. Still other believers see the language of Genesis 1 and 2 as intended to instruct readers of Moses' time about God's character, and not to attempt to teach scientific facts about the specifics of creation that would have been utterly confusing at the time.*[13]

The argument here is an enthymeme — the conclusion is not directly stated but is clearly implied. Dr. Collins has subtly committed the naturalistic fallacy. He is arguing that something is appropriate simply on the basis that many people do it. The argument has the same weight as this one: "Lying can't be wrong. After all, everybody does it." Likewise, Collins seems to be suggesting, "Christians have had many different views on Genesis. Therefore, it is appropriate for Christians to have many different views on Genesis." If he is not suggesting this or something like it, then his comments here are utterly irrelevant to the topic. I don't care about what other people say about the Bible; I care about what it actually says. That's what hermeneutics is all about. And Dr. Collins never deals with the hermeneutics of Scripture at all.

> *Despite twenty-five centuries of debate, it is fair to say that no human knows what the meaning of Genesis 1 and 2 was precisely intended to be. We should continue to explore that!*[14]

If "no human knows what the meaning of Genesis 1 and 2 was precisely intended to be," then Dr. Collins must not know either, since he is a human

13. Ibid.
14. Ibid.

being. But if he doesn't know what the author of Genesis intended, then on what basis can he tell other people what the acceptable interpretations are? He previously affirmed that, "there are probably many valid interpretations of the book of Genesis." But how could he know that if he himself doesn't know what the author intended? Furthermore, if he doesn't know what the author of Genesis 1 and 2 precisely meant, then how can Dr. Collins possibly know that no other human knows this information? We must admit that there are many people who *claim* to know what the author of Genesis 1 and 2 did mean. Now, if Dr. Collins doesn't know what these chapters mean, then how can he say that any of those people are wrong and that they don't really know? If no human knows what Genesis precisely means, then why did Collins state just a few pages earlier that, "There is no question that this is a powerful and poetic narrative recounting the story of God's creative actions." Do you see the absurdity of this way of thinking?

What about Jesus? The earthly ministry of Christ took place within the "twenty-five centuries" of debate over the meaning of Genesis 1 and 2. So did Jesus not know what Genesis meant? Christ quoted from Genesis, and often used the history of Genesis to explain Christian principles. Was Jesus mistaken? Clearly, Dr. Collins hasn't thought through the implications of his philosophy. If we cannot understand the meaning of the first two chapters of the Bible that were written in ordinary, plain, historical narrative, what hope would we have of being able to understand the rest of the Bible?

Christ's words to Nicodemus would seem to apply: "If I told you earthly things and you do not believe, how will you believe if I tell you heavenly things?" (John 3:12). If Christ tells us through His written Word that He created the universe in six days, and we don't accept that simple historical claim, how can we consistently believe in Christ's claims about the future eternal state, and the future resurrection from the dead?

> *If God created the universe, and the laws that govern it, and if He endowed human beings with intellectual abilities to discern its workings, would He want us to disregard those abilities? Would He be diminished or threatened by what we are discovering about His creation?*[15]

Does God want us to disregard our intellect? Not at all! But when people believe in evolution, *they are disregarding their intellect.* There is nothing in

15. Ibid., p. 152.

science that lends itself to an evolutionary interpretation above a biblical interpretation. On the contrary, science would be utterly impossible apart from the preconditions of intelligibility provided by Scripture.[16] It is biblical to be rational (Isaiah 1:18, 55:7–9), and evolution and deep time are about as contrary to rationality as a person can get.

Second, it is not sufficient to merely use our mind. We must use our mind *properly*. You can use your mind to think things that are false, or things that are true. Evolutionists use their minds incorrectly (at least when it comes to origins), irrationally. They don't reason logically because they don't reason biblically. We are supposed to line up our thoughts with God's nature so that our thinking becomes increasingly correct. And this begins with submission to God's Word as our standard (e.g., Proverbs 1:7). A true scholar must begin his reasoning from the truth of God's Word so that he has a foundation to reason properly about anything else. Apart from the truth of God's Word, our human thinking becomes foolish and empty (Romans 1:21–25; Ephesians 4:17–18; 1 Corinthians 1:20, 3:19–20).

Next, Dr. Collins addresses the historical controversy of Galileo's observations and the response of the Roman Catholic Church. Galileo's observations confirmed the heliocentric theory of the solar system — the model that the planets, including earth, orbit the sun. The predominant scientific model of the time was geocentrism — that the (other) planets and sun orbit the earth. Sometimes scientists can become very emotionally attached to a particular model, and resistant to give it up even when contrary evidence is presented. This was certainly the case in the early 1600s. A number of scientists urged the Roman Catholic Church to take a stand on the issue, and denounce heliocentrism as unbiblical.

We saw in chapter 10 that geocentrism cannot be defended on the basis of the Scriptures. Nonetheless, some prominent Catholic priests were persuaded by the geocentrists, and repudiated Galileo. They forced him to recant his view. Galileo was eventually put under house arrest and his books were banned. In 1992, three and a half centuries after Galileo's trial, Pope John Paul II issued a public apology. Dr. Collins summarized the events well, and then drew this conclusion:

16. See my book, *The Ultimate Proof of Creation: Resolving the Origins Debate* (Green Forest, AR: Master Books, 2009) for details on this.

> *So in this example, the scientific correctness of the heliocentric view ultimately won out, despite strong theological objections. Today all faiths except perhaps a few primitive ones seem completely at home with this conclusion. The claims that heliocentricity contradicted the Bible are now seen to have been overstated, and the insistence on a literal interpretation of those particular scripture verses seems wholly unwarranted. Could this same harmonious outcome be realized for the current conflict between faith and the theory of evolution?*[17]

The answer is, "no." The reason is simple: heliocentrism is not contrary to any affirmation of Scripture, but evolution is. There are no specific texts we can point to that, when properly interpreted, deny that the earth orbits the sun. But there are specific texts we can point to that, when properly interpreted, deny particles-to-people evolution and affirm that God created in six days (e.g., Exodus 20:11; Genesis 2:7; Mark 10:6). Dr. Collins has thus committed the fallacy of false analogy.

Often, people use the Galileo incident to show that the Church should not take the Bible so rigidly, and that the Scriptures should be open to re-interpretation on the basis of new scientific claims — whether heliocentrism or evolution. However, I draw just the opposite conclusion. It was precisely *because* the Church (1) had not carefully and properly interpreted the Bible, and because (2) they interpreted the text to accommodate modern (at the time) scientific claims that the Church largely embraced geocentrism in the first place. Had they done proper hermeneutics, they would have recognized that the Bible does not address the topic of Newtonian reference frames, and thus does not endorse or deny either geocentrism or heliocentrism.

Today, people make the *same* mistake in (1) failing to do careful and proper interpretation of the biblical text (e.g., Genesis), and (2) allowing modern claims, such as evolution, to bias their interpretation of the text. Far from learning from the Galileo incident, many Christians simply repeat history. And when modern "Galileos" show powerful scientific evidence that confirms biblical creation and a worldwide Flood, such evidence is often dismissed because it does not fit the prevailing opinion of our time.

17. Collins, *The Language of God: A Scientist Presents Evidence for Belief*, p. 156.

Collins on "Creationism"

In chapter 8 of his book, Dr. Francis Collins goes on the offensive and argues against a literal reading of Genesis 1 and 2. The title of his chapter is "Option 2: Creationism (When Faith Trumps Science)."[18] Collins considers literal creation to be the second of three faulty solutions to his perceived problem of reconciling science and faith. He later offers theistic evolution as the correct solution in which "science and faith" are said to be "in harmony."[19] Dr. Collins describes the position of "Young Earth Creationism" (YEC) as follows:

> *YEC advocates also believe that all species were created by individual acts of divine creation, and that Adam and Eve were historical figures created by God from dust in the Garden of Eden, and not descended from other creatures.*[20]

He's off to a bad start. Dr. Collins begins his case against YECs with a straw-man fallacy — a misrepresentation of the position he is attempting to rebut. I know of no biblical creationist today who believes that God created all *species* by individual acts of divine creation. Rather, the Bible teaches that each *kind* was supernaturally created. There is no reason to assume that the biblical word translated "kind" is the same as our modern word "species." The latter is a recent, man-made convention and has a very different meaning.[21]

From the biblical narrative, we take a "kind" to be a group of organisms that are biologically related to each other — they share common ancestors that could interbreed with each other. Thus, two of each kind of air-breathing land animal was aboard the ark to preserve the created kinds. The definition of species is different: a species is a group of animals that regularly interbreed to produce fertile offspring. If two animals are the same species then they must also be the same kind. However, the reverse is not true; two animals of the same kind can be different species. For example, horses, donkeys, and zebras are classified as three different species partly because they don't commonly interbreed. However, they are *able* to interbreed and are thus part of the same created kind.

18. Ibid., p. 171.
19. Ibid., p. 197.
20. Ibid., p. 172.
21. To make matters worse, the dictionary meaning of the term "species" has changed drastically over the centuries.

The rest of Dr. Collins's description is pretty good — less guilty of straw-man misrepresentations. We do affirm that Adam and Eve were historical figures created by God, and are not descended from other creatures. Adam was made from the dust of the ground and Eve from his side. Isn't this what the Bible directly states (Genesis 1:27, 2:7, 21–22)? Isn't that the historical basis for marriage (Genesis 2:23–24)? Jesus referred to Adam and Eve as historical figures, and used their creation as the historical basis for marriage in Matthew 19:4–6. Is Dr. Collins suggesting that Jesus could have been mistaken about this?

> *Many books and videos can be found in Christian bookstores that claim that no intermediate fossil forms can be found for birds, turtles, elephants, or whales (yet examples of all of these have been found in the last few years), that the Second Law of Thermodynamics rules out the possibility of evolution (it clearly does not), and that radioactive dating of rocks and the universe is wrong because decay rates have changed over time (they have not). One can even visit Creationist museums and theme parks that depict humans frolicking with dinosaurs, since the YEC perspective does not accept the idea that dinosaurs became extinct long before humans appeared on the scene.* [22]

Although this is not a hermeneutical claim, it reveals the same lack of rational reflection evident in Dr. Collins's hermeneutical claims. The claims here are arbitrary. Collins presents not even a bit of evidence to back up his assertions, nor does he seem to be aware of evidence contrary to his claims. He asserts that intermediate fossils have been found recently for birds, turtles, elephants, and whales; but he doesn't mention what they are, or where they were supposedly discovered. He doesn't even provide a footnote to a scholarly article that allegedly documents such discoveries.

Part of the problem could be Dr. Collins's confusion of "species" with "kind." We find lots of "intermediates" *within* kinds of organisms. Variations within a kind are expected in the creation view, both in extant kinds and extinct kinds. But there are no undisputed intermediates *between* kinds — such as an intermediate between a bird and a non-bird. I am well aware of the *claims*, but the *evidence* of evolution between kinds is lacking.[23]

---

22. Collins, *The Language of God: A Scientist Presents Evidence for Belief*, p. 173.
23. http://www.icr.org/article/3763/.

For example, I was taught in school that Archaeopteryx was a transitional form between a reptile and a bird. But we now know that Archaeopteryx was a bird, and not transitional at all. It had fully formed feathers (with an asymmetric quill — indicating flight feathers), hollow bones, a wishbone that is characteristic of birds, and the backwards-directed pubis bone — characteristic of birds. There is even evidence that Archaeopteryx had the reversed-lung design common to birds, but very different from reptile lungs.

Dr. Collins casually dismisses all thermodynamic arguments against evolution with a single parenthetical comment. In reality, the issue of whether evolution is compatible with the laws of thermodynamics is a complicated issue that deserves more analysis than a quick dismissal. Dr. Collins similarly dismisses the possibility that radioactive decay rates have changed in the past with the sweeping claim "they have not." No evidence whatsoever is provided for his claim. No reference is provided.

In fact, it is now well-documented that at least some radioactive decay rates can indeed be accelerated.[24] The rhenium-osmium reaction has been accelerated in a laboratory by a factor of over a billion! There is significant evidence that such acceleration has similarly happened with other elements, as documented in the RATE research project.[25] So Collins's claim is demonstrably false.

Collins seems perturbed that creationists believe that dinosaurs lived at the same time as people. He assumes the commonly repeated story that dinosaurs died millions of years before man. But he presents no evidence at all for this claim. This just isn't scholarly. Would Collins be surprised to learn that there are ancient artifacts (sculptures, carvings, cave paintings) that depict living dinosaurs?[26] Would he be surprised to learn that some dinosaur remains still have soft tissue in them, including red blood cells?[27] When dinosaur remains are carbon-dated they consistently yield estimated ages of thousands of years.[28] How does Collins account for this evidence that seems so contrary to his position?

---

24. https://answersingenesis.org/geology/radiometric-dating/acceleration-of-radioactivity-shown-in-laboratory/.
25. http://www.icr.org/article/helium-diffusion-nuclear-decay/.
26. Vance Nelson, *Untold Secrets of Planet Earth: Dire Dragons* (Vance Nelson, 2011).
27. http://www.icr.org/article/dinosaur-soft-tissues-theyre-real/.
28. http://www.icr.org/article/carbon-dating-70-million-year-old-mosasaur/.

> *Young Earth Creationists argue that evolution is a lie. They postulate that the relatedness of organisms as visualized by the study of DNA is simply a consequence of God having used some of the same ideas in His multiple acts of special creation. Confronted with such facts as the similar ordering of genes across chromosomes between different mammalian species, or the existence of repetitive "junk DNA" in shared locations along the DNA of humans and mice, YEC advocates simply dismiss this as part of God's plan.*[29]

Similarity does not require a biological relationship. The chairs in a room all share some characteristics because (1) they are designed for a common purpose, and (2) they may have been made by the same manufacturer. Living organisms share some characteristics. Is this because they are all biologically related? Or are their common characteristics designed for a common purpose, and designed by the same Creator? Collins arbitrarily dismisses the latter two possibilities and accepts the former. But he gives no reason at all. This is not scientific. Moreover, "junk DNA" is a misnomer, because scientists have increasingly discovered that such DNA is functional.[30]

In science, if two competing models make the same predictions, then verification of those predictions does not establish one model over the other. In this case, creationists predict that organisms that have similar traits ought to have similar DNA, since DNA codes for traits. Evolutionists predict the same thing. So when we find this, how can we claim that it is evidence of one model over the other? Collins has committed the fallacy of affirming the consequent.

He has also committed the question-begging epithet in suggesting without any support that creationists "simply dismiss this [similarity] as part of God's plan." Since creationists *predict* such similarity, we could just as well argue that "evolutionists simply dismiss this similarity as a result of evolution." To be fair and avoid logical fallacies, we ought to honestly say that both creationists and evolutionists expect to find patterns of similarity in the DNA of living organisms. So the discovery of such similarity cannot be used to support one model in favor of another.

The next subsection in Dr. Collins's chapter is entitled "Young Earth Creationism and Modern Science Are Incompatible." What scientific evidence does Collins present to justify this bold claim? Here it is:

29. Collins, *The Language of God: A Scientist Presents Evidence for Belief*, p. 173.
30. http://www.icr.org/article/does-junk-dna-exist/.

> *In general, those who hold these views are sincere, well-meaning, God-fearing people, driven by deep concerns that naturalism is threatening to drive God out of human experience. But the claims of Young Earth Creationism simply cannot be accommodated by tinkering around the edges of scientific knowledge. If these claims were actually true, it would lead to a complete and irreversible collapse of the sciences of physics, chemistry, cosmology, geology, and biology. As biology professor Darrel Falk points out in his wonderful book* Coming to Peace with Science, *written specifically from his perspective as an evangelical Christian, the YEC perspective is the equivalent of insisting that two plus two is really not equal to four.*[31]

Did you spot the evidence that "young earth" creation is incompatible with science? Neither did I. Shouldn't a scientist be able to back up his claims with some kind of evidence? I'm not asking for a complete dissertation on the subject — but provide at least one example of how physics, chemistry, cosmology, geology, or biology would collapse if creation were true. As a matter of fact, all these branches of science are predicated on the uniformity God promises in passages such as Genesis 8:22. But if we reject the historicity of Genesis, then what rational foundation would there be for any branch of science?[32]

Instead of a rational argument, Dr. Collins provides sweeping claims and logical fallacies. The listing of many topics (e.g., "physics, chemistry, cosmology, geology, and biology") to persuade someone when no rational support is provided is the fallacy of "elephant hurling." And we are also treated to the fallacy of false analogy, namely: "The YEC perspective is the equivalent of insisting that two plus two is really not equal to four." The analogy is false because the latter position can be demonstrated to be false in the present, but creation cannot be. Creation is an *historical* claim.

> *For anyone familiar with the scientific evidence, it is almost incomprehensible that the YEC view has achieved such wide support, especially in a country like the United States that claims to be so intellectually advanced and technologically sophisticated. But YEC advocates are serious about their faith first and foremost, and deeply concerned about a trend toward nonliteral interpretations of the*

31. Collins, *The Language of God: A Scientist Presents Evidence for Belief*, p. 173–174.
32. My book, *The Ultimate Proof of Creation*, explores this topic in substantial detail.

Bible, which might ultimately dilute the power of the scriptures to teach reverence for God to humankind.[33]

Again, Collins attempts to use rhetoric, rather than logic, to persuade. He claims that "anyone familiar with the scientific evidence" will believe in evolution. This is a not-so-subtle *ad baculum* fallacy — an appeal to fear. Namely, "you'd better believe in evolution or you will look stupid. Evolution is the view of the intellectually advanced and technologically sophisticated." But from a logical perspective, there is nothing about biblical creation that is contrary to intellectual advancement and technology. On the contrary, many advancements in science were made precisely because people expected God to uphold the universe in a consistent and discoverable way; and they believed this because it follows from the literal history in Genesis (e.g., Genesis 8:22).

The interesting thing about claims like "Believe in evolution or people will think you are stupid" is that there is some truth to them. We live in a time when many people do hold to evolution. And this is especially true in academic circles. Evolution is seen as the "enlightened" position among secular academics, and to reject it is to face ridicule. But this is utterly irrelevant to the issue of *proper interpretation* of the text. Just because it is popular to wrongly interpret Scripture does mean that's what we should do. Part of Christianity is being laughed at and mocked by the opposition (Acts 17:32). That's not fun. But let's get a little perspective. When we consider that many Christians have been tortured and martyred for their faith, when we consider what Christ did for us, how could we be unwilling to accept mere verbal ridicule for His name's sake?

The concern about not accepting liberal interpretations of biblical texts is understandable. After all, there are clearly parts of the Bible that are written as eyewitness accounts of historical events, including much of the New Testament. For a believer, the events recorded in these sections ought to be taken as the writer intended — as descriptions of observed facts.[34]

Actually, *all* Scripture should be taken as the writer intended. That's the definition of the correct interpretation. And, yes, there are clearly parts of

33. Collins, *The Language of God: A Scientist Presents Evidence for Belief*, p. 174.
34. Ibid., p. 175.

the Bible that are written as eyewitness accounts of historical events — including Genesis. We've seen that the text itself indicates this.

> *But other parts of the Bible, such as the first few chapters of Genesis, the book of Job, the Song of Solomon, and the Psalms, have a more lyrical and allegorical flavor, and do not generally seem to carry the marks of pure historical narrative.*[35]

On what *hermeneutical* basis does Collins group the "first few chapters of Genesis" with the poetic literature? We saw in chapter 5 the characteristics of poetic literature, and the characteristics of historical narrative. The first chapters of Genesis have all the indicators of historical narrative and none of the indicators of poetry. In fact, Dr. Collins seems to recognize that Genesis is written historically, because he exempts only "the first few chapters" from literal, historical interpretation. But the first chapters of Genesis are written in the same literary style as the rest of Genesis. *All* the chapters of Genesis have the marks of historical narrative: the introduction to the book, lack of parallelism, paucity of idioms, inclusion of specific details (names of places and people), and copious use of the waw-consecutive. Thus, Collins's claim that these chapters "do not generally seem to carry the marks of pure historical narrative" is demonstrably false. If we are going to end up with a correct interpretation, context demands that we read these chapters as literal history.

> *The insistence that every word of the Bible must be taken literally runs into other difficulties. Surely the right arm of God did not really lift up the nation of Israel (Isaiah 41:10). Surely it is not part of God's nature to become forgetful and to need to be reminded of important matters from time to time by the prophets (Exodus 33: 13).*[36]

Here is a magnificent example of a straw-man argument. Dr. Collins implies that creationists insist that "every word of the Bible must be taken literally." He then shows how easy it is to refute such a silly position. But this is not our position. I don't know anyone who takes "every word" of Scripture literally. We recognize that some types of literature demand a non-literal interpretation. But it is the *text* itself that distinguishes the type of literature, and not modern opinions of origins. Every word of Scripture should be taken

35. Ibid.
36. Ibid.

literarily — according to the type of literature as intended by the author and as indicated by his words. For historical narrative, a literary reading must be a literal reading if we are going to arrive at the author's intended meaning. Dr. Collins expects us to take his words literally due to the type of literature. Why does he not show God the same courtesy?

> *Many believers in God have been drawn to Young Earth Creationism because they see scientific advances as threatening to God.*[37]

Speaking for myself (and I know many other biblical creationists who would agree), I don't see any scientific advances as threatening to God. How could they be, when God is what makes science possible? But there are philosophies that are contrary to Scripture that are sometimes touted as "science" — philosophics like evolution. God is not "threatened" by foolish philosophy (see 1 Corinthains 1:19–28, 3:18–20). He cannot be harmed by it. But we certainly can be. If we love our neighbor, we ought to warn them of the danger of unbiblical philosophy and teach them to rightly interpret God's Word.

> *Most important, is He honored or dishonored by those who would demand that His people ignore rigorous scientific conclusions about His creation? Can faith in a loving God be built on a foundation of lies about nature?*[38]

These comments beg the question. Evolution is hardly a "rigorous scientific conclusion." It is not something that can be demonstrated in a laboratory or observed with the senses. It is a claim about the past and is not directly accessible to the tools of science. Can faith in God be built on lies about nature? No, and this is preciously why we must reject evolution. In fact, our faith in God should be based ultimately not on nature at all, but on His Word. Is God honored when people distort His Word to match pseudo-scientific speculation like evolution?

> *Assisted by Henry Morris and colleagues, Young Earth Creationism has in the last half century attempted to provide alternative explanations for the wealth of observations about the natural world that seem to contradict the YEC position.*[39]

37. Ibid., p. 176.
38. Ibid.
39. Ibid.

What "observations about the natural world" does Collins think contradict biblical creation? He lists not a single example, and so his claim is unjustified. This seems to be a pattern with evolutionary thinking. In any case, I am not aware of any observations that are contrary to creation. How could they be, since creation is a past event and thus not observable in the present? There are interpretations of observations that may be contrary to creation; but interpretations can be wrong. There is nothing wrong with the observations themselves, even when people fail to reason properly about what they observe. What Dr. Morris and others have done is to show how our observations of the present world make sense in light of the literal history recorded in Genesis. Collins states,

> *But the fundamentals of so-called scientific Creationism are hopelessly flawed. Recognizing the overwhelming body of scientific evidence, some YEC advocates have more recently taken the tack of arguing that all of this evidence has been designed by God to mislead us, and therefore to test our faith. According to this argument, all of the radioactive decay clocks, all the fossils, and all of the genome sequences have been intentionally designed so it would look as if the universe was old, even though it was really created less than ten thousand years ago.*[40]

What evidence does Collins present that "the fundamentals of [creation] are hopelessly flawed?" None. His statement is arbitrary and unsupported, and so we need not take it seriously. Furthermore, what biblical creationist argues that the vast body of scientific evidence "has been designed by God to mislead us?" This is certainly not the mainstream position among creationists. On the contrary, we love examining scientific evidence, and would argue that evidence from all fields of science strongly confirms biblical history, and challenges evolution. Notice that Collins does not quote any creationists to illustrate his "straw man" mischaracterization. So on what basis can he claim, without citing any examples, that creationists (supposedly) accuse God of such "deception"? This is not just sloppy misinformation by Collins; it is irresponsible.

And what of Dr. Collins's claim that "all of the radioactive decay clocks" are contrary to biblical creation? First, this is a bit of a reification fallacy.

40. Ibid.

Radioactive decay is not a clock. It might be used to make an estimate of the age of something, but this will involve making assumptions about the constancy of rates, initial conditions, and so on. Second, do all radioactive decay chains support an old earth? As a scientist, Collins should know better. Carbon dating very consistently gives age estimates of thousands of years, even on things that evolutionists believe to be hundreds of millions of years old — like coal. Even the potassium-argon method does not normally give ages of billions of years. The few methods that do sometimes give very old age estimates also frequently give old age estimates on rocks that are known to be young — as from a recent volcano. So they are hardly reliable.

We have pointed out in our various publications (see www.icr.org and Acts & Facts) that there are many earth-processes that cannot last billions of years — from salt accumulation in the ocean, and magnetic field decay, to human population growth rates.[41] The fossils we find are what we would expect given the global Flood described in Genesis 6–8. It is ironic that Collins mentions the genome sequence as an old-age indicator. My ICR colleague Dr. Nathaniel Jeanson has shown that when we compare mutation rates with the number of mutations in the DNA in known species, the genome cannot be nearly as old as evolution predicts.[42] The genome is consistent with the biblical timescale. The data overwhelmingly confirm a "young" earth — thousands, not billions of years old. So I have to ask Dr. Collins, tongue in cheek, "Did God just manufacture all this evidence for a *young* earth to mislead us, or to test our faith?"

> *As Kenneth Miller points out in his excellent book,* Finding Darwin's God, *for these claims to be true, God would have had to engage in massive subterfuge. For instance, since many of the observable stars and galaxies in the universe are more than ten thousand light-years away, a YEC perspective would demand that our ability to observe them could come about only if God had fashioned all of those photons to arrive here in a "just so" fashion, even though they represent wholly fictitious objects.*[43]

41. One of my favorite resources on the geological evidence of a "young" earth is a book by geologist Dr. John Morris, entitled *The Young Earth: The Real History of the Earth — Past, Present, and Future*, available at www.icr.org and masterbooks.com.
42. http://www.icr.org/article/8017/.
43. Collins, *The Language of God: A Scientist Presents Evidence for Belief*, p. 176–177.

No. A "young" universe does not require God to create beams of light that represent wholly fictitious objects. There are a number of ways that God can get light that was actually produced by a star to reach earth within the biblical timescale.[44] These are scientific models, and so I won't cover them in detail here. The point is that Dr. Collins has committed a bifurcation fallacy. He has presented only two options as if they were the *only* two options, and thinks that by shooting down one he has proved the other. "Either God deceives by making light beams of fiction, or the universe is billions of years old." But there is a third option; God gets the starlight here quickly without creating any light beams with fictional images.

More importantly, notice that all of Dr. Collins's arguments are eisegetical. Not one is motivated by considering what the author of Genesis meant to say. Rather, Collins takes his beliefs about the universe, and *imposes* them on Scripture. This is not proper hermeneutics. It's not really hermeneutics at all. Such a method will not consistently arrive at the meaning of a passage.

> *This image of God as a cosmic trickster seems to be the ultimate admission of defeat for the Creationist perspective. Would God as the great deceiver be an entity one would want to worship?*[45]

The irony of this claim is overwhelming. Collins believes that God did not mean even remotely what He said in Genesis, and yet he accuses his *opponents* of making God into a deceiver! What could be more deceptive than creating over billions of years, and then lying about it in Genesis? Wouldn't God have to be a cosmic trickster if He blames man for death when in reality He used death and suffering to bring about man? That's not the biblical God. The imagined "god" of the theistic evolutionist is not only deceptive, but an outright liar — telling us that he made everything in six days and that he made man from the dust of the ground, when in reality he did nothing of the kind.

Would anyone want to worship a "god" who lies about how he created? Would we be drawn to a creator who took billions of years of death, suffering, disease, and bloodshed to slowly evolve the organisms he wanted to

44. https://answersingenesis.org/astronomy/starlight/anisotropic-synchrony-convention-distant-starlight-problem/.
45. Collins, *The Language of God: A Scientist Presents Evidence for Belief*, p. 177.

exist — by trial and error?[46] Would a god who looked at all the pain, death, and suffering in the world and called it "very good" be worthy of praise? The god of evolution seems opposite to the biblical God. I don't mean that theistic evolutionists cannot be Christians, but I suggest that there is great inconsistency in their thinking.

Conclusions

I was disappointed in Francis Collins's book, but not because I disagree with his conclusions — I was expecting that. I was looking forward to applying hermeneutical principles to his analysis of Scripture. My disappointment is that Collins didn't really engage the Scriptures with any depth. He simply dismissed Genesis 1–2 as poetic, without giving any hermeneutically rational basis for that opinion whatsoever. He didn't attempt to resolve any of the theological problems of theistic evolution, such as death before sin. He didn't even mention them. I was hoping to engage a scholarly argument for theistic evolution on the basis of the Scriptures. But Collins provided none.

But that in itself is significant. Perhaps I didn't get a hermeneutical argument for theistic evolution because theistic evolutionists cannot construct one that is even remotely plausible. All arguments for theistic evolution come from outside the text of Scripture. They are not exegetical, and therefore will not be consistently faithful to the author's intention. I submit that theistic evolution stems from shallow thinking. One can be a Christian and an evolutionist only by throwing his brain out the door. Theistic evolution is hermeneutically indefensible.

---

46. See *Creation Basics and Beyond*, chapter 1.

Chapter 14

The Extent of the Flood

> Then God said to Noah, "The end of all flesh has come before Me; for the earth is filled with violence because of them; and behold, I am about to destroy them with the earth" (Genesis 6:13).

The biblical account of the Flood of Noah is a fascinating part of history. In Genesis 6–8 we learn that humanity became increasingly wicked and violent in the 1,600 years that followed creation. But God is righteous and will not tolerate sin indefinitely. God's wrath was kindled against man — all men except Noah who alone found favor with God and was blameless in His sight. Therefore, God instructed Noah to build an ark to carry Noah, his family, and two of every air-breathing land animal to preserve their life from the floodwaters that God would send to judge mankind. The text teaches that the Flood came. The earth experienced 40 days and 40 nights of rain, followed by nearly a year of flooding in which even the highest hills were covered with water. All life on land perished, and only the inhabitants of the ark survived.

Jesus affirmed the historicity of this event, as did other New Testament writers (Matthew 24:37–38; Hebrews 11:7; 1 Peter 3:20; 2 Peter 2:5). So we would expect everyone who professes Christ as Lord to believe in the global Flood, right? Unfortunately, this isn't the case. There are professing Christians who deny that there ever was a global flood on earth. They say that if Noah's Flood was a real event at all, it was merely a local flood — not global. Why?

The answer has to do with fossils. It doesn't make sense to have millions of years of fossil deposition, followed by a global flood. The reason is simple; either the fossil record was caused by hundreds of millions of years of gradual deposition, or it is primarily the result of one catastrophic deposition. It can't represent both because the catastrophic nature of a global flood would destroy any previous fossil record. And so we are left with the option of (1) millions of years of fossil deposition *or* (2) a worldwide flood. Therefore, Christians who have embraced deep time must reject a worldwide flood in order to make sense of the secular interpretation of fossil evidence. In short: belief in millions of years motivates people to reject a global flood.

In a sense, this matter was already settled in chapter 11. We saw that belief in millions of years is not compatible with Scripture, and cannot be hermeneutically justified. Thus, a global catastrophe is required to explain the fossils. And this fits nicely with a natural reading of Genesis 6–8. But those Christians who believe in deep time cannot accept this. Furthermore, they say that those people who believe in a global flood are reading the text improperly. This is a hermeneutical claim, and thus demands a hermeneutical answer.

Once again I turn to Dr. Hugh Ross because he is one of a very few old-earth advocates who argues that the text of Scripture requires us to believe in a *local*, but not global flood. Again, I emphasize that my analysis of his writings is in no way a personal attack. I'm not suggesting here that Ross is a big meanie, or that he is unsaved. That would be irrelevant to the issue. Rather, I wish to critique one of the best arguments for a local flood because if it doesn't stand up to scrutiny, then neither will the weaker arguments. In that light, we turn to chapter 16 of Dr. Ross's recent book *Navigating Genesis.*[1]

Global or Worldwide Flood?

> *For some Christians, belief that the flood covered the entire planet and its highest mountains has become a litmus test of biblical orthodoxy and of belief in the inerrancy of Scripture. This line in the sand is based in large part on the wording used in Genesis 6–8 to describe how the flood impacted all humans, all animals, and all*

1. Dr. Ross's statements are inset in italics throughout this chapter.

> *the mountains. The words, "all," every," and "everything," appear more than 40 times in these three chapters (a few more or a few less, depending on the Bible version). On this basis, it seems no wonder belief in biblical truth demands belief in a global deluge.*

Well said. If Dr. Ross had ended the chapter here, it might have been great. He goes on to explain why he thinks the text does not mean what it appears to say. In principle, I have no problem with that type of investigation. There are Scriptures that don't mean exactly what first impressions might suggest. Translation difficulties or even cultural bias can cause us to draw wrong conclusions at times. And further study is warranted. My point here is that even Dr. Ross notices that the plain, straightforward reading of the text *does* seem to indicate a *global flood*. And hence, it is incumbent upon Dr. Ross to provide a very good textual reason why the text should not be read straightforwardly.

Historical Perspective

In the next paragraph, Dr. Ross begins a section entitled "historical perspective," which might make us think that he is about to discuss the Church's historical position on the extent of the Flood. There would be some value in this because many fine biblical scholars have come before us, and we can benefit from their exhaustive exegetical analysis and their familiarity with the original languages and ancient customs. But ultimately, it is the text itself — not the church — that authoritatively determines what the text means. Unfortunately, Ross does not address the orthodox position of the Church nor exegesis from the text at this point. Instead, he discusses how our modern way of thinking is very global, and suggests that "our global perspective naturally colors our interpretation of Scripture."

We have already seen that bias in interpretation is unavoidable. But that doesn't make an interpretation wrong. We simply need to allow the text to correct our biases as needed. I might just as well point out that Hugh Ross is deeply committed to the secular timeline, and hence his bias is to interpret the Genesis Flood as a local event, regardless of the text, since a global flood would wash away any evidence for deep time. Nonetheless, Christians today should be aware of how ancient cultures might differ from our own, and we must read the text as its original audience would have understood it. So I appreciate that Dr. Ross is considering this:

> *When we encounter such phrases in Genesis 7 as "under the entire heavens" and "every living thing on the face of the earth," we understand "face" as the surface of a spherical body, a planet within a larger system of planets. But what did the people of earlier times understand? What constitutes "the entire heavens" and "the face of the earth" from the perspective of ancient peoples?*

These are fair questions. Unfortunately, Dr. Ross doesn't adequately answer them, as we see below. And we should not place cultural nuances above the clarity of language. Language has the capacity to correct cultural misunderstanding and bias. Some things are so very clear that there is no realistic way that anyone from any culture could reasonably misunderstand. The phrase "under the entire heavens" is clear. In Scripture, "the heavens" refer to the sky, including what we today would call outer space. So the phrase refers to that which is under the sky.

In particular, the text states that "all the high hills under the whole heavens were covered." There is no ambiguity here to conceal under a cultural bias. All (not just some) the high hills (not just local bumps, but the actual elevated hills — mountains) that are under the sky (an indication of universality — in other words, all the hills beneath the sky of earth) and in fact under the *entire* sky (lest anyone think that God refers only to the local, visible patch of sky — God clarifies that all of these high mountains under the entire earth's sky — i.e., all of them) were covered by the rising floodwaters. Context clarifies any misperceptions we may have from cultural biases.

Does "all" always mean "all"? We saw in chapter 5 that the Bible sometimes uses hyperbole — a figure of speech involving the exaggeration of something in order to make a point. We may think of exaggerating as deceptive perhaps because it isn't used quite as much in our culture, and consequently the listener might misunderstand. But the Bible does use hyperbole because that was the custom of the culture, and would not have been considered deceptive or dishonest. And there are examples in Scripture of where "all" doesn't mean "all" in an absolute or universal sense — but context makes them obvious.[2]

---

2. One example of the Hebrew word "all" (*kol*) being used in a less-than-universal fashion is Genesis 24:66. Here the text states, "The servant told Isaac all the things that he had done." But did the servant literally tell Isaac everything that he had done in his entire life? Did he talk about every breath or every step he had made? Did he state what he had for lunch every day of his life? In context, the author intends to convey that the servant told Isaac the *important and relevant events* of his recent journey, and not literally *all* things.

So we must ask, "If God intended to convey the fact that the Flood was global, how could he make clear that it was truly global and not just a local event where the language has been exaggerated for effect?" This is a question that Ross never seems to ask. And that's a shame, because it is a question that must be answered in order to discern the proper interpretation of Genesis 6–8.

One way to indicate that something is truly universal is to repeat universal terms within a phrase. "All the people" might just refer to a local group, as in "all the people said 'amen.' " But the phrase "*all* the people in *all* the world" really can't mean anything other than absolutely everyone. Likewise, when Scripture repeats universal terms, this indicates that they are truly universal, and not merely hyperbole. For example, in Genesis 7:19, the text states that flood waters increased such that "*all* the high hills that were under the *whole* heaven were covered." The words "all" and "whole" are translated from the same Hebrew word *kol*. So *all* the hills under *all* the heaven means absolutely all of them — not just an exaggeration of some hills or all the hills of the local region.

Another way to indicate that something is truly universal is to specify contextual indicators of universality. "All the high hills" by itself might mean just those in the area under discussion. But "all the high hills *under the earth's sky*" clearly means every hill on the planet. And this is the basic meaning of Genesis 7:19. The context eliminates any possibility that the universal-sounding terms are merely hyperbole. God uses exactly the kind of language we would expect to denote a global, world-covering deluge.

Third, a person might use the universal language repeatedly as in "every person on earth — literally every man, every woman, every child, and I do mean everyone, whether at home at work, in between, every person. . . ." The Bible does this in Genesis 6–8 in describing the extent of the Flood — *all* the hills were covered, *all* air-breathing land animals died, and *all* people died except those on the ark. The Hebrew word *kol* meaning "all" is used *50 times* in these chapters. It's hard to avoid the conclusion that God really means "all" when He says "all."

In addition, there are many aspects of the Flood account that make no sense apart from a global flood. The Bible uses a special word for the Genesis Flood (*mabbul*) that is not used for local floods. The word *mabbul* literally means a "cataclysm." The "flood of waters" in Genesis 6:17 may sound redundant in English translations, until we understand that it is literally a *cataclysm* of waters! And why build an ark the size of an ocean-liner for a local flood that Noah knew was coming. Wouldn't it be far easier just to move to another area?

Why take two (or seven in some cases) of every air-breathing land animal — including migratory birds — for a local flood? Think about the absurdity of birds needing an ark to escape a local flood. It makes no sense. The Bible says that the ark was to preserve the kinds of animals (Genesis 6:20), which is why two of each kind (male and female) were brought on board. But kinds would not be eliminated by a local flood. God promised to never again cover the earth with waters (Genesis 8:21, 9:15), but if this was just a local flood and thus God was promising never to send another local flood, then God has broken His promise thousands of times. That wouldn't make sense. All these contextual clues powerfully confirm the global scope of the Genesis Flood.

In summary, *context* is the way we distinguish hyperbolic uses of "all" from global uses. And we see that the context of the Flood indicates a global use of the term. This is important, because Dr. Ross goes on to give examples of places in Scripture in which "all" is used hyperbolically for something that is non-global. But in all such cases, context is very different from that of the Flood. Namely, as we will see below, these examples do *not* have double use of *kol* in the same phrase, nor context that specifies truly global usage, nor copious use of universal language throughout their accounts. And so we have a good reason to interpret them differently from Genesis 6–8. Dr. Ross then states,

> *In addition to the flood of Noah's day, six other worldwide events receive mention in the Bible. The first is Joseph's feeding the whole world. Genesis 41:57 says, "And all the countries came to Egypt to buy grain from Joseph, because the famine was severe in all the world." Genesis 42:5–6 makes clear that the famine had spread to all the nations subject to Egypt's sovereignty and influence, including the land of Canaan. Egypt was a powerful force in Joseph's day, but its sway fell far short of impacting the Maoris in New Zealand and the Incas in Peru.*

And what do we find when we consider the context of Genesis 41–42? We do *not* find *kol* repeated in the same phrase; the text does not say "*all* the lands under *all* the heavens." We do *not* find global details such as "under heaven." On the contrary, we find details indicating a hyperbolic use of "all the lands," suggesting it does not mean "all the lands of planet earth" in passages like Genesis 42:5. This passage states that "the famine was in the land of Canaan also" — a qualifier that would be unnecessary if the author had intended to convey a global famine. And finally, we do not find copious use of universal terms. Context suggests that "all the lands" means all the lands surrounding Egypt — *not* a worldwide event. But this context is the opposite of what we find in Genesis 6–8, where global terminology is used.

> *The second is the coming of foreign dignitaries to receive wisdom from Israel's King Solomon. 1 Kings 4:34 says, "Men of all nations came to listen to Solomon's wisdom, sent by all the kings of the world, who had heard of his wisdom." 1 Kings 10:24 adds, "The whole world sought audience with Solomon to hear the wisdom God had put in his heart." However, we read in 1 Kings 4:31 and 2 Chronicles 9 that these visitors came from as far away as Sheba (modern day Ethiopia) and all the lands of Arabia. Evidently, the whole world of Solomon extended roughly 1,300 miles from Jerusalem in any direction.*

And when we look at the context of this passage, what do we find? Does the text say, "men of all nations under *all* the heavens came. . ."? No, merely one "all" (*kol*) is used for that phrase. The "all" is also used for a different phrase "from *all* the kings of the earth who had heard of his wisdom" but it is used only once for that phrase as well. It's not "*all* the kings of *all* the earth." Nor is there any hint of global context such as "under the whole heaven." And again, we do not have copious use of global terminology. Moreover, we have a qualified restriction — not all kings sent men to learn from Solomon, but only "all the kings of the earth *who had heard of his wisdom*" (1 Kings 4:34). If the kings in South America had not heard of Solomon's wisdom, then there is no reason to think they were included. Dr. Ross seems to have missed that important qualifier. Context again shows that this was *not* a worldwide event, though it was certainly far-reaching.

> *The third is a decree from Caesar Augustus at the time of Christ's birth. In Luke 2:1 we read, "In those days a decree went out from Caesar Augustus that all the world should be registered." (ESV). Given that Augustus' authority extended only as far as the Roman*

> *Empire, this reference to "the world" is understood to mean the Roman world.*

There are several problems with using the above to argue that the Genesis Flood was merely local. We immediately see that this text lacks the three contextual indicators expected of global events. Namely, we don't find "all" repeated within a phrase, nor any contextual suggestion of global usage, nor repeated use of universal terms. So it is evident that the context is the *opposite* of that used to describe the Genesis Flood.

Moreover, Dr. Ross has failed to check the original language, and has instead merely assumed that the "world" refers to the planet Earth; this violates the translation principle. The Greek word translated "world" in Luke 2:1 is *oikoumenê*. Does this word refer to the planet Earth? It can in some contexts, but that is not its primary meaning. If Luke had intended to indicate a truly planet-wide decree, the Greek word *gê* would have been a more natural choice, as this is more readily used of the entire planet Earth. Indeed, *gê* is translated "earth" and refers to the planet Earth in passages like Matthew 5:5, 13, 18, 35, 6:10, 19, 10:34, 11:25, 12:40, 16:19, 17:25, 18:18–19, 23:9, 35, 24:35, 28:18.

In contrast, the primary meaning of *oikoumenê* is the *inhabited world* — the world of humanity.[3] Some English translations even render the word that way. Luke 2:1 in the NASB states, "Now in those days a decree went out from Caesar Augustus, that a census be taken of all the *inhabited earth*." More specifically, the word often indicates the civilized world, in contrast to the lands of the barbarians. So again, the context here is very different from the context of Genesis 6–8, and thus a correct interpretation of each will be different.

> *The fourth is what happened at the time of Pentecost, following Jesus' resurrection. According to Acts 2:5, "Now there were staying in Jerusalem God-fearing Jews from every nation under heaven." According to genetic studies of the Jewish people as well as of other ethnic groups around the world, none of the people mentioned in this verse came from Bolivia or Australia. For Jewish people living in first-century Jerusalem, "every nation under heaven" would likely refer to all the provinces of the Roman and Parthian empires.*

3. As is covered below, a similar Greek word *kosmos* refers to the organized world of human civilization. See Romans 1:8.

I'm tempted to ask Dr. Ross how he could possibly obtain *genetic samples* of the people who were present at Pentecost to perform such a study. A moment's reflection shows that his statement about "genetic studies" cannot possibly be true, and is an obvious bluff. As an additional unsupportable conjecture, Ross claims that " 'every nation under heaven' would likely refer to all the provinces of the Roman and Parthian empires." But what is the support for this claim? What textual evidence does Ross present? Of course, there is none.

Additionally Dr. Ross errs in his analysis of Acts 2:5 by his failure to properly exegete the word "nations." Specifically, he commits the semantic anachronism fallacy[4] in thinking that the "nations" mentioned in the second chapter of Acts are governmental "nations" in the modern sense of the word. But the Greek word translated "nation" in Acts 2:5 is *ethnos*. It denotes a people-group, not a governmental body, and is related to our English word "ethnic." So Acts 2:5 teaches that people from every ethnic group in the world were represented at Pentecost. Although there is no double "all" in this passage, there is also no logical or textual reason to interpret the passage less than globally.[5] Dr. Ross continues:

> *The next is recorded in Paul's encouraging words to the Christians in Rome. He writes, "Your faith is being reported all over the world." Here again, the world of Paul and of the Roman Christians was the vast, but not global, Roman Empire. Paul in no way implied that the Inuit or sub-Saharan people had received news of the Christians in Rome.*

The passage in question is Romans 1:8, where the word "world" is translated from the Greek noun *kosmos*. Again, this word indicates the organized world of human civilization, not the planet Earth. (The "earth" would more naturally derive from the Greek word *gê*). And again, we do *not* see the double use of "all" within a phrase, nor specific contextual indicators of global usages (such as "under heaven") nor copious use of universal terms. This suggests that Paul is using mild hyperbole to emphasize the spread of Christianity throughout the inhabited world.

> *One more appears in Paul's letter to the believers in Colossae. To this group Paul writes, "All over the world this gospel is producing fruit*

4. See chapter 6 for examples and an explanation of the semantic anachronism fallacy.
5. http://www.icr.org/article/5684/.

> *and growing, just as it has been doing among you." Again, the Roman Empire constitutes the whole world of Paul and the Colossians.*

The quoted text is from Colossians 1:6 where the "world" is again *kosmos* in Greek. Again, the text is not necessarily referring to the planet Earth, because the Greek word *gê* is not used. And again, we do not find indicators of literal global action — no double "all" within a phrase, no specific contextual indicators suggesting global activity, and no copious use of universal terms. This again suggests that Paul is using mild hyperbole to describe the spectacular advance of God's Kingdom.

> *Each of these biblical references to a worldwide occurrence points to an area less than earth's entire surface or entire land area. Therefore, phrases such as "the entire heavens" and "the face of the earth" in the context of Noah's flood may also refer to an area or region smaller than the whole of earth's surface.*

Is this argument reasonable? Essentially Dr. Ross's argument is that (1) there are places in Scripture where the "world" is less than global, (2) the Genesis Flood describes the destruction of the "world," and (3) therefore, the Genesis Flood may not have been global. There is an equivocation fallacy hinging on the word "world" which can denote either the planet Earth or something less, such as the civilized world of man. When we consider the context of each passage, we find that those passages that Ross lists as less-than-global always lack the contextual indications of literal global activity, whereas Genesis 6–8 makes copious use of such indicators.[6] When we clarify this issue, Ross's argument becomes:

> (1) There are places in Scripture where the "world" is less than global *that lack contextual indicators of a literal global event.*
>
> (2) The Genesis flood describes the destruction of the world *using contextual indicators that do indicate a literal global event.*
>
> (3) Therefore, the Genesis Flood may not have been global.

If it's still not obvious that this is fallacious, consider the following argument of the same form:

---

6. Additionally, many of the New Testament examples that Ross cites use Greek words for "world" that refer to the human world, not the planet Earth. These passages are therefore logically irrelevant to the issue of how the *Hebrew* word *'erets* (translated "earth") is used in Genesis.

(1) There are places on earth that are tropical where the temperature is very high.
(2) Antarctica is a place on earth where the temperature is very low.
(3) Therefore, Antarctica may be tropical.

Or

(1) The North Star is a star that is very far away.
(2) The sun is a star that is very close.
(3) Therefore, the sun may be the North Star.

It is fallacious to argue that a term in one context must mean the same thing as the term in a different context, because context determines the meaning (see chapter 1). Dr. Ross's argument violates the context principle. He also violates the translation principle when he confuses the distinct meaning of the Greek nouns *oikomenê, kosmos,* and *gê.* Indeed, three of Ross's six examples are from the New Testament and use the Greek word for "world," not "earth." It is particularly absurd to argue for the meaning of a particular Hebrew word (like *'erets* — "earth") on the basis of a *different* word ("world") in a *different* language in a *different* context.

> *With respect to the use of the words "all," "every," and "everything," some interpreters comment that it's their repetition that matters. I agree. But rather than signify anything about geography, this repetition more likely emphasizes that the flood impacted all of humanity.*

If Dr. Ross really agrees that it is the repetition of "all," "every," and "everything" that signifies a truly universal event, then why did he list *six examples of events that do not repeat these words*? By Ross's own reasoning, the examples he just provided of non-global events are irrelevant to the interpretation of Genesis 6–8, because *it's the repetition of such terms that matters*. And not just their repetition, but the double use of a universal term in a single phrase, as well as contextual indicators of global scope, all present a strong and unified message of a flood that is truly worldwide in scope.

In agreeing that these repeated universal terms do indicate universality, Dr. Ross suggests that this universality applies to humans — not the earth. In other words, he believes the Flood killed all people, but did not cover all the earth. Of course, it would take a global flood to kill all people on earth, an issue we will revisit later. Putting that aside, does the text of Scripture apply the repeated universal terms to *humans only*? Or does it also apply these to animals and the earth itself? Consider the following verses (emphasis added):

> Genesis 6:17: "Behold, I, even I am bringing the flood of water upon the *earth*, to destroy *all flesh* in which is the breath of life, from *under heaven*; *everything* that is on the earth shall perish."
>
> Genesis 7:4b: ". . . and I will blot out from the face of the land *every living thing* that I have made."
>
> Genesis 7:11b: . . . on the same day *all* the *fountains of the great deep* burst open, and the floodgates of the sky were opened.
>
> Genesis 7:19b (KJV): . . . and all the high hills, that were under the whole heaven, were covered.
>
> Genesis 7:21–23: All flesh that moved on the earth perished, birds and cattle and beasts and every swarming thing that swarms upon the earth, and all mankind; of all that was on the dry land, all in whose nostrils was the breath of the spirit of life, died. Thus He blotted out every living thing that was upon the face of the land, from man to animals to creeping things and to birds of the sky, and they were blotted out from the earth; and only Noah was left, together with those that were with him in the ark.

The Genesis record applies these universal terms repeatedly, not just to mankind, but to the earth, the hills, and the living creatures of the earth. Indeed, one of the strongest examples of the double use of the Hebrew word *kol* ("all") is Genesis 7:19; here the *all* the high hills under *all* the heavens were covered by the floodwaters. Mankind is not even mentioned in that verse; the extent of the Flood is given in terms of its ability to cover all the hills beneath earth's sky. If Dr. Ross agrees that such repeated terminology indicates literal universality, and since such terminology is applied to the earth and animals as well as man, then he should draw the necessary conclusion that the Flood was global — covering all the earth and destroying all living land animals except those on the ark.

> *Once again, if humans had not yet begun to occupy all of earth's landmasses, the flood could be worldwide, or universal, without covering the globe.*

The text of Scripture — unlike Ross — does not limit the extent of the Flood to any alleged human dispersion. Instead it uses *geological indicators* — "all the high hills that were under the whole heaven were covered" (Genesis 7:19; NKJV). But even if we ignored all the texts with geological data, the argument still doesn't work. Although Dr. Ross has stated this very casually, the antecedent of his premise (that human's had not yet begun to occupy all of earth's landmasses) is extraordinarily dubious. Yet it is essential to his position. In other words, the only possible way that a *local* flood could destroy all mankind is if all humanity lived in a small area. This is an incredible claim, yet Ross gives absolutely no evidence for this condition.

In the 1,656 years between creation and the Flood, are we to believe that not a single person decided to venture out beyond the local area of Mesopotamia?[7] This is sufficient time for humanity to reach hundreds of millions, if not billions, of people. Were they all living in one spot? The proposal is even more absurd if we accept Dr. Ross's timescale. He puts the time between Adam and Noah at 20,000 to 60,000 years![8] This is far more time than has occurred since the Flood, and therefore the population of human beings would have been far greater than it is today — in the tens of billions or more. Are we to believe that each and every one of them lived in a valley in Mesopotamia?[9] By analogy, this would be like thinking that everyone today lives in Kansas, and that not even one person ever had the curiosity to explore what might lie beyond.

Dr. Ross absolutely must demonstrate that all humanity lived in a small region before the Flood in order for his view to even be considered. Yet, there is not even a hint in Scripture of such lack of dispersion before the Flood. It may be that Ross is confusing the Flood account with the Tower of Babel recorded in Genesis 11. Dr. Ross continues,

---

7. The quantity of 1,656 years between creation and the Flood is derived by noting the age of each ancestor of Noah at the time of the birth of the next ancestor in the lineage. The number is only approximate because the ages are given in whole years without fractions. See www.icr.org/article/4124.
8. Ross, *Navigating Genesis*, p. 75.
9. It would have to be a valley to contain the water; otherwise the Flood would be global.

> *The permanence of "dry land" and ocean boundaries is affirmed in Job 38, Psalm 33, 104, and Proverbs 8, all passages elaborating on the creation days.*

Proper hermeneutical analysis refutes Dr. Ross's claim. First, we note that all these are poetic passages of Scripture. Ross has violated the genre principle and the "explicit constrains the implicit" principle in attempting to override the literal clear meaning of historical sections of the Bible, namely Genesis, with poetic passages. Second, Ross has violated the contextual principle in asserting that all these passages are "elaborating on the creation days." In fact, *none* of them even mention the days of creation at all. Let's look at each of these in detail and interpret them in context.

Job 38 records God's response to Job's plea. The synonymous parallelism is clear, and shows that the language is poetic in nature. Consider verses 5–6, in which God asks Job about the creation of the earth: "Who set its measurements? Since you know. Or who stretched the line on it? On what were its bases sunk? Or who laid its cornerstone?" We are not to suppose that God literally stretched a line upon the earth to make sure His measurements were correct. Neither are we to presume that the earth literally has a cornerstone, or sunken bases. The imagery of erecting a house is a fitting metaphor for the creation of the earth. We are supposed to learn from this passage that only God was there to witness the creation of the universe, and only He knows the details of how the universe was made.

Presumably, Dr. Ross's assumption that Job 38 indicates the permanence of dry land comes from verses 8–11. These describe the "doors" of the sea. Verses 10–11 state, "And I placed boundaries on it, and I set a bolt and doors, and I said, 'Thus far you shall come, but no farther; and here shall your proud waves stop.'" Again, we are not to take this as a literal bolt or door, but rather as a metaphor for the boundary of the sea. God sets the limit by which the seas may encroach upon the land. But is that limit fixed and unchangeable even by God? There is nothing in this passage that suggests so. Just as human beings can open a door of their own making, cannot God do the same? Indeed, even our own experience shows that the daily tides cause the interface between land and ocean to change. And we should remember that Job lived sometime after the Flood, at which point God had promised never to again cover the entire earth with water (Genesis 9:11, 15). But there is no such promise during the creation week, and no such promise is mentioned in Job 38.

Psalm 33 says nothing about the permanence of dry land. It only briefly mentions the seas at all, and only in verse 7. This verse states, "He gathers the waters of the sea together as a heap; He lays up the deeps in storehouses." The synonymous parallelism is clear: the ocean is often called "the deep" in Scripture from the Hebrew word (*tehom*) — see Genesis 1:2. This passage seems to refer back to God's gathering the waters to form seas during the creation week (see Genesis 1:9–10). But where does this psalm say anything about the alleged permanence of dry land?

Psalm 104 discusses God's providence in the created world. It doesn't mention the days of creation, but it does occasionally reference the fact that God created what we see today. The sun and moon, for example, are both mentioned briefly in verse 19. But it is equally clear that this psalm is not rehearsing the creation week, because it speaks of the present world; it mentions the ships of the sea in verse 26. But ships would not have been present during the creation week. It also mentions lions roaring after their prey in verse 21. But at the close of the creation week, all animals were vegetarian (Genesis 1:29–30). Psalm 104 describes God's providence since the creation of the world.

Presumably, Dr. Ross is using Psalm 104:6–9 to indicate the "permanence of the dry land." Verse 9 says of the waters, "You set a boundary that they may not pass over, so that they will not return to cover the earth." Does this mean the Flood could not be global? The context shows just the opposite! Psalm 104 was written long after the Genesis Flood, and verse 9 is referring to the promise God made after the Flood — that He would never again cover the earth with water to destroy all life (Genesis 9:11). Indeed, when we read the verse *in context* with verses 6–8, and interpret Scripture with Scripture, we can see that this refers almost verbatim to God's actions during the Genesis Flood:

> Psalm 104:6: You covered it [the earth] with the deep as with a garment; the waters were standing above the mountains.
>
> Genesis 7:19–20: The water prevailed more and more upon the earth, so that all the high mountains everywhere under the heavens were covered. The water prevailed fifteen cubits higher, and the mountains were covered.
>
> Psalm 104:7: At Your rebuke they fled, at the sound of Your thunder they hurried away.

> Genesis 8:1b, 3: . . . and God caused a wind to pass over the earth, and the water subsided. . . . and the water receded steadily from the earth. . . .

> Psalm 104:8: The mountains rose; the valleys sank down to the place which You established for them.

> Genesis 8:5: The water decreased steadily until the tenth month; in the tenth month, on the first day of the month, the tops of the mountains became visible.

> Psalm 104:9: You set a boundary that they may not pass over, so that they will not return to cover the earth.

> Genesis 9:11: "I establish My covenant with you; and all flesh shall never again be cut off by the water of the flood, neither shall there again be a flood to destroy the earth."

Given the obvious parallels between Psalm 104:6–9 and Genesis 7–9, can there be any doubt that this portion of the psalm refers to God's power during the Genesis Flood?[10] Ross assumes it refers to the creation week, but there is no textual basis for that. Far be it from suggesting that a global Flood is impossible, these verses *describe* the global Flood in beautiful poetic language! Verse 9 reminds the reader of God's promise in Genesis 9:11 that the earth will never again be globally flooded as it was in the time of Noah — which would make no sense if the world had not been globally flooded. Dr. Ross had to ignore context and failed to interpret Scripture with Scripture in order to arrive at his interpretation of this passage.

Finally, we come to Proverbs 8. Contrary to Dr. Ross's assertion, this chapter does not so much as mention the days of creation, let alone *elaborate* on them. Rather, it extols the virtue of wisdom by the poetic device of reification. Wisdom is personified, as if it were a woman calling out for people to seek her. In verses 22–31, wisdom is personified as being present with the Lord as He created and shaped the world. Dr. Ross states, "Again, in Proverbs 8:29 we read that 'he [God] gave the sea its boundary.' These

10. The footnotes in the *Henry Morris Study Bible* pertaining to Psalm 104 are very helpful in showing how the global Flood fits perfectly with the text. Dr. Morris literally wrote the book on *The Genesis Flood*. He has thoroughly studied what the Bible states about Noah's Flood — more so than anyone else in recent generations.

verses seem to indicate that Earth would never again return to the watery state in which it began, described in Genesis 1:2."

First, we note that, as with all the proverbs, parallelism abounds. This again reminds us that these passages must not be used to override the literal teaching of historical sections of Scripture, like Genesis. The "boundary" of the sea is mentioned in verse 29, but there is no suggestion that such a boundary is *unchangeable* as Ross supposes. We again note that these boundaries shift slightly every day with the tides. The water will not transgress God's command because God is in control. When He sends a flood of waters to destroy all life on earth, the waters obey (Genesis 6:17, 7:11–12, 19–21). When God commands the floodwaters to recede, they do (Psalm 104:7). It wasn't until *after* the Flood of Noah that God promised never to again cover the earth with water (Genesis 9:11; Psalm 104:9). Proverbs 8 says nothing about the permanence of such a boundary. Even if it did, Proverbs was written long after the Genesis Flood, and thus *after* God promised to never again flood the whole earth.

Dr. Ross closes this section by reminding the reader that God's wrath is limited to the extent of sin. In particular, he uses the city of Sodom as an example of a local judgment of God, and points out that Jesus affirmed this event. Ross states, "Once again he [Jesus] clarifies that God's wrath came against reprobate people and [was] limited to their location." Of course, Sodom was a local event and the context makes this clear. But what does Genesis 6 say about the *extent of sin* at the time of the Flood?

Genesis 6:11–12 states, "Now *the earth was corrupt* in the sight of God, and *the earth was filled with violence*. God looked on *the earth*, and behold, it was corrupt; for *all flesh* had corrupted their way *upon the earth*" (emphasis added). Note that *all* flesh on earth was corrupt. The "earth" is mentioned *four times* in these two verses to emphasize the global extent of mankind's wickedness. Since the extent of sin was planet-wide, the wrath of God was poured out on the entire planet. Genesis 6:13 says as much, "Then God said to Noah, 'The end of *all flesh* has come before Me; for the *earth is filled with violence* because of them; and behold, I am about to destroy them *with the earth*' " (emphasis added).

Furthermore, what was the purpose of the rainbow? According to Genesis 9:11–17, the rainbow was a visible token of God's promise to never again destroy the world by a global flood. But if the Flood were merely a local event as Ross asserts, and the rainbow is God's promise never to send another local flood, then God has broken His promise thousands of times. We do have local floods today. If God keeps His promises — and He does — then the Genesis Flood must have been global.

Failure to Disperse

> *God's earliest command to Adam and Eve was that they "multiply and fill the earth." His plan for humanity called for global occupation. God's later words and actions, as recorded in Genesis 9–11, imply their failure to follow through, Humanity failed to spread out.*

Is there any hint at all in Genesis 9–11 that people before the Flood had "failed to spread out"? If indeed that were the sin that caused God to become angry and flood mankind, it is strange indeed that it isn't mentioned at all in the Flood account. Actually, Genesis chapter 6 does tell us the reason that God sent the Flood — and it has nothing to do with failing to spread out. It was because mankind was *violently wicked.* Genesis 6:11 states, "Now the earth was corrupt in the sight of God, and the earth was filled with violence." Genesis 6:5 states, "Then the Lord saw that the wickedness of man was great on the earth, and that every intent of the thoughts of his heart was only evil continually." In Genesis 6:13 the Lord says, "The end of all flesh has come before Me; for the earth is filled with violence because of them; and behold, I am about to destroy them with the earth." The wicked violence of men is the biblical reason for the Flood — not a failure to spread out.

It is fallacious to assume that because people failed to disperse *after* the Flood in the city of Babel, that this must have been their main sin *before* the Flood. There is no textual support for such a claim. It is arbitrary. We could equally well say, "Many of the religious leaders at the time of Christ's earthly ministry sinned by having Jesus crucified. Therefore, we can conclude that people before Christ's earthly ministry probably also sinned by having Jesus crucified." Since the Fall, people have always been sinners; but they don't always sin in exactly the same way. Indeed, people have found a plethora of ways to rebel against God. Genesis 6 indicates that the wicked violence of man kindled God's wrath, *not* a failure to disperse.

If we hypothetically consider Ross's assertion for argument's sake, we see that it leads to a contradiction. If the failure to disperse was the main sin that kindled God's wrath, then where was Noah and why did he have to build an ark? The Bible teaches that Noah was "blameless" and "righteous" in God's eyes (Genesis 6:9). Therefore, Noah could not have been a participant in mankind's rebellion in allegedly failing to disperse. He and his family would have obeyed God and dispersed; and so they would not be living in the area of rebellious mankind. A local flood would pose no danger to someone who lived far away from it. So why did Noah need to build an ark?

On the other hand, if Noah and his family were living in the same valley as everyone else, and had therefore also *failed to disperse*, then they would be in as much rebellion as the rest of mankind. After all, Noah was 600 years old when the Flood came (Genesis 7:6). In all that time, if Noah never obeyed God's command to disperse, then Noah would have been just as unrepentant as the rest of humanity. How then does God call him "blameless" and "righteous"? Why build an ark the size of an ocean-liner for a *local* flood, when in far less time and with less effort Noah could have simply moved away from the area, and actually obeyed God's original command to disperse? The non-hermeneutical approach that Dr. Ross takes to the Scriptures leads to all kinds of such absurdities.

Geographical Markers

> *Biblical clues to the geographical limits on human habitation can be found in the place-names Genesis records. In Genesis 1–9 all the places mentioned belong to settlements in Mesopotamia and the Persian Gulf Oasis. From Genesis 10 onward, the text refers to places throughout much of the Eastern hemisphere. This sudden shift to a wider geographical focus after Genesis 10 strongly suggests that until the time of the flood (and even afterward), humans and the animals on which they depended remained in and around the area often referred to in textbooks as the cradle of human civilization. Thus, to fulfill God's purpose, the deluge would be as vast as that region but need not go beyond.*

Is it the case that "in Genesis 1–9 *all* the places mentioned belong to settlements in Mesopotamia and the Persian Gulf Oasis"? What about the Pishon River mentioned in Genesis 2:11? Where in Mesopotamia or the Persian Gulf Oasis can we find this river? What about the Gihon River mentioned in Genesis 2:13? This river cannot be found in Mesopotamia or the Persian

Gulf Oasis. Where is the "land of Nod" mentioned in Genesis 4:16? For that matter, where is its primary city — the city named "Enoch" (Genesis 4:17)? What about Eden mentioned in Genesis 2:8? Where in Mesopotamia do we find Eden, and the garden thereof? None of these can be found in the area Ross describes. Clearly, his claim is not true.

In fact, some of the names of places mentioned in Genesis 1–9 are found *far away* from Mesopotamia. Enoch City is located in Utah. Eden is in North Carolina, and there is also an Eden in southeastern Australia. Obviously, these are not the *original* Enoch City and Eden mentioned respectively in Genesis — and that's the point. We know that many of the places named in Genesis 1–9 do not correspond to modern places with those names. And so it would be ludicrous to assume without a good reason that others do. In other words, there is no reason to assume that the names "Cush" (Ethiopia) and "Assyria" mentioned in Genesis 2:13–14 must refer to the modern locations of Ethiopia and Assyria. In fact, they cannot because these two regions are widely separated today and not connected by the river system that Genesis describes.

Likewise, the Tigris and Euphrates Rivers mentioned in Genesis 2:14 cannot refer to the *modern* Tigris and Euphrates because the descriptions do not match. Genesis 2 describes the Tigris and Euphrates as being two of four rivers that split from the single river flowing from Eden. But the modern Tigris and Euphrates do not branch this way. Therefore, modern landmarks that have names matching those in Genesis 1–9 must have been named in memorandum of the originals. No one would seriously argue that Eden, North Carolina, is the same Eden described in Genesis 2. Why then do some people assume that the Tigris and Euphrates are the same as in Genesis 2 when the descriptions do not match?

As Noah disembarked after the Flood, he encountered a very different world from the one he previously knew. The cataclysm of the global Flood radically altered the surface of earth, building new mountains and valleys. Psalm 104:8 states, "The mountains rose; the valleys sank down to the place which You established for them." It seems likely that as Noah and his family explored this new world, they would encounter landmarks that reminded them of various aspects of the pre-Flood world. No doubt they would name some of these after their memory of the originals. This happens whenever explorers settle in a new part of the world. Consider how many towns and cities in the United States are named after locations in England: Birmingham, Canterbury, Norwich, Cambridge, Lancaster, Liverpool, Leicester, Manchester, Dover, Carlisle, Bristol, Boston, Plymouth, Stockbridge, Winchester, Buckingham, and so on, to name just a few.

In fact, geographical markers are strong evidence *against* Dr. Ross's position. If the Genesis Flood were merely local, then it would not have substantially altered earth's geography. Thus, the geographical markers in Genesis should be readily observable today. We should find one river going through the Garden of Eden that splits into four (Genesis 2:10). And one of these four should flow east of Assyria (Genesis 2:11), while another flows around Ethiopia (Genesis 2:13). We ought to find the remains of Enoch City in Nod to the east of Eden (Genesis 4:16). Instead, we find none of these things. Why? The Genesis Flood was global, and radically altered earth's geography. Any pre-Flood rivers or cities were obliterated and any physical evidence of them is buried under a mile or so of sedimentary rock layers that were deposited during the Flood year. Dr. Ross has begged the question in assuming that geographical markers are the same before and after the Flood year; that would only be possible if the flood were non-global — the very point he is attempting to prove.

Furthermore, and aside from all this, Dr. Ross's argument is not reasonable from the start. Even if we grant for the sake of hypothesis that all the location names in Genesis 1–9 correspond to modern Mesopotamia (which they don't) and are readily observable today (which they aren't), would that prove that humanity had not dispersed around the globe? That would be an argument from silence. In Genesis 1–9, the Bible focuses mainly on the lineage leading up to Noah. So naturally we would expect to read mainly of the locations in which that family line lived. It would be folly to assume that other families didn't live in other places, simply on the basis that they are not mentioned. Dr. Ross's reasoning is self-refuting. North and South America are not mentioned at all in the Scriptures — even in the New Testament. Can we therefore conclude that people had not yet dispersed to North and South America?

Highest Mountains

Genesis 7:19–21 indicates that the floodwaters covered all the high hills (mountains) under the entire sky to a depth of at least 15 cubits (about

22 feet), and that every air-breathing land animal, every bird, and every person on earth died. These verses are particularly devastating to Dr. Ross's position, and so he must deal with them. Of this passage Ross states the following:

> *The text would appear to say that all land life on the planet was destroyed and that even Mount Everest was covered by more than twenty feet of water. But is that what the original Hebrew words literally convey? Is it possible that translators have been influenced by tradition or by their own historical context, which includes awareness of earth as a planet? A careful look paints a less (geographically) expansive picture.*

Note first that even Dr. Ross acknowledges that the text *appears to say* that all land life on earth was destroyed. But he cannot accept the text at face value because that would destroy the possibility of deep time. Ross makes another serious mistake in saying that "even Mount Everest was covered" in the global-flood view. But the text only teaches that the mountains that existed *at that time* were covered. Mount Everest was likely *produced* by the tectonic activity associated with the Flood, and therefore would not have existed prior to the Flood year. We know scripturally that many mountains were uplifted at the end of the Flood: Psalm 104:8 states, "The mountains rose; the valleys sank down to the place which You established for them." Dr. Ross has been corrected on this issue more than once, so it is disappointing to see him continue in this error. By the way, scientists have found marine fossils on the top of Mount Everest. It was indeed under water during the Flood year, though it likely was not a tall mountain at the time.

Dr. Ross again brings up the issue of cultural bias. But he seems to assume that people at the time Genesis was written were unaware of the spherical nature of earth. However, the Book of Job which was written *before* Moses wrote Genesis, shows that at least some of God's people already knew that the earth is round and is suspended in space. Job 26:10 describes the "terminator" of earth, the boundary between daylight and night as being a circle. This is only possible on a spherical planet. Job 26:7 states that God "hangs the earth on nothing" — a poetic description of the planetary nature of earth. So Moses and others may very well have known that the world is round, and Ross shouldn't arbitrarily assume otherwise. More importantly,

God has always known that the earth is a spherical planet, and God used copious amounts of global language in describing the Genesis Flood, so that there can be no doubt about the issue.

Next, Dr. Ross quotes from the *Theological Wordbook of the Old Testament* by R. Laird Harris, regarding the Hebrew word *kasah* which means "to cover." Harris states, "In Genesis 7:19–20 the hills were 'covered;' the Hebrew does not specify with what. . . . The Hebrew may merely mean that the mountains were hidden from view by the storm."[11] Apparently, Ross means to suggest via Harris that the mountains were covered with something other than water, so that they were hidden from view. But this doesn't fit the context. Genesis 7:19 states, "The *water* prevailed more and more upon the earth, so that all the high mountains everywhere under the heavens were covered" (emphasis added). It is unnecessary to add "with water" to the end of the verse because the first part of the verse specifies what is doing the covering. Likewise, Genesis 7:20 states, "The *water* prevailed fifteen cubits higher, and the mountains were covered" (emphasis added).

It's hard to imagine that Dr. Ross really believes that the mountains were covered with something other than water. And his next argument seems to reveal as much. He continues:

> *Even if the covering or concealment was by water, three possibilities exist. The water could reside upon, run over, or fall upon the hills. In these scenarios the word* kasa *can be interpreted to mean that more than twenty feet of water stood, that is, remained, over the high hills or mountains; or it could mean that this quantity of water ran over them, as in a flash flood, or fell upon them as rainfall. The context gives no clear indication which of the three meanings to choose.*

I would like to know how Ross thinks that 20 feet of water from a flash flood can sweep over a mountain. Moreover, I would like to know how 20 feet of water can fall on a mountain so as to conceal it from view during a local flood. Such options make no sense and do not fit the context. Contrary to Ross's assertion, context makes this passage very clear. The waters

---

11. R. Laird Harris, *Theological Wordbook of the Old Testament* (Chicago, IL: Moody Press, c1980).

increased to the point that every high hill under the entire sky was covered, and then they increased 22 additional feet, completely covering the mountains. A local flood simply cannot do this.

> *The Hebrew words for "all the high mountains" are* kol heharim hugebohim. *Here again, because of a limited vocabulary the Hebrew words carry a range of meanings. The word* har *is used for "hill," "hill country," "mount," or "mountain." It could refer to a towering peak such as mountaineers love to ascend, or it could mean a small hill that children climb in their playtime. Any landform in between these two extremes is also a possible definition.*

Presumably, Dr. Ross wants to believe that only small hills are being described in Genesis 7:19–21. But context precludes this possibility because Genesis states that *all the **high** hills under the entire heavens* were covered. This important qualifier shows that God is indeed referring to mountains, and not merely a small hill that children climb in their playtime. Indeed, the Hebrew word *har* is the word normally used for "mountain" or "mount" as in Mount Sanai (e.g., Exodus 19:23, 34:2).

> *Genesis 7:19 describes Noah's inability to see anything but water, horizon to horizon, from his viewpoint on the ark's upper deck.*

Here, Ross has violated the text principle — he just hasn't read and represented the text fairly. Genesis 7:19 says absolutely nothing about Noah or his "inability to see anything but water" from the "ark's upper deck." On the contrary, this verse uses global, objective terminology — all the high hills under all the heavens were covered. The phrase "under all the heavens" indicates that all the mountains on earth are included — all those under earth's sky.

> *If the ark were floating anywhere near the middle of the Persian Gulf or the vast Mesopotamian plains on water as much as two or three hundred feet deep, no hills or mountains would be visible from his position.*

This again violates the text principle because the Bible does not say that Noah merely couldn't see the mountains in his local vicinity. Rather, it tells us that all the mountains under earth's sky were covered.

Geographically, Ross's claim doesn't add up. The Mesopotamian valley is not a closed "bowl," but is open on its south-southwestern perimeter where it empties directly to the Persian Gulf. This opening is over a hundred miles wide. So how could a wide-open bowl hold "two or three hundred feet" of water without flooding the rest of the planet as well? Imagine a bathtub with one side missing. Could you fill it with water without flooding the rest of the bathroom?

Additionally, the Bible states that the ark landed on the mountains of Ararat, *not* in Mesopotamia (Genesis 8:4). The word "Ararat" is the Armenian equivalent of "Urartu" and refers to a region surrounding Lake Van, which is located about two hundred miles southeast of the Black Sea, and well north of Mesopotamia. The ark came to rest on the mountains (plural) of Ararat (Urartu). Thus, any mountain in the Urartu region is a possible landing site for the ark — including, but not limited to, Mount Ararat itself. Could a *local flood* deposit an ark on the mountains of this region?

The Urartu region is quite rugged, and has a typical elevation in excess of one *mile* above sea level. Lake Van (which is obviously a local low point or it wouldn't be a lake) has an elevation of 5,400 feet! The region immediately surrounding it varies in elevation in excess of 9,000 feet above sea level. The hills and mountains in the region are higher still, with Mount Ararat itself rising 17,000 feet above sea level. I'm curious how Dr. Ross thinks that a local flood of only 200 to 300 feet of water in Mesopotamia (elevation close to sea level) could deposit the ark on a mountain far north of Mesopotamia in a region with a typical elevation in excess of 5,000 feet. The numbers just don't add up.

> *Further support for belief that the flood covered only the limited, humanly inhabited region of the planet rather than the whole globe comes from Genesis 8:5, which says, "The waters continued to recede until the tenth month, and on the first day of the tenth month the tops of the mountains (or hills) became visible." Although Noah could see land, neither the raven nor the dove he released could fly far enough to reach a landing place. A week later, however, when the dove went out again, it recovered a leaf from an olive tree. Where do olive trees grow? Not on high mountains. We can reasonably assume from this detail that the* har *Noah could see and that the dove was able to reach were low-lying hills or foothills.*

Why Dr. Ross thinks this supports a local flood is perplexing. First, would the waters of a local flood take *ten months* to recede before even the nearby hills become visible again? According to the Scriptures, Noah and his family were on the ark for over one year (Genesis 7:9–11, 8:14). That timescale does not comport with a local flood. Moreover, the literal description of global floodwater drainage movements, provided in Genesis 8:3, matches what creation geologists have analyzed regarding evidences of global mega-sequences that periodically occurred during the global Flood's drainage timeframe.[12]

Second, consider Ross's claim that "neither the raven nor the dove [Noah] released could fly far enough to reach a landing place." Doves can easily fly up to 100 miles, and typically do so even today when they are released at weddings for example. If the "mountains" in Genesis 8:14 were really just hills, and thus relatively nearby in order for them to be seen, then the birds could have easily reached them. Only a genuine mountain could be seen at distances over 100 miles. For that matter, why would *any* bird need to be aboard the ark for a *local flood*?

Third, Dr. Ross seems to have missed the significance of releasing a raven and dove respectively. The raven eats indiscriminately and would readily feed on the carcasses left by the flood. It is not particularly concerned with cleanliness, and was classified as unclean under the Old Testament dietary law (Leviticus 11:15; Deuteronomy 14:14). But doves feed on seeds and plants. The dove is more concerned with cleanliness, is clean under biblical law, and is the only bird considered pure enough to be offered as a sacrifice (Leviticus 5:7, 12:6). The dove is a biblical symbol of purity (Psalm 68:13; Matthew 10:16). As such, the dove would be reticent to remain outside the ark if the land were still muddy. Noah knew exactly what he was doing in releasing these two kinds of birds.

Fourth, what are we to make of Dr. Ross's claim that olive trees do not grow on high mountains? Right from the start, Ross has begged the question. Namely, he has assumed that the mountains were as high then as they are today, which implicitly assumes a local flood. If the Flood was global, and indeed mountains were uplifted toward the end of the Flood and thereafter (e.g., Psalm 104:8), then the mountains would not have been as high as today. In fact, they were below sea-level — by definition

12. www.icr.org/article/6539.

— when the floodwaters covered them. And olive trees can indeed grow near sea-level.

Additionally, when the dove returned with an olive branch, the waters had already been receding for *four months* since the ark had come to rest on the mountain (Genesis 8:4–11). And the waters had been receding for over a month and a half since the mountaintops were visible. So, there is no reason to assume, as Ross did, that the olive branch was from a high mountain. The mountains would not have been high at that time, and the lower elevations may very well have been exposed by that point. Olive trees can grow from rootstock of an otherwise dead tree, or from stem cuttings. They grow well even in poor soil. It makes sense that these would be among the first plants to recover from the Flood year.

> *It is significant to note that from the perspective of the dove as it flew, "the waters were still on the face of the whole earth" (Genesis 8:9; ESV). Right here in the context we have a clear indication the "the face of the whole earth" can and does mean a particular less-extensive-than-global region.*

Here, Dr. Ross seems to suggest that since the Bible says the waters were on the face of the whole earth, and since some of the land was exposed, the "whole earth" must mean just the local area. But that cannot be the right interpretation because it leads to a contradiction. The Bible indicates that portions of the earth were visible at this time (Genesis 8:5). That is, even the *local area* visible to Noah was not entirely covered with water. So what are we to make of the fact that the waters were still upon the land in Genesis 8:9?

The Bible does not say that the waters covered (Hebrew: *kasah*) the earth here, as they did in Genesis 7:19–20. The water was merely "on" the surface of the whole earth at the time that Noah released the dove. In other words, the ground was still wet and sufficiently muddy that the dove was unable to land and rest. The passage does suggest that the entire planet was still in this condition. The land was exposed, no longer covered/concealed by water, but was not yet dry. Hence, the indiscriminate raven had already departed.

> *Genesis 8 also tells us how God removed the floodwaters from the land: He sent a wind. This drying technique perfectly suits what a flooded plain such as Mesopotamia would require. Water of nearly*

> *any depth in such a flat region would flow very inefficiently toward the sea, but a wind would significantly accelerate its movement.*

We find several interpretive problems here. First, does Genesis 8 actually say that the wind God sent was the *cause* of the recession of the floodwaters? I cannot find that in the text. It merely says that "God caused a wind to pass over the earth, and the water subsided" (Genesis 8:1). Dr. Ross may have committed the false cause fallacy in assuming that there is a causal connection between two things simply because they happened around the same time. It may be a very reasonable hypothesis that the wind God sent was the cause of the recession of the waters. But this assumption goes beyond the text.

Second, would wind really be necessary to drain floodwater from Mesopotamia? Recall that the southeast side of the valley opens directly into the Persian Gulf; the opening is over one hundred miles wide. Wind is not required to make water go downhill through an enormous opening. Gravity does that job very efficiently.

Third, wouldn't the ark go along with the water? If the Flood were merely a local event limited to Mesopotamia, and if the waters naturally flowed south into the Persian Gulf, then why didn't the ark end up in the Persian Gulf? In fact, the Urartu region in which the ark landed is North of Mesopotamia, in the *opposite direction* of the Persian Gulf. The ark would have needed to go against the flow of water, *and* uphill to get to the higher elevation of the region of Ararat. And the ark came to rest not in the plain, but on the *mountains* of Ararat, which just adds insult to injury.

Floodwater's Sources

> *Another way in which the flood chapters themselves argue against a globally extensive flood is by reporting where the water came from (Genesis 7) as well as where it returned (Genesis 8). Genesis 7:11–12 says the floodwaters came from "the springs of the great deep" and "the floodgates of the heavens." . . . The first refers to subterranean reservoirs, or aquifers, and the second, to heavy rain clouds. The quantity of water on, in, and around these earthly sources measures vastly less than the quantity required for global inundation — even if the highest preflood hills or mountains were not more than 500 feet above current sea levels.*

The argument here is external to the text and irrelevant to the biblical author's intention. It is therefore non-hermeneutical. Namely, Dr. Ross has concluded — not from textual considerations, but allegedly scientific ones — that there is not enough water to globally flood the earth. But how is Ross's opinion of what is possible even remotely relevant to the author's intention in Genesis? From scientific observations we would have to conclude that pure water cannot be instantly changed to wine. Should we therefore interpret Christ's miracle at Cana (John 2:1–11)? Likewise, if the text of Scripture indicates a global Flood, then it was a global Flood. If Ross doesn't understand the scientific details, then that's his problem — not God's. (See 2 Peter 3:3–6.)

In fact, there is plenty of water to cover the earth globally when we take into consideration that earth's current geological features are largely a *result* of the Flood. As suggested in passages like Psalm 104:8, the mountains rose and the valleys sank as the flood diminished — an increase in topographic relief. Hence, during the Flood year, the earth's surface was smoother than today. A quick calculation shows that earth's current volume of water is more than sufficient to flood all the landmass if the topographic relief is slightly reduced. If there were no mountains or valleys and earth's surface were perfectly smooth, then the entire earth would be covered in water to a depth of 1.6 miles! This puts the upper limit of pre-Flood mountains at 8,400 feet; that is *16 times* larger than the mere 500 feet that Ross suggests.

Meaning of Earth

> *A quick look at a biblical concordance reveals that* 'eres *is an often-used noun — the fourth most frequently used noun in the Old Testament, in fact. . . . It may be used for earth in the cosmic sense, but most often it indicates a specific territory or land area.*

The question is not, "What is the range of meaning of *'erets* (earth)?" Rather, it is "What does the word mean *in the context of Genesis 6–8*?" Again, Dr. Ross has ignored the context completely. The Hebrew word translated "earth" is *'erets* and is the main word that would be used to describe the planet Earth. It is the word used in Genesis 1, when God describes the creation of the universe (the "heavens and the earth"). The same word is used in Genesis 6:13 when God says he will destroy "the earth." It's the same word used throughout the Flood account (i.e., Genesis 7:3, 4, 6, 10, 12, 14, 17, 18, 19, 21, 23, 24).

In fact, this word has a similar semantic range to our English word "earth." This is the term we use for our planet, but can also refer to a small section of land — "earth" as opposed to sky. It can also mean "dirt" or "soil." Context determines meaning. And we have already seen that Genesis uses global qualifiers — not just "earth" but "*all* the earth" (Genesis 7:3) — and *all* the high hills under *all* the heavens. "All" is used *50* times in this passage, so it's hard to imagine that God could have been more emphatic about the global scale of the Flood. I suppose He could have added one more, "And I really do mean *all*," but that hardly seems necessary.

Dr. Ross closes out this section with a comment about the Hebrew word *adamah*, which is translated as "ground" in passages like Genesis 1:25, 2:5, 7, 9, 19, 3:17, 19, 23, 4:2, 3, 10–12, 14, 5:29, 6:1, 20, 7:4, 8, 23 in the NASB. He states:

> *The English equivalents for* 'adama *include "ground," "land," and "earth." Theologian Leonard Coppes points out, "Originally this word signified the red arable soil. From this it came to denote any cultivated, plantable ground and/or landed property." Given that only a fraction of the world's continental landmass may be described as arable, it seems unlikely that* 'adama *could refer to all the land on earth's surface. Rather, the use of* 'adama *in Genesis 6–8 more likely implies that preflood humans limited their habitation to plantable land.*

Here Dr. Ross has begged the question; how does he know what the soil in the pre-Flood world was like and where it was arable? Only by assuming a local flood would it be remotely reasonable to suppose that the soil in various parts of the world was the same before the Flood as it is today. But this is the very topic in question.

Moreover, it is a "root fallacy" to conclude too much from a word's etymology, as that word is analyzed by consulting with extra-biblical usages. In the Hebrew Scriptures the term *'erets* is never limited to "arable" land, nor is it for *'adamah*, so this is yet another red herring distraction from Ross. The Hebrew word *'adamah* is well-translated as "ground" for this is what it means. This is what Adam was made from (Genesis 2:7), what God cursed when Adam sinned (Genesis 3:17), what people return to when they die

(Genesis 3:19), and what animals walk upon (Genesis 1:25). The word is not limited to a particular kind of soil.

In the Genesis record of the Flood, the "ground" is mainly used to describe those animals that were brought aboard the ark, and those that were destroyed by the flood — those that walk upon the ground as opposed to fish or whales (Genesis 6:20, 7:8). It also refers to the surface of the land (Genesis 8:8) as opposed to ocean. Far from indicating a local flood, the use of the word *'adamah* for "ground" or "land" in concert with *'erets* for "earth" precludes any possibility except a global Flood. Here is why.

Apart from context, the "earth" might refer to the entire planet Earth (land and ocean), or it might mean the land only. *'Adamah* by itself just means "ground" or "land" but may or may not mean all land everywhere. In Genesis 7:4, 23, and 8:13 God uses both "earth" and "land" together so that there can be no misunderstanding. All the land of the planet Earth was covered by water — all the high hills under all the heavens. All *land* animals died everywhere on planet Earth, except those that were on the ark. Context is key. Ross continually ignores the context, though he does give lip service to the idea.

Context as Key

> *If we approach Genesis 6–8 from the perspective of both the author and the audience, we can understand why its language seems so strong as to evoke images of a global inundation.*

Yes, we can because that is exactly what the author intended! If Moses had wanted to explain that all the billions of inhabitants of earth were concentrated in a valley that experienced a local flood, he could certainly have said so. But instead, he writes that of all the people and land animals, only Noah and those onboard the ark remained alive (Genesis 7:21–23).

> *The flood was, indeed, a massively cataclysmic event, a total destruction of humanity and the animals associated with them, except those sheltered by Noah's unique craft. It was the most catastrophic event — and potent warning of sin's consequences — ever delivered to humankind.*

This is another instance of the superfluous distinction fallacy. God's Word teaches that the flood was upon all the earth (Genesis 6:13) and covered all the mountains on earth (Genesis 7:19–20), and destroyed all the air-breathing land animals that were not on the ark (Genesis 6:17, 20, 7:21–23). But Ross adds distinctions — all the earth *that humans had settled* was destroyed, and all the mountains *that Noah could have seen from his location* were covered, and all the animals *that had contact with humanity*. The reference is subtle here: "the animals associated with them" — indicating that land animals that had not interacted with humans need not be on the ark and were not destroyed by the Flood. But none of these distinctions are warranted by context or the need for logical consistency. They are hermeneutically unjustified and fallacious.

> *Perhaps because English-speaking, English-reading people have for several centuries pictured earth, its peoples and geographic features, in global terms, we forget that the ancients had no such images in their minds. The world meant people, the land meant the ground under their feet stretching from horizon to horizon. The highest mountains would be those within sight or walking distance of their homes.*

C.S. Lewis referred to this kind of argument as "chronological snobbery" — assuming that ancient people couldn't have understood that the world is round, or that the planet is much more than simply the people on it. How does Ross know what the extent of ancient knowledge was? In fact, the oldest book of the Bible speaks of the roundness of the earth (Job 26:10) and of its global suspension upon the nothingness of space (Job 26:7). So at least some Old Testament believers did know that the earth is round. We have advantages today because knowledge can increase as new discoveries are made and passed on from one generation to the next. But ancient people were highly intelligent as evidenced by the rapid development of tools, culture, music, and so forth (Genesis 4:20–22).

On what hermeneutical grounds does Ross justify his conjecture that the ancients didn't think in global terms and "had no such images in their minds"? What about Isaiah 40:22 where the author describes the "circle of the earth" or Job 26:10 where God is said to have "inscribed a circle on the surface of the waters at the boundary of light and darkness"? This is a perfect description of the earth's terminator — the boundary between day and night that is always a circle due to the earth's sphericalness. How does Ross justify his claim that "the world meant people, the land meant the ground under their feet stretching from horizon to horizon. The highest mountains would be those within sight or walking distance of their homes." The text of Genesis uses repeated global terminology. This not only shows that the Flood was global, but also that people at the time had at least some awareness of the immensity of the planet and were perfectly capable of thinking in global terms.

Conclusion

Throughout the Bible there is not the slightest hint that the Genesis Flood was anything less than a global, planet-altering cataclysm, in which all the mountains under earth's sky were covered, and in which all air-breathing land animals and all people perished, except those on the ark. Dr. Ross has not provided a single hermeneutically cogent argument for his ideas about the Flood. His view cannot be justified hermeneutically, and does not stand up to rational investigation.

I hope that you have enjoyed this book and that it will be helpful in your private Bible study as well as your interaction with others. The Bible really is clear and can be understood by anyone who is willing to work hard at it. Genesis really is the true history of the universe as recorded by the only witness of creation — God. Genesis really means what it states, and no one should be intimidated by arguments to the contrary. It is my prayer that Christians will challenge each other to better understand God's Word by studying and applying the biblically founded principles of hermeneutics. Perhaps the many denominations of Christianity will one day be able to reconcile their differences by careful and humble study of Scripture.

Appendix A

A Dialog with a Heretic, and a Defense of the Trinity

This chapter is an actual written dialog I had with a young man who I will call "Steve" (not his real name). Steve professed to be a Christian, but denied the Trinity. In particular, he denied the deity of Jesus. But the deity of Christ is central to Christianity. To be saved, we must be trusting in the real Jesus — the God-man and the only Savior. Since Steve was not placing his faith in God, but rather in a false Jesus, he is not truly a Christian.

The reproduction below has been organized for clarity. I changed the name so as not to embarrass Steve, and have corrected some typos and grammar, and minor adjustments to points that may have been unclear. Steve and I had lengthy exchanges, and I often copied previous sections for context. I have reordered this when possible so that the reader can see the response and counter-response to each point. Aside from these minor changes and re-ordered structure, the exchange stands as written.

I was very soft with Steve in the first round. But when he continued in sin, I became more direct, though still respectful, of course. I felt that the benefit of leading someone to Christ outweighed the risk of offending a friend. This soft-to-direct adjustment may not be obvious here due to the re-ordered structure. For this chapter I have provided additional commentary in square brackets []. I have also labeled major sections for easy reference.

Our first exchange is lost. But it was short. In summary, Steve originally suggested that there is no evidence of the Trinity in the Bible. He stated that Jesus is indeed the Son of God, but not God. He argued that Jesus must be less than God since Jesus submits to the Father (1 Corinthians 11:3) and since Jesus said "the Father is greater than I" (John 14:28). He thought that Philippians 2:6 indicated that Jesus is not equal to God, but is merely in the "form of God." Many of Steve's arguments are examples of the superfluous distinction fallacy.

This was my response.

My Initial Defense of the Trinity

The Trinity is actually suggested in the very first verse of the Bible; "In the beginning, God created the heavens and the earth." The Hebrew word for God in this verse is *Elohim*, which is a plural word. It literally means "Gods." And yet, the verb form for "created" is singular. The sentence is actually grammatically incorrect, a bit like saying "Gods is good." This construction (the plural word for God with a verb that is singular) is used throughout the Old Testament, and indicates that God is one in one sense, and more than one in another sense.

God is one in nature or essence. But God is three in persons who are eternally distinct from one another. I can show you the texts that demonstrate this if you like. But since your question for the moment is about the deity of Christ, let's concentrate on that issue.

The Bible teaches throughout the Old and New Testaments that Jesus Christ is God. The notion that Jesus is (literally) the Son of God, but not God, really doesn't make sense if you think about it. What is the son of a man? Answer: a man. Indeed, God often calls his human servants "son of man" — see Ezekiel 2:1, 3, 6, 8, 3:1, 3, 4, and Daniel 8:17. Now are we to conclude that Ezekiel and Daniel are not men, but something less than men? Of course not. The fact that each is the son of man means that he is man. Likewise, the Son of God is God. If the Son of God is of a different nature or less than God, then He isn't literally the Son of God.

I can understand how this could be misconstrued in our culture. We tend to think of "son of X" as something less than X. But in the Jewish culture, to be "son of X" means to be equal in value to "X" as is shown in John 5:18. So when Jesus claims to be the Son of God (Luke 22:70), this means

He is God, just as when He claims to be the Son of Man (Matthew 9:6), this means He is man.

The fact that Jesus submits to the Father does not make Him less in value or essence than the Father. After all, wives are to submit to their husbands (Ephesians 5:22), and servants to their masters (Ephesians 6:5–6). But this doesn't affect their intrinsic value to God (Galatians 3:28). This should answer your question regarding 1 Corinthians 11:3. Jesus was humbled in His earthly ministry — made for a little while "lower than the angels" (Hebrews 2:7). For the purpose of His earthly ministry, Christ — the King of kings — took on the nature of a bond-servant and "emptied Himself" (Philippians 2:6–7). He was still divine, but made Himself "lower" for a while. This should answer your question about John 14:28. Don't be thrown by the expression "form of." I'm in the form of a man, and yet this doesn't make me "not a man." The Scriptures are clear that Jesus is fully God. Let's look at just a few examples.

Jesus claims to be God in John 8:58 when He says, "Before Abraham was born, I am." The "I am" is not a mistake, it's one of the names of God (see Exodus 3:14) and indicates that God is self-existent and eternal. Jesus here is applying the name of God to Himself. If Jesus were not God then He blasphemed, and the Jews were right to try and stone Him (John 8:59). Jesus forgives sins in Mark 2:5. But since all sin is ultimately against God, only God can ultimately forgive sins (Isaiah 43:25). If Jesus were not God, then He again blasphemed (as the scribes believed — Mark 2:6–7).

Jesus's disciples recognized that He is God. Thomas called Jesus "my Lord and my God" (John 20:28). The Apostle Paul indicates that Christ is fully God (deity) in Colossians 2:9. The Apostle John tells us that Christ (the Word made flesh — John 1:14) was God from the beginning (John 1:1), and "with God" — another reference to the Trinity! Luke consistently refers to Jesus as "the Lord" (Luke 7:13, 19, 10:1, 39, 41, 11:39, etc.). God the Father refers to the Son as "God" in Hebrews 1:8 and Psalm 45:7. (Was God mistaken? Of course not!)

The Old Testament declares that Christ is God. Isaiah 9:6 teaches that one of Christ's names is "Mighty God." This would be untrue and blasphemous unless Christ really is God. In Zechariah 12:10, referring to the crucifixion (quoted in John 19:37), God says that "they will look on Me whom they have pierced." The "Me" is not a mistake; it's an indication that God

Himself is the one who is crucified. [I ended up mentioning this passage several times to Steve. He had absolutely no comeback.]

There are many descriptions and characteristics that the Bible teaches apply to God alone. Yet the Bible teaches these apply to Christ. If we trust that the Bible does not contradict itself, then Christ is God. Let's look at some of these.

God alone is to be worshiped (Exodus 34:14; Deuteronomy 6:13, 11:16). Jesus is to be worshiped (Hebrews 1:6; Matthew 28:9, 17, 14:33).

God is the Creator of all things (Genesis 1:1; Isaiah 44:24). Jesus is the Creator of all things (John 1:1–3; Colossians 1:16–17).

God is the only Savior (Isaiah 43:11, 21–22). Jesus is the only Savior (Acts 4:12; Titus 2:13; 2 Peter 3:18). Notice the "only" in this argument. Passages like Isaiah 43:11 indicate that the Lord is the only Savior, thereby eliminating the possibility that anyone other than God Himself can be our Savior. Yet the Bible teaches that Jesus is our Savior. This can only be true if Jesus is God.

God is the Lord of lords (Deuteronomy 10:17). Jesus is Lord of lords (Revelation 17:14, 19:16).

God is the Lord of glory (Psalm 24:10, 29:3). Jesus is the Lord of glory (1 Corinthians 2:8).

God alone knows the heart of man (1 Kings 8:23, 39; Jeremiah 7:9–10). Jesus knows the heart of man (Luke 9:47; John 2:24-25).

Knowledge begins with God (Proverbs 1:7). All knowledge is in Christ (Colossians 2:3).

God is the "first and the last" (Isaiah 44:6, 48:12). Jesus is the "first and the last" (Revelation 1:17–18.) (See also Revelation 1:8, 22:13, 16).

God is the only "Rock" (Isaiah 44:8; Deuteronomy 32:4). Jesus is the "Rock" (1 Corinthians 10:4).

God is our Shepherd (Psalm 23; Ezekiel 34:11). Jesus is our Shepherd (John 10:11).

We are God's "sheep" (Psalm 100:3). We are Christ's "sheep" (John 10:14–16, 26–28).

Many others could be listed, but this should get you started at least. The above verses are contradictions if Jesus is not God. One could say with only slight exaggeration that the deity of Christ is on virtually every page of the Bible. It is a very clear and undeniable teaching of Scripture. Whoever was teaching you that Christ is not God is an unsaved person who doesn't know the Scriptures. I would suggest you not spend a lot of time with that person or persons (Romans 16:17). Make sure to be a part of a Bible-teaching church. Be teachable and listen to your pastor.

This is a salvation issue. So please look up the verses I listed above and think through these issues. I'm available if you have any questions. Drop by ICR if you like. But remember that there is no Savior besides God (Isaiah 43:11, 21–22). If Jesus is not your God, then He's not your Savior.

[Steve responded to this below. His comments are interspersed with mine, with his statements in italics.]

Dealing with Jesus as the Word of God — John 1:1

Steve: *As far as Jesus being the "Word of God" I do believe this. However, it takes only Trinitarian assumptions to read a preexisting deity into texts like John 1:1.*

Dr. L.: No, John 1:1 explicitly states "and the Word was God." How much clearer can God make it? The Word is with God, and the Word is God — and this has been the case since the beginning. The text clearly teaches that the Word IS God. Only someone with an "axe to grind" could read "the Word was God" and come away thinking "the Word was *not* God." In other contexts, the "word" can simply mean the Scriptures, however in John 1:1 it clearly refers to God Himself because it explicitly states "the WORD WAS GOD." Furthermore, the text teaches that the Word (in the same context) IS Jesus: John 1:14 tells us that the Word became flesh and dwelt among us and that He is the only begotten from the Father. "The begotten from the Father" is a reference to the only begotten Son — see John 3:16.

Steve: *Yes, you are correct the Word was God. And the Word did become flesh. The wisdom, purpose, and mind of God were indeed revealed among men through Jesus Christ. However, you are taking this passage to mean some sort of preexisting eternal deification of Christ. This is assumed and has nothing to do with the actual context of Scripture.*

[Notice that Steve here has committed the superfluous distinction fallacy in claiming that the "Word" was merely the wisdom, purpose, and mind of God. But the text says that the Word was *God*.]

Dr. L.: The Bible teaches that the person who is Jesus existed before the incarnation (e.g., Philippians 2:6–8). Micah 5:2 teaches that Jesus existed from eternity past: "But as for you, Bethlehem Ephrathah, too little to be among the clans of Judah, from you One will go forth for Me to be ruler in Israel. His goings forth are from long ago, from the days of eternity." Even the very passage we are discussing makes it clear: the Word was with God in the beginning AND the WORD WAS GOD. Remember, Jesus said, "Before Abraham was, I AM." Not "some impersonal aspect that would eventually become me once existed," but rather "I AM." The person of Jesus existed before Abraham did. The person of Jesus existed eternally with the Father (John 17:5). Christ is and always has been the Word of God. The Word of God is not some impersonal aspect of God, but is one of the names of Jesus (Revelation 19:13) and is God (John 1:1).

You are attempting to make the "Word" in this context an impersonal aspect of God — "The wisdom, purpose, and mind of God" — a superfluous distinction fallacy because there is no logical need to reduce the Word to an impersonal force in this context. But this isn't true to the way the text is written. God is sometimes metaphorically labeled by one of His attributes: "God is love." But grammatically, the attribute would always come last. It wouldn't make sense to say, "Love is God." Likewise, if the "Word" were merely an aspect of God, then it would come second in the English translation: "God is Word" — but that's not what the text says.

Was Christ some impersonal force before the incarnation? No — not according to John 1:1. According to this passage, Christ was God from the beginning — not some impersonal aspect of God, but rather GOD. (A mind is not impersonal anyway). The WORD WAS GOD. Therefore, if the WORD was some impersonal force before the incarnation, then it follows logically that GOD was some impersonal force before the incarnation since the "Word was God." But God has always been personal. So the position you are advocating leads to logical contradiction.

The deity and eternality of Christ are throughout the Scriptures. Job knew that his Redeemer lives, and that He would one day stand on the earth (Job 19:25). Job lived around 2000 B.C. — long before the incarnation. He obviously believed that Christ was already alive (my Redeemer lives — present tense) and is a person, not something impersonal that would later become a person. Job did not say, "There is this impersonal wisdom of God that will one day be transformed into my Redeemer." He knew, as did the Apostle John, that his Redeemer was already alive.

John the Baptist knew that Jesus existed before the incarnation. In John 1:15, John the Baptist says, "This was he of whom I spake, he that cometh after me is preferred before me: for he was before me" (KJV). He did not say, "There was this impersonal thing that existed before me, which was then made into a person." No, rather HE (Jesus) existed before John.

Steve: *Notice the text said, "In the beginning was the word" it did not say "in the beginning was the Son."*

Dr. L.: No. It tells us that the Word is God (verse 1), and it teaches that Jesus is the Word (verse 14). Therefore, Jesus is God by categorical syllogism. A person would have to break laws of logic to interpret the passage any other way. Furthermore, the Bible teaches that Jesus is the Son of God (Matthew 16:16–17; John 20:31). Since Jesus is the Word and the Son of God, and since the Word was in the beginning with God and was God, it follows logically that "in the beginning was the Son" and the Son was with God and was God. The argument is deductively conclusive.

Jesus as God the Creator

Steve: *This text in John mirrors the opening verses in Genesis in so many ways because it was God's word that spoke all into existence.*

Dr. L.: Yes — Jesus is our Creator. Colossians 1:16 teaches that the Son (see Colossians 1:13) is the Creator of all things. Genesis 1:1 teaches that God is the Creator. Therefore, the Son is God. Notice what Colossians does NOT say. It does *not* say, "All things were created by something that would later *become* the Son." Rather, it says "for by HIM all things were created." The person of Jesus — the only begotten Son of God — is the Creator of all things. He already existed as God before the creation, and He created everything.

Steve: *First of all, the text actually says (when one reads the original Greek) all things were created IN Him. In fact, even in the KJV, if you do a careful search of the term in the New Testament you will find that the vast majority of the time this Greek term appears in context it is translated as "IN" instead of "BY."*

Dr. L.: Steve, again, you're not reading the text carefully, nor have you done your homework on this. In the King James Version, Colossians 1:16 states that all things were made "by Him" twice, and in the original, the text uses two different Greek words so that there can be no doubt that Jesus is the Creator. Only the first use of "by" uses the Greek word *en* which can mean "in" but can also be rendered "by" or "with." The second one is *dia* and is almost always translated as "by" and occasionally "through" but always indicates causality. It doesn't mean "in." Even if I allowed that the first "by" should be "in," it would still have the force of indicating that Christ is the Creator. All things were made in Him — that is through Him or by his power. All things cannot be made "in Him" if He did not yet exist! John 1:3 also confirms that all things were made by (*dia*) Him and apart from Him nothing has come into being that has come into being. This is further confirmed in Hebrews 1:2. There can be no doubt from the Scriptures that JESUS IS THE CREATOR.

Indeed, speaking of the SON of God, the Father says, "You, Lord, in the beginning laid the foundation of the earth, and the heavens are the works of Your hands" (Hebrews 1:10). Here the author of Hebrews quotes Psalm 102:25 and applies this to the Son. If you read Psalm 102:24–25, you can see that the Psalmist is speaking of God. The author of Hebrews clarifies that this is God the Son. There is no doubt that the Bible teaches that Jesus is God — the Creator of all things.

Hebrews 1:8 confirms that God the Father addresses God the Son as "God": "But of the Son He says, 'Your Throne, O God, is forever.' " So the author of Hebrews understood that Jesus is not only our Savior but our Maker as well.

Since Jesus is the Creator of all things, He Himself is necessarily not a created being. Since all things that were made were created by Jesus, then if Jesus were made He would have to have made Himself. This is logically impossible since He would have to both exist (to be the Creator) and not exist (to be created) at the same time — a contradiction.

Steve: *The fact that the Translators treated this verse [Colossians 1:16] differently shows me their Trinitarian biases.*

Dr. L.: No, they did not treat it differently. Most of them knew Greek and Hebrew better than you know English. These were careful Bible scholars who took very great pains not to introduce errors due to their own biases. This isn't to say that there are no errors at all in any English translation. But when we compare several different English translations and they all agree, we can have confidence that they got it right. All major English translations render *dia* as either "by" or "through" in this passage. And that is the clear meaning of the Greek word. This proves that Christ is indeed the Creator.

Second, you have a low view of God if you think He would allow His Word to be so grossly distorted as to confuse who the Creator is. God is sovereign over history, and He has ensured that His Word has been accurately transmitted.

Steve: *Indeed, I do believe that all things were created "IN" Christ. In other words Paul means that all of creation meets its fulfillment in Him.*

Dr. L.: No, that is not what the passage says. It says, "For by him were all things created, that are in heaven, and that are in earth, visible and invisible, whether they be thrones, or dominions, or principalities, or powers: all things were created by him, and for him." Your claim just isn't faithful to the text. There is nothing about "fulfillment" in the passage. The universe was made by Christ, and it was made for Christ. This is the plain teaching of Colossians 1:16. The Greek text does not allow for any other meaning.

Steve: *John writes in revelation that he is the "Lamb slain from the foundation of the world."*

Dr. L.: Actually, in the Greek text, the referent of "from the foundation of the world" is left ambiguous. It could possibly refer to the lamb. But it could also be those whose name was (or was not) written in the book of life, and some versions translate it as such. For example, the NASB, ". . . everyone whose name has not been written from the foundation of the world in the book of life of the Lamb who has been slain" [Revelation 13:8].

Steve: *Now of course Dr. Lisle I don't think even you believe that Christ literally died before the world began.*

Dr. L.: Nor do I believe that Christ is literally a lamb. This is a tip-off that figurative language is being used here, but the point is still very clear: God knew from the beginning that He would become a man and die on the Cross in order to redeem His people — even before they had yet sinned. [Here Steve has ignored both the genre principle, and the translation principle.]

Steve: *Rather this was something predestined by God himself before time began and so the apostle can make these figurative statements. Consider also what Paul writes in Eph 1:4 "According as he has chosen us in him before the foundation of the world."*

Dr. L.: I can't see much use of figurative language in the Ephesians passage. God is beyond time. So even before we were created, God had chosen His people to be saved in Jesus, even before the incarnation of Jesus.

Jesus Is a Person, Not an Idea

Steve: *Though I am not dogmatic on this point it seems as if John here was talking about the personification of an idea or a character.*

Dr. L.: That's another superfluous distinction fallacy. It's obvious that John is talking about a person — a person who IS God. This is why personal language is used. But since you want to take the Word as "not a person" but some impersonal aspect of God, then you are forced to the conclusion that John is simply personifying an impersonal thing. But there is absolutely nothing in the text of Scripture to suggest that. Moreover, John 1:1 precludes this possibility because it tells us that the Word is God — not an aspect or attribute of God. The Gospel of John is not poetic literature. It is giving us the plain truth that Christ is God.

Steve: *Jesus is the "Word" that became flesh and so gives life to all people.*

Dr. L.: Yes. God gives life to all people (Deuteronomy 32:39; Ecclesiastes 5:18; 1 Timothy 6:13; Genesis 2:7; Acts 17:24–25). Since Jesus is God, Jesus gives life to all people (John 14:6).

Steve: *Yes you are correct; Jesus does gives life to people. But you are assuming this makes him God.*

Dr. L.: Again, I'm not sure if you're just not reading the passages, or if you are not thinking about them carefully. The Bible teaches that it is God *alone* who gives life to men (Deuteronomy 32:39; Ecclesiastes 5:18; 1 Timothy 6:13; Genesis 2:7; Acts 17:24–25). Therefore, if it is actually Jesus who gives life to men, then there are two logical possibilities: (1) Jesus is God, or (2) the Scriptures are wrong.

Steve: *John of course disagrees with you.*

Dr. L.: Hardly. We've already seen that John believed that Jesus was with God from the beginning, and was God from the beginning (John 1:1–1:2) and that Jesus is the Creator of all things (John 1:3). In fact, the Gospel of John is probably the clearest of the four Gospels when it comes to evidence for the Trinity, for example John 14:9, John 10:30, John 1:1–14, etc. Jesus and the Father are the same God — they are the same in nature or essence, which is why Jesus can rightly say, "I and the Father are one" (John 10:30). It is why those who are in the Father's hand (John 10:29) are necessarily in the Son's hand (John 10:28).

Steve: *The Father is the one who granted Jesus life. This was not something inherent to him as life is inherent only in God. John 5:26 For as* *the Father has life in himself; so has he GIVEN to the Son to have life in himself.*

Dr. L.: Again, you haven't read the text carefully, and you have made an equivocation fallacy on the word "life." Jesus, as the Word (John 1:14) was with God and was God from the beginning. So He has always been alive in the same way that God has always been alive. This is why Jesus can rightly refer to Himself as "the first and the last" (Revelation 1:17) — for none were before Him, and there shall be none after Him since He is the eternal God. And again, Jesus calls Himself "the living One" (Revelation 1:18) because He alone as God does not derive His life from another.

But physical life is not the subject of John 5:26, as is obvious from the previous two verses. Jesus here is referring to the gift of eternal life that is granted to repentant sinners. Verse 26 explains that this eternal life is a gift that God the Father possesses that He has authorized God the Son to distribute to those He gives Him. God the Father did not create God the Son. All the persons of the Godhead have existed eternally. "Life" in this passage has to deal with redemption, which Jesus never needed for Himself, since as God He is perfect and sinless. The life here is the gift of eternal life given through Jesus the Lord (Romans 6:23; John 17:2). The text does not say or even hint as you suggested, that Jesus needed to become alive by being created by the Father. He was alive from the beginning. Again, reading the text carefully is the key.

This passage actually confirms the divine nature of Christ then, since God alone can give life to the dead (either spiritually or physically). But it is the second person of the Trinity who accomplishes this as authorized by the Father (John 5:21). God resurrects the dead (1 Thessalonians 4:14; Romans 4:17), but it is the Son who resurrects the dead (John 6:40, 44, 54). Also, God alone is the judge of all the earth, but not God the Father. John 5:22, 27 indicates that it is the Son who judges. These verses would contradict if Jesus were not God.

You also seem to have forgotten something that I mentioned last time: to be the Son of God (literally — not by adoption) is to be God, just as to be the son of man is to be man. The Jews understood this: John 5:18, "Therefore the Jews sought the more to kill him, because he not only had broken the Sabbath, but said also that God was his Father, *making himself equal with God*" [KJV, emphasis added]. If Jesus is the begotten Son of God, then logically He is God. And Jesus is the begotten Son of God (John 3:16).

Steve: *Also the greek [sic] word "autos" that is translated "him" in this passage [John 1:2] was translated "it" in English translations prior to the KJV and a number of French and German translations carry this usage today.*

Dr. L.: In many languages the words "him" and "it" are the same word because even inanimate objects are assigned a gender. Therefore, you must use context to see which translation is correct. This is the same word that is used to describe John the Baptist in verse 6. Clearly "he" is the correct translation in the context of John 1 since it is obvious that God is referring to a person. The same word is used to describe Jesus in verse 14 — the Word became flesh . . . and we beheld his [*autos*] glory. Do you really want to refer to Jesus as "it"?

Steve: *"In the beginning was the word, and the word was with God, and the word was God. The same was with God in the beginning. Through it all things were made, without it nothing was made that has been made. In it was life, and that life was the light of men."*

Dr. L.: This distortion of the text contradicts John 1:1. The "Word was God" — not "the word was some impersonal aspect of God." If the Word is an "it," then so is God, since the Word is God. Such a depersonalization of God (whether God the Father or God the Son) is totally inappropriate and disrespectful. Jesus said that He is the light of the world (John 8:12, 9:5, 12:46), and that He is the life (John 11:25, 14:10) — not some impersonal force.

Steve: *Because the object being discussed here is the "logos" the translation "it" is perhaps best to define "the word" as it does in John 6:60: "Many therefore of his disciples when they had heard this, said, this is a hard saying (logos); who can hear it (autos)?"*

Dr. L.: No, this is terrible reasoning. It is not appropriate to pull a word out of one context and apply it in the same way in a *different* context. The subject of John 6:60 is not the Word of God (Jesus), but rather the *statement* that Jesus had just made. Not every use of the word *logos* is a reference to Christ. Words can have more than one meaning, depending on context. You're supposed to use context to apply the appropriate meaning. This is a very basic rule of hermeneutics. [Steve had violated the "contextual principle."]

Steve: *It is important to note that John further clarifies the meaning to the opening of the fourth gospel in the opening to his first letter. 1Jn 1:2 (For the life* *was manifested, and we have seen IT, and bear witness, and shew unto you that eternal life, which was with the Father, and was manifested unto us).*

Dr. L.: You have not read the text carefully. "It" is a reference to "life" — not the "Word." Moreover, the word "it" is not in the original Greek anyway. The Kings James Version inserted it for grammatical reasons (that's why "it" is in italics); most other versions don't have "it." Moreover, there is absolutely no textual or logical reason to suppose that John's first epistle is meant to clarify his Gospel. That is a non-hermeneutical claim that is unjustified and contrary to context.

Steve: *As far as 1 John 1, you are incorrect; it does in fact mention the "Word" as well as it mentions "life."*

Dr. L.: That's a straw-man fallacy. I never said the word "Word" was not used in verse 1. Rather, I was refuting your claim about verse 2. You claimed that "it" in verse 2 was a reference to the "Word" in an attempt to depersonalize the Word so that you can believe that Jesus wasn't a person before the incarnation. But in fact, the "it" refers to "life" — not the "Word." In KVJ, verse 2 begins "For the life was manifested, and we have seen it. . . ." Clearly the reference is to "life" and not to the "Word" as you had assumed. More importantly, and you seem not to have noticed this though I did mention it, the word "it" is not in the Greek anyway. It was added to make the sentence more readable in English. But the word is not in the original Bible, so this certainly does not support your point. [Steve had violated the text principle; he had not read the text carefully. He had also violated the translation principle by ignoring the fact that the word "it" (upon which he was making his entire case) is not in the original text.]

Steve: *John's letter mirrors the opening to his gospel in nearly every way.*

Dr. L.: No — it really doesn't. This is an example of importing unbiblical ideas into the text based on your preconceptions. This is called "eisegesis" and is the opposite of proper exegesis. The message and point of John 1 and *First* John 1 are very different. It would be erroneous to read them as parallel simply on the basis that both have a few words in common, such as "beginning" and "Word." That's not logical, and thus it is not proper exegesis.

Steve: *Notice his statement, "that which we did behold, and our hands did handle, concerning the WORD of the Life."*

Dr. L.: This is a reference to the gospel of Jesus and His earthly ministry.

Steve: *The passage then goes on to say that it "was with the FATHER, and was manifested to us" this is nearly the exact same word usage as the gospel's opening.*

Dr. L.: You left out a critical portion of the text (and have thereby altered the meaning). The beginning of verse 2 states, "(For *the life* was manifested, and we have seen it, and bear witness, and shew unto you that eternal life, which . . .)" [KJV, emphasis added]. By omitting that, you have twisted the meaning, by implying that verse 2 is continuing to talk about the Word. But it isn't. Verse 2 is addressing the "life" — the eternal life that the Word (Jesus) gives us. So it isn't as similar to John's Gospel as you were thinking. Was the Word with the Father at the beginning? Yes. But that's not what 1 John 1:2 is addressing.

Steve: *However, notice what John says here, he says that the Word was with the "FATHER."*

Dr. L.: No, he states that *life* was with the Father. So you weren't really reading the text carefully. Many hermeneutical fallacies stem from a careless reading of the text. [Here Steve had violated the "text principle."]

Steve: *in other words John explicitly associated "God" in these opening lines of the gospel with the Father himself, because the "Word was with God."*

Dr. L.: Well, again, this just doesn't follow logically. The Father is God — no doubt (as is the Son). But you cannot establish that from these two passages alone because they are addressing two different topics. John 1:1–1:3 addresses creation, and the fact that Jesus (we know from verse 14) was with God from the beginning and was God from the beginning, and that He created all things. On the other hand, 1 John 1:1–2 speaks about the testimony of the eyewitnesses of Christ and the eternal life that had been granted them through Christ — the eternal life that was with the Father. They are two different topics, and it would not be proper hermeneutics to conflate them.

Steve: *Again, there is nothing here [In 1 John 1:1–2] that would require us to read into the text a preexisting Deity, having a nature from eternity as God.*

Dr. L.: No. But John 1:1 does. And the other verses that I sent you previously do. The fact that not every verse in the Bible specifically states that the Word is God, does not in any way diminish those verses that do teach that the Word is God. You have committed the fallacy of denying the antecedent. After all, not every verse in the Bible states that the Father is

God. Can we therefore conclude that the Father is not God? Clearly not. All it takes is one passage to affirm a point. It is enough that even one passage states that the Son is God (e.g., Hebrews 1:8), and there are many such passages as I showed above.

Steve: *Indeed, it is LIFE that was with God from the beginning, life that appeared unto men, and more so, eternal life given to us in His only son.*

Dr. L.: No. If I said, "Joe was with Penny yesterday," and later I said, "Wisdom is always with Penny," would this prove that Joe is not a person? Would it prove that Joe is merely the personification of wisdom? Clearly not. Likewise, that God has life in Himself (and wisdom) and has always had life in Himself does not take away from the fact that Jesus is a person and is God and has always been a person from the beginning.

Steve: *Also keep in mind that the "word" is the only thing that gives true life because Jesus himself said "Man does not live by bread alone but on every word that comes from the mouth of God" — Matt 4:4.*

Dr. L.: Again, the "word" can have different meanings depending on context. The Word made flesh — Jesus — is our only Savior. We learn this through God's revealed written Word — the Bible. [Steve had again completely ignored the "contextual principle," and failed to recognize that a given word can have several meanings depending on context.]

Steve: *It is not necessary to assume that just because Jesus is called "the Word of God" this is equivalent to saying he is God himself.*

Dr. L.: The Apostle John explicitly says in John 1:1, "The *Word was God.*" This is in the same context as the Word becoming flesh (John 1:14) — a clear reference to the incarnation of Christ. It's not hard. Why not just accept what the Bible states?

Steve: *I personally prefer to interpret scripture with scripture and not rely on concepts completely foreign to it.*

Dr. L.: That's exactly the opposite of what you are doing. The notion that Jesus didn't exist as a person before the incarnation is contrary to what the Bible teaches — as I've already demonstrated. Instead, you are relying on a bias completely foreign to the text — that some impersonal force later was shaped into the person of Jesus. The Bible does not teach that in any way, and this is logically impossible if you believe John 1:1, because the text states that the Word *was God* — not an impersonal aspect of God. It is impossible to reconcile the statement "The Word was God" with the position that the Word was an impersonal aspect of God and therefore not God. You cannot reconcile the proposition "The Word was God" with the proposition "The Word was *not* God" because they are contradictory. As I said last time, you'll have to either give up rationality or inerrancy to maintain your belief.

Logic Applied to John 1:1

Steve: *Normally I don't like to use logic on passages that are meant to be poetic and symbolic.*

Dr. L.: This is another huge exegetical error. First, logic *always* should be applied to our understanding of *all* the Scriptures — including poetic passages. "Logic" refers to the principles of correct reasoning. We should always reason correctly; anything less is dishonoring to God. Poetic passages may contain metaphors and other figures of speech that need to be handled properly. But they are not exempt from proper reasoning. Logic still applies.

Second, the Gospel of John is *not* poetic literature! It is historical narrative. [Here Steve has violated the genre principle, and has admitted that he is not being logical.]

Steve: *But since you are so determined to show me my logic is wrong, let's do a little mental exercise to show you where your logic fails. By evidence of John's own writings we know that "God" equals the "Father."*

Dr. L: No — that's a categorical fallacy. The Father is God, and so is the Son. But God doesn't "equal" the Father in the sense that the two terms are interchangeable. For example, Ananias lied to God, but he did not lie to the *Father*. Rather, He lied to the Holy Spirit (Acts 5:3–4). There are other Scriptures that teach that the Father is God, as is the Son, and the Holy Spirit.

Steve: *And since you believe the Word = "Jesus Christ" or the Word = "Son" lets plug these into the text itself.*

Dr. L.: The Bible teaches both of these very explicitly: Jesus is the Word (John 1:1, 14). And Jesus is the only begotten Son (John 3:16). And the Bible teaches that the Son is God (Hebrews 1:8), and the Word is God (John 1:1).

Steve: *"In the beginning was Jesus, and Jesus was with the Father, and Jesus was the Father." Wait a minute, Jesus is the Father!?*

Dr. L.: No, you have committed the fallacy of the undistributed middle, and so your argument is both invalid and unsound. I'll give you an example:

(1) All cats are mammals.
(2) All dogs are mammals.
(3) Therefore, all dogs are cats.

The fallacy is committed when the middle term ("mammals" in this case) is not distributed (does not refer to all its members) in either premise. So if you have a dog, you necessarily have a mammal because a dog is a mammal. But if you have a mammal, you don't necessarily have a dog — cats are also mammals.

You were okay to substitute Jesus in for the "Word" because there is a one-to-one correspondence between the Word (in this context) and Jesus. In other words, the Father and the Holy Spirit are never referred to as the Word. But when you substituted the "Father" in for "God," you committed the fallacy of the undistributed middle. This is because while all references to the Father are necessarily references to God, not all references to God are to the Father. The Bible also refers to the Son as God (e.g., Hebrews 1:8), and to the Holy Spirit as God (e.g., Acts 5:3-4), as I showed previously. Since you've violated the laws of logic, your argument fails. [Since most people (unfortunately) have never studied categorical logic, I explained the fallacy rather explicitly and gave an example. This made for a long reply, but it is often necessary in dealing with our poorly educated culture.]

Steve: *Or let's take it to mean the Son . . . "In the beginning was the Son, and the Son was with the Father, and the Son was the Father." Wait, seriously? The Word is the Son who is the Father!? What !? As you see, such a reading of the text is obviously illogical.*

Dr. L.: Again, you have committed the fallacy of the undistributed middle. You were okay to substitute "Son" for "Word," since there is a one-to-one correspondence. But in substituting the "Father" for "God" you have violated the rules of categorical logic since the word "God" is undistributed. Thus, your argument is invalid.

Steve: *You may refute me, and say that "God" here is meant to be "Godhead" or just the description of the Trinity itself.*

Dr. L.: The text itself refutes you — for it states that the Word was GOD — not the "Father." "God" is the term for the omniscient, omnipotent being who created the universe. We know from the Scriptures I showed last time that all three persons (the Father, the Son, and the Holy Spirit) are referred to as "God" in the Scriptures, and were involved in the creation of the universe. So, if we're going to follow the Scriptures and not violate rules of logic, it is inappropriate to swap out "God" with "the Father" unless we have good textual evidence that ONLY the Father is being referred to in the passage. We don't have that in John 1:1 when it says "the Word was God." In fact, we have clear evidence to the contrary. Since John says that the Word is God, it is clear that God cannot be referring merely to the Father, otherwise we would have a contradiction. John understood that Jesus was the Word and He was with God (the Father and Holy Spirit), and He was God (the Son). The Apostle really couldn't have been any clearer.

Steve: *However, this is a theological presupposition completely independent of scripture and contrary to the writings of the apostle himself.*

Dr. L.: What you are trying to import into the passage is indeed a presupposition completely independent of Scripture and contrary to what John himself has stated. Just think about it logically for a moment. How can it be that A is with B and A is B? In order for A to be with B, there must be some distinction between A and B. Yet in order for A to be B, they must be the same in some sense. A contradiction is avoided only by recognizing that two different senses of the word are in use. Jesus was with God in the sense that He was with the Father and the Holy Spirit, and He was God because He too is the uncreated eternal Creator. See, Steve, it is not the case that people believe in a Trinity because they prefer God to be beyond our understanding (indeed, people always prefer a god they can understand), but rather because it is the only position that is logically consistent with the Scriptures.

The position you are advocating flatly rejects the second part of John 1:1. If the Word is merely the impersonal wisdom of God, then it is not God, because impersonal wisdom is not God. Your view simply cannot be reconciled with the text of Scripture.

Steve: *As I have shown you by John's very statement "was with the Father," we know that in his mind God was unequivocally associated with the Father.*

Dr. L.: Hopefully, you now see why this is wrong. First John 1 is a different topic than John 1, and you had misquoted the text in thinking that 1 John 1:2 was addressing the "Word" rather than "life." So that should be clear now. John believed that the Father is God, and He also believed that the Word (Christ) is God.

Steve: *John knew no such thing as a Trinity.*

Dr. L.: Hopefully, you can now see that you must violate laws of logic to arrive at such a conclusion. John understood the Trinity very well and affirms it in *the very first verse* of his Gospel. John indicates that the Word was Jesus (John 1:14), and that the Word was with God and *was God* (John 1:1). The passage is reduced to nonsense if the Trinity is denied. By my count, John has more references to the Trinity and deity of Jesus than the other three Gospels, excluding all the references to Christ as "the Lord" in Luke. There are also many references to the divinity of Christ in the Book of Revelation (which John wrote), as I showed last time.

It's interesting that both the first verse of the Bible (Genesis 1:1, God, *Elohim*, is in the plural but with a singular action verb) and the first verse of John's Gospel indicates a God that is one in one sense, and yet more than one in another sense. This is clearly a very important aspect of God. Indeed, it is necessary to understand the Gospel.

Christ Has Characteristics That Belong to God Alone — Such as Omniscience

Steve: *The fact is Jesus is called many things in scripture that personifies his character. Paul says of him he is "the Wisdom of God" — 1 Cor 1:24. In Revelation John himself calls Christ "Faithful and True"— Rev 19:11.*

Dr. L.: That's certainly true. And it illustrates the Trinity because many of these descriptions only make sense if Jesus really is God. What mere man can claim to be the wisdom of God, or faithful and true? The Bible says of men, "For all have sinned and fall short of the glory of God" (Romans 3:23). And what mere man can be omniscient? The Bible says that *all* the treasures of wisdom and knowledge are deposited in Christ (Colossians 2:3). Not some – *all.* Christ has all wisdom and all knowledge according to the Bible. Omniscience belongs to God alone. Furthermore, it is Christ who upholds the entire universe by the expression of His power (Hebrews 1:3) — indicating that He is both omnipresent and omnipotent. Only God fills this description (1 Kings 8:27; Genesis 17:1).

Steve: *Yes, Omniscience does belong to God alone.*

Dr. L.: I'm going to hold you to that, and ask you to be logically consistent below.

Steve: *The reality is it only belongs to the Father himself, and this is the direct teachings of scripture. Even Christ himself admitted he didn't know everything.*

Dr. L: Ah, but Christ did indeed know everything (John 16:30, 21:17; Matthew 12:25; Luke 6:8). And all knowledge is in Christ (Colossians 2:3). How do you reconcile this with those verses in which Christ apparently doesn't know something? The Bible answers this. The biblical teaching is that Christ has two natures — one human and one divine. Christ took on human limitations with respect to His human nature during His earthly ministry; the Bible directly states this (Hebrews 2:7; Philippians 2:6–8). He didn't cease to be God, but many of the characteristics normally associated with God were veiled, including omniscience. But with respect to His divine nature, Christ has been and always will be omniscient. Even during the incarnation, Christ remained God and was omniscient with respect to His divine nature (John 16:30, 21:17; Matthew 9:4; 12:25; John 1:48–49).

Steve: *He himself plainly stated he did not know the time of the end. If there is something he does not know then by definition he is not omniscient. Mar 13:32 But of that day and that hour knoweth no man, no, not the angels which are in heaven, NEITHER the Son, but the Father.*

Dr. L.: *In context*, Christ was speaking from His human nature, not His divine nature. This statement was made during His earthly ministry, when He had taken on human nature and human limitations. It was necessary for God to take on human limitations so that He could die in payment for our sins (Hebrews 10:5), since God in His divine nature is immortal. Yet Christ (even during His earthly ministry) also had (and still has) a divine nature. He was and is fully God. The Bible clearly teaches that with respect to His divine nature, Christ knew all things (John 21:17, 16:30) and does not change (Hebrews 13:8). But with respect to His human nature, his knowledge was limited, and increased with time (Luke 19:3). If you don't recognize the biblically warranted distinction between Christ's human and divine natures, then the verses I listed here will contradict each other.

Essentially, what you have shown is that Jesus' earthly human nature was not divine. But no one disputes that. It is with respect to Christ's divine nature that He knows all things. The Scriptures state directly that all knowledge is in Christ (Colossians 2:3). He is indeed omniscient. And there are many specific instances of this, even in His earthly ministry (e.g., Matthew 9:4, 12:25; John 1:47–49; Matthew 17:27).

> (1) Jesus, in the fullness of His deity, knows all things; He is omniscient (John 21:17; Colossians 2:3; Matthew 9:4).
> (2) Only God is omniscient (as you have agreed).
> (3) Therefore, Jesus is God.

Steve: *Jeremiah says of him he will be called "The Lord our Righteousness" — Jer 23:6.*

Dr. L.: It's a fitting name for the Lord, but would be blasphemy for anyone else. God is our righteousness (Psalm 4:1). But no mere man lives up to God's righteousness — not even one (Isaiah 41:26; Psalm 14:3; Romans 3:10; Psalm 53:2–3). If Jesus were a man but not also God, then He could not be called "righteous" and certainly not the "LORD our Righteousness." The Word translated "LORD" in Jeremiah 23:6 is *YHWH* — the name of God. It is blasphemy to apply the name *YHWH* to anyone other than God (Exodus 20:7; Leviticus 24:16). And indeed this reference to *YHWH* — the Lord God Almighty — refers specifically to Christ.

Steve: *Even the Isaiah verse, which Trinitarians love quoting as proof of their doctrine where Christ is called Immanuel which means "God with us" — Isaiah 7:14 is similar to the name Ithiel which means "God with me" — Proverbs 30:1, Neh 11:7.*

Dr. L.: Although I don't use Isaiah 7:14 as a proof-text, it is certainly consistent with the deity of Christ. When Christ was on earth, God literally walked with men. A similar passage that is clearer is Isaiah 9:6 which teaches that one of Christ's names is "Mighty God." This would be blasphemy to apply to anyone other than God.

The Pot Calls the Kettle Black

Steve: *Dr. Lisle, I'll be completely honest with you. It's so frustrating to me sometimes when everyone keeps telling me "Steve be teachable, Steve be humble, Steve accept what the Bible plainly says" and yet these same people aren't showing me that they are willing to be humble themselves.*

Dr. L.: Sometimes when it seems like everyone else is wrong, it is helpful to at least consider the possibility, "Maybe it's me."

Steve: *In my experience, most people start from the perspective that they are right in what they believe about the Trinity, they already know what the Bible* *says, and everyone who doesn't think like them is wrong. To me personally this is not a spirit of humility.*

Dr. L.: This seems to be your attitude. Is it not? You seem to think that you are right, and everyone who doesn't agree with you is wrong, yes? No one believes that he is wrong about what he believes, otherwise he wouldn't believe it. But we need to have some humility and let the Bible correct us. That's true for all of us.

Steve: *Also no one told me to believe these things; it was after reading the Bible for myself and accepting what God's word really was saying that I became convicted of these truths.*

Dr. L.: No. You're repeating arguments that the cults use. So you've read this somewhere. I'm familiar with these claims; I've heard them before. They are not rational. It is certainly not something that a person would come to by reading the Bible and applying proper hermeneutical principles, especially in light of all the Scriptures I sent you in my last message that contradict the theology that you are advocating.

Steve: *I realized that what I had been taught to believe all my life was in fact an incorrect understanding of scripture.*

Dr. L.: What you've fallen into now is not faithful to the text of Scripture and leads to logical contradictions. You've chosen to create a god of your own making — one that makes sense to you. The problem with your god is that he is fictional. He exists only in your mind, and he cannot save you. A "Jesus" who is not God is a "Jesus" who cannot save; only the living God can save (Isaiah 43:11, 45:12; Hosea 13:4). The biblical God has revealed some aspects of His nature to us in His Word. Some of these are hard to grasp. But we accept them by faith because they are what God has said. If God tells me that He is one in one sense, and three in another sense, then who am I to argue? I accept what God says about Himself. Faith in God is a prerequisite to salvation.

Steve: *Dr. Lisle, you are simply wrong here. The truth is you really don't know my spiritual background or what is it that I have read. To be honest with you in the past I actually had no problem believing Jesus was God. Growing up this was just something I accepted because that's just what everyone knew to be "truth." Even before I've read arguments from both Trinitarians and Unitarians it was only after going through the Bible itself that I began to seriously notice problems with the Trinitarian worldview.*

[Notice here that Steve admits that he has read arguments from Unitarians, whereas previously he denied learning this from others, and claimed that he had come to that position "after reading the Bible for myself and accepting what God's word really was saying that I became convicted of these truths." Steve's lie found him out. But I opted not to call attention to his previous deception.]

Dr. L.: So far, you haven't mentioned a single problem with the Trinity. Indeed, we have seen that all the arguments you've listed so far are fallacious — every single one. Each one stems from a misreading of the text, a logical fallacy, a misunderstanding of the Trinity, or a misunderstanding of the nature of Christ's earthly ministry. The reason I knew you had been reading cult material is because I have heard many of these types of eisegesis before. It's no different than when someone claims that the days of creation weren't really days, but long ages and that the Flood was universal but not global, and that the stars merely appeared on the fourth day-age. I know that such a person has been reading Ross because such a view would never stem from proper exegesis from the Scriptures.

Steve: *So regardless of what you may think you know of me, I know where I stand before God and my conscience is clear.*

Dr. L.: You need to learn to rely upon God's Word rather than your conscience. The conscience can be helpful, but it can also mislead since the heart of man is deceitful and desperately wicked (Jeremiah 17:9). In the Book of Judges, every man did what was right in his own eyes (Judges 17:6, 21:25). So they were right in their own thinking, by their own conscience, yet God condemns them. It is God's Word that never fails — including all the references to the divinity of Christ. So while your conscience may be clear, your conscience is corrupt and unreliable. In any case, the Scriptures condemn you. Now I certainly hope and pray that you don't remain in a state of rebellion. But that is ultimately between you and God.

Steve: *Also why is it that Christians are quick to call groups cults that they don't fully understand?*

Dr. L.: A cult is any group that claims to be Christian but denies one or more essential Christian doctrines. Such doctrines include the deity of Christ, the Trinity, the Resurrection, the sufficiency of Scripture, etc. In fact, it is because we *do* understand what such cults are teaching that we must show where their teachings are contrary to Scripture.

Mormons are one example, because they deny that there is one God, and they reject the eternality of God — claiming that God the Father was once a man like us. Jehovah's Witnesses are another example. They also deny the Trinity, and believe that Jesus is a created being, who was resurrected as a spirit only. Based on your answers, the cult you seem to be following is called "Arianism." This view arose in the early fourth century due to the teachings of Arius. It was promptly (and rightly) denounced as heresy by the Council of Nicaea (A.D. 325).

Pagan Practices and the Lord's Day

Steve: *The reality is to this day the overwhelming majority of Christians are still influenced by pagan practices that began centuries ago.*

Dr. L.: As far as I can tell the Trinity is unique to Christianity. Some religions had triads of gods or goddesses, or three modes of a god, but none were like the biblical position of one God in three eternally distinct persons. However, the notion that God cannot be three persons and yet one being is indeed a pagan concept, totally foreign to the Bible.

Steve: *Even those who fervently believe they are completely following all the doctrines of scriptures still yet put tradition over God's Word. For example, the overwhelming majority of Christians reject the 4th commandment by not keeping God's Sabbath. They prefer to go to church on Sunday (a pagan practice that was officially popularize by the emperor Constantine because the pagans in his empire worshiped the sun god on this day) rather than to keep God's Holy Sabbath on the seventh day of the week as God Himself rested on this day. It amazes me how the fourth commandment is quoted all of over the ICR and the Answers in Genesis website in defense of a young earth and yet these individuals within these organizations neglect this commandment before all the rest. They would much rather hold to tradition and try to use verses found in Paul's writings taken out of context to support their predetermined beliefs rather than to accept God's Word plainly. I am convinced that complete orthodoxy even among today's zealous Christians is an illusion. Folks only have themselves deceived.*

Dr. L.: You have made many mistakes here, both biblical and historical. Sunday is observed as the Lord's Day, not because of any pagan practice, but to honor the Resurrection of Christ. Jesus was raised from the dead on Sunday. It was not a result of Constantine — rather the reverse. As a matter of historical fact, Christians were observing Sunday as the Lord's

Day centuries before Constantine decreed it to be the Roman day of rest. Ignatius (A.D. 107) specifically identified Sunday as the Lord's Day, as did Barnabas (A.D. 130), Justin (A.D. 150) and others — long before Constantine. Although there were sun-worshipers at the time, this had nothing to do with the Church, who worshiped God on Sunday to honor the Resurrection. This is why Latin-based languages refer to Sunday as the Lord's Day (e.g., "Domingo" in Spanish). So, wherever you're getting your information, that person is engaging in historical revisionism to support an unbiblical agenda.

There is no doubt that early Christians considered Sunday to be the Lord's Day as a matter of historical fact. Of course, this is separate from the issue of whether or not they should have done so. To see what day Christians should assemble to worship the Lord, we must turn to the Scriptures and do proper exegesis. To support your case, you have tacitly assumed that since the Old Testament has given a law, that it must be kept today in the same way in the New Testament. But this is not necessarily so. Some Old Testament laws have been set aside, others modified. The Bible indicates that there is necessarily a change in the law when the priesthood is changed (Hebrews 7:12).

Many of the Old Testament Laws had a symbolic significance in pointing forward to Christ's coming, or showing the separation between Jews and Gentiles in the Old Testament. These types of laws are sometimes referred to as "ceremonial laws." The Bible teaches that such laws have been set aside now that Christ has come (Hebrews 7:18).

The ceremonial laws were like a tutor to teach Old Testament believers about salvation in Christ (Galatians 3:24). But now that the object of the faith has arrived, we are no longer under that tutor (Galatians 3:25). This is why Paul criticizes the churches in Galatia for trying to continue to follow the ceremonial laws of the Old Testament (Galatians 4:9–11). Paul criticized them sharply for insisting on continuing circumcision, saying that he wished those who taught such things would go the whole way and castrate themselves (Galatians 5:11–12). We don't sacrifice animals today as commanded by Old Testament Law because we are not under the Old Testament administration.

Make no mistake; there are also moral laws, which continue from the Old Testament into the New Testament. The point is this: it is logically fallacious to assume without evidence or reason that a particular law must be followed today simply on the basis that it is found in the Old Testament. We must do our exegetical homework to see if a particular law is to be followed in the New Testament, and if so, if it is to be followed in the same way. And you haven't done your homework on this issue.

Is there New Testament evidence that Sunday is to be observed as the Lord's Day, as a day for assembling together to worship God? Yes there is. We know from Scripture that the early Christians assembled together and took communion on Sundays (Acts 20:7). When the Holy Spirit was given at Pentecost, all the believers were gathered together on Sunday — not Saturday (Acts 2:1). Pentecost always falls on Sunday, because it was 50 days from the Resurrection, which was on Sunday. After the Resurrection, Jesus always came to the disciples on Sunday, not Saturday (John 20:19, 26). Was Jesus wrong to do so?

I have written fairly extensively on the topic of God's Law and have articles online on my blog at www.JasonLisle.com. So I won't go into greater detail here. Much more could be said about the Lord's Day, but the issue is complicated, and you haven't yet got right the very simple things of God's Word — like who God is! Therefore, I will not deal with the meat of the Word, until you are correctly handling the milk of the Word (1 Corinthians 3:2; Hebrews 5:12–13). For me to continue on this topic with you would be like trying to explain calculus to someone who still doesn't understand basic arithmetic. But I felt it necessary to show you the tip of the iceberg so that you could see how proper exegesis is done.

Steve: *So Dr. Lisle, I am curious, are you even a Sabbath keeper? Do you fully keep God's law?*

Dr. L.: I attempt to keep all of God's standing laws in the way specified by the New Covenant. I do not keep laws that God has set aside with the coming of Christ, for it would be unbiblical to do so (Galatians 5:1).

Steve: *If you are then I commend you, but if not I seriously would like for you to question rather you are fully in the faith. I don't say this to change the subject: I only mentioned this because you have written quite boldly in your previous post. And if you are bold enough to dish out rebuke then hopefully you will have no problem receiving reprove yourself. As the apostle himself so eloquently writes . . . Rom 2:21 "You then who teach others, do you not teach yourself? . . . You who boast in the law dishonor God by breaking the law."*

Dr. L.: We should keep God's standing laws. The same Apostle chastises the Galatians for trying to keep laws that God has set aside (Galatians 4:9–11, 5:6–12). To live under the Old Testament administration today is to misunderstand that Jesus is the Christ. In a way, this is connected to your other mistakes. You don't really know Jesus, and so it makes sense that you would misunderstand the Old Testament ceremonial laws that pointed forward to Him.

The Bible Teaches the Concept of the Trinity

Dr. L.: If God tells me that He is one in one sense, and three in another sense, then who am I to argue? I accept what God says about Himself.

Steve: *Would you please backup your statement with scripture?*

Dr. L.: Steve — I've provided Scripture, upon Scripture, upon Scripture. Read my previous comments, and look up the passages.

Steve: *Please show me one place in the Bible where it plainly says God is three in one sense. In fact out of the nearly 4,000 occurrences of "God" in the Bible you wont find a single verse that even mentions "three" and "God" in the same location.*

Dr. L.: This is the fallacy of denying the antecedent. It would be like saying, "you think it's okay to read your Bible on Wednesday? Then show me one place in the Bible where it plainly says that it's okay to read your Bible on Wednesday. In fact, out of all the verses in the Bible, you will not find a single verse that even mentions 'Wednesday'!" That reasoning is ridiculous. I could equally well ask you Steve, "Can you show me one verse in the Bible where it specifically says 'God is *not* a Trinity?' Or that there is one and only *one person* in the Godhead?" God expects you to take what the Bible does explicitly say, and to believe it and logically derive other truths from. The Bible teaches that there is one God — that the Father is God, the Son is God, and the Spirit is God. I've shown you the verses. The doctrine of the Trinity is scriptural, and is shown in verse, after verse, after verse, after verse, after verse, after verse. But you continue to harden your heart.

[Steve stated his argument as an enthymeme — a shortened version with one or more unstated premises. The formal version of Steve's argument is this: (1) If the Bible explicitly stated "God is three in one sense" then it would prove the Trinity. (2) The Bible does not explicitly state "God is three in one sense." (3) Therefore, the Bible does not teach the Trinity. This is the fallacy of denying the antecedent. Rather than explicitly teaching

Steve about this fallacy, I refuted his example by a logical analogy. That is, I used the same form of argument to conclude something that is absurd. This proves that Steve's original argument is also absurd.]

In the KJV, the word "God" is used 3,893 times in total, 2,697 of which are in the Old Testament. Of those, around 2,300 use the plural term *Elohim* with a singular verb, indicating that God is one in one sense, and more than one in another sense. In other words, over 85 percent of the Old Testament references to GOD are to a God who is one, and yet more than one! So there is just no excuse for denying it.

And it's not just with that word either. The Hebrew word *Adonai* which is translated "Lord" is also plural and yet used with singular verbs when applied to God. Indications of plurality within the Godhead are *ubiquitous* throughout that Old Testament. For example, Genesis 1:26 says, "And God said, 'Let *Us* make man in *Our* image, according to *Our* likeness" (emphasis added). Who is He talking to? In case you are wondering, yes, the plurality is in the Hebrew. Genesis 3:22: "And the Lord God said, 'Behold, the man has become like one of *us*, knowing good and evil" (emphasis added). The phrase "one of us" used here makes absolutely no sense in a Unitarian view. There are many others (e.g., Isaiah 41:21–22). Unitarian religions (e.g., Islaam, Jehovah's Witnesses, Arianism, Christadelphians, Associated Bible Students) are very uncomfortable with such passages, whereas polytheistic faiths (e.g., Mormons) are uncomfortable with those passages that teach one God. Christians are comfortable with both.

The Trinity Is a Salvation Issue

Steve: *Also, may I ask that you refrain from calling individuals an "unsaved" person because of their position on this topic, because you are indirectly talking about me as well since these are my beliefs.*

Dr. L.: No. I cannot honor that request — it is unbiblical. I was very gracious last time, hoping that you would be teachable. But I will be more direct in this post. Steve — you are unsaved. There is absolutely no question about this. You are not a Christian. I pray that you don't remain that way. But make no mistake, if you continue to reject the biblical God, you will not see heaven. You might think this is harsh of me to say, but it is because I do care about you that I must warn you of the danger you are in. I like you, Steve. If I didn't, I wouldn't waste my time. But I wouldn't be a friend to you if I didn't tell you that whoever you are following or reading is not a Christian, but a false teacher.

Belief in Christ as God is necessary for salvation. We must confess Christ as LORD (Romans 10:9). Not just "a" Lord, but the Lord God. To prove this, the Apostle Paul goes on in verse 13 to quote Joel 2:32 — those that call upon the name of the LORD will be saved. It is clear that "Lord" must refer to the Lord God because in the quoted passage (Joel 2:32) "Lord" is *YHWH* — which only ever refers to the true God. If Jesus is not your God, then He is not your Savior. Only God can save (Isaiah 45:21, 12:2, 43:3; Hosea 13:4; Luke 1:47, 2:11; Titus 1:3, 2:10). "I, even I, am the LORD; and there is no savior besides Me" (Isaiah 43:11). It's not God plus some other being. It is God alone who saves. Only by placing our faith in the God of Scripture can we be saved. Salvation is found in no one else.

I must also point out that since you are not a believer, there will be limitations to what you are able to understand about the Bible (1 Corinthians 2:14). The unbeliever does not think rightly about spiritual things because his spirit is "dead" and must be made alive by God (Ephesians 2:1, 5). You will have *some* ability to understand by God's common grace. But unless and until the Holy Spirit grants you repentance, you may find that there are perfectly logical concepts that you simply cannot grasp because they are spiritually discerned. The Trinity may very well be one of those concepts. Even though it is on virtually every page of Scripture, you will not see it unless the Holy Spirit opens your eyes (Acts 26:18). Pray that God grants you this.

Steve: *I realize that your words are meant with good intention therefore I am not offended by them, its just that in the future words like these are not helpful to your cause if you want to reach people who may be easily angered by them.*

Dr. L.: Proverbs 27:6 is very relevant here. An enemy will tell you that you're doing just fine. He will flatter you and say nice things so that you won't get angry. But a friend is willing to tell you the truth even if it hurts because he cares about you.

Christ Is the Perfect Image of God Because He Is God

Steve: *Before I respond to your points let me further clarify what I believe. I do believe that Christ is the perfect image of God because his Father was actively working in him.*

Dr. L.: The Bible indicates that Christ is the perfect image of God because He is God. Otherwise He couldn't be a *perfect* image. And it's not just God's image, but the *exact* representation of His nature (Hebrews 1:3), which a mere image never is. The fullness of deity dwells in Christ (Colossians 2:9). Not partial deity: Christ is not just partly God, He is fully God.

Steve: *Yes, the fullness of deity or God does indeed dwell in Christ. Since when does that make him the Almighty God?*

Dr. L.: By definition, "deity" means "God." That's what the word means. The full nature and essence of God is in Christ. Christ is God with flesh. This is what Colossians 2:9 is telling us. It is logically impossible to have the fullness of deity without being God, for to have fullness of deity is to be fully God — by definition.

Steve: *Consider what Paul says in Ephesians 3:19 And to know the love of Christ, which passeth knowledge, that you might be filled with all the fulness of God. As you can see, Paul also says that "ALL" the fullness of God is to dwell in us, does that make us God?*

Dr. L.: Again, you are not carefully reading the text in context. The context of Ephesians 3:19 is love — specifically, the love of Christ. And it is the love that Christians are being filled with — not God. The love is given by God. The KJV words the passage slightly awkwardly by strangely translating *eis* as "with" — a very unusual choice. But it is still incumbent upon you to do your homework, read a few other translations, or look up the words in a lexicon, etc. The NASB renders the verse more naturally from the Greek, "and to know the love of Christ which surpasses knowledge, that you may be filled up to all the fullness of God."

So, we are being filled with love (not God) to the fullness of God — that is, we are filled with love to the full level that God intends us to have. It's not even remotely suggesting that we are filled with deity. Christ alone is the fullness of God. Jesus is the only man who is also deity.

Christ Is Called God Because He Is — It's Not an "Honorary" Title

Steve: *Christ in at least two scriptures of the NT is given the honorary title of "God" because he was the exact representation of his Father (John 20 and Hebrews 1).*

Dr. L.: No. Calling a non-God by the Holy Name of God would be blasphemy. (I will deal with the text that you seem to think supports your idea below.) You have committed the "superfluous distinction fallacy" by asserting without any textual support that "God" doesn't really mean God, but that it's just "honorary." No. Jesus is called God because He is God. Why don't we let the Bible mean what it says? That is the straightforward reading of the text. And it's not just in those passages either. As I showed you previously, it is throughout the entire Bible. There are those who are called "gods" in the generic sense — even idols are called this. But never by the name that is above all names.

You have to do intellectual gymnastics to say, "well yes, He is called God throughout the Scripture, but He's not really God because ______." The same logic could be applied to God the Father. Is the Father's title of "God" merely honorary? How do you know? The correct approach to historical narrative or doctrinal teaching in Scripture is to take it literally unless there is an obvious and necessary reason to not take it so. So when the Bible teaches that Jesus is God, we need to accept that teaching, even if it is contrary to our intuition or preferences. [Steve here had violated the "literal principle."]

Steve: *Christ makes this point very clear when the Jews accused him of blaspheme in John 10.*

Dr. L.: Not at all. Consider first, why did the Jews accuse Him of blasphemy? John 10:33: ". . . because You, being a man, make Yourself out to be God." The Jews understood that Jesus *was indeed claiming to be God.* Their mistake (the same as yours) was in arbitrarily assuming that claim to be false. Jesus did not blaspheme when He claimed to be God because He really is God.

Before we look at how Christ responds, it is very important to note what Christ does *not* say. He does not deny being God. Now wouldn't that be conspicuously strange for someone who is not God? If someone said to me, "You are claiming to be God," my response would not be to pontificate on honorary titles. Rather, I would adamantly deny it as all (non-divine) Christians should (Acts 14:12–18).

If Christ really were not God and were not claiming to be God it would make sense for Him to correct the Jews, "Oh no — that's not what I'm claiming at all." When the Jews accuse Him of claiming to be God, He doesn't deny the claim — instead *He defends it*! So, even before we look at the details of Jesus' response, it is clear that His response confirms that *He was indeed claiming to be God.* Instead of denying the claim, Christ makes an *a fortiori* argument — pointing out that those sent by God were sometimes called "gods" by the Jews; thus, how much more appropriate to call God the one who was not only sent by God but is God as well!

Steve: *Rather than to focus on what Christ did not say, I focus on what Christ DID say. When they accused him of blaspheme he only said, "I am God's SON" This is perfectly consistent with my Unitarian beliefs.*

Dr. L.: It isn't, and I guess you didn't read what I wrote or at least didn't think about it carefully. Christ *defended* His claim to be God. Recall, the Bible teaches that to be literally God's Son is to be equal to God (John 5:18). Maybe you're not looking up the verses? I'll quote it and then comment. John 5:18 states, "For this reason therefore the Jews were seeking all the more to kill Him, because He not only was breaking the Sabbath, but also was *calling God His own Father, making Himself equal with God*" (emphasis added). The inspired text of Scripture clearly states that when Jesus called God His own Father, He was making Himself equal with God.

In fact, in the verse we were discussing, Jesus isn't just calling Himself God's Son (though that would be sufficient to establish Him as deity); rather, He's calling Himself God directly when He says, "I and the Father are one" (John 10:30). His statement would indeed be blasphemy if He were not God. But since God the Son and God the Father are the same in nature/essence, Jesus can truthfully say, "I and my Father are one." The Jews understood that he was claiming to be God (John 10:33). When they accuse Him of claiming to be God, Jesus does not deny the claim. He defends it. *Jesus defended His claim to be God* (John 10:33–36).

Jesus — God with a Capital "G"

Steve: *Here [John 10:34] Christ is quoting from Psalms 82 where humans themselves are called God (Elohim) in the honorary sense.*

Dr. L.: No. He calls them "gods," plural — (little "g" in English). The Hebrew term *Elohim* has a range of meanings. It can refer to false gods — idols (Leviticus 19:4; 1 Chronicles 16:26; Psalm 96:5). It only necessarily refers to *the God* when used with the singular verb. It is not used with a singular verb in Psalm 82. Steve, you must learn to use *context* to discern what a passage means if you are ever going to have biblical theology.

God occasionally calls those who are acting under His authority as *elohim* — but never as "God." And we have other scriptural reasons to understand that the judges are not truly God (for example, they sin, but God does not). God never applies His Holy Name *YHWH* to any sinful man, but He does apply His Holy name to Christ (Jeremiah 23:6; Isaiah 54:5; Isaiah 60:19–20; Revelation 21:23).

Steve: *As you have already noted, big "G" and little "g" only appears in the English. It does not appear in the original language. Therefore translators decide this based on the context and that is completely dependent on their biases.*

Dr. L.: No — it is dependent on *context*, and the translators knew that. My argument had nothing to do with how the word appears in English, but rather how it is used in Scripture. *Elohim* can mean "gods" (in the sense of so-called "gods": idols, angels, or judges), but there it would be used with a *plural* verb. When referring to the Living God, it is used with a singular verb. This itself is indicative of the Trinity, because God is one in one sense, and more than one in another sense.

Steve: *This is a classical case of circular reasoning. Because it is assumed that Jesus is the Almighty God translators capitalize the G whenever it is associated with him. So you assume that Jesus is God, add caps to the letter, and then turn around and argue because it is capitalized in these passages that proves Jesus is God. But you have only assumed the very thing you are trying to demonstrate.*

Dr. L.: Here you have committed another straw-man fallacy. I've never argued on the basis of English capitalization. I was merely using the common English nomenclature to help you understand the difference between *elohim* when used with a plural verb to denote so-called gods, and *Elohim* when used with a singular verb, which means "God." To be clear, you are correct that someone who makes the argument you refute above is indeed reasoning in a circle. But that wasn't my argument — it never has been. We can tell whether the word refers to God or gods based on the biblical context. And it is the biblical context that you continue to ignore.

That being said, I again point out that the Bible scholars who translated the text of Scripture from its original language into English were highly skilled at Hebrew and Greek. Their recognition of the deity of Christ comes from their decades of scholarship and careful study of the text in its original language. And they were right to capitalize references to Christ as they are indeed references to God. The Arian heresy arose out of a desire to make god more comprehensible to the human mind, not from careful scholarship.

Steve: *Now, you are correct, God does occasionally call those acting under his authority as "gods" and yes even the singular "god" as is used with Moses.*

Dr. L.: Actually, the term is plural when used with Moses — literally "gods." There is no verb associated it, so it is ambiguous as to whether it refers to the *God* who is one and yet more than one, or "gods" in the lesser sense of the word. But it doesn't strongly matter to the meaning of the text. God does *not* call Moses God or a god, but would make him as God or as gods *to Pharaoh* — according to Exodus 7:1.

I wrote this before, but I'll repeat it here in a different way since apparently it wasn't clear. The Hebrew word *elohim* is a generic term for "gods" and includes false gods, and very, very rarely people who act under God's authority in the Old Testament. When used with a singular verb, however, it is always a reference to *the* God.

The New Testament does not use the word *Elohim*, because the New Testament was written in Greek, not Hebrew. Instead, *Theos* is the New Testament word that is translated "God." The singular form of *Theos* always denotes deity.

Steve: *This also appears occasionally with Christ in 2 places in the NT for sure. Compare that with the occasional passages within the OT attaching "god" to human agents, and contrast that with numerous texts throughout the NT only applying God to the Father.*

Dr. L.: You are repeating an error that I have already refuted. "God" is not only applied to the Father, but also *explicitly* to the Son (e.g., Hebrews 1:8; John 20:28) who is the Word (John 1:14) and explicitly God (John 1:1), and also to the Holy Spirit (Acts 5:3–4). The Greek word *Theos* is used here in the singular form, which always indicates deity. [Here again, Steve violates the text principle. He just isn't reading the Bible carefully.]

When the term God is used of the Son in Hebrews 1:8, can it merely mean "gods" in the lesser sense of the word, or must it mean Almighty God? The author of Hebrews is quoting Psalm 45:6 where the Hebrew Word for "God" is *Elohim* used with singular verbs. This is never used of human agents. Remember, when *Elohim* (plural) is used in the singular sense, it refers to *the God.* So there is no doubt that the author of Hebrews is teaching that the Son is *the God*. I know you really don't want to believe that. But the Scriptures are clear.

There are many other references to God that you have assumed refer to the Father only, but this is merely your bias — the Scriptures do not indicate such. In logic, you are supposed to provide a reason for your claim, and not just state it over and over. But you haven't provided any reason to think that Jesus is not God. The best you've been able to do is point out that when He was in His earthly ministry, His human nature was less than God. But no one denies this. Jesus was with God in the beginning and was God from the beginning (again, John 1:1).

Both in the Old and New Testaments, the Almighty is referred to as either Lord or God or both. The vast majority of references to the "Lord" in the New Testament are to the Son — not the Father. Isn't that interesting? Only rarely is the "Father" explicitly referred to as "Lord" in the New Testament. Would it then be rational to say, "Therefore, the Son is the Lord, but not the Father. The very few times that the Father is called Lord are merely honorary." Wouldn't that be absurd?

***Steve:** Compound that with the fact that Christ himself said very clearly he has a God greater or above himself. To me it is obvious; the Father is the only Almighty God.*

Dr. L.: You are again repeating an error that I've already refuted. It was only with respect to Christ's human nature and His submission to the Father that He was less in that sense to the Father. I showed you some verses that teach this, do you remember? (e.g., Hebrews 2:9; Philippians 2:6–8). Yes, Christ humbled Himself in His earthly ministry. His earthly nature was less than the Father's divine nature. That's not disputed.

But you seem to be forgetting that Christ also asserted *equality* with the Father. In John 10:30, Jesus says, "I and the Father are one." He said, "He who sees Me sees the One who sent Me" (John 12:45), which is only logically possible if Jesus is the same being as the One who sent Him. These verses contradict the view that you are currently following.

***Steve:** Joh 10:34 Jesus answered them, Is it not written in your law, I said, You are gods? Joh 10:35 If he called them gods, unto whom the WORD of God came, and the scripture cannot be broken; Joh 10:36 do you say of him, whom the Father sanctified, and sent into the world, you are blaspheming; because I said, I am the Son of God?*

Dr. L: Jesus' argument here is called an "*a fortiori*" argument. He is arguing from the lesser to the greater. An example is: "You respect your parents, right? How much more should you respect God?" Jesus uses this type of argument to refute their claim and show hypocrisy in the Jews. If they were willing to accept that the judges could be called "gods" (not *God*, but "gods") (the judges being wicked sinners, though guided by God and acting for Him in making judgments), then how much more should they be willing to accept the actual begotten Son of God, who is literally God, the one of whom the judges merely represent? Jesus' argument would lose its power if He were not really God, the One whom the judges merely represented.

Steve: *Even Moses and the judges are given the honorary title of "God"* (Elohim) *in the OT because God was working through them. Surely Trinitarians themselves aren't willing to expand the Godhead to include these individuals, all of whom are called "God" in the Bible. These titles are to be understood in their proper context. Exo 7:1*

Dr. L.: No — they are called "gods" in the lesser sense of the Word. They are never referred to as "Mighty God" or "the Almighty" or "the First and the Last" or *YHWH* — but Jesus has all these titles. In the Exodus 7:1 passage, God makes Moses *as* a god *to Pharaoh*. He's not saying that Moses is "God" as He does with Jesus.

You have committed the hermeneutical error of the "unwarranted expansion of an expanded semantic field." Though the term *Elohim* can refer to something that is not the Living God in some contexts, it cannot mean this in other contexts. There are other terms for God that only apply to God — and these are applied to Christ, never to anyone else. Incidentally, the fact that you are trying to make Christ's status as God merely "honorary" shows that you really do see that the Bible teaches that Jesus is God. So the deity of Christ is found throughout the Bible; you are simply trying to explain why such passages don't really mean what they say.

Steve: *Exo 21:6 then hath his lord brought him nigh unto the judges (God) (Elohim), and hath brought him nigh unto the door, or unto the sidepost, and his lord hath bored his ear with an awl, and he hath served him — to the age.*

Dr. L.: Again, the term *Elohim* has a range of meanings depending on context. Judges are implied, but not actually mentioned. The servant was brought to the Lord via the judges who were operating under His authority.

The Bible never refers to the judges as "Mighty God" or "the First and the Last." That would be totally inappropriate. But Jesus is God and is rightly referred to as such (e.g., Isaiah 9:6; Revelation 1:8, 17). God is the First and the Last (Isaiah 41:4). Jesus uses this Name of God to identify Himself (Revelation 1:17, 22:13).

The Trinity Is a Monotheistic Concept

Steve: *Also the vast testimony of scripture indicates there is only one God. Monotheism is the central creed of the OT and of Christ himself.*

Dr. L.: Yes — it certainly is. The fact that you brought this up strongly suggests that you don't understand the doctrine of the Trinity. The Trinity is *not* the teaching that there are three Gods. Rather, the Trinity is the teaching that there is only one God. The Father is God, the Son is God, and the Holy Spirit is God. These three persons are eternally distinct (the Son has always been the Son, the Spirit has always been the Spirit, the Father has always been the Father). These are the same God in nature or essence. But they are three in persons. So there is only one God. The Father, Son, and Holy Spirit are three persons, but one God. This isn't easy for us to understand. But since it is what the Bible teaches, we accept it by faith. Who are we to tell God He cannot be what He claims to be?

Steve: *No, I understand this position. I have heard it time and time again and it is not based on scripture neither is it genuine monotheism.*

[Steve's statement here reveals his extreme ignorance of the topic. Apparently, Steve thought that the Trinity somehow involves more than one God. That shows that he hasn't bothered to study this topic at all.]

Dr. L.: Your statement here proves conclusively that you do not understand the Trinitarian position. I say that not to belittle you, but to encourage you to study the position before attempting to argue against it. The Trinitarian position is *by definition* monotheistic because it asserts that there is only one God. That's what *monotheism* is. Mono = One; Theism = God. The issue is not therefore about the number of Gods — there's only the one. The issue is about the *nature* of that God. Do we accept what God has told us about His nature, or do we insist that God cannot be triune because it's hard to understand? God is infinite, and as such, not entirely comprehensible by the human mind. But He has revealed some aspects of Himself to us.

Steve: *Furthermore the very language, "three persons one God" is completely foreign to scripture.*

Dr. L.: Your enthymeme is ridiculous as a moment's thought reveals. The phrase "If you don't trust in Jesus for salvation, you will spend eternity in hell" is also not found in Scripture. Does that mean the *concept* isn't there? You have conflated a verbal token with a referent. This is a logical fallacy because *terms* are not the same as the *concepts* they convey. To be clear, my defense is not of the terms, but of the biblical doctrine. You are welcome to come up with your own terms as long as you don't deny the biblical truth that:

1. The Father is God (John 6:27)
2. The Son is God (Hebrews 1:8; John 1:1; 20:28)
3. The Holy Spirit is God (Acts 5:3-4)
4. There is one God (James 2:19)

Steve: *I know of not one verse that even remotely hints at this language.*

Dr. L.: Straw-man fallacy, because the "language" is not what is at issue. In fact, the language we use is English, whereas the Bible uses Hebrew and Greek, with some Aramaic. The English word "Jesus" is not found in the original Hebrew and Greek Bible, nor is "God." But are the concepts there? Of course.

Steve: *Rather it is a philosophical idea invented by man that is completely unreasonable and completely unbiblical.*

Dr. L.: Arianism is the philosophical idea invented by man that is completely unreasonable and completely unbiblical. It denies what God has said about Himself, and we have already looked at the verses. [Since Steve made an arbitrary claim, all that was necessary to refute it was to make the opposite arbitrary claim. I went a little further and pointed out that my opposite claim isn't actually arbitrary, but is backed up by Scripture.]

Christ Is Both God and Man

Steve: *"1Ti 2:5 For there is one God, and one mediator between God and men, the man Christ Jesus" Notice here how Paul used "one God" ONLY with the Father.*

Dr. L.: No, he doesn't; just read the text. The word "Father" is not mentioned; you've imported that. [Steve had violated the "text principle."] First Timothy 2:5 affirms that there is one God, which is what the Trinity affirms. And it affirms that Christ is the one mediator between God and man. It is precisely because Christ is both man and God that He alone is qualified to be the mediator between man and God. He has both natures, and can therefore represent both parties. So the Trinity is illustrated, at least in part, in this very verse.

On the other hand, your interpretation leads to a contradiction. If you are arguing that Christ cannot be God since He is a mediator *between God and man*, then by the same reasoning you must conclude that Christ is not a man. Yet this very passage teaches that Christ is a man (as do many other passages). It is because Christ is both man and God that He alone can reconcile man to God.

Steve: *Dr. Lisle, you are incorrectly reading this versus. Christ is not mediating between man and himself.*

Dr. L.: He's mediating between God and man — which He can do precisely because He is both God and man. Christ reconciles men to the fullness of God. And since Christ is God, that necessarily includes reconciling men to Himself (Colossians 1:20). The reason that Christ can mediate between God and man is because He has both natures. He is God and man, thus he can represent both parties. If Jesus were not God, then He could not mediate between God and man. If Jesus were not man, then likewise, He could not mediate between God and man.

You are supposed to apply logic to see if your interpretation is internally consistent. For example, if you conclude that Christ cannot be God since He is the mediator between God and man, then logically you must conclude that Christ cannot be man by the same reasoning. This of course contradicts the texts that indicate that Christ does have a human nature, as well as the texts that indicate that Christ has a divine nature.

Steve: *Rather he is mediating between two parties, God and man. This is obvious by the Paul's own writings.*

> *Gal 3:20 Now a mediator is not a mediator of one, but God is one.*
>
> *Heb 8:1 Now of the things which we have spoken this is the sum: We have such an high priest, who is set on the right hand of the throne of the Majesty in the heavens;*
>
> *Heb 8:2 A minister of the sanctuary, and of the true tabernacle, which the Lord pitched, and not man*

Heb 8:6 But now hath he obtained a more excellent ministry, by how much also he is the mediator of a better covenant, which was established upon better promises.

Rom_8:34 Who is to condemn? Christ Jesus is the one who died — more than that, who was raised — who is at the right hand of God, who indeed is interceding for us.

These scriptures convincingly demonstrate to me that Christ is mediating or interceding between man and the majesty on High whom he is sitting at His right hand. I have no clue where you are getting this from that Christ is interceding between man and himself.

Dr. L.: Another straw-man fallacy, perhaps because you don't understand the Trinity. I did not say that "Christ is interceding between man and himself" even though Christ is God. Nor did I say that "Christ is interceding between *God* and Himself" even though Christ is a man. Rather, Christ intercedes between God and man. He is uniquely qualified to do so because He is both God and man. He has both natures: He is God and He is man, thus He can represent both. This is why Christ alone can be that mediator — He is the only person who has both natures. The Scriptures directly teach in many places and ways that Jesus is deity and, after the incarnation, a man as well; indeed, they would make no sense if Christ were not divine since He would not be able to be a mediator.

Christ Is God and Lord

Steve: *Also since it is not clear to you from the Timothy passage that the one God is the Father perhaps the Corinthians text will better express this. 1Co 8:6 Yet for us there is ONE God, the FATHER, from whom are all things and for whom we exist, and one Lord, Jesus Christ, through whom are all things and through whom we exist.*

Dr. L.: Since you don't yet understand the doctrine of the Trinity, you have inadvertently made a straw-man argument here. You keep attempting to refute the notion that there are three gods, but this is not the Trinity. The biblical position is that there is indeed one God (James 2:19). Moreover, the Father is God (John 6:27), the Son is God (Hebrews 1:8; John 1:1, 20:28), and the Holy Spirit is God (Acts 5:3–4). I've shown you the verses. This text affirms that the Father is that one God, which is also affirmed by the Trinity. So the fact that you brought up this verse suggests that you *still* have a misunderstanding of the Trinity.

Perhaps you think that since this particular verse only mentions the Father in relation to being God that you can conclude that the Son and Holy Spirit are not God. Is that your reasoning? It would be the fallacy of denying the antecedent to deny that the Son and Spirit are also the one God merely by virtue of the fact that they are not mentioned in that context in this particular passage. In Hebrews 1:8, only the *Son* is mentioned in relation to God. Should we therefore conclude from Hebrews 1:8 that the Father is *not* God? By your reasoning, we should. But that would be fallacious.

Again, you are supposed to apply logic to your interpretation to see if it stands up to scrutiny. Let's assume for argument's sake that the passage means what you suggest, that the one God refers *only* to the Father and not to Jesus (even though the text doesn't actually say this). Read the rest of the verse "and one Lord, Jesus Christ. . . ." Then by the same reasoning, the "one Lord" must apply only to Jesus and not to the Father, since the same grammatical construction is used for both. One God = Father (*alone*), thus one Lord = Jesus (*alone*) [by your reasoning]. *Therefore, you must conclude that God the Father is not the Lord.* But that leads to a contradiction since there are verses that refer to the Father as Lord (e.g., Matthew 11:25; Luke 10:21; 2 Corinthians 6:18).

Logically, if Jesus and the Father are two different beings, and if the first is the only one who is *Lord*, and the second is the only one who is *God*, then the expression "Lord God" is a logical contradiction and would never occur. Yet the Bible speaks of the "Lord God" in a number of places (e.g., Luke 1:32, 68; Jude 1:4; Revelation 4:8, 11:17, 16:7, 19:6, etc.) and uses Lord and God as the same being (Matthew 4:7, 10, 22:37; Mark 12:29–30; Luke 1:16, 20:37; Acts 2:39, 3:22, 4:24, 7:37, 17:24; Revelation 19:1). Although the word "lord" is very occasionally used in a lesser sense than God, it is clear that "Lord" in most contexts is a reference to God, particularly when it is a reference to *the* Lord. First Corinthians 8:6 tells us that there is only *one Lord.* So my question for you Steve is: *who is this one Lord?*

Logically, if Jesus is the Lord, and the Lord is God, then Jesus is God. So we have yet another confirmation of the divinity of Christ in all of the above verses. In Acts 17:24, God is called the Lord of heaven and earth. Since Jesus is God, the Bible rightly says in Acts 10:36 that Christ is Lord of all. See, that would all contradict if Jesus were not God.

Jude 1:4 (esp. NASB) states that our *only* Master and Lord is Jesus Christ. Does this mean that God is not our Master and Lord? If Jesus is not God, then it does. But the Bible teaches that God is our Master and Lord (Mark 12:29; Acts 4:24 ["Lord" = same Greek word for Master used in Jude 1:4]). This contradicts unless Jesus is the Lord God. There is only one God, only one Lord. The Bible teaches that the Father, the Son, and the Holy Spirit are this one God and Lord. We've already looked at the verses, so I won't repeat them here. You might say, "But that is hard to understand, and doesn't make sense to me." But God is not limited to human understanding. He is infinite and we are finite. Thus, we should trust Him, even when we don't fully comprehend.

Jesus — The Only True God

Dr. L.: So 1 Timothy 2:5 actually confirms that Christ is God. I tend to not use this passage as a proof text, because of the grammatical ambiguity in English. But if you look up two verses earlier, 1 Timothy 2:3 clearly indicates that God is our Savior. There can be no doubt that Jesus is God, if indeed He is our Savior.

Steve: *This to me rules out the possibility that the Son and the Spirit are somehow a part of this eternal Godhead.*

Dr. L.: Why? The passage confirms that Christ is God. It says nothing about the Spirit one way or the other. But we do know from the other Scriptures that the Holy Spirit is God. In Acts 5:3–4, when Ananias and Sapphira lie to the Holy Spirit, the Scriptures say they have lied to God. Jesus is the Son of God. But He was conceived by the Holy Spirit (Matthew 1:18). This is only possible if the Holy Spirit is God. Jesus said that He is of His Father. The Bible also teaches that Jesus is of the Holy Spirit (Matthew 1:20). This is only possible if the Holy Spirit is God. The Holy Spirit is a person, which is why He counts as a witness under the law of God (Acts 5:32).

Steve: *Notice how Paul excludes Christ from the statement "one God" or "one theos."*

Dr. L.: No — Christ cannot be excluded because He *is* the one God. This is *why* He is the one mediator between God and men. Even if the first phrase were referring to the Father alone there is no logical reason why Jesus cannot also be God so long as it's the same one God (which it is)! After all, Jesus is a man — and that doesn't preclude Him from being the one mediator between God and *man*. So, logically, how could being God preclude Him from being the one mediator between man and *God*?

Steve: *How then can anyone argue that "one" in the Bible naturally means a complex unity.*

Dr. L.: That's another straw-man argument. Please stop misrepresenting the position you are castigating. The Trinity affirms that "one" means "one." But "one being" does not logically equate to "one *person*." It might happen that for every mortal man one person is also one being, but that is not a requirement of logic. There is one God and only one God. But there is nothing in logic or Scripture that precludes the one God from having characteristics that are more than one, such as "persons." After all, I am one man but I have many positions — speaker, author, writer, researcher, etc.

[Steve's argument is tantamount to saying, "No, Dr. Lisle, you can't be a writer *and* a researcher, because you are one person. There's only one Dr. Lisle, therefore the researcher cannot be Dr. Lisle if the author is Dr. Lisle. Are you saying that 'one' naturally means a complex unity?" No. I am one person, with several positions. That doesn't make the number "one" a complex unity. It just means that I am one in one sense and more than one in another sense. Likewise, God is one being, but three persons.]

Steve: *To do so is to utterly destroy the meaning of language.*

Dr. L.: No, the opposite is true. To fail to recognize that God is one in nature or essence, yet three in persons is to ignore the Scriptures and impose your own preferred god into the text — a god that is easier for you to understand. *That* would destroy the meaning of language because you are not attempting to ascertain the author's intention. The biblical God is one. But as I said earlier, the fact that God is one in one sense and more than one in another sense is built into the very first verse of Scripture. So there is absolutely no excuse for those who would deny this scriptural truth.

[Frankly, God has built into the universe many things that are one in one sense, and more than one in another sense. The universe itself is one universe, yet with many diverse aspects. That's why it is a universe ("uni" = "one," "verse" = "many" as in "diverse"). Space is one space, but is three in dimensions. Time is one in dimensions but three in perspectives. Matter is three in particles, but one in essence. Space, time, and matter are three in one sense, but comprise one universe. Now these are not exactly the same type of trinity as God of course. But the fact that God has built into His creation so many examples of things that are one in one sense and many in another sense makes it absolutely inexcusable for us to deny the Triune God.]

Steve: *Consider John 17:3, these are the words of Christ himself: "Joh 17:3 And this is life eternal, that they might know thee the ONLY TRUE God, and Jesus Christ, whom thou hast sent." Again notice here, how "only true God" is applied to the Father whom Jesus is praying to, again, this cannot be argued by Trinitarians that "theos" here is plural because Christ as the speaker is excluded from the statement.*

Dr. L.: Why do you think that "the only true God" is applied *only* to the Father? The text does not say this, and there is no chain of logic by which you could reach that conclusion from any biblical text. The Bible affirms that the Father is the only true God. The Bible affirms that the Son is also the only true God. The Bible affirms that the Spirit is also the only true God. This is because these persons are the *same* God; and there is only one true God. Christ does not exclude Himself from the statement. John 17:3 is perfectly consistent with the Trinity.

Steve: *Furthermore, notice how at the beginning of Revelation, Christ as the speaker, in addressing the Christian churches uses the term "My Father" three times and "My God" four times in his powerful message to the people.*

> *Rev 2:27 And he shall rule them with a rod of iron; as the vessels of a potter shall they be broken to shivers: even as I received of MY Father.*
>
> *Rev 2:28 And I will give him the morning star.*

Dr. L.: Yes — all confirmations of the Trinity. God the Father is God. Jesus is right to refer to Him as such. To think that this somehow proves that Jesus is not God is without any logical merit whatsoever. (When I refer to my father as a man, this does not prove that I am not also a man.) Jesus and the Father are the same God (John 10:30).

The Holy Spirit Is God

Steve:

> *Rev 2:29 He that hath an ear, let him hear what the Spirit saith unto the churches.*

Dr. L.: I'm a little surprised you quoted this one, since it shows that the Holy Spirit is also God. Jesus is speaking, and yet He tells people to listen to what the *Spirit* says. What Jesus says is also what the Spirit says, and is also what the Father says, since these three are one in nature. Was Scripture inspired by God (2 Timothy 3:16; Matthew 22:31; Romans 3:2), or by the Holy Spirit (2 Peter 1:21; Hebrews 3:7, 10:15–16; Acts 28:25, 1:16; 2 Samuel 23:2)? The answer is both, because the Holy Spirit is God.

Steve: *I don't understand why this surprises you. We Unitarians don't see the Holy Spirit has being something entirely separate from God. Rather we see the Spirit as being the power, presence, and influence of God himself. The Holy Spirit is part of who God really is. As the Apostle John declares through Jesus "God is Spirit."*

Dr. L.: The Bible treats the Holy Spirit very differently from the view that you are following. The Bible treats the Holy Spirit — not as an impersonal aspect or part of God (as in the power, presence, or influence of God), but rather as a person who is God. Indeed, Jesus refers to the Holy Spirit as the comforter who would teach the disciples (John 14:26, 16; Luke 12:12; John 15:26, 16:7). Moreover, Christ says that the Spirit will testify of Him (John 15:26). The thing about impersonal attributes or qualities like power, presence, or influence, is that they cannot testify. Only persons can. In Acts 5:32, the Holy Spirit is invoked as a witness; under biblical law, only *persons* can qualify as a witness (e.g., Deuteronomy 19:15; Numbers 35:30). See also 1 John 5:6 (1 John 5:7; NASB). The Holy Spirit speaks (e.g., Acts 21:11, 28:25), which impersonal attributes obviously cannot do.

The Son Is the Same God as the Father

Steve:

> *Rev 3:5 He that overcometh, the same shall be clothed in white raiment; and I will not blot out his name out of the book of life, but I will confess his name before MY Father, and before his angels.*
>
> *Rev 3:12 Him that overcometh will I make a pillar in the temple of MY God, and he shall go no more out: and I will write upon him the name of MY God, and the name of the city of MY God, which is new Jerusalem, which cometh down out of heaven from MY God: and I will write upon him my new name.*

Dr. L.: Yes, God the Son refers to God the Father as His Father. A begotten son is always of the same nature as his father. So each of these verses confirms the Godhood of Jesus. Jesus could not be the begotten Son of God if He is not the same nature as God. "But aren't Christians referred to as sons of God? And yet we're not gods, right?" We are not *begotten* children of God as Jesus (and only Jesus) is (John 3:16). Rather, Christians are *adopted* sons of God (Romans 8:15; Galatians 4:5; Ephesians 1:5). An adopted son need not be the same type of being as a parent. You can adopt a pet. But you cannot "beget" one. A begotten son is always of the same nature as his father. Jesus is the only begotten Son of God, which is why He is necessarily God in nature. And the Scriptures clearly address Him as such (e.g., Hebrews 1:8; Isaiah 9:6; Hebrews 3:1–4; Psalm, 45:7).

Steve: *So since we are adopted sons and therefore cannot claim to be of the same nature of God then what are you to make of the angels? They are called "Sons of God" (Job 1:6, 38:7) and there is no indication that they are adopted as we are. So in what way are they Sons of God?*

Dr. L.: I can certainly understand your confusion here. Some godly men that I respect have made the same error; but it is an error. Angels are never referred to as sons of God — see Hebrews 1:5. Believers are referred to as "sons of God" by the spirit of adoption. This is what Job 1:6 and Job 2:1 are referring to. Even in Job 1:3 when it states that Job was the greatest of all the men in the east, the word translated "men" is the Hebrew word *ben*, which is literally "sons" and is the same word used in verse 6. Job was a man of God, and thus one of the "sons of God." It was He and other believers who had gathered together for worship in Job 1:6 and Job 2:1.

Job 38:7 is a poetic passage, as indicated by the synonymous parallelism in that verse and throughout that chapter. This means you should have been expecting an increase in figures of speech and poetic imagery. I used to think that the "sons of God" in this verse might mean angels, but I now find that view impossible to reconcile with Hebrews 1:5. It seems to be a poetic reference to the luminaries, since the synonymous parallelism requires that "sons of God" must be a synonym for "stars." The sun, moon, and stars can metaphorically be called "sons of God," since God is the Father of lights (James 1:17). Other poetic literature describes the luminaries as praising God (Psalm 148:3, 89:5, 148:4; Nehemiah 9:6). Again, the only literal begotten Son of God is Jesus. Thus, He is of the same nature as God the Father.

Steve: *Futhermore, the term begotten which is the Greek gennaō means to procreate (properly of the father, but by extension of the mother); figuratively to regenerate: — bear, beget, be born, bring forth, conceive, be delivered of, gender, make, spring. Or the Greek, monogenēs only born, that is, sole: — only (begotten, child).*

Dr. L: *Gennao* is the Greek word which means to cause to be born. Of course, Jesus was born. But His Father is God; He has no human biological father. This makes Christ different from the rest of us who all have an earthly father, and can only be sons of God by adoption. Jesus is the begotten Son of God — He is not adopted. Just as we are of the same nature as our father and mother (e.g., human), Jesus is of the same nature as His Father (God) and mother (human).

Though He existed as God from all eternity (e.g., John 1:1; Micah 5:2), He took on human nature by being born into the world as a human being. *Monogenes* is the Greek word for "begotten" used in John 3:16, 18, 1:14 and 1 John 4:9. It has the meaning of "single of its kind, only." Christ is unique because He is the only God-man in existence. The term would not make sense if Jesus were just a man, but not also God. If Jesus were just a man, then He would be one of many.

Steve: *There is nothing in these definitions that would require me to believe that Christ has to be the exact same nature as God to be begotten of God. This is a philosophical argument on your part that ultimately does not satisfy me.*

Dr. L: This is only because of the hardness of your heart. The Bible teaches that Jesus is of the exact same nature as His Father (Hebrews 1:3). As I showed you previously, in the Jewish culture, the son of X is always equal in nature and value to X. Thus, to be called the Son of God, or to call God your Father (in a literal sense) is to call yourself God. The Bible very clearly teaches this: Jesus "said also that God was his Father, making himself equal with God" (John 5:18; KJV). It's not a mere "philosophical argument," but a direct teaching of Scripture.

God Is Tempted, But Never "Tempted"

Steve: *Futhermore, if you really want to work off of philosophical arguments then you will find there is an abundance of support for the Unitarian perspective. Although, I am not using these as proof texts because like I said, they* *are philosophical, but they nevertheless lend support to the Anti-Trinitarian perspective. Consider what the writer of Hebrews says*

> *Heb 4:15 For we have not an high priest which cannot be touched with the feeling of our infirmities; but was in all points tempted like as we are, yet without sin.*

But James then says

> *James 1:13 Let no man say when he is tempted, I am tempted of God: for God cannot be tempted with evil, neither tempteth he any man:*

Jesus was tempted, but God cannot be tempted. Therefore how can he be God?

Dr. L: Here you have committed an equivocation fallacy on the word "tempted." Proper exegesis involves paying close attention to the meaning of words and how they are used in context. To be "tempted" has two different meanings depending on the context. It can either mean (1) to be tested or (2) to be enticed. The first is external; the second is internal. If a homosexual man offers to sleep with me, I have just been tempted — in the sense of being tested. But I wouldn't for a moment be tempted — in the sense of being enticed.

If you conflate these two meanings, or fail to distinguish them, then the Bible will contradict itself. In Numbers 14:22, God Himself says that He was tempted (ten times!). The Bible refers to God being tempted in Exodus 17:7, Psalm 78:18, 41, 56, 95:9, 106:14, and Hebrews 3:9. Do these passages conflict with James 1:13 which says that God cannot be tempted? God was externally tempted in the sense of being tested, but God was never internally tempted in the sense of being enticed. Likewise, Jesus was externally tested, but never enticed.

In context, the passage in Hebrews is dealing with the external/testing form of temptation — Jesus was tested in all ways, and yet He never sinned. In context, the passage in James is dealing with internal temptation, as is made clear by the very next verse: "But every man is tempted, when he is drawn away of his own lust, and enticed." There is no Scripture that indicates that Jesus was ever enticed by sin. Indeed, as God, He could not have been. Thus, He never sinned.

It's almost too obvious to mention, but the fact that Jesus never sinned is also proof of His deity. The Bible states, "For all have sinned, and fall short of the glory of God" (Romans 3:23), and the concept is found throughout the Scriptures. Obviously "all" refers to everyone who isn't God (God would not fall short of His own glory). Thus, if Jesus isn't God, then He is not excluded from the "all" and He too must have sinned, and therefore would fall short of the glory of God. But this contradicts Hebrews 4:15. Do you see the tangled web of contradictions that follow from heretical teaching?

Can God Die?

Steve: *Consider how Paul describes God,*

> *1 Timothy 6:16 Who only hath immortality, dwelling in the light which no man can approach unto; whom no man hath seen, nor can see: to whom be honour and power everlasting. Amen.*

The word immortality is the Greek athanasia which literally means deathlessness or one who cannot die. Now since Jesus died, and God cannot die, then Jesus cannot be God.

Dr. L.: Philippians 2:5–9 refutes your claim. (It also refutes almost all your other points, so it would be a good passage to carefully read.) God — in the fullness of His glory and with respect to His divinity — cannot die. (Though, the verse you cited does not demonstrate it. This verse indicates that God possesses immortality, in the sense that eternal life is His to give.) So can Jesus die? In the fullness of His glory and divine nature — no. But did Jesus exhibit the fullness of His glory and divine nature in His earthly ministry? According to Philippians 2:7, Jesus "emptied Himself, taking the form of a bond-servant, and being made in the likeness of men." Though the Son is equal to the Father in divinity, glory, and power, the Bible teaches that He emptied Himself during His earthly ministry. It's not that He ceased to be God, but rather the characteristics normally associated with God, such as omnipresence, and immortality, were suppressed. But Jesus gave up (temporarily) His immortality with respect to His human nature by His own divine choice (John 10:17–18).

Jesus took on a human nature precisely so that He could die! This was the whole point of the incarnation, Steve. See Matthew 20:28 and Mark 10:45. Before the incarnation, Jesus existed only as God, and not as man.

In the fullness of His divinity, apart from His humanity, He cannot die; therefore, he took on human nature and was given a physical body so that He could die (Hebrews 10:5) in payment for sin. This is foundational to the Gospel.

We've all sinned against an infinitely Holy God, and hence must pay an infinite penalty. But no one other than God's life is of infinite value. Only He is worthy to pay that penalty. God took on human nature so that He could die for our sins.

Does God Repent?

Steve: *Consider what the writers of Numbers says,*

> *Num 23:19 God is not a man, that he should lie; neither the son of man, that he should repent: hath he said, and shall he not do it? or hath he spoken, and shall he not make it good?*

Not only is God not a man but he is not the son of man. Jesus was the son of man, and he was a man, therefore he cannot be God.

Dr. L.: Numbers 23:19 is an Old Testament passage. Jesus did not have a human nature *at that time* — it was before the incarnation. Also, the passage exhibits synonymous parallelism, indicating poetic usage. So you need to exegete it appropriately. God in His essential nature is not like a man who lies or repents of something. The passage does *not* say that God would never take on human nature. And so it doesn't support your view. Jesus, as God, cannot lie. Indeed, as God in the flesh, He is the very embodiment of truth (John 14:6).

Steve: *Like I said, these arguments tend to be philosophical and I realize that since you are a Trinitarian they will not ultimately sway you. I only write this to show you that anyone can make a philosophical argument they feel exists on biblical grounds to satisfy their own worldview.*

Dr. L.: Hopefully, you now see that these arguments are not at all cogent. They stem from a very sloppy reading of the text, and logical fallacies. When the passages are read in context, and logic is applied properly, these texts all affirm the Trinity very strongly.

Steve:

> *Rev 3:21 To him that overcometh will I grant to sit with me in my throne, even as I also overcame, and am set down with MY Father in his throne.*

Dr. L.: Likewise, what Jesus says is what the Holy Spirit says, since these two persons are one with God the Father in nature and essence.

What Did the Jews Believe, and Is This Relevant?

Dr. L.: The Trinity is actually suggested in the very first verse of the Bible: "In the beginning, God created the heavens and the earth." The Hebrew word for God in this verse is *Elohim* which is a plural word. It literally means "Gods." And yet, the verb form for "created" is singular."

Steve: *I am already aware of the plural form of* Elohim. *The truth is so have the Jewish people for thousands of years and there is no univocal theological position in all of their history showing they believed God to be Triune in nature.*

Dr. L.: That's the fallacy of irrelevant thesis. The Jews did all sorts of things, and not all of them were biblical. The men who wrote under the inspiration of the Holy Spirit (i.e., under the inspiration of God) did indeed have at least some knowledge of the Trinity. David's reference in Psalm 110:1 is to both the Father and the Son — both as his Lord. And He mentions the Spirit in many other places (e.g., Psalm 51:11). Job knew that his Redeemer would one day stand on the earth (Job 19:25) — an indication of the incarnation of Jesus.

Steve: *Yes, they did do all sort of things that were unbiblical, but on this point they were not mistaken.*

Dr. L.: You seem to have forgotten the point that you were trying to make. You were suggesting that the Jews of the Old Testament did not accept the Trinity. I pointed out that (1) this is not the case, and (2) if it were the case it would have been sin on their part. But those who wrote the Scriptures under the inspiration of the Holy Spirit affirmed the Trinity. I've already listed a number of examples. Just as a reminder: Job professed that His Redeemer lives (that's the Lord Jesus) and that He would one day stand upon the earth (a reference to the incarnation) (Job 19:25). Isaiah speaks of the coming Christ as "Mighty God" (Isaiah 9:6). God the Father specifically refers to the Son in the Old Testament as God (Psalms 45:6–7). (This also shows that the Son already existed as a person before the incarnation.)

Steve: *They believed strongly in one God and they worshiped that one God with zeal.*

Dr. L.: I wish that were so, since the Bible affirms (as one crucial aspect of the Trinity) that there is one God. But as a matter of historical fact, the Jews fell into all sorts of idolatry and worshiped many false gods (e.g., Numbers 25:1–3; Judges 2:11–13).

Steve: *This is evident by Christ's own words, "John 4:22 You worship what you do not know; we worship what we know, for salvation is from the Jews." In other words Christ states very clearly that the Jews knew whom they worshiped when he was speaking to the woman at the well.*

Dr. L.: Again, it is important to pay attention to what the text actually says. Jesus did not affirm that all Jews worshiped the Lord. Indeed, most Jews rejected the Messiah. From context, the "we" is referring to the faithful Jews. If it weren't, then it would contradict the many places where Jesus rebukes the unbelieving Jews (e.g., Matthew 23:13, 33).

Jesus affirms that there is one God (Mark 12:29). And He affirms that He is the same in nature as the Father (John 10:30), and that He is equal with God (John 5:17–18). I know you don't want to believe that. But the Scriptures are clear.

Steve: *He then goes on . . .*

> *John 4:23 But the hour cometh, and now is, when the true worshippers shall worship the Father in spirit and in truth: for the Father seeketh such to worship him.*
>
> *John 4:24 God is a Spirit: and they that worship him must worship him in spirit and in truth.*

Notice how in the mind of Christ "the Father" is once again unequivocally associated with "God" whom even Christ's worships.

Dr. L.: I have already refuted the claim that only the Father is God by pointing to verses where the Son is called God. Do I really need to relist them? Moreover, the Son is called "Lord," which is also a term for God. John 4:23–24 affirms that it is appropriate to worship the Father. It would be the fallacy of denying the antecedent to conclude that it is not appropriate to worship the Son or the Spirit. There are many passages of Scripture which state that "God" is to be worshiped — not just the "Father" (e.g., Exodus 3:12; Deuteronomy 6:13).

Steve: *Futhermore, the Shema, which is the central creed of Judaism, was also the creed of Christ himself.*

Dr. L.: The Shema is a beautiful confirmation of the Trinity. It is *not* consistent with a unitarian (or polytheistic for that matter) view of God. Here is why: Deuteronomy 6:4 states, "Hear, O Israel! The LORD is our God, the LORD is one!" The word "one" is *echad* in Hebrew, and suggests something that is one in one sense, and more than one in another sense. It is the word used for a single (*echad*) cluster of grapes in Numbers 13:23. It is the word used for the *first* day in Genesis 1:5, which was comprised of two parts — evening and morning. It is the word used for *one* group of people in Genesis 34:22. When Pharaoh has two dreams that both contain the same message, Joseph says that the two dreams are "one" (*echad*) in Genesis 41:25. All these are one in one sense, and more than one in another. And this is the same word used for the "one" God in the Shema.

The word translated "God" in Deuteronomy 6:4 is *Elohim* — the plural form. Again, it is not plural of majesty, which is of more modern invention. But the term for "Lord" is *YHWH* — the special name of God that is only ever applied to God. So the Shema tells us that the Lord (singular) our God (plural) is one (singular but complex) Lord (singular), which is only logically possible if God is one in one sense, and yet more than one in another sense.

Another interesting tidbit: the Jews did not believe it fitting to say out loud the Holy name of God (*YHWH*) — it was only written. So when they read aloud the Shema, they substituted the word *Adonai* which is also translated as "Lord" in a number of Scriptures. The interesting thing about *Adonai* is that it too is plural, and yet is used with a singular noun (as it is in almost all references to God in the Old Testament). It's literally "lords." (*Adon* would be the singular form). So when the Jews read aloud the Shema, it would be "The Lord [plural] our God [plural] is [singular] one [singular but complex] Lord [plural]." So for those who believe that the Bible really does mean what it says, there can be no doubt that God is one in one sense and more than one in another sense. This type of usage (mixing of singular and plural when it comes to God) is ubiquitous throughout the Old Testament.

Steve: *Consider the conversation between a Jewish scribe and Jesus*

> *Mar 12:29 Jesus answered, "The most important is, 'Hear, O Israel: The Lord our God, the Lord is one.' "*

Mar 12:30 "And you shall love the Lord your God with all your heart and with all your soul and with all your mind and with all your strength."

Dr. L.: This confirms that Jesus too affirmed the Trinity, since He affirmed the Shema. We get an even greater confirmation of the divinity of Jesus when we compare this very passage with other New Testament passages. Since Jesus has just affirmed that the Lord our God is one Lord, it is interesting to take a look at 1 Corinthians 8:6 which tells us who that one Lord is. That's right. It is none other than Jesus Christ.

Steve:

Mar 12:31 "The second is this: 'You shall love your neighbor as yourself.' There is no other commandment greater than these."

Mar 12:32 And the scribe said to him, "You are right, Teacher. You have truly said that he is one, and there is no other besides him."

Mar 12:33 "And to love him with all the heart and with all the understanding and with all the strength, and to love one's neighbor as oneself, is much more than all whole burnt offerings and sacrifices."

Now there is no indication at all that this scribe believed in some Triune Godhead.

Dr. L.: Since he affirmed the Shema, he obviously did have at least some understanding of the Trinity, or at least of the fact that God is one Lord, and yet more than one in another sense.

[It is clear from his comments that Steve still did not understand the Trinity. He thought that by listing verses that show that there is one God that He was somehow disproving the Trinity. But the Trinity is one God.]

Steve: *Instead his understanding of the one God is exactly the same understanding of the Jews of his day.*

Dr. L.: That's probably true. Most of the Jews at that time did have some understanding of the Trinity. They used plural words for God (in the Hebrew language) with singular verbs — confirming that they understood that God was one in one sense and more than one in another sense.

[Steve here had arbitrarily assumed that the Jews rejected the Trinity. He then argues that Christ agrees with the Jews. Steve then concludes that the Trinity is false. But this was the very assumption with which he began his argument. He has begged the question.]

Steve: *Immediately after that Jesus commends him for his correct understanding of the central creed of Israel.*

Dr. L.: I agree.

Steve: *Mar 12:34 And when Jesus saw that he answered wisely, he said to him, "You are not far from the kingdom of God." And after that no one dared to ask him any more questions. Now in case you may try to advance any argument that goes beyond the plain meaning of this creed notice very careful what Jesus says in versus 29. He says the Lord OUR God is one. In other words the one God mentioned is unambiguously the God of Christ as well.*

Dr. L: That's true. And it is perfectly consistent with the Trinity. The Father, Son, and Holy Spirit have enjoyed fellowship from all eternity, as one God. It is perfectly logical for one person of the Trinity (who is God) to refer to another person of the Trinity as "God" since all three persons of the Trinity are the one God. Psalm 45:7 refers to one member of the Trinity referring to another as "God." It may be counter-intuitive to your carnal mind. But there is no contradiction.

God Refers to the Other Members of the Trinity as "God"

Steve: *There is nothing you or any other theologian can say to make me possibly believe that "one" here is some sort of complex unity that includes Christ when clearly Christ is speaking of an entity apart from himself.*

Dr. L.: It's really a shame you won't let the Bible correct your thinking on this issue. God often refers to God as God, particularly when one member of the Trinity addresses another (Psalm 45:7; Hosea 1:7; Amos 4:11; Jeremiah 50:40; Malachi 3:1; Micah 5:2; Zechariah 2:8–11, 3:2). These verses must be very perplexing to those who deny the Trinity. In the first listed Zechariah passage, the Lord of hosts says that He was sent by the Lord of hosts. That must be a tough pill to swallow for those who deny what God has said about His own nature. David is clearly addressing God the Son in Psalm 45:1–2, because he says of His King that He is fairer than the sons of men, and that God has blessed Him forever, and yet He called Him God in verse 6. This is *Elohim* with the singular verb, and thus must mean the God. Verse 7 must be another hard pill to swallow since David says, "Therefore God, thy God hath anointed thee." All that to say, Jesus' remarks are perfectly consistent with the Old Testament passages in which more than one person of the Trinity is mentioned.

I have previously pointed out that Zechariah 12:10 demonstrates that Christ is God, since God refers to Himself as the one who is pierced on the Cross. But this passage also confirms the Trinity. It refers to the same being both as "Me" and as "Him," which makes utterly no sense apart from God's Triune nature. God says, ". . . they will look on Me whom they have pierced; and they will mourn for Him. . . ."

[Steve again had no answer to this verse.]

Steve: *Whatever speculation you may add to rescue your unbiblical world-view will not convince me when compared to plain statements of scripture.*

Dr. L.: That's such an ironic statement Steve, because I've shown you Scripture after Scripture that indicate that Jesus is God. You've not listed even one verse that even so much as hints that Christ isn't God. The best you've been able to find are those verses which refer to the limitations that Christ placed on Himself during His earthly ministry (Philippians 2:6–8). But when God places limitations on Himself, or choses to take on human nature, or willfully submits to the Father, or humbles Himself to the point of being obedient to death for our sakes, He doesn't cease to be God.

You haven't heeded the Scriptures that directly and explicitly teach that Christ is God (e.g., John 1:1; Hebrews 1:8; John 20:28). And you've just ignored all the Scriptures by which you can logically deduce that Jesus is God. So what else can I say?

Steve: *This position is also entirely consistent with what he told Mary which further verifies that I am reading the correct understanding of the scribe and Jesus from this verse.*

> *John 20:17 Jesus saith unto her, Touch me not; for I am not yet ascended to my Father: but go to my brethren, and say unto them, I ascend unto my Father, and your Father; and to my God, and your God.*

Dr. L.: If you think that person A calling person B "God" proves that person A is not God, then you cannot consistently believe that God the Father is God. In Hebrews 1:8, the Father calls the Son "God." (This is a quote from Psalm 45:6, where "God" is *Elohim* (plural) but used in the singular, which is only ever used of *the* God.) By your reasoning, we would have to conclude that the Father is not God, since He calls the Son "God." Applying the same reasoning to Psalm 45:7, you would have to conclude that God isn't God (since God refers to God as God). In that case you would be committing an obvious violation of the law of identity.

Psalm 45:7, "Therefore God, Thy God has anointed Thee with oil of joy about Thy fellows." So it's not clear why you think that John 20:17 is somehow evidence against the Trinity. God the Father is God, and Jesus rightly refers to Him as such. But Steve, you continue to commit the fallacy of denying the antecedent in thinking that this somehow proves that Jesus isn't God. That just doesn't follow logically. God refers to God as God — and this is easily seen in Psalm 45:7. It wouldn't make sense apart from the Trinity.

Steve: *In other words, to the extent that the Father was the God of Mary he is also the same Father that is the God of Christ, exactly as he meant when he quoted the Shema.*

Dr. L.: God the Father is the Father of God the Son as He is the Father of all who believe. However, He is a father to those who believe only by the spirit of adoption. Jesus is the only begotten Son of God, and the only one therefore that shares in the Father's divine nature. It's not clear why you think this is a problem. It's certainly not a logical problem for the biblical doctrine of the Trinity.

Steve: *Consider also what Christ told the Jews . . .*

> *Jesus answered, If I honour myself, my honour is nothing: it is my Father that honoureth me; of whom ye say, that he is your God.*

This makes it very clear that in the mind of the Jews and in the mind of Christ, that the Father of Christ is understood to be the exact same God of the Jews as they knew him.

Dr. L.: It's not clear to me why you think this is somehow evidence against the Trinity. Jesus is correctly applying Proverbs 27:2. God the Son says that if He honors Himself, it is nothing, but God the Father honors Him, which the Jews acknowledge to be their God. But God the Father is God (as is the Son), thus there is no difficulty here. It's not clear to me why you think otherwise.

[The fact that Steve thinks that these kinds of arguments and verses are evidence against the Trinity is further evidence that he does not understand the Trinity. It is crucial when refuting a position that you correctly understand that position.]

Steve: *Peter, who thinks as a Jew proclaims . . .*

> *Act 5:30 The God of our fathers raised up Jesus, whom ye slew and hanged on a tree.*

Dr. L.: Who raised up Jesus? "The God of our fathers" — yes? Just to be clear, it is God who raised up Jesus. Jesus was resurrected by God. I reiterate because this is yet another proof of the Trinity. Jesus said this about His death and Resurrection in John 2:19, "Jesus answered them, 'Destroy this temple, and in three days I will raise it up.'' (The temple he spoke of was His body — John 2:21.) Yes, you read that correctly. Jesus said, "I will raise it up." He taught that He would raise Himself! Was He mistaken? He reiterates this in John 10:18: Jesus says of His life that "I have power to lay it down, and I have power to take it again" (KJV). Indeed, Jesus even claims that He *is* the resurrection (John 11:25).

So the Scriptures teach that God raised Jesus from the dead. And they teach that Jesus raised Himself from the dead. I'll leave the logical conclusion to you.

In fact, all three persons of the Trinity were involved in the Resurrection of Christ. The Father (Galatians 1:1), the Son (John 2:19), and the Holy Spirit (Romans 8:11). Rightly then do the Scriptures teach that God raised Him from the dead (Acts 3:15, 4:10, 13:30; Romans 10:9; Colossians 2:12; 1 Peter 1:21) since all three persons of the Godhead were involved.

Peter Affirmed the Deity of Jesus

Steve: *Please show me any indication that Peter believed "God of our fathers" was to include Christ or some sort of Plural deity. If you can do that Dr. Lisle then I will concede any claim of mine.*

Dr. L.: Okay — I can do that. And I will hold you to your word that, "If you can do that Dr. Lisle then I will concede any claim of mine." Just to be clear (and because I'm convinced that you don't yet understand the concept of the Trinity), it is only the persons within the Godhead that are more than one. There is only one God. Did Peter believe this? Yes. I'll show you some verses that indicate this.

In Acts 2:25, Peter quotes Psalm 16:8 and applies the passage to Jesus. Peter refers to Christ as the "Holy One" both in Acts 2:27, and John 6:68–69, which is one of the names of God used throughout the Old Testament (e.g., 2 Kings 19:22; Job 6:10; Psalm 78:41, 77:22, 89:18; Proverbs 9:10, 30:3; Isaiah 5:19, 24, 10:17, 20, 17:7, 29:19, 23, 43:3, 14–15, etc.).

The disciples were with Christ (John 2:12–22) when He claimed that He would raise Himself from the dead (John 2:19). Jesus said He had the power to take up His life again (John 10:18). Yet Peter attributes the power of Christ's Resurrection to God (Acts 2:24, 32), which indicates that He understood that Jesus is God.

In 1 Peter 1:10–11, Peter says that the prophets of old prophesied according to the indications of the Spirit of Christ within them. Peter was undoubtedly aware that the Old Testament teaches that it is by the Spirit of the Lord (*YHWH*) that prophets spoke (e.g., 2 Samuel 23:1; Zechariah 7:12). Peter recognized that this is not a contradiction since Christ is *YHWH*.

Peter believed that Christ, as God, was omniscient. In John 21:17, Peter says, "Lord, *you know all things*; You know that I love you." Specifically, Jesus knew the heart of man (John 2:24–25). But this prerogative belongs only to God (1 Kings 8:39; 2 Chronicles 6:30; Jeremiah 17:9–10). And Peter acknowledges this in Acts 1:24 and Acts 15:8. Peter is praying to Jesus in Acts 1:24, because it is Jesus who chooses His disciples (John 6:70).

Peter knew that it was God who pours out His Holy Spirit since He quotes Joel in Acts 2:17. But He also knew that Jesus (as God) gave people the Holy Spirit (e.g., Acts 2:33).

Peter quotes Joel 2:32 that "whoever calls on the name of the Lord shall be saved." The Hebrew Word translated "Lord" is *YHWH* — the divine name of God. Peter understood that people must call upon the name of *YHWH* to be saved. And what name does Peter say is the only name by which men can be saved? Acts 4:10, 12, ". . . by the name of Jesus Christ. . . . And there is salvation in no one else; for there is no other name under heaven that has been given among men by which we must be saved." The only way this does not contradict is if Jesus is *YHWH*.

Peter called Jesus the Christ — the Son of the Living God. And as we have already seen, in Jewish thinking (and really anyone who is reasoning rationally), the begotten son of X is always of the nature of X. So clearly, Peter understood and embraced the fact that Jesus is divine. Much more could be said, but any one of the above should suffice. [Steve did not honor his word to concede his claims.]

Steve: *On the contrary, the God of Israel RAISED up Jesus. The God of Israel is not believed to include Jesus.*

Dr. L.: You may not believe that the God of Israel is Jesus, but the Scriptures would contradict otherwise, and that's the point. The God of Israel raised up Jesus; yet, Jesus raised up Jesus (John 2:19–22, 10:17–18). The God of Israel was already known to have a one and more-than-one nature at the time of Christ. We've already looked at some of the Old Testament passages, so I won't repeat them here.

Steve: *This is a post biblical idea that cannot be defended with scripture.*

[Steve provided no support for his claim, and simply ignored the verses that contradict it.]

Steve: *Still not convinced?*

Dr. L.: Actually, the notion that Jesus was not God is foreign to the Scriptures, (there is no Scripture that teaches that Christ is not God, and many that teach that Christ is God) and was never a part of the early church, but can be traced back to the heretic Arius (~A.D. 250–336). Whomever you are reading does not know his history — or his Bible — or basic logic.

Jesus Is Good. But God Alone Is Good. Therefore . . .

Steve: *Consider the words of Christ here*

> *Mar 10:18 And Jesus said to him, "Why do you call me good? No one is good except God alone.*

Clearly Christ is contrasting himself from the One God of Israel.

Dr. L.: Not at all. He was asking a question of the rich ruler to get him to think about the implications of what he had just said. Good teachers do this. God *alone* is good (Mark 10:18). And Jesus is good (John 10:11, 14). What is the only logical conclusion we can draw?

Steve: *He is saying that there are qualities about God that is inherent to God alone.*

Dr. L.: Think this through Steve. It's not hard. If God alone is good, and if Jesus is not God, then it follows logically that Jesus is not good. But if Jesus is not good, then He cannot atone for our sins on the Cross. Moreover, Jesus claims that He is good (John 10:11), and the Father confirms that He is well pleased with the Son (Matthew 3:17). This contradicts Mark 10:18

unless Jesus is God, for God alone is good. Contrast Christ with those men who are not God — our righteousness is like filthy rags (Isaiah 64:6).

It is because Christ was sinless that He could be our substitute on the Cross (2 Corinthians 5:21). He takes on our sin, and we are imputed with His righteousness. But this is only possible if Jesus is inherently righteous. If He were a sinner too, then His death could only atone for His own sins. So the heretical theology that you are following leads to an inescapable problem: there is no salvation.

Since God alone is good, if Jesus were not God, then He would not be good — and could not atone for our sins. If Jesus is merely called "good" by imputed righteousness, then He too needs a savior, and cannot atone for our sins. If Jesus is truly good and sinless (which is necessary for our salvation), then He must be God, since God alone is good. So once again, we see that a careful reading of the Scriptures and an application of logic forces the rational Christian to embrace the Trinity.

Steve: *He was pointing his listeners not to himself but to the God above himself from whom Christ derives his goodness and righteousness. Are you going to argue here that the "God" in this text is the plural Godhead as well?*

[Note that Steve's reference to the "plural Godhead" suggests that he still has a false conception of the Trinity, and continues to argue against that straw-man position.]

Dr. L.: From the Old Testament Scriptures, we know that God is one in nature, and yet more than one in persons. Therefore, this theology extends to the New Testament as well. We are to take "God" to be all three persons of the Trinity, unless we have clear contextual evidence to the contrary. In the case of Mark 10:18, it is clear that Jesus must be included as God, otherwise He could not be good since God alone is good. Christ alone is Holy — He is *the Holy One* (John 6:69; Acts 2:27, 13:15, 3:14; 1 Peter 1:15; 1 John 2:20).

1. God *alone* is good/Holy, and there is none else (e.g., Revelation 15:4)
2. Jesus *alone* is Holy (e.g., Acts 3:14 – *the* Holy One)
3. Therefore, Jesus is God.

Any alternative to this conclusion must violate logic, or deny one of the premises.

Is There any Biblical Evidence *against* the Trinity?

Steve: *As you can see the abundance of evidence in scripture for my position is univocal.*

[Steve seems to think that by asserting over and over that his claim is biblical, that this will somehow make it so. But he hasn't provided any logically cogent arguments from the Scriptures.]

Dr. L.: So far, none of the arguments you have listed have turned out to be sound or cogent. In every single case, there is a major (1) misreading of the text, (2) logical fallacy, (3) a misrepresentation of the Trinity, or (4) a failure to distinguish between Christ's respective states of humility and exaltation. So the position you are advocating is absolutely without any scriptural support whatsoever. It stems entirely from a lack of understanding of the Bible, and bad reasoning. It is a false gospel.

Steve: *To speculate that Christ is making these statements about him having a God above himself only in the sense of voluntary submission is just that, speculation. You cannot find any biblical support for your beliefs*

Dr. L.: Actually, Philippians 2:6–7 directly states this.

Steve: *nor one single text that's says Christ was fully God from past eternity,*

Dr. L.: Micah 5:2 does. "But as for you, Bethlehem Ephrathah, too little to be among the clans of Judah, from you One will go forth for Me to be ruler in Israel. His goings forth are from long ago, from the days of eternity." So does John 1:1 really (and John 8:58, as we have already seen). Isaiah 9:6 calls Christ the *eternal* Father, which at least suggests eternality. Christ says that He had the glory of God before the world existed (John 17:5). This is yet further proof that Christ is God, since God has promised that He will not give His glory to another (Isaiah 48:11).

Steve: *and then freely gave up his nature only to call the Father God for an eternity after that.*

Dr. L.: No — Christ never gave up His divine nature. He was, is, and will always be God (Hebrews 13:8). Rather, at the incarnation, Christ took on an additional nature — that of man. During His earthly ministry, Philippians 2:6–8 teaches that Christ emptied Himself of His visible equality with the Godhead; thus His divine attributes were suppressed, but not lost. Christ's humiliation ended at the Crucifixion, and He now exhibits the full, unveiled glory of God, as He did before the Incarnation. There is one difference: Christ retains His human nature (something He had not yet taken on before the Incarnation), and will forever be the God-man. Thus, He was glorified after the Resurrection, not only as God, but as the Messiah as well.

Elohim — God or gods?

Steve: *I have actually heard that this plural usage is similar to the usage of "we" as used in the Koran to describe God, indicating the plurality of majesty.*

Dr. L.: No. From what I can discern, the plural of majesty is a more modern concept, apparently not in use at the time Genesis was written. The Old Testament does not contain any evidence of royalty (e.g., David or Solomon) using the plural of majesty to refer to themselves. Moreover, God sometimes switches from singular to plural within the same sentence, which is not consistent with plural of majesty (e.g., Isaiah 6:8). Additionally, the Hebrew always uses the *singular* verb form with the plural noun for God. It is a unique grammatical construction which indicates the unique one-and-more-than-one nature of the living God — and this construction is only applied with any regularity to God.

Steve: *Furthermore, when the NT writers wrote in the Greek they rendered "*Theos*" singular demonstrating they understood the proper usage of their original language.*

[Steve here committed the fallacy of denying the antecedent. Essentially, he seems to be arguing that:

(1) if the New Testament writers used a plural noun for "God," then that would suggest a Trinity.
(2) But they did not use a plural word for God
(3) Therefore, they did not believe in a Trinity.

The fallacious nature of the argument is clear. Since the triune God is one in nature, but three in persons, it is not surprising to find some references to the one-ness aspect, just as we find references to the more-than-one aspect. The existence of one aspect does not disprove the existence of the other.]

Dr. L.: There is no doubt that God is one (based on the verbs used with *Elohim*) and there is no doubt that God is more than one (based on the fact that *Elohim* is plural). The translators had to make a choice, and it was a very reasonable one. "God" in the singular is the best translation into

English just as *Theos* is in Greek because there is one God, even though the Godhead is three persons. So although the plural aspect in the word "God" cannot be captured in the Greek language in which the New Testament was written, there are nevertheless many other references to the Trinity: to Christ as God, to the Spirit as God, and to the Father as God, and references to the fact that there is only one God. So the Trinity is clearly seen in the New Testament as well as the Old Testament. The biblical authors simply had different ways of expressing the concept since they wrote in different languages.

Steve: *Who is talking about translation into English? I specifically was talking about the NT writers themselves who rendered* "theos" *singular in the Greek.*

Dr. L.: Just as in English, Greek has no way to fully encapsulate the Hebrew use of the plural *Elohim* used with singular verbs. Since there is only one God, the plural word *Elohim* is rendered as singular in Greek (and in English) when it refers to the one God. The Trinity is still obvious throughout the New Testament. But the unique grammatical construction used in the *Hebrew* does not carry over into the Greek (or English) use of *Theos* (God).

Steve: *Also, even if I give you the argument that God is plural [from Genesis 1:1], since when does plurality mean solely three? Plurality could mean two or three or more.*

Dr. L.: You shouldn't expect to find a complete elucidation of a biblical doctrine in just one verse. The 3-in-1 nature of God isn't proved in Genesis — but it does disprove 1-in-1. And that was my point. The first verse of the Bible refutes Unitarianism (as well as many of the verses that follow, of course)! Genesis 1:1 gives us enough information to know that God is one in one sense, and yet more than one in another sense. We will need additional Scriptures to find out how many persons are in the Trinity, though, we need not look very far to see a glimpse of the 3-in-1 nature of God. All the persons of the Trinity are present by the third verse in the Bible. The Spirit moves over the surface of the waters in verse 2. God speaks light into existence in verse 3. This is an indication that Jesus is present — for He is the Word that is made flesh and by whom God made the universe (Colossians 1:16). The rest of the Bible gives us more information on the Trinity.

Steve: *The fact that you read these verses and walk away believing they describe some triune deity shows me your Trinitarian biases are assumed rather than read from the actual context of scripture.*

Dr. L: No — I've shown you the verses where the *text* teaches that the Son is God, and the Spirit is God. You are the one trying to claim Christ's title as God doesn't really mean that He is. I'm just letting the text say what it says.

Steve: *It is important to be aware that not every Trinitarian agrees with you that this speaks of a definitive Trinity. The following was taken from a commentary that already subscribes to a Trinitarian perspective.*

> *"Some interpreters think that the plurality within God is seen in the Hebrew word for God, 'Elohim which is plural in form (though others disagree that this is significant, the word is used with singular verbs and all agree that it has a singular meaning in the OT.)" ESV Study Bible*

Dr. L.: Well, that's a bad argument coming from the ESV Study Bible. Essentially, "Some people don't think it's significant because it's used with a singular verb." That's precisely the reason why it *is* significant!

Steve: *I only quoted this because you keep trying to make the point that the plural form of* Elohim *is an obvious reference to the Trinity. And I am trying to show you that if it is so obvious then it would be readily obvious to those who already agree with your theological position.*

Dr. L.: It *is* obvious. That's why it is disappointing that some people just haven't done their homework on this issue. But their lack of scholarship doesn't make the obvious any less obvious.

Steve: *But if it is not even obvious to them, do really think it will convince me?*

Dr. L.: It's not my job to convince you of the obvious — and I can't do that anyway. It is up to the Holy Spirit to enable you to see that Jesus is Lord (1 Corinthians 12:3). My job is simply to refute every argument that exalts itself against the knowledge of God. Arianism is certainly an attack on the Christian faith.

Steve: *Therefore, I don't think anyone can be dogmatic on these points [that the plural word used for God suggests He is more-than-one in some way].*

Dr. L.: We can rule out Unitarianism for certain in the very first verse of Genesis. The fullness of the doctrine of the Trinity is clarified and solidified in the rest of the Scriptures. Jesus does what only God can do, and there are numerous places where Jesus is referred to as deity.

The Son of God Is God the Son

Dr. L.: The Bible teaches throughout the Old and New Testaments that Jesus Christ is God. The notion that Jesus is (literally) the Son of God, but not God, really doesn't make sense if you think about it. What is the son of a man? Answer: a man. Indeed, God often calls his human servants "son of man" — see Ezekiel 2:1, 3, 6, 8, 3:1, 3–4 and Daniel 8:17. Now are we to conclude that Ezekiel and Daniel are not men, but something less than men? Of course not. The fact that each is the son of man means that he is man. Likewise, the Son of God is God. If the Son of God is of a different nature or less than God, then He isn't really the Son of God.

Steve: *I don't find your argument here convincing. "Son of God" is also applied to men throughout the Old and New Testament. Are you willing to make the huge leap in saying they are exactly equal to God himself because a son of God is God?*

Dr. L.: No — because they are not *literally the begotten* Son of God. Only Jesus is (John 3:16). You didn't read what I wrote very carefully, or think about it very carefully. A begotten son must be the same type of being as his father. This is universally true. Are any men ever referred to as the begotten Son of God besides Jesus? No. The Bible teaches that Christians are called the children (or sons) of God by the spirit of adoption (Romans 8:15; Galatians 4:5; Ephesians 1:5). An adopted son is not a begotten son, and need not be of the same nature as the (adopting) father. The Bible teaches that Jesus is the only begotten Son of God. Christ is both Son of man, and Son of God; therefore he is fully man, and fully God. The begotten son of any living being is always of the same nature as the parents; there are no exceptions.

Jesus — The Great I AM

Dr. L.: "Jesus claims to be God in John 8:58. The "I am" is not a mistake, it's one of the names of God (see Exodus 3:14) and indicates that God is self-existent and eternal. Jesus here is applying the name of God to Himself."

Steve: *The "I am" used by Christ here is the greek word* "ego eimi" *If you do careful search of it in the NT you will find it is used multiple times without an* *expressed predicate by more than just Christ. Only Trinitarians who are already preconditioned to believe in their position read OT passages into this text such as that found in Exodus.*

Dr. L.: Incorrect. This is the only place in the New Testament where the present tense "I am" is used to express past action (where it has the meaning "I was"). This passage should have leapt off the page at you for its grammatical strangeness. "Before Abraham was born, I AM." Why did Jesus not say, "Before Abraham was born I *was*"? This would be the expected grammatical construction. And by the way — even *that* would be sufficient to show that Jesus was a person from the beginning — with God and was God. He didn't say, "Before Abraham was born, there was this impersonal Logos, which eventually became me." The fact that Jesus closes the sentence with I AM seals this as a clear reference to the self-existent God. Only someone who is adamant to deny the deity of Christ would take the passage to mean anything but that Christ was claiming to be the eternal God by invoking the name that God calls Himself in Exodus 3:14. The Jews understood exactly what He was saying. He was claiming to be God. That's why they tried to stone Him (John 8:59). By your reasoning, the *Jews were right*!

Steve: *No, this is only clear to you because you read the text in English and you already have a predetermined Trinitarian bias.*

Dr. L.: With respect, you are just not thinking, Steve. If Christ did not mean to identify Himself as the I AM, then He would have said, "I was," since this is the grammatically correct way to close the sentence. His grammatical choice was a mistake if He didn't intend to identify Himself with the I AM — which is one of the names of God.

Steve: *This would not have been clear to a Jew of Christ's day who may have picked up the Septuagint.*

Dr. L.: The Scripture *explicitly* refutes you here. Yes, the Jews of Christ's day did indeed recognize that Jesus was identifying Himself with God in saying, "Before Abraham was, I AM," because they immediately tried to stone Him. This is stated in the very next verse: "Jesus said to them, 'Truly, truly, I say to you, before Abraham was born, I AM.' Therefore they picked up stones to throw at Him" (John 8:58–59). Why would they try to stone Him if Christ was not claiming to be God? Once again, a careful reading of the text confirms the deity of Christ.

Steve: *which by the way was widely in use around this time and the source-book for the Apostles own OT references. Consider what the Septuagint translates of Exodus.*

> *Exo 3:14 And God spoke to Moses, saying, I am THE BEING; and he said, Thus shall ye say to the children of Israel, THE BEING has sent me to you.*

Even in the Hebrew Bible, the same term that is translated "I AM" is the Hebrew hâyâh *which means to exist, that is, be or become.*

Dr. L.: You've strayed from the issue and have lost your point. The Septuagint translation of Exodus 3:14 is best rendered into English as "I am the one who is." But the Septuagint is not infallible as the original text is.

God actually uses the term "I AM" as one of His names by which He is referred to: Exodus 3:14. Perhaps you didn't realize that the Holy name of God *YHWY* is actually connected to the Hebrew word *hayah*. God is the only being who exists without being dependent on anyone else. He has always been and required no one to create Him. Thus, He can call Himself, "I AM" as Jesus does in John 8:58. The Jews tried to stone Him because they understood that He was identifying Himself as God (the "I AM"). They took this to be blasphemy because they failed to understand that Jesus really is God. But it's not blasphemy for God to refer to Himself as God.

Hypothetically, if Jesus were not God, then it would indeed have been blasphemy for Him to refer to Himself as the "I am." In that case, the Jews would have been right to stone Him, *and thus you really should be defending their actions if you are consistent.*

Christ — The Object of Our Worship

Dr. L.: God alone is to be worshiped (Exodus 34:14; Deuteronomy 6:13, 11:16). Jesus is to be worshiped (Hebrews 1:6; Matthew 28:9, 17, 14:33).

[The argument here is of an inductive nature — it's probabilistic rather than deductively conclusive. To "worship" means to "bow down." This can mean bowing in the sense of religious worship and surrender (of which God alone is worthy), or it can mean to bow in respect (which would be appropriate for humans). Since the word is used in either sense, a deductively conclusive argument would be difficult to make. Nonetheless, it is significant that Jesus never declines to be worshiped when people bow to Him; yet, the

Apostles and angels do not allow people to bow to them since they are not God (Acts 10:25, 14:13–14; Revelation 19:10, 22:9).]

Steve: *Understand that the term worship as is used in the NT within these passages is the greek word* "proskuneo" *which is sometimes translated "worship" to someone that is honorable. We see this same term applied to humans as found in Rev 3,*

> *Rev 3:9 Behold, I will make them of the synagogue of Satan, which say they are Jews, and are not, but do lie; behold, I will make them to come and worship* (proskuneo) *before thy feet, and to know that I have loved thee.*

Dr. L.: Not quite. "Before thy feet" indicates a state of humility, not the object of worship. They are not going to worship the feet of people! They worship (in the religious sense) God — *at* the feet of the people (in a state of humility) that they had formerly persecuted. I agree, by the way, that worship can in some instances mean simply to bow in respect.

Steve: *Because humans receive worship in an honorable context are you going to argue they are God as well?*

Dr. L.: No, that's not correct. Sinful humans are not permitted to receive worship in the religious sense. I will give more explanation below. [Steve here is confusing worship in the modern sense of the word with bowing in respect. The original biblical languages used the same word for both, so the specific meaning is determined by context. Only God is to be worshiped as God.]

Steve: *I personally subscribe to Christ's own words: "Mat 4:10 Then Jesus said to him, "Be gone, Satan! For it is written, " 'You shall worship the Lord your God and him only shall you serve.' " The word here translated "serve" is the Greek* latreuo. *It means the highest sense of worship. It is one that is applied only to God the Father himself. If you do a careful search of* latreuo *in the NT you will find that in no instance in scripture is it applied to Christ.*

Dr. L.: No, and no, and no. First, the word *latreuo* is *never* applied to the Father alone. It is applied to *God.* From the other verses we've already looked at, we know that the Son is God, the Holy Spirit is God, and the Father is God. It is the fullness of the Godhead that is to be served and worshiped. There is no verse in the New Testament that applies this word to the "Father" only.

Second, the word *latreuo* means "to serve" or "to minister" and so it is well-translated in Matthew 4:10. It does *not* mean the "highest sense of worship," and in fact would be the term used for slaves who "serve" their masters, or free men who "serve" for hire, who obviously are not worshiping as they would God (e.g., Hebrews 8:5).

Third, in context, this isn't what Satan is tempting Jesus to do. Satan uses the word *proskuneo* in Matthew 4:9. Satan wants Jesus to worship him. And Jesus responds using both *proskuneo* and *latreuo*. Only God is to be served *and* worshiped, indicating that this is in the religious sense. Thus, when Jesus accepts worship from others, either He is God, or He is contradicting what He said in Matthew 4:10.

To some extent, I can understand your confusion since "serve" can mean to serve in a less-than-ultimate sense, such as a worker serving his employer. Likewise, "worship" can simply mean to bow, or it can mean religious worship as we understand the term today. (The meaning depends on context.) This latter use is only appropriate for God, and this is the meaning of Jesus' response to Satan. In the New Testament, *proskuneo* usually refers to worship in the religious sense. And this is only acceptable for God — as Jesus indicates in Matthew 4:10. Let's look at some examples.

Cornelius inappropriately worships (*proskeneo*) Peter in Acts 10:25–26. Peter responds: "But Peter raised him up, saying, 'Stand up; I too am just a man.' " Peter refused worship because he was just a man — not God. In Revelation 19:10, John falls down to worship (*proskeneo*) an angel, but the angel replies, "Do not do that; I am a fellow servant of yours and your brethren who hold the testimony of Jesus; worship God." The angel redirects the worship to God. In Revelation 22:8–9, John again falls down to worship the angel who replies "Do not do that. I am a fellow servant of yours and of your brethren the prophets and of those who heed the words of this book. Worship God." Again, the angel refuses to be worshiped, and redirects the worship to God. These are certainly consistent with Exodus 34:14: "— for you shall not worship any other god, for the LORD, whose name is Jealous, is a jealous God."

But when Jesus is worshiped, He *never* redirects it to God because He is God (e.g., Matthew 2:2, 2:11, 14:33, 15:25, 28:9, 28:17; Luke 24:52; John 9:38). It's perfectly appropriate to worship the Son, and Hebrews

1:6 indicates that the angels worship the Son — and this must be in the religious sense, as angels cannot physically bow down since they are not physical beings.

Steve: *Dr. Lisle, that's not the perspective of the Bible.*

Dr. L.: Did you read the verses? Matthew 4:10, Revelation 19:10, 22:9. How can the verses of the Bible not be the perspective of the Bible?

Steve: *Since it's not clear to you from Revelation*

Dr. L.: Actually, it *is* clear from Revelation that only God is to be worshiped (Revelation 19:10, 22:9). Thus, the people who are brought to the feet (an indication of submission and humility) of the church of Philadelphia are worshiping God along with the Philadelphians. They're not worshiping the Philadelphians!

Steve: *then consider other examples in the OT where humans receive worship.* Shâchâh *is the Hebrew equivalent of* proskuneo.

> *1Ch 29:20 And David said to all the congregation, Now bless the Lord your God. And all the congregation blessed the Lord God of their fathers, and bowed down their heads, and worshipped (*Shâchâh*) the Lord, and the king.*

Notice here how the Lord and David both received worshiped.

Dr. L.: It appears that you did not read carefully what I wrote. To "worship" means to "bow down" — this can either mean to (1) physically bow in respect, (which would be a perfectly acceptable way for one human to honor another), or (2) religious worship which is only appropriate for God. We know that it is in the second sense that Jesus is worshiped, for the reasons I gave last time. But the examples you give are all of the first type — physically bowing in honor of a man.

The Greek word translated as "worship" is *Proskuneo* and is usually used in the second sense of "worship" — divine worship. The Hebrew word that is translated as "worship" or "bow down" is *shachah* which is primarily used in the first sense — as in bowing in respect to a person. I note that all the examples you listed are from the Old Testament, where "bowing in respect" would be the main use of the word. But the topic of discussion was whether or not worshiping Jesus is appropriate in the religious sense, and thus, the Greek word is the one at issue.

Steve: *Consider other examples from the Bible*

> *Gen 19:1 And there came two angels to Sodom at even; and Lot sat in the gate of Sodom: and Lot seeing them rose up to meet them; and he bowed himself (*Shâchâh*) with his face toward the ground*

And I can go on to cite other examples but I think the above should suffice. Clearly the term "worship" or Shâchâh *applies to humans as well.*

Dr. L.: Yes — the Hebrew word does. But that wasn't the point at issue. So this is another red-herring fallacy. By the way, I fully agree that even the New Testament word *Proskuneo* can — in some contexts — refer to bowing (not "worshiping" as we would say it in English) in respect for a person who is not God. But I gave reasons why this is not the way the term is applied to Jesus. I guess you didn't read what I wrote very carefully. [People who don't read the Bible carefully often do not read letters carefully either. I found this to be the case with Steve.]

Steve: *Of course though, we know that God alone receives the highest sense of worship. Because you assume Jesus is God every time you see "worship" associated with him you assume this is the same as the highest sense of worship given only to God. Then you turn around and argue because Christ is associated with the term worship he must be God. But once again, this is circular reasoning; you assume your beliefs only to argue the meaning of the word "worship" in its context.*

Dr. L.: Another straw-man fallacy, since this wasn't my argument. I showed why *Proskuneo* must be in the divine sense by a making a case for it, which you have merely ignored. In the temptation of Matthew 4, Satan tempts Jesus to worship Him (*Proskuneo*). If this were an appropriate (physical) bowing of respect, then Jesus' response would be a mistake! He indicates that it would be inappropriate, and that we should worship and serve God only. Clearly the divine sense of *Proskuneo* is in play, otherwise Jesus' rebuttal makes no sense.

When Proskuneo is applied to the Apostles or an angel, the person who worshiped is sharply rebuked — which wouldn't make sense if it were merely bowing in respect. Angels are not physical beings — they are spirits, and thus cannot physically bow in respect. Thus, when they are told to worship God the Son, it is *necessarily* in the religious sense of the word (Hebrews 1:6). It's a cogent case.

The Trinity Is ONE God, in THREE Persons — not Three Gods

[This is moved from another section, where I had pointed out that the Bible teaches that we have only one Savior.]

Steve: *Wow, I find it funny here that you are arguing ONE here means only numeral one, but with the Trinity you take "one" to include plurality.*

Dr. L.: That's another straw-man fallacy. It reveals that you don't understand the concept of the Trinity. The Trinity affirms that there is one God. One God. I'll repeat this in case you missed it again: *One God.* But logically, this doesn't mean that this one God cannot be more than one in persons. Many things are like this. A church is one church. But it is more than one in persons. Time is one in dimensions, but three in perspectives (past, present, future). These aren't exactly the same as the Trinity, but it should be obvious that things can be one in one sense and more than one *in another sense.*

If you insist that everything that is one cannot be more than one in some other way, then you are logically reduced to a monistic worldview ("all is one"). After all, the universe is one universe. But if it is not also more than one in another sense, then the universe cannot have any diversity or plurality within it. And so you would be like the Hindus who believe that everything is one, and that distinction is merely an illusion.

Steve: *You can't have it both ways.*

Dr. L.: Respectfully, you could benefit very much from a class on logic. The law of non-contradiction states that A and not-A cannot both be true at the same time *and in the same sense*. Apparently, you are confused about the last part of the law, so I will give an explanation and some examples. There are many things that are A in one sense, and not-A in another sense. Joe is three inches taller than his older brother Mike. Who is the "big brother"? In one sense it is Mike, but in another sense it is Joe (not-Mike). "Betty just got a new truck," says Person A. Person B says, "No she didn't. That truck is ten years old." Is the truck new? "Yes" in one sense — new to Betty, but "no" in another sense — in terms of bluebook age. Steve, many of the errors in reasoning that you have committed involve a simple misunderstanding of this very basic principle.

Of course something can be one in one sense and more than one in another sense. A man is one in terms of personage, but (at least) two in natures (since He is both flesh and spirit). An atom is one in terms of its essential properties, but three in terms of its constituent particles. The entire universe is one in one sense (it's one universe) and many in another sense (it contains many things). That's where the word "universe" comes from: uni = ONE, verse = many (as in "diverse").

In Genesis 1:1 when God (*Elohim* — plural) created (*bara* — singular) the heavens and the earth, He made it a type of "trinity" as well — not exactly the same type of Trinity that He is, but nonetheless, a three-in-one. Space, time, and matter are three, and yet one universe. Each of these is also a type of trinity. Space is three in dimensions, but one in nature. Time is one in dimensions but three in terms of perspective (past, present, future). Matter is one in nature, but three in constituents (protons, electrons, neutrons) and is found as solid, liquid, or gas. And so when the Bible speaks of God as one in one sense, and more than one in another sense, we have absolutely *no excuse* for denying this principle, since God has given us a universe full of examples. Indeed, the Bible states that from the creation of the world God's invisible attributes, His eternal power and divine nature (Godhead) have been clearly seen, being understood through what has been made, so that those who would deny it are without excuse (Romans 1:20). There is literally no excuse for denying the triune nature of God.

Jesus/God Is Our Only Savior. The Logical Trilemma

Dr. L.: God is the only Savior (Isaiah 43:11, 21–22). Jesus is the only Savior (Acts 4:12; Titus 2:13; 2 Peter 3:18).

Steve: *Yes, God is the only Savior, he accomplished this through Jesus Christ. Christ himself said he did not act on his own accord but God gave him the power to do so. I don't see anything here that would conflict with my Unitarian beliefs.*

Dr. L.: With respect, you apparently haven't read this carefully or thought about it very carefully, Steve. The Bible teaches that there is only *one* Savior. Since you deny that Jesus is God, I must ask who is the Savior, Jesus or God? If you say "Jesus but not God," then you deny Isaiah 43:11, 21–22 and Titus 2:10. If you say "God but not Jesus," then you deny Acts 4:12, Titus 2:13, 2 Peter3:18, Ephesians 5:23, and 2 Timothy 1:10. If you say "both Jesus and God — two different beings" then you deny Isaiah 43:11, 21–22 which state that God is the *only* Savior, and Acts 4:12 which teaches that there is only *one* name that brings salvation. The Bible teaches explicitly that there is exactly *one* Savior — not two. The only way to avoid contradiction is to recognize that Jesus is God. The Bible teaches that Jesus is our God and Savior (Titus 2:13, 3:4, 6).

Steve: *In response to your point, God is the only savior.*

Dr. L.: I'll hold you to that. Then it follows logically that Jesus must be God. The Bible explicitly states that Jesus is our Savior. It does not say that Jesus is merely the conduit through which our Savior works, as you seem to want to believe. Rather, the text says that Jesus is our Savior (KJV):

> Acts 13:23 "Of this man's seed hath God according to his promise raised unto Israel a Savior, Jesus."
>
> Philippians 3:20 "For our conversation is in heaven; from whence also we look for the Savior, the Lord Jesus Christ."
>
> 2 Timothy 1:10 "But is now made manifest by the appearing of our Savior Jesus Christ, who hath abolished death, and hath brought life and immortality to light through the gospel."
>
> Titus 1:4 "To Titus, mine own son after the common faith: Grace, mercy, and peace, from God the Father and the Lord Jesus Christ our Savior."
>
> Titus 3:6 "Which he shed on us abundantly through Jesus Christ our Savior."

Steve: *He accomplished this salvation through Jesus Christ. Christ as the savior of mankind. . . .*

Dr. L.: Oops! Here you just contradicted yourself. You've stated (1) that God is the only Savior, (2) Christ is the savior. (So far, so good — no contradiction yet). But your third premise is (3) Christ is not God. Now you have a logical impossibility. No matter how you combine these premises, your view is self-contradictory. Let's try the other combinations to see this:

> From premise (1), God is the only Savior,
> and (your) premise (3), Christ is not God,
> we can conclude that Christ is not the Savior — which contradicts premise (2).
> Alternatively, from premise (2), Christ is the Savior
> from (your) premise (3) Christ is not God,

we must conclude: God is not the only Savior — which contradicts premise 1.

Lastly, we take premise (1) that God is the only Savior,

premise (2) Christ is the Savior,

and conclude: Christ is God. This, of course, is the correct answer, but it contradicts your premise (3).

So, you see, Steve, you are in a logical bind. The Bible does teach premise (1), God is the only Savior, and premise (2), Jesus is the Savior. The logical conclusion is that Jesus must be God, which contradicts your theology. Thus, you have three choices:

(1) Give up your theology.

(2) Give up inerrancy (reject those Scriptures that teach either (1) or (2)).

(3) Give up logic.

As I mentioned last time, you will have to give up either rationality or biblical inerrancy to maintain the theology that you are following. And this has now been very clearly demonstrated.

Steve: *. . . constantly pointed to his Father who gave him the power and strength to accomplish his will in giving salvation to mankind.*

Dr. L.: Jesus said that He and His Father are one, and that to see Him is to see the Father. In His earthly ministry and human nature, Jesus humbled Himself, and emptied Himself of the outward appearance of equality with the Father as the Bible teaches in Philippians 2:6–8.

You didn't really ask, but just in case you are wondering, the biblical position on salvation is that it is a gift from God. It was accomplished through Jesus who is God. Jesus was sent from the Father to accomplish salvation, and it is the Holy Spirit who enables us to say that Jesus is Lord. Salvation involves all three persons of the Trinity. The biblical Christian can say with confidence that Jesus Christ is our God and our only Savior. This is the only way to avoid logical contradictions in the above passages, and the ones which you previously listed (below):

Steve:

Jud 1:24 Now to him who is able to keep you from stumbling and to present you blameless before the presence of his glory with great joy,

Jud 1:25 to the only God, our Savior, THROUGH Jesus Christ our Lord, be glory, majesty, dominion, and authority, before all time and now and forever. Amen.

Dr. L.: These verses make sense in light of the fact that Jesus is God the Son. This is why the Bible can say that God is the only Savior, and in other passages that Jesus is the Savior, and yet there is only one Savior.

The Lord Is My Shepherd

Dr. L.: God is our Shepherd (Psalm 23; Ezekiel 34:11). Jesus is our Shepherd (John 10:11).

Steve: *Various times in the OT are the leaders of Israel called shepherds. Since when does that make them God himself? Indeed God does appoint people to "shepherd" his flock, but he himself is the ultimate Shepherd.*

Dr. L.: The problem (for the position you are advocating) is that the Bible teaches that there is only ONE ultimate shepherd (Ezekiel 37:24). It teaches that God is that ultimate Shepherd (Ezekiel 34:12; Psalm 23:1, 80:1), and it teaches that Jesus is the ultimate Shepherd (Hebrews 13:20; 1 Peter 5:4), which makes sense since He is God. Remember, Jesus says that He is the Good Shepherd (John 10:11, 14). He is *the* good Shepherd. He does not say, "I am one of two Good Shepherds." There is only one Shepherd who is absolutely good, and that Shepard is the God-man Jesus. By the way, Jesus also said that "No one is good except God alone." So if Jesus really is the GOOD Shepherd, then He is God. If Jesus is not God, then He is not good by His own statement. There just isn't any way around it.

Steve: *I am actually surprised you quoted from Ezekiel because Ezekiel definitely is in contrast to what you just said.*

Dr. L.: Not at all. It's what I based my statement on.

Steve:

Eze 34:23 And I will set up over them one shepherd, my servant David, and he shall feed them: he shall feed them and be their shepherd.

Eze 34:24 And I, the LORD, will be their God, and my servant David shall be prince among them. I am the LORD; I have spoken.

Notice here that it is the one God that SETS UP his SERVANT David (Jesus) as the one shepherd over the people.

Dr. L.: Oops! You've got another contradiction. Is Jesus the one Shepherd or is God the one Shepherd? In your view, you can't have both. But the Scriptures teach both! God is the Shepherd (e.g., Psalm 23:1, 80:1). Jesus is the Shepherd (John 10:11). The heretical teaching just cannot bring those verses into harmony.

Steve: *He then goes on to say that He shall be their God, and Jesus shall be the prince. Where are you getting this idea that Jesus is the highest shepherd of the people if he is appointed by the one God of Israel?*

Dr. L.: The Bible. Specifically 1 Peter 5:4 which speaks of Christ as the Chief Shepherd. Hebrews 13:20 also seems fitting. And although you conveniently ignored this, I'll remind you that Jesus used the definite article: He said that He is *the* Good Shepherd (John 10:11, 14). *The Good Shepherd.* Jesus did NOT say, "There are two Good Shepherds, myself, and God." He said that He is "The Good Shepherd." Now if Jesus was telling the truth and He really is *the* Good Shepherd, and not merely "a" good shepherd, and if we assume for argument's sake that Jesus is not God, then it follows logically that God is NOT a good shepherd (because then Jesus couldn't be THE Good Shepherd). But we've already looked at the verses which show that God is a Shepherd. So we must conclude either that Jesus is God, or that God is not good — which is contradictory. So once again, we see that by denying the Trinity, we are forced into irrationality.

Steve: *In response to your statement, "No one is good except God alone," I have already mentioned this above. You clearly must have missed what Christ said before this, "Why do you call me good?" in other words it is not him he is referring to but instead he directed his listeners to the one God Himself.*

Dr. L.: I've already shown that your interpretation of what Christ is saying is self-refuting. Think about it, Steve. Was Christ's sentence true? Is there no one good except God alone, or was Jesus lying? If (1) Jesus was telling the truth and God alone is good, and if (2) Jesus is not God, then it follows conclusively that (3) *Jesus is not good.* But if He is not good, then He cannot atone for sin. Alternatively, if Jesus was lying, then He is not good and cannot atone for sin. Salvation is not possible in a Unitarian system. And it contradicts dozens of verses that describe the sinless nature of Jesus. So again, the heretical view simply cannot stand up to logical scrutiny. People deny the Trinity because it's easier, not because of the Scriptures.

Steve: *Also a verse found in Micah conclusively demonstrates that though Christ is Shepherd over his flock he still is in submission to God Almighty.*

> *Mic 5:4 And he shall stand and shepherd his flock in the strength of the Lord, in the majesty of the name of the Lord HIS God. And they shall dwell secure, for now he shall be great to the ends of the earth.*

Dr. L.: That's certainly true. Since Jesus is God, the Scriptures can rightly refer to God as the Shepherd, and Jesus as the good Shepherd without contradiction. However, the verse you cited is in conflict with the view you espouse.

The Names of God Are the Names of Christ

Steve: *I would be happy to respond to all of your points in the future but I don't want to say too much and the meaning gets lost in everything.*

Dr. L.: You'll have to give up either rationality or inerrancy to stay with your current position. Denial of the deity of Jesus explicitly contradicts the Scriptures (e.g., Colossians 2:9) and will lead to internal contradictions of the Scriptures as I showed previously. Who is our "Rock"? The Bible teaches that God is our *only* Rock (Isaiah 44:8; Psalm 18:31, 62:2, 6; 1 Samuel 2:2; 2 Samuel 22:32; Deuteronomy 32:4; Psalm 18:31). Yet it teaches that Jesus is our Rock (1 Corinthians 10:4; Romans 9:33). This contradicts, unless Jesus is God.

In Zechariah 12:10, referring to the crucifixion (quoted in John 19:37), God says that "they will look on Me whom they have pierced." The "Me" is not a mistake; it's an indication that God Himself is the one who is crucified. This makes sense since Jesus is God. One of the names of God is "the Holy One" (Psalm 71:22, 78:22; Isaiah 30:15). God is THE Holy One because He alone is Holy (Revelation 15:4). And since Jesus is God, He is also referred to as the Holy One (Psalm 16:10; Acts 2:27, 13:35; John 6:69). If Jesus were not God then He would not by THE Holy One, and the Bible would have contradictions. We can only be called holy by Christ's imputed righteousness.

One of God's names that He says of Himself is, "I am the first, I am also the last." (Isaiah 48:12). Isaiah 44:6 says, "Thus says the Lord, the King of Israel and his Redeemer, the Lord of hosts: 'I am the first and I am the last, and there is no God besides Me.' " God the Son repeats this in Revelation 1:17: "I am the first and the last," and this is clearly Jesus speaking given what He says in the next verse. Jesus again calls Himself "the first and the last" in Revelation 2:8. In Revelation 22:13, God the Son says, "I am the Alpha and the Omega, the first and the last, the beginning and the end." The Lord God Almighty is the One "Who is and who was and who is to come" (Revelation 1:8).

Here is an interesting one. God is the judge of all the earth (Psalm 7:11, 50:6, 94:2; 1 Chronicles 16:33; Psalm 82:8, 105:7; Romans 3:6; Revelation 19:2; Isaiah 26:9; Genesis 15:13, 18:25; Hebrews 12:23). The Scriptures are clear, yes? But God the Father does not judge anyone (John 5:22). It is the Son who judges (John 5:22; Acts 10:42; 2 Corinthians 5:10; Matthew 16:27, 25:31; 2 Timothy 4:1; 1 Peter 4:5). Therefore, all the verses that speak of God judging must be referring to God the Son, since the Father does not judge.

Steve: *Dr. Lisle why do you only quote from John 5:22? Even though Christ does say the Father judges no man in this verse three chapters later he then goes on to say that he judges no man.*

> *Joh 8:15 Ye judge after the flesh; I judge no man.*
>
> *Joh 8:16 And yet if I judge, my judgment is true: for I am not alone, but I and the Father that sent me.*

Therefore it is clear to me that both of these verses are context dependent and not meant to be used as some sort of overarching hermeneutical principle in interpreting the roles of action by the Father and the Son.

Dr. L.: Again, you have not paid attention to the context. The meaning is context dependent — that's always the case. But I guess you didn't look at the context of these verses. John 5 is an extended discourse on the relationships and responsibilities of the Father and the Son. We learn from this passage that while God is the judge, it is the second person of the Trinity specifically who has the authority to execute judgment (John 5:27) since He is also the Son of Man. This is confirmed in Acts 10:42. John 8 in context is referring to Christ's earthly ministry — His purpose in taking on human nature and coming to earth in the flesh was not to judge the world, but to save it. This is explained in John 3:17.

This being answered, my point remains. God is the judge. But God the Father does not judge apart from the Son. It is the Son who is given authority to judge. If the Son is not God, then the Scriptures contradict. So once again, you must decide whether to give up your theology, or the verses that contradict it, or logic.

Steve: *By the way, I just thought I let you know that the term "God the Son" is completely absent from scripture. This is purely a Trinitarian invention. Now, you can find the term God the Father mentioned in the Bible.*

Dr. L.: The term "Wednesday" is completely absent from the Bible. Shall we then conclude that the Bible teaches that there is no such thing as Wednesday? The Bible never says that the Apostle John used the bathroom. Should we conclude therefore that he didn't? Come on Steve, you're smarter than this. In the Jewish culture, to be the begotten "son of" X is to be equal in terms of nature. I have shown the verses that prove this. Thus, all references to Christ as the "Son of God" are logically equivalent to "God the Son." Jesus, the Son of God, is directly called God in a number of verses (e.g., John 20:28; Hebrews 1:8; John 1:1).

Christ Is the LORD

Steve: *In regards to your comments on Romans 10:9 this is incorrect. Confessing Christ as Lord is not the same as addressing him as YHWH. Consider how David addresses Christ in Psalm 110:1.*

Dr. L.: No. This is a red-herring fallacy, because Paul does not defend Romans 10:9 with Psalm 110:1. Rather he defends it by quoting Joel 2:32. So you are not reading the text in context, nor comparing texts contextually. Paul argues that we must call upon Jesus as Lord to be saved (Romans 10:9). To support this, Paul quotes Joel 2:32, which teaches that all who call upon the name of the Lord shall be saved. And what is the word used for "Lord" in Joel 2:32? It is *YHWH*. Thus, only by calling upon Jesus as *YHWH* can we be saved.

Steve:

> *Psa 110:1 A Psalm of David. The LORD (*yehôvâh*) said unto my Lord (*âdôn*), Sit thou at my right hand, until I make thine enemies thy footstool.*

*Christ here is addressed by the Hebrew word "*adon*" which is Lord as applied to human masters. He is not addressed as "*ădônây*" which is Lord that*

ONLY applies to God alone. For sure he is not addressed as YHWH. *On the contrary it is* YHWH *speaking to the Lord of David.*

Dr. L.: Here, you got one thing right, but several other things wrong. Let's start with the good news. *Adonai*, being a plural form of *Adon* is indeed a reference to God when used with a singular noun. Like *Elohim*, it shows that God is one in one sense, and yet more than one in another sense. (*Adonai* can be used for men, but only with a plural verb, as in Genesis 19:2, 18).

Adon often refers to humans, but it can refer to God as well, as in Exodus 34:23 where the "Lord God" is "*Adon YHWH.*" Other passage where *Adon* clearly refers to Almighty God include Joshua 3:11, 3:13; Nehemiah 8:10, 10:29; Psalm 8:1, 8:9, 97:5, 114:7, 135:5, 147:5; Isaiah 1:24, 3:1, 10:16, 10:33, 19:4, 51:22; Micah 4:13; Zechariah 4:14, 6:5; and Malachi 3:1 (in the Masoretic text — see below). So again, whoever you are reading really doesn't know his Bible, and is a sloppy researcher. [Here I am giving Steve a way to "save face" in the midst of his ridiculous claim. He can blame the error on another if he likes. But it is a bad error nonetheless.]

Most significantly, the term translated as "Lord" (the second term) in Psalm 110:1, is in fact *Adonai* in the most ancient extant Hebrew texts — which as you pointed out is only applied to Almighty God. It is rendered as *Adoni* ("my lord" — essentially *Adon*) only in the Masoretic text (~A.D. ninth century). The Masoretes of the 9th century were Jews who rejected Jesus as Messiah and God. But older manuscripts, such as the Qumran scrolls (~1000 years older than the Masoretic text) have it as *Adonai.*

Actually, it doesn't really matter whether the word is *Adoni* or *Adonai* in verse 1 (vowel points were not in the original text anyway), because context demonstrates that it is a reference to Almighty God either way. (It's a pity that whoever you're reading did not continue reading to verse 5; he might have avoided his error.) Psalm 110:5 refers to David's Lord as *Adonai* in both Masoretic and older scrolls. Yes, David's Lord who sits at the right hand of *YHWH* is unquestionably referred to as the Lord (*Adonai*) in verse 5. Again, many errors in exegesis can be avoided by simply reading the text carefully.

Moreover, we have the context of the rest of the Bible. Since Psalm 110:1 speaks of David's Lord, we should ask, "According to the Scriptures, who is David's Lord?"

> Psalm 16:2, "I said to the Lord [*YHWY*], You are my Lord [*Adonai*]; I have no good besides You."

> Psalm 35:23, "Stir up Yourself, and awake to my right and to my cause, my God [*Elohim*] and my Lord [*Adonai*]."

> Psalm 38:15, "For I hope in You, O LORD [*YHWH*]; You will answer, O Lord [*Adonai*] my God [*Elohim*].

Even in the Masoretic text, it is clear that David's lord (*adon*) is the Lord God: Psalm 8:9, "O Lord [*YHWH*] our Lord [*adon*], how majestic is Your name in all the earth!"

Steve: *Clearly I am well within my biblical allowances to confess Christ as Lord as my ruling authority and not as the Lord God.*

Dr. L.: No, you are not. No man can serve two masters (Matthew 6:24; Luke 16:13). If Christ is not your God, then He is not your Lord and He is not your Savior. If Christ is just a man, and not also God, then He is a sinner, and thus cannot redeem you.

> Ecclesiastes 7:20, "Indeed, there is not a righteous man on earth who continually does good and who never sins."

> Romans 3:10, "As it is written, there is none righteous, no, not one."

> Romans 3:23, "for all have sinned and fall short of the glory of God."

> Psalm 14:2–3, etc.

If Christ is not your God, then He is not your Savior, because God alone is the Savior. Isaiah 43:11, "I, even I, am the LORD, And there is no savior besides Me."

> Isaiah 45:21, "A righteous God and a Savior; There is none except Me."

> Hosea 13:4, "Yet I have been the LORD your God since the land of Egypt; and you were not to know any god except Me, for there is no savior besides Me."

> Isaiah 63:8, "For He said, 'Surely, they are My people, sons who will not deal falsely.' So He became their Savior."

Thus, if you continue to deny Christ as God, (and I sincerely pray that you don't) you will spend an eternity separated from Him in the lake of fire. This is the ultimate end for people who refuse to allow the Scriptures to inform their theology. [This may sound harsh. But it is truth that Steve needed to hear. He still did not realize that he was worshiping a false messiah — a Jesus who is not God and who exists only in his mind. And he had not responded to my earlier more subtle correction.]

Steve: *Furthermore, who is it that gets the glory by confessing Christ as Lord? Well Paul makes that clear "to the glory of God the Father." — Philippians 2:11*

Dr. L.: Only when Christ is confessed as Lord (*YHWH*) is it to the glory of the Father. And this was the point I made last time, which you failed to answer, or even address. The Bible states that we must confess Jesus as Lord in order to be saved (Romans 10:9–10). You want to take this to mean "lord" in a sense less than God. But is this what Paul really means? Does he mean that we must confess Jesus as *a* lord, or as *the* Lord (*YHWH*)? Look at the context! To prove his point, Paul cites the Old Testament passage, "Whoever will call on the name of the Lord will be saved" in Romans 10:13. Clear? Paul is saying that we must confess Jesus as Lord, because whoever will call on the name of the Lord will be saved. The Old Testament passage Paul is quoting is Joel 2:32. In this passage, the "Lord" being referred to is *YHWH*. Paul proves His point, that we must call upon the name of Jesus to be saved, by showing that the Old Testament claims that we must call upon *YHWH* to be saved. So obviously, Paul is using "Lord" in the sense of *YHWH*, otherwise He would be taking the Old Testament out of context.

Steve: *Lastly, Christ was MADE Lord by God. If Christ is inherently the LORD God as you proclaim then the statement "made Lord" is pointless. If he is "made" Lord then by definition he was not Lord before.*

> *Act 2:36 Therefore let all the house of Israel know assuredly, that God hath made that same Jesus, whom ye have crucified, both Lord and Christ.*

Dr. L.: <<Sigh>>. Again, this just isn't good reasoning. The meaning of a term depends on its context. Although Jesus was God from all eternity, he was only made Messiah and messianic King at the time of the incarnation. Psalm 2 teaches this in regard to Christ's kingship — and this is the sense of "Lord" in this passage. Yes, He was Lord God from all eternity. But He was installed as the King of Zion at the incarnation.

Characteristics That Apply Only to God Are Applied to Jesus

Dr. L.: Isaiah 45:23, God says "To Me every knee will bow, every tongue will swear allegiance." But this is clearly God the Son speaking, because it is to Jesus that every knee shall bow (Philippians 2:10).

God is called the "husband" of His people (Isaiah 54:5). The New Testament clarifies that it is Christ who is the husband of God's people (2 Corinthians 11:2–3; Ephesians 5:25–32; Revelation 19:7). This will contradict unless Jesus really is God.

Zechariah 14:9 teaches that the LORD will be king over all the earth and the only one. God is the sovereign Kings of kings and Lord of lords (1 Timothy 6:15). But other Scriptures teach that Jesus is the King of kings and Lord of lords (Revelation 17:14, 19:16). Are you beginning to see how many verses would contradict if Jesus were not truly God? Many others could be listed. These are just the tip of the iceberg.

Steve: *As far as the texts you've quoted which makes direct similarities between God and Christ proves nothing to me. If I said today, "Job is a man who is perfect and blameless" and if I turn around tomorrow and say, "God is perfect and blameless." Would this prove Job is God? No it only would prove Job is perfect and blameless.*

Dr. L.: That's the fallacy of the undistributed middle (again.) That is quite different from the argument I had made. I was *not* merely pointing out similarities between descriptions of Jesus and descriptions of God. Rather, I showed that the Bible teaches that there are some characteristics that apply *only* to God. And the Bible attributes many of these to Jesus. This contradicts unless Jesus is God. These were of the same form as the "only Savior" point I made above. Similarly, the Bible states that Jesus/God is our *only* Rock, Lord, God, etc. It appears that you did not carefully read my arguments. Take a look at them again with this in mind. They have the following formula:

1. God is our **only** (X)
2. Jesus is (X)
3. Thus, Jesus is God, (otherwise there would be *two* Xs, which contradicts 1.)

The logic is really not difficult. Why do you not want to accept the necessary conclusion?

Faith and Prayer

Steve: *Please though, I ask that you not think down on me because I disagree with you on this topic.*

Dr. L.: I don't look "down" on you — not at all. Christians are not superior to anyone else. We're just forgiven. I am concerned for you though. You're following a cult at the moment, and that path doesn't end well.

Steve: *I have prayed day and night over this issue and have asked God to guide me spiritually in correctly understanding his word.*

Dr. L.: Do you suppose it is possible that God has answered your prayer through this very text? Sometimes God answers our prayers, and we don't even realize it because we were expecting Him to answer in a different way.

Steve: *I hope that you believe me.*

Dr. L.: I do believe that you are sincerely having trouble seeing the unmistakable evidence of the Trinity found throughout the text of the Bible. This goes back to what I said earlier. It is obvious to any Christian that Jesus is God. No one else is worthy to pay for our high treason against God — no one else's life has sufficient value to pay an infinite penalty. But to those who don't have saving faith, there are some things that they simply cannot understand. The Trinity may very well be one of them. Faith must precede understanding, for it is by faith that we understand (e.g., Hebrews 11:3). In other words, you will have to trust in Christ as Lord God on the basis of the text of Scripture *before* an understanding of the details will become clear.

Steve: *I have tried my best to be humble and accept what the Bible says.*

Dr. L.: I appreciate you writing that. But you need to accept what it says about the Son. For example, in Hebrews 1:8, God the Father says to the Son, "Your throne, O God, is forever and ever." The deity of Christ is in the other verses I listed, and many that I didn't. If you say, "That doesn't make sense to me. Therefore, I will not accept it," then you do not have saving faith. God doesn't require us to understand everything about His nature — we can't. But He does require us to have faith in what He says about Himself.

Steve: *Please don't view me as someone "unsaved" because it personally hurts a little when people whom I respect for their Godly convictions see me this way.*

Dr. L.: I wouldn't be a friend if I called you "saved" when you deny Jesus as Lord (*YHWH*). Because I do accept what the Scriptures teach about

Christ and about salvation, I know that salvation is only found in the Lord (*YHWH*) Jesus. And confessing Jesus as Lord is a requirement for salvation (Romans 10:9, 13). But this will only be possible if God grants you a saving faith in Him, because "no one can say 'Jesus is Lord' except by the Holy Spirit" (1 Corinthians 12:3).

Steve: *As I told my former pastor, I understand your perspective differs from mine, but yet I do believe we will see each other in heaven.*

Dr. L.: That will only happen if you repent, and confess Christ as Lord (Romans 10:9, 13). I pray that you do, but that is between you and God. I believe that I have fulfilled my obligation to be ready to give a defense of the faith (1 Peter 3:15).

Steve: *Once again, I am really sorry to grieve you Dr. Lisle. I personally don't wish this on any good friend. However, my faith compels me to be true to scripture.*

Dr. L.: Thank you for that kind thought. I'm concerned for you of course. You've been taken in by a cult; they are using really bad arguments (logical fallacies) and are not taking Scripture in context. But people get pulled in psychologically and it can be difficult to break away from such things. Nonetheless, perhaps the Lord will help you out of this, and perhaps He will even use some of what I've written as part of the process. I pray so. But He will do as He pleases.

Regarding faith and being true to Scripture, I would just point out that Muslims, Mormons, Jehovah's Witnesses, and any other cult members all believe that they're faithfully following the Scriptures. People read the Scriptures with "rose-colored glasses" so that they only see what they want to see. You've accused me of that (I'm not offended — I'm saying the same thing about you anyway), but my point is that this should give us all pause, because clearly these contradictory systems of faith cannot all be true. Moreover, we cannot appeal to our conscience or our feelings of personal contentment since these are unreliable. But we know that God does not deny Himself. Thus, a correct understanding of Scripture will be one that is non-contradictory. And we've seen that the Unitarian position contradicts verse after verse after verse.

To be clear, correct theology will have some paradoxes (paradoxes seem contradictory on the surface, but do not genuinely break any rules of logic — like the twin paradox of relativity) since God is infinite and since His ways and thoughts are infinitely higher than ours (Isaiah 55:8–9). If you can comprehend every aspect of God, then He isn't God. This is why it is so important that we do not try to make God fit our finite and fallible sense of what is possible.

Steve: *I must harmonize myself completely to the faith of the Lord Jesus Christ. He himself submitted to the one God of Israel who is the Almighty Ruler of the Universe.*

Dr. L.: Which Jesus? The one who is God (John 1:1; Hebrews 1:8), and who, as God, created the universe (John 1:3; Genesis 1:1; Colossians 1:16; Hebrews 1:2) and upholds all things by the expression of His power (Hebrews 1:3)? Or a Jesus of your own making who is not God? That latter cannot save you.

Steve: *Am I perfect? By no means! As a human I realize I am subject to error. I can only trust in God to deliver me from my imperfections and create in me the complete image of His son. This is my prayer daily. Hopefully you can understand my convictions.*

Dr. L.: Perhaps the Lord has answered your prayer in allowing me to give you a very explicit response to each and every one of the mistakes in exegesis that you had been claiming. It is between you and Him as to how you will respond.

Are Christians and Unitarians brothers in Christ?

Steve: *Your brother in Christ, Steve*

Dr. L.: I like you very much, but again I must point out that we are not brothers in Christ. My Jesus is the sovereign, uncreated King of kings, the Creator and Almighty Lord of all, the omniscient, and all-powerful God of heaven and earth, who upholds the entire universe by the expression of His power. My Christ is my Creator and my Savior. He is perfectly holy and true to God, since He is and always has been God. My Christ, as God, is infinite in power, knowledge, and majesty. And that is very different from your Christ. Even if I (for argument's sake) assume that you are right, and that I'm wrong in believing that Jesus is God, it should be obvious that we do not have the same Christ. One of us is trusting in a false Messiah. Indeed, if you genuinely believe that I am worshiping someone as God who isn't actually God, then you shouldn't consider me a brother in the faith, but an idolater.

[The fact that Steve considered me a "brother in Christ" shows that the he really hasn't thought through his position. I worship as God someone who Steve thinks is not God — that should be idolatry from his perspective.]

The Scriptures indicate in many places that God is one, and that there is only one God. And yet, in just as many places the Scriptures teach that there is a more-than-one aspect to God's nature. The Scriptures teach that the Son (the Word, Jesus Christ) is God, that the Father is God, and that the Holy Spirit is God, and that it has always been that way. This makes people uncomfortable, because it's hard to understand. People are inclined therefore to eliminate this tension by slicing off either the plural aspects of God's nature, or the single aspects of God's nature. Both of these positions are mistakes; both lead to a grievous misunderstanding of who God really is. This is why the Trinity is a non-negotiable Christian doctrine.

Summary and Conclusions

I have not included here my closing comments to Steve, as they are not directly relevant to the debate. I basically pleaded with Steve to repent and I presented and explained the gospel, showing why only Christ as the incarnate God is worthy to pay the penalty for our sin.

In reviewing our exchange, I must note that this is *not* a debate between two Christians who have a legitimate disagreement over an obscure or difficult doctrine. Rather, it is a debate between a believer and an unbeliever over whether the Bible is true in something that it directly teaches throughout. Steve was adept at coming up with excuses as to why the text does not really mean what it says; that is, that the title of God is merely "honorary" when applied to Christ. But there is no logical warrant or textual basis for such a claim. It is the fallacy of the superfluous distinction. Such arbitrariness violates the most basic principles of hermeneutics.

If arbitrary distinctions were acceptable, we could "prove" absolutely anything from Scripture — no matter how insane. We could argue that God the Father is not really God, and that His title as "God" is merely honorary. We could argue that the Apostle Peter was actually a *housecat*, and that any personhood attributed to him was merely honorary. But how could a cat write two epistles? No problem — we could just claim that God supernaturally enabled the cat to write them. Once we drop the requirement that claims must be backed up by good reasons, *anything* can be claimed, no matter how absurd or heretical.

Additionally, we saw no shortage of logical and hermeneutical fallacies in Steve's thinking. But one particular error in reasoning stands out: a failure to recognize qualified distinctions. This fallacy occurs when a person falsely claims that two statements are contradictory because he or she has ignored the last part of the law of non-contradiction. The law states that it is impossible to have both A and not-A at the same time *and in the same sense*. Steve did not seem to understand those last five words. And this resulted in faulty theology.

Can a person be heavy and also light at the same time? Yes, if the person is heavy in the sense of weight, and also light in the sense of complexion. There is no contradiction here because the sense is different. Can a feather be dark and light at the same time? Certainly — if the feather is light in terms of weight, and dark in terms of color. Can a person be an older brother and also a younger brother? Sure, Logan can be older than his brother Andrew, and younger than his brother Collin. He is older with respect to one brother, and yet not-older with respect to another. There is no contradiction.

Could Jesus be both immortal and mortal? Certainly, Jesus was mortal with respect to His human nature, yet immortal with respect to His divine nature. Can God be one and yet not-one? Of course, God can be one being, and yet three in persons. There is no contradiction regardless of our ability to "picture" the situation. Can Christ be both omniscient and limited in knowledge? Yes, He can be omniscient with respect to His divine nature, but limited with respect to His human nature.

Philippians 2:5–8 explains that Jesus existed as God, but for our sake "emptied Himself" and took on the nature of man, and voluntarily humbled Himself even to the point of death on the Cross. In light of the fact that Jesus has two different natures, we must ask whether a given attribute is applicable to His divine nature, His human nature, or both. Steve missed this crucial distinction, and that resulted in the bulk of his errors.

On the other hand, we have seen that there is copious evidence of the deity of Christ in both the Old and New Testaments, and that genuine contradictions would occur if Christ were not God. God is the only Savior (Isaiah 12:1–2, 21-22, 43:11;). Yet, Christ is the only Savior (Acts 4:10–12).

Note that salvation is in the *same sense* of redemption in both instances. And so this would genuinely contradict if Christ were not God. The Bible directly calls Christ "God" in a number of instances (Hebrews 1:8; Isaiah 9:6; Psalm 45:6–7, 102:25; John 1:1, 14, 20:28). The eternality of Christ is indicated throughout (John 8:58; Revelation 1:11, 17–18; Micah 5:2; Isaiah 9:6). Christ is the Creator, not the created (John 1:1–3; Colossians 1:16).

Most importantly, only those who call upon Christ as Lord can be saved (Romans 10:9–10). And that doesn't just mean calling Christ a lord, but rather as the Lord God. We know this because in Romans 10:13 Paul quotes Joel 2:32 to establish his point that we must call upon Christ the Lord to be saved — and Joel 2:32 refers to the Lord as *YHWH* — the special name of Almighty God that is applied to no one else.

The Trinity may be bothersome to people on an emotional level. But how is that relevant to the truth of the matter? I am bothered when people put anchovies on a pizza; but my displeasure does not cause the anchovies to cease to exist. People may not want to believe in the Trinity because it is difficult to visualize. But that is not a rational reason to reject a claim. After all, many true things are difficult to understand. Consider quantum mechanics or higher-level mathematics. A person's ability or lack thereof to fully understand a given claim has absolutely no bearing whatsoever on the truth of that claim. Moreover, a person's unwillingness to accept a claim also has no bearing at all on the truth thereof.

The Lord knew that we would not be able to fully comprehend His nature. He is infinite and we are finite. His ways and thoughts are infinitely above ours, and so there will always be things about Him that we will not understand (Isaiah 55:8–9). The Lord therefore has not made our salvation and fellowship with Him contingent upon a full understanding of Himself — otherwise none could be saved. Rather, He has given us the gift of *faith*, and it is through faith that we are saved (Ephesians 2:8). That faith necessarily includes trusting in what God has written in His Word about His own nature. God does not require people to fully understand the nature of the Trinity, or the details of how Christ can be both fully God and fully man. But He does expect us to trust what He has written in His Word on these issues (Proverbs 3:5).

Appendix B

Formal Fallacies

Logical fallacies of the formal variety can be a difficult subject to cover. Although the concepts are not hard, there is much terminology that is necessary in order to identify the various kinds of errors. There is no easy way to sidestep such terminology. So we will have to cover some background information before moving on to the specific fallacies. But this information is valuable to know!

The fallacies discussed below occur often enough that I felt they deserved a chapter in this book. On the other hand, I didn't want any readers to get bogged down in the details here and put the book aside. Hence, I felt that this subject should be included as an appendix. I'm providing this section for the courageous souls who want to be as sharp as they possibly can be in reasoning from the Scripture and who are willing to work hard for it.

Formal fallacies are errors in reasoning where the *structure* of the argument is faulty, regardless of the specific content. The structure of an argument is its "form," which is why fallacies involving structure are *formal* fallacies. The form can be represented using a type of "algebra," where either nouns or the various claims being made are represented by a letter. For example, "if p then q." The letter "p" represents a claim, such as "the sun is visible in the sky" and "q" represents another claim such as "it is daytime."

Here is an example of a formal argument with a correct structure:

1. If the sun is visible in the sky, then it is daytime.
2. The sun is visible in the sky.
3. Therefore, it is daytime.

This argument consists of three *propositions* — truth claims. The first two are called *premises*. The third proposition is called the *conclusion*. The conclusion is the thing a person is trying to prove, and the premises are the supporting statements that are supposed to lead a person to believe the conclusion. A good formal argument is said to be *sound*; it has true premises and the conclusion follows logically from them. In the above argument premise 1 is true by definition. Premise 2 is true if you happen to be reading this on a sunny day — in which case you can rightly conclude that "it is daytime."

This argument has the following form:

1. If p then q.
2. p.
3. Therefore, q.

If a formal argument has a correct structure, as this one does, then it is *valid*. In a valid argument, the conclusion follows logically from the premises. So, in a valid argument, if the premises are true then the conclusion must be true as well. However, a valid argument might have a false premise, in which case the conclusion might *not* be true. But the argument is still valid *if the structure is correct*. If a formal argument has an incorrect structure, it is "invalid" and contains a fallacy. This is the case regardless of whether or not the individual premises are true.

A correct argument must be valid *and* also have true premises. In such a case, the argument is called *sound* and its conclusion must be true. Our goal should be that all of our formal arguments are not only valid, but sound as well. If an argument has either a false premise *or* is structurally flawed (invalid), or both, then it is unsound. With an unsound argument, the conclusion is *unreliable* (though it might in some cases turn out to be true by accident).

Here is an example of a valid, but unsound argument:

1. If the sun explodes, then all life on earth will die.
2. The sun has exploded.
3. Therefore, all life on earth will die.

The structure of the argument is good — so it is valid. But the second premise is false, so the argument is unsound. Its conclusion is unreliable.

There are two primary types of formal arguments: categorical and propositional. Categorical arguments use words like "All, some, no, not." Propositional arguments uses words like "If-then, or, and, not." There is a way of combining these categories, but that goes beyond the scope of this book. We begin with propositional arguments and their corresponding fallacies.

Section I. Propositional Fallacies

The examples of logical arguments above are all of the propositional type, and they are all an example of *modus ponens*:

1. If p then q.
2. p.
3. Therefore q.

They begin with a hypothetical proposition "if p then q." In a hypothetical proposition, the "if" part is called the *antecedent* and the "then" part is called the *consequent*. The second proposition is not hypothetical, but affirms that "p" is true. Since "p" is the antecedent, this form of argument is called "affirming the antecedent" or "the method of affirming" which in Latin is *modus ponens*. This form is valid. So if premises 1 and 2 are true, then the argument is sound and the conclusion must be true.

To see examples of how this works, simply substitute a claim for "p" and another claim for "q," such that all the premises are true. And behold, the conclusion will always be true as well. As before, we can let "p" mean "the sun is visible in the sky" and we can let "q" mean "it is daytime."

Modus ponens is one form of a mixed hypothetical syllogism. It's "mixed" because the first premise is hypothetical and the second one is not. Another example of a mixed hypothetical syllogism is as follows:

1. If p then q.
2. Not q
3. Therefore, not p.

In this argument, the second premise denies that the consequent (q) is true. So this is called "denying the consequent" or "the method of denying" which in Latin is *modus tollens*. It is valid. And so if the premises are true, then the conclusion will necessarily be true as well. Once again, we can illustrate this by plugging in expressions for each term such that the premises are true:

1. If the sun is visible in the sky, then it is daytime.
2. It is not daytime.
3. Therefore, the sun is not visible in the sky.

The Fallacy of Denying the Antecedent

Modus ponens and *modus tollens* are the only two standard form mixed hypothetical syllogisms that are valid. There are also two mixed hypothetical syllogisms that are invalid. And these are what we must watch for when examining hermeneutical claims. Here is an example of such a fallacy:

1. If p then q.
2. Not p.
3. Therefore not q.

In this argument, the second premise denies the antecedent. And so this fallacy is simply called "denying the antecedent." We can see that it is fallacious by coming up with terms that make each premise true, and yet still reach a false conclusion. Suppose for example that it is daytime, but overcast. Then we would have:

1. If the sun is visible in the sky, then it is daytime. (true)
2. The sun is not visible in the sky. (true)
3. Therefore, it is not daytime. (false)

Since the conclusion can be false even if both premises are true, the argument is a fallacy. In chapter 6 we saw that an argument from silence is fallacious. We can now see why — it is one form of the fallacy of denying the antecedent:

1. If the Bible stated that Noah had daughters, then Noah had daughters.
2. The Bible does not state that Noah had daughters.
3. Therefore, Noah did not have daughters.

Notice that the conclusion is not necessarily false. But neither is it necessarily true. In a fallacy, the conclusion is unreliable. Baptismal regenerationists commit the fallacy of denying the antecedent when arguing that water baptism is a requirement for salvation.

1. If you repent and are baptized, then you are saved (Mark 16:16).

2. It is not that case that you have repented and are baptized (because you have only repented and have not yet been baptized.)
3. Therefore, you are not saved.

The conclusion is unreliable — and in this case is demonstrably false because we know from other Scriptures that salvation is by God's grace received through faith and not by works (Ephesians 2:8–9). And the Bible reports that people have been saved after repenting without ever having been baptized in water (Luke 23:39–43).

The Fallacy of Affirming the Consequent

The other fallacious form of the mixed hypothetical syllogism is called "affirming the consequent" because the second premise affirms the consequent of the first premise:

1. If p then q.
2. q.
3. Therefore p.

Again, we can demonstrate the fallacious nature of this form by substituting propositions that make the premises true but the conclusion (potentially) false, as follows:

1. If the sun is visible in the sky, then it is daytime. (true)
2. It is daytime. (true)
3. Therefore, the sun is visible. (false)

If the sky were overcast during the day, then premises 1 and 2 would be true, and yet the conclusion would be false. So the argument is invalid. The fallacy of affirming the consequent is at the root of many faulty scientific claims. People will sometimes claim that since their favorite scientific theory predicts X, and since X is observed, it follows that their theory is true. But this doesn't follow. Consider the following.

Evolution predicts that the DNA of closely related organisms ought to be more similar than DNA of more distant organisms. But relatedness of organisms is judged largely by their physical characteristics. And creationists and evolutionists both agree that physical characteristics are largely determined by DNA. So creationists would *also* predict that organisms with similar traits (those that are assumed by evolutionists to be more closely related) would have similar DNA. Both models make the same prediction. Thus, the following argument is fallacious:

1. If evolution is true, then organisms with similar traits should have similar DNA.
2. Organisms with similar traits do have similar DNA.
3. Therefore, evolution is true.

Premises 1 and 2 are true. But the structure of the argument is faulty — it's an example of affirming the consequent. The fallaciousness of the argument is particularly evident when we see that it could equally well "prove" creation:

1. If creation is true, then organisms with similar traits should have similar DNA.
2. Organisms with similar traits do have similar DNA.
3. Therefore, creation is true.

Again, premises 1 and 2 are true. If the form of this argument were valid, then we could prove that creation and evolution are both true! Sometimes this fallacy is employed in old-earth creationist arguments:

1. If the seventh day was a long period of time, then God must still be resting.
2. God is still resting.
3. Therefore, the seventh day is a long period of time.

The argument is fallacious since premise 2 affirms the consequent.

One of the strange things about scientific procedures is that they seem at first to be based on the fallacy of affirming the consequent. That is, a scientific model predicts X. We observe X. And then doesn't the scientist say that this supports his or her model? But this isn't strictly so. Science is generally probabilistic in nature, and is based on *repeated* observations.

That is, a scientific model predicts X where competing models predict Y or Z. When we observe X, these competing models are eliminated by the correct logical formal argument of *modus tollens*. By repeating the experiment under a variety of conditions, the scientist seeks to eliminate all possible competing models. In practice, it is normally impossible to eliminate all competing models; and so the scientist can only eliminate what are likely to be the most probable alternatives. Repeated observations that are consistent with the predictions of a model (and contrary to competing models) give the scientist confidence that his or her model is *likely* to be correct. But strictly speaking, they do not prove the model unless all possible alternatives are eliminated.

Can the fallacy of affirming the consequent be avoided simply by making the argument probabilistic rather than deductively conclusive? In other words, would it be rational to argue, "1. Evolution predicts similarities in DNA. 2. We observe similarities in DNA. 3. Thus, evolution is *probably* true"? No. Creation equally well predicts similarities in DNA. Thus, the observation that similarities exist in DNA does not eliminate any competing models. This kind of analysis is helpful not only in science but in theological claims as well. *Observations cannot be used to distinguish between two models that make the same predictions.*

The Fallacy of Affirming a Disjunct

The following argument is valid. It is called a *disjunctive syllogism*:[1]

1. p or q.
2. not p.
3. therefore q.

Assuming the premises are true, the conclusion must also be true. Substituting phrases for each proposition, we can see that this argument makes sense:

1. Either Bill is at least 35 years old, or he is disqualified for the office of U.S. president.
2. Bill is *not* at least 35 years old.
3. Therefore, he is disqualified for the office of U.S. president.

The corresponding fallacy is called *affirming a disjunct*, and has the following form:

1. p or q.
2. p.
3. therefore, not q.

The reason this is fallacious is because the first premise (p or q) would still be true *if both p and q are each true*. And so the truth of p does not guarantee that q must be false. For example:

---

1. In logic, a *disjunction* is a compound proposition where its two components are connected by the word "or" as in "p or q." When connected in this way, p and q are each called a *disjunct*.

1. Either Bill is at least 35 years old, or he is disqualified for the office of U.S. president.
2. Bill is at least 35 years old.
3. Therefore, Bill is *not* disqualified for the office of U.S. president. (He is qualified).

But that conclusion is not guaranteed from the truth of the premises. Both premises could be true, and yet the conclusion could still be false if, for example, Bill is not a U.S. citizen. In that case, he could be both 35 years old and also disqualified for the office of U.S. president.

Here is a common theological error based on this fallacy:

1. Either God sovereignly controls the universe, or men make free choices.
2. God sovereignly controls the universe.
3. Therefore, men do not make free choices.

The argument is fallacious because the possibility exists logically that God is sovereign *and* men make free choices. That may be hard to grasp, but the two simple propositions are not contrary. Since the compound proposition [p and q] may be true, the truth of either p or q does not falsify the other one.

The Fallacy of Denying a Conjunct

The fallacy of *denying a conjunct* can be thought of as the "negative" version of the previous error.[2] It is structurally identical to *affirming the disjunct*, but with the truth value of all terms reversed, and "or" replaced with "and":

1. Not both p and q.
2. Not p.
3. Therefore, q.

If the double negative is confusing, consider this clarifying example:

1. It is not the case that it is both sunny outside and nighttime.
2. It is not sunny outside.
3. Therefore, it is nighttime.

---

2. In logic, a *conjunction* is a compound proposition where its two components are connected by the word "and" as in "p and q." When connected in this way, p and q are each called a *conjunct*.

The conclusion is unwarranted, because it could be overcast during the day. In that case, both premises would be true, and yet the conclusion would be false.

The Fallacy of Commutation of Conditionals

The commutation of conditionals is a common error in reasoning with this form:

1. If p then q.
2. Therefore, if q then p.

The first premise indicates that the truth of p guarantees the truth of q. However, from this we cannot conclude that the truth of q guarantees the truth of p. For example:

1. If it is snowing then it must be cold outside.
2. Therefore, if it is cold outside then it must be snowing.

Although the premise is true, the conclusion is not warranted since the possibility exists that it could be cold outside and yet not snowing. Snow requires cold temperatures, but cold temperatures do not require snow. Theological errors can stem from this fallacy.

1. If you love Jesus, then you will keep His commandments (John 14:15).
2. Therefore, if you keep Jesus's commandments, then you will love Him.

The conclusion is not guaranteed because some people might obey certain laws, not out of love, but for fear of the penalty. Just because someone doesn't go around murdering others does not necessarily imply that the person loves Jesus. The person may simply fear incarceration.

The Fallacy of Improper Transposition

Similar to the fallacy of commutation of conditionals is the fallacy of improper transposition.

1. If p then q.
2. Therefore, if not-p then not-q.

The argument is fallacious because the premise only guarantees that q will be true if p is, but it does not guarantee that q will be false if p is false. Here is an example:

1. If it is snowing then it must be cold outside.
2. Therefore, if it is not snowing, then it must not be cold outside.

Of course, cold weather does not guarantee snow. Since the premise is true and yet the conclusion can be false, the argument is a fallacy. The proper form of transposition reverses the order of the conjuncts (p and q) in the conclusion, and results in the following valid argument:

1. If p then q.
2. Therefore, if not q then not p.

This argument is valid, and is similar in essence to *modus tollens*.

Section II. Categorical Fallacies

A categorical syllogism is a short argument consisting of three statements (propositions), and deals with which types of things belong in a particular category. As before, the first two propositions are assumed to be true; these are *premises*. In standard form, the first premise is called the *major premise* and the second is called the *minor premise*. The third is what the person is attempting to prove and is called the *conclusion*.

1. All mammals are air-breathers.
2. All cats are mammals.
3. Therefore, all cats are air-breathers.

The above argument is valid — meaning that if the premises are true then the conclusion will also be true because it follows logically from the premises. The argument is also sound — meaning that it is valid and the premises are indeed true. The conclusion of any categorical syllogism will have a subject ("all cats") and a predicate ("are air-breathers"). By convention, the premise that contains the predicate term ("air-breathers" in this case) is placed first and is called the *major premise*. For example, "All mammals are air-breathers" is the major premise of the above argument. The premise containing the subject term ("cats") is placed second and is called the *minor premise*. Of course, the order of the premises has no bearing on the validity. The argument would be just as valid (and sound) if I had stated "all cats are mammals" first and "all mammals are air-breathers" second. It just wouldn't be in *standard form*.

There are three terms in this argument: mammals, air-breathers, and cats. The term found only in the major premise and the predicate of the conclusion is called the *major term* (air-breathers). The term found only in the minor premise and the subject of the conclusion is called the *minor term* (cats). The term found in both premises but not in the conclusion is called the *middle term* (mammals).

Each term also has a *quantifier* that indicates the extent of the term, and a *qualifier* that indicates whether the term is used in a positive or negative way. The above argument used only the "all" terms as the quantifier and qualifier. This is a *universal affirmative* — "universal" because "all" refers to each-and-every member of the referent, and "affirmative" because it refers to them in a positive way. The term "some" (as in "some mammals are cats") is a *particular affirmative*. This is because "some" refers to some specific members of a class, but not necessarily all of them, and it does so in a positive way. The phrase "some ___ are not" (as in "some mammals are *not* cats" is a *particular negative* because it refers to specific members of a class, but in a negative way. The term "no" (as in "no dogs are cats") is a *universal negative* — it refers to all dogs, but in a negative way (denying that they are cats).

There are 256 possible forms for a standard-form categorical syllogism.[3] But only 15 of these are valid on the Boolean interpretation (described below). The remaining 241 forms commit one or more of the fallacies listed below.

---

3. In a categorical syllogism, the middle term can be either the subject or predicate (2 options) in each of the 2 premises, for a total of 4 (2 x 2) possible order-combinations, each of which is called a "figure." The subject in each proposition will be used in 1 of 4 possible ways — universal affirmative, universal negative, particular affirmative, or particular negative. Since there are 3 propositions in a syllogism (2 premises and 1 conclusion) each of which has 1 of 2 possible quantifiers and 1 of 2 possible qualifiers, then there are 64 (4 x 4 x 4) possible combinations of quantifiers and qualifiers for each figure. And since there are 4 figures, there are 256 possible forms for a standard categorical syllogism (64 x 4). Of these, only 15 are valid on the Boolean interpretation.

On the older, classical interpretation, there are 24 valid categorical syllogisms. The additional 9 are considered fallacious on the Boolean system because they commit the existential fallacy. That is, they conclude that at least one member of a category exists when that is not implied by the premises (based on current linguistic convention.) These 9 syllogisms ***would be valid*** if, in addition to the syllogism itself, we added a premise that at least one member of a category exists. Five of these forms presuppose that the minor term has at least one member that exists, 3 presuppose that the middle term has at least one member, and 1 presupposes that that major term has at least one member.

The Fallacy of the Undistributed Middle

There are only six possible categorical fallacies.[4] By far the most common is the fallacy of the undistributed middle. I will briefly discuss the other five fallacies below just for completeness. But they seldom come up in actual debates because most people can easily recognize the error. But this one is more subtle. The fallacy of the undistributed middle is any categorical syllogism where the *middle term is not universal* (does not refer to all of its members) in either premise. Here is an example:

1. All cats are mammals.
2. Some dogs are mammals.
3. Therefore, some dogs are cats.

The middle term is the noun that occurs in both premises but is absent from the conclusion. In this case, the middle term is "mammals." This term is undistributed in premise 1, because the statement "all cats are mammals" does not refer to each-and-every mammal — only to those mammals that happen to be cats. (By contrast, the term "cats" *is* distributed in this premise, because the premise refers to *all* cats.) In premise 2, the statement "some dogs are mammals" does not refer to each-and-every mammal — but only those that are dogs. So the middle term is not distributed. (Neither is the term "dogs" distributed, because the claim references *some* dogs, not all.) Whenever the middle term is undistributed in both premises, the argument is fallacious. Here is another example.

1. Some mammals lay eggs.
2. All dogs are mammals.
3. Therefore, some dogs lay eggs.

Premises 1 and 2 are true. A duck-billed platypus is an egg-laying mammal. And all dogs are mammals. But the conclusion is false. The argument is fallacious — the fallacy of the undistributed middle — because the middle term "mammals" is not distributed in either premise.

Some faulty interpretations of Scripture are due to the fallacy of the undistributed middle:

4. Any standard-form categorical syllogism that does *not* commit one of these six fallacies is guaranteed to be valid.

1. The Father is God.
2. Jesus is God.
3. Therefore, Jesus is the Father.

Here, the term "God" is not distributed in either premise because it does not refer to all three members of the Trinity. The conclusion is false. Sometimes old-earth creationists commit this fallacy when attempting to argue that since the Hebrew word for day, *yôm*, can sometimes mean a long period of time rather than an ordinary day, that the days of creation were not ordinary days. The argument could be expressed as follows:

1. Some instances of *yôm* are long periods of time.
2. The days of Genesis 1 are instances of *yôm*.
3. Therefore, the days of Genesis 1 are long periods of time.

In this case, the noun *yôm* is undistributed in both premises. The first premise explicitly states "Some instances of *yôm*" — not all. Hence the term is undistributed. The second premise refers only to the days of Genesis 1 as instances of *yôm*, and hence not every *yôm* is implied, since most of them occur after Genesis 1. The argument is therefore fallacious.

Is the following argument an example of the fallacy of the undistributed middle?

1. All men are sinners (Romans 3:23).
2. Jesus Christ is a man.
3. Therefore, Jesus Christ is a sinner.

This argument is valid, but unsound. The structure is correct, but the first premise is subtly false because when the Bible states that all have fallen short of the glory of God, this implicitly and necessarily excludes the one man who is also God — namely Jesus. Therefore, this is not an example of the undistributed middle, but rather an example of an unsound argument due to a false premise. With a slight change, the argument becomes:

1. *Some* men are sinners (those men who are not also God).
2. Jesus Christ is a man.
3. Therefore, Jesus Christ is a sinner.

This argument does commit the fallacy of the undistributed middle because the term "man" (or "men") does not refer to all its members in either premise.

In the second premise, only one man is referred to, and in the first premise only some men are addressed (all but one). The argument is invalid, and therefore unsound.

1. Things that are possible sometimes occur today.
2. God speaking through prophets is possible.
3. Therefore, God speaking through prophets sometimes occurs today.

The above argument commits the fallacy of the undistributed middle because "things that are possible" is not distributed in either premise. In the second premise, "God speaking through prophets" is a subset of "things that are possible," and does not refer to the entire set of "things that are possible." In the first premise, "things that are possible" is also undistributed, because clearly not *all* things that are possible today actually occur today — only *some* of them. Even though premise 1 and 2 are both true, the conclusion is unreliable since the form of the argument is invalid.

Often fallacies can be "hidden" by stating the argument in a non-standard way:

1. God rested on the seventh day.
2. God is still resting today.
3. Therefore, we are still in the seventh day.

This argument commits the fallacy of the undistributed middle, which becomes obvious when we rephrase the premises in standard form. The argument becomes:

1. The seventh day of Genesis is a day in which God is resting.
2. Today is a day in which God is resting.
3. Therefore, today is the seventh day of Genesis.

The middle term "a day in which God is resting" is undistributed in both the major and minor premise. So the conclusion is unreliable. Sometimes, it is easiest to refute a fallacious argument by giving an argument with the same form with true premises and an obviously false conclusion:

1. I rested last Monday.
2. Today I am resting.
3. Therefore, today is last Monday.

The Fallacy of Illicit Process

Illicit process involves asserting a distributed (quantitatively universal) term in the conclusion when it is undistributed (quantitatively particular) in the premises. Namely, if a term is distributed in the conclusion, it must also be distributed in at least one of the premises — otherwise, the conclusion has asserted more than is warranted in either premise. Since there are two terms in the conclusion, there are two ways in which this fallacy can be committed. If the major term is distributed in the conclusion, but is undistributed in the major premise, then this is "the fallacy of the illicit process of the major term" — or more briefly, "the fallacy of the illicit major." Here is an example:

1. Some mammals are dogs.
2. No cats are dogs.
3. Therefore, no cats are mammals.

The term "mammals" is not distributed in the major premise because only some mammals are also dogs. But the term "mammals" is distributed in the conclusion, which asserts that *all* mammals fall outside of the class of "cats."

The other way this fallacy is committed is when the minor term is distributed in the conclusion, but undistributed in the minor premise. This is the "fallacy of the illicit process of the minor term" or more briefly, "the fallacy of the illicit minor." For example:

1. All dogs are mammals.
2. Some four-legged animals are dogs.
3. Therefore, all four-legged animals are mammals.

The term "four-legged animals" is distributed in the conclusion, which refers to all of them. But the term is undistributed in the minor premise, which refers to only some four-legged animals. The argument is therefore fallacious, even though the premises are true.

The Illicit Negative Fallacy

The illicit negative fallacy occurs when an argument has a positive conclusion ("all" or "some"), but at least one negative premise ("no" or "some ____ are *not*"). This is fallacious because any syllogism that has a negative premise must also have a negative conclusion. For example:

1. All housecats can purr.
2. No dogs can purr.
3. Therefore, all dogs are housecats.

It is also the case that the reverse situation is invalid — when the conclusion is negative, but both premises are positive:

1. All mammals are air-breathers.
2. All dogs are mammals.
3. Therefore, no dogs are air-breathers.

This is sometimes referred to as the "illicit affirmative fallacy." But it is not generally included as one of the standard six categorical fallacies, because it is unneeded on the standard Boolean system. That is, any illicit affirmative fallacy also commits one of the standard six fallacies. The above argument, for example, also commits the fallacy of the Illicit major — defined above.[5]

The Fallacy of Exclusive Premises

The fallacy of exclusive premises occurs when both premises in a syllogism are negative. *No valid conclusion* can be drawn in such a scenario.

1. No people have tails.
2. No dogs are people.
3. Therefore, no dogs have tails.

It wouldn't matter what the conclusion (3) states about dogs and tails — it would be fallacious. From premises (1) and (2), there is no conclusion we can legitimately draw about the relationship between dogs and tails.

The Existential Fallacy

As a matter of convention, most modern logicians use a Boolean interpretation of categorical logic. On this system, particular terms like "some ___" or "some ___ are not" have what is called "existential import." That means that they imply that at least one member of that class does exist. In other words, if I say, "Some dogs have long fur," then by convention we agree that I am implying that dogs do exist — they are not merely hypothetical.

5. The term *air-breathers* is distributed in the conclusion because it asserts that all air-breathers fall outside the class of dogs. But the term *air-breathers* is undistributed in the major premise, which implies that some air-breathers are mammals, but does not refer to all of them.

However, universal terms like "all" or "no" do not have existential import — they do not necessarily imply that any members of their class exist. So, if I say, "All ghosts can pass through solid matter," this does not imply that any ghosts necessarily exist. The category of "things that are ghosts" need not have any actual members in order for me to discuss the category. Likewise, if I said, "No Klingons are eligible for salvation," then we cannot conclude that I'm claiming that any Klingons actually exist. They may be hypothetical only.

The Boolean interpretation is therefore a linguistic convention. On this convention, a valid syllogism cannot have a particular conclusion if both premises are universal. The reason is that universal terms do not necessarily imply that their categories have any members, but particular terms do. And it would be inappropriate to conclude that something exists when neither premise asserts this. For example:

1. All things with a horn on their head are potentially dangerous.
2. All unicorns have a horn on their head.
3. Therefore, some unicorns are potentially dangerous.

The argument is fallacious on the Boolean interpretation because the conclusion implies that some unicorns do exist, yet neither premise asserts this. The conclusion is particular — "some" — and thus has existential import, but both premises are universal: "all." The fallacy is very subtle because it uses a linguistic convention and not a direct statement to fallaciously conclude that something exists.

The Fallacy of Four Terms

A proper syllogism has only three terms: a major term, a minor term, and a middle term. If an additional term is introduced then the conclusion is not reliable. Consider this ridiculous example:

1. Some cats can purr.
2. Some people get married.
3. Therefore, some married people can purr.

The fallacy is rarely so obvious. Instead, it is usually the case that the fourth term is disguised by having the same *name* as one of the three, while nonetheless having a different *meaning*.

1. Things that are light are never dark.
2. Feathers are light.
3. Therefore, feathers are never dark.

In the first premise, "light" means "brightly colored or highly reflective," whereas in the second premise "light" means "having very little weight — the opposite of heavy." The fallacy of four terms is the formal equivalent of the fallacy of equivocation. Here is a heretical example of the fallacy of four-terms:

1. God cannot be tempted (James 1:13).
2. Jesus was tempted (Hebrews 4:15).
3. Therefore Jesus is not God.

This commits the fallacy of four terms (equivocation) because the middle term, "tempted," means something different in the first premise than it does in the second premise. In the first premise "tempted" means to be enticed — drawn away by lust (James 1:14). In the second premise, "tempted" means to be "tested" as in a trial. God can indeed be "tested" in that sense (Deuteronomy 6:16; Psalm 78:18), though He is never enticed. I have often heard that very example used by heretics who claim that Jesus cannot be God.

Conclusion

A study of formal logic may seem abstract and academic. But in reality it is *extremely* practical. The ability to spot logical fallacies in arguments is one of the most useful tools in the apologist's toolbox. It is an acquired ability — one that can be *learned.* And it is well worth the time investment. It guards us against errors in our own thinking, and can help us to gently correct unbiblical thinking in others. Learning to be rational is one aspect of our calling to be conformed to the image of Christ. We are to think, insomuch as is possible for finite creatures, in a way that is consistent with God's thoughts (Isaiah 55:7–9).

Index